FORTUNE'S FOOL

FORTUNE'S FOOL

....

The Life of
John Wilkes Booth

TERRY ALFORD

OXFORD
UNIVERSITY PRESS

OXFORD

UNIVERSITY PRESS

Oxford University Press is a department of the
University of Oxford. It furthers the University's objective
of excellence in research, scholarship, and education
by publishing worldwide.

Oxford   New York

Auckland   Cape Town   Dar es Salaam   Hong Kong   Karachi
Kuala Lumpur   Madrid   Melbourne   Mexico City   Nairobi
New Delhi   Shanghai   Taipei   Toronto

With offices in

Argentina   Austria   Brazil   Chile   Czech Republic   France   Greece
Guatemala   Hungary   Italy   Japan   Poland   Portugal   Singapore
South Korea   Switzerland   Thailand   Turkey   Ukraine   Vietnam

Oxford is a registered trade mark of Oxford University Press
in the UK and certain other countries.

Published in the United States of America by
Oxford University Press
198 Madison Avenue, New York, NY 10016

Library of Congress Cataloging-in-Publication Data
has been applied for.

ISBN 978-0-19-505412-5

1 3 5 7 9 8 6 4 2

Printed in the United States of America
on acid-free paper

Dedicated to James O. Hall,
Historian, Mentor, Friend

CONTENTS

· · · ·

FORTUNE'S FOOL

INTRODUCTION

WHEN THE AFRICAN AMERICAN educator John E. Washington was a boy walking home in the 1880s, he quickened his step when he passed Ford's Theatre. In fact, he ran past the building. Eyes locked straight ahead, he refused to look in that direction. The old folks said there were ghosts there, and Washington could feel them. Restless spirits, begging for release, they flowed around the theater. After midnight one might be unlucky enough to encounter a specter face-to-face. It was well known that John Wilkes Booth, his eyes glowing like hot coals, prowled the alley behind the theater as he cursed his phantom horse.

Years later, in 1942, Washington published *They Knew Lincoln*, a collection of anecdotes about the great president from the previous generation of city residents—the cooks, seamstresses, draymen, street vendors, and laborers whose voices often went unrecorded. Mostly former slaves, these people revered Abraham Lincoln, and Washington himself imbibed the spirit of their freedom as fully as if he, too, had been a personal beneficiary of the Emancipation Proclamation of 1863.

"Lincoln's life to these humble people was a miracle," he wrote. "To the deeply emotional and religious slave, Lincoln was an earthly incarnation of the Savior of mankind. Was he not also a carpenter's son, born in a humble log cabin? Was he not a worker in the field, unlettered and unsung?

Was he not despised and rejected by men, and did he not know by experience their sorrow? Did he not yearn for the day when he might learn to read and write, and enjoy the pleasures of life for himself and his children? Upon whom could he depend in his hour of need but the Almighty God for comfort and guidance? Was he not inaugurated as President amidst the waving of flags and the sounds of trumpets, only to be martyred, as Christ was, because of his services for the lowly?"

Washington had learned Booth's name almost as soon as he learned Lincoln's. That was because wherever history carried the great president, his assassin was not far behind. Booth left a different legacy. He was a killer of a most special kind. He wanted more than the life of one man. He wished to murder a nation and the freedom of a people.

Not surprisingly, the assassin preyed on Washington's childhood imagination. One night when the boy was in bed, he realized that Booth was in the room with him. Booth pulled a dagger and lunged at him, chasing him over the bed. Washington dove under it, and Booth followed. Crying in fear, Washington leapt toward the ceiling and clutched onto a spiderweb. Booth flourished his knife and came after him. "I was suddenly awakened by my Grandmother, just as the dagger was approaching my heart. She found me nearly suffocated by a large bundle of bedding with which I had covered my head and screaming at the top of my voice." It was only a nightmare.[1]

No one would have been more surprised by Washington's dream than Booth himself. During the New York City draft riots of 1863, mobs rampaged through Manhattan. African Americans, a principal target of their fury, were attacked both north and south of the Booth home on East 17th Street and from river to river. "Booth spoke with detestation of the murdering of inoffensive negroes," wrote Adam Badeau, a federal officer living with the Booths at the time. At one point the rioters burned the Colored Orphan Asylum on Fifth Avenue. Randall, Badeau's African American servant from Louisiana, was in the Booth house that day. When it appeared that he might be in danger, Booth vowed to hide the youngster in the cellar. If the rabble came after him there, he said, he would protect the boy with his own life. Booth vigilantly watched over Randall for a week, until the riots ended.[2]

"John Wilkes Booth meant well to every human being," his contemporary Joseph Howard Jr., a top reporter for the *New York Times*, told his readers. "None of you who judged him knew him."[3]

"THE PRESIDENT WAS SHOT in a theater tonight and perhaps mortally wounded."[4] When Lawrence A. Gobright, agent of the Associated Press in Washington, D.C., telegraphed this brief message to his subscribers in New York only moments after the assassination, one hundred and fifty years of writing on the death of Abraham Lincoln commenced. A vast literature on the death of the president has appeared over that time. Yet, oddly enough, *Fortune's Fool* is the first full-length biography of John Wilkes Booth ever written.

Historians have long recognized the need for such a book. It would fill an important gap in the assassination record as well as help dispel some of the absurd theories about April 14, 1865, and its aftermath. The old standby, Francis Wilson's *John Wilkes Booth: Fact and Fiction of Lincoln's Assassination* (1929), was written by an author born in 1854 and is out of date. The books that came along in subsequent decades were a mixed lot, many written by special pleaders or conspiracy junkies. Recent titles, the best of which are mentioned in "Notes on Sources," have been much better. Still, no Booth biography appeared. That was surprising, not only because there was an amazing—if disturbing—story to be told, but it was apparent that without a thorough understanding of Booth our knowledge of the murder of Lincoln was lacking. After all, as Booth's friend and co-conspirator Samuel Arnold explained, everything that happened was due to him. "He alone was the moving spirit," said Arnold.[5]

The story of Booth's life is complex and the task of researching it formidable. There is no comprehensive collection of John Wilkes Booth papers with which to start, for example. Like many other highly verbal individuals, Booth was not much of a writer. His surviving letters are few and seldom revealing. Beyond a short memoir by his older sister Asia, his family members, horrified by what he did, left little about him. Government investigators compiled an invaluable mass of information in 1865 about Booth's role as a conspirator, but the material focused on the assassination and did not give a broad picture of the man's life. If Booth had not been an actor and public figure before the murder, it would be impossible to recover his life in any meaningful depth.

The best source for learning about Booth before the assassination—about his family, childhood, education, career as an actor, personality, and public life—turned out to be the recollections of his friends. As time passed following Lincoln's death and they felt safe to do so, these friends spoke. It says something about Booth that although they shrank from what he did, they did not shrink from him. Much of what they remembered is surprisingly positive.

Born in 1838, Booth was the fourth son of Junius Brutus Booth and Mary Ann Holmes, an immigrant couple from London. His inheritance was complex. His father was a brilliant actor whose alcoholism, scandalous behavior, and lapses of sanity cast a disturbing shadow over the future assassin's childhood. His mother was an indulgent parent whose unqualified love formed a wholesome counterweight to the unpredictable father. The son seemed a mix of the two. Excitable, erratic, and reckless, he was loveable, congenial, and kind-hearted as well.

Detesting the wear and tear of theatrical life, Junius wanted another vocation for John, but it is unsurprising that the youth followed his father's footsteps. He served his apprenticeship at the Marshall Theatre in Richmond, where he learned the daily ins-and-outs of his profession. Equally significant was the welcome that Richmond society extended to him. He loved the city, and as the crisis between North and South intensified in the late 1850s, he identified fully with the people and the customs of the future Confederate capital.

This was shown when he volunteered with the Virginia militia in 1859 to ensure the peace at Charlestown and carry out the execution of John Brown, whose abolitionist raid at nearby Harpers Ferry had convulsed Virginia in fear and anger. Booth was fascinated by Brown—attracted by his indomitable spirit yet repelled by his abolitionism, a movement the young actor believed would tear the country apart. When Brown was hanged, Booth stood only feet from the gallows and told friends he considered the moment the proudest of his life.

Booth hoped to become a traveling star in the spring of 1861, but the outbreak of the Civil War brought theatrical life to a halt, and he was swept up in the conflict. Like most others in the Upper South, he had hoped this moment could be avoided through sectional compromise, but when events dictated otherwise, Booth decided to become a Confederate soldier. He and his widowed mother, fearful for his life, discussed the topic exhaustively. She reminded him tearfully of his childhood promise that, in return for the love and encouragement she had given him, he would always strive to make her happy. Devoted to the kindest of mothers, he yielded to her frantic pleas for him to live in the North and keep away from trouble. This decision, which went against both his beliefs and his instincts, was fraught with ill consequences for the future.

As the Civil War raged in the early 1860s, and hosts of young men his age wrote the history of their generation, Booth acted. He performed Shakespearean classics and melodrama. His impetuous personality had a spark of genius that shone onstage and, added to his superb good looks, wonderful voice, and exciting acting style, brought him stardom within a matter of months. Some critics complained that he was hurried, inarticulate, and crude at times. Others saw him as uniquely gifted. The public embraced him without reserve, and he played successfully throughout the North, being particularly popular in Boston and Chicago. For many he had the potential to become the greatest actor of his day, if he did not already deserve the title.

Despite professional acclaim and material success, Booth was a deeply troubled man by the summer of 1864. "For four years I have lived (I may say) a slave in the north—a favored slave it's true, but no less hateful to me on that account," he wrote his mother. "Not daring to express my thoughts or sentiments, even in my own home. Constantly hearing every principle dear to my heart denounced as treasonable, and knowing the vile and savage acts committed on my countrymen, their wives and helpless children, I have cursed my willful idleness and begun to deem myself a coward and to despise my own existence."[6] To rescue himself from self-reproach, he concocted a plot to abduct Lincoln and present him to the Confederacy as a bargaining chip to force the North to exchange of prisoners of war. He recruited a small cadre of former school friends, Confederate operatives, and Southern sympathizers to assist him. Twice—in January and again in March 1865—he put his scheme in motion, only to fail both times. Doubts flourished about his leadership, and some of his associates drifted away.

Even as Booth and his team worked to abduct the president, there was always a possibility that, given the proper opportunity and inspiration, he might murder Lincoln on impulse. He appeared ready to do so on March 4, 1865, at Lincoln's second inauguration. Booth had grown up in a home where the self-sacrificing heroes of antiquity were honored. Subsequently, his study of plays like *Julius Caesar* confirmed that Brutus and Cassius were men of high principle, not common cutthroats. These convictions, held by an individual as unsettled as Booth, spelled tragedy.

As the war came to an end in the spring of 1865, he was moody and misanthropic. He drank heavily, acted oddly, and lashed out at friends. Fixated on Lincoln, he saw the president as the cause of the nation's woes.

"Our country owed all her troubles to him," Booth wrote.[7] When the rebel army in Virginia surrendered on April 9, 1865, he was stunned. He never considered such a thing possible. Goaded by the celebrations that followed in Washington and incensed by Lincoln's pledge of limited voting rights for African Americans, he assassinated Abraham Lincoln on the evening of April 14, 1865, at Ford's Theatre. Escaping from the rear of the theater, he became one of only two presidential assassins who successfully fled the scene of the crime.

The twelve-day manhunt for Booth that followed mesmerized the nation. The assassin simply disappeared, and there was fear he might escape into the chaos into which the Southern states had descended. But on April 26, 1865, he was cornered in a Virginia barn and shot to death during a standoff with federal troops. So ended, at age twenty-six, the life of one of the most remarkable personalities of his era.

Booth's friends were nearly speechless with astonishment at this turn of events. The comedian William Warren, on a train traveling to Boston, heard that Booth had shot the president from a conductor rushing down the aisle. *That's a lie*, thought Warren, and, leaping to his feet, he contradicted the man. Booth was a generous and affable person. He could not be a murderer. "Alas," wrote the comedian in his diary, "it proved too true."[8]

Perhaps Booth was a better actor than Warren realized. Although the men were close, the friend had never seen Booth's other, more sinister side. Few had. Adam Badeau also failed to detect it. "I had seen him several times under unusual circumstances," Badeau wrote, "and he never displayed any trait or indicated any sentiment that made it probable he would end his career with this appalling catastrophe." Since Badeau was a Union officer, Booth would not have been open with him, but even politically congenial fellows like the actor Frank Drew were no less dumfounded. "I knew he was a Southern sympathizer, of course, but so was I. He never even hinted or gave me the slightest reason to suppose he intended to commit such an atrocious crime," Drew recalled in 1899.[9]

One can say in defense of these men that Booth didn't look dangerous or irrational. There were his heated political outbursts, of course, but, as William Ferguson of Ford's Theatre wrote, "they were accepted without analysis as part of his high-spirited nature. In the excitement of Civil War times this trend of his mind passed without attracting particular attention."[10] Why should it? "Booth looked the part of neither the lunatic nor villain, but seemed to be a most likable fellow," said the sculptor Edward

Valentine.[11] J. B. McCormick, whose hands were scarred by injuries inflicted by Booth in stage combat, recalled in 1901, "Before he shot Lincoln, I never heard anyone say he was crazy. Even now I don't think he was."[12]

Badeau thought such statements were absurd. It was evident that "the awful act was the result of a disturbed brain." Consider its staging. "It was so theatrical in plan and performance—the conspiracy—the dagger— the selection of a theater—the brandishing of the weapon—the cry 'sic semper tyrannis' to the audience—all was exactly that a madman brought up in a theater might have been expected to conceive." Wrong, countered Ferguson. What happened at Ford's Theatre, where Ferguson was backstage the night of the murder and no more than a foot or two away from the murderer when he escaped, proved Booth was entirely rational. The assassin carefully arranged everything he did to make certain he could both get to the president and escape when his bloody work was done. "It was the act of a man in full possession of all his undiluted faculties, working with speed and precision according to a well-laid plan."

The actress Anne Hartley Gilbert, a family friend, wrote, "I never felt it was madness that carried him into the plot to assassinate the President. I know how high feeling could run in those days. Whatever drew Wilkes Booth in, if the lot fell to him to do the thing, I feel sure he went through it without a backward thought. He had that kind of loyalty, that kind of courage." While there was room for light and shade in his personal life, there was none in his politics, and he fixated on his fear that Lincoln would become a king. He reacted, continued Gilbert, "with the devotion of a high-strung nihilist" who lives—and dies—for his beliefs.[13]

ON HIS SIXTIETH BIRTHDAY in 1898, the actor Owen Fawcett was in a reflective mood. Sitting down at his desk in his Manhattan apartment, he took up a blank octavo scrapbook with black-and-white marbled board covers and a brown leather binding. Nearby were scissors and a glue pot. In spidery letters on a title page he wrote the words "John Wilkes Booth," then set to work pasting in a pile of clippings he had saved over the years.[14]

Booth would have been sixty that year as well. He and Fawcett had often performed together. Once they played before Lincoln at Ford's Theatre. On another occasion they shared the stage before a vast crowd of America's cultural elite at the Winter Garden in New York City to raise money for the Shakespeare statue in Central Park. How handsome, charming, and fun Booth had been, Fawcett recalled. How talented. And yet how odd.

It was difficult to know how to measure such a man. So Fawcett turned to the sacred canon of his profession—to Shakespeare. Below Booth's name on the title page he added three lines from act five, scene two of *Othello*—a caution for himself and an exhortation for those of us who would come after:

> *When you shall these unlucky deeds relate,*
> *Speak of me as I am; nothing extenuate,*
> *Nor set down aught in malice.*

1

. . . .

BRIGHT BOY ABSALOM

ON AN OCTOBER MORNING in 1934 a short, stocky man with a long face and a crown of thick black hair walked along a country lane in Maryland. Rows of maple trees flanked the road and formed an autumn canopy of orange and red over his head.[1] The setting was so beautiful that the traveler paused. Stanley Kimmel—author, musician, and self-described soldier of fortune—wanted to experience it. He wanted to take in everything. His footloose life had convinced him that "we are nothing more than tiny rubber balls bouncing about a world. Other worlds exist, too. Other people on them. Whoever is responsible [for our existence] is keeping us in mystery. So why fuss about it? When the end comes, we are like an autumn leaf blown across a graveyard."[2]

Even so, there was one leaf Kimmel intended to revivify. In Paris in the twenties he had met Ernest Hemingway, F. Scott Fitzgerald, John Dos Passos, and Ezra Pound. He thought they were all amazingly talented, but the writer he most admired was Carl Sandburg. A friend and fellow Illinoisan, Sandburg was well into his multivolume Lincoln biography, and Kimmel was stirred. While it might be unfair to say he envied the older man, he admired and emulated him. Like Sandburg, Kimmel sang and played the guitar and wrote poems and smoked pipes, and now he would attempt some history of his own. He wanted to write a biography of the Booths, America's great acting family.

The tree-lined lane led to a gate. Beyond it a gravel drive wound up to a quaint-looking brick house shaded by a sycamore. Ella V. Mahoney, a severe-looking white-haired woman, lived here, and she answered his knock. Yes, this was the Booth home, she told him. Her husband, Sam Kyle, had purchased it from the family in 1878. She married Sam the following year and came here when she was a bride of twenty. Sam was long dead, as was a second husband, but she still lived on the old place. Her entire life had been spent within one mile of this house. She was now seventy-five years old.

Mrs. Mahoney welcomed Kimmel inside, built a fire in the dining room, and fixed the traveler breakfast. She knew little about the Booths when she came here, she explained, but over the years she met neighbors who remembered them, actors who shared their stages, even Booth family members. Most were strangers who just wanted to touch base with their own past and knocked on the door as he had. Once Woodrow Wilson came by. H. L. Mencken, too. Each visitor had a memory, and her interest grew. She began to read, collect relics, and write down stories she heard. Back before the Depression she had even published a little book about the Booths and Tudor Hall, as the house was known. Time and circumstance had made her the custodian of their legacy, and she was proud of it, proud of the Booths, proud even of John Wilkes. One thing more. She was "tired of hearing so many good things about Lincoln," she told Kimmel. The man was crude and uneducated. Were he alive, he could never be elected president today. "Wait till this country has to put down its first great uprising of the blacks against the whites," she warned. "Then people will not have the regard for Lincoln they have. The people will then see that J. W. B. was right." As a journalist Kimmel was trained to listen to all sorts of nonsense, so he heard her out with the politeness required of an uninvited guest. Little wonder, he thought, that people called Mrs. Mahoney "the Keeper of the Flame."[3]

There were a few locals around who still remembered the Booths, and Mrs. Mahoney offered to take Kimmel to interview them. Their first stop was the home of Elijah Whistler, a former schoolmate of John Wilkes Booth. At ninety-three, the retired dairy farmer retained a sharp mind and strong opinions. His older brother William had died while serving in the Union Army. Understandably, he was no unreflective Southerner like

Mrs. Mahoney. Lincoln's assassination was terrible, he told Kimmel. "Everybody was stunned—couldn't believe Booth would do such a thing," he said. Well, Kimmel speculated, the assassin was probably bad from the start. Some people just were. After all, "he once shot a Negro on the farm."

"That's a damn lie!" exclaimed Whistler, visibly upset at the statement. The old man was so agitated that Kimmel feared he might work himself up to a heart attack or stroke. Settling back in his chair, Whistler jabbed a finger at Kimmel and said, "Johnnie was kind and gentle."[4]

MRS. MAHONEY'S FARM WAS LOCATED twenty-seven miles northeast of Baltimore between the hamlet of Churchville and the village of Bel Air in Harford County. John Wilkes Booth was born here on Thursday, May 10, 1838, in a log house no longer present at the time of Kimmel's visit.[5] Mary Ann (or Anne) Holmes Booth, the baby's mother, was thirty-five at the time. Junius Brutus Booth, his father, was forty-two—and drunk at a local tavern. He was hauled home "in a very jolly condition" to meet the newborn.[6]

It was erroneously reported in 1865 that the name Wilkes was given to the baby to honor the Baltimore merchant Jim Wilkes, a friend of the father.[7] In fact, the name was long established in the Booth family. The baby's great-uncle was Wilkes Booth, a London silversmith. This man had a son named John Wilkes Booth, Junius's contemporary and first cousin, who handled annuities that Junius inherited from their grandmother. These family members were named for John Wilkes, a relative who was a noted political radical and onetime Lord Mayor of London. The Wilkes name attached to the family because the mother of Richard Booth, the baby's grandfather, was a Wilkes. Richard lived most of his life in London, admired Wilkes greatly, and imbibed the politician's potent democratic principles. It was said that he brought Junius as an infant into Wilkes's presence for a benediction toward the end of the great radical's life. John Wilkes Booth grew up of proud of his middle name. "It meant liberty," he would say.[8]

Junius was a noted English actor, and Mary Ann the daughter of a Lambeth seed merchant. She was selling flowers outside a theater the night they met. The two fell in love and married at a friend's home on January 18, 1821. A few weeks later they sailed for Brazil, but during a stopover on Madeira, they decided instead to go to the United States. Over the next year Booth performed as far north as Boston, as far south as

Charleston, and as far west as New Orleans. Having sized up his new country, he settled in Baltimore. The city was attractive and centrally located to his work, but when outbreaks of yellow fever and smallpox hit, Junius's proclivity for reclusiveness took over, and he searched the countryside for a place of refuge.[9] Outside the village of Bel Air he leased a tract of 150-plus acres for a period of one thousand years.[10] (As a legal alien he couldn't own the land outright.) Junius knew no one here, nor did he care to. "They wished to be retired from so much company and only have a few acquaintances in this strange land," recalled Elizabeth Rogers, one of their new neighbors.[11]

The young couple chose an isolated spot. The property was located off the rough coach road connecting Bel Air and Havre de Grace. A narrow track of white clay, still looking more like a gulley than a lane when John was born sixteen years later, led off the road into thick woods. One-quarter mile down this crooked trail was a clearing with a strong spring. At this sheltered site the Booths put down their American roots. "A sharper contrast to life on the stage, with its travel, glare, and tumult, could scarcely be fancied, and this was no doubt what the actor sought," wrote Walter E. McCann, one of John's contemporaries.[12]

Junius erected a two-story log house here. A kitchen was added on the east side of the cottage, and another addition, never finished, was begun on the west side. The cabin was plastered and whitewashed, with window-sashes, shutters, and doors painted red. The result was unpretentious but snug. The four-room interior was equally simple. Furnishings, like a rustic chair made of tree roots, were odd or old-fashioned. Heavy pewter plates dressed a well-worn maple table. Two or three shelves of books of history and literature formed a library; a few engravings on historical themes adorned the walls. There was a spinning wheel, a corner cupboard, and a row of wall pegs on which hung coats, newspapers, and an almanac. A high brass fender screened the large fireplace. Over the next few years, at intervals in his acting tours, Junius planted fruit trees and built a dairy, a barn with stables, a cider-press, and a pond. A traditional zigzag fence enclosed the property.[13]

Mary Ann, a native of London, the largest city in the world in the 1820s, did not like this pioneer-like existence, but her husband did, and that was all that mattered to him. "Anything is better than a nagging shrew," he warned her, and she took his words to heart.[14] Mary Ann never argued with him, recalled Elizabeth, their neighbor. It startled her to see how unprepared the newcomer was for such rough rural conditions. She found the family eating hardtack out of a barrel since Mary Ann did not know how to bake. Elizabeth jumped in, teaching her how to make cornbread, wheat bread, and beaten biscuits, consoling her for her frequent and laughable failures at the round Dutch oven. The two women, who were the same age, became best friends. "Aunty Rogers," as the Booth children called her, helped deliver John into the world and nursed him when he was a baby.[15]

Richard Booth, Junius's father, arrived at what he termed "Robinson Crusoe's Island" in 1823 to join the family.[16] Tall, thin, with long white hair worn in a queue, he was an antique dressed in knee breeches and buckle shoes.[17] The elderly London lawyer had no aptitude for farming, but when his son Junius was away, he was competent to pass along orders to the hired hands as well as provide an additional adult presence at the farm. He could also be counted on to help slaves run away to Pennsylvania, forcing Junius on occasion to compensate their owners in an effort to keep the old man out of trouble. In addition to his well-known crutched walking stick, Richard had obviously brought from England a hatred for despotism that ensnared his idol John Wilkes in trouble with the British government. A love of classical heroes showed in his naming Junius for a Roman general who put to death two of his own sons who favored monarchy. John T. Ford of Baltimore, later a famous theatrical manager, termed these beliefs "French or red-republican ideas." As a child Junius had been steeped in these ideas, forced to copy down as sacred truths any stray political thoughts that occurred to Richard. John was one year old when the grandfather died and had no memory of him, but he did receive as a legacy a disposition toward political extremism. "John Wilkes Booth had the family trait the grandfather had," continued Ford, who worked with three generations of Booth family actors. "Some called it 'an eccentricity of genius.' It was akin to madness, if not actual insanity. Thousands can recall it."[18]

John was the ninth of ten children born to Junius and Mary Ann. Junius Jr.—called June—was the eldest, born in Charleston, South Carolina, in 1821. Thereafter the floor cradles at the farm filled with clocklike regularity—Rosalie (1823), Henry (1825), Mary Ann (1827), Frederick (1829), Elizabeth (1831), Edwin (1833), Asia (1835), and John Wilkes (1838). Joseph, the final child, was born in Baltimore in 1840. Four of this number died of illnesses in childhood. Henry died a few years before

John's birth when Junius was on a visit to London, and he was interred there. Mary Ann, Frederick, and Elizabeth died at the farm within weeks of each other and were buried in a hillside meadow west of the house.[19] Born after their deaths, John knew these siblings only by their small mounds behind a cast-iron fence that enclosed the family cemetery. Later, when he farmed the property in the 1850s, he mowed carefully and quietly around the burial plot, never speaking about his long-dead sisters and brother.[20]

"SO LOVABLE," EDWIN said of his younger brother. "He was of a gentle disposition, full of fun. All his family found a source of joy in his boyish and confiding nature."[21] The playful youngster was the hands-down favorite of both parents. He delighted Junius.[22] "But," wrote their contemporary Frank A. Burr, a journalist who studied the family, "John developed too early and was too restless and emphatic to suit the grand old man."[23] Edwin was more tractable, so Junius turned to him for companionship. While Mary Ann always thought June was the handsomest of her sons, perhaps because he looked the most like his father, she said John "was the most pleasure and comfort to me of all my sons, the most affectionate."[24] Over the years a special, some would say psychic, bond developed between them. "The love and sympathy between him and his mother were very close, very strong," wrote Anne Hartley Gilbert, a character actress who knew the family well. "No matter how far apart they were, she seemed to know, in some mysterious way, when anything was wrong with him. If he were ill, or unfit to play, he would often receive a letter of sympathy, counsel, and warning, written when she could not possibly have received any news of him. He has told me this himself."[25]

As John toddled into childhood, he grew much attached to his sister Rose. Handed much of the household management, as eldest daughters in large families often were, Rose busied herself in the dining room, the kitchen, the pantry, and the springhouse, where everyone took it for granted that the uncomplaining teenager belonged. Peaceful and sympathetic, she was a sort of unbeatified saint, and her little brother followed her around like a puppy. "John was her idolized favorite and pet," recalled Mrs. Mahoney.[26] On Sundays she would dress him, take his hand, and walk with him the half mile along the post road to Mount Zion Methodist Church, where the Reverend John S. Gorsuch was visiting pastor. They went often enough for John to earn a book as a reward for faithful attendance.[27]

John's favorite outing with Rose was a visit to Aunty Rogers. A stout woman with a happy face and smile wrinkles at the corners of her eyes, she was the Booths' immediate neighbor, and the trip across the fields to her kitchen was always rewarded with a slice of buttered bread with sugar. The two women would watch in amusement at how quietly he sat while eating it. When trouble with John arose on the farm, Aunty Rogers came, like the day he got a large cut on his head and she was called to dress and stitch the wound. "John was so kind, tender-hearted, and good," she remembered. "A light-hearted, happy little boy. Full of jokes and fun."[28]

Not long before her death in 1899, she told Mrs. Mahoney that "when JWB was a fugitive [in 1865], she baked a ham and kept other food cooked to give him if he should come to her, for provisions to eat in hiding or on a flight to Canada. She sat up all night watching for him with a light placed as a signal in her window to guide him." As Aunty Rogers explained, "I loved him."[29]

With Junius often absent on tour and Mary Ann overwhelmed with household and family responsibilities, two other people helped keep the farm—and to some extent even the family—on an even keel. Ann Hall was an African American woman in her twenties when John was born. She was described as having "an ample figure, serious face, and long yellow cheeks." Her husband, Joseph, was a tall, dark-skinned man who wore a broad hat and carried a spelling book in hopes of learning to read. He handled the chores of field and barn while Ann took care of domestic matters. Joseph was free when John was born, thanks to Junius, who hired him and allowed him to work for wages. Joseph saved the money, hiding it behind a sill along the back wall of the stable, until he had enough to purchase the freedom of Ann and their children. Rowland Rogers, her owner, would not permit Ann, while still a slave, to live with Joseph, and once he refused to summon her when her child was choking to death. She was understandably bitter about her bondage, but Junius was kind, and she was profoundly loyal to the actor and his family. She spent so much time tending to John that he was jokingly referred to as her foster child. When a neighbor asked Ann after Lincoln's death if she would give the assassin food and shelter should he come her way, her answer made clear that John had won her heart as surely as he had Aunty Rogers's. "Indeed, I would, honey," she replied. "Give him all dat I have."[30]

JUNIUS EXPLAINED TO HIS CHILDREN that he made his living in a very simple way. "I amuse," he said.[31] At this he was exceptional. During the

1820s and 1830s he was the leading tragedian on the American stage. When on point, he was a uniquely gifted performer capable of powerful emotion and excitement. When distracted or disinclined, he mumbled lines, dressed inappropriately, annoyed audiences, refused curtain calls, walked out on performances, or failed to appear for them.

Added to these eccentricities was something darker and more ominous. Edwin traced it to an episode in June 1824, when his father was acting in New York City. Believing a false report that Mary Ann had died, Junius went mad and attempted to stab another actor, Henry John Wallace, who happened to walk by.[32] This was the first in a series of disturbing incidents that brought the father and the family shame and notoriety. By the time John was born, Junius had compiled an unenviable résumé of trouble. He had shot one man in the face, assaulted others, attempted suicide on three occasions, and been jailed in four states. With the deaths of the children in the mid-1830s, Junius grew even odder and the number of disturbances increased. In 1835 he wrote to Andrew Jackson threatening to cut the president's throat.[33] He wandered naked in a snowstorm, sought Christian burial for a bushel of pigeons, and tried to sell his son Edwin for five dollars. The father's torments were at flood tide at the time John was born. Two months before the event, Junius made an unprovoked attack on the comedian Thomas Flynn, a friend. He seized an andiron and attempted to kill Flynn with it while he slept. Flynn fought back, breaking Junius's nose.[34] A leading newspaper in Baltimore published a rebuke of the actor. Its headline asked a question on many minds: "Is this man a maniac?"[35]

Alcohol was the catalyst for most of these incidents. Junius claimed he drank to buffer the emotional wear and tear of acting. Unfortunately he had a taste for what his friends called the jolly god.[36] Liquor pushed his delicately balanced mind out of kilter, and he became a potential danger to himself and others.

The demons waned on occasion. There were extended periods when he was entirely lucid onstage, a pleasure to live with, and a delight to know. His behavior was best at the farm. He purposely kept no liquor there, and, free of the need to please others, he could regain his peace of mind and expend his energies by hoeing in the turnip patch.[37] Here he was at his happiest. Still accounted peculiar, he was accepted as an industrious person with a conscientious wife and good children, a man who paid his bills on time and left others alone. Said Aunty Rogers: "He was a gentleman and a gentle man." Even at the farm, however, the storm could rage, as she well knew. When his favorite horse, Peacock, died, he broke down completely. Convinced that Mary Ann could bring the horse back to life, he forced her to wrap herself in a sheet and mount the dead animal. As she sat riveted with fear, he marched around her with a gun, reading from a book. Joseph Hall ran to fetch the Rogerses, who disarmed the father and led the terror-stricken mother to safety.[38]

Mary Ann never attempted to fix her wreck of a husband. How could she? She simply tidied up after him. Declining to question anything he did or said, no matter how extravagant, she picked up the pieces and carried on. John and his siblings were taught to follow her example and "regard these periodic tortures of mind, these seasons of abstraction, with sad and reverent forbearance."[39] Conventional, placid, and long-suffering, Mary Ann held things together, wrote James Young Jr., a friend of Aunty Rogers, through her patience and her ability to contend with whatever came next.[40] Remarkably, she remained upbeat. "My mother was like sunshine," recalled Asia.[41] The journalist George Alfred Townsend felt her struggles ennobled her and lifted those around her. "The realities of a new country and a sinister, timorous life in a forest patch, her love for her handsome brood, and her despair of her husband raised Mrs. Booth. *She made men out of mimes*."[42]

JOHN'S FORMAL EDUCATION started before a small rectangular blackboard in a one-room schoolhouse across the road from the entrance to the farm. "He was by no means a studious boy," recalled George Y. Maynadier, a classmate. "He was not deficient in intelligence and brains—very much in fact the other way—but he was not bookish, not devoted to his studies."[43]

Better opportunities awaited at Bel Air Academy, where Edwin Arnold, a former Anglican minister with a doctorate in civil law, was principal.[44] The strong-minded Arnold was a no-nonsense teacher who considered education a higher calling than the ministry, and he meant business when he tolled the deeply resonant bell in the cupola atop the fortress-like school to summon his pupils.[45]

John perplexed Arnold. The principal believed that young minds should feel a natural pleasure in learning, yet John was no case in point. Classes were difficult for him. Memorization was challenging, spelling problematic, and math nightmarish. Hunched forward over his desk, his mouth firmly set, John clasped his brow with both hands as if he could push knowledge into his head. The problem was that, unlike his brothers, he was a slower learner. "He had to plod," recalled his sister Asia. "His was not a quickly receptive mind." As a result he often lagged behind his classmates.[46] These childhood struggles were reflected in an adulthood of mediocre writing and orthography. In one modern collection of fifty-five of his letters—the bulk of his known correspondence—he apologized in two-thirds of them for inelegant grammar or misspelling or blamed a bad pen, poor light, haste, or low spirits. "I am, at the best of times, the worst letter writer in the world," he lamented to a friend.[47]

On a certain Friday night, when Arnold was believed to be safely out of the way, John participated in a memorable school "blow-out." Deciding to throw themselves a party, members of the debating society spent the club's dues on "pitchers of hot stuff" purchased by the larger boys at a hotel. They played cards, sang songs, and drank. As the hot stuff disappeared, so did self-restraint. "Pandemonium broke loose," recalled Maynadier, a happy participant in the near-riot that ensued. Hijinks and blood-curdling screams startled the sleepy village. John and a few others were caught, saved only by the fact "that so many were engaged in the affair, equally guilty, that expulsion as a punishment would have broken up the school."

Though he was popular at the academy, John hated being there. He preferred hanging about the stable and watering the horses. "He was fond of the saddle and learned to ride with his first pair of boots," wrote James Shettel, a historian who spoke with John's classmates.[48] Delighted when Rose gave him a saddle for his birthday, he quickly displayed the balance, coordination, and quiet attentiveness characteristic of a natural-born rider. "Booth, sitting his horse like a centaur, was no common horseman," wrote the actor Charles Warwick. "His head erect, his riding whip more for ornament than use, his slender steel spur scarcely seemed to touch the stirrup as he rode."[49] He was exceedingly fond of Cola di Rienzi, his beautiful black colt, and taught him to neigh, stamp, bow, follow, and lie down as if dead.[50] Cola provided John a power and sense of independence comparable only to that experienced by a modern-day youth with his first car. Riding the open country, plunging through streams, and exploring forest trails brought a sense of profound happiness to the boy, said his friend Thomas Harbin, later a famous Confederate agent.[51]

Early on it was clear that John loved excitement.[52] "He had a twinkle in his eye that seemed to say, 'If I could only think of a good joke to play on you, I should be supremely happy,'" recalled H. Stearns Smiley, who knew him professionally later in life.[53] Maynadier caught the receiving end of his humor one July afternoon as he and others lounged on a porch in Bel Air. What seemed like a land mine suddenly went off under their feet. John had thrown fireworks at them from a nearby hotel just to shake things up. Another prank involved Cola. When John rode to Bel Air, he would lean out of the saddle with the colt at a gallop and snatch up any small child walking along. It was all in fun, and he never hurt anyone, but it was reckless, and he was ordered to stop it.[54] "John was a wild and impetuous youth," said Robert Hanna, a schoolmate who recalled these occasions in a 1906 interview. "The older folks just shook their heads."[55]

Junius tried to channel this energy into something productive. The father had always admired furniture makers, whose artistry produced results more tangible than his own, so he fitted out a workshop for John with hammers, saws, and planes. Happily, the practical nature of woodworking appealed to the boy. He made a set of chairs with laurel wood bent cleverly into curves for the arms and back. He also built a handsome pine sewing table as a gift for his mother. The piece featured triangles of oak bark forming a six-pointed star inlaid in the center. Around the three-cornered base of the table were symmetrically spaced sycamore knots with laurel branches twining up like vines.[56]

The wood for these projects and even for the fireplaces and stove at the farm came from trees downed by age or storms. Junius ordered that no live tree on the property ever be cut and no animal killed for food. Horses and cattle employed for farm work were to be treated humanely. The livestock were to be watered twice a day, the dogs given clean bed-straw weekly. Hunting and fishing were strictly forbidden. Even snakes could not be harmed or flies swatted. Here, in one little corner of Maryland, the boar, the deer, and the partridge existed free from fear of man. The world was cruel enough, declared the father. "Let the poor devils live."[57]

IN 1845 BALTIMORE drew Junius back. Its railroad connections were convenient for his professional travels and its opportunities superior for his children, so he purchased a house in the city, and the Booths split their time between there and the farm.[58] The move had a profound effect on John. Baltimore, bigger than Philadelphia or Boston, was the second-largest city in the United States. It was a dynamic and enterprising warren of docks, factories, mills, colleges, banks, roundhouses, and hospitals, all dominated by a skyline thick with church steeples. The contrast with the Harford countryside was striking. As a result John's childhood was more cosmopolitan than that of most others who made their way to the Confederate cause. While their roots tended to be exclusively rural, his mixed the country with the most sophisticated city life the South offered.

The Booth house at No. 62 North Exeter Street was located in Baltimore's "Old Town" just east of the city's commercial core. It was a substantial brick town house with a roomy attic and a side passage leading to a sizable backyard. The house nestled unobtrusively into the neighborhood of residences and small shops. The Booths had a banker living on one side and a grocer living above her business on the other. The street before the house was tree-lined. Nearby residences were adorned with colorfully painted shutters, and doors had large brass door-knockers.[59] The overall feeling along North Exeter was quiet, settled, and middle-class. Although their house looked plain (except for the Italianate touches in the door surround and cornice), Mary Ann and Rose worked hard to give it a cheery and comfortable interior. How proud they were when the actress Rosalie Pelby exclaimed, "This is a *home*, not merely a habitation."[60]

John's education continued with Susan Hyde, who ran a small school on nearby High Street. Preceptress Hyde was a young woman with glasses, corkscrew curls, and a handy rattan cane. As modest as her establishment, she was described by Edwin as "a woman all through—in the true sense of that word—gentle in manner, soft in heart, and low in her estimation of her worth."[61] Asia, also a pupil, met her future husband, John Clarke Sleeper, at the school. Irish-born Martin J. Kerney, John's next teacher, was an energetic and civic-minded Catholic layman. Kerney encouraged his students in public speaking.[62] This suited John, who was always ready to have his say. "From early boyhood he was argumentative and fervid in debate. His discussion was didactic," recalled Asia. "When his turn came, he would wear his argument threadbare. He meant what he cared to utter."[63]

When John was nine, he helped Edwin fit up a latticework arbor in the backyard as a playhouse. With a gaily patched bed quilt for a curtain and a row of tallow candles for footlights, the Theatre Royal, as it was cheerily called, opened for business. One large copper cent secured a seat in the best part of the house—the yard. Jack Sleeper, whose mother ran a small hotel, was lead support. Edwin fancied a career in comedy, Sleeper in tragedy. Ironically, they switched genres as adults and made fortunes.

Nevertheless, Sleeper looked a perfect villain. Wrapped in a dark cloak and wearing a tall hat, he waved a dagger and threatened destruction, only to be dragged away and thrown over "yonder cliff," namely a box on the edge of the stage.[64]

Since Edwin and Sleeper were older and larger, "they were wont to put on airs over us younger boys," recalled Theodore Hamilton of himself, John, and their friend Henry Stuart (later known as Stuart Robson). "There was a great gulf between us."[65] When John stuck his head through a window to annoy them, one of the big boys threw an oyster shell, which whacked him on the forehead.[66] He would not be deterred, however, so Edwin permitted him to play a triangle. Soon John graduated to speaking roles. On one occasion at the arbor playhouse, Edwin's villainous Gessler forced John's William Tell to shoot an apple off the head of his own son, played by a trembling youngster named Marion Kerner. John did this successfully, only to be asked by Gessler what he would have done if his arrow had missed and killed the boy. "I would have aimed an arrow at thee, my King," John replied in a monotone.

"No, no!" exclaimed the elder Booth, suddenly bursting forward. "That is not the proper rendering. This is the way Tell would answer. 'I would have killed *thee*, my King!'" the father said, emphasizing the pronoun.[67] John required no second lesson about putting passion into his parts.

"Wilkes was immensely popular," recalled George L. Stout, one of the childhood company. "All the boys liked him," even after John, Stuart, and Hamilton stole the set-piece in an effort to start a rival theater. Stout and Sleeper tracked the miscreants down and won the scenery back in a fist-fight. John enjoyed such rough-and-tumble. Edwin, who had a lamb for a pet, did not and often let others stand up for him. Stout remembered when Edwin was returning home with several of his father's foils that he had borrowed, and a local bully grabbed and broke them. Edwin began to cry, and Stout was obliged to confront the offender. John would have pitched head-long into the troublemaker. "Wilkes was always ready for a fight."[68]

Stuart was having breakfast one morning when he heard a tap on the window. "Looking up, I saw John, his nose flattened against the pane, motioning vehemently for me to come out." The two went to a nearby wheelwright's lot, where "he showed me two cats that he had tied up in such a way that a movement of the one would produce pain to the other. He seemed to thoroughly enjoy their discomfiture." On another occasion Stuart saw John chase a cat up through an attic and out onto a roof so steep "that if he had made the least slip he would have fallen and probably killed himself. But he never stopped till he got the cat!"[69] At the farm these poor animals fared no better. "He was always shooting cats and killed off almost the entire breed in his neighborhood."[70] Stuart observed that John, who was about twelve at the time, "had a mania for killing cats and went about it with enthusiasm that was quite remarkable."

Behavior of this nature by a child is exceptionally troubling. It has been recognized for centuries as an ill omen. In 1693 the philosopher John Locke wrote of children who acted in this manner that "the custom of tormenting and killing beasts will, by degrees, harden their minds even toward man, and they who delight in the suffering of inferior creatures will not be apt to be very compassionate or benign to those of their own kind."[71] Modern researchers note an association between repeated intentional abuse of animals and a later disposition toward a variety of antisocial behaviors, including all kinds of violence. The disorder is classically interpreted as the abusing child's way to vent frustration and anger, often in response to parental cruelty, neglect, or mental illness. A child who exhibits such behavior is disturbingly insensitive to the suffering of other living things.[72]

Oddly, John's ability to experience feelings of empathy with other animals was not compromised. He was fond of dogs. Once, when a fellow passenger on a ferry threw a setter into the river, "Booth pulled him [back] on board, caressed the dog, and bitterly denounced the fellow who would treat a dumb animal so cruelly." Protective of butterflies and lightning bugs, "he would go out of his way to avoid injuring them," recalled Asia. When she attempted to skewer a katydid for her insect collection, he rescued it, walked over to a tree, and placed it safely on in a leaf. "Katy shall sing tonight out in the sycamores," he told her. His love of horses was unbounded. When he was in his twenties, John saw a teamster beat a horse that was unable to pull a wagon out of a mud hole. He was so incensed that he seized the whip from the man's hand and punched him.[73]

"THERE WAS A skeleton in the father's closet," wrote the playwright and poet John Hill Hewitt. "It haunted him. He hoped, and so did the members of his family, that the rattling dry bones would not be exposed to public view." Unfortunately, in 1846 that occurred. A woman named Adelaide Delannoy approached Hewitt's desk in the business office of Baltimore's Howard Athenaeum. She stated in accented English that she needed to speak to Booth. The woman was tall and refined and wore a black lace cap. She had once been pretty, but hard times had taken their toll, and both her beauty and her fortunes were as faded as her silk dress. Only a sense of dignity remained.[74]

Adelaide had a secret. The Brussels native was Junius's legal wife. She had married him in 1815 and gave birth to two children, a son and a daughter, fathered by him. Junius then quit Minnie, as he called her, for Mary Ann. The couple never divorced. He did send her an annual stipend faithfully, but when this payment was insufficient, Adelaide sought charity from Junius's brother actors and friends in London. The daughter died, and the son, named Richard for his grandfather and Junius for his father, came to America in 1843. The intelligent and delicately built young man sought out Junius, saw his prosperous condition, and learned of his second family.[75] The trans-Atlantic wife, as Hewitt, struggling for words, titled her, was apprised of the facts and came to see for herself. She spied out the Exeter Street house where John Wilkes *Holmes* and his family lived. (No one there was entitled to the Booth name, she insisted, since the father was not legally married to Mary Ann.) With such a home as well as a large estate in the country, Junius obviously was thriving. "My lawyer will fall on his back like a bomb," she promised her sister Therese.[76]

"You here!" Booth exclaimed in a growl when he saw Minnie in Hewitt's office. Adelaide, her arms folded, met his gaze defiantly and reminded him in a scornful tone that he had a son named Richard. Hewitt realized he was in the wrong place, hastily excused himself, and heard no more. All he knew was that a short time later a hackney cab was ordered and the visitor departed in it.

Adelaide went to the farm. Furious and menacing, she announced, "I am the wife of Junius Brutus Booth. I have come with my son to claim our rights."[77] Mary Ann was stunned. She knew that her husband had been married before, but she also thought he had been properly divorced and was free to marry again. It never occurred to her to question that.

Shy and nonconfrontational, Mary Ann was not curious by nature, a characteristic that pleased Junius, who believed—and proclaimed in her presence—that a woman's job was to stay home and keep quiet.[78] Mary Ann realized instantly that her own wedding had been a legal sham, her husband was an adulterer, and her children were illegitimate. Her trust had been terribly abused. Rose, the only family member home when Adelaide appeared, watched Mary Ann wither before the fiery stranger. "This

was a crushing blow, an exquisite chagrin to her fine mother," recalled
Mrs. Mahoney, who learned the story from Ann Hall.

Weary and chastened, yet finally relieved of a guilt that had haunted
him for twenty-five years, Junius acceded to the inevitable. On May 7,
1847, the disgraced husband gave Adelaide one thousand dollars, and she
settled in for the residency period required for a divorce, at the end of
which time additional rewards could be harvested.[79]

The matter did not end there, however. Adelaide liked the jolly god as
much as Junius did, and when drunk she engaged in a distressing pattern
of behavior. "It was a custom with her to haunt the Baltimore markets for
a chance meeting with the woman who had usurped her place," noted
Eliza Mitchell Ward, Mary Ann's niece. "These encounters were as much
avoided by the one as sought for by the other. She assailed [Mary Ann]
with violent, often coarse language and opprobrious epithets, which the
other never resented but cut short by the speediest exit." A crude revenge
for Adelaide, it was painful public humiliation for Mary Ann.[80]

In February 1851 Adelaide filed for divorce on the grounds of deser-
tion. "Booth came to the United States in company with a woman with
whom he has been in the habit of adulterous intercourse," she alleged to
the Baltimore County Court. This woman had a large number of children,
"the fruits of said adulterous intercourse." Junius offered no defense, ad-
mitting the truth of her statements, and two months later the divorce was
granted. On May 10, 1851—John's thirteenth birthday—the father obtained a license to marry Mary Ann and appears to have done so on that
day.[81] "It was tardy justice to the mother of the Booth children," wrote a
New York journalist who dug up the story forty years later.[82]

Although John could hardly miss the strange tension in the household
or the grim faces of his elders, he was too young to understand the scandal
convulsing his family. Told nothing, he realized only that he and his siblings had suddenly become the objects of gossip, "objects nonetheless vulnerable for not knowing why they were attacked," said Mrs. Mahoney.[83]
In time he learned scraps of the story and finally got the details from Rose
when he was twenty.[84] The odd reality was that he did not feel illegitimate. He did not feel extraneous or neglected. He enjoyed a childhood in
which he was wanted, loved, and admired. Therefore, whatever the facts,
it was understandable for him to join Edwin and insist that their father
had only one wife: their mother.[85] The truth, thought cousin Eliza, was
locked behind "gates so securely closed and guarded by the children, in

their struggle for professional rank and social position, that even a legal inquisition could hardly have forced them ajar."[86]

Nevertheless, in his heart of hearts, John was angered by Junius's misconduct toward his beloved mother, and he moved in a boyish way to distinguish himself from his father. He began putting his initials on things. He carved them on the big beech tree near the springhouse at the farm and scattered them throughout the woods on the property. He even branded himself. On his left hand he tattooed his initials, surrounded by a wreath of stars, in India ink.[87] The initials affirmed his identity as a Booth, but they also asserted his individuality. He was himself and not his father. Junius was a great actor—the greatest—but John could be a better man.

SOME RESPITE FROM scandal came when Booth was sent to Milton School for Boys, a boarding school in Sparks, Maryland. A classical academy for boys ages ten to thirteen, it was operated by John Emerson Lamb, an elder of the Society of Friends. Lamb expected students "to exhibit in their social intercourse a pleasant and obliging disposition, to avoid turbulent and quarrelsome behavior, and to adhere strictly to the truth on all occasions."[88] The school was academically demanding, but its homelike atmosphere— warm yellow pine floors, low-beam ceilings, and large fireplaces gleaming with brass cookware, all managed in a pastoral setting by a headmaster as gentle as his name—made the time pass pleasantly. John liked being there and put his initials on the stone step leading to the back porch, on the building wall, and on the large rock in front of the schoolhouse.[89] "Jack, as he was called, was very popular, a good swimmer, ball-player, tree-climber, etc," said his fellow student Clarence Cobb. "But he would not study. He was very slow at his books." Cobb also claimed that John bullied the smaller boys cruelly until one fought back and put him in his place.[90] Cobb's statement does not square with either the ethos of the school or the fond feelings that Lamb entertained for John. Lamb's granddaughter Esther recalled, "He held him in such esteem that he referred to him as one of *his* boys."[91]

Mary Ann visited on the day of the annual school picnic. She wore lilacs and a dress of pale gray so as not to appear too conspicuous among the Quaker company of lisse caps, plain kerchiefs, and broad-brimmed hats. A dinner for three hundred was held on the grounds, followed by the awarding of school prizes and recitations. Alone on a platform, John did several scenes as Shylock from *The Merchant of Venice* and was warmly applauded. Smiling and blushing, he bowed repeatedly.[92]

In the woods near the school were English Gypsies. John saw them, and curiosity led him to go over and have his fortune told. He learned that he had been born under an unlucky star. "You've a bad hand," an old crone told him. "It's full enough of sorrow. Full of trouble. You'll die young and leave plenty to mourn you. You'll have a fast life—short, but a grand one. Young sir, I've never seen a worse hand. I wish I hadn't seen it." John copied her troubling message in pencil on a strip of paper. When he showed it to Asia, she told him to forget it. "It was only a Gipsey's tattle for money," she said reassuringly. He agreed, laughing dismissively at the prophecy, but the words lingered in his mind. He was superstitious by nature, and he studied the paper so often that it grew tattered through folding and unfolding. Well, he concluded, "the Gypsey said I was to have a grand life. No matter how short, then, so it be grand."[93]

Gypsies aside, John felt personally unlucky. This self-perception showed early in his life. When he and some friends were setting off fireworks in Exeter Street, they annoyed an adult who sent a constable after them. Everyone escaped the dragnet but John. He was collared, hauled off to the watch-house, lectured, and fined. "That is my luck," he told his sisters.[94] No matter what game or mischief was afoot, he was the one sure to be scraped, kicked, nabbed, trounced, or trampled. His saving grace was his resilience.

On a September evening in 1850 John, along with Lamb and his son Eli, climbed the hill to Gunpowder Meetinghouse, a gray fieldstone building near the school, to attend the wedding of Abraham Scott and Ann Price, two Friends from Baltimore County.[95] After the simple ceremony, a queue formed. Traditionally, Friends have no clergy, so those present signed the marriage certificate as witnesses. John came forward to write "John W. Booth," his customary signature when young.[96] The name affirmed that, as a member of a loving community, he pledged his support of the young couple in their life together. It was an eye-opening example of how marriage was meant to be—open and joyous, not tardy and furtive.

John liked Eli Lamb but grew particularly close to another fellow student, Thomas Gorsuch. Tom's older brother was the Gorsuch who preached at Mount Zion Church near the farm. Both were sons of Edward Gorsuch, a prosperous farmer who lived near the school. A hospitable figure in the academy neighborhood, "the father was all that a man of honour should be," wrote John. On September 11, 1851, the elder Gorsuch was killed and a third son, named Dickinson, was severely wounded at Christiana, Pennsylvania, while attempting to reclaim four runaway slaves. No one was ever punished for Edward Gorsuch's death. The incident created a firestorm of sectional controversy, pitting the rights of slave-owners under the Fugitive Slave Act of 1850 to reclaim their human property against the "higher law" rights of runaways to seek their freedom. Connected socially with the family, thirteen-year-old John was deeply disturbed by the incident. The Christiana tragedy was the first political incident to catch his attention.[97]

Writing about these events nine years later, Booth expressed great sympathy for the Gorsuches, but none for the slaves. John did not hate African Americans. An insubstantial people, "Nigs" (as he called them) were lucky to live in the United States even in bondage. "Witness their elevation in happiness and enlightenment above their race elsewhere," he wrote. Their basic problem was they did not belong here. "This country was formed for the *white*, not the black man. And, looking upon African slavery from the same standpoint held by those noble framers of our Constitution, I for one have ever considered it one of the greatest blessings (both for themselves and us) that God ever bestowed upon a favored nation." As far as alleged cruelty to slaves went, he claimed to have seen worse treatment by father to son.[98]

John could be kind to individual African Americans like the Halls. He bought candy for the children and listened patiently to old Joe, their garrulous father. But, as Mrs. Mahoney wrote astutely, "this close association gave occasion for understanding, but also for an arrogant, contemptuous paternalism toward Negroes with all the dangers implied in such an attitude."[99]

ASIA, IN BIOGRAPHIES of her father published in 1865 and 1882, painted a picture of happy family life. Her niece Blanche, who had no emotional investment in such tales, presented a different take on life with the Booths. Blanche was June's daughter and nine years old in 1851 when her father brought her to live with the family after his marriage to the comedienne Clementina DeBar failed. During the two years she stayed with them, she grew to adore Mary Ann and to learn that "John had a disposition as beautiful as can be imagined." Her grandfather Junius, with his closely cropped iron gray hair and darting hawklike eyes, frightened her. He was naturally glum, silent, and unapproachable.[100] Worst of all, he was violent when opposed. On occasion he belittled Blanche. When she was unable to spell the word *sugar*, Junius told Mary Ann that the girl did not possess the intelligence natural to a Booth. The comment was doubly hurtful, as June had doubted aloud that Blanche was his biological child.[101]

John left no record of what he thought of his father as a parent. Predictably, however, two such obstinate natures clashed. Sometimes Junius, whose actor eyes could bore a hole into a child, used a cold silence as a punishment. This ominous shunning continued until the offender came to heel. On other occasions Junius employed a belt. John's playmate Stout recalled an incident when the father discovered that someone had cut the decorations off his Shylock costume. He went immediately to John and began beating him. He wanted a confession or the name of the guilty party. Finally little brother Joe cried out that Edwin had ruined the costume, and John confirmed it. The fact that the father reached instinctively for John when something was amiss speaks for itself.[102]

Happily, Junius was often absent on tour. At such times the regime he forced on his largely indifferent family collapsed, and they all did as they wished. Mary Ann abandoned the kitchen, Edwin fished, Rose read, Asia sulked, and Joe moped. John practiced his marksmanship, setting bottles on a fence and learning to shoot through the mouth and knock out the bottom. He boasted that his aim was so good he never wasted a bullet. In a grievous violation of his father's rules, he went hunting.[103] Mary Ann did not try to stop him. She had enough to do and was content so long as her children were.[104]

Although John was a loving child to his mother, he was often headstrong and willful even with her. "Seldom contentious, he was obstinately bent, and what he willed, he did," wrote Townsend. He skipped school, chased fire engines, wrecked sleighs by riding them in summer, and nearly drowned in a reckless escapade with friends. Once he ran away from home with Billy Andrews, one of the juvenile players, to join the oystermen on Chesapeake Bay.[105] Mary Ann, who had had a vision that he would die an early and unnatural death, was frantic. Upon his return from such misadventures, he was always genuinely and profoundly remorseful for worrying her, and the indulgent mother, relieved to see him unscathed, routinely forgave him.

One day she sat the youngster down for a talk. She told him that to be well and favorably known was just about the best thing in life. Such an achievement started with a belief in one's self. John had wonderful potential, she thought, but it meant little if he did not develop it. If he would—if he would make that effort—he could become an exceptional adult. Work to be who he could be and she would always be there to help him, she promised. The words of the sweet-tempered mother had a profound impact on the boy. He thanked her and made a vow of his own in return. When he grew up, he said, he would take the greatest care to see that she was happy.[106]

JUNIUS WANTED A residence at the farm more suitable to his age, station in life, and family size, and he found a design he liked for a house in Gothic Revival style in William H. Ranlett's *The Architect* (1847–49). At a spot within fifty yards of the front of the old cabin, and at the foot of locust trees that he ordered left untouched, work commenced on a cellar in October 1851. Above it rose a one-and-a-half-story redbrick villa. The building had clustered chimneys, four gables, and a roof of heavy block tin. One distinctive feature was the diamond-shaped panes of glass in the windows. Not a mansion, the building was a sort of grand cottage with small homelike rooms and simple interior finishes.[107] Asia named the house Tudor Hall.[108]

John, together with Joe, was packed off to St. Timothy's Hall, a boarding school in Catonsville, Maryland. Located a six-mile, one-hour horsecar ride into the countryside from Baltimore, the Hall was a military academy operated under the auspices of the Protestant Episcopal Church. Students wore gray uniforms and were organized along military lines. The Reverend Libertus Van Bokkelen, a native of New York City and a closet abolitionist, served as rector. A flute-playing Episcopal priest, he was known to his students as Mr. Pan.[109] Irreverently, John, who also played the flute, called him Van.[110]

St. Timothy's Hall was a middle and high school whose purpose was to prepare students for college or a business career. Discipline was strict. Van Bokkelen published ninety-nine rules that included prohibitions on drinking, smoking, playing cards, coarse language, firearms, truancy, food from home, novels, group study, absence from chapel, whispering in study hall, and singing in quarters.[111] Living conditions reflected his goal of instilling toughness. The rising bell sounded at 6:30 in the morning; during the winter months, students in the three-story frame barracks woke to find their overcrowded rooms so cold the water in their pitchers had frozen. They had to crack ice to wash their faces.[112]

Although St. Timothy's Hall had a strong academic program and the most professional teachers John had encountered, his classroom struggles continued. Courses were challenging, and there were times when he felt like a dullard.[113] He did best in presentations and debates, particularly in recitations on tragic and classical themes. His study of history, as well as his individual temperament, gave rise to a hatred of kings, and ridding the world of tyrants was a favorite theme in his declamations.[114] While John impressed no one as a scholar, his learning style showed two important adaptations. He picked up memory tricks, able to hold on to anything he fully understood, and he developed as an auditory learner. "He liked to hear persons of reading and information converse, listened earnestly, and afterwards appropriated much that fell from their lips," said a friend.[115]

With 130 boys, St. Timothy's Hall was a hive of adolescent energy, and John was initially cowed in the presence of so many older and better students. Samuel Arnold, one of the senior boys, remembered him as timid.[116] Schoolmates laughed at the bowlegs he inherited from his father and teased him as their own Billy Bowlegs, the nickname of the Seminole leader Holato Mico, who was in the news at the time.[117] John, however, soon made friends. Fitzhugh Lee, nephew of Robert E. Lee, was one of the older students whom he knew and admired.[118] The self-confident Arnold was another appealing character, as was the underclassman Prentiss Ingraham, who would gain fame as the author of hundreds of postwar dime novels as well as a historically important account of John's death.[119] These three youths were representative of the student body—Maryland sprinkled with Virginia and a touch of Deep South seasoning. There were few Northerners at the school. John heard nothing at St. Timothy's Hall to challenge his rapidly solidifying social beliefs and racial attitudes.

Wednesday and Saturday afternoons were free time for students, and John and two friends usually headed to a nearby wood where they had built a bush house. Each boy had a Colt revolver, and they purloined a rifle from the school, so the well-armed trio hunted rabbits, stole eggs, and cooked dinner. Afterward John settled back to smoke his red-clay pipe with its yard-long stem and to speak of his aspirations for the future. "He thought only of being a man admired by all people," wrote one of the friends. "He would do something that would hand his name down to posterity—his name, known in history, to live forever." There was nothing dark in John, who seemed cheerful and full of life, or in his remarks. "John was kind, generous, and affectionate in his nature," the boy continued. "He was never a vicious or bad-minded boy; on the contrary, he was noble in mind and honorable in all his actions."[120]

Food was always on the minds of students at St. Timothy's Hall, and it led to a crisis. One of Van Bokkelen's less popular ideas was to have classes *before* breakfast. When students got to the dining tables, they found "foul meat, eaten with silver forks," as John wrote home.[121] Little wonder the school was named for Timothy, patron saint of individuals suffering from stomach ailments.

Troublesome youngsters who might have respected Napoleon or Wellington had less fear of Father Libertus, parish priest. Three or four bolder ones killed several of his chickens, tied them to a pole, marched around the grounds, and placed the birds against the window of the school's housekeeper for her to cook. Foolishly, Van Bokkelen punished the entire school by suspending the twice-weekly afternoon holidays. When he did, the place erupted. Students took rifles from the clapboard armory building and set up camp one mile away in a patch of woods. Although the rebels were led by older boys like Arnold, John joined in, as did most of the rest of the student body. The headmaster was exceedingly frustrated with them; as he explained, he wasn't running a reform school on behalf of the parents of young delinquents. Nevertheless, given the number of boys involved, he was unable to end the rebellion. The standoff continued for three days until Arnold's father, George, a prominent Baltimore baker, and several other notables were brought to campus and negotiated an end to the trouble.[122]

JOHN SAW HIS brother Junius Jr. infrequently. June was seventeen years older and launching his own acting career when John was born. His rare visits home were delightful to John, whom he taught to use a foil and broadsword. June had neither the taint nor the talent of their father, but he was a master swordsman, and he taught John to fence equally well with both arms.[123] June also taught him how to box, a skill not only street-smart but valuable in giving a performer self-confidence in the use of his hands.[124] John admired him greatly, and "Junius dearly loved this one of his brothers," wrote Asia, "admired his athletic beauty, loved him for his nature, his disposition."[125]

After a season of managing a theater in San Francisco, June came home for a break in the spring of 1852 and filled his father's head with tales of the wealth to be earned in the West. When he departed for California after a two-month stay, Junius Sr. accompanied him, as did eighteen-year-old Edwin, who had been traveling with his father for three years.[126] It was the final time the family saw the father alive. Returning home after his tour, Junius died onboard a Mississippi River steamboat just below Louisville, Kentucky, on November 30, 1852. The cause of death was apparently enterophthisis, also known as consumption of the bowels. His remains were embalmed in Cincinnati and placed in a massive airtight iron coffin. Mary Ann went alone to retrieve the body and arrived with it in Baltimore on December 9.[127]

For three days the remains lay in state in the Exeter Street house as visitors called to pay their respects. Junius reposed in the parlor, where the walls were draped in white. The coffin had a closed glass plate beneath which his face could be seen, and a marble bust of Shakespeare placed above it seemed to be peering down for a look. Junius's gray eyes were partly opened, his lips curled in a half-smile, his brown hair thickly streaked with white. He looked just as he did when he took naps, and the children became uneasy. Perhaps their father was not dead after all but only in a trance.[128] John and Asia grew frantic at the thought. Bolting from the house, they ran down the street screaming that their father was still alive.[129] A physician came and established the obvious, but for John it was a traumatic moment. "I cannot look upon the dead," he later told a friend. "It is a terrible sight to me. It sends a chill through my body."[130]

On Saturday, December 11, 1852, a funeral cortege left the house with the body and wound its way on foot some two miles through the city to the Baltimore Cemetery. The day was raw and wet, with patches of snow on the ground, but a large party from all social classes showed its respect by trudging along with the family. At the cemetery a band in the distance played the death march as services were held. On the outskirts of the funeral party hovered a small woman, standing alone. She was obviously poor, as she was too thinly clad for the weather, yet she stayed and watched until the grave closed over Junius. It was Adelaide.[131]

AMONG THOSE WHO called at the house to express their condolences were Elisha and Ann Browne, the elderly couple who lived next door. Pillars of the Light Street Methodist Church, the mouselike pair informed the Booths that the father's death was a judgment on the family's wickedness. They urged Mary Ann "to cease following after evil." She should at least try to teach John and his siblings—"poor things"—to be good. The couple had some missionary tracts for her. Mary Ann replied coldly that the family was content with its own Episcopal faith.[132]

Embarrassed by the visit, Mary Ann took an overdue step. When John and Joe (then fourteen and twelve respectively) returned to St. Timothy's Hall, she had them baptized at the Episcopal church in Catonsville. The Reverends James Stephenson and Henry Onderdonk, two professors at the school, stood as sponsors.[133] While this made John a nominal Episcopalian, Asia, who converted to Catholicism following her attendance at a school operated by the Sisters of the Carmelite Convent, insisted her brother preferred that faith.[134] He was wearing a small Catholic medal, said to be an Agnus Dei medal, at the time of his death in 1865. Where the medal came from and, more importantly, what it meant to him are unknown.[135] It may have been little more than a talisman since Booth went to a variety of Christian churches. As a rule he disliked preachers and their histrionics. They were "Bible thumpers," he protested, so called for the way they slammed their fists on the Bible or slammed the Bible itself down on the pulpit to emphasize a point.[136]

John's mature beliefs resembled those of his father. On long rambles in the Pennsylvania hills with his friend Robert Brigham, Booth spoke freely about his faith. "In religion Booth was what is called a 'free thinker,'" said Brigham. "He tied himself down to no one dogma or creed. He believed in an all-powerful head and master of all the universe, but reserved for himself the right to think out and live according to the teaching of the Bible and of nature, as he himself understood it, and to draw his own conclusions as to the meaning and intent of the Almighty."[137] As for ethics, John declared that there was no greater teacher of morality and virtue than Shakespeare.[138]

WITH THE FATHER went his annual income of over five thousand dollars, and trouble followed immediately. James J. Gifford, the builder of Tudor Hall, had not been paid. A hard-looking man with a perpetually furrowed brow, Gifford took the roof off the house—literally tore it off—to make it plain that he wanted his money.[139] Every actor's family fears losing the roof over its head, but this was a literal case in point. The house was made livable again, but, since no one in the family was capable of earning an outside income, it was clear that big changes were at hand.

Mary Ann decided the way forward was to rent the town house and attempt to farm the country property. The home place had eighty acres of arable land, a good garden, a small vineyard, fenced fields, and milk cows.[140] With a decent manager, good hands, and economy, it might be possible to make a living there. Accordingly, just off the Bel Air highway, John built a new gate for the property. Well balanced on stout wooden posts, it swung at a touch, and the Booths moved through it and back to the farm.[141]

At age fifteen John could hardly be a proper farmer, but he did what he could. Up with the sun, he could be found by the sound of his ax in the woods or his shouts in the fields. He learned about dry cows, the price of oats, the positioning of fence rails, and the driving of cattle to market. At night, when he came in, he was often too tired to wash or eat.[142]

As the oldest male family member at Tudor Hall, John was protective of the physical safety and social reputations of Mary Ann, Rose, and Asia. When the white laborers came to the house for their midday meal and cider during harvest season, he did not want them associating with the women at table, and he invented excuses to explain their repeated absence. Such class snobbery, which never would have been countenanced by his father or grandfather, did not escape the workmen's notice. "We were not a popular family with our white laborers," Asia recalled, "because, as they said, 'They'd heer'd we had dirty British blood, and being mixed up with Southern ideas and niggers made it dirtier.'"[143]

George B. Hagan, a Virginian hired on shares in 1854 to oversee the farm, learned the hard way about John's sensitivity on this matter. Tension had risen at Tudor Hall over Hagan's demanding dawn-to-dusk schedule of working the stock and hands. Mary Ann was pained to see her pet horses too tired to drag themselves to the barn at day's end, and on July 30, 1854, a warm, cloudy summer day, she spoke to Hagan about it. "The man became very insolent and called her vile names," said Asia. Absent from home when this unpleasantness occurred, John learned of it upon his return.

Cutting a stout stick and carrying it like a riding whip, he and his friend Herman Stump, a law student, confronted Hagan at his lodgings. John demanded that Hagan come to the house and apologize to the ladies. The manager not only refused; he said there were no *ladies* at Tudor Hall to whom one might apologize.[144]

John exploded in anger at his remark and clubbed Hagan on the head and shoulders. "I knocked him down, which made him bleed like a butcher," he boasted to a friend.[145] At that point Stump decided the mother was properly avenged and intervened. The next day Hagan limped to the home of James A. Fulton, Churchville's justice of the peace, and filed a complaint against John. The result was a rather comical trial held at Tudor Hall. In attendance were Mary Ann, dressed in her widow's weeds, a placid Rose, a belligerent Asia, an indignant John, and a half-dozen Halls of all ages who looked on helpfully. John was not arrested for assault or fined. He was simply bound over to keep the peace, the lightest punishment he could have received short of a dismissal of the charge. He and his mother signed a fifty-dollar bond, essentially a promise under penalty to behave, and the affair ended.[146]

Although burdened with responsibilities at the farm, John was still a teenager and enjoyed a busy social life. A series of eight of his letters written in the mid-1850s to a Baltimore friend tells of picnics, fairs, hunting trips, camp meetings, strawberry pickings, and rides to the Rocks of Deer Creek. He visited the city occasionally and kept up with friends there. Of the latter he wrote light-heartedly, "Give my regards to all who ask after me, and to those that don't, tell them to kiss my Bumbelbee." Girls were always on his mind. "I've got my eye on three," he confessed. Drinking figured in the correspondence as well. "I whent to a Champaign drinking and you had better believe that the road home seemed longer that night than it ever did before."[147] Nothing in the badly written letters was sinister or misanthropic or left reason to doubt the remark of his boyhood friend Charles Harward, Ella Mahoney's father: "Stories about John Wilkes were jolly ones with a laugh at the end."[148]

John manifested a strong interest in nativist politics at this time. The heavy immigration of the period produced fears among many of Maryland's native-born that foreigners were taking over the state and the nation. George Alfred Townsend described their reaction in two concise sentences: "The cold German and the mettlesome Irishman had swarmed upon the land, the power of their naturalization felt at the ballot box. It was not in the nature of American boys to submit."[149] Street violence and electoral fraud occurred in Baltimore, where immigrants formed 25 percent of the city's population, while in Harford County, with far fewer newcomers, the nativist effort centered more peaceably on winning state and federal elections.[150]

"Three Cheers for America!" John wrote to a friend, and he crossed two American flags and fixed them over the door at Tudor Hall.[151] Attracted by the rituals, oaths, and secret doings of the American Party (often called the Know Nothings), he attended its conclaves held a few miles away. When the former Whig and future Republican radical Henry Winter Davis campaigned for the U.S. House of Representatives in the county in the fall of 1854, John volunteered as a rally steward and banner-bearer. Dressed in dove-colored trousers, pale buff waistcoat, dark claret-red cloth coat, and broad Guayaquil straw hat, he adorned himself in party decorations. "On this particular occasion he looked remarkably handsome," thought Asia.[152]

Later in his life John had many immigrant friends. John McCullough of Coleraine in Ireland's County Londonderry was his best and most intimate comrade. Obviously, John managed to make a distinction between individuals like McCullough and the generality of Irish immigrants, just as he did between the Hall family and African Americans as a whole. In the 1860s he was angered to see newly arrived Irish pour into the federal army. He called them "bastard subjects of other countries, false-hearted unloyal foreigners who would glory in the downfall of the Republic."[153]

THE BOOTH LAND was "the worst of bad farms, in a bad piece of country," thought one visitor, and no one had ever made it pay.[154] Not surprisingly, Mary Ann couldn't either. Inexperience, lack of capital, severe weather, poor planning, hard luck, and the difficulty of securing first-class help doomed Mary Ann's efforts. Equally vexing were certain neighbors. The farm often played host to the turkeys and chickens of William Woolsey. The prosperous Woolsey had stealthily moved the farm's boundary marker to take for himself a sizable piece of meadow. Now his flock fed on what grain the buzzards left in the Booths' best field. When John shot one of his turkeys, Woolsey came to the house in a rage.[155] Later John noticed a strange sow heading to the barn for lunch. Exasperated with these intrusions, he sat in a gable window of the house and shot the sow, as he did a trespassing dog belonging to Stephen Hooper, a free black who lived nearby.

Clearly, some of the neighbors showed no respect for the family—perhaps because there was no adult male on the place, perhaps because the Booths were unconventional—and when John assassinated President Lincoln ten years later, they made their feelings plain. Hooper told journalists that the Booths were shiftless people who frequently stole poultry, cattle, grain—"anything rather than do a stroke of honest work." A German immigrant who lived nearby agreed, adding, "None of the neighbors ever liked the family. They were the devil's own play-acting people and would do anything bad."[156]

Edwin returned home from the West in October 1856. The slender, graceful brother looked almost ethereal. He had oddly luminous eyes, an improbably oriental face, and hair so long and thick that it looked like a mane. The porters who carried his trunk into the house winked knowingly at its weight and said it was filled with gold. Unfortunately that was not true, but the twenty-two-year-old had brought back something valuable. Knocking around the California mining country, managing a theater in Honolulu, and acting in Australia, he had often been down to his last dollar. The vicissitudes had been instructive. As his friend William Winter wrote, "He had four years of the most severe training that hardship, discipline, labor, sorrow and stern reality can furnish, and when he came east again, he was on the right road and in fresh exultant vigor."[157]

When Edwin had left for California in 1852, his farewell look at John had revealed "a rattle-pated fellow, filled with Quixotic notions," charging through the woods mounted on Cola, shouting heroic speeches, and waving an old lance—"a good-hearted, harmless, though wild-brained boy." The lance had been replaced by a rifle, but John was still the same irresponsible creature he had always been and clearly in over his head at the farm.[158]

Focused and determined, Edwin took charge. Before he picked up his father's acting mantle, he needed to get the family on a stable financial footing. He ended Mary Ann's effort to farm.[159] The family would sell the stock, put the farm up for rent, and return to the city.[160]

John agreed to the proposal. "Buried here, torturing grain out of the ground for daily bread, what chance have I?" he asked.[161] The preceding year he had played one night as Richmond in Shakespeare's *Richard III* in support of Asia's beau Jack Sleeper at a Baltimore theater, and he had done well.[162] Stuart Robson and Ted Hamilton, friends from the brothers' boyhood company, were already onstage, and he was eager to follow them. Sleeper, now calling himself John Sleeper Clarke, was the lead comedian at the Arch Street Theatre in Philadelphia. Edwin arranged for John to live with Clarke and his mother, Georgiana, in Philadelphia. Clarke would try to get him a position at the theater.[163]

"The seriousness of life had come," said Asia. "The last happy days of childhood were recollections only, and each of us children went out of the solemn old woods forever."

In parting with John she thought how singular he was in his combination of gay and grave qualities. Everyone knew the happy side. The somber side showed itself more privately in things like his love of sad songs. The sound of the mouth harp plucked by one of the Hall children was like the buzz of an insect to Asia, but not to John. He seemed attuned to its plaintive melody. He would listen abstractedly for a while, then pull himself away as if struggling against a dark emotion.

"Don't let us be sad," he told her as he roused himself. "Life is so short, and the world is so beautiful."[164]

2
. . . .

THE MUFFIN

JOHN SLEEPER CLARKE was as good as his word. When Booth arrived in Philadelphia in the summer of 1857, he found that Clarke had secured him a professional engagement—his first—as a "walking gentleman" for the Arch Street Theatre's resident acting troupe, or stock company.[1] Advertisements in the city newspapers introduced the nineteen-year-old as a veteran of the New York stage.[2] Not true, but the management could hardly boast that he was direct from a cabbage patch in Maryland. Booth's salary was eight dollars per week, average for an actor of his grade. For the sum Booth was expected "to play in any piece or part for which he might be cast and to appear every day at rehearsal."

It was agreed that Booth would be billed as "J. B. Wilkes." He performed under this name in Philadelphia and Richmond for the next three years. "All knew he was 'old Booth's son,'" wrote Townsend, who first met Booth at this time, but ordinary playgoers might not.[3] Booth had two reasons for this disguise. "Doubtful as to his meeting with that success which his ambition had pictured for him," he feared disgrace.[4] He confided to his friend Edwin A. Emerson that if he failed, he did not want the family name tarnished by it.[5] Also, "Booth" on the marquee would invite comparisons to his father. "It is a name which awakens old memoires and revives past triumphs," a theatrical critic asserted, and Booth wished to be judged on his own merits. As his confidence grew, he bragged to the actor James Pilgrim that he would make the name of Wilkes as famous as that of Booth.[6] But he was unwilling to trade on his father's reputation. June's playbills proclaimed him "the Father as He Lived!" By 1862, when John returned to his hometown of Baltimore as a star, he had resumed use of his last name, but his passion for individuality was unchanged. His bills boldly declared, "I Am Myself Alone!"[7]

Booth's boss was William Wheatley, the lessee and manager of the Arch.[8] Wheatley had been on the stage for thirty years, mixing in business adventures on Wall Street and in Nicaragua. An actor with a huge ego, Wheatley had a declamatory style ill suited for tragedy but quite funny in comedy roles. As a manager he was an industrious impresario with a quick eye and good judgment.[9] Wheatley encouraged young stock players, called "muffins," but only if they worked hard.[10] He had no patience with slackers. Long runs and good houses were his watchwords. A handsome man, Wheatley struck some as pompous and shallow, but he was unquestionably a dynamic leader with a gambler's inclinations. The Arch would need both his skill and his luck to contend for the entertainment dollar in Philadelphia against two rival theaters, an opera house, and numerous music, lecture, and variety halls.

Twenty-nine men and women formed the Arch's stock company.[11] Wheatley promoted them as "the Celebrated Star Company" even though many were beginners or little more. They had been hired for their ability to fill specialized lines of work. There was the "leading man," E. L. Davenport, a veteran actor who took the principal male part in productions. Fanny Vining, his wife, made an accomplished "leading lady." Clarke, the "low comedian," took the star roles in his line or in farces presented as afterpieces to the featured plays. Wheatley performed in support of these three and at other times played the lead himself. Other stock characters included a "heavy," who was the play's villain or tyrant; an "old man" and an "old woman," who played older characters and persons of consequence; a "juvenile lead," who was the theater's young hero and lover; "walking gentlemen and ladies" (like Booth), who served a tutelage by playing small roles; "utility actors," or "utes," who took what scraps remained; and "supernumeraries," the actors in crowd scenes who might be permitted to shout "Hurrah!!" when Davenport concluded a stirring speech. The walkers, utes, and supers were naturally ambitious to move up the ladder, and Junius Sr., John's father, had predicted that these lower orders would eventually disappear. *They'll all be stars!* he had said derisively.[12]

Booth and the rest of the company assembled on Wednesday, August 12, 1857, at the call of William S. Fredericks, acting and stage manager.[13] They met in the theater's greenroom, a common room near the stage where performers customarily gathered to chat, read announcements, and check themselves in long mirrors before going onstage. Wheatley had a plain message for them: "The end and purpose of the stage is, in the language of Shakespeare, 'to hold, as 'twere, the mirror up to nature, to show virtue her own feature, scorn her own image, and the very age and body of the time his form and pressure.' To do this, and do it well, will be our earnest aim and endeavor."[14] Wheatley was justifiably proud of the Arch. Its exterior looked like a classical temple, while the interior had been beautifully remodeled over the summer with gilded decorations, new wallpaper, oil paintings, and plush cushions on the seats. An open house for the press produced the opinion from journalists that the Arch was the prettiest theater in the city.[15]

The season began on the intensely hot evening of Saturday, August 15. *The Belle's Stratagem*, a popular old-fashioned comedy, was presented to an overflowing house.[16] Booth took the tiny role of Second Mask.[17] A guest at a masquerade ball, Booth had only a few sentences, the longest—delivered to one of the male leads—being "How the devil came you here?" Reaction to this brief appearance is not known. On the following Monday he made a definite impression, however. He played the Courier in a drama titled *The Wife*. He had several little speeches to make, but when he came before the footlights, he looked startled and ill at ease. "Such was his nervousness that he blundered continually," recalled Townsend. And the problem persisted. On three subsequent nights Booth flubbed his lines and was hissed by the audience.[18]

Stage nerves are common in beginners. Edwin suffered so badly from them in his earliest efforts that he stood about shyly and spoke his lines like a schoolboy.[19] Embarrassed friends reminded him that there were other good trades available to a promising youngster like himself. Edwin overcame the problem in time, but younger brother Joe could not. While performing with Edwin in 1859, Joe seemed thunderstruck. He stumbled over his lines repeatedly. Edwin finally whispered to him, "Get off the stage!"[20] The remark was no cue; it was career advice.

Long concerned about his lack of grace and difficulty in memorizing lines, John was frustrated by these episodes. Occasionally he did well. In February 1858 he performed selected scenes from Shakespeare's *Richard III*,

41

taking the role of Richmond while Clarke played a comic Richard. As straight man to the comedian's clownish villain, "Booth showed some energy and obtained some applause."[21] But failure followed. The very next week Booth was cast in the role of Ascanio Petrucci in Victor Hugo's *Lucretia Borgia*. Toward the end of the first act, he came onstage with a number of other young noblemen to find his companion Gennaro, played by Wheatley, in conversation with Mary Ann Farren's Lucretia. The comrades introduced themselves in turn to the evil duchess. "Madame, I am Maffio Orsini, brother to the Duke of Gravina, whom you caused to be stabbed in his dungeon," said the first. "Madame, I am Beppo Liveretto, brother of Liveretto Vittelli, whom your ruffians strangled while he slept," the second continued.

Booth was to have said, "Madame, I am Ascanio Petrucci, cousin of Pandolfo Petrucci, Lord of Sienna, who was assassinated by your order that you might seize his fair city." His head swimming with names, Booth exclaimed, "Madame, I am Pondolfio Pet—, Pedoflio Pat—, Pantuchio Ped—. Damn it, what am I?!"

The audience roared with laughter, Townsend reported, as Booth stood there mortified. Realizing the absurdity of the situation, there was little he could do but laugh with them.

Presented the next night was *The Gamester*, a "moral tragedy" about the destructive effects of gambling upon a family. John Dolman of the stock company took the character of Stukely, a villain seeking to ruin a wealthy friend. Booth was cast as Dawson, Stukely's companion in crime. The role called for Dawson to dress like an aristocrat. Davenport had always advised novices like Booth to spend what they could on a wig or bit of wardrobe to enhance their performances, even if it meant skipping a meal. "There is very much in appearance," he counseled.[22] Dutifully, "Booth bought a new dress to wear on this night and made abundant preparations to do himself honor." So confident was he in his ability to acquit himself, he invited friends to the theater to witness the triumph.

Dawson does not come onstage until the final act of *The Gamester*, but the part of this henchman is important to the conclusion of the play. When Booth appeared, some in the audience recognized him as "Pondolfio Pet—" of the previous evening. They burst into laughter and hisses. The young actor, out to plot villainy with Dolman, was dumbstruck at their behavior. Unable to utter a word, he stood there like a mannequin. The audience rewarded him with a round of cynical mock applause.

To bring the play to a conclusion, Dolman had to strike Booth from the piece.

These episodes upset and embarrassed Booth, whose ambition to excel in his profession was boundless. "I must have fame!" he cried in exasperation to acquaintances.[23] His boardinghouse near the theater, to which he had moved after leaving the Clarkes' home, was filled with young men his age—aspiring medical students, artists, actors—each hoping to win a place in the world. None craved distinction more than Booth, yet none seemed idler. "He was not without ability and might, with study, have succeeded in earning a reputation in his profession; but he was both lazy and inordinately vain," an unnamed fellow boarder recalled. He would not apply himself. "Booth protested that he studied faithfully," Townsend wrote, "but that his want of confidence ruined him." Whatever the case, Fredericks, whose job was to form the actors into a cohesive troupe, complained constantly about him. Booth was late to rehearsals, social instead of studious, and failed to take advantage of his opportunities. He was often worthless to the company.[24] He must either find his stage legs, or, as Joseph Whitton, the theater's treasurer, put it, join that crowd at the bottom who never go beyond "'My Lord, the carriage awaits,' and six dollars a week."[25]

Booth bemoaned his fate to John McCullough, one of the utes who was doing nicely in his small parts. McCullough was a young Irishman who immigrated to the United States in 1847. While at work in his uncle's chair-making shop in Philadelphia, he loved listening to a coworker recite Shakespeare and gladly submitted to murder by paintbrush in *Julius Caesar*. Enraptured by the make-believe, McCullough fled to a nearby alley and joined the Boothenian Dramatic Association, an amateur acting club named for the elder Booth. Fredericks saw him there, and, although McCullough looked dreadful acting Othello, he was so perfect in his lines that the stage manager hired him for the utility corps. He made his debut on the same August evening as Booth, and they became fast friends.[26] Broad-shouldered and full of fun, "Genial John" had a happy nature. "McCullough was the sort of man Booth wanted for agreeable companionship, and Booth would fight for his friend," Townsend remembered. For his part, McCullough found Booth lovable and sincere. The two were kindred spirits.[27]

Booth was well liked in and about the theater, making friends like McCullough readily.[28] "He had the most superb masculine beauty I ever saw—was, in fact, a young Apollo in face and figure," his boardinghouse critic conceded.[29] "All who knew him well were captivated by him," wrote Henry V. Gray, a medical student. "He was the most hospitable, genial fellow to be met," quick at the tables with a bit of poetry or Shakespearean quotation.[30] For William A. Howell the captivation was complete. One of the Boothenians, Howell recalled that the young actor "was that sort of man that if you ever came within range of his personal magnetism and fascination, you would involuntarily be bound to him as with hooks of steel."[31] Another Philadelphian felt "he was neither cruel nor murderous by nature, and I always doubted whether he was the monster of vice which men [would later] deem him," yet at times he appeared ridiculous. Blustering that a young man at the boardinghouse had wounded his honor, he wrote out a challenge to a duel. Unfortunately, "the writing was that of a boy of seven." It was so wretchedly spelled that when word of it got around Booth became the laughingstock of the house.[32]

Developments at the theater were less amusing. The economic downturn known as the Panic of 1857 was raising unemployment and driving prices down nationwide. Places of amusement were highly vulnerable to such developments, and by October it was reported in theatrical circles that "there is not probably in the Union two theaters earning expenses."[33] The Arch felt the pinch. In November hard times and strong opposition from the rival Walnut Street Theatre forced Wheatley to cut admission prices to all parts of the house except the choicest seats.[34] Advertising was severely curtailed, and salaries were threatened. Then in February 1858 Davenport fell out with Wheatley, and "like a chap on board a ship in a storm at sea, he took his carpet bag and stepped ashore," as a trade paper put it.[35]

The departure of Davenport was a personal setback for Booth. He had learned much from the older actor, whom he admired for the polished nature of his performances.[36] Davenport had been an encouraging mentor, bringing even utes like McCullough before the curtain for applause. The remaining seniors were not congenial. Clarke never praised the efforts of the youngsters.[37] Wheatley was hemorrhaging dollars, while the hot-tempered Fredericks displayed "that reputation for crabbedness that struck terror in the hearts of the entire profession."[38] The managers reorganized upon the decamping of Davenport, bringing in new faces and reshuffling others. Booth suffered in the shake-up. Theater playbills that occasionally list his name below that of McCullough (who made half his salary) suggest a demotion.[39] Clearly, Booth had lost some of the management's confidence just as the management was losing the city's. "With nobodies acting the principal male characters and women as leading actresses who are incompetent, the Arch seems in a sad way," a critic in the *Philadelphia Sunday Dispatch* complained in April.[40] The resourceful Wheatley recovered some ground by bringing in name talent from out of town, but it was with relief that Booth saw the long theatrical year close on June 19, 1858.

Clarke, who would comanage with Wheatley in the fall, believed Booth would make a good actor and wanted him back. "He don't want too," Mary Ann wrote June. "He is for trying another City." John left the Arch without a backward glance, telling friends he had been unsuccessful there. He mother believed that he secretly wished he had done something else for a living but would not acknowledge it.[41]

A much-needed vacation followed. John, Edwin, Asia, and Jean Anderson, a family friend from Baltimore, took a trip to Niagara Falls.[42] On their return they stopped in New York City at the St. Nicholas Hotel, an elaborately furnished house on Broadway popular with Southerners.[43] As Jean grew up, she had grown interesting to the young actor. "John has an eye on you," Asia teased her. He stole a kiss from Jean, whispering that it was her own fault that he did it: she was too sweet for him to resist. Asia hoped the two might become attached. That was not to be, but Jean liked John very much. Years later, after the assassination had made her brother notorious, Asia began praising John in a letter to Jean, then stopped herself in midsentence. "I won't speak of his qualities," she stated. "You knew him."[44]

Booth seemed revitalized by his time off. He appeared to one female admirer "like a new blown rose with the morning dew upon it" when he returned to Baltimore.[45] He responded eagerly when John T. Ford, manager of the Holliday Street Theatre, suggested a joint appearance with Edwin in *Richard III*. John played Richmond to Edwin's title role. "Both performances were superb," wrote the actor James H. Stoddart. "I shall never forget the fight between Richard and Richmond in the last act, an encounter which was terrible in its savage realism."[46] John surprised everyone favorably. Edwin wrote their niece Blanche, "I think he will make a good actor."[47] Ford thought so, too.

THE MARSHALL THEATRE of Richmond, Virginia, stood on the corner of Seventh and Broad Streets in the heart of the city's business district.[48] Named for the great jurist John Marshall, a Virginian who had been a theater buff and stockholder in the business, it was a handsome brick structure designed to seat one thousand people. There was nothing special about the large building except perhaps its unusual number of doors and windows. They were the deliberate legacy of a stampede of theatrical patrons during a horrifying fire in 1811, when seventy-two people (including the governor of the state) had died. The new building design was to ensure that that would never happen again. There were other halls in the city that could be rented for special events, but the "Old Marshall" was Richmond's only full-time theater. Unlike the Arch, it operated without competition, serving the needs of Virginia's capital city until 1862 when it, too, was destroyed by fire.

Kunkel and Company were the lessees and managers of the Marshall. The partners in this concern were John T. Ford, George Kunkel, and Thomas L. Moxley, all Baltimore-based friends of the Booth family.[49] Ford recruited John Wilkes for the Marshall ensemble but was otherwise an absentee, living in Baltimore, where he managed the Holliday Theatre for the partnership. Day-to-day operation of the Marshall fell to Kunkel and Moxley. These showmen, both only in their thirties, had already performed together for years. Kunkel started his working life as a typesetter, but he soon learned there was money in his bass voice and skill with the accordion. He joined with Moxley to form a series of minstrel troupes that toured nationally for a decade. Kunkel was a talented singer and composer. Moxley was an exceptional dancer, often impersonating female characters to Kunkel's male lead. The keen mimic abilities of this pair, who did blackface comedy and musical pieces, fed the racial stereotypes of the period, yet it should be noted that the two burlesqued white as quickly as black if the routine could get a laugh or make a dollar.

Kunkel and Moxley, having made "plenty of tin" on the minstrel stage, settled into the stationary life of management in Richmond.[50] By the fall of 1858 they were entering their third year at the Marshall. The two had spent July in New York City recruiting talent for the stock company. Having paid full salaries during the height of the preceding year's financial panic, they had an excellent reputation and no difficulty gathering some two dozen actors, dancers, vocalists, and comedians for the coming season.[51] A substantial number of the new company was from Baltimore. Booth was signed, again to be billed as "J. B. Wilkes," at a salary of eleven dollars per week. The amount, a three-dollar raise over Philadelphia, indicated that his year at the Arch was not a complete loss professionally.[52]

During the summer months, while the theater was closed, the Marshall was renovated inside and out. New stucco, wallpaper, and frescoes went up.

Sets were retouched, and the drop curtains were repainted. Ticket prices remained unchanged from the previous year, however. Seats in the dress circle or parquet, both on the main floor, cost fifty cents. Those in the family circle on the second tier were a quarter. The "Eastern Gallery for colored persons" had seats for 37½ cents each. Doors to the theater opened at 7:00 p.m., and the curtain rose promptly at 7:45.[53]

The season began on the evening of Saturday, September 4, 1858. George C. Boniface, an actor who worked with Kunkel and Moxley, recalled the managers' routine: "A popular play was selected and all the company appeared in it. When the curtain rose, we were standing in a row and sang 'The Star Spangled Banner.' Then the curtain fell for a minute, and the play began."[54] The attraction for opening night was a double bill, *Town and Country; or, Which Is Best?*, followed by *1,000 Milliners Wanted for the Fraser River Gold Diggins*. As the titles suggest, both plays were lightweight comedies. Interspersed throughout were orchestral pieces, jokes, singing, dancing, and musical burlesques. The evening pleased the critic of the *Richmond Dispatch*, who wrote that "the theatre [was] uncomfortably crowded from the parquette to the highest gallery—the audience being the largest on the first night in four years." The cast was young and attractive, the writer continued, and "about fifty percent better than that of last season."[55] They were so well received that the Marshall's audience not only clapped but also pounded sticks and canes on the floor.

Booth's contribution to the entertainment is unknown. Even his roles cannot be determined. Both were apparently as insubstantial as were the evening's featured plays. The *New York Clipper*, the nation's leading theatrical newspaper, failed to mention the young actor in its notice of opening night. Nevertheless, the lengthy bill had accomplished the managers' purpose. All the old hands and all the fresh muffins had been brought forward and introduced. A new season was under way.

"I would have written to you before this," Booth reported to Edwin on September 10, "but I have been so busily engaged, and am such a slow writer that I could not find the time. I have played several good parts since I have been here [and] believe I am getting along very well. I like the people, place, and management, so I hope to be very comfortable." Unhappily, "I have heard my name—Booth—called for one or two nights," he lamented. "Everyone knows me already."[56]

Booth also added that he had been ill since his arrival in Richmond. He did not explain further, saying only that the sultry climate did not agree with him.[57] Unable to shake the sickness, Booth called on Dr. James Beale, a prominent city physician, who put him on an unnamed medication. Although Booth's illness was not severe enough to keep him off the stage, it was apparently recurrent and the medicine one he had taken before. Unfortunately the drug caused him to feel languid and thickheaded, making things tough for a young actor needing all his wits to establish himself in a new city.

An acquaintance of the elder Booth, Dr. Beale was to become an important friend of the young actor. When Beale was a boy working in his family's blacksmith shop, he had been rebuked by his father for being too fond of books. Chief Justice Marshall, overhearing the remark, took an interest in the child and provided for his education. Dutifully Beale studied law but later found his vocation in medicine, becoming a man of wealth in his profession. His home, opposite Capitol Square, was a beautifully furnished mansion with winding stairways, artwork, and an outstanding library. From here "Beale dispensed elegant hospitality to nearly every visitor of any note," assisted by his wife, Isabella Pallen, and their little daughter, Mary Bella. "Dr. Beale was a very entertaining and congenial man," recalled Herbert T. Ezekiel, a historian of Richmond's Jewish community. His lively nature made him particularly popular with young people.[58] His knowledge of literature and the arts was daunting, his nature cosmopolitan. Although his ancestry was Italian, he became a Presbyterian, whereas Isabella and Mary Bella attended Beth Shalome Synagogue, to which he contributed liberally.

Unlike most Presbyterians, Beale held no prejudice against the stage. "Almost every night my father would drop in [at] the Richmond theatre, where he had a box, and it was very seldom that he came home alone," Mary Bella reminisced years later. "Many a night [John Wilkes Booth] would return home with my father after the play was over. There was always a warm supper and a warm welcome after the theatre doors were closed."

Booth's affection for children, observed by all his friends, was apparent at the Beale home. The first thing he did upon arriving was make for the nursery to rouse Mary Bella. The girl's birth mother had died when she was born, and she was adopted by her aunt Isabella. Although she was much loved and well treated, there was a touch of sadness about her that aroused Booth's sympathy. "He would hold me up aloft and straddle me across his shoulders," she recalled. Off they went, her pigtails flying.

"I remember one night his taking me downstairs and sitting me on a silver butter salver that stood embedded in flowers in the center of the table." That was too much for the girl's nurse, who came to her rescue, muttering, "Them play actors is the debble."[59]

BOOTH QUICKLY MADE FRIENDS among the Marshall company. "Booth's personality was most attractive," said Jimmy Wells, one of the theater's musicians. "He was well set up, of medium height, courtly to a degree, and possessed a magnetism which attracted all who came in contact with him." The New York actor Benjamin Ringgold, a fellow newcomer to the city, thought him a man of extraordinary beauty and charm. Edwin F. Barnes, a novice actor, found him "a handsome, grave-eyed man, with a quiet, dignified and determined air, and strangely gifted with personal charm."[60]

One of the company grew especially close to Booth. Sam Chester was an acquaintance from boyhood days in Baltimore. As an apprentice in a city printing shop, Sam was sent around to the theaters to pick up their advertising copy. A chance meeting with Edwin awakened a fascination for the stage that grew into a calling.[61] Sam's birth name was Samuel Chester Knapp, but as *Knapp* sounded somnambulant for an actor in the age of melodrama, he reversed his middle and family names, being reborn in the profession as Samuel Knapp Chester.

Now in the fourth year of his career, Sam had grown into a stout young hulk, imposing enough to play the heavy. Appearances aside, he was a mild, quiet sort offstage, much attracted to the effervescent Booth. "I was on terms of close friendship with him ever since I knew him," Sam recalled in 1865.[62]

Harry Langdon, the Marshall's leading man, was another key friend. The two were roommates, in fact, and that posed a problem. Harry was a heavy drinker. A *New York Times* critic quipped that the actor had a "predisposition to indisposition."[63] In retrospect it is astonishing that he was able to postpone until 1910 his death from cirrhosis of the liver. Struggling to be a teetotaler at this time, Booth was highly sensitive to anything that brought the family curse too close. Happily, Harry himself was attempting to reform, starting the new season sober, and Booth was able to spread the word that Langdon had stopped drinking and they got along well together.[64]

Ten years John's senior, Langdon was a model for Booth since he, too, had commenced his career at the Arch Street Theatre and gone on to play leading roles. Langdon was a handsome man with a deep voice and was a capable actor up to any role when not "indisposed" for the evening. He had much to teach about the world of the theater, both in what to embrace and in what to avoid. Young Booth was a project, and Langdon, lacking any petty jealousy over newcomers, decided to give him a hand. "I took a fancy to him," Langdon explained. "He had a manly side to him."[65]

"John Wilkes Booth was a country looking boy," Langdon recalled in an 1883 interview. "His clothes, style, and everything were countryfied. I showed him how to read [his lines], got him a grammar, and made him commit [to memory] every day a certain number of words from the dictionary and pronounce and define them." It was a struggle, Langdon remembered, "as he always had trouble committing his lines to memory." Booth, in turn, annoyed his roommate by sitting up most of the night smoking cigars.[66] Nevertheless they persevered, and "it was very pleasing to see his growth." Since Booth's stage success in time exceeded Langdon's significantly, it was with pride that the older actor claimed, "I taught John Booth the rudiments of acting."

The "star system" under which the Marshall players operated was quite different from that Booth had known at the Arch, where the resident senior actors always took the key roles. In this arrangement Kunkel and Moxley brought a steady stream of traveling stars to Richmond. These actors would stay for two weeks generally, performing their most popular plays. It was often not until the conclusion of an evening's play that Booth and the other stock members were assigned their individual secondary, minor, or walk-on roles for the following night. While the city slept, they studied. One stock actress recalled, "It meant very hard work for the beginners, as there were six new parts a week to study, and frequently the farces [which followed the plays] as well, but it was great practice."[67] With a new play or two each night, and with another star with a different repertoire on the way, the pace at the theater was brisk and the demands on the company challenging.

Kunkel promised that he would bring the leading entertainers of the nation to the Marshall during the 1858–59 season. To a large extent he did. Julia Dean, James W. Wallack, James E. Murdoch, Barry Sullivan, and A. J. A. Neafie appeared, all highly competent dramatic actors. Avonia Jones, a fine tragedienne, came to town, as did the Florences, a pair of first-class comedians. Wheatley brought laughter from Philadelphia, as did John S. Clarke, recently announced in the family as Asia's fiancé. The amazing Maggie Mitchell and brother Edwin rounded out the visitors. Unfamiliar as these names would become to later generations, they were the nation's top entertainers in their day. They knew the elements necessary for success, even directing the plays in which they starred. During rehearsals they drilled the company, showing the cast any special business they required, from where to stand to how a key line should be delivered. The process was a tutorial in the craft of acting. "The stock theatre was a college in itself," recalled William Seymour, who performed with Booth in 1864.[68]

Booth developed a profound admiration for several of these players. James E. Murdoch, who performed in March of 1859, was an intelligent and versatile actor connected with the stage for thirty years.[69] Murdoch had known Booth's father, with whom he acted in 1832, and he managed June's early performances in Boston ten years later. Amazingly, after reaching his thirties, Murdoch succeeded in adding an extra octave to the range of his voice, allowing him to produce some startling vocal effects onstage.[70] His performances were highly polished and inclined to the ideal. "He was a natural and most effective, though not always a patient, teacher," recalled one Kunkel employee.[71] Although Booth's mature style was quite different, he had great respect for Murdoch's acting. "Murdoch was his ideal of grace and perfect elocution," wrote Asia.[72]

Few playbills from the Marshall during the two years of Booth's residence survive, but one of these is for a night when Murdoch and Booth shared the stage.[73] On Monday, March 21, 1859, *De Soto, the Hero of the Mississippi,* was presented. This play was written expressly for Murdoch by George H. Miles of Baltimore. The star had performed the play dozens of times throughout the country, and it was a proven applause-catcher for him. Styled a "Grand Romantic Tragedy," the five-act drama featured Murdoch in the title role. There were also five tableaux vivants in which historic scenes were represented by Booth and his castmates costumed and posing silently without movement. To ensure a complete success, Murdoch even brought with him to Richmond the costumes he wished the company to wear.

Langdon was cast as the lead heavy, De Soto's vengeful adversary the Indian chief Tuscalooza. Booth played the part of Gallegos, a soldier in De Soto's army. As the seventh name in order of prominence on the playbill, "J. B. Wilkes" had a minor role. "My horse, Gallegos!" orders De Soto in one act, sending the younger man scrambling off the stage. But in truth every actor except Murdoch must have disappeared in this riot of fur and feathers. The play commenced with an ambush and went on to a hostage-taking, the marching of troops, a triumphal entrance, "Indian vengeance," a solemn oath scene, treachery, a "View of the Mississippi by Sunset," and a grand battle in which Tuscalooza is defeated and his village destroyed. The tableaux vivants were interspersed among the acts, and there were frequent parades of "Pages, Knights, Banner Bearers, Priests, &c., &c.," no doubt recruited from any loiterers found sober in the alley behind the theater. A chorus or two were thrown in, and the play ended with all the characters, red and white, joining in a dirge at the burial of De Soto. Before the audience was let out for the evening, Moxley had Kate Pennoyer pop out and dance. Kate and her pretty "stems" were completely unrelated to the play, but Moxley knew it was bad business to allow patrons to leave the theater in a glum mood.

During this time together Murdoch was startled to observe Booth's excessive love of applause. The younger actor would do anything to obtain it.[74] But Booth was not the actor his father had been, in Murdoch's opinion, nor did he or his brothers ever achieve his father's greatness. "Without belittling any other genius known to him in his career," Murdoch felt, the elder Booth was the greatest actor he had ever seen. When the son of his beloved mentor and friend murdered Lincoln six years later, "the revulsion of feeling in Murdoch's heart was profound." He was bedridden for weeks. "It is the truth that afterwards life was never the same for him," wrote Murdoch's family friend and biographer Edmund Russell.[75]

Glimpses of the Marshall days are few. Isabella Pallen recalled Booth standing in the wings during a production of *The Sea of Ice*. A small child had a role in the play, and Booth was so tender to the little thing "that she would nestle in his arms until her time came to go on stage."[76] James Pilgrim remembered seeing the youthful actor in the character of the majestic General Putnam, an odd bit of casting.[77] Far more people saw another side of Booth shortly before Christmas 1858, when he stopped a farce from becoming a tragedy. During the play *Our Gal* the young comedienne and vocalist Kate Fisher, wearing a large, loose-fitting merino dress, came too near the gas footlights, catching her skirt on fire. Audience members, seeing what was happening, shouted to the actors to help her. "Mr. Wilkes Booth promptly extinguished the fire," reported the next morning's *Richmond Whig*. In true theatrical tradition "the performance progressed as if nothing had happened."[78]

"There is a young gentleman named Wilkes, a good deal like Edwin Booth in face and person," read a notice in the *Richmond Examiner*. "He is a man of promise, and might, with the approbation of the audience, be cast for a higher position than he usually occupies."[79] Others agreed. Walking home from one disappointing performance, O. Jennings Wise, a diplomat recently returned from France, told his brother John that "the only performer of merit in the [cast] was the young fellow John Wilkes Booth. In him, he said, was the making of a good actor." Knowing Jennings to be familiar with the best theaters in Paris, John Wise wrote that "the criticism made an impression on me, who remembered the man and the name."[80] John T. Ford of the Kunkel partnership was equally pleased, feeling John's early performances were better than Edwin's, and Edwin had become a star.[81] The management relented on occasion and gave Booth better roles, but generally he played those small parts that the second juvenile man must.[82] The names of these characters—Sir Benjamin Backbite, Lord Tinsel, Cool, Trueworth—indicate the limited nature of the parts. Booth was often frustrated since his ability was unquestionable.[83] His mother wrote to his brother June, "John is doing well at Richmond. He is very anxious to get on faster. When he has a run of bad parts, he writes home in despair."[84]

Booth raised his spirits in part by making friends, although he knew that Richmond society was not fully open to the city's actors. The false reality of the theater, as well as its risqué themes, morally ambivalent characters, emotionalism, extravagance, dancing, coarse audiences, and historic association with prostitution, led some families to oppose the institution on principle. As late as 1860 the General Assembly of the Presbyterian Church of the United States reaffirmed its opposition to "stage plays and all kindred amusements calculated to awaken thoughts and feelings inconsistent with the Seventh Commandment" on adultery.[85] Evangelicals considered the theater fire of 1811 a clear judgment and built a church on the spot of the disaster to underscore the point. The dead theatergoers were entombed below the sanctuary—a bizarre sort of caution.

Proud of the stage, Booth defended it as best he could. While performing subsequently in Louisville, Kentucky, he had a polite disagreement over the morality of the stage with a Virginia-born woman named Mary Brown.[86] A pious person, Brown was a fifty-year-old schoolteacher raising two nephews and a niece. William Booth, one of the nephews (and no relation to John's family), became friends with the actor. Star-struck, William decided to become an actor, too, "but shuddered to think what my family, who were intensely religious people, would think of it, for the stage was then in disrepute—under the ban, I may say—with most of the better class of people." William implored Booth to go and "try his powers of persuasion upon my aunt, as I had great faith in his imposing appearance and agreeable manners to set aside her religious scruples." Booth agreed and called at the Brown home. There he met "with a most frigid reception, a complete throw-down of such a sinful idea," and left the house in defeat. When William gathered the courage to creep home that evening, his aunt was waiting for him. "I got a lecture I shall never forget," he recalled. William became a bookkeeper.

Friendlier voices urged these nontheatergoing critics like Miss Brown to come and witness what they condemned without seeing. The overwhelming majority of plots rewarded virtue amply and punished evil with a vengeance. *The Sea of Ice*, for example, was acclaimed by one Richmond critic as "a moral lesson of the most impressive character," a play suitable for the most scrupulous Christian.[87] Such plays refined and civilized the community.[88] The theater is "the literary gratification [most] within the reach of the multitude," wrote the French traveler Alexis de Tocqueville. "It is the most democratic side of literature."[89] As Joseph Whitton put it, stage characters awaken "the lively emotions of the heart, excite curiosity, and arouse sympathy." In a weary world, actors "serve as time-killers and care-quellers for humanity, to prod the tedium of our idle hours and quell the worries that may rise from out our busy ones."[90]

The Richmond stage had able advocates, and few attacks on it went unanswered. Prominent in support was William Ritchie, editor of the influential *Richmond Enquirer* and a strong supporter of drama. Married to Anna Cora Mowatt, a former actress, Ritchie defended the stage from personal as well as philosophical motives.[91] Robert Ridgway of the *Richmond Whig* was also friendly. He permitted the publication of a witty reply to the complaint of several young ladies on their way to church that they had been gawked at by rude boys lounging in front of the Marshall. One of the loungers replied that in this case a church was little different from a theater, since the young ladies went to church expressly to be stared at in the first place.[92] High spirits like the "boys," together with the large number of young professionals in the city, theater-friendly European immigrants, sophisticates like the Wise brothers and the Beale family, and that portion of the city's residents who had never shunned the theater, were always a source of encouragement for actors like Booth.

The young actor found no shortage of friends in these groups. Among that crowd of young bucks like himself he was highly regarded.[93] Harry Watkins, a fellow actor, claimed that "Booth's leisure hours were devoted to sporting with young men about town, with whom his athletic prowess and exuberant spirit made him a natural leader." He was the pet of the city, thought Edwin Hunter Brink, a standabout at the Marshall. "He led a very wild life, being allowed to do almost as he pleased," and became well acquainted with the leading citizens of Richmond.[94]

Booth's expanding social circle included the sculptor Edward V. Valentine. Moxley had introduced Edwin Booth to Valentine early in October 1858, when Edwin was filling a star engagement in the city. Edwin sat for a bust for eight sessions in Valentine's studio. Valentine lived only two blocks along Broad Street from the theater and met John during a Saturday evening stroll toward the end of the month. They had a long talk about the theater, John telling the sculptor that Kunkel and Moxley were about to send the company to Lynchburg. He later visited the sculptor at his studio. "Booth looked the part of neither the lunatic or villain, but seemed to be a most likeable fellow," said Valentine. Departing for study in Europe the following year, the sculptor never saw Booth again. But since he had known John in the springtime of his life, Valentine was one of the people with whom Edwin would speak, in later years, about his brother. When he visited Edwin in New York in 1891, Valentine wrote in his diary that the older brother talked among other things about John's great physical strength.[95]

Another new friend was Edward M. Alfriend, a young Richmonder who was, like Valentine, the same age as Booth. Ned was an insurance underwriter in the family business. He mixed business with the study of law, but the theater was his true love. He sought out the companionship of actors and over the ensuing decades came to know most of the principal players in the nation. Booth, he believed, was an actor with unlimited gifts and potential—a genius—and "his future assured."[96] Ned watched Booth become "a great social favorite, knowing all the best men and many of the finest women." As Alfriend explained: "With men John Wilkes was most dignified in demeanor, bearing himself with insouciant care and grace, and was a brilliant talker. With women he was a man of irresistible fascination by reason of his superbly handsome face, conversational brilliancy and a peculiar halo of romance with which he invested himself, and which the ardent imagination of women amplified."

The trip to Lynchburg occurred in November 1858, one of several out-of-town tours undertaken by the company to that city, Petersburg, and Norfolk. Hosts to circuses, balls, concerts, and lectures, these smaller cities had no full-time theater and were usually eager to see Kunkel and his "masters of the histrionic profession," as the Marshall stock actors were described by one Lynchburg editor, presumably without sarcasm.[97] Since traveling stars of Murdoch's stature rarely came along, these trips gave "masters" like Booth an opportunity for better parts. At Dudley Hall in Lynchburg he took the roles of Paris in *Romeo and Juliet* and of Count Florio in *The Wife*. In both plays his character loves and loses the leading lady. Buckingham, the wily and faithless ally of Richard III, was another substantial role. These were good parts, as was Traddles in a dramatization of Charles Dickens's *David Copperfield*. A hapless student, Traddles drew laughs with his custom of brushing his hair up on end, giving him a look of perpetual surprise.[98]

In late December 1858, Booth and the company played Petersburg's Phoenix Hall, a theater where his father had performed shortly after immigrating to the United States. Since that time the present structure, owned by one of the Alfriends, had been largely rebuilt following a fire, hence its name.[99] Theatrical tradition attached to a large slab of granite at the foot of the steps near the stage door. "On that stone all the great actors before us had stepped," wrote Booth's friend John M. Barron, "and we poor players held it in great reverence." The interior of the Phoenix produced less reverential emotions. The stage was dimly lighted. Scenery was limited. There was no gallery or parquet, simply a gloomy auditorium where hard chairs were the only seats. It was indeed just a plain room, and Booth felt challenged by its bare environment.[100]

Nevertheless he won applause as an actor and welcome as a visitor in the city. James Read Branch, member of a prominent Old Street merchant family, and his wife, Martha, saw dramatic genius in him.[101] Martha treasured a small, sweepingly inscribed photograph of Booth showing him "with more than ambrosial curls, a horn-handled cane, and a wholly implausible amount of watch chain" festooned about his waistcoat, as the author James Branch Cabell, her grandson, described it. Booth thought fondly of the Branches, and the couple in turn reared their descendants to think of him charitably. When the Civil War commenced, Booth sent to Branch, then a lieutenant colonel in the Confederate army, a pack of English-made playing cards. The backs of the paper cards bore the national flag, the battle flag, and the seal of the Confederacy. Booth sent the cards through the blockade that had been proclaimed by the federal government around the rebellious states. The deck of cards was inherited by Cabell, who always grew reflective when handling the time-yellowed artifacts. He published a letter to Booth in his book *Ladies and Gentlemen* (1934) in which he declared that the tangibility of the playing cards was reassuring proof that such a fantastic character as Booth had actually existed and walked the same Southern streets as himself.[102]

The new year of 1859 brought more stars to Richmond, and none was more appealing than Maggie Mitchell. Actress, singer, and dancer, the diminutive Maggie had worked her way assiduously up the ladder from children's parts to the ballet corps to stardom. "She is young, pretty, has a good bust, good arms, and 'a knee round as a period,'" declared one admirer. "A cunning wee thing," said another, "she was so handsome and exquisitely formed as to remind one of a fairy."[103] Seen around town, little Maggie did not look like a tireless and disciplined professional, but that she was, "and with talent and courage, not to say audacity, enough for a giant."[104] "I was startled when that little elf came on the stage," Barron recalled of her debut. She gave directions with an exactness that startled the old-timers, while the utes stood with their mouths agape. Maggie demanded much, "but she never required more of the ladies and gentlemen than she herself was willing to do. Accordingly, she was the inspiration that infected the entire company."[105]

Booth was fascinated by her. Petite and animated, Maggie embodied characteristics observable in most women who bewitched Booth over the years. He spoke admiringly of her to Jimmy Wells, with whom he passed time in the theater dressing room. The two were discussing the relative attractiveness of certain women. Booth agreed that all the women were beautiful, said Wells, but "he always laughingly exclaimed that not one compared with Miss Mitchell."[106]

Booth supported Maggie in her February appearances. She needed no help in *The French Spy*, in which the star stripped down like a pugilist, shaking the house in the process, but Booth drew positive notice in another play.[107] He took the role of Uncas in a stage adaptation of James Fenimore Cooper's novel *The Wept of Wish-ton-Wish*. Maggie starred as

Narra-Mattah, a beautiful white girl who had been abducted and raised by Indians, eventually marrying the noble Conanchet. After various plot twists, Conanchet is betrayed and delivered to his enemy Uncas, who executes him. Narra-Mattah dies of shock. Leonard Grover, later an important manager, went to the show and read in the evening bill that the role of Uncas had been undertaken by one John Wilkes. "Later I learned that he was John Wilkes Booth," Grover wrote in 1909. "He seemed the most talented actor in the company."[108]

John S. Clarke took the first two weeks in March, playing *Our American Cousin* with Wheatley. Barron was unimpressed with Clarke, writing that "to see him in one part was to see him in everything," but the comedian was popular.[109] *Our American Cousin* was performed for eleven of Clarke's twelve nights in Richmond, the longest run of any single play that year in the city.[110] Playing the insufferable Lord Dundreary, Booth proved himself adept at light comedy.[111] It was the first time Booth performed in the play to which his name would soon be forever linked.

Clarke liked Booth, but the young actor did not reciprocate his feeling. This was clear when Booth took a brief leave the following month to attend the comedian's wedding to Asia at St. Paul's Episcopal Church in Baltimore.[112] Edwin had pushed hard for the match between his sister and his longtime friend, and she wrote frankly to Jean Anderson that she married to please him.[113] John feared that Clarke, who was exceptionally ambitious, was using her. When Asia fretted over how little she brought into the marriage, John reassured her. "Our father's name is a power—theatrical—in the land," he responded proudly. "It is dower enough for any struggling actor [like Clarke]."[114]

Back in Richmond, Barry Sullivan followed in April 1859 to play Shakespeare and melodrama. Born in England of Irish parents, "the English-Irish tragedian" was making his first American tour. Despite stilted mannerisms and a harsh voice, Sullivan was an energetic and original performer. A stage historian of the following generation wrote that he was "regarded with esteem by intelligent playgoers," a cautiously worded compliment.[115] Contemporaries were more enthusiastic. Barron loved him, Richmond praised him, and the *Clipper* pronounced him one of the world's greatest actors. Sullivan was hot-tempered, jealous, and difficult. His business agent quit him, unable to endure Sullivan's "insulting, arrogant, oppressive, and otherwise generally objectionable [behavior] to the numerous dramatic artists in the United States (of both sexes and every grade)."[116] The obnoxious tragedian mitigated the problem by altogether avoiding stock actors like Booth and hiring a stand-in to rehearse in his place.

This martinet earned forbearance from Booth by the respect he showed for the memory of the young man's father. During a Baltimore engagement he made a special pilgrimage to Bel Air, then on to Tudor Hall. There he walked the grounds, soaking up inspiration. "It was a source of great interest to Barry Sullivan to roam through the old farmstead where for nearly thirty years Booth had constantly resorted," wrote a friend.[117] The plays Sullivan performed—*Richard III*, *Hamlet*, *The Merchant of Venice*, *King Lear*, *A New Way to Pay Old Debts*—were key pieces of the elder Booth's repertoire. In *Richard III* Sullivan (as Richard) made rapid thrusts with an empty hand after being disarmed by his rival Richmond, a piece of business identified with the elder Booth.[118] One newspaper connected the two directly during Sullivan's visit by stating that he was "the best Shakespearean actor that ever visited Richmond since the illustrious Junius Brutus Booth first trod their stage thirty-eight years previously."[119] Since John never witnessed his father perform, the opportunity of seeing his plays acted by a mature admirer to full and appreciative houses was eye-opening.

Edwin Booth followed directly on Sullivan's week. Praised as "Richmond's favorite," Edwin was popular and his performances well attended. He played a number of his father's pieces, several just done by Sullivan, plus *Macbeth* and melodrama. The engagement reunited the brothers onstage for the first time since the preceding fall. Edwin's visits meant better roles in support, and John was billed as "Wilkes Booth" for these occasions. Edwin was favorably impressed. "I don't think he will startle the world," he wrote June, "but he is improving fast and looks beautiful on the platform."[120] He had talent, Edwin continued, although he did not like to be corrected.[121]

Before Barry Sullivan departed for an engagement in Philadelphia, the tragedian took a private box at the Marshall to study Edwin and size him up as a competitor. "No actor in England can play against *those eyes*," he worried. His presence, however motivated, was a gratifying mark of respect for the Booths. As the play progressed, John was upset to see that Edwin had been drinking.[122] He looked anxiously at Sullivan and "saw, or thought he saw, a sneer on the face of the Englishman." When the curtain fell, John flew at Edwin and demanded "how he dared disgrace his position and his country by appearing before the English actor in his condition." "Is it not enough," shouted John, "that our father's reputation should follow us without such an exhibition as you have given tonight? When I saw the Englishman look at you, I could have killed you where you stood. Have you no shame, no pride in your profession, no thought of the disgrace you bring upon your country?"

Edwin was in no mood for a lecture. Less than five years John's senior, he had seen much more of the world. He had often been near the bottom. To a drunken actor who apologized to him for marring a play, Edwin replied knowingly, "I've been there." Edwin, who threw up during a Cincinnati performance of *Richelieu*, made a sarcastic reply to John's outburst. When he did, the younger brother exploded. "John seized the first weapon that came to hand and dashed at his brother." Edwin wisely sought safety in his dressing room.[123]

John had finally put on display his sensitivity to the mixed legacy of his father's life. His words showed that he understood, even early in his career, the dignity of his vocation and the necessity of performing its demands credibly. It was also clear that in his mind the father's alcoholism was a formidable obstacle with which the sons had to struggle. No less striking was John's intense nationalism. To be embarrassed before a foreign actor offended his pride of country. The incident stirred that mixture of personal and patriotic elements so potent in the young man. Those who witnessed the scene between the brothers did not forget it. For one evening, at least, the action at the theater was as exciting behind the curtain as onstage.

Amiably, Edwin was forgiving. John continued in his support and on Edwin's final night played Horatio to Edwin's Hamlet. When the play concluded, the audience called Edwin out to take a bow. Alfriend recalled that when the curtain went up, Edwin came downstage leading John by the hand. Pointing to him, the older brother said generously, "I think he has done well. Don't you?" Cries of "Yes!" "Yes!" and thunderous applause came from the audience.[124]

The season was closing, and John prepared to take his benefit night. On this highly important occasion, Booth was given the opportunity to star. He also got the proceeds of the evening (after minimal expenses) to supplement his salary. John was announced to play on Monday, May 2, 1859. His mother noted in a letter to June that Edwin remained in the city over the weekend to perform with him.[125] This ensured a bigger take and was another kindness by Edwin, who received nothing from Kunkel for the performance. John was billed as "J. Wilkes Booth," the form of his name under which he would become widely known as a star. He decided to attempt Othello for the first time with Edwin as Iago.[126] A good idea, the *Clipper* dryly observed, if the younger brother could sustain his part.[127] It is amusing to imagine the twenty-year-old, whose stage nervousness still drew comment, playing the formidable and self-confident Moorish general. Edwin's friend William Winter, a noted critic, believed that the role called for a master actor of large physique who conveyed at a glance a rugged warrior.[128] Nevertheless the performance was well received by a full house.[129] After the other actors took their benefits, the Marshall ended its theatrical year on May 16, 1859, with a brass band, song, dance, a patriotic tableau representing George Washington, and comedy by the company.

The theater closed until September, the actors taking vacations or heading home to rest, study, and pinch pennies over three long summer months. It meant farewells to some of the company who would seek greener pastures. Ben Ringgold would not return to Richmond, but he carried away impressions of Booth as a youngster with wonderful dramatic genius to develop.[130] Ike Mortimer, also departing, thought him a person of great promise, more spirited than Edwin and ultimately much finer.[131] Harry Langdon said his good-byes as well and advised Booth to make money by assuming his family name.

"Now, John, you go off into the farther south and take your father's name," Langdon counseled. "You are as much entitled to the use of your father's name as your brother. If you play in the far south as John Wilkes Booth, the son of the old tragedian, they will come to hear you, and you can make a good stake."[132]

Booth listened politely but declined. He would make it, all right, and, when he did, no one would carry him. He would be great on his own.

3

· · · ·

LIONS AND FOXES

"WHEN JOHN WILKES BOOTH was in the Richmond Stock Company, he was very young," wrote his friend Ned Alfriend. "In his early twenties he weighed about one hundred and seventy-five pounds, was a little taller than his brother Edwin, possessed marvelously intellectual and beautiful eyes, with great symmetry of feature, an especially fine forehead, and curly black hair. He was as handsome as a Greek god. It is saying a great deal, but he was a much handsomer man than his brother Edwin. He possessed a voice very like his brother's, melodious, sweet, full and strong, and was like him, a consummate elocutionist."[1] Thus Booth appeared as the young actor returned to Richmond in the late summer of 1859 to commence his second year at the Marshall Theatre.

Important changes had been made in the company during his absence.[2] Edwin Adams, a spirited actor who excelled in romantic drama, was the new leading man. "A handsome dashing sailor lad" in type, he did wonderfully clever parodies, including one of the elder Booth as Iago.[3] For a time Booth and Adams were quite friendly. They may have visited Boston together at some point, as letters written by Booth to friends in that city often send greetings to Adams's relatives who lived there. But the relationship cooled. The pair was too close in age, looks, and ambition. After the assassination, Adams readily offered information about Booth, then a fugitive, and told unflattering stories of "this horrid monster," his erst-while friend.[4] Also new to the Marshall was Clementina DeBar, June's ex-wife. Her divorce from John's brother had been bruising, but John re-mained cordial to Clem and fond of her daughter, Blanche, who had lived with the family ten years earlier. Other newcomers included George, Ella, and Eliza Wren, English-born actors and singers. The delightful Ella caught Booth's eye immediately. Finally there was the youthful Oliver Doud Byron. It amused Israel B. Phillips, the corpulent stage manager of the Marshall known as "Old Phil," to call this youngster "Old Doud." Since Byron was a neophyte, nothing could have been more absurd, but the handy youth "was the right hand and both feet [of Phillips,] who was not active on his pedal extremities," recalled John Barron.[5] Byron spent a great deal of time with Booth, liked him, and thought him a fine actor.[6]

Booth made his home at the Powhatan Hotel, sharing his room occa-sionally with Byron. Not the best hotel in the city, the Powhatan was com-fortable and convenient to the theater, accommodating the late hours and irregular mealtimes of the actors. Kunkel, Moxley, and Adams also lived there, as did James W. Collier, the Marshall heavy. The fraternity felt at home at the Powhatan, even putting on a special performance at the hotel during the Christmas season. Significantly, the Powhatan was a temper-ance house. Its prohibition of alcohol reinforced Booth's determination to stay clear of liquor.[7] In this and other ways life at the hotel brought a semblance of stability to Booth's life. Here he was known under his own name, and here, for the first and only time in his life, he was stationary enough to be listed in a city directory.[8]

THE HEIR-AT-LAW, a popular five-act comedy, opened the season on Saturday, September 3, 1859. An immense throng mobbed the theater to see it, so numerous that the critic for the *Dispatch* complained he could not get within seeing or hearing distance of the stage. "From floor to roof there was one dense mass of mankind, wedged down, packed and driven into the pit as close as matches in a matchbox, tight as nails in woodwork, [their mouths] open as so many hungry fellows around a free lunch." Even a good place to stand was unavailable.[9] This large crowd received the actors enthusiastically. Booth appeared as Henry Moreland, one of the male leads, with Adams, Chester, DeBar, "Old Doud," and the others taking their appropriate parts. As the evening progressed, an audience member briefly stole the show.

Forced to perch in a gallery window, he slipped and fell out of the building a distance said to be eighty feet to the sidewalk. Amazingly, he walked away from the accident, remarking only that the bricks on Seventh Street were rather hard.[10] Back onstage, Booth's Henry, the beloved of Ella Wren's Caroline, embraced her, exclaiming, "Let me clasp you to my heart and shelter you there forever." She fainted into his arms.[11] The play concluded with the cast, in turn, speaking an epilogue in verse. Ella sang a ballad, and her brother George costarred in a short farce, concluding the evening's entertainment.

Kunkel and Moxley were shrewd to feature their stock company for the first week of each new season. During this shakedown interlude the players worked with each other before the traveling stars arrived. The *Enquirer* reported that the new cast was the best dramatic company with which the managers had ever opened in Richmond.[12] As a bonus, it possessed enough musical talent to produce an opera, "each and every performer sustaining their role with marked ability."[13] The theater was crowded nightly, and Booth was well received. The *Enquirer* stated, in a characteristically brief notice of the resident actors, that he was very good, popular, and well known.[14]

It was generally believed that Southern cities like Richmond were friendlier to actors than cities in the North and were therefore better liked by them. This was the opinion of George Alfred Townsend, the Philadelphia journalist who witnessed Booth's Arch Street efforts. "I have never wondered why many actors were strongly predisposed toward the South. There, their social status is nine times as big as with us. The hospitable, lounging, buzzing character of the southerner is entirely consonant with the cosmopolitanism of the stage and that easy 'hang-up-your-hatativeness' which is the rule and the demand in Thespianship," he wrote.[15] Stripped of its regional bias, Townsend's sentiment would certainly have been endorsed by Kunkel's employees. "Richmond and your beautiful hills," soliloquized John Barron in 1907 at the end of his career, "for my companions still abiding with me and for those who have passed away, I salute you. We lived many happy days enjoying your delightful hospitality and with your generous applause urging us to achievements which otherwise would not have been ours. No people ever paid more devoted homage to dramatic art than the citizens of Richmond. No city in the Union was ever dearer to the heart of the young aspirant for dramatic fame."[16]

Barron's observations explain Booth's growing affection for Richmond, but only in part. As Booth won his way in the city, it was not solely by being an actor. Many Richmonders would receive an actor socially, but, as Barron observed, the actor had to do the rest himself. Booth made friends because he had what Ned Alfriend termed a facility for social success.[17] The young actor entered easily into the world beyond the stage. "He had always been 'one of the boys' in Richmond, ready for a fire or ready for a fray," recalled Mary Bella Beale. She thought Booth had three particular qualities that were claimants upon the Southern heart: "He was brave, ardent, and affectionate."[18] Barron, who occasionally bivouacked in Booth's room at the Powhatan, was highly impressed with his quickness in action and his generosity. And, "as to determination, he was all that the term implies." He presented himself well and impressed acquaintances as a respectable person, neat and careful in his dress, "but never at all gaudy or flashy," stated Joseph W. Southall, a medical student who lived at Booth's hotel.[19] George Crutchfield, a bank clerk, believed Booth's handsome face was an asset, although his close friends teased him about his slightly bowed legs. Crutchfield summed up the common feeling about Booth when he wrote years later to the sculptor Edward Valentine, "He was a man of high character and social disposition and liked by everyone with whom he associated."[20]

Many of Booth's friends, like Crutchfield, were members of city militia companies. These companies provided civic-minded individuals an opportunity for fraternal bonding while supporting public ceremonies and performing actual military duty in times of civil disorder or invasion. Crutchfield, whose father was a city councilman, served in the Richmond Light Infantry Blues, considered by its members to be the socially elite unit in the city. O. Jennings Wise, the governor's son, was a member of Company F, another troop with claims of social distinction. Booth was attracted to a third unit, Ned Alfriend's Richmond Grays.[21] Its members were a varied lot. Some were Christian, some Jewish, some native, some immigrant, and this at a time when such distinctions were matters of great significance. These differences meant little in the Grays, a people's company representative of the military-minded young men of Richmond's white middle class. Known officially as Company A, 1st Regiment of Virginia Volunteers, the Grays were commanded by Captain Wyatt M. Elliott, an attorney and editor. The company enjoyed the honor of traveling to New York City in 1858 to escort the body of President James Monroe home to Virginia for reinterment. Later the Grays spent a week in the city, where they were entertained as guests of New York's celebrated 7th Regiment.[22]

Philip Whitlock, a Polish immigrant who was a private in the Grays, boasted that "our company was considered one of the best drilled companies in the country."

The public musters and dress parades of the Grays were highly attractive to Booth, as were the company's balls, suppers, and encampments. Social as well as military occasions, these events turned heads and caused hearts to flutter. The Grays looked grand parading in their gray jackets trimmed with black above gray winter trousers, each soldier wearing a black varnished knapsack and sporting a brass letter *A* on his cartridge box. The company's distinction, camaraderie, and military virtues captivated Booth.

Several of the Grays were personal friends. Louis J. Bossieux was the first lieutenant of the company; his son Cyrus was a corporal and his son Louis F. a private. The Bossieux family had connections to the theater going back a generation when it owned an entertainment hall at the rear of the Marshall.[23] Alfriend, an aspiring playwright, was a private in the Grays, and so was Miles T. Phillips, who worked evenings in the theater box office. The family of Quartermaster Robert A. Caskie were noted theater aficionados. Individual Grays like Whitlock attended the Marshall frequently. Fond of Shakespeare, Whitlock rarely missed a performance, and when he was a very old man he could still rattle off the prices of seats in different parts of the house.[24]

Booth never enrolled in the company. The theater demanded odd hours and a transient lifestyle that made such commitments difficult. Indeed, the stage tolerated no rivals. Booth understood that. And he knew that Richmond, while delightful, was not home to him as it was to Crutchfield and Alfriend. But Booth socialized with friends in the company and often joined them at their outings. He was a regular when they mustered for fun at Schad's Garden, a rural park in a grove of trees on West Broad Street. There was bowling and target shooting there, and a ballroom with music, dancing, and beer. On these festive occasions Booth generally wore a magnificent velvet vest with large pockets, wrote Herbert Ezekiel, a friend of Whitlock and the Beale family. In one pocket he carried a derringer. In the other, a dirk.[25]

OCTOBER 16, 1859, was a Sunday, and there were no performances at the theater that day. It was just as well. No show could have competed with a real-life drama being enacted elsewhere in Virginia. John Brown, an abolitionist notorious for his activities in the Kansas Territory, launched an antislavery raid into Virginia. Emerging from a staging area on a secluded Maryland farm, Brown and eighteen followers crossed the Potomac River and seized the U.S. government armory in the little town of Harpers Ferry. Hostages were taken and efforts made to liberate slaves. Shooting erupted in the streets. Outraged citizens and local militia besieged Brown and his raiders in the fire-engine house of the armory. On Tuesday morning, October 18, a force of marines under the command of Brevet Colonel Robert E. Lee stormed the building. Wounded, Brown was taken prisoner along with six of his men.

News of the raid produced outrage and anxiety in Richmond. Doubly alarming were initial reports of the size of Brown's force. Rumor had a biracial army of up to 750 abolitionists in the attacking party. Fearing the worst, Governor Henry A. Wise ordered out the 1st Regiment of Virginia Volunteers, the state's first line of defense. The Grays and other units readied themselves throughout the night of October 17, and on the following morning, cheered by a large crowd standing in a heavy rain, they boarded a train and headed north. When they arrived in Washington, D.C., that afternoon, the soldiers learned that the raid had been suppressed; orders were waiting to return home. Their mission superseded by events, the Grays departed for Richmond, never having reached the site of the insurrection.[26]

The entire raid lasted less than forty-eight hours, but the shock of the event was profound and long-lasting. Brown and his little army of black and white abolitionists, woefully inadequate to accomplish anything practical, had achieved one extraordinary thing. They had taken the argument over slavery from distant western prairies and brought it home to Virginia. Slavery was to be overthrown by violence, Brown declared in a speech, "and it would be war to the knife and knife to the hilt."[27] "It seemed to me," wrote William Fellows, a student who lived near the scene of the attack, "that this shaggy bearded man Brown was about as near a human fiend as one could be."[28] In the wake of the raid Fontaine Beckham, the mayor of Harpers Ferry, and three citizens lay dead, as did of ten of Brown's own party and one of Lee's marines. As John H. Claiborne, a Virginia doctor, wrote, the event "opened the eyes of the Southern people to the great gulf which separated them from the North, a gulf not wide enough nor deep enough to insure them safety or to secure them from rapine and murder."[29]

Booth, performing in Lynchburg at the time, was deeply disturbed by the raid. "He was always an intense Southerner in all his feelings and thoughts, on all the questions that were dividing the North and South," wrote Alfriend, and his reaction to the raid was predictable.[30] Brown was a common cutthroat and murderer.[31] Back in Richmond, Booth visited the hotel bars, loudly declaiming what manner of punishment Brown deserved.[32] He told friends he desired to go to Harpers Ferry "and help shoot the d-d Abolitionists."[33] For the chance of a dustup with the radicals, "John Wilkes was in a perfect fever of delight," recalled Edwin Hunter Brink of the Marshall. These feelings were shared by many others. Isabella Pallen, "one of Virginia's most devoted admirers and one of the most rebellious of rebels, gave Wilkes Booth her blessing," recalled her daughter, Mary Bella. She offered him for the purpose the use of a rusty old carbine from the War of 1812.[34]

Brown was promptly tried and convicted of murder, treason against the Commonwealth of Virginia, and "conspiring with negroes to produce insurrection." On November 2, 1859, he was sentenced to hang. The execution was set for December 2 at Charlestown, county town of Jefferson County.[35]

In response to this extraordinary situation, Governor Wise's office was flooded with mail from across the nation. Much of it was sympathetic to the old abolitionist. One writer, signing himself "John Brown" and dating his letter on the scheduled day of execution, told Wise that on arriving in heaven, he had been greeted by Saint Peter with the words "Welcome, John Brown, you are the first man from Virginia in 20 years." Most letters were less good-natured. They were characterized by one Richmond journalist as "full of all manner of threats at vengeance from raving abolitionists and marauders."[36] The letters promised new raids into Virginia or vowed revenge on the commonwealth if Brown were executed. Several writers threatened Wise personally. Expressing outrage at Brown's sentence, one writer signed his letter "Brutus," a name whose menace could not be lost on any head of government. Meanwhile, anxiety mounted in Charlestown, where Brown was jailed. Strangers were seen in the area, prowling arsonists burned barns, and Brown received letters declaring that he would be rescued. This situation was reported to Wise along with rumors that a large force of armed men was marching on the town. Colonel J. Lucius Davis, the commander of troops in the area, telegraphed his alarm to Richmond and asked for help.[37]

Surprised once by fanaticism, Governor Wise reacted decisively. "The military of this city were ordered to pack knapsacks," wrote George W. Libby of the Grays, "and to be ready at the sounding of alarm from the bell in the Old Bell Tower" in Capitol Square near Booth's hotel.[38] A feeling of crisis spread through Richmond. Early in the evening of Saturday, November 19, 1859, the great bell, customarily reserved for fire alarms, began a distinctive toll. Six strokes followed by a pause, then six more. The noise threw the city into tumult. An excited mass of people surged onto the grounds around the governor's mansion. Mounting the portico of the building, Mayor Joseph Mayo harangued the crowd with the latest facts and rumors from Harpers Ferry.[39]

Part of the audience broke away and headed for the Broad Street depot of the Richmond, Fredericksburg, and Potomac Railroad, located directly opposite the Marshall Theatre. The 1st Regiment gathered in the street to entrain. There with the Grays were Alfriend, Whitlock, Libby, and the Bossieuxs. Perspiring profusely, Miles Phillips rushed over from the theater to join them, having bid farewell to his five young daughters. The girls clung tearfully to him as Phillips told his boarder Charlie Brooks about a shotgun and a musket he had left behind at home in the event trouble spread to Richmond. "Load them up," Phillips ordered. The feeling along the street was intense, wrote an acquaintance of Phillips, "for not knowing the exact nature of the summons, and supposing that actual fighting was going on at Charlestown, the parting of the volunteers from their families had all the semblance, and in fact reality, of the departure of soldiers to a bona fide, acknowledged, and declared war."[40]

Joseph Southall, the medical student living at Booth's hotel, was heading toward the depot with a group of his friends when he noticed the young actor walking just ahead of him. Near the theater he "saw Booth, who had been walking at a brisk pace, stop suddenly as if he had forgotten something." Just as Southall reached Booth, the actor wheeled about and hurried off. "I have ever since been convinced that when he stopped and stood for a moment in thought that he then and there decided that his duty to the State had first claim on his allegiance in an emergency like that," Southall concluded, "and that when he turned back, he had made up his mind as to his course."[41]

Face flushed and deeply agitated, Booth burst into the theater dressing room. Collier and Edwin F. Barnes, one of the supers, looked up at him in surprise.

"What is the matter?" exclaimed Collier.

"I'm off to the wars!" Booth exulted. Hastily snatching his overcoat and hat, he rushed from the building.[42]

He left without a word to the management, added the actor James E. Murdoch.[43] Kunkel would be furious. Attendance at the Marshall had suffered considerably since Brown's raid, while those present were distracted. There were brawls in the audience during performances and arrests of patrons "raising a rumpus." The actors were equally preoccupied. One critic lamented that Barry Sullivan was miserably sustained by the company, with Booth named as among the few exceptions who played well. The current star, William E. Burton, was ill and had canceled his engagement. The coming week would have to be taken by the company, one of whose most popular members had just bolted madly out the door.[44]

Back in the street Booth found the train ready to start. Running up to the baggage car, where Libby and Louis F. Bossieux were stowing equipment, he told the privates that he wished to go along. "We informed him that no one was allowed on that train but men in uniform," Libby explained. "It was a soldiers' train." Down the line exceptions were being made, however. Southall's party was pushing one of its number onboard. Shouts came from the train for Booth to get on.[45] The actor pled again for the privilege, saying he was so anxious to go that he would buy a uniform if necessary. This was too much for Libby. "After some consultation with him, Bossieux and I each gave him a portion of our uniform." Libby provided a coat, Bossieux a cap and accoutrements. The result was nondescript but adequate, and the men pulled Booth onboard.[46] Surprisingly, the elder Bossieux, a very strict disciplinarian ("and therefore unpopular"), made no objection to his presence, and Captain Elliott, in temporary command of the regiment, granted him permission to stay. Duties would be found for him.[47] Welcomed aboard, Booth wandered the densely crowded train, mingling with the soldiers. They were surprised to see him. Crutchfield asked the young actor how Kunkel could possibly get along without him. Booth replied that he didn't know and didn't care.[48]

The engine idled a moment longer, awaiting the arrival of Governor Wise, who would accompany the troops. Bathed by the gas streetlights, an immense crowd stood in Broad Street, "nearly the whole male population appearing to have turned out to witness the departure of the volunteers," and many women, too, wrote Henry Hudnall of the Richmond Howitzers.[49] By now the Marshall Theatre's audience had joined them. A roar of approval announced the governor. At about ten o'clock the long train jerked forward at last. Soldiers pushed to the windows to wave good-byes. The street came to life, Hudnall continued, and "sent up cheer after cheer, which seemed to shake the very heavens," as the cars pulled off into the night.

The trip to Charlestown was roundabout. It took Booth and the Grays north through Fredericksburg to Aquia Creek. Here the rail line ended and the soldiers left the train to board a steamer that carried them the remaining forty miles to Washington. They arrived in the nation's capital around daybreak. "The regiment was then formed and marched down Pennsylvania Ave.," recalled John O. Taylor of the Grays. Washingtonians, throwing open their windows at the sound of drums, "were not a little surprised to find nearly 400 Virginia troops (who 12 hours before, were not even in uniform), marching through their streets, fully equipped for action." Wise, wearing his high beaver hat and large silver spectacles, walked prominently with them. Booth was directly behind the governor, his overcoat thrown over his arm. They marched past the White House, a deliberately intimidating act, and headed for the depot of the Baltimore and Ohio Railroad. A train had been ordered and should have been ready to take them north to Relay House in Maryland, where the lines split and one branch headed west toward Harpers Ferry. Wise was livid to find no connection waiting, but he did what any good politician would do with a crowd at hand: mounted a wagon and gave a speech.[50] The soldiers ate breakfast and milled about until their transportation finally appeared, and the regiment left for Harpers Ferry, arriving there in the late afternoon of Sunday, November 20. Wise stationed several companies at the approaches to Charlestown and traveled on the eight additional miles to the county seat with the Grays and three additional companies.

It was dark and threatening rain when the men arrived in Charlestown. Colonel Davis had informed the citizens of the soldiers' coming, adding obsequiously that they were led by Wise, "our Great Chief who at the first alarm threw around you an impregnable wall of chivalry and himself stood ready to shed his blood in your defence."[51] Charlestown greeted the governor and his troopers as if they were just such a set of deliverers. Eighty-four hot dinners were ready for the Grays at a local hotel, but the grateful public intervened and led the soldiers away to private homes.[52] Later the Grays found quarters at a large stone warehouse.[53] Booth bunked down on a straw pallet that he shared with his fellow soldier Wirt Harrison. Alfriend put his bed next to Booth's.[54] This warehouse, an old tin factory, would be home for the duration of their stay. The Grays had to share the simple structure with the Black Horse Cavalry of

Fauquier County, but it was a happy association. The supply wagon of the Black Horse, parked in the rear yard of the building, contained a store of whiskey. The cavalry shared it liberally with their Richmond comrades.[55]

Over the next two weeks Booth became a frequent sight in the area. Joseph E. Whiting, an actor who played a supporting role in John and Edwin's *Richard III* performance in Baltimore in 1858, noticed him on sentry duty in front of the jail where Brown and his companions were confined.[56] Alfriend remembered him taking night duty as a sentinel.[57] Booth was also said to have assisted the cavalry in guarding the road to Martinsburg.[58] Booth's official duties were those of a sergeant in the regimental quartermaster's department.[59] He was put to work under the direction of Robert A. Caskie, the theater buff who had done quartermaster duty for the Grays during their summer visit to New York City. Pedestrian as the job was, Booth could have done nothing more helpful to his friends. Caskie's first order was to procure overcoats to protect the soldiers from the chilly night air of the mountains.[60]

Although Wise found the region quiet, he continued the precautionary buildup of soldiers, pouring in militia from every part of Virginia—the Alexandria Rifles, Clarke Guard, Shepherdstown Cavalry, Woodis Riflemen, Mount Vernon Guards, Winchester Rifles, Petersburg Artillery, Newtown Cavalry, Wheeling Rifles, Montgomery Guard, and cadets from the Virginia Military Institute. This imposing concentration swelled to twelve hundred armed men or more, nearly doubling the size of the town. Additionally, several hundred federal troops secured the armory at Harpers Ferry. It became apparent that no attempt to rescue Brown could succeed. "Perfect quiet prevails," Major General William B. Taliaferro, who had superseded Davis in command, reported to the governor.[61]

Nevertheless, tensions remained high. The woods were feared full of "land-pirates, barn-burners, Brownites, and assassins."[62] Nervous pickets reported seeing rockets streak over nearby hills, presumably fired by abolitionist fanatics. Wise worried that if these friends of Brown could not rescue him, they would seize others as hostages for him or kill people in revenge. Sure enough, one night a shot rang out. Alarm swept the town, shutters were slammed, lights extinguished, and soldiers filled the streets. The excitement was extreme until it was learned that a sentry had opened fire on a cow.[63] "New troops are very apt in the novelty of their situation to mistake objects," explained Taliaferro. When these alarms occurred (and they occurred frequently), the Grays would dash to the jail double-quick and form a hollow square around it to repel any rescue attempt.[64] No "Brownite" ever appeared. Alfred Collier, one of the Grays, finally saw a dark presence charging his way. He opened fire—at a horse. His shot missed, and the animal trotted nonchalantly past Collier, through a gate and into a barn. It was bad enough to fire at a horse, but in that event, one must certainly hit it. Collier became the laughingstock of the company.

One night scouts came in to report that a party of Northern raiders had crossed the Potomac and established a signal light on a mountain outside town. "The report created intense excitement," recalled W. H. Caskie, the brother of Booth's commanding officer. Subsequent investigation confirmed the presence of the light but could not determine its source. Eager to learn the nature of these pyrotechnics, Booth secured permission from Taliaferro to make a personal reconnaissance. He crawled under cover of darkness to the location, where he discovered to his surprise "that the so-called signals were merely sparks from the chimney of a little cabin occupied by an old couple who were burning large chunks of wood to keep comfortable." Booth spoke to the husband and wife and learned that they were guilty of no more than living a life so isolated that they had never heard of John Brown. When the actor reported his findings to Taliaferro, the general did not believe him. Booth replied indignantly that if the general would not take his word, he should send him back to the spot with someone in whom he had more confidence. The following night Booth returned to the cabin with a scouting party. The scouts asked the elderly pair if they had seen anyone unusual in the neighborhood. The old couple replied that they certainly had. A soldierly-looking man had been prowling around their place in the wee hours of the morning asking questions. In fact that very man was in the cabin with them now, they exclaimed, and the pair pointed dramatically at Booth. Once the laughter died down, Caskie wrote, "the excitement blew over as suddenly as it had appeared."[65]

As Taliaferro's little army settled into place, Charlestown became a garrison town ringed with infantry pickets and patrols of cavalry. Cannon commanded the streets, schools were closed, ordinary business was suspended, and strict military law was observed. Drums beat reveille early each morning, assembling soldiers in the streets where roll was called. In squads of ten or fifteen, the men trooped to a hotel or private home for breakfast. A dress parade might follow, after which orders were read to the soldiers. The remainder of the day was employed in cleaning weapons, policing barracks, discussing the merits of firearms, lining up at the post office, or visiting one another's camps. Toward dark those going on picket duty, wrapped well against the weather, received the password and affixed bayonets to their rifles before setting out. The remaining soldiers made themselves comfortable in their quarters. Four companies filled the courthouse, one of which, Richmond's Company F, occupied the courtroom where Brown's trial occurred. Units were also stashed about here and there in churches, halls, and other vacant spaces. December approached, and warm stoves were the focal point of each barrack. Around them music and laughter sounded in the night.[66]

The inconveniences and temporary loss of freedom attendant to the presence of so many soldiers annoyed some residents. One wit published a "PROCLAMATION!" filled with biting satire. Anonymously issued on November 30, the broadside appeared at first glance to be an official document. In it, however, the writer expressed contempt for "the mushroom, corn-stalk military now quartered among us" and resentment at what he felt was the overly numerous retinue of self-important officers, staff, and "toot horns" who were their bosses. He went after both. "Soldiers, for fear of an attack by Brown's men, will remain in their Barracks, as in case they expose themselves on the streets, they may run the risk of being hurt," the proclamation read. "The General commanding, the Mayors, Attorneys, Colonels, Majors, Captains, Lieutenants, and Corporals being more numerous than the rank and file, and therefore of more importance, are hereby particularly warned to remain in their Quarters, as in case of attack, especially during the night, the citizens who are able and willing to defend the town from all attacks, either by Brown's men or anybody else, may be incommoded in the performance of their duties."[67] "Gen. Tumblebug" signed the document as commander in chief and "Bob Dunghill" as military secretary. Taliaferro was not amused by the broadside, possibly because its author touched a nerve. The five Richmond companies and their regimental staff carried sixty-five men above the rank of private, including Quartermaster Sergeant Booth.[68]

Most Charlestown citizens reacted more positively to the soldiers. Reassured by their presence, the public welcomed them into nearly every home. Lucy Ambler, daughter of the town's Episcopal minister, wrote that the soldiers' impact on Charlestown society reminded her of a Jane Austen novel when a regiment comes to camp in a small town. "It must be owned that the young people experienced a series of delightful thrills when they heard that an invading force of the flower of Virginia chivalry was about to be quartered among them," she wrote. "It is safe to hazard a guess that every young woman in the neighborhood was at the station [when they arrived] unless restrained by parental authority." One of the village belles passed an immediate verdict on the Grays as they marched up the muddy street. "Beautiful," she announced.[69]

While the crisis disrupted the ordinary course of life in Charlestown, the army compensated the region by flooding it with dollars, and Booth was at the center of all the action. His office was responsible for the daily needs of some four hundred soldiers of the 1st Regiment. The department purchased everything these men required, from tin cups and twine to nails and blankets. The men were active eaters as well.[70] Food and supplies were brought from Baltimore, Washington, and Richmond, or purchased locally.[71] Booth helped sort, label, and deliver the largesse, and he was regularly in and out of village shops.[72] John O. Taylor of the Grays wrote, "He proved to be a good man for the place."[73] Some merchants and farmers, reprimanded for price-gouging, were difficult to deal with. Nevertheless, Booth, in the area of his limited responsibility, was reported in both Charlestown and Richmond to be an efficient soldier well versed in military matters.[74] Caskie wrote, in a barbed compliment many years later, that "the actor, by strict attention to duty, natural modesty, and gentlemanly conduct, wormed himself in the good graces of the officers."[75]

While at work in the quartermaster's office, Booth was introduced to John Yates Beall, a local farmer who lived at Walnut Grove plantation.[76] Beall was in Charlestown to sell farm products and became a familiar figure at headquarters. He provided the soldiers a ton of fresh beef and for their horses seven tons of hay and hundreds of bushels of oats.[77] In time legend would say that Booth and Beall were devoted friends, college roommates at the University of Virginia, even cousins. None of it was true, nor was Booth engaged to Beall's sister Mary.[78] But the two became acquainted, as Booth told his friend John McCullough.[79] The pair had an additional opportunity to rub elbows at the home of Beall's aunt Louisa, where a number of the Grays boarded.[80] After Booth left Charlestown, he never saw Beall again. Their brief friendship would prove fateful, however.

Bored in the absence of danger, the troopers enlivened things on their own. "Our boys are playing all kinds of Deviltry at the Barracks," wrote Isaac Cocke, referring to the fiddling, singing, dancing, burlesque opera, and other antics he heard and saw.[81] Soldiers became "Fox and Hounds," chasing each other about the streets like boys. Nine Grays crowded into a mule cart and toured the village, presenting an appearance they would have blushed over at home in Richmond.[82] Lewis Dinkle, a local photographer, took ambrotypes of Booth and several of his comrades in playful poses near the jail.[83] But the Woodis Riflemen outdid everyone. One afternoon they marched hurriedly down the street to the train station, shaking hands along the way and receiving hurried cheers, adieus, and farewell wishes of onlookers. Citizens and soldiers were taken aback, however, when a short time later the Riflemen returned to their barracks, laughing at them, pointing and shouting, "Sold!!"[84] "The military aspect of the town yesterday was very gay," wrote a reporter for the *Baltimore American* about November 24, 1859, "the weather being fine, and the troops availing themselves of the opportunity of making an exploration of the streets and alleys, many going beyond the suburbs. The Richmond Grays and Company F, which seemed to vie with each other in the handsome appearance they present, remind one of uncaged birds, so wild and gleesome they appear. Amongst them, I notice Mr. J. Wilkes Booth, a son of Junius Brutus Booth, who, though not a member, as soon as he heard the tap of the drum, threw down the sock and buskin and shouldered his musket and marched with the Grays to the reported scene of deadly conflict."[85] Newspapers in Richmond, Petersburg, and New York City reprinted this flattering notice.

Back in his barracks home Booth had an audience quite as captive as Brown, and like the professional he was becoming, he worked it. Nearly every night before taps, this "remarkably handsome man would regale us around the camp fire with recitations from Shakespeare," recalled Libby. "Entertaining chap, he was—amused us every night." [86] Alfriend recalled that Booth was very fond of reciting, "which he did in such a fiery, intense, vigorous, brilliant way as to forecast that great genius he subsequently showed on the stage."[87] Watching Booth's winning personality at work, Libby wrote many years later, no one could have imagined he would commit the act that he did.

The troops were not alone in requiring some enjoyable distraction. "Booth sensed the need for diversion and entertainment to help ease the tension," according to local lore, so he agreed to give several evening performances as part of an effort to calm the townspeople.[88] The diarist Susan Keys stated that these entertainments occurred in the Zion Episcopal Church, then serving as soldiers' quarters. Others place them in the Episcopal Lecture Room. Calming or not, Booth's presentations were memorable.

Arthur Hawks, a local boy approaching his twelfth birthday, was so delighted with Booth's dramatic readings that he spoke of them with anima-
tion six decades later.[89]

Stellar as his performances may have been, Booth was a mere super in
the great drama under way. John Brown, star of this show, awaited his fate
in the jail across from the courthouse. Booth was anxious to see the lion in
his lair, encouraged by knowledge that the old abolitionist received all
manner of visitors in his cell. Brown lectured one proslavery minister that
the man did not know "the A B C's of Christianity," but he greeted most
callers with remarkably good nature.[90] Once an entire militia company
from Frederick, Maryland, trooped in. Brown rose and dutifully shook
each man's hand.[91] At length, worn out by such visits, Brown asked Sheriff
James W. Campbell to protect him from morbid curiosity.[92] This slowed
but did not stop the visitors. John Avis, the jailor, admitted Taylor of the
Grays, and Taylor decided that Brown was "about the meanest looking
man you would care to see, a very low order of a man."[93]

Booth wished to form his own opinion. The day before the execution
he sought out Sheriff Campbell, a person who treated Brown with such
consideration that he would be remembered in the condemned man's
will. Campbell was favorably impressed with Booth, whom he described
to family as "a handsome, fresh, black-eyed youth of 20 years," and he
admitted the young man to the jail.[94] Booth found Brown confined in a
narrow cell off a heavily guarded corridor on the left as one entered the
jail. Here the actor spent a moment "visiting the old pike-man," as
Townsend whimsically expressed it.[95] No details of the meeting survive.
Booth's subsequent writings only make apparent that he perceived himself in the presence of a man of heroic dimension. Years later even Governor Wise expressed pity for Brown, who had suffered such hardships in
life that he seemed "as much sinned against as sinning," and Booth felt a
qualified sympathy, too. "Poor John Brown," he wrote in 1864, "poor old
Brown." "He was a brave old man," he told Asia.[96]

The morning of Friday, December 2, 1859, was cool and clear.[97] Reveille
sounded at daybreak. Booth had breakfast at the Carter House and joined
the Grays as they assembled.[98] Special orders had been issued to each company. Some were sent to the jail to form Brown's escort, others fanned out
along the roads and into the woods, alert for mischief-makers, and Sergeant
Booth and the Grays marched directly to the field of execution. Although
the entire town was in motion by 9:00 a.m., the mood seemed subdued.

There was no military band music, drumbeat, or bugle blast, wrote one officer, "no saluting by troops as they passed one another, nor anything done for show."[99] The long-anticipated day proved to be a somber one.

Brown's gallows, erected earlier that morning, stood on a small knoll in a large meadow. Passing a piece of artillery commanding the road, the Grays marched through a gate and onto the field. Small white flags marked their position. In front of the gallows were the cadets of the Virginia Military Institute, conspicuous in red flannel shirts crossed by white belts. They were flanked by the cadet howitzer detachment commanded by Major Thomas J. Jackson, later known as "Stonewall." The Grays formed before the gallows obliquely on the cadets' left. To enhance their appearance the company had been ordered by height down the ranks. Company F gathered across on the right. It was clear that the best-equipped and -trained companies had been deliberately placed near the scaffold. The two Richmond companies, their soldiers shoulder to shoulder in solid squares, looked so impressive that Major J. T. L. Preston of VMI felt that, while "inferior in appearance to the cadets, they were superior to any other company I ever saw outside the regular army." By ten o'clock all was ready.

His arms pinioned, Brown was led out of the jail door shortly before eleven. He was dressed in the worn black suit of ordinary business clothes he had had on since the night of the raid. With his old slouch hat and stubble of beard, he looked seedy and shopworn. Brown's face was prison-bleached, his eyes turning from side to side at the spectacle before him. A mass of soldiers—six infantry companies and a cavalry troop—awaited him in the street. Impressed, Brown remarked, "I had no idea that Governor Wise considered my execution so important." The undertaker George Sadler was present with a furniture wagon. Brown, Avis, and Campbell climbed aboard and took seats on a pine box that contained the condemned man's coffin. Soldiers surrounded the wagon, the team of horses was stirred, and the eight-minute procession to the gallows began.

The chill was gone with the dew, and the morning had become as balmy as a day in May. Brown talked freely on the ride. To the east and south of Charlestown were the Blue Ridge Mountains, covered with the slight haze that gave them their name. Farther south and west were farms and rolling tracts of forest. "What a beautiful country," exclaimed Brown wistfully. "I had no idea it was so lovely." Elijah Avey, an eyewitness, thought Brown owned the lightest heart in Charlestown that day.[100] Fate was permitting him to die publicly for a cause to which he had given everything. "I cannot say what was in his heart," Avis declared, but Brown was no coward.[101] He appeared perfectly composed and determined. Major Preston thought his demeanor was intrepid. Sadler summed up their common opinion when he said, "Capt. Brown, you are a game man."[102]

Booth was standing in rank next to Philip Whitlock when Brown's wagon arrived at the scaffold. Whitlock estimated that the Grays were about thirty feet from the gallows, giving the actor an extraordinarily good vantage point from which to watch the condemned man as he approached the steep steps to the scaffold.[103] "Brown mounted as calmly and quietly as if he had been going to his dinner," recalled Parke Poindexter, a soldier in Company F. "He did not exhibit the slightest excitement or fear."[104] At the top, Brown bid farewell to Sheriff Campbell, whom he had made executor of his will. To Avis he said, "I have no words to thank you for all your kindnesses to me."[105]

Now bareheaded, Brown stood alone. "A dead stillness reigned over the field," wrote one reporter. Governor Wise feared the old man would use the moment to deliver an antislavery lecture.[106] Brown said nothing, however, merely looking out, about, and beyond. Booth, despite confidence in the justice of Brown's sentence, experienced a rush of sympathy on seeing him, feeling "a throb of anguish as he beheld the old eyes straining their anxious sight for the multitude he vainly had thought would rise to rescue him." Among the eight-hundred-plus soldiers and officials on the field, Brown did not have a single friend. Booth thought he was searching the distant hills for them. "His heart must have been broken when he felt himself deserted," Booth later told Asia.[107]

The condemned man's feet were tied together and a white linen hood pulled over his face. His noose adjusted, Brown was brought forward onto the drop. "I am ready now," Brown said to Campbell, his executioner. "I do not want to be kept standing here unnecessarily long." All waited, however, as the escort party from the jail maneuvered into position. Five, perhaps ten interminable minutes of tramping about continued. Brown stood with the rope around his neck, unsure which second would be his last. His bony fingers drummed impatiently behind his back. "Be quick," he urged Avis. Brown continued resolute through the delay. "Once I thought I saw his knees tremble," wrote Major Preston, "but it was only the wind blowing his loose trousers."

At 11:15 the military authorities gave their signal. Campbell immediately took a hatchet and with one swift blow cut the rope holding up the trap door. It fell away with a screech of its hinges. Brown plunged three feet, then jerked to a halt. His arms thrashed up, his knees bent, and his fists clenched violently. The body quivered and struggled. In seconds it grew still. Death came quickly for the old abolitionist. Soon the only movement of his form came from the wind blowing it to and fro.

Booth suddenly felt weak and light-headed. "He got very pale in the face and I called his attention to it," wrote Whitlock. "He said he felt very faint."

"I would like a good, stiff drink of whiskey," Booth added. Booth's reaction would be exaggerated as others retold it, until he was staggering and catching hold of a support to stand erect at the mere sight of Brown walking to the gallows.[108] Whitlock's own handwritten account of the episode, stating simply that Booth grew pale and said he "would then give anything for a good drink of whiskey," is credible for its lack of embellishment. Whitlock added that Booth was distressed.

A deliberate death was a difficult thing to stand and watch, and Booth was not the only person struggling with his feelings. A crude comment or a chortle was heard here and there, but there was an almost oppressive silence on the field. Sheriff Campbell was so troubled he would not even look at the body, keeping his eyes deliberately turned away. His nephew William Fellows, a guard at the jail, said that after nearly four decades he had "never quite recovered from my personal sorrow at his execution, legal and necessary though it might have been." "A very solemn scene," thought Major Jackson, who sent up a prayer for Brown's soul. Major Preston broke the stillness around him by declaring, "So perish all such enemies of Virginia! All such enemies of the Union! All such foes of the human race!" Yet he wrote to his wife, "It was a moment of deep solemnity and suggestive of thoughts that make the bosom swell. The mystery was awful—to see the human form thus treated by men—to see life suddenly stopped in its current, and to ask one's self the question without answer —'And what then?'"

Soldiers were kept on the field until Brown was pronounced dead; then they returned to quarters. Booth dined again at the Carter House and that night kept an engagement at the home of Wells J. Hawks, a local politician. Owner of a carriage-making business, Hawks had opened his house to entertain officials, and Booth was in demand. Hawks's son Arthur, Booth's most enthusiastic fan in the village, greeted the actor at the door. The boy had been on the gallows field but missed the fatal moment when, perched on a fence in a distant corner, he had lost his balance and toppled off. Tea was served in the Hawks family parlor as Booth performed "Shakespeare and other poems."[109] The Sadler family was present and remembered his rendition of the poem "Beautiful Snow" by John Whitaker Watson.[110] Arthur was most taken with the quarrel scene from *Julius Caesar.* "Surely," Arthur later reflected, "John Wilkes Booth was the greatest Brutus who ever lived."[111] In 1925, more than sixty-five years after that evening, Arthur wrote to Edward Valentine, "I am a great admirer of all the Booth family including John Wilkes Booth," underlining his name for emphasis.[112]

Booth departed with the Grays for Richmond the following day (Saturday), spent that night in Washington, and arrived in Richmond on Sunday afternoon, December 4, 1859.[113] He traveled well supplied with mementos of his remarkable experience. From Sadler he secured a section of the wooden box that contained Brown's coffin—the box upon which Brown sat on the way to his hanging. "That piece of John Brown's coffin [container] Wilkes Booth cherished religiously, distributing bits of it to his particular friends," recalled an associate.[114] He also had one of Brown's impressive spears. Made in Connecticut, this pike had an iron blade two inches wide and about eight inches long, screwed onto a handle made of ash. Down the handle in large ink letters was written "Major Washington to J. Wilkes Booth." The weapon had been presented to Booth by B. B. "Bird" Washington of the Continental Morgan Guard of Winchester, the great-great-nephew of George Washington. Booth delighted in showing to family members this memento linking him to the first president.[115]

Booth's most lasting keepsake was not material, however. It was a set of beliefs consistent in all his future writing and conversation. These were few and simple. Booth rejected a claim circulating in the North that Brown's trial had been hasty or irregular. The old abolitionist "was fairly tried and convicted before an impartial judge & jury," he believed.[116] For his own part, "I may say I helped to hang John Brown," he wrote proudly in 1860, "and while I live, I shall think with joy upon the day when I saw the sun go down upon one trator [*sic*] less within our land." Four years later, after Brown had been embraced by the North, Booth remained proud of his contribution to events in Charlestown. "I was helping our common country to perform an act of justice," he said. He mentioned his role often over the years, although never in boast. Townsend, described in Charlestown as "a John-Brown admirer and negro worshipper," was no friend of Booth or admirer of his role in the Brown affair, but the journalist was quite perceptive in realizing that "Booth never referred to John

Brown's death in bravado."[117] Although he despised Brown's cause, he idolized heroic characters, and Brown fit the mold perfectly. "John Brown was a man inspired, the grandest character of this century!" he exclaimed to Asia. An abolitionist, yes, but no coward hiding behind a New England pulpit. Brown was a lion, and since "open force is holier than hidden craft, the Lion is more noble than the fox." By 1869, when time had seasoned Townsend's understanding of Booth, the journalist wondered if the actor had not learned from Brown the secret of plots and conspiracies he displayed at Ford's Theatre. Indisputably, Booth's service completed his identification with the Old Dominion. "Booth's going to John Brown's execution was the pride of his life. Booth learned in the companionship of that episode to sympathize with Virginia. From his connection with the militia on this occasion, he was wont to trace his fealty to Virginia."[118]

Home in Richmond, Booth had to face a person hardly less formidable than Brown—Kunkel. Often called "Major" for his military-like command of the theater, Kunkel could be six feet of raging *basso profundo* when provoked.[119] The Marshall was his house. It had rules, some strict, but even then the theater was "as good an organization as an actor could care to belong to," the tragedian George C. Boniface pointed out.[120] Booth had crossed the line. "'Tis a great pity he has not more sense," wrote his future sister-in-law Mary Devlin.[121] Booth had joined the Grays, forgetting that he was already enrolled in another company. "He left [that] company in the lurch in the way his father used to do before him."[122] When the runaway returned to the theater, Kunkel fired him.[123]

Richmond newspapers had threatened to expose any businessman so unpatriotic as to discharge an employee on duty in Charlestown.[124] O. Jennings Wise of Company F, a Booth acquaintance who returned on the train with him, was an *Enquirer* editor, and Captain Elliott of the Grays was an editor of the *Whig*. In some manner, perhaps through one of them, word of Booth's predicament spread through the city. Alfriend recalled that in response militiamen gathered, not merely from the Grays but from the entire regiment. A large contingent mustered and marched through the city streets to the theater. There this imposing troop *demanded* that Booth be reinstated.

Horrified, Kunkel complied.

"IT WAS STUDY! STUDY! study! rehearse! rehearse! rehearse! act! act! act!" recalled John Barron of stock life at the Marshall.[125] Two parts a night, then home with two more for the next evening. The pace was exhausting; Booth and the other actors were often discovered asleep behind the scenery, their manuscripts lying beside them.[126] Stars like Murdoch and Clarke came through, and then came the vivacious Lucille and Helen Western. These lovely sisters "understand perfectly how to 'fetch the boys,'" declared Frank Queen of the *New York Clipper*.[127] They drew fine houses with *Hot Corn Girl*, *Three Fast Men*, and *Satan in Paris*. "Tell the public a play is vulgar, not fit to be seen, and it will rush to witness it," lamented the comedian Joseph Jefferson.[128] The Westerns earned a good living on that truth. Richmond thought Helen, a beautiful brunette, simply perfect, and Booth agreed. Less talented than Lucille, black-eyed Helen "likes to show much of her person, swings plenty of curls, and can do a little of everything (if only passably well)."[129]

The actress Mary White was another friend. When illness forced her retirement from the company, Booth indulged a fondness for poetry in the following inscription in her autograph album:

> *Miss White;*
> *May all good angels guard & bless thee.*
> *And from thy heart remove all care.*
> *Remember you should ne're distrest be.*
> *Youth & hope, can crush dispare.*
> +
> *Joy can be found, by all, who seek it.*
> *Only be, right, the path, we move upon,*
> *Heaven has marked it; Find & keep it*
> *Ne're forget the wish of —John.*
>
> *Richmond, Feb 18th 1860*
> *He who will ever be your friend*
> J. WILKES BOOTH

The first letter of each line, as an acrostic, formed a special message: MARY + JOHN.[130]

Booth's most complicated relationship involved Ella Wren, one of nine brothers and sisters, all players.[131] Ella had joined the company the preceding fall with her brother George and sister Eliza. She was an actress, singer, and composer. Her vocals, sung sometimes with sweetness and at other times in

thundertones, later earned her the sobriquet "the Mockingbird of the Southern Theatres." Lacking Helen Western's beauty, Ella had other assets. She
was attractive, unaffected, and vital. Booth was now twenty-one, Ella a year
younger, and they grew infatuated with each other. Marriage was mentioned,
no surprise to her brother Fred, who thought Booth the handsomest man he
ever saw. Brother George, with whom Booth occasionally shared his hotel
room, seemed positive about the actor. "There was no one of my friends that
was better liked," George said. The Booth family also heard of the rumored
engagement, and later Edwin Booth asked Fred, with whom he was performing, "many questions regarding my family, especially of my sister Ella
Wren, who was at one time engaged to be married to his brother."[132]

The Wrens constitute a link to an unsettling event that occurred in
February 1860. Booth and Pat Redford, a handsome clerk, had a fight in
the theater box office. Redford was a ticket agent at the theater, and the
management had staged a benefit performance for him the preceding
winter. Incredibly, Kunkel permitted Redford to take a lead role in the
production.[133] Rose wrote to the family that John had trouble with the
man for some reason. Insults were exchanged, and fists flew.[134] Redford
did like the Wren sisters, and a rivalry over the young women, then being
featured with Booth in a light comedy, may have been the cause. Clearly,
when the dust settled at the end of the season, the romantic landscape had
altered. Booth and Ella went their separate ways. Redford married Ella's
sister Eliza.[135]

Meanwhile, affairs at the theater took an unhappy turn with the withdrawal of John T. Ford from the partnership.[136] Ford had been with
Kunkel since the latter was touring the boondocks with his Nightingale
Minstrels. The departure of the talented administrator and businessman
was a troubling development. Ford handled bookings for all the company's theaters. Without him the Major experienced difficulty in engaging
star power. He was forced to place urgent advertisements for "first class
stars" in the New York newspapers. Exasperated, the normally friendly
Whig lost patience with him. "The present low condition of drama in this
city," it stated, was due largely to Kunkel's lamentable decision to parade
actresses like the Westerns and their ilk before the public. "This place of
amusement has presented so little of strictly intellectual amusement for
some time past that a large number of most respectable patrons have kept
away from it." To win them back the theater should present performers of
artistic merit. More *Hamlet* and less *Hot Corn Girl*. The management was

also challenged to close the bars in the theater and put a stop to activities in "the third tier," theatrical shorthand for prostitution in the upper gallery. "If the theatre can't succeed under reforms such as these, then it ought not to succeed," opined the *Whig*.[137]

Booth was restless and broke. Anxious for something better, he stirred the family in his behalf. Mary Devlin thought of Joe Jefferson, "Old Phil's" predecessor as stage manager of the Marshall. Though Jefferson was not in management at the time, she believed he could procure Booth a better engagement.[138] Jefferson agreed to look into the matter and write Booth about it. On April 14, 1860, the actor received $64.58 from the Commonwealth of Virginia for his service at Charlestown.[139] It was timely money. Richmond was expensive, particularly for a young man inattentive to dollars, and Booth generally lived beyond his means. James Pilgrim thought him extravagant: "He gave no thought to money and was constantly in debt."[140]

Booth's benefit, shared with James W. Collier, was held on May 31, 1860, the last night of the season. The *Enquirer* promoted the pair, annoyed that the management had not given each actor his own individual night. "Our stock company has not been appreciated, even by Manager Kunkel, as they ought to have been. Then, again, 'tis with a manager as with a merchant. He is 'boss' and gets the lion's share, while the poor actor or the poor clerk, jogging along like horses going 'round and 'round at a mill, come out in the evening exactly where they go on in the morning." Since "half the stars that come here are humbugs," the newspaper continued, the public should support these local artists. "Pray do, reader, encourage them. They are good actors and good fellows, too." By way of advice to Booth for his big night, "we would say, 'a little more grape, Captain Bragg,'—that is, have a little more confidence."[141]

The house was well filled for the evening. Booth and Collier took roles in three plays. They opened with the action-packed fifth act of *Richard III*. Booth as Richard and the red-faced Collier, an athlete and boxer, as Richmond provided an excellent fight scene. *The Son of Malta* and *My Fellow Clerk* followed. The *Enquirer* was satisfied. "Booth has proved, as we always thought he one day would, that he inherits no small share of his father's genius, but he has never had sufficient confidence in himself to show it. On Thursday night, however, he got over that to a considerable extent, and his success was proportionate, as was manifested by the hearty and sincere applause bestowed on him. But Booth is young in years, and as he grows older he will gather more pluck, and pluck more laurels."[142]

Booth's two years in Richmond were ended, and he decided to move on. While his immediate future was uncertain, his progress as an actor had been substantial.[143] "He was become very popular in the South," wrote Asia. "Yet he sadly felt in need of a less enthusiastic school."[144] The challenge again was his father. The actress Kate Reignolds believed that the memory of a theatrical generation lasted no more than ten years.[145] For truly great performers like Junius Brutus Booth Sr., that number seems too low. The memory of the elder Booth loomed large in Richmond, the city where his American career commenced. Friends of the son were often family friends. Thomas P. August, colonel of the 1st Regiment, for example, had signed a petition imploring the management to forgive the father a drunken episode in 1850 and restore him to the stage. Miles Phillips and other acquaintances signed, too.[146] If these friends loved the son, John feared they loved him for his father's sake.

James Pilgrim bought an earful when he trespassed on these feelings. Doling out advice, Pilgrim echoed the counsel given by Harry Langdon the previous year and suggested that the young man drop the name Wilkes and play as a son of the elder Booth.

"Damn my father's name!" Booth exclaimed.[147]

His ambition remained intense. "When next you hear of me, I will be famous," Booth told Mary Bella. He slipped onto the little girl's finger a gold ring with the word *Regard* in blue enamel on it. It was his farewell present.[148] Booth left her home, as he did Richmond itself, in some esteem.[149] "Indeed, it would have been strange had it been otherwise," wrote the actor Francis Wilson, a friend of Edwin's who wrote a biography of John. "He was in absolute sympathy and harmony with his surroundings."[150] Richmond had become an ideal city to him. Here he had been reborn socially and professionally. He was fond of saying that to these years he dated his nativity.[151]

4
....

THE UNION
AS IT WAS

EDWIN BOOTH AND MARY DEVLIN were married in New York City on the afternoon of Saturday, July 7, 1860. The simple wedding took place at the home of the Reverend Samuel Osgood, one of the nation's leading Unitarian ministers.[1] Brown-eyed, brown-haired Molly, as Edwin called her, was an actress who retired from the stage to become his wife. She was lovely, affectionate, and intelligent, thought Sam Chester, and the couple blessed with love at first sight.[2] Asia despised her, calling the bride "a deep designing artful actress, a bold-faced woman who can strut before a nightly audience, a poor obscure girl, the lowest Irish class."[3] She did not attend the ceremony, nor did Mary Ann, Rose, or Joseph. John was the only family member present, a gesture of brotherly solidarity and affection that impressed his friends.[4] The younger brother joined a small wedding party composed of Adam Badeau, Mary's sister Catherine, and her husband, Henry Magonigle. When the ceremony was over, John threw his arms around his brother's neck and kissed him.[5] Years later, when their friend Ned Alfriend brought up the topic of the assassination, Edwin pressed his lips together and said, "I could not approve what he did, but *he was my brother*!" The latter words were uttered with great emotion.[6]

Edwin's happiness secured, the brothers looked to John's future through an association with Matthew W. Canning. A good-natured Philadelphian with thin brown hair, mustache, and goatee, Canning was an attorney who had abandoned the law for the stage.[7] He acted briefly before turning to management. When John Wilkes Booth commenced his career at the Arch in 1857, Canning was treasurer of the rival National Theatre. He had an army of friends in the profession, and Booth became one of them. During the actor's Richmond years Canning had been busy establishing theatrical connections in the Deep South. Profits were smaller there than in the North, but general opinion felt "the Southern cities are usually safe cheeses,"[8] and Canning developed a circuit with Montgomery, Alabama, as his hub of operations. He seemed to prosper. Certainly no one looked more successful. Elegantly dressed and dripping diamonds, Canning was the most fashionable man imaginable.

"Edwin Booth asked me to give his brother Wilkes a start," recalled Canning. The manager was intrigued. Edwin had done well reviving the Booth name on a Southern tour the preceding year. But Edwin was a star. John, though able in support and a favorite in Richmond, was young and entirely unproven at the head of a bill. The manager agreed to take the younger brother on the condition that John would be given the opportunity to star for six weeks, with a benefit each Friday, but he would be paid stock wages only. "He was not, strictly speaking, a star," Canning explained. "He was a member of my stock company and played as a star, but of course he did not get the profits a star would receive." Canning claimed in an 1886 interview that he had one additional requirement of his fledgling. "I made it a point with Edwin that he should play under his family name. It would draw me money," he said candidly.[9] When Booth began his appearances for Canning, he ignored the demand and continued playing under the name of Wilkes. Canning gave no indication that this caused friction between them. The pair remained friendly, and from this time on Canning was identified with Booth in the public mind.

Canning's company had talent. John W. Albaugh was its stage manager and male lead. A Baltimorean like Booth, he had worked for the Kunkel-Ford partnership in that city, sharing Booth's hotel room on occasions when he helped out in Richmond. Booth and Albaugh were rivals for the unofficial title of handsomest young actor of the day. Albaugh's future wife, Mary Mitchell, was Canning's leading lady. Half-sister of Maggie Mitchell, Mary had just divorced the Marshall's Jim Collier, whom she discovered making visits to a New York City house of prostitution.[10] James Lewis and James M. Ward provided talent in comic and character roles. The Irish-born Ward performed often with Booth during the latter's career, once before Lincoln. Finally, Sam Chester signed on as leading heavy. "He is a particular friend of mine," Booth explained to Canning.[11] Youth marked this troupe. Booth, Albaugh, Lewis, Ward, and Chester were in their early twenties, and Canning was scarcely older.

"Canning's Dramatic Company" opened its tour at Temperance Hall in Columbus, Georgia, on October 1, 1860. Booth and Mitchell took the title roles in *Romeo and Juliet*. The beau monde of Columbus attended, a large number of whom were debutantes.[12] One wonders how well Mitchell, a single parent nearing thirty and recovering from a painful divorce, played Juliet, a thirteen-year-old girl in the blush of first love. Equally curious is the question of whether Booth, while closer in age to the youthful Romeo, played the part with a mustache. Except in a pair of photographs taken in November 1864, every likeness commonly agreed upon as that of Booth shows the actor with one.[13] Booth had other concerns, however. "I can never be a nimble skip-about like Romeo," he confided to Asia. "I am too square and solid."[14] Nevertheless, his performance was well received. A critic for the *Daily Sun* made allowance for the fact that he was portraying the character for the first time and, while pointing out that John was not as experienced an actor as Edwin, felt he "bids fair soon to equal him. He has all the promise and in personal appearance is handsome and prepossessing."

Ably backed by the company, Booth undertook a new lead character each night for six nights a week. Notable among his roles in this demanding schedule were Pescara in *The Apostate*, Phidias in *The Marble Heart*, Claude Melnotte in *The Lady of Lyons*, and Richard in *Richard III*. These plays in time became the most popular and successful pieces in his repertoire. Such major parts required Booth to study assiduously, and he did. "He works hard," reported the *New York Clipper*.[15]

On Friday, October 12, Booth and Albaugh were with Canning in a room at Cook's Hotel in Columbus when a pistol shot rang out. Canning had shot Booth! The bullet struck the actor in the thigh and, traveling downward, lodged in the upper leg. The wound looked grave. "We thought he would die," recalled the manager. Dr. Francis A. Stanford was summoned. The physician, who fortunately was one of the best-trained doctors in Georgia, examined the patient and found that the bullet had "escaped the important [blood] vessels lying near its course." In other words it missed the femoral artery, a wound that might have killed him in minutes. Booth was seriously injured, but his life was not in immediate danger. Unwilling to risk the complications of surgery, Dr. Stanford left the ball in the leg. He dressed the wound and put the actor to bed.[16]

All accounts agree the shooting was accidental, but there were conflicting stories told as to what actually occurred. In an 1865 biographical sketch of Booth that he prepared, Canning wrote simply that he shot Booth by accident.[17] Twenty years later, in an interview with George Alfred Townsend, Canning elaborated, putting the blame for the incident on Booth. Canning recalled that he had been exhausted that day and went to his room to rest. Booth saw him and said, "Now, you must let me nurse you. You are fagged out." Replying that he needed only sleep, Canning lay down on his bed. He had a pistol in his pocket. "Everybody carried weapons down in that country, and so did I." Noticing it, "Booth yielded to his passion for arms, and he drew it out of my pocket." Canning then claimed that Booth pointed the pistol at a mark on an opposite wall and fired it right there in the room. The manager sprang up and protested, but Booth insisted on firing again to prove his marksmanship. The pistol being rusty, it was difficult to fit a new cartridge. Canning claimed that as he held the pistol, Booth took a knife to scrape it and the cartridge clean. "While in the act of doing it," he alleged, "down came the lock in my hand and discharged the pistol," wounding Booth.

Albaugh remembered the incident quite differently. It was about an hour before curtain on the night of Booth's weekly benefit. *Hamlet* was announced, and Booth and Albaugh were practicing their lines in the former's room. Suddenly Canning appeared at the door with a pistol in his hand. In a teasing temper, he had every manager's fantasy in mind. He announced playfully to the actors that he was there to shoot them. According to Frank P. O'Brien, the assistant scenic artist, Booth caught the good-humored spirit of the remark, and the two began to tussle. Each claimed to be the stronger, but who was? They wrestled, and as the manager threw Booth onto the bed, the pistol accidently discharged.[18]

This mishap, however caused, proved costly. A painful convalescence followed, occupying nearly half the time Canning had promised Booth. The show went on in his absence. Albaugh played Hamlet that night, earned a curtain call, and continued creditably in Booth's subsequent pieces. He was a quick study who, when he forgot his lines, could improvise in the style of a play's dialogue so skillfully that only the other actors were aware of what was happening.[19] Canning, having nearly killed his protégé, paid the invalid's debts when they moved on to Montgomery.[20] His generosity was only fair, but it was also characteristic. Alex Johnston, Canning's brother-in-law, said the manager coined money in Georgia and Alabama, "but like all of his kind he gave it away."[21]

On its final night in Columbus the company staged a benefit for Booth. The *Daily Sun* reported that although he was still too feeble to take part in any performance, Booth came to the theater. "Curiosity to see the rising young tragedian and sympathy for his late misfortune" drew the largest audience in two weeks. Halfway through the entertainment Booth made his way onstage and recited Mark Antony's oration over the body of Caesar from Shakespeare. His pain and weakness were evident to observers, but Booth's voice was finely controlled and his presentation well received.[22]

The company departed for Alabama the following morning, but it was several days before Dr. Stanford permitted Booth to follow. He rejoined the troupe in Montgomery on October 23. A new building had been constructed there over the course of the summer at the cost of forty-five thousand dollars. African American slave women carried bricks for the walls on specially designed hods so fitted to their heads as to allow each person to carry ten bricks at a time up to the masons.[23] Canning leased the second floor of their handiwork, put carpenters, painters, and upholsterers to work, and brought in decorations from New York. The result was a splendid playhouse with seats for up to two thousand people.[24] The theater's festive opening found Booth still sidelined, however, and Albaugh continued as star. Booth's wound was a serious matter. He was suffering its effects two months later when Asia saw him in Philadelphia.[25] Booth did not recover fully from the accident until February 1861.[26] Canning recalled that it "left a large scar on his person, not to be mistaken."[27]

Booth's final week with Canning commenced with *The Apostate* on October 29. One critic noted that, while it was evident that Booth was not back to normal, "his performance still stamps him as a chip off the old block and was received by the large audience with outbursts of applause." A positive review in the *Weekly Post* also made a family comparison: "Mr. Wilkes is a young man of very fine appearance, resembling very much his talented brother Edwin Booth. True, his manner is not so graceful, his voice is not so full; nor his pronunciation so distinct as that of his brother, but this may be attributed to his limited practice rather than to any inferiority of ability."[28] *Hamlet* and *Richard III* relined Canning's pockets, "his large theater full from pit to dome." Booth drew no individual notice in either play from city newspapers. They did announce that in *Romeo and Juliet* "Mr. John Wilkes was all that could be desired. His rendition was received with applause and approbation by the large number present."[29]

Overall, Booth's Montgomery reviews were mixed, and there is no evidence that his reception in the Deep South was so flattering that it sparked in him an uncritical love of the region. James Pilgrim claimed he played only tolerably, and Canning chose not to renew his engagement.[30] Pilgrim, the agent for J. B. Roberts, a tragedian playing many of the same parts as Booth, was not a neutral observer, however. James Lewis stated that Booth enjoyed tremendous success in Montgomery.[31] One wonders if they saw the same man perform. "He played a highly successful engagement," wrote Canning in a statement that may be considered authoritative.[32] "It is a mistake, however, to say that he was chiefly a favorite in the Southern States," Canning cautioned. "They did not take to him down there as much as they [later] did in the West and in the North."

Lewis, Canning's witty low comedian, maintained in an 1875 interview that U.S. Senator Jefferson Davis of Mississippi saw Booth play in Montgomery.[33] Davis sat quietly in the audience "like a grey wolf, and with a solemn sort of manner." This is the sole occasion on which they are placed together by a credible witness—if Lewis were not mistaken. Davis's whereabouts are well documented for this period. He had a series of speaking engagements in Mississippi during the week of Booth's Alabama performances and returned to Washington, D.C., by November 27, 1860. Davis's usual route north was not through Montgomery but by a more expeditious way through Memphis.[34] It is probable, as Lewis also stated, that Booth played before Georgia senator Robert Toombs and former Alabama congressman William L. Yancey, two fiery advocates of Southern independence. Yancey lived in Montgomery, and Toombs was in town to speak at the time. That Davis saw or knew Booth is doubtful.

Booth remained in Montgomery after his engagement ended, and on November 16, 1860, he played *Romeo and Juliet* for the benefit of Kate Bateman, who followed him as star. Kate was a former child actress making the transition to adult leads under the management of her father, H. L. Bateman. A shrewd fellow with stiff wiry hair, Papa Bateman believed his daughter to be the greatest actress of the century, and from a strategically placed seat in the audience his large hands resounded loudly as he led the applause for her. Parental solicitude aside, Kate was elegant and beautiful onstage.[35] It was exciting to theatergoers when the bill was announced because Booth would be the first actor to whose Romeo Kate ever played Juliet. The *Daily Mail* declared the play, promoted "by a large number of our families and leading young men," would be the most fashionable night of the season. Therefore the newspaper urged the audience to dress stylishly and make the occasion brilliant.[36]

The evening came off well, declared the *Mail* in its notice of the following day. Its reviews of Booth continued mixed, however, in the vein of "Mr. Wilkes showed that he can learn to play Romeo with great power, though as yet his conception is crude." Kate was positive about her costar, saying that "he was really a beautiful creature—you couldn't help admiring him—so amiable, so sweet, so sympathetic." Papa Bateman grew interested in him. A man of quick insight, Bateman boasted that he only required five minutes to know the measure of a man,[37] and in Booth he saw something special. Booth was "so good in the part that Mr. Bateman had serious thoughts of engaging him for the *jeune premier* character and bringing him to England to act with Miss Bateman." Booth never went to England or acted again with Kate. "Some trifle interrupted this engagement," recalled a journalist. "This purpose, if it had been carried out, would have saved a great actor to the stage and possibly changed the political destiny of a nation."[38] Booth seemed relieved to have escaped Papa's clutches, writing a friend, "Thank God, I am not yet a Bateman, and may I never be."[39]

Booth's social life was active in Montgomery, bearing out the validity of Lewis's observation of the Deep South that "the people in that section uniformly treated actors with a sense of both their social and professional worth."[40] The affable and romantic young actor was besieged by the attentions of the citizens.[41] The odds and ends that constitute Booth's effects, found after his death, include an invitation to attend the anniversary dinner of the St. Andrew's Society of Montgomery on November 30, 1860.[42] It is unknown if he went, but this stray piece of paper is evidence of the welcome of which Booth was deemed worthy. His problem was not a shortage of such invitations. Rather, like countless other young people with places to go and things to do, he had no money. "I am very hard up," he complained to a friend. "Extravagant habits," the friend thought.

Help arrived when Maggie Mitchell rotated in to star. The ever-popular Maggie volunteered her services for a "Grand Complimentary Benefit" for

Booth on December 1, 1860. Booth took two roles. He played the title character in the two-act drama *Rafaelle*. At the close of this piece he was summoned before the curtain to acknowledge the audience's favor. Maggie followed in the comedy *Katty O'Sheal*, and Booth closed with the roof-raising fifth act of *Richard III*.[43] "Booth, Booth, Booth!!" ran the advertisements, and he performed this night for the only time on his Southern tour under his own name. Booth told friends such as George Crutchfield of Richmond that he would use his family name only when he made his reputation as an actor.[44] Pilgrim believed that he finally assumed the Booth name when "he was made to understand fully his financial difficulties." Both explanations may be true in part and are not mutually exclusive. Be that as it may, John Wilkes was retiring after three long years of apprenticeship. From this night forward, J. Wilkes Booth would star.

It is unclear how much money the big benefit earned him. Canning's actors customarily took in from thirty to one hundred and fifty dollars on their nights;[45] Booth would have been on the high end of such sums. He did net enough money to return north. No less important to Booth's future was a report published in the *Clipper*, a newspaper read by every important manager in the nation. "Mr. Booth's engagement was very successful, and his friends predict for him a brilliant future. Nature has done much for him, and he will soon be on the uppermost round of the ladder."[46] Finally, there was the cane. It was customary for the regular patrons of the theater to present the leading actor at his final performance with the gift of a gold-headed cane. Montgomery presented a cane to Booth, and he was exceedingly proud of it. He showed it to the comedian Stuart Robson, who had been awarded a cane of his own and readily appreciated its significance. A fashionable accessory, the cane was more importantly a badge of esteem and respect to a young actor like Booth, and he would part with it only under dire circumstances. Pawn a velvet coat but never a cane, Robson advised.[47]

Booth had known Maggie Mitchell from his first year in Richmond. There was a steadily increasing attraction between them. Speaking of Booth with a reporter in 1882, Maggie was asked, "Was he a very handsome and agreeable man?" "Oh, very," she replied. "Indeed."[48]

For the moment a young Montgomery woman named Louise Wooster occupied Booth's affections.[49] When Louise was a child, a Gypsy read her fortune and told her, "Were your life a written book and you could look half way into its pages, you would say, 'Let me die tomorrow.'" The forecast proved true. Her rare physical beauty "made men rave and in the end proved her ruin." The orphaned girl was seduced by a family friend. Other predators followed. By the fall of 1860, when Booth visited the city, she was living a self-described "life of shame" with seven other women in a house of prostitution in Montgomery.[50]

Eighteen-year-old Louise, who loved poetry and amateur theatricals, was naturally drawn to Booth, whom she considered wonderfully gifted. Her profession was older than his, but he talked theater with her, sharing his dreams and encouraging hers. "Booth became infatuated with the beautiful young Southern girl, and she with him," wrote one of her friends, and the two became lovers. "I was madly in love with J. Wilkes Booth," she reminisced in her *Autobiography of a Magdalen* (1911). "He was my ideal man, handsome, generous, affectionate, and brave. He was my idol." Booth had nothing to give her but an embroidered handkerchief, but she treasured it, as well as a forget-me-not, the floral emblem of faithfulness and friendship, which she pressed in her keepsake book. Kindness was his best gift, she felt. Employed in an occupation in which she ran a daily danger of mistreatment, Louise wrote that "he was ever kind to me, and for that kindness I will ever love and cherish his memory."

Meanwhile the presidential election of 1860 threatened the unity of the nation. Abraham Lincoln, nominee of the Republican Party and a great favorite in the North, frightened white Southerners. Responding to a speech by Senator Toombs, the *Daily Mail* of Montgomery editorialized that if Lincoln was elected, he must be resisted at all cost. "If the South could be stupid enough to submit to such an administration as Lincoln's for one moment, it ought to be plundered and mulattoized both—made no better than the North!" the newspaper declared.

Illinois senator Stephen A. Douglas, Lincoln's leading rival, brought his presidential campaign to Montgomery on November 2, 1860, and the actor went to hear him speak. "This Union is the greatest blessing ever conferred upon a free people," Douglas told an audience of about four thousand. Its safety was more important than any other thing, including the fate of slavery. Laying into extremists of both sections, he explained the obvious—that Alabama had more security for its institutions within the Union than without. Later that day, as he made farewell remarks at the Alabama River wharf from the deck of the steamer *Virginia*, the floor upon which he stood gave way, hurling Douglas and those nearby to the planks below. Douglas was not seriously injured, but some wondered if the incident was not an omen.[51]

Booth had formerly admired Douglas, recalled Fred Ferguson, an extra at the theater, but the Little Giant's moderation did not suit him. "He was convinced that Douglas was simply a professional politician and a rank opportunist," said Ferguson. The actor retired to Yung's restaurant, where, in the low-ceilinged dining room just past the oyster bar, he expressed his disgust with what he had heard.

"Yung's was John Wilkes Booth's favorite tippling place," recalled Lorenzo F. Woodruff, a Montgomery native. "There gathered the wealth, the brains, the culture, the beauty, and the chivalry of Alabama and the South." When Congressman Yancey announced a speech at the statehouse to rebut Douglas, Booth, Ferguson, and Yancey's eldest son, Ben, walked from Yung's to the capitol to attend. "Yancey's oratory swept the young actor off his feet," said Ferguson, "and he left the meeting in a delirium of enthusiasm. From that time until he left Montgomery he was constantly with Ben Yancey and at every opportunity sought conversation with Ben's father." Stirring his hot toddy, Booth sat and gazed in adoration at the Roman features of the great Fire-Eater as he spoke. Looking at Booth's face, Ferguson realized that it defined fanaticism.

Second thoughts soon set in, however. It took no great intelligence to see that the Yanceys of the world would break up the Union, and that would lead to war. That was fine with Fred and Ben, both future Confederate officers. But Booth had been bred to revere the nation's permanence. While he appreciated Yancey's defense of states' rights, he recoiled from the consequences of disunion. One night at Yung's, as a party of young hotheads pushed back their dinner plates and drained their glasses, Booth stood up at the table. He had strayed from the temperance path and was drinking now—in fact, he was "the hardest drinker of the crowd of hard drinkers," recalled James V. Ashurst, one of those present. Steadying himself by holding the edge of the table, Booth was downcast. "This is a night for us all to remember," he said somberly. "It is fraught with portent." Booth threw back his black hair. It seemed to frame his pale face. Turning his eyes upward, he recited the Lord's Prayer, which Edwin always said was the most all-embracing petition for deliverance from evil that the mind of man could conceive. "He did nothing else. He said nothing else," recalled Ashurst. "The effect of his power and elocution was amazing. That crowd—gay, noisy and disorderly a few minutes before—was hushed into silence. Before the roll of that wonderfully modulated voice, every man about the table including myself was weeping. Booth dropped back into his seat and with his head on the table covered his face with his hands."[52]

Lincoln was elected on November 6, 1860, and secession was shouted for in the streets of Montgomery and elsewhere. The legislature of South Carolina called a convention to consider withdrawal of that state from the Union. Alabama and five other states in the southernmost part of the United States authorized similar meetings.

Booth was deeply troubled by Lincoln's victory, recalled Louise. He would later write that the event was essentially a declaration of war against the South. But his cheerfulness soon returned. "All will be over in a few weeks," he told her. Like most other Americans he simply did not believe that the unthinkable was possible. "There will be no war," he assured Louise. "It would be too terrible, and neither side will dare begin it."

As the crisis deepened, however, so did Booth's anxiety. He studied the newspapers, following political developments closely. Yancey's statement that if Alabama left the union he would go with it drew a rebuke from Booth: "The whole union is our country and no particular state. We should love the whole union and not only the state in which we were born. We are all one people." Booth at this time held views more common in the Upper South than in deepest Dixie. Deploring Lincoln's election, that region sought a compromise between the sections to keep the nation together. If the people of Alabama wanted to divide the nation, Booth did not. "He loved the union, though from his mad act the world would judge that he did not. His love for the union was one of his strongest passions. I knew him and know that he did," Louise, a secessionist in feeling, said.

In Booth's view the abolitionists were the worst sinners, but Southern radicals were falling into their game. "He was as bitter against secession as he was against abolition," recalled Louise. Both extremes imperiled the nation. "Men have no right to entertain opinions which endanger the safety of the country," he wrote. "So deep is my hatred for such men that I could wish I had them in my grasp and I had the power to crush. I'd grind them into dust!" Louise saw that his feelings were as violent as his words. Once, reading a newspaper, Booth became enraged. Throwing the newspaper down, he exclaimed, "If I could I would kill every d—— Abolitionist in the North and every d—— Secessionist in the South, then there would be no war. This is too grand a country to be plunged into a civil war by such fanatics!"

It is not solely through Louise's recollections that his Virginia-brand unionism is known. Booth began to draw unfavorable notice from others in Montgomery. "Young, impetuous, fearless, true," as his friend John Ellsler described him, Booth spoke his mind openly and with the naïveté of one who felt his opinions were so just that, properly explained, they had to be accepted by others. Yes, the South was grievously provoked, he told one secessionist, and "he was a Southern man and liked the people of the South who had been kind to him, but he could not for all that admit they had any right or occasion to secede. That they had had it all their own way in Congress, and that if they insisted on fighting, they should take the American flag and fight under that."[53]

Suddenly Yung's was no longer congenial. Booth had spoken too boldly in a secessionist furnace like Montgomery. "Poor Wilkes had foolishly expressed himself in regard to the rebellion," Louise declared. "I felt very uneasy about him." Canning was concerned, too. "Booth's sympathy for, and utterances on behalf of the Union, were so unguarded in their expression that his life was in jeopardy."[54]

Tormented by the anathema of national disintegration, his views unpopular, and his person threatened, Booth underwent an emotional crisis. He became moody and erratic, alternatively haranguing Louise, then falling silent for hours. At moments his eyes swam with tears. Such behavior led one acquaintance to consider him "a trifle crazy."[55] Another contemporary employed the adjective *crazy* without the kindly qualifier of *trifle* before it.[56] Louise recalled more sympathetically, "I often thought that off the stage his mind was not just right. I don't mean that he was insane, but there was something about him."

Having had no engagements in a month, it was time—perhaps past time—for Booth to depart. He came hurriedly to Louise one evening and said, "I must go home tonight or I cannot get away at all." Canning found it "necessary to resort to strategy and spirit Wilkes Booth out of the city to save his life," said John Ellsler. "This I had from the lips of the manager himself."[57] To save face, Booth announced publicly that he intended to return to the South at a later date to fill engagements.[58] The sectional crisis, he asserted, "cannot last longer than a few weeks or a few months at the longest. Such a glorious country as ours cannot be broken up by a few fanatics."[59]

With the help of his fellow actor Sam Chester, who Booth thought saved his life on this occasion, the star left Montgomery on December 3,

1860. He took a four-hundred-mile rail trip to Savannah, Georgia, where he secured a cabin on the steamer *Huntsville*. He arrived in New York City on Sunday, December 9.[60] Edwin was playing in the city, and John lingered long enough to be noticed by *Wilkes' Spirit of the Times*, a weekly newspaper whose theater columns were eagerly read. "He was looking well," the editor stated. "The press and public in that section of the country [the Deep South] hold him in the very highest estimation. He is several years younger than his brother Edwin Booth, and the resemblance between them in person, voice, and manner is very striking."[61] By December 16 Booth had joined his mother and Rose, who lived in a rented residence in Philadelphia near Asia and Clarke.[62]

John was, oddly enough, now homeless. However warm his welcome on Marshall Street, the house there scarcely deserved the title of home. After the family left Tudor Hall in 1857, Booth had, in fact, no such special place in his life. He lived with Edwin, with Asia, with friends, in rented rooms, or at hotels. He traveled constantly in his profession. Wardrobe items were stashed here, papers there. A deteriorating relationship with Edwin compounded his rootlessness when Mary Ann and Rose moved to New York City in 1863 to live permanently with the older brother. John came to feel unwelcome there. This lack of roots mirrored an inner disconnection in the young actor. He told one person he might move to Canada, then told another he might move to Virginia. "I am a northern man," he wrote in 1860. Yet he contradicted Asia when she said the Booths were a Northern family. The question was well worth asking: where did John Wilkes Booth belong?

Philadelphia provided the young actor with no refuge from the escalating national collapse. The city voted for Lincoln, but the president-elect was not universally popular. Conservatives and moderates backed the call of Mayor Alexander Henry for a nonpartisan Grand Union Rally on December 13, 1860. One of the rally organizers was David Paul Brown, a Booth family attorney and author of *Sertorius*, a play whose title role the elder Booth had often performed.[63] Booth joined the thirty to forty thousand people who crowded around historic Independence Square for the event. Magnificent banners that floated above them from the upper-story windows of the nearby Continental Hotel provided the rally theme. "Concession before Secession," they read, and the words captured the feeling of most present. Professing loyalty to the Union, speakers offered olive branches to the South.

Despite such conciliatory gestures, South Carolina declared its independence from the United States on December 20, 1860. There could be no such thing as peaceful secession, Booth knew. Soon after, the Senate rejected the Crittenden Compromise, a measure proposing a series of constitutional amendments to protect slavery and secure its existence in a share of the western territories.[64] The bill's authors hoped to allay Southern fears, and Booth believed, along with many others in Maryland and Virginia, that this measure was the one compromise that could have saved the nation.

As events ominously unfolded, Booth hit upon the idea of making a speech of his own, perhaps to some mass meeting like the Grand Union Rally. Shortly after the failure of the Crittenden Compromise, he penned an extensive address on the national crisis.[65] Known as the "Allow Me" speech, it is more properly the "Alow Me," as Booth misspelled the initial word of his address. The manifesto was twelve and a half pages long with an additional six-plus pages continuing the themes of the first section and perhaps to have been incorporated into it. At some five thousand words, it is the lengthiest surviving document written by the actor.

It has been stated that Booth used the basic structure of Antony's funeral oration from *Julius Caesar* to frame the arguments of his speech. By addressing his listeners as "fellow countrymen," Booth opened his remarks in a style reminiscent of Antony. But Booth lacked the subtlety with which Shakespeare endowed that orator. Booth's address calls more readily to mind the bold remarks of Brutus on the dead Caesar. Brutus asserted that he acted for love of country alone, appealed directly to his listeners' patriotism and honor, and offered himself and his views to their judgment. So did Booth. Like both Brutus and Antony, Booth made use of rhetorical questions. He would frame a question and record a cry of assent from his listeners. Booth actually wrote shouted *ayes* and *noes* in his text, a device that gives the speech elements of a theatrical script. But most of the address was in a more traditional form of political argument.

Since Booth disliked writing, the speech represented a major undertaking. He poured himself into the effort, quoting from the Bible, Shakespearean plays, and Edward Bulwer-Lytton, paraphrasing Andrew Jackson and Stephen Decatur, and invoking the names of the revered sectional peacemakers Henry Clay and Daniel Webster. On the plus side, Booth produced an address that was natural and energetic, and he avoided the excessive formality so fatal in novice speechwriters. But, as was true in all of his writing, Booth struggled in vain for poetic language and for dignity.

Unoriginal, ill-organized, and repetitive, the speech had a turbulent and violent tone. It was an odd combination of harangue, lamentation, and threat. It had only one shining quality: it was deeply sincere.

The crisis of the age was at hand, declared Booth. "Can you with unmoved souls see the land, where once dwelt love and joy, fretted by internal dissentions? To see the land where dwell our fathers our mothers, our hearts, our loves, our all, upon the fearful brink of self-distruction. O what a triumph for the crowned world will it be to see this once proud union bend its head unto the dust!" The end of nationhood was an unthinkable disaster. Economic depression and social upheaval would follow in the North, chaos and violence in the South. Monarchy would be vindicated, and European nations would take advantage of the nation's fragments. Horribly, civil war would follow.

In Booth's view the South wished only to tend its own business and maintain its traditional rights. It held an unassailable moral high ground in any such calamity as civil war. Coercion would be the fastest way to precipitate this catastrophe, uniting the South and making the North "greater Tyrants! Than George the 3d ever was towards our fathers!" Should war result, "I will not fight for cesession. This union is my Mother. A Mother that I love with an unutterable affection. No, I will not fight for disunion. But I will fight with all my heart and soul, even if there's not a man to back me for eaqual rights and justice to the South."

"You all feel the fire now raging in the nations heart," he continued. "It is a fire lighted and faned by Northern fanaticism. A fire which naught but blood & justice can extinguish. I tell you the Abolition doctrine is the fire which if alowed to rage—will consume and crush us all beneath its ruins." Abolitionists had caused all of the nation's problems. "Continually preaching and crying" over slavery, they were fanatics who abused freedom of speech to whip up sectional hatreds. They were a set of ignorant hypocrites. "I have been through the whole South and have marked the happiness of master & man.... True I have seen the Black man wiped but only when he deserved much more than he received. And had an abolitionist used the lash, he would have got double." Being "so good so gospell," they declare slavery a sin. "You never saw it such until it became unprofitable," Booth chided the North. "And you would even now share in that sin if it was necessary to you and could be made to pay.

"What is to be done with such men who are cold to all the blessings of freedom they possess? Who laugh at our country as it is. Scoff at her

institutions as they are, And who not only would cry for a King, but endeavor to lead others to their views and spread their d——d opinions
throughout the land. Now I call it treason to our common country, and it
should not be alowed.... Such men I call trators and treason should be
stamped to death.

"Now that we have found the serpent that madens us, we should crush
it in its birth," he urged. The crisis could be ended only by an explosion
of antiabolitionist outrage so intense and universal that antislavery advocates would alter their views or be shamed into silence. "The Abolition
party must throw away their principals. They must be hushed forever."
They must either agree to this or be compelled. "God grant, it may be
done in a peaceful way. If not, it must be done with blood. Ay with blood
& justice. I tell you Sirs when treason weighs heavy in the scale, it is a
time for us to throw off all gentler feelings of our natures and summon
resolution, pride, justice, Ay, and revenge, to take the place of those nobler
passions in the human heart, respect, forgiveness, and Brotherly-love."

The American people, he concluded, "are too wise, too good, too just"
to refuse the South its rights. "Ill speak no more, think upon what I have
said. For we can not live without the union as it was. The Union our
fathers made. The union which God has blessed, And the flag of that
union forever."

Notably, the name of Abraham Lincoln is absent from this lengthy
document. Although Lincoln had become the most widely discussed man
in the nation, Booth had yet to focus on him. Only two antislavery figures
are mentioned. One was John Brown, whose execution Booth acknowledged attending. Brown died "attempting in another way, mearly what
these abolitionists are doing now," wrote Booth. The Reverend Henry
Ward Beecher of Brooklyn, New York, also drew Booth's ire as a man
"who takes shelter behind his white cravat! to belie his profession. And
speak his treason." The bedrock principle of Booth's political philosophy
was hence laid bare. He loved the Union as it was, and he hated the abolitionists who were destroying it. Before Lincoln ever drew Booth's notice,
the young actor loathed abolitionists.

A close reading of the speech reveals an interesting point. Booth stated
that he wrote the address "to vindicate myself in the steps I intend to
take." He was contemplating some action. The "Alow Me" speech does
not state what that was, and his meaning remains a mystery. It is improb-
able that he refers to joining the rebel army. He states specifically that he

would not fight for secession. Given the tenor of the speech and the temper of the speaker, the possibility of an attack on a prominent abolitionist figure cannot be ruled out.

Whatever Booth intended to do, he apparently did nothing. His mother's presence was always restraining, and no record of any rash act at this time has surfaced. It does not even appear that Booth found an occasion to deliver his "Alow Me" speech. Rapidly moving events made his ideas, unachievable as they were, obsolete as well. The speech disappeared into a pile of playbooks and clothes that in time were moved to Edwin's home in New York. The older brother discovered it there many years later.

Unable to save the nation, Booth decided to salvage something for himself. He arranged a series of star engagements in several small Northern cities. To his Southern pieces he added *Othello*, *The Merchant of Venice*, *Macbeth*, and two swashbucklers titled *The Corsican Brothers* and *Don Caesar de Bazan*. Such additions to his repertoire required much preparation and indicate that not all of his time could possibly have been absorbed by politics. He opened for two weeks at the Metropolitan Theatre in Rochester, New York, on January 21, 1861. The best notices of his budding career followed. "He has played here for ten nights to full and crowded houses," stated the *Union and Advertiser*. "This fact speaks more than anything else that can be said as a tribute to this genius. His Othello, Richard III and Romeo were as faultless as the same characters in the hands of his illustrious sire at the same age, and there is no reason to doubt that he is destined to fill his place upon the stage and add new luster to the name he bears." The *Evening Express* was particularly taken with his Richard. "There was but one opinion expressed—that nothing had ever excelled it in our theatre," it asserted. "Mr. Booth was most warmly and deservedly applauded through the entire piece, and at the close was loudly and persistently called for. On his appearance before the curtain, he was greeted with a perfect storm of applause."[66]

Booth split the next eleven weeks, from February 11 to April 26, 1861, between Albany's Gayety Theatre and the Portland Theatre in Portland, Maine. Reviews continued favorable, and "the reception he met with was no doubt most flattering to his professional pride," declared an editor.[67] Booth clipped and mailed to June in San Francisco one particularly positive notice of his Othello, and the older brother pasted it into his own scrapbook.[68] How much such acclaim meant in terms of dollars remains unclear, however. At Rochester, for example, houses said in the local press to be crowded were described in the New York trades as so-so and unfavorable to an extended run.[69] Albany's little Gayety, formerly a carpet store, was a gamble even for veteran stars, while in Portland, Booth was known to be short of cash. Horace C. Little, editor of the latter city's *Advertiser* newspaper, alleged that Booth left town without paying his printing bill. When a collector called upon him to settle the small account, Booth referred the man to an agent, the agent referred him back to the actor, the actor back to the agent, "and so like a shuttlecock our collector was batted backward and forward between their falsehoods, wearing out more shoe leather than the whole thing was worth. We wish merely to say to our brethren of the press that when 'J. Wilkes Booth' may appear on the boards in their vicinity, if they make any contracts with him, the safest way is to adopt the advance principle." In other words, get the cash up front.

Rebuked as irresponsible and ungentlemanly, Booth was also having bad luck in the form of a succession of stage accidents. Acting was a physical profession and the theater a hazardous workplace. Performers held swords, daggers, and pistols, and they worked around props, drops, platforms, ramps, gas footlights, smoke, and even horses at times. Space limitations could compound the problems. The stage at the Gayety was a laughably small seven by nine feet. Into this space were crowded actors who might be inexperienced, anxious, or exhausted. Amid the mad energy of a play, the recipe was always at hand for real-life drama. In Rochester, Booth was in combat with R. E. J. Miles when his sword broke. Its point flew down, striking Miles just above the eye and inflicting a severe wound. In Albany, Booth's rapier cut J. A. Leonard on the head as the two dueled. Later in the same play Booth fell on his own dagger. The blade, "glancing from the ribs, cut away the muscles for some three inches" under his right arm, and Booth bled freely onstage. The ugly wound cost him several nights of his engagement. Frank Queen of the *Clipper* observed aptly, "In respect to these occurrences, Mr. Booth has been rather unfortunate."[70]

Convalescing in his room at Stanwix Hall, Booth caught up on the deepening national crisis. The cotton states seceded and convened in Montgomery to form a new national government. To Booth their action was a justifiable measure of self-defense. He expressed this view openly on the morning of his arrival from Rochester, and he did so with a passion that H. P. Phelps, a contemporary journalist and historian of the Albany stage, described as violent. Friends of the theater alerted the management, and the Gayety's treasurer, Jacob C. Cuyler, set out to track down the star. Cuyler found Booth at breakfast and explained to him that this far north, discretion was the better part of employment. "If Booth persisted in expressing his sentiments in public," Cuyler cautioned, "not only would he kill his engagement, but endanger his person." The choice being clear, "Booth accepted his situation and thereafter kept quiet." The actor held no ill will toward Cuyler for the advice and remained friends with the treasurer during his stay there.[71]

In Montgomery on February 18, 1861, Canning and Albaugh witnessed the inauguration of Jefferson Davis as president of the Confederate States of America, an event crowned with Yancey's memorable utterance "The man and the hour have met." Abraham Lincoln arrived in Albany that same day en route to his own inauguration. Artillery boomed a welcome from Observation Hill as the mayor and common council went down to meet his train. An immense throng greeted the president-elect with cheers and enthusiasm.[72] The streets were lined with people, the windows and balconies filled.

Baffled, Booth asked Cuyler, "Is this not a Democratic city?" Lincoln had not carried Albany County in the previous year's election, so the question was a fair one. "Democratic? Yes," replied Cuyler, "but disunion, no." That evening, while Booth starred in *The Apostate*, Lincoln received the citizens of Albany at the Delavan House not half a mile away. Cuyler's friend Phelps reflected, "How little did either then dream of the tragedy that was to link their names together in all coming time."[73]

Lincoln was inaugurated in Washington on March 4, and on April 12 Confederate forces attacked Fort Sumter in the harbor of Charleston, South Carolina, starting the Civil War. Booth was in Portland at the time. His reaction to the event is not recorded. On April 19 soldiers of the 6th Massachusetts Infantry Regiment, passing through Baltimore to reinforce the capital, were forced to fight it out with pro-Southern civilians. At least twelve citizens and four soldiers were killed and dozens wounded. In 1865 Booth claimed to have taken part in the April 19 riot, one of the most famous events in Baltimore history. This could not have been true.[74] Booth remained in Portland until April 14 and was back in Albany in time to play on April 22. Since Marylanders destroyed railroad bridges connecting Baltimore with the North in an attempt to isolate the city, it would have been impossible for anyone to travel normally in this chaotic period.[75]

The *Albany Evening Journal* declared that Sumter required every person to show colors, and Booth unfurled his.[76] "Booth at that time openly and boldly avowed his admiration for the rebels and their deeds, which he characterized as the most heroic of modern times," declared Albert D. Doty, a news dealer. Booth stated "that the Southern leaders knew how to defend their rights and would not submit to oppression."[77] The incautious remarks drew indignation and threats in the New York capital. "People became incensed," Doty wrote, "threatening him with popular violence." Cuyler chronicled the distress these weeks caused Booth by noting the steady transformation in his personality as the war came on. "Each time he came here (his engagements commenced on February 11, March 4, and April 22), it was noticed that he grew more morose and sullen." Cuyler watched Booth change "from a genial gentleman into a soured cynic."

Booth's final run at the Gayety was fittingly brief. He shared the bill with Samuel Canty, who performed as "Signor Canito, the Man-Monkey." It seems absurd to later generations that *Richard III* would be followed immediately for the same audience by an acrobat dressed as an orangutan climbing trees and cracking nuts.[78] Such was the variety of the nineteenth-century theater, however. The two entertainers held court for less than a week before the Gayety closed for lack of patronage due to the wartime distractions. After four nights, Booth's first tour as an independent star came to a close. A painful postscript to the engagement was added by Booth's leading lady.

Henrietta Irving, who began her acting career in 1855, was a capable theatrical hand and an ambitious and volatile young woman. Rarely described as beautiful, she was pretty enough to keep the boys on the benches interested. Praise of a performer's art and person are often fulsome in sources of the period, but such references to Henrietta are infrequent. Perhaps a remark by the theatrical gossip Harry Hill reveals why. Replying in the 1880s to the charge that actors of the Civil War era were more high-minded and generous than those of his day, Hill cited Irving to prove his point that the earlier generation had been equally cunning and selfish. No reader rushed to defend the woman whom Hill teasingly termed "the Irving."[79]

A correspondent of the *Clipper*'s Frank Queen quipped that many actresses like Henrietta went about playing under the title of Miss despite having from one to three husbands each.[80] Where husbands one to three might have been was unknown when "the Irving," along with her sister Maria, supported Booth in his Rochester and Albany performances. Sparks flew, and the intimacies of their Romeo and Juliet continued after hours in the less Shakespearean setting of Booth's hotel room at Stanwix Hall. There John and Henrietta "were as tender as love without esteem can ever be," as the journalist Townsend, who dug out every scrap of Booth gossip he could mine, struggled with propriety to phrase it.[81] When Booth tired of the relationship, Irving protested. He grew cold. She grew angry. On Friday, April 26, 1861, the situation exploded.

A Midwestern newspaper summed up the action:

All for Love and Murder.—Miss Henrietta Irving,
well known as an actress in Buffalo, entered the room
of J. Wilkes Booth, at Stanwix Hall, last Friday, and
attacked him with a dirk, cutting his face badly. She
did not, however, succeed in inflicting a mortal wound.
Failing in this, she retired to her own room and
stabbed herself, not bad enough to 'go dead,' however.
The cause was disappointed affection or some
little affair of that sort.[82]

Canning knew the story behind the story. Booth was not simply tired of Henrietta, the manager reported; he was interested in Maria. "There were two sisters in the company, and neither one was very considerate. One of them was Booth's temporary mistress, and he got a fancy for the other one, and the first sister kept watch on him." Canning believed Henrietta placed herself outside Maria's door and ambushed Booth when he emerged.[83] Most other accounts agree that the attack occurred in Booth's room. The actor was lying down when he heard a knock at the door. On the other side was Irving, frenzied and armed with a knife. When Booth opened the door, she stabbed him in the face. Grappling with her, Booth forced her out of the room and wrested the knife from her hand. Irving fled to her own apartment, found another knife, and stabbed herself. "She meant business," reported a tattletale for the *New York Sunday Mercury*, "but she made a botch of it." Her injuries kept her off the stage for a time, "but she recovered, got over her infatuation for Wilkes Booth, and made a clever, popular actress of herself at last, which was a heap better than suicide."[84]

Booth nursed his wound at his mother's residence in Philadelphia. Edwin, he learned, intended opening the fall season in London. This interesting news would leave him as the only Booth available for the big-city stages. For his twenty-first birthday on May 10, 1861, Mary Ann gave him a set of books inscribed in his stage name of "J. Wilkes Booth."[85] It was her acknowledgment of his career and promise. She also proved a tender nurse for the painful souvenir from Irving. For once Booth had been lucky. The wound on his face was on the forehead at the hairline, which could be covered with a tousle of hair and no loss of good looks.[86] The injury pained Booth for weeks, and the notoriety gleefully given the incident by the *Clipper* and *Wilkes' Spirit of the Times* added embarrassment. The former claimed that the young actor trifled with Irving's affections, while the latter called him faithless and deceptive.[87] Booth learned his lesson. His amours continued, but he would not disgrace himself or the family again by giving occasion for a similar story.

As he recuperated, Booth was deeply disturbed by the news from Baltimore. Events of April 19 had initiated the "Three Glorious Days" in which the pro-Southern element showed its muscle. "The very air was lurid with rebellion," wrote James Hall, a Maryland physician.[88] To prevent the violence that would attend passage of additional troops through Baltimore, Mayor George Brown and Governor Thomas H. Hicks ordered the railroad bridges north of the city destroyed. Exclaimed one Marylander at work on the business, "God damn them, we'll stop them from coming down here."[89] Tracks were pulled up, telegraph lines cut, and mails stopped. U.S. flags disappeared, even from federal buildings. John T. Ford lowered the Stars and Stripes and raised the Maryland state flag at his Holliday Street Theatre.[90] Unable to enter Baltimore, soldiers from Massachusetts and New York flanked the city. Washington, D.C., was reinforced by water via Annapolis, and on May 13 large columns of federal soldiers arrived in Baltimore from the south. Occupying Federal Hill, they overlooked the city and were in a position to devastate it with artillery fire. "It's *our* turn now," U.S. Treasurer Francis Spinner jubilantly declared to Lincoln's assistant secretary John Hay as the tide turned.[91]

The most severe threat to national authority ended at this time, although that fact was not apparent to those involved, least of all to Booth when he arrived in the city. He ran into William A. Howell, an actor friend of Arch Street days. Graduate of an amateur acting club in Philadelphia, Howell was employed in the utility corps at the Holliday and boarded at a house on High Street. Booth asked if he could share Howell's room, and the latter gladly consented. Each evening Booth attended the theater, and when the play concluded, the pair walked home together. "After getting into bed, we would talk for hours of our prospects, both present and future," recalled Howell. "He would crayon out for me his hopes and desires in a way that was irresistibly fascinating." Few men admired Booth as much as Howell, who found him "quick, impulsive, fiery, big-hearted, generous, captivating, and magnetic."[92]

While Howell did not say, the ambitions Booth imagined for himself were apparently still as personal as they were political. His money problems had grown perilous. Hard times compelled Booth to take a few secondary roles at the Holliday, where his old mentor Harry Langdon was manager.[93] He was even forced to pawn his Montgomery presentation cane. Lack of cash could not, however, interfere with his preoccupation with the ladies. Enamored with one young woman, he followed her about, stared at her through shop windows, and even attended church to catch her eye. To impress another enchantress, he borrowed money from Stuart Robson to redeem his cane and so present an elegant appearance for an afternoon rendezvous in the park.[94]

Ultimately war fever intruded. Howell was a Northerner and Booth a border state man who had declared himself unwilling to fight for secession. "Yet the excitement and turbulence grew so prodigious as to become contagious and infect Wilkes Booth and myself," Howell recalled. Booth told Howell that he would go to Harford County and raise a company for the Confederate army. Howell, who expected a lieutenancy out of the arrangement, would stay in Baltimore to look after their prospects there. The spreading Yankee presence doomed the plan. Political arrests were being made, weapons seized, local government shoved aside, and open recruiting for the South no longer safe.[95] "I have often tried to conjecture what the outcome might have been had Wilkes Booth and myself raised a company and donned the gray," fancied Howell as an elderly man in 1899. "We might have won the bubble reputation at the cannon's mouth and, in case we had come out alive, have gone to Congress and been Governors."

The fate of George P. Kane, Baltimore's police marshal, demonstrated the new state of affairs. A former Whig Party leader, Kane was a militia officer, businessman, city official, theatrical investor, and Booth family friend. During the April 19th riot he placed himself fearlessly between the Massachusetts troops and the citizens in an effort to stop the bloodshed. Kane's Southern sympathies were undisguised, however, and Unionists in Baltimore complained to Washington that he commanded the bridge burners. When soldiers from Federal Hill, acting under orders of Major General Benjamin Butler, attempted to seize city arms from a warehouse, Kane refused to hand over his key, demanding to know their authority for such an action. "By authority of my sword!" a Northern colonel responded. The weapons were seized, and shortly thereafter so was Kane. Troops arrested him without a warrant in a 3:00 a.m. raid at his home on June 27. Major General Nathaniel P. Banks explained, "The government cannot regard him as otherwise than the head of an armed force hostile to its authority and acting in concert with its avowed enemies." The marshal was hauled away to a military prison.[96]

Kane's arrest enraged Booth, and he remained angry about it for months. In March 1862 Kane's name came up in a discussion of public events during a rehearsal at Mary Provost's Theatre in New York City. One cast member declared that the person who ordered Kane's arrest should be shot. Booth, who had been silent as the company debated the war, was still so angry at the marshal's treatment that he erupted: "Yes, sir, you are right! I know George P. Kane, he is my friend, and the man who could drag him from the bosom of his family for no crime whatever, but a mere suspicion that he may commit one some time, deserves a dog's death!" One startled but perceptive eyewitness to Booth's outburst recalled, "It was not the matter of what he said, it was the manner."[97] Said another: "I don't think J. W. is all o.k. in his nut."[98]

Kane spent more than a third of the entire war in prison. When he was released in November 1862—without charge, trial, explanation, or apology—he did not blame Lincoln for his incarceration. He blamed Secretary of State William Seward. On his way south, Kane wrote of Seward in a public letter, "All that is bad in a man, unpatriotic in a citizen, and corrupt in an officer finds itself concentrated in this individual."[99] The Confederate element in Maryland loathed Seward, whom it held chiefly responsible for its miseries. Booth fully shared this opinion.

Large and unfriendly crowds continued to line the streets and hurrah for Jefferson Davis as Northern troops passed through Baltimore, but the trickle of soldiers became a flood, and they passed unopposed.[100] The crackdown on the Southern faction accelerated. "Violent and unwarrantable searches and seizures, illegal arrests and imprisonments of citizens in military fortresses and dungeons, the subversion of state laws, the displacement of lawful authorities, and the substitution of an illegal and unauthorized force" were the order of the day, complained the editor Samuel S. Mills shortly before his own arrest.[101] Mayor Brown joined Mills in prison, while Governor Hicks threw in with the Union. Baltimore, the nation's third-largest city, was being subdued. The reflexively anti-Lincoln *New York Day-Book* lamented, "If secession be ever so wrong, the means resorted to to put it down are infernal and infamous."[102]

Booth passed a large Maryland flag flying on the Harford Road as he made his way to Bel Air, his mind struggling with these events and his role in them.[103] His family worried that his abhorrence of abolitionists would carry him south. Asia knew that he had always considered it his fate to be a soldier and to die for his country, and she was relieved when her brother took rooms at Bel Air's Eagle Hotel to spend the summer studying for the fall season.[104]

Asia mentioned no military ambitions on her brother's part, but he had them. He purchased as a birthday present for himself a copy of C. M. Wilcox's *Rifles and Rifle Practice* (1859), a treatise on the theory of rifle firing published by an army lieutenant who taught military tactics at West Point.[105] He also renewed his perilous friendship with the Bel Air lawyer Herman Stump.

Stump, alleged to have taken part in the April 19 riot in Baltimore, was captain of a volunteer infantry company named the Harford Rifles. This militia troop was customarily called (and may be best understood as) "the Home Guard." Booth joined them, drilling under Stump's command. This little-known fact was revealed by Stump one winter evening in 1886 at a meeting of the Harford Historical Society. When fellow member E. M. Allen suggested the importance of preserving a record of events that occurred in the county during the Civil War, Stump began to reminisce. This was unusual because Stump was customarily silent, even with his own family, on his relationship with Booth. That night he was expansive, however, acknowledging that he had organized a militia unit to blow up the Conowingo Bridge over the Susquehanna River leading toward Philadelphia and that Booth had been a member of his company. Feeling awkward about what he was hearing, Allen ended Stump's reminiscence by saying that "it was not his intention to revive unpleasant recollections but no man whose opinion was worth having would think less of a man now for the part he took in the late war."[106]

The Harford Rifles had been organized in the village early in 1860. Months later, after Lincoln's election, they were still unarmed, and Stump appealed to Governor Hicks for weapons. The governor promised to furnish arms to the company, adding playfully that he wondered if Stump's soldiers would "be good men to send out to kill Lincoln and his men." Stump read Hicks's letter to the militiamen, and it elicited laughs of approval from them. Hicks seemed solidly pro-Southern at the time, declaring "Maryland was indissolubly connected with the Old Dominion, and should act when and as she acted." But when Virginia joined the rebellion in May, the governor adhered to Washington after all. Livid, Stump accused Hicks of wanting to "disarm the citizens of the State and give the arms to Northern militia, notoriously wanting them for war upon the South or outrage on our own citizens." Stump declared that Hicks had reversed his jest. "Lincoln and his men should be the sportsmen and men of Maryland the game."[107]

Federal authorities declared Stump "an ardent advocate of the rebel cause in Harford County, attached to a volunteer military association recruiting and getting under discipline there with a view to entering the rebel service."[108] General Banks ordered a raid to arrest him and secure militia arms. Before dawn on the morning of July 13, 1861, two to three hundred men of the 12th Pennsylvania Volunteer Infantry Regiment poured into the village. "Northern fanatics in Bel Air!" noted a local diarist. "Half-starved, ill-clad, woebegone-looking wretches."[109] The soldiers fanned out, occupying the hamlet and picketing the roads. A search for weapons commenced. The Pennsylvanians took axes and chopped down the door of the town hall, an act of frightening symbolism for the future of local government. Other soldiers searched homes and made arrests. The roads out of Bel Air were closed, and no one was permitted to leave except slaves on their way to work.[110]

The military strike trapped Booth in Bel Air, but Stump was more fortunate. He had attended a ball the preceding evening and afterward had escorted a young lady home and spent the night in the country. Unaware of this, soldiers raided the Eagle, where Stump boarded, and searched for him. They found Booth, in whom they had no interest, but no Stump. The federals decided to post a reward of ten dollars for him. The laughably small amount was war on a budget.

Booth left the hotel and hurried up the street. Seeing the roads blockaded, he entered a shop and said to the owner, "I want you to let me go out through your back door." Booth crept out and crawled on his hands and knees through a garden. Once clear, he went to a friend's house near Bel Air Academy, borrowed a horse, and galloped to Thomas Run, where he found Stump and warned him of his danger.[111] Stump fled to the Big

Woods, a tract of heavy forest where the militia was gathering. Booth went to Tudor Hall. During all the derring-do, he had been shot at. Catherine Quinn, who was visiting at the house with her family, saw Booth rush in exclaiming that "he had been fired on by the soldiers and meant to defend himself." Booth went to the old log house, got his rifle, and headed to the Big Woods.[112]

For the young Marylanders who assembled in the dense forest, the gloom of the setting was apt. They had lost more than the day; they had lost the moment, the state, and now even their own community. They were indeed the desperate people their former friend Hicks claimed they were, and the time for life-transforming choices was at hand. Go south and throw in with the Confederacy or submit to the new regime? It would be an intensely individual decision because Marylanders would not be carried forward in a body by action of their state government as soldiers to the north and south were.

Every man in the Big Woods agreed on two things. All opposed coercion of the seceding states, and all objected to the presence of Northern troops in their own. Beyond that, opinions varied. Some were solidly Southern. Stump's first cousins James and Robert Archer entered the Confederate army, the former becoming a brigadier general. Others joined them, taking militia arms to Virginia. Stump opted for Canada. Some chose to stay home in Harford County and mind their own business. They became malingerers in Lincoln's reunion crusade. Still others may have joined or been drafted into federal service. More than one thousand men from the county would ultimately wear the blue. Like Maryland itself, Harford County was divided.

Booth's feelings were unmistakable. "He was," wrote Asia, "what he had been since childhood, an ardent lover of the South and her policy, an upholder of Southern principles."[113] On the slavery issue he was entirely Southern in feeling.[114] Knowing that, friends urged him to join them in a company that ultimately became part of the Confederacy's famous Stonewall Brigade. To their surprise he refused. When they renewed their appeal, he rebuffed them again. In Richmond he would be denounced "as a 'turncoat' from the Southern cause." Could one love Virginia and not share her peril? One theatrical acquaintance in the future Confederate capital "never lost an opportunity of excoriating this actor for his apostasy against the South."[115]

The *New York Herald* reported in 1865 that "many of his friends have wondered why he did not join the rebel army, in which his sympathies were already enlisted."[116] In the early months of the war, before the brutal nature of the conflict became apparent, a multitude of romantic spirits enlisted in both armies. As a child Booth dreamed of military glory, and the conflict offered the chance to earn it. How could a healthy young man desirous of distinction and passionate of view not be swept away by the urge to volunteer? Even Asia wondered about it. Provoked by one of John's outbursts in favor of the South as he loitered around her home in Philadelphia, she lost patience and snapped, "Why not go fight for her then? Every Marylander worthy the name is fighting her battles." Asia saw that her remark stung and she regretted it, but the question was a fair one.

Family tradition, a powerful influence carrying young men into the army in 1861, had no force in the Booth family. The Booths had no military legacy.[117] The father deserted a British ship during the War of 1812. "He was never a friend to gunpowder," it was explained.[118] Junius believed that actors should stay clear of politics, and Asia often reminded John of their father's opinion. "No actor should meddle with political affairs," she said. "The stage and politics did not go hand in hand." June, Edwin, and Joseph felt the same. The brothers had neither military aptitude nor interest.

Some writers later wondered if cowardice was a motive for Booth's nonenlistment. B. F. Morris, compiler of tributes to President Lincoln, wrote that Booth was an individual "whose chivalry could induce him to murder but could never summon courage to fight in the ranks of his brother rebels."[119] The problem with this interpretation was that Booth had raw fortitude in abundance. His instinct in times of danger was to charge it head-on. Proud of his well-conditioned body, Booth had the self-confidence of an athlete. Added to that he was "a dead shot, a fine fencer, a thorough horseman, and a master of the dagger or bowie knife," claimed New York's *Play Bill*, a stage paper, in 1865. "Ninety-five men out of a hundred would be no match for him at fighting." He was bold, even reckless with his person. Whatever his faults, he was no coward. When the *Play Bill* reported after the assassination that "his personal bravery has been unquestioned," it expressed the opinion of all those who knew him well.[120]

Paradoxically for someone who often rushed toward danger, Booth suffered from hemophobia. The sight of blood might cause him to pass out. In 1864, when his friend Richard M. Johnson asked Booth to accompany him inside a funeral parlor to visit Johnson's business partner who had been stabbed to death, Booth exclaimed, "My God, man, no, no." Ironically, the man who slew hundreds onstage and became a murderer in real life could not stand to see the real thing. "I cannot bear to see blood nor a dead face," he told Johnson. "They make me wild." Johnson noted that Booth no sooner said those words than his countenance began to change. "He sank in a corner, and his face grew dark. His features worked violently. His eyes took on a wild look. He raised his hands as though warding off a blow. He trembled with the intensity of his excitement." This extreme fear of blood, often caused by direct or vicarious trauma in childhood, was also displayed in his frequent references to blood in the "Alow Me" speech and his description of the stripes on the nation's flag as bloody gashes.[121]

The family never mentioned hemophobia as a factor in John's failure to enlist in the rebel army, but they did bring up something else. Edwin informed historian Nahum Capen in 1881 that—given John's politics—he had been curious about John's lack of service and asked him point-blank about it. John gave an excuse that rang true to the brother: "I promised mother I would keep out of the quarrel if possible."[122]

This explanation has met with skepticism, but it is undoubtedly the principal factor for his wartime neutrality. Booth had "a pure, fervent and indescribable affection and love of a son for a mother," and a vulnerability to her pleading, said Joseph R. Bradley Sr., a contemporary who studied his personality.[123] Mary Ann needed him. She was a widow with no income beyond rents from the farm. June had not been home from California since 1854. Edwin and his wife, Molly, were about to depart for England. Clarke and Asia would follow them. Joe, having dropped out of medical school, was at loose ends and would soon wander off to Australia. The only other family member left within three thousand miles of Mary Ann would be Rose, who had no life outside the home. Who was there but John?

Mary Ann's premonitions of an early and violent death for him petrified her. Fearful of losing her favorite child, she refused to give her blessing to his enlistment. They discussed the topic exhaustively. "He begged his mother to allow him to go south," wrote John T. Ford. "She most earnestly refused."

"You will not let me go," he protested. "You know my heart is there."

He was packed and ready to depart, but she pled, she prayed, she wept, and, in the end, she won. "Ah," he said resignedly as he put his hands on her shoulders. "You are no Roman mother."[124]

"John Wilkes is crazy or enthusiastic about joining for a soldier," Asia wrote Jean Anderson. Then she added a sister's special insight: "It has been his early ambition—perhaps it is his true vocation."[125] Booth might have made a good soldier, fighting well and filling a cavalryman's grave by midwar. But the conflict would go on without him. To fulfill an obligation to his mother that he considered sacred, he made a fateful decision that went against his nature. "With all his faults he *was* devoted," observed Ford.[126]

He regretted the choice more and more as time went by. "I am sorry that I said so," he later lamented to Edwin.[127] But the die was cast. He would stay north and act. In August 1861, as friends and classmates filled out the rebel armies in Virginia, Booth gave his miniature silk eleven-star Confederate flag to Hannah Hanna, the wife of his landlord.[128] When next heard from he was in Boston, bidding farewell to Edwin as he left for England.

Back in Maryland, Stump packed hurriedly for exile, Yankee soldiers swept the Big Woods for hidden weapons, and a federal officer ripped down the Maryland flag flying on the Harford Road.[129]

5

....

SHINING IN
THE ROUGH

JOHN WILKES BOOTH'S friends were not surprised that he became an actor. After all, it was the family business. His father was legendary, and Edwin possessed gifts that would take him nearly that far. June, while not as talented as Edwin, made a decent living onstage. Even Mary Ann had done a bit of acting before John's birth.[1] The young man came of age in the shadows of these seniors. Around him were promptbooks on the tables, rehearsals at the fireplace, poetry on the stairs, and songs in the parlor. In the background Rose stitched patiently away on costumes. In a sense John did not choose acting as a profession. It chose him.

He had star-quality good looks. "His father's finely shaped head and beautiful face were reproduced in him," wrote Asia. "He had the black hair and large hazel eyes of his mother. These were fringed heavily with long up-curling lashes, a noticeable peculiarity as rare as [it was] beautiful."[2] Hazel is commonly a light brown, yet John's friends described his eye color as dark (without specifying a color) or even black. Booth wore his hair in what the playwright Augustus Thomas termed "Civil War standard"—full, long, and parted on one side.[3] His tresses were soft, dark, and inclined to curl without the use of hot irons or pomatum. His mustache added a rakish dash. The features of his face were regularly proportioned and classically molded. Booth's complexion was unblemished. His teeth were white and perfect. He smiled often.[4] "He is a rare specimen of manly beauty," thought a New York acquaintance.[5]

Booth was five feet eight or eight and a half inches tall—average for his time.[6] This was the average stature of a Civil War soldier. With his well-developed arms and shoulders, his finely formed neck, and the fact that he *acted big*, Booth found his height no impediment in playing heroic characters. Of course, one could always improve on nature with heels and lifts if needed. (Edwin, who was shorter than John, measured five feet nine inches when dressed.[7]) As muscular as John was, however, he feared appearing square and solid. A natural grace, enhanced by fencing, boxing, and dancing lessons, allayed that worry. He also lost weight over the course of the war years, dropping ten pounds or more due to constant travel, an irregular lifestyle, and stress. An exercise fanatic, he burned calories at the gym as well. Once he stripped away his coat before a fellow actor and "showed the magnificent physical condition to which he had brought himself. He was trained to perfection, hard as iron, without an ounce of superfluous flesh anywhere. His eyes were bright and keen as razors, his head in fighting trim."[8]

More than a good face and figure were required of an actor, however. Certain personal qualities were indispensable, too. An actor must be smart, attentive, and energetic. An actor must be reliable, collegial, and versatile. An actor must be studious, hardworking, and authentic. An actor must speak well and understand that, as the comedian Joe Jefferson said, one employs the voice "as if you are quite sure the man in the last seat is a little deaf." And John M. Barron, who played with Booth in Richmond, thought that an actor must also have passion. "Fire! Fire! My boy, give them fire— dramatic fire!" exclaimed the tragedian J. A. J. Neafie to Barron.[9]

Booth's father told him he did not have the stuff to become an actor, but he had proven the old man wrong.[10] By the end of 1861, Booth had the benefit of three years of apprenticeship at major theaters in Philadelphia and Richmond. He had performed with the nation's finest actors. He had worked for some of the best and most professional managers in the business. To this tutelage Booth added a season of leading roles in the Deep South and at small Northern theaters before the war. The twenty-three-year-old had learned a great deal. He had earned his wings. Now he would try them.

WHEN THE ACTOR Charles Krone first met Booth in St. Louis, where the aspiring star would fill two weeks at DeBar's Theatre, he was highly impressed.

"Young Booth was tall and graceful with a charm of personality that was dominated by dark and brilliant eyes that took fire in character or discussion," recalled Krone. "He was very much liked by his colleagues. His manner was frank, manly, and cheerful. In the fullness of youth, life, and passion, with the glorious record and talents inherited from his father at his command, he gave promise of achieving the highest. Most men predicted great things in his future."[11]

Ben DeBar, Krone's boss, had brought Booth to St. Louis. A veteran actor-manager, DeBar was a heavyset fellow with a full, rosy face.[12] The editor Frank Queen combined DeBar's hardworking nature and potbelly frame into a one-word tease. The manager was "inde-*fat*-igable."[13] True enough. But the portly showman was also family, at least of a sort. He was the brother of Clementina DeBar, June's ex-wife. Their daughter, Blanche, after her stay with the Booths, had been handed over to Ben to raise. He did well at the task, becoming (in the girl's own words) "both father and mother" to her. Twenty-year-old Blanche was a beauty, with her striking face, fine figure, and lustrous dark eyes and hair. While she looked like a Booth, June was convinced she was not his daughter and insisted she not use the family name. Asia was equally unyielding, writing her friend Jean Anderson that Blanche was her brother's stepdaughter. "I call that nothing," she added. John was less hardhearted. He loved Blanche's high-spirited nature, so much like his own, and he was proud to be her uncle.[14]

Booth had wanted a Boston and not a St. Louis engagement, but managers like Davenport considered him a novice not yet ready for the big cities and brushed him off.[15] Hence he turned west to prove himself. It would be tough work. DeBar had a reputation for being cheap. His theater was a rat-hole, complained the comedian William Warren, a Booth friend. The musty backstage, as cold as the street in winter, had a reputation among actors for being unhealthy. Perhaps that was why Ben's company was loaded with scrubs. Kindhearted Ben tolerated no criticism of them, however. "Would you let them starve?" was his reply. "They had to get work *somewhere!*" The manager did frustrate them, however. Once his company cornered him dining on quail in a restaurant and insisted he pay them their wages. Ben exclaimed in mock surprise that it was astonishing they would demand salary when blackberries were in season.[16]

To escape the drafty theater, Booth took his promptbook and rehearsed his lines at Billy Gleason's saloon, which adjoined the theater. As needed, he called in the players and drilled them there.[17] When show time approached,

DeBar appeared on the stairs from his office above the saloon. Dressed in an old black velvet coat and vest, short trousers, and a pair of carpet shoes, he marched around behind the curtain, whistling Irish ballads. When the orchestra struck up the overture, he took his usual seat—not in a box, but *on* a box—near the stage. "My curtain waits for nobody," he barked.[18]

As was now his custom, Booth opened with *Richard III*. Its inevitable success would set the town talking. *Hamlet*, *Macbeth*, and *Othello* followed, along with *The Apostate*, *The Robbers*, *The Marble Heart*, and *The Lady of Lyons*. This was the same package Booth offered the previous spring during the secession crisis, but the quality of his performances was much better. His months of study at the Eagle Hotel in Bel Air, where landlord Hanna heard him pacing in his room above the dining hall reciting his lines, had paid off.[19]

The *Daily Missouri Democrat* and rival *Missouri Republican* agreed on little, as their names suggest, but they were of one mind about Booth. He was a fine actor. "Mr. Booth, as Hamlet, took the house by storm," declared the *Republican*. "This gentleman is an artist of the highest order." The *Democrat* reported, "Mr. Booth had a most rapturous reception as Richard III. He is an actor with all the fire and enthusiasm of his father or brother Edwin, being taller and better formed [and with] a fine expressive face."[20] Krone felt these compliments were fairly won, and he disputed the opinion later in the century that critics of the Civil War era were too easy on actors, particularly critics in western cities who allegedly knew little about good acting. "The critical spirit of those days was more severe than it is at present," he said in 1906. "A set of hyper-critics were then on hand who could not have been satisfied with anything short of a theatre where Forrest and Booth were the boot-jacks and the archangels played the leading business."

Less than forty-eight hours after he closed in St. Louis, Booth was Richard again on the stage of James H. McVicker's theater in Chicago. Fresh triumphs followed. "J. Wilkes Booth is a very youthful actor and as a consequence has hardly reached the point at which a full appreciation of his powers can be arrived at, but to judge from a single hearing, we would at once pronounce him a genius," declared the *Chicago Tribune*. During his combat scene with Edwin C. Prior's Richmond, Booth broke the other player's heavy stage sword. The scene was so lifelike that the *Tribune*'s critic recorded in the huge notebook ostentatiously displayed in his lap that half the audience thought Booth actually intended to kill the other player. Booth's Pescara, for which he received several curtain calls, was so popular that three newspapers asked McVicker to repeat it, and his Hamlet was declared the equal of Murdoch's, considered by many to be the gold standard. "Young, ambitious, resolute, and unswerving in honest integrity, we bespeak for him a future in the history of the drama to which few may aspire and but one or two in a generation attain," wrote the *Evening Journal*.[21]

Offstage, Booth was also well received. John F. Stafford, a wealthy Chicago businessman and patron of the arts, took him in. "As a man he was a noble, generous-hearted fellow, full of honor and good purpose," recalled Stafford. "With the exception of the faults of all young men, which he would have outgrown in time, he was in all respects a good citizen and a splendid actor."[22] The most recent "fault" was an after-hours drinking bout, a reference to which made its way obliquely into print.

Highly pleased with his success, Booth kept his feet on the ground. His houses were crowded—and McVicker's house could seat twenty-five hundred people—but Booth had no illusions about how far he had to go. He was attending a charity event when an organizer requested he sign autographs that could be sold as part of the fund-raising. He responded that his signature was worthless.[23]

There was still no encouragement from Boston when Booth arrived in Baltimore for a three-week engagement at the Holliday Street Theatre. He was tired and lethargic. "As usual I began with excuses. I do not think my success here will be very great," he confided to his Boston friend Joseph Simonds. "One's native place is the last place in the world to look for such a thing."[24]

The Doric-fronted Holliday was a magnificent temple of a theater with three tiers of boxes and could seat as many people as McVicker's in Chicago. Its acoustics were marvelous, its stage was deep, and its wings were wide enough to afford all the space needed for the complicated fixtures and machinery required for scenic display.[25] John T. Ford owned the house. He had brought Edwin here two years earlier, and, notwithstanding the fact that Ford spent more than one thousand dollars on costumes alone for Edwin's appearance, the response to his performance was only so-so.[26] The impresario decided to give John a try. "He had more physical beauty and intellectual power than [Edwin or June]. He had a magnificent mind, great originality of thought, and he threw the vitality of perfect manhood into every character he impersonated. He was wonderfully energetic when acting," stated Ford, "and spoke as though a whole army was listening to him." Good looks never hurt, and "Booth was one of the handsomest men I ever saw."[27]

On February 17, 1862, Booth opened with *Richard III*, already being recognized as *his* play. Despite the poor weather, the theater was filled. Ford promoted the young actor to the city as an heir to the father, and the public came, curious to see this new scion of the great Booth. Familiar faces dotted the audience, casting the father's troubling legacy about them. Even the stage on which Booth stepped was the one upon which many of them had seen the elder Booth bid farewell to Baltimore ten years earlier. Would the ghost of the father hover above it, directing him on, as spiritualists proclaimed?[28]

Performing with Booth required all of one's wits. Billy Ballauf, the property boy, discovered this when, "standing in the wings reading the plot-book and not giving any particular heed to the scene," he narrowly missed being gashed in the face by Booth's outstretched sword as Richard and his followers dashed from the stage.[29] Booth then aimed a club at Thomas A. Hall, the play's King Henry, and threw it at him. Owen Fawcett, one of the company, thought enough of the incident to record it in his diary, although he did not explain Booth's behavior.[30] This star did throw things. The following year he hurled a wooden wedge used to plumb scenery just above the head of an inattentive prompter to wake him up during a production.[31]

Despite these stumbles and the fact that Booth was playing with a severe cold, his Richard was highly satisfactory. Audience members noticed some similarities to his father, but the acting was not derivative. It was dynamic and original. Ballauf thought that "Booth played with a fire and an earnestness that has seldom, if ever, been equaled. He was a remarkable figure." "A bright and glorious success," wrote another. "Booth received an ovation of genuine and continuous applause from an audience tremendous in numbers and brilliant in fashion."[32]

"Richard's himself again!" exulted Ford in the next day's advertising. He meant, of course, that the son was a worthy chip off the old block. Booth hated such statements. He told a friend, "Had the Almighty vouchsafed me whatever ability I now possess, and permitted me to have made for myself a name without the weight and prestige that my father has thrown about me, I should have been infinitely better satisfied."[33] He insisted that his uniqueness be stressed in the bills. Booth wanted to be judged as himself and had a fierce dislike of hearing comparisons between himself and others.[34] Ford thought that Booth's sense of individuality was so intense that it had a touch of irrationality to it.

His success at the Holliday was indisputable. Richard Cary, an intimate friend of Edwin's, complained that the actor ranted, and at least one critic agreed, writing more amiably that John overworked certain scenes.[35] Generally, however, the press embraced "the pride and pet of Baltimore," as Ford put it. "Mr. Booth has every reason to be grateful with his reception in his native city," wrote one Baltimore newspaper. "Seldom have we seen more enthusiastic audiences."[36] Any rough edges were set down to youthful enthusiasm. A second journal opined, "He is making out a course of great originality. The force and timely discrimination with which he renders his characters are peculiarly his own, and stand forth strong, bold, and refreshing."[37] Reported a third, "That this young tragedian is destined to achieve great distinction and possibly peculiar eminence in his profession there can be no doubt."[38]

On a visit to his family in Philadelphia the actor looked up Matthew Canning, the manager of Booth's 1860 southern tour. Canning had been trapped in Montgomery, Alabama, when the war commenced. Departing for the North, he lost his property and was able to get away with only three thousand dollars in unenthusiastically accepted Confederate bonds for everything.[39]

Now working as a theatrical agent, Canning proposed to take Booth as a client and find engagements for him.[40] He could place Booth in New York, an idea with much appeal. "As all good Jews look towards Jerusalem for the realization of their fondest hopes, so do the actors of England sigh for a London engagement, the actors of America turn to New York as their Mecca," wrote Fawcett.[41] Success there, and the acquisition of what the journalist Junius Henri Browne termed "a metropolitan reputation," assured acceptance in the provinces.[42] Canning contacted the managers Samuel Colville, J. Lewis Baker, and George Ryer, all California friends of June. They were unwrapping a new theater, named the Mary Provost Theatre for Colville's wife, on Broadway near Broome. Their idea was "introducing stars who had made a reputation throughout the West and South but were unable to obtain a hearing at the older and so-called legitimate houses." They had heard good things about Booth, deemed him a strong draw, and offered him a chance. "He snapped readily at the opportunity," recalled J. J. McCloskey, one of the Mary Provost company.[43] Edward L. Tilton, who had just played the heavy at the Holliday with Booth, and

Mary Ann Farren, who did the leading lady business there, would come along with him. Together the trio formed an experienced team.

John hired his brother Joe as an assistant. This was a mistake. "Joe was brimful of romantic, dreamy, unpractical ideas," wrote their mutual friend William Howell. "He was a builder of air castles, an indolent young fellow who was always hoping for something out of the usual routine of events to turn up for his special benefit."[44] Joe had been a medical student in Charleston when the war broke out. Swept up by events, he served on the medical staff of Confederate forces attacking Fort Sumter. Returning north, he showed Howell a trunk full of shell fragments, musket balls, splintered bones, and skulls—a combination of military trophies and deposit from his studies. War fever raged, and Joe decided to become a Union officer. Rumor was that when he heard the guns at Fort Henry on February 6, 1862, he deserted.[45]

Joe returned home moody and anxious. "I was troubled in mind and worried," he would say, and he lapsed into a bout of what his doctors labeled as melancholy insanity. To escape his mother's incessant babying, Joe left with John for New York, only to discover that he was expected to work hard. On the cusp of a professional breakthrough, John was charging hard and had no time for a gloomy woe-is-me. "If Wilkes was not cut out for an actor," Joe complained to his friend Edward Westall, "he should have been a merchant for he is a regular money-grabber." After one bitter argument over business, Joe walked out. In fact, he vanished. John grew frantic, worried that Joe might commit suicide. He searched Manhattan for him, visiting police stations to leave Joe's photo and plead for help.

He would learn that Joe, with money from their mother and some of John's own dollars that Joe considered his due, sailed for Europe to join Edwin. Eventually the younger brother traveled on to Australia and finally to California, where June got him a job delivering letters for Wells Fargo in San Francisco. Despite the trouble between them, John reached out, writing him letters of encouragement, and "Joseph always manifested more affection for his brother Wilkes than for any other member of the family," said Westall. "He thought more highly of Wilkes than either of his other brothers."[46]

ON THE MORNING of March 17, 1862, the cast at the Mary Provost Theatre were awaiting the arrival of the star when one player said, "I am an old man in the business and have seen and played with some of the greatest tragedians. But in all my long years of professional experience, this young man Wilkes Booth is the first actor that ever knocked me off my pins, upset and completely left me without a word to say! Yes, sir, an old actor like me that you would suppose an earthquake could not move was tongue-tied, unable to speak his lines."[47]

There was a stir behind the actors, and Baker was heard to say to someone, "Oh, not waiting long. You are on time."

Booth strode forward on the darkened stage. "The foot and border lights were suddenly turned up and revealed a face and form not easily described or forgotten," recalled McCloskey. "You have seen a high-mettled racer with his sleek skin and eyes of unusual brilliancy, charging under a restless innocence to be doing something. It is the only living thing I could liken him to."

A chance reference to the latest war news ignited a debate among the actors. McCloskey was pro-Southern, as was Jim Collier, the muscle man with whom Booth acted in Richmond. Tilton favored the North. The men began to argue over military arrests in Maryland. Words grew hot, tempers short, "and when the denunciation of [Lincoln and Seward] reached fever heat, Booth, who had been listening to it at the back of the stage, strode down trembling with rage and ashy pale and quivering like an aspen leaf."

"It is a damnable outrage," shouted Booth, referring to the federal suppression of Maryland.

Baker cut him off. "We will have no more of this. Let us get along with the rehearsal," Baker said. "Pardon me, Mr. Booth. The stage is no place for political discussions."

Booth bowed to Baker, forced a smile, and responded, "I quite agree with you, sir. Let us proceed with the rehearsal."

The star commenced work abruptly, eager to get past the incident. McCloskey watched him closely and concluded "the encomiums passed upon him by the old actor were not in the least exaggerated. Reading entirely new to us—he gave. Business never thought of by the oldest stager—he introduced." Booth was very particular in telling those around him not to be frightened by the passion with which he would act that evening. "He might, he said with a smile, throw a little more fire into the part than at rehearsal." Booth issued the caution, McCloskey believed, because he knew his own strength.

Opening night found a packed house for *Richard III*, with hundreds of would-be patrons turned away at the door. The critic for the *Herald*, the city's leading newspaper, fought his way inside and watched Booth deliver a performance of great maturity and extraordinary self-possession, as he informed his readers the following morning. "In the last act he created a veritable sensation. He seemed Richard himself. Mr. Booth's Richard Third ought to crowd the theatre for a month."[48] Onstage, McCloskey thought, "whether it was in the gentle wooing of Lady Ann, the hypocrisy of the king, or the malignant joy at Buckingham's capture down to the fight and death of the tyrant, originality was stamped all over and through the performance. It was a terrible picture."

Booth had warned Collier to take care in the fight scenes, and the brawny player took offense at the remark. He shot a look back at Booth that seemed to say, "You have been frightening everybody tonight. Try it on me."

"A dreadful lay. Here's to decide it," Booth's Richard cried out as he pitched into Collier.

McCloskey recalled, "The shower of blows came furious from Richard's sword. Now was Collier's turn and bravely did he return them. With renewed strength Richard rained blows upon blows so fast that the athletic Jim began to wince as if to say, 'How long is this going to last?'" Undaunted, Collier recovered. Grasping his sword with both hands, he pounded back. At length Richard was mortally wounded, and after lamenting that with his death the world was no longer his stage, he expired.

When the curtain fell, the other actors milled about, but Booth lay motionless on the boards. Only his hard breathing revealed he was still alive. "Could it be possible this was the man who only a few moments before nobody could withstand in his fury—now a limp mass of exhausted nature, his nerves all unstrung and whom a child might conquer?" wondered McCloskey. Booth might remain prostrate five or ten minutes "before he recovered strength or even full consciousness."[49]

Collier enjoyed better roles after Ned Tilton suffered an accident on Friday, March 21, 1862. In a fight with Booth near the footlights Tilton stepped off the stage and fell into the orchestra pit. The musicians retrieved him from among the drums and fiddles and lifted him back up. Sword in his left hand, he gamely resumed the fight to cheers from the house. It was later discovered that Tilton had broken his shoulder (or possibly his arm). The actor told a colleague that he believed that Booth, wielding a double-handed broadsword weighting seven pounds, knocked him off the stage. If true, it was a serious indictment of the star.[50]

This incident caused a great deal of talk at the time, wrote T. Allston Brown, a *New York Clipper* reporter, and even more after the assassination.[51] It was offered as evidence of Booth's malicious nature. Heedless of another's safety, he injured a fellow performer in order to demonstrate his own prowess as a fencer. John T. Ford clipped and saved an account written a quarter century after the event that expressed this view: "Booth made a wild lunge at Tilton, forced him over the footlights, and fairly hurled him into the orchestra. Then he madly tried to kill his fallen foe, amid the shrieks of the ladies and the shouts of some of the men in the audience who now began to dread a tragedy in earnest."[52]

McCloskey, the only cast member to leave an account of the evening, saw something quite different. Tilton was a large and powerfully built man capable of delivering blows as well as taking them. He was one of the best fencers in the business.[53] He had practical experience dueling with Booth in Baltimore. That night, however, "nothing could withstand the trip-hammer blows of Richard," McCloskey felt. "Watching for his head's protection, [Tilton] was too unmindful of his heels." In an instant he was on his back in the orchestra. The accidental nature of the mishap was confirmed by critic Brown, a friend and biographer of Tilton, who stated that the actor "accidently stepped off the stage, dislocating his shoulder, which was the groundwork of the story about Booth's getting so excited that he knocked him off."

In 1890 the novelist John Paul Bocock wrote an essay on stage dueling for the *Boston Herald*. Bocock believed that "the most realistic stage duel of this generation was fought between John Wilkes Booth and Tom Connor at DeBar's in St. Louis. The audience rose to its feet night after night in an agony of suspense as first Richmond and then Richard would be driven at swords' points over the footlights. [They] would try, it seemed, to cleave each other to the chin. Fire would fly from their broad blades as sparks from a blacksmith's anvil. Both men were athletes and [played] for the love of the fight, pure and simple." Booth's routine was single and double primes (fencing parries with the blade down and to the side and the wrist pronated), followed by ups and downs, circles, shoulder blows, and a thrilling snake-like crawl upon one knee from upstage center to downstage left.[54] As realistic as the combat appeared, however, " 'Connor and Booth were both *faking*,' " an old hand explained to Bocock. Stage duels were not free-for-alls. They were rehearsed. Each night before they went on, Booth and Connor discussed who would be driven where.

"Wilkes, it's your night," Connor would say.

"Why, Tom, you miserable rascal, I went off first last night, and then I've got to get killed," Booth responded. "You'll have to make that break yourself and mind you do it well, too!"[55]

Despite stories that later emerged, Booth was not insensitive to the safety of other actors. When things went wrong, he was duly distressed. Once his blade came perilously close to Charles Krone, slicing out the back of that actor's velvet armhole coat. Krone carried on, giving King Henry's dying speech. Thinking that he had stabbed him, Booth stood nearby and asked Krone repeatedly in a low voice if he was hurt. Booth was trembling in alarm. "When the curtain fell, he raised me. I knew not whether I had been hurt or not but a brief examination revealed that a small hole in the cloak had been the only damage done, at which he was highly delighted."[56]

His two weeks extended for a third, Booth continued at the Mary Provost Theatre through early April 1862. The public wanted *Richard III*, and he gave it to them, playing the title role eleven times in eighteen appearances. Edwin's friend William Winter thought John "raw and crude and much given to boisterous declamation and violent demeanor."[57] The public was more receptive. Charles B. Seymour in the *New York Times* found "his presence intellectually impressive, his delivery natural and unstrained, his perception of character clear and vigorous. We cannot name a better Richard." The *Times and Messenger* thought "his intellectual appreciation of the part is somewhat wonderful for so young an actor. It is acknowledged to be without a rival upon the American stage." The *Tribune* was less enthusiastic, although its review acknowledged his abilities and the fact that he was still fighting the cold he had brought with him from Baltimore. Booth's Charles de Moor in *The Robbers* was also well received. The star was called before the curtain repeatedly by sustained applause. At the end of the second act he received several floral tributes from the audience. As Shylock, however, critics thought he failed. "He neither looks, conceives nor acts the character in a style to increase his reputation or satisfy his audience," wrote the *Herald*. "Youth is an excellent apology for so unfinished a rendition, but none for offering it to the public." In general his New York engagement concluded with much critical encouragement and back-patting. "The public have had an opportunity to witness the efforts of a genius who acts without being an actor," declared the *Evening Express*. It went on to announce that Booth had indeed earned his "metropolitan reputation," employing the phrase as if it were handing over a tangible gift. The *World* agreed and stated the obvious: "This gentleman has in an incredibly short space of time become a general favorite with playgoers."[58]

Something about Booth would always puzzle Manhattan know-it-all Isaac G. Reed, however. With good reviews and popular favor, why did the actor not take a subsequent engagement in the city? Why did he never return to New York? Writing thirty years later about the young star, Reed reflected, "He was probably the handsomest actor ever seen on the New York boards, gifted not only with beauty of features but of expression. It is very rarely that good-lookers among actors are man-like but Wilkes Booth was a 'manly man.' His form was simply perfection, his manners winning yet dignified, his dark eyes were twin souls, his voice was music. Had Booth been true to himself and remained in New York, he would have made a bigger hit here than was ever made either by his father before him or his brother after him." And yet, continued Reed, the actor's appearance at the Mary Provost Theatre "was, strange to say, the only engagement ever played by Booth in New York."[59]

Reed understood the importance of the city. Its population was almost four times that of Baltimore, five times that of St. Louis, and seven times that of Chicago. Additionally, tens of thousands of strangers visited the city daily, many seeking amusement. "There is incalculable advantage in gaining favor here," wrote Browne, a student of city life, "and the advantage is not merely apparent. It is actual." Gold lined the city's canyons. As Edwin told his fellow actor Barton Hill, "I *must* play in New York."[60]

Did Edwin intend to own Manhattan? "Edwin, as is well known, has always been opposed to any kind of rivalry," wrote a critic. "He always wants the fat for himself."[61] According to one story, when John came on as a star, Edwin decided to divide the country.[62] He would take the North, June the West, and John the South. But if there ever was such a plan, which is doubtful, the arrangement was untenable by 1862. The war forced actors, like other citizens, to make critical choices. Since his family lived in Philadelphia, John came north. "He by no means sought to place himself in opposition to Edwin," wrote Asia. "He never wanted to try to rival Edwin." The older brother was "an inspired machine," John said.[63] But it seemed unreasonable for Edwin to monopolize the most lucrative market in the nation when he was off seeking a London reputation.

Edwin's unhappiness with John crossed the Atlantic, and it frayed the bonds between them. "It was the first wearing away of family affection," lamented Asia.[64] Dutifully, John withdrew. Except for two days across the river at Brooklyn's Academy of Music in 1863 and one benefit evening at the Winter Garden in 1864, John kept away from the Manhattan stages as if they were cursed. Before long Edwin sailed for home to fence his property more properly. Since June had lost Edwin's savings in a California mining speculation, he had to borrow money for his return trip to the United States—from John.[65]

THE COVETED BOSTON INVITATION came from Edward F. Keach. A native of Baltimore, the highly capable Keach was an actor-manager like DeBar. Autocratic and high-strung as a boss, he was popular as a player and notable for the thick black sideburns, cascading down to his collar, that he wore in every part from Caesar to Romeo.[66] His theater's odd name—the Boston Museum—came from the fact that the owner, Moses Kimball, a veteran showman, had a collection of a half-million curiosities on the first floor and a wax statuary on the second. These exhibits made the place respectable for those who, for moral reasons, did not wish to be considered theatergoers. If their steps led them to the auditorium on floor three, "they could visit it without a blush," laughed the actress Kate Ryan.[67]

Tea with Boston literati before his opening found Booth anxious about the challenges before him, such as adjusting his voice to the acoustics of a new house and performing with a new cast. But at least the Museum was a fine hall with a wonderfully professional company. Booth was most concerned with and perhaps a bit frightened of opening with *Richard III* in a city whose audiences could be cuttingly critical. "Still, he believed he could bring out whatever power was in him better in Richard and make a better first impression." The young actor's modesty in the face of these difficulties created a favorable first impression.[68]

On May 12, 1862, Booth's Boston debut, thirteen-year-old Frank Stanwood passed under the large white-globed lights that lit Tremont Street and threaded his way up the stairs to a balcony seat. "All the dramatic interest of the city centered at the house on that calm spring evening," noted the Boston Latin School student, "and the curtain rose upon an audience as large as the house could hold. Every seat was occupied as well as the aisles and every spot from which a glimpse of the stage could be obtained." Even members of the company who would appear late in the play or in the afterpiece came out to watch from behind the gallery seats. William Warren, the beloved Boston comedian, stood among them.

This assembly had great expectations, and tension in the auditorium was so palpable that Stanwood realized "that the hero of the evening must gain either a great triumph or an ignominious defeat."

When act 1, scene 2 commenced, there was a pause and then Booth entered downstage to the audience's right. It might be better said that he *appeared* there, thought Stanwood, for "he possessed an ability to glide on and off the scene with an incomprehensible movement." The star's arms were crossed. In them he carried a sword. The front of the house erupted in applause and shouts, which continued for several minutes. Booth acknowledged the ovation with a bow and began: "Now is the winter of our discontent/Made glorious summer by this sun of York." His voice was firm, his tone even, and "it did not take long to convince those before him that he and not they ruled the situation. His rage, sarcasm, and blasphemous defiance seemed to make his fellow artists shrink away from him without the necessity of assuming a horror they did not feel. Richard's jests [were] more terrible than other men's imprecations."[69]

There had been whispers along the rows as to what Booth would do in the last act. "For once rumor fell short of fact," recalled the youngster. "The combat was truly terrific." Bostonians were not given the traditional "one up, two down" duel. Center stage and close to the footlights, Booth fought furiously with William H. Whalley, "a very tough and very big man." Their combat no sooner began than Whalley broke Booth's sword close to the handle. Picking up the blade from the stage floor, Booth fought on with it to waves of applause. "The clash of steel was almost continuous. Sparks flew from the blades," observed the actor William H. Crane. "Most actors who have been through Richard up to that scene are willing to die after a few exchanges. But not so John Wilkes. The audience began to fear that either or both of the contestants might receive injury. Even the boys in the gallery squirmed."[70]

"It was decidedly a crescendo performance," honored by two curtain calls, wrote Stanwood, "and there was in it this much, at least, of the great artist, that he conveyed to his auditors a sense of on-coming doom and a belief there was to be no halting or falling off until 'the spark of life went out upon the field of Bosworth.' After witnessing a great number of performances of the tragedy, no occasion can be recalled when it was so effectively given as on that May evening."

For his two weeks in Boston, concluding May 23, Booth presented a more varied menu than he had in New York. He gave them three Richards, two Romeos, two Charles de Moor (*The Robbers*), and single nights of Hamlet, Pescara (*The Apostate*), Claude Melnotte (*The Lady of Lyons*), and the title character in *The Stranger*. "Booth won great favor," recalled Crane, "drawing the largest audience ever assembled within the walls of the Museum." A critic for the *Evening Transcript* wrote, "There are strong indications of genius in his acting. He is perhaps the most promising young actor on the American stage."[71] "W.F.P." in the *Clipper* agreed, writing, "Young Booth created a very favorable impression during his visit. He is one of the 'coming men.'"[72] "X.Y.Z." declared, "With him the present is full of merit, the future big with promise. He has in no way mistaken his profession."[73]

Boston was a theater-savvy city, however, and Booth did not escape the critics unscathed. Most found some flaw in his work, and one of them delivered a real punch to the gut that called into question Booth's basic understanding of his business. Howard Malcolm Ticknor was a poet whose father ran Ticknor and Fields, the publishers of Emerson, Thoreau, Hawthorne, Longfellow, and Dickens. Well centered in the Boston arts scene, he was an expert on the voice, as he made clear.

"In what does he fail?" Ticknor asked. "Principally in knowledge of himself—of his resources, how to husband and how to use them. He is apparently entirely ignorant of the main principles of elocution. We mean the nature and proper treatment of the voice. He ignores the fundamental principle of all vocal study and exercise—that the chest, and not the throat or mouth, should supply the sound necessary for singing or speaking." Grunts and groans were no substitute for proper modulation. Furthermore, Booth's enunciation, ranging from gratingly southern to Cockney, was inelegant, and he had a proclivity to a nasal quality. Ticknor concluded, "These are not trivial faults, and to point them out is not necessarily carping criticism."[74]

It is difficult to know what to make of this opinion. A critic like Ticknor might identify an actor's salient strength or weakness, but surely he would have much company in doing it, especially in so important an area as the voice. Yet few writers made such observations. Most were highly positive about the actor's vocal assets. "X.Y.Z." said that Booth "has a voice very much like Edwin's—the same smooth, silvery tone, with no nasal twang, no mouthing of words, no disposition to rant." T. Allston Brown of the *Clipper* asserted that "Booth had a musically full and rich voice of rare compass and modulation." Indiana congressman Albert G. Porter, a noted student of rhetoric, heard "a clear, ringing voice of good range and compass, of rich and melodious tone, singularly free from rant." And Isaac G. Reed felt "his voice equaled in its melody that of Forrest," the highest sort of praise.[75]

Ticknor's fellow critic R. M. Field spoke for a wider audience. Writing in the *Boston Post*, the most popular daily newspaper in New England, Field said that "Booth has laid a firm, substantial, enduring foundation for a brilliant Boston reputation. There are crudities here and there which time alone can soften, and faults of elocution which it is impossible to get the better of in a day. The towering reputation of his father and elder brother is [also] rather a disadvantage. But we see genius blossoming into beautiful flower, surmounting difficulties which only veterans in years gone by could overcome, and we have no stomach whatever for a host of your *ifs* and *buts*. We accept John Wilkes Booth most joyfully as a gift which the patrons of the stage cannot prize too highly or encourage too generously."[76]

BETWEEN MID-OCTOBER 1861 and the end of June 1862 Booth gave 163 performances in eleven cities. This included a Christmas-night play and appearances every Saturday. In need of a break, he returned to the old homestead in Maryland.

Tudor Hall, put up for rent when the family left in 1857, had been occupied only intermittently. The house was drab and musty and the fields untended. Weeds had overtaken the flower beds, and wood had been stolen from the property. "The grounds and whole place wear a look of desolation that would lead you to suppose an army had passed over it," wrote a visitor. The old cabin where Booth was born was on its way to ruin. A leaking roof dumped water on the second floor, where mildewed books and a damp theatrical wardrobe were left to rot. Ann Hall, the longtime family servant, kept an eye on the premises, but Ann, now widowed, and her children could hardly take proper care of such a large farm, and the place had an unwholesome energy that Adam Badeau sensed on a visit. "I can readily imagine how the brain might become disturbed in the midst of these suggestive garments and weapons and memories," he wrote.

In this forlorn setting Booth spent much of the summer of 1862. Here he raged. His rehearsals for the fall season had an unsettling level of violence. His ravings and brandishing of weapons frightened Ann. Booth's family worried about him, too, notably "his talking and muttering to himself."

He displayed a "rattling, nervous, incoherent manner" and a mind that might fly off in any direction. Said Ann's son Joe: "Mr. John rode wild and hollered and thought there was people when you couldn't see nobody."[77]

At least "John Stone" was diverting company. That was the name that Herman Stump assumed during his Canadian exile. Injured in a sword fight, the Bel Air lawyer was permitted by federal authorities to return to Maryland in February on promise of good behavior. His homecoming represented no change of opinion, of course. Stump merely joined the anti-Lincoln opposition known as the Copperheads. Oakington, his estate, was a handsome stone manor house with sweeping views of the Chesapeake Bay, and Booth visited regularly. As headstrong younger sons in large families, the men were well matched. They hunted, fished, and caroused together. Politically they were peas in a pod.[78]

On September 4, 1862, the rebel army crossed into Maryland. Confederate columns marched into Frederick, sixty miles west of Bel Air, and scouting parties ventured even closer to Westminster. The Baltimore area shuddered with excitement and anxiety, while Southerners like Booth were thrilled. Robert Hanna, the Bel Air hotelkeeper, knew Booth was a daredevil, but he could hardly believe what the actor did at the time. He climbed atop a tower of barrels where no sane man would have thought of going. Taking a knife, Booth cut letters out of a large circus poster and arranged his own message: "Jeff is coming!" The gaping citizenry broke out in applause and laughter.[79]

"This place must be nearer the pure, unadulterated Secession article than can be found in the extreme South," wrote a *New York Tribune* correspondent who spoke to Hanna. Jefferson Davis never appeared, as the Confederate army was rebuffed at Antietam on September 17 and withdrew into Virginia.

EDWIN RETURNED TO THE UNITED STATES in August 1862, with Molly and their baby daughter, Edwina. The delicately built wife was pregnant, so the family moved into a large two-story house in the Boston suburb of Dorchester, and Molly went under the care of Dr. Erasmus Miller, a specialist in obstetrics and gynecology. Dr. Miller could do little for her, however. Over the course of the winter Molly wasted away from an inflammation of the bowels. Acting in New York, Edwin drank to divert himself from worry. "Ned at his old wild ways again," Asia complained to Jean Anderson. When Molly's friend Lucy Pry lectured Edwin about his behavior, he laughed in her face and made silly remarks, or so the aptly named Miss Pry informed their circle. "Already half a spirit," as Julia Ward Howe phrased it, Molly died on February 21, 1863.[80]

Edwin, who failed to make it to his wife's deathbed in time, was filled with sorrow and self-loathing. "The shock almost unbalanced his mind," recalled Badeau. "He was crushed and saw no hope, no reason for living." John, who was scheduled to commence an engagement at the Arch Street Theatre in Philadelphia, worried his brother might commit suicide.[81] Postponing his appearance, John hurried north with Asia's husband, Clarke, to join his mother in Boston and attempt to comfort the widower. At the funeral service held in the chapel of Mount Auburn Cemetery in Cambridge he stood beside Edwin as the older brother, his long coat over his arm, slumped against a column. Despite political differences between them, "he was devotedly attached to his brother," recalled John T. Ford.[82]

Booth commenced his run at the Arch on March 2. This was the theater where he had begun his professional career six years earlier, but William Wheatley, his first boss, was long gone, and Louisa Lane Drew held the lease. Drew was matriarch of a theatrical dynasty even more extended than the Booths, being the grandmother of film and stage stars Lionel, Ethel, and John Barrymore. A versatile artist, the Duchess, as she was known to her company, was an excellent manager as well.[83] The actress and author Rose Eytinge described Drew's theatre as "without exception, the best-conducted, cleanest, most orderly and most all-around comfortable theatre that I ever acted in."[84] A consummate professional, Drew expected the best of anyone who stepped on her stage, be they stock or star. Actors knew a storm was brewing when she donned a certain red paisley shawl and began to pace.[85]

The shawl was out for Booth. He had risen too far too fast, in her opinion. Since the Arch had to cater to a wide variety of taste, from Shakespeare to rustic comedy to spectacle play, she brought him in to sell tickets. Still, "Mrs. Drew did not take very kindly to the idea of his coming to her theatre and appearing in a leading role," recalled the actor Stuart Robson. For his part, continued Robson, "Booth, like all of us, had the greatest respect and fear of Mrs. Drew," noted for her slashing sense of humor.

During rehearsal the Duchess decided to rattle Booth by pretending to look to him for advice and suggestions.

"Where do you want me to stand, Mr. Booth?" the veteran actor asked with mock sweetness.

Hesitant to give direction to a grand lady of the theater, the twenty-four-year-old stammered, "Why—er—where—er—ever you have been accustomed to, Mrs. Drew."

"Mr. Forrest," she continued, "used to want me to stand here, but not all *great actors* agree, Mr. Booth."

"Well, you might—" he stuttered.

"Yes?" the Duchess asked in a tone of false excitement.

"Come here —"

"Yes, yes?" she continued breathlessly.

"A—a—and if you—"

"Yes, yes, yes, yes?"

Booth was enormously embarrassed.[86]

Clarke had had a recent engagement with Mrs. Drew that lasted sixty consecutive nights. Booth had no illusions of such success. The day before his opening—a dull rainy day that suited his mood—Booth wrote to his friend Simonds that he didn't expect much success as the city theaters contained empty benches each night.[87] The forecast was apt. The winter travel to Boston had given him another cold; his voice had a husky quality that interfered with its clearness and melody. The audience could tell that he struggled to make his points.[88]

To compound his challenges, Edwin Forrest was playing at the New Chestnut Street Theatre a fifteen-minute walk away. It made little sense for a rising star to compete with a setting one for the drama market, particularly in the latter's home city. Booth had the utmost regard for Forrest, touted by the *Clipper* as the greatest living tragedian and successor to the elder Booth, but the aging giant did not return the feeling. He came over to see Booth "try to act" and left disgusted. Some months later, when Forrest's Iago was ill, Ford suggested that Booth fill in. "Forrest ripped out a frightful oath," recalled a friend, "and said he would not 'tread the boards with the G—— d—— spad.'"[89]

Booth won at least one friend in the city, however. Mrs. Drew had told ten-year-old Roland Reed that his Cyrano-like nose would make his fortune. So the boy, later a famous comedian, sat night after night faithfully tending the stage door. One evening as Booth left the theater, he looked closely at the slightly built child, as if noticing him for the first time, "and seeing what a small boy I was for such a position, turned back and shook hands with me." As Booth walked away, Roley found a dollar in his hand.[90]

Booth was fond of children, perhaps because he was childlike himself in some ways. In Clarke and Asia's grand home on Race Street he frolicked with his niece Dolly, age three, and nephew Edwin, age two. "He lays on the floor and rolls over with them like a child," the sister wrote Jean Anderson. "John laughs outrageously at me for having babies—he can't realize it, he says—to think that our Asia should be a mother."[91]

While Booth's Confederate sympathies were not displayed at the Arch, it was a different matter around his sister's house. "He expressed himself bitterly against the North," Asia wrote. " 'So help me holy God!' he told her, 'my soul, life, and possessions are for the South.' "[92] One day Clarke began to lambast the rebels. Booth listened sullenly, frowning and drumming his fingers. But when his brother-in-law added personal insults about Jefferson Davis, Booth erupted. He leapt forward like a maniac onto Clarke, caught him by the throat, and swung him from side to side like a rag doll. Bystanders attempted to intervene but could not pry Booth loose. Slowly the actor recovered his senses, paused, and threw the funnyman back into his seat. As Clarke gasped for breath, Booth stood dramatically over him, threatening, "Never, if you value your life, speak in that way of a man and a cause I hold sacred!"[93]

The star's Philadelphia appearances generated mixed reviews. "Without having Edwin's culture and grace, Mr. Booth has far more action, more life, and, we are inclined to think, more natural genius. He is a good actor and may become a great one," thought the *Philadelphia Press*. The *North American Gazette* disagreed, declaring Booth's engagement an unequivocal failure. The Arch's expanse of empty red plush-velvet seats proved it.[94] Even Mrs. Drew, with her terms of $175 off the top each night before Booth saw his first dollar, struggled to make money.[95] And there were times when "Mr. Booth's abominably bad acting must have [made it] extremely unpleasant for Mrs. Drew" to share the stage with him. "We are positive were his name Smith or Mulligan instead of Booth, he would be booed off the stage."

Little wonder Booth was ready to move on. When June later acted in Philadelphia, John wrote him, "I don't know how the Phila. papers will use you, but if they are as kind to you as to me, why god help you say I."[96]

THE WAR BROKE some but made others. Leonard Grover of Springwater, New York, was a college dropout who toured the country in the prewar years producing amateur musical entertainments. He first noticed Booth during the latter's days at the Marshall and thought him an exceptional actor. Grover operated one of the principal theaters in Washington as rival to John T. Ford, and Booth was now a star. When Booth asked for an engagement, Grover readily agreed. The manager believed in kismet, and this proved it. "What is written is written," said Grover.[97]

Booth played seven nights for Grover, starting April 11, 1863, at the manager's New National Theatre, on Pennsylvania Avenue near the White House. He offered his usual fare of drama and melodrama. Critics were kind and none more so than John Coyle. One of the owners and editors of the *National Intelligencer*, Coyle was an aesthete, theatrical investor, and Peace Democrat. He had known the actor from his boyhood and took a deep interest in his career. Booth had the one indispensable ingredient Coyle demanded in every would-be star: the ability to strike fire in the hearts of theatergoers. Intelligence could not create it. Study could not produce it. Practice could not fashion it. "It is the lightning of the soul and cannot be taught. This young actor plays not from stage rule but from his soul, and his soul is inspired by genius."[98]

About this time Booth grew annoyed by a lump on his neck. It had been increasing in size and had become painful. He was scheduled to play *The Marble Heart* on Monday, April 13, and the role of Phidias called for him to dress in a slate-colored tunic that hung on the shoulders and would, of course, expose the blemish to the audience. "On his fine youthful skin it made a bad impression," thought Canning. So the agent drove him that morning to the home of Dr. John Frederick May, arguably the finest surgeon in Washington.[99]

May's examination revealed the lump to be a fibroid tumor located about three inches below the left ear on the neck's large muscle. "You will have to submit to an operation to be relieved of it," he told Booth. The procedure was a fairly simple one, barring complications. The actor "desired to know if the removal of the tumor would prevent him from fulfilling [his] engagement. I told him if he would be careful not to make any violent efforts, he would not open the cicatrix" formed after the removal.

Do it now, Booth said.

May hesitated, reluctant to proceed due to Booth's physically demanding schedule, but Booth brushed away the doctor's concerns. His mind had been made up. "You cut it out right now," Booth ordered. "Here is Canning who will be your assistant."

All of Booth's friends knew he carried the agent's bullet in his body from the accidental shooting in Georgia, and now at last, or so the yarn would go, they could exorcise it. Booth and Canning would say in the future that by some miracle the ball had "migrated" from his rear end to his neck—a fine joke. Canning later told Townsend this preposterous tale, and the star said the same to anyone silly enough to believe it. Booth even attempted to recruit May into their hoax by asking him to inform inquirers that a bullet was found at the spot.

Declining to respond to such an odd request, the doctor readied himself. His thirteen-year-old son, William, stood by with a basin to catch blood while Canning was told to pull back the skin as the doctor cut it.[100] There was no anesthetic. Booth threw himself into a chair, leaned his head to expose the neck, and said, "Now cut away."

May sliced, and black blood gushed out. Gasping at the sight, Canning thought, "He seemed to have cut the man's head partly off." Booth blanched but remained motionless. The doctor carved on, complimenting Canning for his ability as a nurse, but the agent felt his stomach give way. The next thing Canning knew he had collapsed to the floor. Weak from loss of blood, Booth swooned and fell out of the chair.

May's stitching closed the wound tightly, and the doctor was pleased with the result. "I congratulated him upon the slight scar which would be left," recalled May.

Trooper that he was, Booth played the dual roles of Phidias and Raphael in *The Marble Heart* that evening. When he repeated the performance on Saturday, a special guest was in the audience: Tad Lincoln, the president's ten-year-old son. The play was a boy's delight; Booth's character screamed, wept, shuddered, tottered, threatened, collapsed, jumped about, argued with invisible people, threw clothes on the floor, laughed maniacally, ran about on a spooky darkened stage, and finally fell dead. The passions of the love-struck leading man ran wild in this "emotion drama," as it was called.

"I'd like to meet that man," said Tad. "He makes you thrill." Between acts Grover took Tad and his companion Gus Schurmann backstage.

"Mr. Booth, this is the president's son," said the manager.

Booth smiled and shook hands with the boys. "He continued his makeup, asking us how we liked the play, and we telling him the parts we most admired," recalled Gus. "On our leaving he handed us each a rose from a bunch that had been presented him over the footlights. Booth shook hands with us and smiled in the pleasantest fashion imaginable."[101]

It is unclear when the president first saw Booth act. Joe Whiting, a cast member, said that Booth, playing Richard at Grover's, accidentally knocked a dueling opponent into a stage-level box where Lincoln was sitting. The following day's newspapers, however, reported that the president spent the evening three blocks away at the Washington Theater. This tale is typical of stories placing the president and his assassin together in 1863. Another putative Lincoln watched Booth perform Richelieu and give a secessionist reading of a certain line, directed personally at Lincoln, while the Bourbons in the gallery cheered at the president's discomfort. But Booth never played Richelieu in Washington. Mary B. Clay of Kentucky alleged that she attended a play with the Lincolns in which Booth's character put a threatening finger near Lincoln's face, causing the president to remark, "He looks pretty sharp at me, doesn't he?" There are chronological flaws in her account, however.[102]

There is no doubt, though, that the president saw Booth act at Ford's Theatre on November 9, 1863, when a party of the Lincolns, presidential secretaries John G. Nicolay and John Hay, and several other guests attended. Once again *The Marble Heart* was the featured play. Set in ancient Greece and modern France, it was refreshingly nonpartisan for war-weary American audiences. In fact, it lacked a single redeeming political or social virtue—with one incongruous exception. Booth's Raphael is mocked by a rival for shedding tears over the fate of the slaves.

When Raphael ignores the jibe, the antagonist continues his insults. "Yes, I see I am right. I presume from the ardor with which you applauded the liberal sentiments [of *Uncle Tom's Cabin*] that you are in favor of the emancipation of the blacks."

"Death and dishonor!" cries Raphael, and he moves threateningly toward the man. The sudden appearance of Raphael's lady love averts a fight, however, and the incident passes. But the stage moment let Booth do something remarkable. He had, in character, rebuked emancipation before Lincoln from the stage of Ford's Theatre.

John Hay found the evening rather tame. *Tame* is an adjective no one applied to a Booth performance, particularly the role of Raphael, which was an explosion of emotions. Hay meant that the play had no blasting trumpets, dancing banners, tramping soldiers, and clanging swords. Booth looked daggers in *The Marble Heart*, but he did not brandish any.[103]

While Hay was unimpressed, Lincoln admired Booth's acting, stated Joseph Luckett, an old hand on the Washington theatrical scene.[104] Grover and Ford said the same thing and added that the president returned to see him act on multiple occasions, always applauding his efforts.[105] The actor was coldly indifferent to Lincoln, however. "Booth said he would rather have the applause of a negro."[106]

"I *know* President Lincoln was an admirer of the man who assassinated him," said Frank Mordaunt, who worked for McVicker in Chicago. Tad introduced Mordaunt to his father, and the actor had several conversations on drama with the president. Mordaunt discovered that Lincoln knew exactly who Booth was and liked his acting. "He told me that he desired to meet him, and I said I could arrange it." It was a promise Mordaunt could not keep. He approached Booth several times on the topic, but the star found excuses to avoid an introduction.[107] So the president and the actor never spoke. Lincoln knew him on sight, of course. He would smile in greeting as they passed.[108]

CHARLES CULVERWELL, an Englishman acting under the name of Charles Wyndham, was hired by Grover to support Booth. When the relatively inexperienced Wyndham came onstage for his first rehearsal, he settled in at a little table that afforded a good view of the set. "John Wilkes noticed me there and smiled," recalled Wyndham. A few moments later the stage manager saw Wyndham and rushed up in agitation. "It seemed I had been sitting at the star's table whereas my proper place was far back in the wings. I apologized, of course, but Booth didn't seem to mind."

Socializing with Booth after hours, Wyndham was captivated. "A most charming fellow, a man of flashing wit and magnetic manner, he was one of the best raconteurs to whom I ever had listened. As he talked, he threw himself into his words, brilliant, ready, enthusiastic. He was unusually fluent. He could hold a group spellbound by the hour at the force and fire and beauty of him. And yet, throughout the spell he wove upon his listeners, there were startling breaks, abrupt contrasts, when his eccentricity and peculiarity cropped to the surface. No one pretended to have an understanding of this strange man."

Dismissed for incompetence by Grover, Wyndham soldiered on in the profession, ultimately earning acclaim as an actor and manager and becoming a giant in the English-speaking theatrical world. As such he had seen hundreds of players come and go over the decades, but one of them lingered. "There was but one John Wilkes," he mused, "sad, mad, bad John Wilkes. As an actor [his] natural endowment was of the highest. His original gift was greater than that of his wonderful brother Edwin—more spontaneous, possessing a higher degree of inborn inspiration. He was one of the few to whom that ill-used term of genius might be applied with perfect truth. He *was* a genius and a most unfortunate one. His dramatic powers were of the best." But he was an unpolished jewel. "His was not a nature to submit to discipline, adversity, or a long routine of study. When he achieved some notable triumph of his art, it was a divine flash, a combustion of elements within him. What he had he could use, but he never brought his gift to flower because, it may be, his race was destined to quickly run."[109]

"He had no master to form his style upon," explained Asia in her brother's defense. True, there were actors whom he greatly admired. Booth loved listening to Murdoch. No one spoke more clearly or beautifully. Davenport was equally magnificent, so elegant and exact onstage. As for Forrest, Booth's admiration of him was unbounded. Yet, he lamented, "these are not [to me] as father was to Edwin. If I shine at all, it must be in the rough. Whatever talent [I] possess will be nature's own legacy."

What he had to do, he told his sister, was to persevere in all things.[110]

6

. . . .

LIFE'S FITFUL FEVER

MAY 27, 1859, was a pleasant evening in Centreville, Rhode Island, and Albert Slocum, a farmer, took advantage of the weather for a stroll. Friends were out as well, carrying groceries, entering churches, and popping into shops. In the midst of their familiar faces Slocum noticed a stranger. Dressed in a loose-fitting overcoat and a low crowned cap, the man loitered nearby and watched. It was none other than John Wilkes Booth, disguised in heavy whiskers. Before him a streetlamp illuminated the storefront of the merchant Burrill Arnold. Under its light Booth observed Arnold seated with his back to a window. When the street cleared for a moment, Booth stepped up to the window and at a distance of two or three feet raised a pistol and fired. The bullet shattered the glass and struck Arnold between the shoulders. "My God!" the shopkeeper gasped and then fell dead.

Before anyone could realize what had happened, Booth bolted into the shadows and disappeared.

Slocum told this story in 1904. He wished no publicity for doing so, he insisted. He only wanted the truth to come out at last, and the truth was this. Booth was visiting his uncle, who lived in the village. When the actor discovered that Arnold was prosecuting the uncle for trafficking in illegal liquor, he committed the murder in revenge. It was the future assassin, beyond doubt, his false whiskers trimmed to a theatrically villainous point. Thousands of old Union soldiers read Slocum's account in the leading veterans' newspaper.[1]

In fact, Slocum was mistaken. Booth had no family in Rhode Island. In 1859 his only surviving uncle was James Mitchell, widower of his late aunt Jane, his father's sister. Mitchell lived in a tenement in Baltimore, where he eked out a living as a peddler. He had no connection with Rhode Island. The Booth arrested in Kent County for violating Rhode Island's prohibition laws was one Hiram Booth, a man entirely unrelated to the Maryland family.[2]

Slocum's story fit a pattern, however. It was one of dozens of postassassination accounts telling some dreadful tale about Booth. The young actor was said to be an opium addict, a sexual predator, a home wrecker, a thief, a cutthroat, and a debauchee. These fictions found ready readers. Since history had proved that Booth was capable of the unthinkable, it was tempting not to add to a truth already disturbing enough.

But the question is well raised—who was John Wilkes Booth?

MATHEW CANNING KNEW Booth well. In 1886 the star's longtime friend and manager sat down for an interview with George Alfred Townsend and told him an unappreciated fact. For all Booth's fame on the stage and infamy in public life, neither the theater nor politics was his chief passion in life. First, last, and always it was the ladies. "Booth was a very slave to his almost insatiable amorous propensities."[3]

Booth's attitude toward women was generally chivalrous. When in Montgomery, Alabama, in 1860 he was said to have stepped in to protect several actresses from the insulting behavior of Henry Thomas, the drunken son of a prominent planter. Thomas pulled a knife and slashed Booth severely. Yet this is another event that never happened. Thomas did stab two theater employees who attempted to defend the actresses, but that incident occurred the year before Booth arrived in Montgomery.[4] The story seemed believable, however, because friends knew it was just the sort of thing he would do. "I have nothing to say in favor of Booth, because he committed one of the worst crimes in history," said the actress Kathryn Evans, "but I cannot refrain from telling those who never saw him that he was the finest gentleman I ever met."[5]

Evans and countless others were attracted to Booth's polished manner. The Washington publisher D. C. Forney found him "a thorough master of all the graces and courtesies of high-born life which he naturally inherited as well as acquired."[6] He spoke intelligently, correctly, and cleanly. "I have heard him talk by the hour but never heard a vulgar, obscene or ungentlemanly expression fall from his lips," said James P. Ferguson, who kept a tavern adjoining Ford's Theatre. When a reporter replied skeptically that he heard Booth was something of a cad, Ferguson grew agitated and snapped, "Don't believe a word of it! Wilkes Booth was a gentleman."[7]

When Booth became a public figure, his romantic life grew complicated, and he struggled at first to find his footing. While acting in Richmond, he received scented letters from a young woman from one of the city's elite families. When Booth did not reply, the writer grew bolder, telling him she was ready for anything. A wrong move here would damage his reputation in a city he had grown to love, so the young man, away from home and the counsel of his mother, turned for advice to Isabella Pallen, the family friend and stalwart of Beth Shalome Synagogue. She arranged for Booth to meet the woman in a public place. There, at the foot of the Washington statue on Capitol Square, "he appealed to her better nature," recalled Isabella's daughter, Mary Bella, "disabused her mind of the idea that everything and everybody was jolly behind the scenes, and sent her back to her father's house a wiser virgin."[8]

In time Booth's self-confidence in these matters grew. As it did, he acted on his own inclination, pulling women in or pushing them away as suited the moment. Nevertheless, "he was licentious as men, and particularly as actors go, but not a seducer," thought Townsend. If anything, the opposite sex pursued him.[9] "I *have* to communicate," an unidentified woman wrote him. "I make use of the only means of approach to you. I am about your own age, possibly a few months younger. You will probably wonder that a woman . . ."[10] The remainder of this missive is torn away, leaving the imagination free to fill in the rest, but the letter had the hallmarks of a regular correspondence Booth received. "Booth's striking beauty was something which thousands of silly women could not withstand," wrote the actress Clara Morris, who met him in 1863. "His mail each day brought him letters from women, weak and frivolous, who periled their happiness and their reputations by committing to paper words of love and admiration which they could not refrain from writing." Since he did not like being chased, "a cloud used to gather upon his face at the sight of them." Booth cut off the signatures and tore them into tiny pieces, then piled up the unread letters. "Harmless now," he said to

Morris. When a fellow actor picked up one of the neutered notes and started to read, Booth said sharply, "Lay that letter down please!"[11]

"It is scarcely an exaggeration to say the sex was in love with Booth," Morris wrote in *Life on the Stage*, her best-selling autobiography published in 1901. "At depot restaurants those fiercely unwilling maiden-slammers of plates and shooters of coffee-cups made to him swift and gentle offerings of hot steaks, hot biscuits, hot coffee, crowding around him like doves about a grain basket. At the hotels maids have been known to enter his room and tear asunder the already made-up bed that the turn-over might be broader by a thread or two. At the theatre, good heaven! as the sunflowers turn on their stalks to follow the beloved sun, so old or young, our faces smiling turned to him." Some of these fans became pests, and he was forced to change his address to escape them. Two of them became stalkers, or "lunatic adorers," as they were known at the time.[12]

Actresses were no more immune to his charms than anyone else. The effervescent Maggie Mitchell became a star during the war years, invited to the White House for tea with the Lincolns. She had looks, brains, and personality fired by a vitality so impressive that it was said she was still in her twenties when she died at the age of eighty-one in 1918.[13] In the small world of traveling actors her path often crossed Booth's. Maggie found him smart, fun to be with, and unbearably handsome. He dressed like a prince, owned the body of an athlete, and had the most beautiful hair in the world. Booth was intrigued, as were many others, by the sprite-like woman with bewitching gray eyes. In St. Louis their time overlapped, and they went horseback riding together. He followed the rides with gifts of forget-me-nots. She was soon wearing the flowers as a decoration, and their intimacy began. Since Booth had often played Romeo, and now Maggie was his Juliet, there was some good-natured teasing between them. Nevertheless, the relationship seemed serious, and word reached the East that the pair was engaged. Maggie admitted up front that she couldn't sew and couldn't cook—but who expected such things from a sunbeam? The two would never wed. They did remain friends, however. Booth sent Maggie flowers from time to time, and on the night Lincoln was shot she dreamt of Booth, handsome as ever and dressed stylishly in a short Spanish coat lined with crimson satin.[14]

The close physical and emotional association of actors working in the same company also led to temptation. John Barrymore, Mrs. Drew's grandson, made this point in a legendary riposte. A society matron cornered him backstage and asked him if, in view of his knowledge of Shakespeare, he thought Hamlet had a sexual relationship with Ophelia. Barrymore famously replied: "Only in the Chicago production, madam."[15]

Short, small-featured, dark-eyed, fair-skinned, and exquisitely shaped, Fanny Brown was said to be the loveliest woman on the American stage. "Beautiful and bewitching," sighed Queen of the *Clipper* when she played with Edwin at the Winter Garden in New York. While not as gifted as Maggie, she was a talented vocalist, pantomime, ménage rider, dramatic artist, and dancer.[16] Her wonderful physicality matched Booth's own. She could wield a sword better than most men, leading one critic to suggest that "Fanny would distinguish herself as a light cavalry officer in Sherman's army."[17]

In the fall of 1863 Booth organized a company to visit some of the smaller New England cities, and he invited Fanny to join the troupe. "When on his theatrical tour through the country, accompanied by Miss Brown, he exhibited some little regard for her shaky reputation," wrote a busybody. "When they stopped at hotels, Miss Brown, for the sake of appearance, was wont to room with an accompanying female friend." The women would then pretend to have a falling-out, "the affliction of which she found comfort for in the adjoining chamber of the handsome and enticing John."[18] Once again an engagement was rumored; once again no wedding bells rang.[19] But Booth remained fond of Fanny and carried her photo with him.[20]

Booth's revolving courtships did not preclude visits to prostitutes at the same time, and often close relationships with them. In addition to Louise Wooster, the Alabama woman who a quarter century after his death would permit neither friend nor stranger to say a disparaging word about him, Anne Horton and Sally Andrews, both of New York City, were attached to him.[21] His final relationship along this line was with Ellen Starr. A native of Baltimore, Ellen was expelled from that city's Ladies Literary Institute (Asia's alma mater) after accusing the Reverend John Jarboe, her principal, of sexual harassment. When Jarboe later saw her in the city and warned about the dangers of the street, she asked him what he expected. Her mother and sisters were in the business. Joining them, she became "a fashionable courtesan traveling over the country."[22]

"She was one of the most beautiful women I ever saw," said barkeep Ferguson about her.[23] He also found the small, dainty blonde cold, but she was warm enough to Booth. "My darling Baby," Ellen wrote to him in early 1865, "please call this evening or as soon as you receive this note. I'll not detain you five minutes—for gods sake come." After Booth shot Lincoln, she attempted to kill herself.[24] "She was as fierce as a tigress in her devotion to Booth," Ferguson added. "After the assassination, when she heard that I was the first man to report the murder at the police station, she sent me word that she would blow my head off the next time she saw me."

When Booth was interested in a woman, he pulled out all the stops—poetry, flowers, jewelry, even sentiments etched on glass. Isabel Sumner was a sixteen-year-old student at Bowdoin School whose father owned a grocery market in Boston. She was a smallish brunette with blue eyes, soft pretty features, and a lively manner. Booth wrote a stream of letters to her over the summer of 1864. Six notes survive, affording a glimpse of the actor in full pursuit. "How shall I write you, as lover, friend or brother?" he began. She must know, he continued, how much he respected her goodness and purity. That was why it was agony to see so little of her. "I was about to say, *I love you*, well perhaps I do. But do you think the least little bit of me? Forgive me for asking such a question, but I know the world and had begun to hate it. I saw you. Things seemed changed." It was hard, he explained, for him to express himself in the manner he wished. Would she help him learn to write a proper love letter? He knew he could trust her, trust her to keep his little secrets.[25]

Mother Booth had seen all this before. "You have so often been *dead in love*, and this may prove like the others—not of any lasting impression," she cautioned her son. "A young man in love does not stop to reflect, and like a child with a new toy, only craves the possession of it. Think and reflect. You are aware that the woman you make your wife you must love and respect beyond all others, for marriage is an act that cannot be recalled, without misery, if otherwise entered into—which you are well aware of." Knowing his probable reaction to her words, she closed, "I expect you will turn round and laugh at my preaching."[26]

Isabel lived with her family above her father's shop. To facilitate the romance, Booth checked into the Bromfield House, a hotel directly across the street from the Sumner dwelling, giving him a full view of her home. Earlier in the century another romantically minded young man loved a maid who lived at the same address. The suitor arranged for a hay wagon to drive by the house. His adored jumped from her room into the hay, and the pair hurried off to the altar. History would not repeat itself. Booth went all out, even sending Isabel a ring with a pearl set with tiny diamonds. The gift should have sent the young woman's head spinning. But Isabel was a cautious girl. She had had Booth direct his letters to her to the post office, not her home, for example. Although details are murky, it appears that ultimately she decided to keep things merely friendly. According to neighborhood lore, "she lived, it was said, to give devout thanks, after the murder of Lincoln, that she had ignored Booth's attempts."[27]

The sheer number of Booth's courtships and dalliances suggests that he enjoyed the chase as much as the catch—just as his mother said. In other words, he was in love with being in love. There was no headier intoxicant. A passion for passion pushed every other thought out of his head. Because of this, the playwright Addie Norcross, a Boston friend, believed Booth belonged to that class of individuals whom society indulged for their extravagances. "We forgive men of his type much for their exuberance and vitality," she wrote. "They were handsome and clever and full of life. They lived and loved."[28]

Men were drawn to him as well as women. Booth's biographer Townsend, speaking with him for the first and only time over drinks at Washington's Metropolitan Hotel in the spring of 1865, recalled his manner. The actor leaned on the bar, fingered his mustache, and "drew his face very near to mine, like a lover to a woman. There was not a foot between us." Booth's breath was sweet despite the actor's years of drinking and smoking. "His white brow and dark eyes and excellent address were captivating. He looked the full man, gave his heart as well as his head, and seemed to admit me to his inner circle. He was soft as a duke, modest as virgin genius, without antagonisms, making himself like my old acquaintance yet without familiarity, as friendly as if he had taken an affectionate interest in me. The trait he left upon my mind was amiability. What an agreeable fellow!" Townsend thought.[29]

There was a naturalness to him. "One may know an actor off the stage by the formal strut, the affected manners he uses," said Charles M. Wallace, who served with Booth in the Richmond Grays. "Booth was an exception to the rule." John Deery, who operated a saloon in Washington during the war, agreed. "In common intercourse he was utterly devoid of that artificiality and 'staginess' so common to men of his profession. He never used to gossip about his professional work nor boast of his stage career as it is the general custom of actors." In fact, Booth rarely spoke of the theater with those outside of it.[30]

Ordinarily Booth was quiet, even reserved in public. With people around him, he lit up, "convivial in his habits, and sprightly and genial in conversation." That was why the Ford's Theatre callboy William J. Ferguson disliked photographs of the actor. "Pictures in the main disclose him as saturnine. They show little of his quick excitability, nothing of his love of fun, no trace of his joyousness. For these qualities, which completely concealed the dark side of his character, I held him in admiration and high esteem. With me the extent of my regard and respect for Booth fell nothing short of hero-worship."[31]

Booth got along well with all classes of people. "He was extremely popular with everybody," wrote Norcross. "Simple and democratic, he joked with everyone he came in contact with, even the girls in the laundry where he left his collars and cuffs. They always saw to it that Mr. Booth's package was ready when he came in for it and vied with each other as to who should have the honor of delivering it. He joked with the cabmen at the stand corner of the Tremont House. In his quiet quizzical way he made friends everywhere." It was easy for him to like Norcross, whose father was a wealthy journalist, but Booth's friendships extended to the bottom of the social ladder as well. "By the unlettered and ignorant who came in contact with him he was almost idolized," recalled John T. Ford. "His graciousness to that class was proverbial, his liberality unstinted. He astonished them with his strength, fearlessness, and wonderful gymnastic feats." Said one: "He was a man to be liked because *he* enjoyed *you*."[32]

The variety of these associations seems contradictory. The poet Thomas Bailey Aldrich, a friend so sweet he was described as "a stick of sugar candy," told Annie E. Field at the time of the assassination that "we should not have been more astonished to hear he himself had done the terrible deed than he was Wilkes Booth. He was so gentle, gentler than I."[33] Yet Aldrich spoke of the same man who cleared out barrooms when angered and drinking.[34] Townsend explained this contradiction by asserting that Booth was "hollow." This is a tantalizing reference to the "empty vessel" syndrome common to some great actors in which a dazzling exterior with little beneath is lost without director or script.[35] That was why Booth got along well with everyone, argued Townsend. "He had very little to communicate and therefore harmonized well with people."[36] He could sing sweetly with the poets or crack heads with the rowdies as the moment demanded.

Townsend quickly rejected his own thesis, however. He knew as well as anyone that Booth's problem was not that he was empty. The problem was that he was full. His powerful personality harbored consuming likes and dislikes. Surpassing all was his hatred of abolitionists. He never lost an opportunity to excoriate antislavery leaders like Wendell Phillips and William Lloyd Garrison for their extremism. "And yet," wrote a Chicago friend, "he was precisely of that nature." In an odd way he reminded the friend of John Brown. "These two murderers reached extremes. Both became permeated with the spirit of the faith which they adopted, each carried this belief into his whole life and brooded over it and nursed it till it became the absorbing controlling idea and he a monomaniac and murderer."[37] The result did not surprise Marcus M. Pomeroy, one of the nation's most notorious Copperhead editors and a Chicago drinking crony of the actor, who said, "Booth was a very impassioned man, as we all know, and he never did anything by half."[38]

Friends realized it was pointless to discuss certain things with him. He might listen and even pick up information from those whose knowledge he respected, but it was impossible to change his mind. "To argue with him would have been as effective as trying to widen the Royal Gorge of the Colorado by whistling in it," said the actor John M. Barron.[39] This closed-mindedness had a serious downside. In contrast to Lincoln, who showed an ability to learn and grow as a person, Booth never had a new thought after his core opinions were formed in his teenage years.

Compounding this defect was an inability to let go of his troubles. "While Booth was a very likeable young fellow, very courteous in his manner, he was quick tempered—also quick to forgive—unless the offence was of a grave character. Then he would brood over it," said a Baltimore friend.[40] For example, anger over the imprisonment of Baltimore police marshal George P. Kane roiled for months. Such worrisome thoughts lingered, festering away. When he lost his temper, "he would snap you up like anything," said William Withers, Ford's Theatre's musical director.[41]

Booth developed the habit of rationalizing away bad war news. As his brother Junius knew, John did not hear what he did not want to. "Whenever I would mention any success of the federal arms, he would say that he had not heard it," June wrote after the assassination, "or that it was a false report &c., and would soon be corrected." The younger brother claimed that for each fact in a newspaper, there were a hundred lies.[42] If Booth liked a person of differing views, he redirected the conversation. On late-night walks with Forney, who ran the Lincoln-friendly *Washington Daily Chronicle*, Booth seemed happy unless the topic of the war came up. Then he fell silent. "Forney," he would finally say, "let's talk about something else."

Not surprisingly, he hated losing. Like most athletes, Booth was highly competitive, and hence he puzzled John Deery, operator of a classy billiard parlor above Grover's Theatre in Washington. Deery regularly invited Booth to play, but the actor never picked up a cue. Since Booth loved the game, Deery was baffled. The fact was that Booth knew he could not beat Deery, who was the national billiard champion in 1865, and he did not want the embarrassment of losing before a roomful of people.[43]

With a few such exceptions, Booth was not unduly egotistical. "He was in general a modest man," recalled his friend Thomas Harbin, a noted Confederate agent. "The only thing he was proud and almost boastful about was his physical strength. As a good spreer, fighter, good shot, good jumper, and lover of the open air, he felt supreme." He was bold and self-confident in all things physical. A sweet-tooth for trouble got him into difficulties, but once in them he was composed and steady.[44] The comedian John E. Owens expressed a common view when he declared, "He was all man from the child—and the feet—up."[45] Yet "all men at times are cowards," as Booth put it. He was traveling on a Mississippi River steamboat once when rebel guerrillas opened fire on the vessel. A bullet whistled through the bonnet of Henrietta Vallee, Ben DeBar's wife. When the gunfire turned his way, Booth jumped for cover as fast as anyone else, a fact he freely admitted.[46]

The "Booth full of fun and pranks" was very familiar figure to his friends such as Frank Drew. The two men were sharing a room at the National Hotel in Washington when their sleep was interrupted one night by hackmen quarreling below on Pennsylvania Avenue. The former occupant of the room had been a hard-drinking congressman who had left the bureau drawers full of empty whiskey bottles. Booth retrieved one, quietly opened a window, and dropped it on the street between the cabbies. Far from ending their ruckus, this raised it to a higher level as the hackmen accused each other of the attack. Booth then retrieved an armful of bottles and dropped one after the other out the window. As the missiles exploded like bombs on the icy pavement about their feet, the drivers scattered left and right while Booth stood at the window in his nightdress and laughed himself silly.[47]

"He loved fun of a rather rough sort," wrote a journalist from his hometown of Baltimore.[48] "This love sometimes carried Booth to extremes," continued Ferguson, the callboy. The youth had dropped into a billiard hall near Ford's to deliver parts when an argument broke out between two men at a table. Also present to observe the spat was Booth, an excited look on his face. "To egg on the altercation Booth found a bound book and threw the book at one of them. It reached its mark, square in the middle of the man's back." The victim wheeled around and accused a bystander of the assault. The accusation was resented, and a free-for-all started. Suddenly the lights were turned out to quell the melee as Booth fled the scene with Ferguson on his heels.[49]

Despite such incidents, a Philadelphia journalist asserted that "the disposition of this 'star crossed' murderer of the President was not vicious, nor was he, as has been represented, savage and morose. His address was remarkably winning and insured the friendship with all with whom he came in contact." Willful and impetuous, yes, "but tempered with a general kindness of heart." An employee at the Arch Street Theatre believed "he was not a bad man and after all was an innocent kind of fellow who would not do a mean action for the love of meanness."[50]

It is no surprise that Booth had devoted friends who, in later years when they felt safe to do so, spoke freely of his better qualities. Despite the trouble he brought upon the Ford family, Harry Ford, a younger brother of John T. Ford, always insisted that "Booth was one of the simplest, sweetest-dispositioned, and most lovable men he ever knew."[51] "Booth was a most winning captivating man," agreed John Mathews. "That was the opinion of everyone who came in contact with him."[52] Deery felt him to be "the most charming of men, the most fascinating personality I have ever met in my long life. In his way, with his intimates, he was as simple and affectionate as a child. That much at least in his favor can with truth be averred over his grave, dishonored as it is over that of any other American."

"He is, all in all, a strange compound of a man," said a Chicago journalist, "a peculiar combination of mind and nature."[53] All who crossed his path agreed. "There were many things connected with this man which I was unable to understand," said Forney. These friends could do no better than embrace the perspective of young Ferguson of Ford's when he took stock of Booth six decades after the war. "I now can trace back through my memories of him and note *tendencies*, but they were then accepted without analysis as part and parcel of his high-spirited nature, of the dashing buoyancy I so much admired."[54]

Clara Morris added thoughtfully, "Who shall draw a line and say— here genius ends and madness begins?"

Family members understood him no better. June worried that a "crack runs thro' the male portion of our family, myself included," as he wrote Edwin in 1862. "Father in his highest had it." But June did not have John in mind when he wrote these words. Joe, he believed, was the most troubled member of the family, and Edwin agreed that Joe bore watching. "Strange, wild, ever roving," Edwin wrote of the youngest brother, "he causes us all some degree of anxiety."[55]

Edwin adored John, wrote their friend Norcross. "Meeting him in the street his long refined face would light up and he would smile." And yet Edwin never knew what made his brother tick. "I cannot understand why my brother did this," he said at the time of Lincoln's murder, unless John had driven himself mad over politics.[56]

Edwin was still perplexed a quarter century later. He was standing in the wings with his fellow player Frank Oakes Rose awaiting an entrance when the talk turned to the ill-fated brother. "Yes, indeed, that was very sad," Edwin said. "He was so peculiar. I never seemed to know him.

"Do you know, Rose," he continued, "I believe I am as well acquainted with you as I ever was with John."[57]

JAMES HENRY HACKETT, one of Lincoln's favorite actors, wrote that young people constituted the great majority of Civil War playgoers.[58] Of that number women formed an increased percentage of the audience, since the war allowed them more latitude to go to places of public amusement at night,[59] and Booth was the recipient of their new freedom. "Ladies flocked to his performances," recalled the actor Henry A. Weaver. "It was no unusual sight to see numbers *standing* all over the house."[60] During his second visit to Boston, in February 1863, he entranced them with his acting.[61] "John, at any performance, could be counted on to draw into the house three-hundred chambermaids, three-hundred wet nurses, and a score of widows," teased his friend John McCullough.[62]

His sister-in-law Mary saw him in the dual roles of Fabien and Louis in *The Corsican Brothers* and found him overly melodramatic. " 'Look at his arm!' " she quoted the audience as saying, and explained, "His sleeves were rolled up—the muscles eclipsing everything else. [Yet] highly delighted the audience seemed at this exhibition."[63] For such scenes Booth was occasionally compared to Forrest, who William Warren thought would make a good boss in a slaughterhouse.[64] Like Forrest, Booth won applause by his physicality and swordplay, but he excelled the great man in one important additional particular, which Mary did not mention. Joined to his physical work was the ability to enact scenes of great tenderness. Said another way, Booth wrung tears from his audiences.[65]

The result was predictable. "The stage door was always blocked with silly women, waiting to catch a glimpse, as he passed, of his superb face and figure," wrote Kate Reignolds.[66] At the Boston Museum a wave of crinoline surged toward the star as he left the theater for his hotel after the play. Keach came out to remind the women that they were ladies and furthermore to say that he would permit no such behavior at his theater. The wave parted, and the star, dressed impeccably and wearing kid gloves, strode forward, his overcoat slung casually over his arm. He looked as if he were sitting for a picture.[67] His eyes darted among those in the crowd until he saw a pretty face, and then he smiled, tipped his hat, and nodded. Some admirers asked for the privilege of touching his cloak. Others did not ask, and Booth became the first actor known to have his clothes shredded by enthusiastic fans.[68]

The relentless attention of strangers in such a manner should have induced a state of absolute self-centeredness in Booth. "It is not surprising that stars feel entitled to exceptional treatment when that privilege is constantly reinforced by acquaintances and strangers alike," wrote a perceptive observer of stage life.[69] Happily, Booth maintained an honest view of his accomplishments. When an admirer gushed, "You're great! You're wonderful!" Booth suggested the young man go onstage himself—as a comedian.[70]

This down-to-earth nature earned the esteem of his colleagues. He had his moments of petulance, such as the time in Detroit when, after an argument with the stage manager G. P. De Groat, he refused to appear until De Groat's name was struck off the playbill. Generally, however, "Booth was universally liked upon the stage," recalled a Chicago friend. "His manner to all of the profession with which he was thrown together was urbane and gentlemanly, and from supernumerary (or extra) to manager he treated all with courtesy and consideration."[71] When he cued them in rehearsal with a blast on his silver whistle, "he was always considerate of the other actors and if he had a suggestion to make, made it with the utmost courtesy, prefacing it with, 'Now, Mr. ——, don't you think that perhaps this might be a better way to interpret that?'" recalled Edwin A. Emerson.[72] Martin L. Wright, starting his career at Cleveland's Academy of Music in 1863, felt that "any supernumerary could go to him for advice. Whoever went to him was received with gentle courtesy and generally came away an admirer. Of all the stars that came to play with us the one we loved and admired the most was John Wilkes Booth. He was not high and mighty like most of the stars. There was never a better fellow."[73]

Booth's sense of humor relieved many of their anxious onstage moments. Sometimes the humor was spontaneous, as in Buffalo when he was playing Richard III and his Norfolk embarrassed him by coming in from the wrong entrance. Booth greeted him with "What thinks thou, Norfolk?—*and why the devil didn't you come in on the other side?*" The house shook with laughter for five minutes at the remark.[74] At other times his wit was prankish. William Ferguson recalled a night at Ford's when Booth, in *The Taming of the Shrew*, had a prop ham covered on the underside with moist lampblack. Playing an angry Petruchio chastising his servants at the dinner table, the star seized the ham and smudged it against the cheeks of the actors. "Magically, on one cheek and then on the other dusky smears appeared until we all looked like darkies," recalled Ferguson. "The audience shrieked with laughter, shouts rising louder and louder as each black smudge was added."[75]

When things turned serious, Booth could be considerate. He was in stage combat with James Clarke McCollom when the latter lost count of the number of head blows he had delivered. As Booth shifted to parry a thrust, McCollom brought his sword down across Booth's forehead, cutting one eyebrow cleanly through. "Blood spurted and flowed down over his face," wrote an eyewitness. Flinging the blood from his eyes with his left hand, Booth insisted they finish the combat and then shrugged off the incident when the curtain fell. "You couldn't help it, Mac. It was my fault," Booth said. Ice and vinegar paper were applied to the star's wound. "Now if my eye had gone, that *would* have been bad. But don't worry. It's all right, old man," he remarked matter-of-factly, and he shook McCollom's hand reassuringly as a physician arrived with needle and thread. Later, led faint and nearly blind to his dressing room, Booth reflected upon the sanguinary spectacle they had just given the audience. "That was splendid!" he muttered.[76]

Backstage Booth was a good colleague. He recommended Ben DeBar take in George DeVere and his wife, Nellie Mortimer, an English couple refused permission by Secretary of War Edwin Stanton to travel south and play in Richmond. He encouraged Matilda Vining Wood, a New York manager, to hire Charles Wyndham, the struggling actor fired by Grover. And he bucked up Joseph Wheelock at a discouraging moment for the youngster by encouraging him to persevere in his craft. Wheelock went on to become a fine professional and president of the Actors' Society of America, an organization formed to protect actors from predatory producers.[77]

HOW GOOD AN ACTOR was Booth? Stuart Robson believed it was impossible to evaluate an actor whom one never saw perform. If an actor's work is known only by a description of it, one might by analogy try to appreciate a symphony by reading about it. In fact, it is more difficult than that. At least a composer leaves a score, just as an author leaves a book and an artist leaves a painting. An actor of Booth's generation leaves only a memory.[78]

Compounding the difficulty of assessing his work was the short time Booth spent onstage. There were three years as trainee, one as fledging lead, and three as star. "Three little years," as Morris phrased it with deliberation. John McCullough played for twenty-seven years, Clarke for thirty-six, and Edwin, June, and Maggie Mitchell each for forty-plus. These performers had time to mature as artists, unlike John. Considered that way, he was less a star, with its fixity, than a comet. "His rise was as sudden as his fall. We scarcely knew him before we lost him," reflected the manager John Ellsler.[79]

To understand his stature as an actor, one must first acknowledge his special gift. "There was a spirit in Booth such as made actors," said McCullough.[80] At its highest level the spirit was a concoction of intelligence, spontaneity, vitality, and, as Plato said, a dash of madness. His friend John M. Barron believed it akin to a divine spark.[81] It was intuitive, not studied. "In his soul the fires of genius burned brightly," Clara Morris told a reporter in 1890.[82]

The gifts were a legacy from his father, or so these friends believed. Early in his career the father and son's bold, above-the-fold styles were recognized as remarkably similar. "He comes nearer to the fire and passion of his renowned father than any [other] actor," wrote Judge Theodore J. Barnett ("Erasmus") in the *National Intelligencer*.[83] The manager Leonard Grover thought of this style as that of the earlier English actor Edmund Kean—all fire.[84] With the sizzle came episodes of eccentricity, excitability, and moodiness. But at least the son was more disciplined on stage than the father, more reliable, and more appealing.

That Booth was kissed by genius was a given. The New York correspondent of the *Washington Evening Star*, collecting Broadway gossip in the 1890s, wrote, "It is an odd circumstance that nearly every old-time actor, actress, and manager believes firmly that John Wilkes Booth was the greatest star of his day. His crime has not shaken their belief in his genius. There is still no faltering in their worship of his brilliant and meteoric stage achievements, which, after a lapse of a quarter century, have gained rather than lost luster."[85] Charles B. Jefferson, one of those old-timers, knew the truth of that. "Booth was a genius whose dramatic powers were little less than marvelous. At its best the art of Wilkes Booth was like a divine flash—an inspiration—that wonderful gift of nature."[86]

Booth approached acting by attempting to identify himself with the characters he played.[87] "He told me that when playing," recalled Louise Wooster, "he forgot his own identity completely and for a time would feel that he was really the character."[88] Charles Krone believed that his success lay in his ability to effect this transformation.[89] "He seemed to live the character," confirmed actor Louis James. "While I personally do not believe in such methods, it seemed to fit the man."[90]

A better education would have improved his work. Even the minimally educated Forrest conceded that "a higher sense of an author's intentions could be best conveyed by a richly stored mind." But Forrest also knew that a player could become a fine actor without being a scholar, adding—almost proudly—that he was ignorant of grammar long after he played the principal characters of Shakespeare with success.[91] Booth's indifferent education showed itself most notably in the way he mispronounced certain words. This was the only blemish in his performance, thought Robson, "but his voice was so beautiful and his intensity so great that when he became aroused, these mispronunciations were not noticed."[92] Such defects were no more fatal in him than they were in his brothers. None of the sons, however, was the intellectual equal of the father.

To what brains he had, Booth added his wonderful physique. "He was the most remarkable actor we probably had on the stage for hardiness, endurance, and strength," said Canning. "We sometimes called him the cast-iron man from the crown of his head to his feet."[93] He was also a fine gymnast.[94] "Full of impulse, like a colt," John Ellsler told Clara Morris, "his heels are in the air nearly as often as his head."[95] Beyond the leaps and bounds he was one of the best fencers of his era, once crossing blades in a rehearsal with two actors and disarming both in seconds.[96] Since nature gives a reckless impulse to the born artist, Booth got as good as he gave, "and he generally slept smothered in steak and oysters to cure his bruises," wrote Reignolds.[97]

It has been said that the hallmark of brilliance is not perfection but originality. "If originality *is* a virtue," wrote a Chicago critic, "Booth is virtuous to an extreme degree. No actor ever displayed more independence of, or disregard for, the old beaten path than he does."[98] He often inserted completely unstudied effects into a play. When the curtain rang down one night in Cleveland, Ellsler questioned him about something he had done during the performance. "Did you rehearse that today, John?" "No, I didn't rehearse it," was the reply. "It just came to me in the scene and I couldn't help doing it. But it went alright, didn't it?"[99] Booth could be original without being eccentric, said one old hand, "and he made telling points in his plays that no other actor of his time would dare to attempt."[100]

He had considerable talent in the invention of stage business. In *Richard III* he had the stump of a tree set in the center of the stage as far back as possible. "After parrying the first blow of Richmond, he deliberately turned and ran up the stage, his foot tripped against the stump, and he fell headlong backwards," recalled Weaver, who supported Booth in his Cincinnati engagements. "Richmond ran up after him and, as he fell, aimed a blow at his head. This was immediately caught by Richard who was on his feet in an instant, raining blow after blow at his adversary and driving him down the stage to the footlights. This had an electrical effect on the audience." John T. Ford stated, "He introduced into some Shakespearean plays some of the most extraordinary and outrageous leaps. In the play of Macbeth, in the entrance to the witch scene, he jumped from a high rock down on the stage, nearly as high as from the top of the scene. And he made the leap with apparent ease. He excelled in everything of that kind."[101]

His innovations extended to his characters' look, where he sought realism. When Booth reached for the chalk, Chinese vermillion, and ochre, the results were startling, but he wanted his villains deeply dyed, outside as well as in, for he intended their external appearance to reflect their inner demons. His *Richard III* was a ragged, dirty, bloodstained madman.[102] "He looked as though he had been run through the business end of a sausage machine," recalled J. B. McCormick, who acted with him in Philadelphia.[103] The look exceeded anything his contemporaries had seen. "With most tragedians it was a custom to rush on the stage while the fight was going on, looking as if dressed for court. Wilkes Booth made a terrible feature of this part of the performance. His face was covered with

blood from wounds, his beaver was lost in the fray, his hair flying hel-
ter-skelter, his clothes all mussed, and he panted and fumed like a prizefighter. He was truly original," wrote T. Allston Brown of the *Clipper*.[104]

Versatility was another strong point. Although drama was always his
mainstay, "Booth was exceedingly good in light and eccentric comedy,"
thought Weaver.[105] He frolicked about as Petruchio in *The Taming of the Shrew*
with a supper scene so lively and amusing that props from the table flew into
the audience. As Romeo Jaffier Jenkins in *Too Much for Good Nature,* he paro-
died his own romantic staples as a laughably inept young lover. "I remember
that Booth kept the audience in a roar of laughter all the time he was on
stage," Weaver continued. Booth could even clog dance if required. "Actors
like Booth were trained in those days to play a part a night, to do anything at
all on the boards from dancing a measure to battering down a broadsword
guard, and what they did, they did as well as it could be done. They didn't act
on a capital of good looks, dress coats, Broadway promenades, and one change
of parts a season!" growled a veteran Manhattan manager in 1890.[106]

It is beyond dispute that Booth was a hit onstage. Most critics liked
him, and even if they had not, it was not the critics who made a star. It
was the audience. But while an audience can make an actor successful, it
can't make one great, so the question remains: Was Booth truly distinguished? Was he among the best of the best? There were as many answers
to this question as there were people with opinions, but Edwin Forrest
provided a definition of acting greatness that is useful for making such a
determination. While arbitrary, the definition has the merits of being
both contemporary and provided by an individual universally acknowledged as a theatrical giant. Forrest believed that an actor was great if he
could play three major leads better than anyone else in the nation.[107]

Performing no fewer than twenty-two different roles between late
1861, when he commenced his star career in earnest, and 1865, Booth
had a sizable repertoire in which to find three such parts. Lear was his favorite Shakespearean character. Booth lacked the maturity and gravitas to be
top-notch in that role, however.[108] He played Hamlet well but felt Edwin's
performance superior to his own and gave first place to his brother's Macbeth as well.[109] As Romeo, Judge Barnett thought he had no equal.[110]
Others raved over his dual roles as Fabian and Louis Dei Franchi in *The
Corsican Brothers.* The Boston critic Benjamin Guild dissented, writing
acerbically that if a Corsican brother was indeed the way Booth played
him, it was regrettable there were two of them. Theatrical commonplace

had it that one bad notice was worth five good ones, and Booth was so angry with Guild that he threatened to horsewhip him.[111]

Setting these roles aside, Booth gains admittance to Forrest's pantheon for his work in three other plays. Not unsurprisingly, they were among the key pieces he played.

His Raphael in *The Marble Heart* was exceptional. Booth played a sculptor who had the misfortune to love a hard-hearted and materialistic woman. The play appealed to younger audiences who identified with Raphael's hopeless passion. Since openness and sincerity were required for this character, the role was markedly different from the villainous Richard—its opposite, in fact—and it showed Booth's range that he could realize it.[112] Coyle wrote in the *National Intelligencer* that the part was peculiarly well suited to him, "and it is not to be wondered at that he has achieved in its embodiment his richest distinctions. By his earnestness, his vigorous grasp of genius, and his fervor of style, he claims the most brilliant honors of his art."[113] "His Raphael was simply matchless," concurred John T. Ford. "He was ideal. He was the greatest that was ever seen."[114]

Booth's friend John Mathews thought Pescara in *The Apostate* was Booth's finest role.[115] An inheritance from his father, this dismal tale of the Spanish Inquisition was considered old-fashioned when Booth toured it in the 1860s, but he gave new life to the villainy, plots, counterplots, and gloomy ending in which all the leading characters perish. Pescara was a malignant and bloodthirsty villain. He was the biggest fiend on the Civil War stage, and Booth made that evident in every way. Even his makeup for the character was so frightening that he was once forced to pause his performance and reassure the youthful actress Kathryn Evans that it was just Johnny underneath.[116]

As Booth reached for the great dramatic intensity that the role required, his onstage demeanor astonished the audience. "The human face is my study," Booth said, and his features as Pescara appeared supernaturally employed.[117] Louis Weichmann, a government clerk who saw him play the part at Ford's, was dumbstruck by "the hideous, malevolent expressions of his distorted countenance, the fierce glare and ugly roll of his eyes which seemed ready to burst from their sockets. I cannot use language forcible enough to describe Booth's actions on that night."[118]

A Boston critic wrote that while "Richard is doubtless his most popular effort, Pescara is certainly his most artistic one." A New York scribe said, "His Mephistophelian sneer, his demoniac glare, and pity-murdering

laugh, fairly curdle the blood and haunt one like the spectres of a dream."[119]
Coyle felt Booth was without competition in the role. "He had made the
part peculiarly his own and has excited the greatest enthusiasm in every
city where he has played it. In this great character Mr. Booth is said to
stand without a rival."[120] Edwin saw John's Pescara at the Boston Museum
on January 21, 1863, and theatrical tradition has it that he presented the
younger brother with his own costume for the role. "I shall never play it
again after seeing you.'" Edwin told him.[121]

The third role in Forrest's required trio for greatness was the one Booth
performed most often during his career, the title character in *Richard III*.
"As Richard he was different from all other tragedians," wrote the *Clipper's* Brown, reflecting on his own decades as critic, agent, manager, and
theatrical historian. "He imitated no one, but struck out a path of his
own, introducing points which older hands at the business would not dare
to attempt. In this character he was more terribly real than any other actor
I ever saw."[122] The *New York Tribune* joined the praise, noting, "Booth is
head and shoulders above those who ordinarily attempt Richard III in
intellectual breath and powers of concentration." The *New York Times and
Messenger* felt that "his Richard is acknowledged to be without a rival
upon the American stage."[123] Ford thought Booth's Richard was une-
qualed by any contemporary.[124] "He did not *act* Richard," explained Isaac
G. Reed. "He *was* Richard—hump and all."[125]

When John Ellsler penned his memoirs late in life, he was hesitant to
include too much about his friend Booth in the text. He paused the
writing for a moment, then continued. "It is with a feeling of reluctance
that I proceed further," he stated. "Still I feel I may be pardoned for intruding my memories of him, whom I hold in such dear estimation."
Ellsler hoped that Booth's great crime would not entirely efface his legacy
as an actor. "It must be understood that young Wilkes was not finished.
Far from it. He lacked age, experience, and discretion—attainments only
to be acquired by time, study, and conscientious labor. In all his acting
one was reminded of a blooded colt; full of action, full of fire, necessitat-
ing a master hand to hold him in check and keep him down to good work.
It required time to remedy these defects. Unfortunately the period never
came. He died in the very springtime of his life. But those who saw him
still speak of him as an actor who, had he lived, would have stood head
and shoulders above all the artists of his time.

"It is no disparagement to them to say so."[126]

SUCCESS MEANT WEALTH. "To those stars who hit the popular taste and become public favorites," wrote the theatrical agent Wardle Corbyn, "the United States is an El Dorado and wealth flows in upon them in a golden stream."[127] Booth told Keach in December 1862 that his gusher averaged more than $650 per week for the season. In Chicago that month his weekly take soared to nearly $900. His profits upon his return to Boston in January 1863 are unknown, but it was reported that "his engagement was one of the greatest pecuniary successes known in the history of the Museum." In the spring of that year Ford paid him $700 for six nights in Washington.[128] Canning believed that Booth totaled $40,000 in one fifteen-month span.[129] Such a sum was possible. The popular comedian John Owens made $52,000 over a similar period, and Laura Keene once took home $17,000 for eleven nights.[130] The best guess is that during his peak earning years Booth averaged at least $20,000. That is what Asia thought, and a friend to whom Booth showed his bankbook recalled a figure in that range or higher.[131] The star, who had never had his hands on real money before, was giddy with success. "My goose does indeed hang high," he laughed.

"Wilkes hoarded, saved, grew miserly at last," recalled Asia. And he invested. He purchased stock in the Boston Water Power Company, a business whose name hardly suggested that it made money selling lots of land created as the tidal flats of the Back Bay were filled in.[132] He also bought bonds, purchasing three thousand dollars' worth of U.S. Treasury 5-20s. These bonds had an interest rate of 6 percent (paid half-yearly) and were redeemable in gold after five years and payable in twenty years from date. Given his political views, it is ironic that he owned federal bonds designed specifically to finance the war, but such were his contradictions.

These investments show the influence of Joseph H. Simonds, a Boston bank teller about Booth's age. A theater aficionado, Simonds knew Booth early on, even before the actor's first appearance in the city, and they became close friends. Simonds was organized and precise and so fastidious that a speck of dirt on his coat or a blot of ink on his letter paper horrified him.[133] Clearly, the two were an odd couple, but the clerk was honest and Booth trusted him. "I think I will have to make you my banker," Booth wrote him early in 1863, "and give you an interest in my speculations, so that if we are lucky, you may be able in a few years to throw aside those musty ledgers."[134]

Simonds's guiding hand was shown in facilitating Booth's purchase of a lot on Boston's Commonwealth Avenue. Delighted with his reception in the city, Booth thought about building a house there, and this lot was located only two blocks from the Public Garden and a brisk ten-minute walk to the Boston Museum. The property cost about $8,200, which the actor paid in four installments in 1863 and 1864. He had his eye on other lots as well, telling Simonds to look out for good investments.[135] Despite this expense, Booth had money enough left over to help Edwin buy a house for the family in New York City. With it their mother and little Edwina, Edwin's daughter, would have a permanent place to live. "It will be a home for John," the older brother promised.[136]

THE WAR GROUND ON, claiming the life of Booth's first cousin George Mitchell. George was a teenager living at the Booth farm when John was born. When his parents were evicted by Junius, he moved with them to Baltimore, where he made a living as a newsvendor. Enlisting at the war's outset in the 2nd Maryland Infantry Regiment (U.S.), George served faithfully until shot in the thigh at Petersburg in June 1864. His death at a soldiers' hospital in Washington followed a few weeks later.[137]

One of Booth's preoccupations was the fate of prisoners of war, and it is notable that George had earlier been a prisoner, captured at Second Manassas in August 1862. But Booth's concern over this issue was not sparked by George's bad luck. In fact, family letters have nothing to say about George, living or dead. Booth's distress grew from the arrest of Marylanders such as Marshal Kane. In the first year of the war the largest number of civilian prisoners from any state came from Maryland.[138]

One of those swept up by federal forces was Jessie B. Wharton. A resident of Clear Spring, Wharton was arrested shortly before Christmas 1861 for aiding the rebels by wrecking a feeder dam on the Chesapeake and Ohio Canal above Washington. Confined in Old Capitol Prison, he proved to be a handful. On April 20, 1862, he allegedly lingered at a prison window in violation of the rules. When a sentry, Private Ambrose Baker of the 91st Pennsylvania Infantry Regiment, ordered him to step back, Wharton unleashed a string of curses, "calling him 'a d———d Yankee son of a b———h, a Northern son of a b———h, a d———d hired scoundrel.'" Baker repeated the order. Wharton threw open his coat, bared his breast, and exclaimed, "Shoot, you coward, shoot! I'm nothing but a prisoner." The sentry did just that, wounding Wharton fatally.[139] Baker was arrested, but when his comrades petitioned President Lincoln on his behalf, the soldier was immediately freed.[140]

Wharton's death was reported in St. Louis newspapers on the same day, and the same page, as Booth's second engagement with DeBar was announced.[141] It was shocking news for the star. He and Wharton had been classmates at St. Timothy's Hall. Wharton's father, Dr. John O. Wharton, registrar of the Maryland Agricultural College (later the University of Maryland at College Park), was one of the parents brought in to broker an end to the student rebellion of 1853. After he left school, Wharton was a guest at Tudor Hall, where he flirted with Asia, writing her poems that he had published in the local newspaper. She looked encouragingly at the handsome visitor as he and John smoked and swapped stories, the former's arm draped affectionately around the latter's neck. Later she heard their laughter running down the narrow stairs to John's room.[142]

Asia always feared her brother would become a martyr of some sort, but now Wharton had earned that distinction among Lincoln's opponents. An unarmed civilian arrested in his own home, he had been shot on a peaceful Sunday afternoon when, after reading the Bible, he sought a ray of sunshine at the window of his dreary cell in which to stand and lift his heart in song. That is what his fellow inmates swore had happened, at least, and the Copperhead press believed it. Booth was incensed by the shooting, joining Wharton's relatives in their conviction that Wharton had been murdered.[143]

Among those appalled by Wharton's death was the Wisconsin editor Marcus M. Pomeroy. Booth was introduced to Brick, as he was known, in the bar under McVicker's Theatre in Chicago. The turbulent journalist, who believed the war to be inhuman and corrupting, agreed with Booth that abolitionists were first-class sinners. Little wonder that Lincoln's proposal to free the slaves in the rebel states was turning Pomeroy into a hater of the president. Brick liked Booth, however. The actor had ideals and lived by them.[144] When his friend later murdered Lincoln, Brick wrote and published a pair of sentences that were surprisingly casual in tone for a time when the president's death was still a painful topic for most Northerners: "One fine evening in 1865 a gentleman of the name of Lincoln, whose misfortune it was to be a tyrant as well as a fool, a despot as well as a blackguard, while taking his royal ease in a one-horse theatre of Washington, was waited upon rather unexpectedly by another gentleman by the name of Booth, whose misfortune it was to hate tyranny and love liberty. Booth invited Lincoln to *git*, and, using very persuasive arguments, Lincoln concluded he would accept the invitation!"[145]

Lincoln's emancipation plans confirmed Booth's worst fears. The entire war was nothing more than one gigantic John Brown raid, directed again at Virginia, a state he loved. June, who had returned from San Francisco to New York City to live, was disturbed to learn the depth of these feelings. "Knowing his sympathy for the South, I was very much afraid he might go over the lines, and I begged him not to be so foolish," June later told authorities. "I feared he might join the South, tho' he promised me that he would not for his Mother's and his family's sake." While June wrung a renewal of that pledge out of him, their conversations were troubling, and so was the younger brother. One night in a Washington street, June noticed tears in John's eyes as the latter turned his face toward Richmond and said sorrowfully, "Virginia. Virginia."[146]

"The trouble with Booth, in my opinion," thought Martin Wright of the Ellsler company, "was that he felt too keenly."[147] John Mathews saw the star's emotions so engaged when speaking with his fellow actors E. L. Davenport and J. W. Wallack. The men described the suffering they witnessed at a soldiers' hospital. The talk then turned to the war in general, Booth joined in, "and all of them expressed, more or less, feeling against the war," recalled Mathews, who was present. "It was a feeling not of bitterness but of sorrow, that brothers should be engaged in killing each other." Wallack and Davenport were uncommonly eloquent in expressing their desire for peace, and Mathews noticed that the power of their words made a profound impression on Booth.[148]

"It is terrible for a man to shed the blood of another," Booth said. "The sight of blood drives me wild, and this war has been nothing but blood—blood. The land runs with blood!"[149]

Empathy had its limits, of course. On the evening of December 31, 1862, African Americans gathered at churches to await the day of liberation. At one "watch night" held at the Union Bethel Church not far from Ford's Theatre, a minister exhorted his congregation to get off their seats and on their knees in gratitude to God and to Abraham Lincoln. The following afternoon—New Year's Day 1863—the president signed the official copy of the Emancipation Proclamation. At about the same hour Booth finished a rehearsal of *The Corsican Brothers* at DeBar's in St. Louis. Standing in the dressing room with the singer Con Murphy, he suddenly seized a large prop pistol and shoved it into the man's ribs. "By ——, Murphy, if you were Lincoln, what a chance I'd have."[150]

BOOTH TOURED WIDELY during his final year on the stage. Christmas 1863 found him in Leavenworth, Kansas. Although well received, he failed financially due to the weather. A blizzard, "believed to be the heaviest ever known in the plains," pounded the area.[151] The trip from Leavenworth to St. Joseph was an ordeal. To catch the steamboat he had to run four miles from the fort to the Missouri River, then help cut ice to allow the vessel to approach the dock. Booth was a self-described "dead-man" when he fell into a cold bed at the Pacific House in St. Joe.[152]

Michael F. Tiernan, an attorney, lived at the hotel. A former actor and admirer of the elder Booth, Tiernan joined in signing a public letter inviting Booth to give a reading at Corby's Hall. Short of cash, Booth agreed. He excelled in reciting in intimate, salon-type settings. This would be a more formal affair for a paid audience, however, and call attention to his elocutionary (as opposed to his acting) skills. The result disappointed Tiernan. "The room was uncomfortably cold, the audience restless and at times annoying," and Booth untrained and stagy. Nevertheless, the evening put $150 in the actor's pocket.[153]

The brutal weather continued, with St. Joe recording a bone-chilling twenty-five degrees below zero and the Mississippi River at St. Louis locked in ice from bank to bank. Booth got as far as Cameron on the Hannibal and St. Joseph Railroad line before snowdrifts closed the track to the east. Stranded, he became acquainted with Weston Bassett, the station's telegraph operator. Since the one small hotel in this hamlet was overwhelmed by snowbound travelers, Bassett offered to share his room at the depot with Booth. Neighborhood children discovered "Mr. Boots" and drew him outside for snowball fights. "Sometimes they would all join against him and give him much the worst of it, but he took it all in perfect good nature and was as rollicking and boisterous as the best of them," recalled Bassett. "He played games with them and romped until dark."[154]

Impatient to get to St. Louis, where he was overdue, he ultimately took matters into his own hands. Booth found a sled owner fool enough to drive in the frigid weather if the man could find someone fool enough to pay, so the two struck a deal. The driver would carry Booth down the line to the point where the tracks were clear enough for the trains to operate. Attaching four horses to the sled, they stuffed it with straw. Wrapped in a buffalo robe, Booth climbed in, waved a cheery good-bye to Bassett, and whirled away, "laughing and shouting, red-cheeked and happy over [his] release from the blockade." There was danger in the trip, and, as Booth wrote Ellsler, "I never knew what hardship was till then," but he reached St. Louis in time to perform on January 12, 1864. He had lost over a week of his engagement in a city where he always minted money.

Later in the month, while performing in Louisville, Kentucky, Booth still seemed shell-shocked by his frontier adventures. Krone of St. Louis met him on the street and thought "he looked worn out, dejected, and as melancholy as the dull, grey sky above us." Colleagues reported troubling signs. Booth drank, spoke, and behaved more extravagantly than before. Krone was concerned. When the star remained quiet and gloomy over a beer at Dannerman's Tavern, it was clear that more than good company would be required to cheer him up. Krone asked what was wrong. "Booth smilingly answered that no doubt it was the rough experience he had passed through lately." His old bad luck had tracked him down, he felt.[155]

Booth never crossed the lines to perform in the Confederacy, but he did perform in Union-occupied areas of the South like New Orleans, where he began a run at the St. Charles Theatre on March 14, 1864. The city's oldest and largest theater, the St. Charles had been closed by the war. The citizens of New Orleans were in no mood to watch the imaginary woes of actors when they had trouble enough of their own. Grant's capture of Vicksburg in July 1863 reopened the river and improved the economic life of the city, however, and DeBar decided to revive the St. Charles, with Booth to headline.[156] The star played nineteen nights to mixed houses and reviews. One critic complained that his combat scene in *Richard III*—the physical highlight of the play—was so protracted as to be ludicrous. The remark calls to mind Ellsler's observation that "John Wilkes as Richard never knew when he was conquered; consequently he was never ready to die. In many instances he wore poor Richmond out, and on one occasion Richmond was compelled to whisper, 'For God's sake, John, die! Die! If you don't, I shall.' "[157]

Booth had caught a bad cold in Leavenworth, and by the time he played in Cincinnati en route to New Orleans, he was quite ill with bronchitis. Two physicians were called in, treating him with pills, mustard baths, and a throat cauterization. Severe hoarseness continued in New Orleans, marring his engagement. Two nights at the end of March had to be canceled. Booth just couldn't go on. "My dear boy," he wrote Joe Simonds, "you have no idea how sick I have been."[158]

His extended time in the city gave him the opportunity to look around, and what he saw shocked him. Booth had always pointed to the forlorn appearance of Alexandria, Virginia, across the Potomac River from Washington, as an example of the cruel inflictions of the war, but New Orleans exceeded anything he could have imagined. "This great Hydra of Rebellion," as Navy Lieutenant David D. Porter phrased it, was seized early in the war.[159] A heavy hand kept the South's largest and most prosperous city subdued. "I have never been upon a battlefield, but, O my countrymen," Booth wrote a few months later, "could you all but see the *reality* or effects of this horrid war, as I have seen them, I know you would think like me. And would pray the Almighty to create in the northern mind a sense of *right* and *justice* (even should it possess no seasoning of mercy), and that he would dry up this Sea of blood between us—which is daily growing wider."[160]

At the home of Thomas W. Davey, manager of the St. Charles, he ripped into the occupation, "was very vitriol in his talk as to Pres't Lincoln, and called the Union soldiers all manner of evil names." An old friend of Davey, First Sergeant James Peacock of the 8th Regiment, Indiana Volunteer Infantry, was present. Peacock, a Canadian native, was a recently naturalized citizen as unionist in his views as Booth was rebel, and the soldier exploded in anger at what he heard.

"Cowardly dog," he shouted at the actor. He exclaimed that "if Booth had one spark of manhood in him, he would be in the Confederate ranks with a gun on his shoulder." There, at least, he and his views might be worthy of notice.

Enraged, Booth reached into his hip pocket for a pistol. Peacock seized a carving knife from the dining room table and told Booth that "if he attempted to draw a pistol on me, I would eviscerate him." Before the situation turned tragic, Davey and his wife, Lizzie Maddern, rushed into the room and calmed the men.[161]

This far south Booth did not care to disguise his views. Standing on the unevenly laid granite blocks that formed the pavement of St. Charles Street, Booth let out a cheer for the Confederacy. His companions dared him to follow that up by singing "Bonnie Blue Flag," a popular rebel tune that military authorities had banned in the city. Without a moment's hesitation he broke into song. "The rest of the party was too scared to think," recalled Edward Curtis, who lived in Booth's boardinghouse. "It was treason to sing that song, so they ran away." Quickly surrounded by excited soldiers, Booth informed them that he knew nothing about the ban. He was a stranger to the city, had heard the tune, and liked it. The soldiers released him. "Booth had a way about him which could not be resisted, the way which permits a man to overstep the boundaries of the law and do things for which other people would be punished," Curtis believed.[162]

Between April 25 and May 27, 1864, Booth made his fourth and final appearance in Boston. At the start of this five-week marathon he had a lingering cold, but he was able to complete his engagement without losing any nights. The press declared his vocal problems temporary and his engagement highly successful.[163] And yet, less than a year later, Richard Frothingham Jr. of the *Boston Post*, which had celebrated his performances, stated that Booth was washed up. He was suffering from an incurable bronchial affliction. "The papers and critics have apologized for his hoarseness," wrote Frothingham, "but it has long been known by his friends that he would be compelled to abandon the stage because of this throat disease."[164]

This is a serious allegation, and Frothingham was not the only one to state it. An unidentified actor friend of Booth's informed Harry Hill, who operated a legendary Houston Street bar for sporting clientele in Manhattan, that the worst was indeed at hand. The star had consulted an elocutionist and a physician about his condition, this friend said, only to be informed that "his voice was permanently gone, for stage purposes at least." Stunned at the news, Booth hinted darkly that there were other ways a man might win fame. "It is one of the strange ideas that are suggested by the possibilities of real life that had Wilkes Booth not lost his voice, Abraham Lincoln might not have lost his life," Hill reflected in his 1884 series "Thirty Years in Gotham."[165]

This claim must be taken with skepticism, as it provides an overly simple explanation of the assassination. Every traveling actor suffered from colds, sore throats, and bouts of bronchitis. Booth compounded his problems by smoking and drinking. But the assertion that he was finished would have astonished his family. Asia believed her brother had a wonderful future before him, and Edwin wrote that if John had not gone mad and shot the president, "he would have made a brilliant mark in the theatrical world."[166]

At the same time, an unspecified throat problem did spoil June's career, and one sees signs that John, too, was concerned about his voice.[167] He put aside the pungent Louisiana perique and loaded his meerschaum pipe with kinnikinnick, a mixture of dried sumac leaves and the inner bark of dogwood or willow smoked for centuries by Native Americans. The ingredients of these leaves had astringent and antiseptic properties and were used for treating fevers. Booth found the aromatic blend soothing on his throat.[168]

Brown, of the *Clipper*, who knew more about the public and private lives of Civil War actors than any other person, believed that chronic bronchitis did drive Booth off the stage. He could do the occasional benefit, of course, and he could manage, but he could not act as before. He was being forced to the wings.[169] Booth acknowledged a problem in a seldom-noticed remark to the playwright Augustus Cazauran. When Cazauran asked him to look at a new play, Booth replied, "I have left the stage. My voice goes back on me." Surely not, Cazauran responded. "I cannot act," Booth said bluntly. "I have quit the stage and am out of the business."[170] While the severity of his trouble remains undetermined, his remarks conceded that a cloud had appeared on the horizon.

Was it related—or only coincidental—that at about this time Booth made an effort to earn money outside of the profession? He formed the Dramatic Oil Company with Ellsler and a second Clevelander named Thomas Y. Mears. Their goal was to make a fortune in the oil country of western Pennsylvania. The men purchased drilling rights on a three-and-a-half-acre farm lot near Franklin. Mears, an inventor, prizefighter, fireman, salesman, gambler, and knockabout, would boss the job site, with Simonds coming on from Boston to manage the office. Mears hired Henry Sires, a local driller, to work the property. When Mears introduced Sires to Booth, the driller apologized for the oil-covered hand he extended in greeting. "Never mind," laughed Booth. "That's what we are after."[171]

Franklin was a boomtown. Its streets bustled with entrepreneurs, dreamers, and hustlers infected with oil-fever, and Booth, as intoxicated as all the rest, spent a happy, expectant season here. As Sires worked the rig, he scouted the district for new properties. When the weather was poor, he loafed at his hotel, read, or joined an impromptu club of literary spirits who gathered to drink and talk. On the weekend he attended Bible classes with Simonds at the local Methodist church. He was quiet on these occasions but quite lively at dances and at taverns, where his spirits were truly engaged. One night, watching a ruckus on the street outside a bar, Booth suddenly threw out his chest, drew back his shoulders, and cried out, "My God, I would like to be in a fight!"

Booth nearly got his wish on the Allegheny River ferry. His fellow passenger Titus Ridgway, a sawmill owner, made a derogatory comment about Southerners.[172] "Booth was a man who would not willingly offend or injure a living soul," recalled the ferry operator, whose name was McAninch, but he was also quick-tempered, and he retorted in kind. Ridgway replied that Booth's remarks were lies. "I will never allow a man to call me a liar," shouted Booth. Ridgway grabbed a hand spike, and Booth reached for his pistol. McAninch jumped between them, seized Ridgway, forced the spike out of his hand, and turned him aside. Ridgway was an ignorant loudmouth, McAninch later explained, while "Booth was a thorough gentleman [who] always treated the ferryman with great kindness and the greatest respect."

Meanwhile troubles abounded at the well. The irrepressible Mears found his position one sweet deal, and "Mears took good care of Mears," as Sires saw it. The partner spent company money as if it were his own, purchasing a watch, presents, and other personal items. When Simonds finally caught up with him, Mears cursed the accountant into the ground.[173] Booth took over, confronted the brawny scoundrel, and got cut with a knife for his effort. At the rig things were equally vexatious. "They always had a great deal of trouble from one cause or another," recalled J. H. Lee, an oilman. Casing had to be pulled and replaced repeatedly, and an explosive charge intended to remove an obstruction down the bore hole actually decreased production. What should have gushed merely trickled. "Not enough to grease the working barrel," said Sires.[174] Expenses soared, and Booth, far from making a fortune, was losing one.

Heading back to his lodgings after one discouraging day, Booth noticed a litter of stray kittens. He bought some milk and took the cats home to Sarah Webber, his landlady. Would she care for the little creatures, he asked, until a good home could be found for them?[175]

JOHN WILKES BOOTH had great respect for his vocation, recalled Louise Wooster.[176] "Why cannot the world understand the true nature and dignity of our noble profession?" he asked. "The world will think better of the actor some day and treat him more liberally."[177] Booth felt that Lincoln's frequent attendance at the theater indicated that the president appreciated the stage and earned three kind words—"God bless him"—from his assassin.[178] A humble and anonymous tramp understood as well. One winter day the man knocked on John Mathews's door in Washington.

The shabbily dressed vagabond, who had been over at Ford's looking for actors, said, "I have nothing to eat or drink, no place to sleep, and hardly shoes that will stay on my feet. I thought if I could see some of the actors they would set me up a little."

Mathews fetched a basin of water in which the man bathed his feet. "As he was washing, I looked in the glass opposite me and saw John Booth looking down at the man with an expression of interest and pity." Mathews outfitted the tramp with shoes, socks, and an old suit and sent him on his way.

"What a compliment that was to actors, Johnny," Booth said to Mathews. "Did you mark that, my boy? He didn't go to one of those Bible-thumpers, did he? He went to the theater. He asked for the actors."[179]

Booth was proud of his trade. It gave him fame, wealth, and a sense of self-esteem. But he walked away from it. After his final Boston appearance ended in May 1864, he refused all future engagements. It was a pivotal decision and therefore worth a hard look, but, as in many transforming moments, his motives were complex, even setting aside the significance of a throat problem whose severity is indeterminable.

First of all, Booth found performing around the country hard and lonely work. He had never liked touring.[180] A star was a nomad with a nomad's wandering and rootless life. The money was great, it was true, but the dollars were earned "by a life of toil and travel, sleepless nights, tedious journeys, and weary work."[181] It was a routine of cold and drafty theaters, indifferent hotels, and indigestible meals. These were kitted together with constant travel, often at night, on jolting, swaying trains and the attendant ordeal of banging doors, loud voices, importuning nutsellers, milling passersby, and cramped seats. One particularly irksome trip from Boston to Chicago took Booth fifty-one hours to complete.[182] And, when he arrived, he was expected to be fresh and engaging, of course, and ready to tear his heart out and hand it to an audience of strangers.

Success came, but at a high cost to the mind and body that produced it. Booth suffered a terrible strain in acting colossal characters. After playing Lear, for example, he would remain Lear half the night and wake next morning weary, nervous, and unrefreshed.[183] Added to that was the weekly accumulation of sprains, cuts, and bruises. While Booth impersonated supermen, he wasn't one himself, and he often felt bludgeoned. Given his playing style, no actor in America put more blood, sweat, and tears into his work than he did. The routine was punishing.

Every star tired of this grind from time to time. Edwin believed that he was little more than a trained monkey. "I wish to God I was not an actor," he wrote a friend in 1863. "I despise and dread the damned business."[184] Equally exasperated on occasion, John left no remark so impassioned, but he did tell Weston Bassett shortly before he quit acting, "To be candid with you, the profession is a very uninteresting theme with me. I like its great climaxes the same as I do the great upheavals in nature or the meteoric flashes in human life, but the almost endless details, the commonplaces, weary me."[185] The grind was like a leaden weight on someone so naturally restless. Edwin felt he had to endure such things. John embraced no such destiny. "Fate takes hold of some men, but with me I do not wait for Fate," John told Frank Jerome, a scenic painter at the theater in Leavenworth. "I make my own fate, and have to thank no man for it."[186]

The actor Harry Weaver felt that when Booth first entered his vocation "he had made up his mind to devote all his energies to the task, was most thoroughly in earnest, most sincerely devoted to his profession."[187] The effort was now spent, and his longtime friend Harry Langdon felt Booth abandoned his good acting habits toward the end. Even John Mathews, in his childlike apologies for Booth, had to admit that "he would not get down to study and bring himself into shape."[188] He had reached the limits of his willingness to slave for his art. Simply put, he did not live to act. Accordingly he never made that final and supreme effort to do what may have been within his grasp—establish himself as the very best.[189]

"Have you lost all your ambition, or what is the matter?" Simonds asked him not long after the actor left Franklin. "I hardly know what to make of you."[190] The withdrawal from his former world and friends confused and concerned Simonds. The business manager foresaw that retirement, with nothing else to do, would lead to trouble. Booth would grow depressed and would have too much time on his hands in which to think, or more accurately to stew.[191] A helmless ship, he would be less able to curb the drinking. "None knew better than Booth himself," thought a Chicago friend, that alcohol was trouble. The star always believed that if he could only find the right woman she could help him banish the temptation. "With him it was an often expressed hope that should he ever marry, he might obtain for a wife someone possessing sufficient influence over him to restrain him from this accursed excitement."[192]

Above all, and at every occasion, hovered the war. Wherever he went, it intruded. One afternoon in Cleveland, not long before his trip to New

Orleans, Booth was in rehearsal when a noise on Bank Street drew the company to the windows. The 29th Ohio Volunteer Militia, having just received its colors, was marching past to the cheers of the city. "I was the first to return to the stage," recalled Martin Wright. "There was Booth striding back and forth like a caged lion. His face was white and convulsed with rage. He was swearing horribly. This was the only time I ever heard an oath pass his lips."[193]

Toward the end of his life Booth wrote to his mother, "For four years I have lived (I may say) A *slave* in the north (A favored slave its true, but no less hateful to me on that account.) Not daring to express my thoughts, even in my own home. Constantly hearing every principle dear to my heart denounced as treasonable. And knowing the vile and savage acts committed on my countrymen their wives & helpless children, I have cursed my willful idleness. And begun to deem myself a coward and to despise my own existence. For four years I have borne it mostly for your dear sake. And for you alone have I also struggled to fight off this desire to be gone."[194]

Mary Ann did not read this letter until it was too late. She found it a few days after the assassination. Clarke took it away from her and gave it to federal authorities, and they suppressed it. The letter was rediscovered at the National Archives in 1977. Those who knew Booth well, like John T. Ford, did not need to read it, however. They knew the story it told. As long as the South was winning, or at least not losing, he could live with his promise to his mother to stay out of the war. But as things grew critical for the Confederacy in 1864, Ford believed, "he brooded over it and fretted at the thought that, after all his warlike talk, he was acting a coward in the eyes of the world in keeping back from deeds. His promise preyed upon his mind."[195]

On occasion he was called out and embarrassed for his inaction. Langdon found him wrapped in a large white coat and reveling with Sam Chester at the House of Lords in New York. He was drinking heavily. When the talk turned to politics, as it did increasingly, Langdon lost patience. "John, you ought to be ashamed of yourself. To stay on our side and help the other."[196] The remark hit Booth like a well-directed punch. Little could have been more hurtful.

Free of the stage, he could now atone. Did he do so from a simple sense of duty? Or was it more complex—a sort of self-conscious performance with himself as star? These opposing viewpoints will be endlessly debated. One thing will not. John Wilkes Booth had reached a turning point. He would stop playing history. From now on he would make it.

175

7

· · · ·

MISCHIEF, THOU
ART AFOOT

SAMUEL B. ARNOLD IDLED AWAY the warm summer. Finding farm work monotonous, he intended to spend his time in pursuit of big-city pleasures. As the hard-living Arnold knew from personal experience, these were considerable in Baltimore. Starting his rounds one day after breakfast, he reached his father's house about noon, where he found his brother William. A habitué of the Holliday Street Theatre, Willie had news. John Wilkes Booth was at the Barnum City Hotel and wished to see him.[1]

A dozen years had passed since Arnold and Booth were classmates at St. Timothy's Hall. The two had not seen each other in all that time. Arnold remembered Booth well, however. Like his classmates, he had witnessed his old school chum's rise to stardom. So it was with a light step that he made his way that day in early August 1864 to the Barnum. Arnold had not "the remotest idea of the result which would follow the visit," he recalled in a memoir published in 1902. "I merely called upon him as a companion and friend of my boyhood."

Booth received him warmly. The pair sat at a table, the actor calling for cigars and wine. Smoking and drinking, they talked of old times and of the less happy days of the present. Booth remarked that he had heard Arnold had been in the Confederate army.

As Booth spoke, Arnold could scarcely believe the transformation that had taken place in his friend. "Instead of gazing upon the countenance of the mild and timid schoolmate of former years, I beheld a deep thinking man of the world before me, with highly distinguishing marks of beauty, intelligence, and gentlemanly refinement, different from the common order of man and one possessing an uninterrupted flow of conversational power."

What Arnold had become over the years was not as apparent. Taller than the actor and well built, with dark brown hair and gray eyes, Arnold had a frank, open face. He gave the impression of being "a good man in a knock-down, quite a fighting man," thought a Baltimore acquaintance. Not so evident were the psychological scars that Arnold bore. He had enlisted with the rebels in May 1861, serving until discharged for ill health that fall. After a convalescence at home, he returned south in 1862, met up with an older brother who was a Confederate captain, and served the Southern war effort as a civilian clerk until returning to Maryland a final time in February 1864, to attend to his seriously ill mother. During his absence, the war had changed many attitudes in the state, and the proud ex-soldier was mortified by the coldness and hostility with which former friends received him. He resented their behavior bitterly. Now at loose ends as an occasional farmhand, Arnold was a troubled veteran in need of friendship.[2] Booth's kindness and gracious manners infatuated him completely.

There was a knock at the hotel-room door, and Michael O'Laughlen was admitted. O'Laughlen was Booth's close friend and confidant, whose acquaintance, going back to childhood days on North Exeter Street, antedated even Arnold's. A former Confederate soldier who had returned home when ill in 1862, he was twenty-four (Booth was now twenty-six, Arnold twenty-nine). With black hair, mustache, and imperial, O'Laughlen possessed "a warm, friendly disposition and a fine comprehensive intellect," wrote a friend. Genteel in appearance, he did not have the look of a doer of daring deeds, but he was pluckish and smart, a keen observer, and talented with his hands. Although he and Arnold were both Baltimoreans and had served together in the 1st Maryland Volunteer Infantry, CSA, a regiment engaged at Bull Run in 1861, they were strangers to each other.[3] Booth introduced the two, and O'Laughlen joined the festivities.

"We drank and freely conversed together about the war," Arnold recalled, "the present condition of the South and the non-exchange of prisoners." It was common practice to exchange captured soldiers in the early years of the war. The practice gave a boost to Southern manpower, however, and rebel abuse of the system led the federal government to limit it in the autumn of 1863. On April 17, 1864, General U. S. Grant declared a formal stop to exchanges except in certain hardship cases, and he reaffirmed the policy on August 18, stating that it fed men to the Confederate army and prolonged the war. U.S. military prisons, stretching from Camp Douglas at Chicago to Fort Pickens, Florida, bulged with nearly sixty-six thousand rebel prisoners, a number nearly as large as the size of the Confederacy's principal fighting force, Robert E. Lee's Army of Northern Virginia. The Southern need for these men was critical. During the summer Lee was desperate enough to authorize an attack on Point Lookout Prison, a camp in southern Maryland where nearly fifteen thousand rebel soldiers were held.[4] If exchanges could only be revived, Arnold reasoned, "it would strengthen the force of the Confederate army and be the means of filling up to some extent their depleted ranks."

Arnold had no idea of Booth's views on the war when he entered the actor's room, but he was rapidly enlightened. "For the success of the Southern cause every pulsation of his heart throbbed," wrote Arnold years later. Booth was Southern to the core, and that went to the point of their reunion. He had an extraordinary proposal to make—"to undertake the abduction of Abraham Lincoln, convey him to Richmond, turn him over to the Confederate States government, to be held as a hostage for the exchange of prisoners." Booth felt it was perfectly honorable to the South "to make for her a prisoner of this man to whom she owes so much of misery."[5]

It is impossible to determine how Booth got this idea. Clearly it was not unique to him. Confederate General Bradley T. Johnson made plans to abduct Lincoln in June of the same year as part of operations in the Washington area. His effort was capsized by larger military events. It has never been shown that Booth knew anything of Johnson's plan.[6] Booth's idea may perhaps be traced back to wild talk by Southern hotheads during the secession winter of 1860–61 that President James Buchanan "was to be kidnapped and made off with [to] throw the country into confusion and revolution, defeating the inauguration of Lincoln and the coming in of the Republicans."[7]

The notion of abducting Buchanan antedates even that, however, and involves a figure of great personal significance to Booth. Hugh Forbes, an associate of John Brown, speculated on the éclat that would have been produced if Brown and his crew "made in the night a descent on the White House and carried off the President to parts unknown before the marines could have had time to open their eyes."[8] Forbes's statement was reported widely in the *New York Times* and elsewhere. One wonders if Booth, fascinated by Brown and details of his quixotic raid, knew of the idea. George A. Townsend, Booth's biographer, seldom failed to mention the inspiration the actor took from Brown. Suffice it to say that no one needed to suggest an abduction plot to Booth or recruit him for it. Such an idea, in the air as it were, might occur naturally to an individual with what Arnold termed Booth's "visionary mind." Added Arnold: "He alone was the moving spirit."

Arnold does not share his immediate reaction to Booth's proposal, but John H. Surratt Jr., who would join the abduction team in December, did. "I was amazed—thunderstruck—and in fact I might also say frightened at the unparalleled audacity of this scheme," he recalled in an 1870 lecture. Nevertheless, "I was led on," Surratt continued, "by a sincere desire to assist the South in gaining her independence." The goal of independence resonated deeply among some Marylanders. When Surratt informed a sympathetic postwar audience in Rockville, Maryland, that he agreed to help Booth because he "had no hesitation in taking part in anything honorable that might tend towards the accomplishment of that object," he was greeted with tremendous applause from his listeners.[9] Arnold wrote similarly that "patriotism was the motive that prompted me in joining the scheme, not profit." He felt "the contemplated design within itself was purely humane and patriotic in its principles" if it would liberate prisoners, shorten the war, or advance the Southern cause. Lincoln, the federal commander in chief, was a legitimate military target, after all. As a reasonably neutral observer, the theater impresario John T. Ford, later put it, the plan could be seen as a fair stroke in war.[10]

Booth explained to Arnold and O'Laughlen that the president was known to visit wounded soldiers at St. Elizabeth's Hospital across the Eastern Branch (or Anacostia) River in Washington. Lincoln was often accompanied only by his carriage driver. And the president was exposed even more frequently on trips to the Soldiers' Home, a government facility for invalid and disabled soldiers three miles north of the city. A Gothic cottage there, located on a hilltop, provided an escape from the heat, humidity, and crowds of the city and served as a presidential retreat. Lincoln and his family spent a considerable amount of time at the cottage each summer and fall. The president commuted to the White House by carriage or horseback in the morning and returned late in the day. Lincoln's route along Seventh Street Road, leading from Washington to the Soldiers' Home, took him through relatively secluded farm country, often in the dim twilight.[11] On one of these trips, Booth said excitedly, the three young Southerners could pounce on him, "take him, coachman and all, drive through the lower counties of Maryland, place him in a boat, cross the Potomac to Virginia, and thence convey him to Richmond."[12]

The trio discussed the idea through most of the afternoon, debating bridges to cross and measures to foil pursuit. They drank as they talked. Predictably, the more they drank, the more promising the scheme appeared. Arnold would claim in later years that he drank too much to consider the matter properly. He gave statements in 1865, 1867, and 1902 on his plotting with Booth. He mentioned the drinking in all three, but only in one did he bring up another highly pertinent topic. What if Lincoln resisted? What if he attempted to flee? What if he were injured, wounded, or even killed in a melee? Joseph W. Taylor, a Confederate officer, had presented a Lincoln abduction plan to Jefferson Davis in 1862. Davis listened but rejected the proposal. He explained that if physical harm befell Lincoln, the reaction in the North and overseas would be counterproductive to Southern interests.[13] In Arnold's 1902 recollections he wrote, "There was no violence contemplated in the execution of the design other than the seizure. Violence would have been in flat contradiction to [Booth's] avowed purpose and the object to be attained." Arnold was a battered old man when he wrote these sentences and may be suspected of seeking some measure of exoneration with an insincere afterthought. Subsequent events make clear, however, this was truly how Arnold and even Booth saw the project at this time. If they struck a blow both sufficiently daring and unexpected, Davis's concerns would never arise.

Booth returned repeatedly in his conversation to the ease with which the abduction could be accomplished. In doing so the actor displayed from the outset a failure to appreciate the time, expense, and frustrations that would invariably beset any such undertaking. For one thing, Lincoln was not as accessible as Booth imagined. The president did travel occasionally without a military escort, but these were spur-of-the-moment occasions offering no opportunity for an orchestrated ambush. Lincoln was far more likely to be heavily guarded. The poet Walt Whitman saw the presidential entourage passing to and fro and observed that Lincoln was always accompanied closely by "twenty-five or thirty cavalry, with sabres drawn and held upright over their shoulders."[14] Waiting to receive Lincoln at the Soldiers' Home was an entire infantry company detailed as guard. Such security seemed oppressive to Lincoln. "I do not myself see the necessity of having soldiers traipsing around after me wherever I go," he said, "but [Secretary of War Edwin] Stanton, who knows a great deal more about such things than I do, seems to think it necessary, and he may be right."[15] As the fighting front moved farther away from Washington in 1864, Lincoln managed to evade his escort from time to time. Then, about a week after Booth's meeting with Arnold and O'Laughlen, an unknown assailant shot the silk hat off the president's head one night as Lincoln, riding alone, turned his horse from the Seventh Street Road toward the Soldiers' Home. The incident was hushed up, but "after that the President never rode alone," recalled John W. Nichols, one of the Lincoln bodyguards.[16]

If Booth knew any of these details, his enthusiasm seemed a match for them, and his sincerity showed when he told the men that he would bankroll the abduction effort personally. "He showed me the different entries in his diary of what his engagements paid him in his profession," Arnold wrote, "and I judged from what I have heard his income therefrom to be from $25,000 to $30,000." If money was in supply, however, time was not. The abduction had to be undertaken before the presidential election of November 8 returned Lincoln, an implacable foe of Southern independence, to a second term in the White House. "The enterprise being deemed feasible and productive of good, we jointly entered into the plan as an act of honorable purpose, humanity and patriotism," wrote Arnold. Booth, Arnold, and O'Laughlen took "an oath of secrecy and good faith," binding themselves "not to divulge [their plan] to a living soul."

It was late when the meeting broke up. Booth informed his friends that he would go north to wind up his business and personal affairs. They should hold themselves ready. He would return to Baltimore in one month to set the plan in motion.

Some weeks later Arnold was threshing wheat in a neighbor's field when he was handed a letter from Booth. Inside was twenty dollars, leading Arnold to remark that he was now "flush." With some pride Arnold showed Booth's letter to Littleton Newman, a coworker, who read several lines and failed to grasp their meaning.

"I handed it back to him and asked him what it meant," Newman said.

Arnold replied enigmatically that "something big would take place one of these days."[17]

SHORTLY AFTER HIS RETURN to Edwin's house in New York, John fell ill with erysipelas, a streptococcal infection, in the right elbow. The course of the disease is sudden fever, powerful chills, and a spreading zone of swollen, burning hot, and tender skin that appears brilliantly red. Edema follows, along with weakness, headaches, loss of appetite, and restlessness. In the nineteenth century the disease could be highly dangerous.

John fainted from the pain of the attack. June picked him up and carried him to bed. Asia, there on a visit from Philadelphia, was struck by how pallid her prostrate brother looked. She recalled that "as he lay there in his shirt-sleeves so pale and death-like, we all felt how wondrously beautiful he was." As a premonition of John's death, which none of the family was to witness, "we were to ponder it all our lives."[18]

Physicians of the day divided erysipelas into two categories. Simple erysipelas produced fever, slight acceleration of pulse, and reddened swelling. It was treated by bleeding, purging the bowels, and applying cold or evaporating lotions to the affected area. Phlegmonous erysipelas was more serious, causing high fever, nausea, vomiting, and an acutely painful zone of swelling. If the condition grew grave, gangrene and symptoms familiar in cases of typhoid fever might appear and the patient sink into an often-fatal coma. An aggressive treatment of bleeding, active cathartics, dressings of the diseased area with nitrate of silver, blistering of the surrounding tissues, and opiates to rest the sufferer was undertaken. In extreme cases amputation of the affected limb might be necessary as a lifesaving measure.[19]

Booth appears to have had the more serious stage of the disease. He suffered the intense pain characteristic of phlegmonous erysipelas and displayed suppuration, "the burrowing of pus among the muscles [below the skin]." It was advisable in such cases to cut the skin and draw the pus out. On or about August 28, 1864, a Dr. Smith called on Booth and "cut in my arm about two inches long," the actor wrote Isabel Sumner. "I am sure I will be in bed all day tomorrow."[20] In healthy young men of Booth's age—for example, soldiers infected during the trauma of gunshot wounds—the disease lasted on average from nine to eleven days. June noted in his diary that John was ill for three weeks, another indication of the severity of the attack.[21]

John's extended convalescence permitted him to discuss the war in detail with his eldest brother. Devotedly neutral, June implored John to stay clear of the trouble and let events take their course. "He would listen," the older brother wrote, "but would not change his ideas."[22] Nevertheless, because June heard him out respectfully, the younger brother was touched by his fraternal interest.

With Edwin it was a different story. That brother, long exasperated with John's politics, laughed in his face whenever the younger brother frothed up on politics. Little could have been more hurtful to John, who craved Edwin's respect. Edwin, a Unionist, declared, "If each wish of mine could lead an army, the C. S. of A. would swing as high as Haman." Unsurprisingly, political disagreements with John finally grew violent.[23] An explosive argument occurred between them toward the end of August 1864. "There were stormy words between the two brothers," Asia noted, "the first, and, I believe, the last unkind ones that ever passed between them."[24] It commenced at breakfast one morning, was briefly adjourned, then renewed with a fury a short time later.[25] Incensed, Edwin ordered him out of the house. Finally back on his feet from the illness, John left in a rage.

This "severe family quarrel," as Junius characterized it, became a watershed moment in John's life. Most writers point out political differences between the brothers, but few have paid proper attention to the consequences of this single transformative encounter. In a statement given to federal authorities in 1865, June said John later told him that as a result of this quarrel, he decided to leave the North. He would ship his theatrical wardrobe south and play there in the future. He even intended to dispose of all of his property, "for he did not mean to take anything he made in the North" with him. In this way he could wash his hands of the time he had spent there. He would go south and, as June phrased it portentously, "commence the world anew."

Booth was back in Franklin, Pennsylvania, on September 7, 1864, to close out his oil affairs. After paying two thousand dollars to Tom Mears as his share of the purchase price for the Allegheny River land, he surprised Joe Simonds by announcing that he intended to give his property away.[26] He wished two-thirds deeded to June. The other third was to go to Simonds himself in consideration of his attention to Booth's business affairs in Venango County. Booth told Simonds nothing more than that "he wished to dispose of every interest he had in this section as they served to draw away his mind and attention from his profession to which he intended to devote all his faculties in the future." An interest in a property called Pithole was conveyed to Rose. Booth expressed the hope that the properties would one day be valuable. He seemed concerned that the assignments be properly done, taking the precaution of carrying them personally to the registry office.[27] Simonds subsequently mailed him the final papers, and Booth signed them while in New York City on October 29, 1864. John chose not to mention the gifts to June or Rose, however, perhaps for fear of alarming them. With these transfers Booth's oil adventures came to a close. Contrary to stories of exaggerated wealth that he himself encouraged, Booth made no money in oil. "From neither of these interests did he ever derive a single dollar benefit," wrote Simonds. Booth's investment, about six thousand dollars, was a total loss.[28]

"My old luck," as Booth said.[29] During his visit to Franklin, Booth seemed changed.[30] Normally agreeable, the actor appeared downcast and distracted to his barber, James Lawson. "Towards the end of his stay here, this preoccupation was noticeable," Lawson felt. "Something was evidently weighing heavily on his mind." While one might imagine that Booth was devoting thought to the abduction plot, these episodes appear instead to be periods of genuine mental abstraction. Lawson would observe him "often fall into a deep study or reverie during which he would pay no attention to what was going on around him."

Booth was, in a measure, in shock. What he had begun three months earlier in such optimism was blasted as Booth met the fate of most small-time speculators. The actor had always taken pride in making money, and even defined himself by it. Now, "morose and nervous," he was left with an experience that shook his self-image and estranged him further from the North. The truth was so painful that in the future he deceived friends about his success in oil, boasting to them of how well things were going.[31] If he acknowledged a loss, it was not his fault. Rather it was bad advice or flooding or something else.[32]

Increasingly only one thing aroused him. Booth was in Lawson's barbershop in Franklin, standing with his back to the wall, when Caleb Marshall, an African American brick mason, came in. Marshall, a refugee from North Carolina and a bit of a hothead, began to rejoice over a recent Northern victory. Booth listened for a moment, pointed his finger at Marshall, and asked sternly, "Is that the way you come among gentlemen, and with your hat on, too?"

"When I go into a parlor among ladies, I take my hat off," replied Marshall, "but when I go into a bar-room or a barber shop or any other public place, I keep my hat on."

Lawson saw Booth's face go "white as a sheet." The actor shoved his hand into his hip pocket to retrieve a pistol. Mears, sitting in a chair near Booth, leapt to his feet. Pinning Booth's arms against his side, he and another man succeeded in getting Booth outside and down the street. Booth was intensely excited, and Lawson felt that he would have killed Marshall except for the prompt intervention of Mears. Jerry Allen, a local awning maker who also recalled the incident, agreed that Booth would have shot Marshall on the spot if he had not been stopped.

Booth departed Franklin for the final time on September 29, 1864. He left behind many friends and a good opinion, as he did wherever he went, but also some perplexity. When acquaintances asked him where he was going, Booth gave a memorable reply.

"I am going to Hell," he said.[33]

BOOTH PACKED THE ACCOUTREMENTS of his professional life into two trunks and one long box. The trunks contained his dressing case and wardrobe of velvet suits, crowns, caps, plumes, doublets, shoes, and accessories. Also included were fifty-six bound and pamphlet volumes of plays, many with stage notes in his hand, together with correspondence, photographs, and clippings of old reviews. The large box was filled with stage swords and pistols.[34] He was off to Canada to fulfill an engagement, he declared to the family.[35] No one had reason to doubt him. Such preparations and departures were common with the Booths.

He arrived with his cargo in Montreal by train on October 18, 1864. A principal order of business was to seek out Patrick C. Martin, a former Baltimore merchant engaged in blockade-running. Martin made his home a resort for Southern refugees, and Booth called, hoping to find George P. Kane, the former Baltimore police marshal whose arrest in 1861 had so angered the actor. Kane had returned to the Confederacy earlier in the year, however, and Booth was greatly disappointed not to find him in Montreal. The Martin family welcomed Booth nevertheless, and "he became intimate at my house with my wife and daughter," Martin informed Kane. The blockade-runner agreed to arrange shipment of Booth's trunks to Nassau in the Bahamas. From there they could be slipped past the Yankee fleet and be sent on to Richmond.[36]

Montreal was a friendly place to Southerners. It swarmed with Confederate agents, exiles, fugitives, escaped prisoners of war, adventurers, spies, and ne'er-do-wells. John F. Potter, the American consul in Montreal, characterized

this jetsam as "enemies of the United States, scoundrels [who are] too cowardly to stay at home and fight, too indolent to labor."[37] It infuriated Potter
that these villains were "harbored, entertained and treated with consideration" in the city, but the reality was that Southerners enjoyed a necessary
sympathy from Canadians anxious over the size and growing power of the
United States. Officials and citizens did little to stop (and some abetted)
smuggling, intrigue with the Copperheads, plots to liberate prison camps or
steal ships on the Great Lakes, and worse.

Like most Southerners with any money, Booth checked into the St.
Lawrence Hall, a hotel whose owner, Henry Hogan, described as the unofficial headquarters of Confederate agents and refugees.[38] A picturesque coterie
of twenty to thirty of these men could always be found here. Settled into
room 150, Booth was therefore immersed into a cauldron of Canadian rebel-
dom. Then, on the morning following his arrival in Montreal, an event
occurred that electrified the hotel's residents. Confederate soldiers based in
Canada dashed across the border, raided St. Albans, Vermont, and fled back
across the frontier for sanctuary. A diplomatic uproar ensued, filling the Hall
with judges, lawyers, detectives, and civil and military authorities of every
description. The excitement was intense and the hotel accommodations so
taxed that "three and four guests to a room was the rule," recalled Hogan.[39]
Booth followed these developments closely, good news sending him "scattering small silver pieces round among the newsboys and bell boys."[40]

Fond of actors, Hogan liked Booth. "He was a most genial gifted man
in many ways, a fine actor, and a great favorite," recalled Hogan.[41] The
owner's reminiscences and an article titled "When Wilkes Booth Was in
Montreal," both of which appeared in the *Montreal Star* in 1902, reveal
that Booth made friends quickly at the Hall. Notable among them was
the former Florida senator James D. Westcott, "a most bitter hater of everything 'Yankee' who thoroughly despised every soul from the North,"
according to Hogan. Westcott, his hair pulled behind his head in an
old-fashioned queue, joined Booth at cards together with Dr. Luke Black-
burn of Kentucky, later accused of plotting to send infected clothing to
President Lincoln; Dr. Montrose Pallen of Missouri, observed spying on
the American consulate office; and Beverly Tucker of Virginia, an American diplomat turned Confederate purchasing agent. These uncompro-
mising rebels were happy company. There was no need for Booth to argue
the justice of the Southern cause with them, but he impressed upon
any Canadian or British friends who joined the table his hope "that the

'Redcoats' would soon be on the march across the border to attack the Federal forces in the rear."

Booth also met with George N. Sanders, a Kentuckian who was perhaps the most radical of the Confederate principals in Canada. Sanders, stopping at the Hall to arrange the defense of the St. Albans raiders, was seen frequently in Booth's company by Hosea B. Carter, a federal detective living at the hotel.[42] The two were also observed in confidential conversation by John Deveny, an American draft dodger. "They were standing outside of the hotel, talking on the portico," Deveny stated, Sanders leaning against a pillar and Booth directly in front of him. Deveny also saw them drinking together at Dolly's Chop House, a nearby tavern.[43] The burly, piratical-looking Sanders was dangerous company. He had associated intimately with European nationalists in the 1850s, once engaging in a plot to assassinate Napoleon III of France. America had no more ready defender of tyrannicide. He told George Augustus Sala, an English journalist visiting Montreal at this time, "of the plotting of atrocities which would make the world shudder." Regrettably, no eavesdroppers overheard what Booth and Sanders discussed. As Deveny admitted, Sanders's "conversation [was] always confidential, always whispered."

First among equals in the Confederate junta was Jacob Thompson, a former Mississippi congressman and secretary of the interior under Buchanan. Thompson was one of three so-called commissioners sent to Canada by Jefferson Davis. He controlled a purse believed to contain up to one million dollars for use in freeing prisoners, buying friends, staging counterrevolution in the North, and waging retaliatory warfare.[44] Thompson was heard at his headquarters at the Queen's Hotel in Toronto declaring that Lincoln "was not fit to be President of any country and never would be President again—the people had had enough of such Presidents."[45] Thompson's prominence and his ability to endow mischief later led to his name being connected with Booth's in Lincoln's death. Booth never visited Toronto, where Thompson was based, however, and probably never met Thompson. The senior commissioner passed through Montreal on a return visit from Quebec in mid-October, but it has not been established that he was in the city at the same time as Booth. Thompson later denied any connection with the actor. "I have never known, or conversed, or held communication, either directly or indirectly, with Booth, the assassin of the President, or with any one of his associates," he wrote in a public letter to the *New York Tribune* six weeks after Lincoln's murder.[46]

Booth had time on his hands, according to George Iles, an errand boy who met the actor. James Baillie, Iles's pro-Southern employer who was a regular at Westcott's card parties, lent Booth several of Walter Scott's romances. Once, to break the boredom, Booth donned a heavy coat and yellow fox-skin cap and rode to Lachine, eight miles below the city. He returned chilled to the bone, Iles recalled.[47] Billiards were also diverting for the actor, and Booth enjoyed playing with Joseph Dion, manager of the billiard room in the basement of the Hall, or with fellow guests.[48] He struck one opponent with "the wandering character of his conversation and the wild ideas." Seeing that Booth had been drinking, the man put his erratic talk down to that and to "a slight mental derangement or excitement."

The topic of the American presidential election came up over the billiard table. Booth remarked with great feeling that "it made d——d little difference [who was elected], head or tail—Abe's contract was near up, and whether re-elected or not, he would get his goose cooked." Meanwhile Booth's opponent made a good run, drawing from the actor the observation that his rival seemed to have a "partiality for the pockets." Inspired by the analogy, Booth raised his own cue and said excitedly, "Do you know I have got the sharpest play laid out ever done in America? I can bag the biggest game this side of —— . You'll hear of a double carom one of these days."

Accompanied by Martin, Booth went to the Ontario Bank on October 27, the morning of his departure for the United States. He opened an account in his own name, depositing $455. He also purchased a bill of exchange for sixty-one pounds, twelve shillings, and ten pence. The bill of exchange may be thought of as a nineteenth-century traveler's check. Made payable to him, it could be cashed only by Booth himself, as he took pains to determine from a teller, Robert A. Campbell.[49] Innocuous in themselves, these bank transactions demonstrate a revealing line of thought. The funds on deposit would give Booth a nest egg if he needed to make a hasty retreat across the border to Canada, a notion that had already crossed his mind. The bill of exchange would be welcomed anywhere. Safer than gold, which could be lost or stolen, it was better than Northern greenbacks and far superior to Southern paper money.

With this business done, Booth's visit to Montreal concluded. He left with helpful letters of introduction from Martin to rebel agents living along the route by which an abducted Lincoln would pass through southern

Maryland.[50] Other than that, nothing is definitively known of other arrangements he may have made or understandings reached with Confederate officials. Cautious in speaking about his plans to outsiders, he could keep his mouth shut. John Deveny experienced his wariness when Booth brushed off his fellow Marylander's question as to what he was doing in Montreal with the reply "A little business." When Deveny repeated his question, Booth repeated his answer.

Back in the States, Booth stopped in New York to visit his mother. He was still seething over his August run-in with Edwin. "If it were not for mother I would not enter Edwin's house," he told Asia. "She will leave there if we cannot be welcomed, and I do not want her to be unhappy for me." On November 8, the day of the presidential election, he ran into June in Baltimore. The older brother knew that John was not acting, but, when questioned, John directed the conversation to oil, stating he could make more money doing that. To explain the time he intended spending in Washington, he told June that he was also forming a company to purchase farmland along the Potomac River. The brother was satisfied with their talk, relieved that the topic of the war did not come up when Baltimore was in a state of political excitement. It is not known if John voted. When he learned that Edwin, in New York, cast a ballot for Lincoln, "he expressed deep regret and declared his belief that Lincoln would be made king of America," that brother wrote in 1881.[51]

On November 11 Booth took the stagecoach from Washington to Bryantown, a village some thirty miles south of the capital, in Charles County, Maryland. Booth once boasted, "Maryland is true to the core—every mother's son."[52] That claim, never entirely correct, was less so now than ever. Incredible changes were taking place around Booth, changes that redefined what it meant to be a Marylander. Deemed a loyal state and thus unaffected by the Emancipation Proclamation, Maryland adopted on its own a new constitution on November 1, 1864, which abolished slavery without compensation to slave-owners.[53] Lincoln's reelection followed with a predictable sweep of the Northern states. But the weary president, who received less than 3 percent of Maryland's 1860 vote, won the 1864 vote with 55 percent of the total over George McClellan, his Democratic rival. Smuggled through Baltimore in 1861 when "not one hand reached forth to greet me," Lincoln now received cheers and applause in the city. "The change from then till now is both great and gratifying," Lincoln remarked at a charity event for soldiers in Baltimore. "We cannot fail to note the world moves. When the war began, three years ago, neither party, nor any man, expected it would last till now. Each looked for the end, in some way, long ere to-day. Neither did any anticipate that domestic slavery would be much affected by the war. But here we are."[54]

Nowhere were these changes more deeply resented than in southern Maryland, where Booth now traveled. Occupying a peninsula formed by the Potomac on the west and the Chesapeake Bay on the east, it was the oldest settled region in the state. A farming district, it was Catholic in religion and conservative in politics. Slavery had been long established. Close to Washington in terms of miles, the area was relatively isolated, unbroken by a railroad track or even a telegraph pole until the military strung a line for its use during the war. George Alfred Townsend referred to one neighborhood through which Booth's stage passed, the hamlet of Surrattsville, as "a suburb of Richmond, ignorant and rebel to the brim."[55] His charged phrases provided to Northern minds an accurate social and political description of southern Maryland as a whole. Contraband goods, mail, and passengers flowed through this peninsula across the river into Virginia while Confederate agents came and went. Raids by the authorities disrupted their activities periodically but angered residents profoundly. Emancipation had substantially diminished the net worth of many farmers in the blink of an eye. Already disloyal, white citizens were embittered by the new state of affairs. Since the federal government had bigger fish to fry elsewhere, it never took the time to overawe the region. Townsend concluded that this had a most tragic consequence. "One single hanging at the roadside might have saved the life of Mr. Lincoln," he believed.[56]

Booth arrived in Bryantown bearing letters of introduction to Dr. William Queen, Dr. Samuel A. Mudd, and possibly a third local physician.[57] Martin had plugged Booth into the "Doctors' Line," a network of pro-Southern doctors whose profession gave them plausible excuse for traveling at odd hours to carry out underground activities.[58] Queen's son Joseph, a medical student, met Booth at the hotel in Bryantown and escorted him to the Queen home several miles away. Arriving about dusk, Booth met Queen, who introduced him in turn to his son-in-law John C. Thompson.[59] The pair looked over Martin's letter. Through it or in person, Booth made his needs known to the men. Queen and Thompson were Marylanders of Southern stripe and had suffered for it. Queen owned more than a dozen slaves when the conflict started, but now those who had not fled previously were emancipated. As for Thompson, the war had swept away his fortune.[60] Booth was at the right house.

The actor spent one or two nights at Queen's. He "personified the handsome debonair gentleman, dressed to perfection, and had a charming manner," said Queen's youngest son, Billy. His granddaughter Mary, nineteen, thought Booth was the handsomest man she had ever seen.[61] Booth spun fiction on his oil investments for the family, informing the impoverished Thompson "that he had made a good deal of money out of those operations." When the talk turned to the war, Booth was adamant in his hatred of Lincoln. He produced a newspaper clipping containing the lyrics of a Copperhead song contrasting the happy prewar period with the dreary present. "Then and Now" could be sung to the tune of the spiritual "Kingdom Coming." Booth knew the melody and hummed it for Mary, who picked out the tune on the piano. Their combined talents provided an impromptu entertainment. When Mary, as an octogenarian in the 1920s, recounted the evening for a grandson, her eyes filled with tears at the memory of the ill-fated guest.

The text of the song had appeared during the recent presidential campaign.[62] One can see why its identification of Lincoln with a host of wartime controversies so appealed to Booth. The election may have been over, but the issues it raised, such as Booth's fear of a Lincoln dictatorship, lived on. Two stanzas show the purport of "Then and Now."

> *Time was, we had our free discussion*
> *With the press, the tongue, the pen,*
> *Nor had we learned to ape the Russian*
> *With his spies and dungeons, then;*
> *But now, unless one sings the praises*
> *Of the Lincoln-Stanton crew,*
> *Some Bastille yawns as quick as blazes,*
> *And the poor soul's lost to view!*
> *There's no more liberty,*
> *Our rights are all a sham,*
> *And this must be the kingdom's coming*
> *In the days of Abraham!*
>
> *We love the War, and all are burning*
> *For the cause we hold so dear,*
> *That conscript-wheels are kept a-turning*
> *In the country far and near;*

Our taxes and our debt are bigger
Than we are likely soon to pay,
But Ab'rm wants to free the nigger,
And we let him have his way;
       Our chance for Liberty
       Is hardly worth a d———n,
But there's a nigger kingdom coming.
And the king is Abraham!

Booth wished to accomplish two important things on his visit. He needed to purchase horses for his men to ride, and he needed to know the roads leading to the Potomac and the landings on the river from which crossings into Virginia might be made. Unfortunately neither Queen nor Thompson could be much help. A native of Georgia, Thompson was relatively new to Charles County, while Queen, at seventy-five, was inactive and in uncertain health.

The problem was taken care of on Sunday, November 13, when Booth accompanied Queen and Thompson to St. Mary's Church near Bryantown. As was customary, a group of men gathered just in front of the church door to talk before the service. Among them was Dr. Samuel A. Mudd, an intelligent-looking man with a high forehead, thinning hair, blue eyes, and reddish mustache and beard. An 1856 graduate of the University of Maryland Medical School in Baltimore, the thirty-year-old Mudd was a married farmer with four young children. He was described by those who knew him as everything from "a man of most exemplary character, peaceful, upright, kind and obedient to the laws" to "an ill-balanced man of very slight force of character and but little moral courage." Two Mudd family slaves informed federal authorities that the doctor fed and hid Southern soldiers, delivered contraband mail, secreted weapons, and assisted in attempting to carry both slaves and free persons of color into Confederate lines for enforced service to the rebel army. Although never a soldier, he was resolutely pro-Southern in his views, fueled (just as in the case of Booth) by a hatred of abolitionists. Mudd wrote early in the war to the Catholic intellectual Orestes Brownson, "The North, on account of its pride, shortsightedness, hypocrisy, and mock phylanthropy [*sic*], has caused the destruction of one of the most glorious nations upon the face of the Earth."[63]

Since Mudd was a communicant of St. Peter's Church near his home in the country, his presence at St. Mary's that morning seems prearranged.

At any rate, Thompson introduced the doctor to Booth, and they spoke.[64] Controversy has flourished over the years about the nature of Mudd's involvement with Booth. Subsequent events make it plain that Mudd was ready to help. It might take time to arrange, but the doctor could also connect Booth to a level of operative beyond that of mere Southern sympathizer. Within the next several weeks Mudd would introduce him to Thomas Harbin and John H. Surratt, two resourceful Confederate agents whose appetite for danger matched his own.

Inside the church the actor sat in the Queen family pew as Father John T. Gaitley of County Galway, Ireland, said the Mass.[65] Booth had reason to feel satisfied. He had come into Charles County like an apparition, thought a contemporary, with no companions or acquaintances.[66] He could depart in confidence, having crossed a threshold. From this point on his conspiracy assumed momentum.

RETURNING TO NEW YORK, Booth took part in one of the most celebrated theatrical events of his generation. To mark 1864 as the tercentenary of Shakespeare's birth, Edwin, John, and June had agreed to play *Julius Caesar* as a benefit for a fund to erect a statue of the Bard in Central Park. Originally scheduled for July, their performance "did not take place on account of J. Wilkes' absence hunting up oil-wells in Pennsylvania," Edwin wrote a friend.[67] Rescheduled for August, it was postponed a second time due to hot weather and the absence of the fashionable crowd who were at the beaches. The play was at last slated for Friday, November 25, at the Winter Garden, a theater where Edwin, Clarke, and William Stuart were co-lessees and -managers.[68] Although relations with Edwin continued strained, John had promised to do the benefit and kept his word.

Great interest attended the announcement of this performance. For one thing, *Julius Caesar* was seldom presented in New York. Critics believed it was more effective to read than to produce onstage and accordingly ranked it below *Hamlet* or *Othello* as an acting play.[69] *Julius Caesar* also lacked strongly interesting female parts. But it was wonderfully written and had powerful male roles if actors of quality could be found to fill them. The fact that three brothers, sons of a famous father and fine actors in their own right, would take the leads seemed inspired, as did the fact that this would be the first—and only—time they performed together.

Stuart beat the drum: "Junius Brutus—Edwin—John Wilkes—have come forward with cheerful alacrity to do honor to the immortal bard, from whose works the genius of their father caught its inspiration, and of many of those greatest creations he was the best and noblest illustration the stage has ever seen."[70] "What a cast!" declared Henry Clapp, dramatic critic of the *New York Leader*, "the three best tragedians in the land, and brothers at that, and sons by psychological as well as genealogical descent, all brought together on one stage and in one play! What wonder the town is excited."[71] Ticket prices reflected it. A seat in the family circle went from twenty-five cents to one dollar, in the dress-circle and parquet from fifty cents to a dollar and a half, and in the orchestra from one to five dollars. Aware these were stiff prices, Stuart begged potential playgoers to remember "that in addition to the value they receive in intellectual enjoyment, they are contributing to a great national work and not to the personal advantage of any individual."

Stuart, known for a quick tongue that earned him the hatred of Edwin Forrest, was a large and enterprising Irishman with a genius for promotion. He entered theatrical management in 1856 and soon joined Edwin and Clarke at the Winter Garden.[72] Stuart ran the theater in a manner that reflected his own hospitable nature, "taking rehearsals the easiest probably of any manager that ever lived," thought the gossip Harry Hill, while committing the sacrilege of allowing individuals unconnected with the theater to lounge in the greenroom during performances. At Stuart's Winter Garden "there was no stage discipline whatever."[73]

John disliked Stuart, and the manager returned the feeling. In fact, Stuart held all actors in contempt, thought Edwin's friend William Winter. John's problem, Stuart believed, was that his "early education had been entirely neglected, and he really had no conception of character, but sailed in for strong points." Edwin was the rising star, and Stuart had signed on for the ascent. "Edwin was head and shoulders, as an actor, above the other two," said the manager.[74]

Stuart found John and June fencing when he came around to hand out parts. Edwin, the brothers could see, would play Brutus, the central character in the play, with June as Cassius and John as Mark Antony. "Give me the part," snapped John, snatching the script from Stuart. Suspicious how his role might be cut, he studied the text for a full ten minutes. "I will play that fellow," he said finally. The manager thought that John and June were unwarrantably jealous of their brother. The pair knew, however, that Stuart was Edwin's man. Edwin was scheduled to commence an engagement of *Hamlet* the evening following the benefit. When Stuart informed him the advertisements would read simply "Booth as Hamlet!" Edwin protested that there were three Booths. The manager replied that there would be only one in the public mind when *Hamlet* closed.[75]

The house doors opened that evening at 7:15 p.m. "So great was the crowd," wrote the critic T. Allston Brown, caught up in the throng, "that a strong force of police had to be sent for to preserve order and force every one back into a line."[76] The theater filled quickly, including five extra rows of orchestra seats run back into the parquet. Well before the eight o'clock curtain, "there was not a seat to be had in the house for love or money." Well, maybe for money. Ten to twenty dollars was being offered for any seat, one hundred for a box.[77] "The theatre was crowded to suffocation, people standing in every available space," recalled Asia, who herself was relegated to standing room.[78] Great excitement prevailed. "It was a very large, cultivated, and critical audience," wrote one playgoer, the dress circle filled "with proper people and handsome women, the parquette and orchestra stalls with Boothites, Shakspere [*sic*] men, artists, authors, actors, the men of taste of the city generally, and bohemians, of course, without number."[79] Brown, savvy veteran of the theatrical world, recalled, "When the curtain rose, there was an audience of over two thousand persons present, composed of the elite of the city, and one of the most intelligent I have ever seen in any theatre."

Owen Fawcett, who took the role of Second Plebeian, wrote that no actor of note wished to be discovered onstage as the curtain rose. He preferred an entrance in order to secure a reception from the audience.[80] *Julius Caesar* provided the brothers with a fine opportunity along that line. In act 1 Cassius, Brutus, and Antony came on side by side in a dramatic joint entrance. A torrent of applause greeted the trio. Asia stated, "The eldest [was] powerfully built and handsome as an antique Roman; Edwin, with his magnetic fire and graceful dignity; and John Wilkes, in the perfection of youthful beauty." John had shaved off his mustache for the performance. "Our Wilkes looks like a young god," Asia overheard someone say. The brothers paused and bowed to Mary Ann, who sat in a private box. It was a proud moment for their mother, one of the grandest in her difficult life.[81]

The performance, interrupted frequently by applause and curtain calls, proceeded smoothly until the second scene of act 2. Edwin Varrey's Caesar was delivering the lines "Cowards die many times before their death/The valiant never taste of death but once" when a commotion was heard at the rear of the theater.[82] The immense audience stirred.

Incredibly, a Confederate agent from Canada was attempting to set the adjoining Lafarge House on fire. It was part of a plot to destroy the principal hotels of the city and bring to New York a share of the wartime terror that Southern towns were feeling. John T. Ashbrook, a rebel lieutenant from Kentucky, set a fire in his third-story room just over the entrance of the theater.[83] Ashbrook fled, and hotel employees extinguished the flames. Nevertheless, with their bells ringing, fire engines arrived as summoned, their lanterns gleaming up and down Broadway. Firemen burst into the Lafarge House, dragging their pipes and hose and shouting orders. "Several of them with hose in hand came rushing pell-mell into the vestibule of the theatre," recalled Brown. The smell of smoke penetrated the Winter Garden.

"Fire! Fire!" shouted someone in the rear of the theater. "The great audience rose to its feet as one man," Charles Walcot, the play's Octavius, remembered. They did not know that the danger was over, but they were well aware that the Winter Garden was too crowded to permit a rapid exit. "The wildest confusion, amounting to a panic, pervaded the vast audience," wrote Frank Kernan, a fireman on the scene.[84]

Varrey stepped forward and urged the audience to remain calm, shouting what could only have been his hope that all was perfectly safe. Edwin hurried onstage to repeat the assurance. From the orchestra seats Police Inspector James Leonard attempted to pacify the crowd, while Judge John H. McCunn sought to quell the dress circle.

Heedless, hundreds rushed for the doors. Shouts and screams ripped the air. The crowd pushed the critic Brown, standing near the parquet exit, into the lobby, then hurried him forward, then knocked him flat. There he "saw several magnificent dresses completely stripped from ladies, also bonnets and fur lying underfoot. For several minutes the scene beggared description," he wrote. The danger now was that "hundreds of others would have followed to choke the passage-ways and crush each other to death."

Behind the stage the scenic artists were at work. "With a huge brush and lightning strokes [they were] painting on a piece of canvas ten feet high, in letters that could have been read for a mile, *THERE IS NO FIRE. IT HAS ALREADY BEEN EXTINGUISHED.*'" The sign, its letters wet and glistening before the footlights, reassured many in the audience. Meanwhile Inspector Leonard and a squad of police took charge of the exits and enforced order. Leonard, a heroic former "fire-laddie" himself, yelled at the top of his voice that there was no fire. "IT IS ONLY A DRUNKEN

MAN!" he roared. "KEEP YOUR SEATS!" Leonard's words "produced the effect of a cup of ice water poured into a boiling cauldron." The cry was repeated through the house, and the panic began to subside, the audience slowly composing itself and drifting back to its seats. In thirty minutes the entire excitement passed, and the performance was able to resume.

John's most celebrated scene followed in act 3. He delivered Mark Antony's funeral oration. Journalists alleged immediately after the assassination that he interpolated into the play the expression "Sic semper tyrannis," the motto of Virginia, which he would later make memorable.[85]

"I heard the words plainly," said the economist Alexander Del Mar. He turned to Judge McCunn, who sat on his right, and asked if the lines were in Shakespeare. The judge whispered that it was an acceptable emendation of the text.[86]

Varrey later recalled an amusing story of the Forum scene. As John commenced his oration over Varrey's prostrate body, he came down to the bier and suddenly stuck his fingers into Varrey's ribs.[87]

"Don't!" Varrey gasped under his breath. Varrey, playing Caesar for the first time, was understandably nervous, and John decided to have some fun with him. Playfully and out of sight of the audience, John tickled him. As discreetly as possible Varrey hitched up his knees for protection and whispered, "If you don't stop, I'll have to get up and walk off stage." Varrey recounted this episode in an interview in 1900, adding, "That would have been a funny sight—to see a dead man walk away from his own funeral." The joke enjoyed, John stopped.

At the play's end "the three brothers stood side by side, again and again, before the curtain, to receive the lavish applause of the audience mingled with waving of handkerchiefs and every mark of enthusiasm," wrote their adoring sister. Walcot believed John "carried off the honors of the occasion," and even Stuart acknowledged that he garnered the largest share of applause. Critics spread their praise equitably. The *Times* reported that John possessed "an elan and fire which at times fairly electrifies the audience and whirls them along with him." The *Tribune* lauded Edwin, while Brown in the *Clipper* raved for June.

An unfortunate misunderstanding marred the conclusion of the evening. Stuart arranged a postplay reception in "the Barracks," his parlor over the stage, a celebrated scene of many good times—but neglected to invite June and John. The former had already left the Winter Garden to escort Mary Ann home. Edwin, learning of the oversight, sent Jim Brown, his black valet and dresser, to find John and request that he join the party. Chagrined at what he considered to be an intentional slight, John left the theater.[88]

The unpleasantness continued at breakfast the following morning. The topic of the arson plot came up, and John "justified the deed as an act of war in retaliation for Union atrocities in the Shenandoah Valley." Edwin and June disagreed, and a heated argument ensued. John grew infuriated with the pair and expressed anew his fear of a Lincoln dictatorship.[89]

The brothers patched it up sufficiently by Sunday, November 27, to go together with the artist Rufus Wright to be photographed in their *Julius Caesar* costumes. June had commissioned Wright, who painted portraits of Stanton and Seward, "to paint a picture of the three as they appeared in this play."[90] They were posed in the scene from act 3 in which Antony offers his hand to the scowling Cassius while Brutus, expostulating with his fellow assassin, lays his hand on Cassius's shoulder.[91]

Two photographs were taken at Jeremiah Gurney's gallery on Broadway, the only known pictures showing the brothers together. The sons secured Wright's promise to guard the negatives, authorizing only a single print from each for his use. The painting was intended as a gift for their mother. Wright did not complete the commission but later would present the photograph to Mary Ann as a memento.

This benefit and two others in 1865 for friends constituted the final stage appearances of John Wilkes Booth. His career was truly ending. He refused new engagements, turning away McVicker in Chicago and others. His thoughts were elsewhere.

He left indelible memories behind, thought Charles Pike Sawyer, a veteran journalist who sat down during the hot Manhattan summer of 1930 to peck out on a rusty old typewriter "Sixty Years and More of Shakespeare," his recollections of the New York stage.[92] Sawyer had been in the audience for *Julius Caesar* that night. Now, wrapping up his career as the dramatic critic and music editor of the *Evening Post*, he found his memory of Booth's Mark Antony ineffaceable. "His fine pose and manly figure with that unruly shock of black hair surmounting a finely cut face stamped him the great Roman. His piercing eyes still flash as he urges the mob on to fury."

Applying one of Antony's lines to Booth's own future, Sawyer concluded, "In the end it is a veritable demi-god who closes the scene with,

'Mischief, thou art afoot.
'Take thou what course thou wilt.'"

Junius Brutus Booth, Sr. John's father was a brilliant actor, but his alcoholism and erratic personality cast a troubling shadow over his family. Author's collection.

Mary Ann Holmes Booth. A loving and indulgent mother, Mary Ann was the central emotional influence in John's life. "He was the most pleasure and comfort to me of all my sons," she said. Painting attributed to Thomas Sully, Timothy Hughes Rare and Early Newspapers.

Birthplace. Booth was born in this log house near Bel Air, Maryland. Taken in 1865, this photograph, as well as the one below, shows an unrelated family who were renting the property at the time. Courtesy of Anne King Sehlstedt Feild.

Tudor Hall. Built near the log house, this villa became the new family home when completed in 1852. Booth lived here during his teenage years. Courtesy of Anne King Sehlstedt Feild.

Booth City Home in Baltimore's Old Town Neighborhood. John and his brothers performed amateur theatricals in the backyard. Memorial Library, University of Wisconsin-Madison.

Junius Brutus Booth, Jr. "June," oldest of the Booth sons, admired his younger brother and begged him to stay neutral in the war. "He would listen but would not change his ideas," recalled June. Courtesy of Jonathan H. Mann.

Edwin Booth.
"Ned," a prominent actor, argued with John over politics. He never understood his handsome younger brother but couldn't help loving him. Courtesy of Edward Steers, Jr.

Asia Booth.
Asia was the wife of comedian John S. Clarke, whom her brother John once attacked for insulting Confederate president Jefferson Davis. She wrote a secret memoir of John's childhood.

Booth viewed abolitionist **John Brown** (left) as a dangerous fanatic and was among those who rallied to the call of Virginia governor **Henry Wise** (right) to defend the Commonwealth at the time of Brown's 1859 antislavery raid at Harpers Ferry. From *The Southern Literary Messenger*, Virginia Historical Society.

Canton of the flag of the Richmond Grays, flown at Brown's execution seven weeks after his failed raid. Booth marched under this militia banner with its memorable phrase *sic semper tyrannis*, Virginia's official motto. Virginia National Guard.

With his large-check
trousers and contrasting
loosely cut dark frock
coat, Booth was in the
forefront of fashion in
this early photograph
taken in Boston. TCS 18,
Harvard Theatre Collec-
tion, Houghton Library,
Harvard University.

Booth is shown in
Chicago about 1863
at the height of his
acting career. Play-
wright Edward M.
Alfriend wrote, "He
was as handsome as a
Greek god." TSC 18,
Harvard Theatre Collec-
tion, Houghton Library,
Harvard University.

1864

J. W. Booth

Booth. Tack holes (top, bottom, sides) distinguish this likeness, posted at the Aqueduct Bridge leading from Washington to Virginia, in order to help guards identify Booth if he passed that way after the assassination. Massachusetts Historical Society.

Fanny Brown. One of the most beautiful actresses of the Civil War generation, Fanny toured with Booth in 1863. She was one of his lovers and rumored to be his fiancée. Princeton University Library.

Maggie Mitchell. The captivating Maggie, a fairy-like actress, singer, and dancer, had a passionate wartime affair with Booth. Author's collection.

Isabel Sumner. A lovely Boston teenager, Isabel was romanced by Booth in the summer of 1864. His courtship letters to her still exist. Collection of Louise Taper.

The bewitching **Lucy Hale** (left, with her head on shoulder of older sister Lizzie) was the daughter of a prominent antislavery politician. She was secretly engaged to Booth at the time of the assassination. Courtesy of Richmond Morcom.

John, Edwin, and **June Booth** (left to right) pose in their theatrical costumes for the play *Julius Caesar*. Jeremiah Gurney of New York took this photograph in 1864 as a study for a portrait intended for Mary Ann, their mother. TS 932.8.6, Harvard Theatre Collection, Houghton Library, Harvard University.

Herman Stump.
Booth's boyhood companion, this Maryland lawyer shared in his plots against Lincoln. Like the friend he was, Stump took their secrets to the grave. Courtesy of John W. Stump.

Thomas Harbin.
A fellow Marylander, this daring Confederate agent schemed with Booth to abduct Lincoln and later helped him escape after the assassination. Southern Maryland Studies Center, College of Southern Maryland, Thomas A. Jones Collection.

ASSASSINATION OF
PRESIDENT LINCOLN
APRIL 14, 1865.

FORD'S THEATRE DRAPED IN MOURNING

The assassination is melodramatically depicted in this postcard produced
by M. W. Taggart Co., of New York in 1909, the centennial of Lincoln's
birth. A Byronic-looking assassin poses before an enraged audience after
leaping to the stage floor at Ford's Theatre. Courtesy of Edward Steers, Jr.

Scenes from a Lincoln commemorative fan sold by Bartolomé Crespo de Borbón of Havana, Cuba, for the Latin American and European markets. A series of theatrical depictions chronicle the history of Booth's plot. National Defense University Library, Special Collections, Archives, and History Division

Flourishing a dagger at a meeting with fellow conspirators.

Shooting the President.

Fleeing Washington, D.C., on horseback.

Fatally wounded in a Virginia barn twelve days after the murder.

Lewis Powell. An ex-Confederate soldier from Florida, Powell considered Booth his superior officer and carried out orders to attack Secretary of State William Seward on the same evening that Lincoln was shot. He was executed for his role in the conspiracy. Courtesy of the Surratt House Museum/MNCPPC.

Thomas A. Jones. After hiding and feeding Booth and his companion David Herold following the assassination, Jones, a die-hard Confederate, provided the boat by which they crossed into Virginia and continued their flight south. Southern Maryland Studies Center, College of Southern Maryland, Thomas A. Jones Collection.

The wages of friendship—and of greed. **David Herold** (left) and **George Atzerodt** (right) are prepared for their executions on July 7, 1865, in Washington, D.C. Library of Congress.

Abraham Lincoln. Lincoln, holding his spectacles and a pencil, was photographed by Alexander Gardner on February 5, 1865, in his last photo session. At the time the President was the focus of an abduction plot by Booth. Library of Congress.

Boston Corbett. A New York cavalryman, Corbett shot Booth through the neck in the early morning hours of April 26, 1865. "God commanded me do it," he explained. Surratt House Museum/MNCPPC.

8

. . . .

THE FIERY
FURNACE

BOOTH TOOK OUT A SHEET of fine embossed paper. "Dearest Beloved Mother," he wrote. It was time at last to retract his promise to Mary Ann to stay clear of the war, yet he was struggling as he always did when he took pen to hand. The proper words would not come. Characteristically, he included a line of apology to her for his inarticulateness.

"I have always endeavored to be a good and dutiful son, and even now would wish to die sooner than give you pain," he stated. "But, dearest Mother, though I owe you all, there is another duty, a noble duty, for the sake of liberty and humanity due to my country. For you alone have I struggled to fight this desire to be gone, but it seems that uncontrollable fate, moving me for its ends, takes me from you, dear Mother, to do what work I can for a poor, oppressed, downtrodden people. I cannot longer resist the inclination to go and share the sufferings of my brave countrymen, holding an unequal strife (for every right human and divine) against the most ruthless enemy the world has ever known.

"You can answer for me, dearest Mother (although none of you think with me) that I have not a single selfish motive to spur me on to this. Nothing save the sacred duty I feel I owe the cause I love, the cause of the South, the cause of liberty and justice. So should I meet the worst, dear

Mother, in struggling for such holy rights, I can say, "God's will be done," and bless him in my heart for not permitting me to outlive our dear bought freedom and for keeping me from being longer a hidden lie among my country's foes.

"Should the last bolt strike your son, dear Mother, bear it patiently and think that at the best life is short and *not at all times happy*. My Brothers and Sisters (Heaven protect them) will add my love and duty to their own, and watch you with care and kindness, till we meet again. And if that happiness does not come to us on earth, then may, O may it be with God. So then, dearest, *dearest* Mother, *forgive* and pray for me."[1]

Lacking the heart, and perhaps the courage, to deliver the letter, Booth folded it twice, sealed it inside an envelope addressed to Mary Ann, and put it among personal papers he kept in a safe in Asia's Philadelphia home.[2]

By Sunday, December 18, 1864, Booth was back in Charles County, Maryland, riding the countryside with young Billy Queen and swapping spurs with him as a token of friendship.[3] The actor had been busy. While in the North Booth purchased arms for the plot. These included two of the impressive seven-shot Spencer carbines, three pistols, ammunition, knives, canteens, and two sets of handcuffs. Since this weighty arsenal might draw attention in transit, Booth left most of it with Arnold and O'Laughlen in Baltimore to bring into Washington discreetly.[4]

Booth attended church with the Queens and met again with Samuel Mudd. After Mass the two went over to the hotel in Bryantown, where Mudd found a tall, well-built man with gray-brown eyes and florid complexion. This was Thomas Harbin, a former village postmaster. Mudd introduced Harbin to Booth and informed him that they wished to have a word. The trio headed upstairs to a private room.[5]

Quiet and mild-mannered, the curly-headed Harbin looked innocuous, as any good secret agent should, but looks were deceiving. Harbin was the Confederacy's principal spy in lower Maryland. He was the linchpin in a broad network of official and unofficial rebels on both sides of the Potomac. Such was the confidence placed in him that he carried messages into enemy lines for Jefferson Davis himself. Delivering a set of recent dispatches, Harbin had been surprised and surrounded in Bryantown by two dozen Union cavalrymen. Pistols blazing, "Bold Tom" shot his way through them and outran the lot.[6] Here was no mimic hero. Here was the real thing. It would be of immeasurable assistance to secure the cooperation of a man like Harbin. He knew all the little tricks of the dangerous game Booth wished to play.

"Hush," the actor whispered to Harbin as he motioned him along the hallway. "Silence."

What melodrama! thought the veteran agent as he watched Booth pace about nervously to examine the hall and exits.

"Mr. Booth has engaged me," declared Mudd, getting down to business. "We want you to join!"

Booth then outlined the abduction scheme to Harbin. As he spoke, Harbin realized the stranger was a serious person. "He knew Lincoln well, and described him to me," Harbin recalled. "He hated him." Booth explained that he and his associates planned to seize Lincoln. They intended to take him over the Potomac the same night, thwarting all effective pursuit. Harbin was not needed for the capture. But would he meet them on the road and keep the party moving south?[7]

Harbin was an exceptionally private individual, according to his friends. He would later be so alarmed at his possible liability for the death of Lincoln that it was said he fled to Europe to escape the aftermath. It was not until a few months before his death in 1885 that he consented to an interview with George Alfred Townsend. "Harbin was a cool man who had seen many liars and rogues go to and fro in that illegal border [region]," Townsend wrote, and he was rightly wary of the exotic Booth. It was clear that the actor drank too much. He was "possibly crazy" as well. But Harbin was a Southerner. When Townsend spoke to the ex-spy at his home twenty years after the war, he noticed hanging on Harbin's wall something one rarely saw. It was an engraving of Jefferson Davis taking the inaugural oath as president of the Confederate States of America.

Harbin pledged his cooperation.

While this was happy news, Mudd had begun to share Harbin's reservations about Booth, and these were reinforced that evening when their new friend, unannounced and uninvited, showed up at Mudd's door. The doctor had mentioned there might be some good horses for sale in the neighborhood, and Booth came to investigate.[8] He arrived quite late. Dinner was already over and the house crowded with guests. Nevertheless, it would have been poor manners to turn Booth, standing in his overcoat, back into the winter darkness, so Mudd yielded to the conventions of hospitality and invited Booth to stay overnight. The actor joined the family banter until bedtime was called at about 9:30.[9]

"Pushy," thought Mudd, who felt imposed upon by this incident. His wife, Frances, also grew unhappy with "the handsome face" when she discovered a letter in a woman's hand that Booth inadvertently left behind the following day. She found its contents unflattering to the actor's moral character.

After breakfast on Monday, December 19, 1864, Booth and Mudd called on George Gardiner, who lived on the adjoining farm. Booth told Gardiner that he wanted to buy a buggy horse. Gardiner recommended one of two mares. Declining the suggestion, Booth selected a large brown saddle horse, rather old and blind in the right eye but "a very fine mover," thought Mudd. Booth paid eighty dollars for the horse, and Gardiner's nephew Thomas agreed to deliver it to him at the Bryantown stable the next morning.[10]

Peter Trotter was pounding a bar of glowing iron thirty years later when a correspondent for the *Philadelphia Press* sought a word with the blacksmith on the topic of Booth's visit to Bryantown.

"Yes, I shod Booth's horse for him," said Trotter. "He stood around while I was at work. He was a dark, handsome man. I'll bet he was a great one with the women." The actor had little to say to Trotter, a Scottish immigrant, although he did manage some charm for the locals who soon collected around him in Trotter's shop. By the time he purchased a saddle for the brown horse from Henry A. Turner, a clerk in the village store, he had fallen quiet again.[11]

Mudd performed another service for the abduction plot on December 23 in Washington. He agreed to introduce Booth to John H. Surratt, a Confederate courier. The two set out up Seventh Street toward the Surratt home. It was a delightful night for a stroll. The weather was pleasant, and the shop windows along their way were gaily decorated for the holiday season. Booth and Mudd had not gone far, however, when they chanced upon Surratt and his college friend Louis Weichmann walking past them on the sidewalk. Introductions were made, and at Booth's suggestion the quartet headed for Booth's room at the National Hotel, Surratt and Mudd arm in arm, Booth and Weichmann trailing.[12]

At the hotel Booth pulled a call bell, ordered refreshments, and bade his guests make themselves comfortable. Room number 84 was large and well kept, with a center table and chairs, writing desk, and settee. Senator Morton S. Wilkinson of Minnesota had recently occupied it. The senator, a member of the Manufactures Committee, had left a pile of published government reports and pamphlets on a shelf. Booth picked up several of these. "Congressional documents!" he laughed. "What a good read I shall have when I am left to myself!"

Cigars and wine arrived, along with milk punch, a concoction of brandy and milk flavored with sugar and nutmeg. Brandy was always Booth's drink of choice.

After some socializing, Mudd rose and went out the door into a dim passageway, calling Booth after him. In a few moments they returned to ask Surratt to join them. Several more minutes passed before the three returned. Mudd apologized to Weichmann for leaving him alone, explaining that he and Booth were dickering over the price of Mudd's farm, which the actor wished to purchase.

Booth, Mudd, and Surratt gathered at the center table. Booth pulled an envelope and pencil from his pocket and drew a series of lines, probably roads in southern Maryland leading to the river. A conversation ensued. Weichmann, on the settee by the window, understood their talk was private and made no attempt to overhear it. He merely noticed that as Booth drew, Mudd and Surratt looked on intently.

Mudd was expecting friends from Baltimore, so the party adjourned to his hotel, the Pennsylvania House, several blocks away. Weichmann, a government clerk, was dressed in the blue uniform of the War Department Rifles, a regiment organized from among the employees of the different bureaus for the defense of Washington. When Mudd joined him on a couch to chat about current events, a revealing game began. Mudd, the embittered ex-slave-owner, spoke like a Union man, remembered Weichmann, while the doctor thought the clerk sounded more like a Southerner than he did.[13]

The men were disguising themselves from each other, but these were uncertain times. Whom could one trust? Mudd still had his doubts about Booth, and he whispered a warning to Surratt.

There seemed little concern there, however. Sitting together before a blazing fire, Booth and Surratt were having a merry time. The actor—handsome, faultlessly dressed, and "a man of the world and a gentleman," thought Weichmann—retrieved letters and photographs from his pocket and, sharing them with his companion, regaled him with stories. Surratt, tossing his head in the air, replied with laughter. "Very lively there," observed Weichmann jealously. Booth was the first to depart, but not before arranging to see Surratt again.

Six feet tall, with a goatee and light brown hair, John Surratt had a face distinguished by a prominent forehead and sharp aquiline nose. His piercing, rather sunken gray eyes bespoke a certain cunning.[14] He was well educated, having attended St. Charles College west of Baltimore, a Catholic institution preparing students for seminary and the priesthood.[15] Lacking the call for that vocation, Surratt left school in the summer of 1862 at about the time of his father's death in order to help his mother, Mary, operate the family tavern and farm in Prince George's County. Their red-colored frame house, which also served as the neighborhood post office, sat on the road from Washington to Bryantown. Booth passed by it on his trips to see Mudd and the Queens.

"I was a red-hot rebel and dearly loved my native state," Surratt recalled in an 1898 interview in the *Washington Post*. These opinions led to his dismissal from the postmastership he inherited from his father. He passed time hauling the farm's produce for sale in Washington, but an inevitable process occurred. The family tavern, sitting on the smuggler's highway to Richmond, was a way station for the illegal and the disloyal. Surratt found himself delivering rebel mail, handling contraband goods, and ferrying people across the Potomac. When Weichmann saw his formerly boyish-looking friend for the first time after half a year of this roving life, he was surprised at the brusque air and bronzed appearance of the ex-classmate.

Surratt, when engaged on these clandestine missions, avoided anything that appeared furtive.[16] He dressed as an ordinary business traveler, rode the trains, and dined in the hotels. He hid dispatches in his boot heels or between buggy planks. Surratt carried one set of messages to agents in Canada concealed inside a copy of James Redpath's biography of John Brown. The book was an excellent hiding place. No self-respecting rebel would be thought capable of touching Redpath's abolitionist eulogy. Passing time in traveling, Surratt opened the book and started reading. As he later told a friendly audience to uproarious laughter, "I learned, to my utter amazement, that John Brown was a martyr sitting at the right hand of God."[17]

The greatest danger the twenty-year-old faced in all this work was getting over the Potomac. Since the river was heavily patrolled, Surratt preferred to make the attempt on dark or rainy nights. As a precaution against capture by prowling federal gunboats, he weighted secret messages and towed them in the water astern his boat so that, if overhauled, he could sink the dispatches quickly.

"It was a fascinating life to me," he said in 1870. "It seemed as if I could not do too much or run too great a risk." He was never apprehended, and his self-confidence grew. "Never in my life did I come across a more stupid set of detectives than those generally employed by the U.S. Government."

Anxious over her son's perilous life, Mary Surratt leased out the tavern and moved the family to a home on H Street NW in Washington. The country place provided a bare living, and, burdened by her late husband's debts, she felt the opportunities for herself, John, and her daughter, Anna, would be superior in the city.[18] At least a change of residence would remove her son from the disordered countryside. The Surratt town house opened for boarders, Weichmann moved in, and John sought employment with the Adams Express Company, a business that shipped boxes and packages to soldiers at the front.[19]

Surratt estimated that in all his derring-do he had been shot at a score of times by cannon and rifle. He had always been lucky—until now. Earlier in the week Booth, returning to Washington from Bryantown on the one-eyed horse, had taken a wrong turn and rode miles out of his way, arriving in the city exhausted. He simply did not know this area well enough to use it as an escape route for a captured Lincoln. On the other hand, Surratt boasted that he knew "every cross road, bypath, and hiding place in Northern Virginia and Southern Maryland." Added to that, he was an expert rider and marksman, he was unmarried, and he had a home in the city. Booth intended to have this young daredevil.

A series of meetings between the two men followed.[20] These were highly vexatious. Booth attempted to draw information from Surratt without revealing his purpose. Surratt determined to give nothing away until he understood what Booth really wanted. Surratt still feared that he might be a spy. To Booth, at this point, Surratt was only a friend of Harbin's who was a friend of Mudd's who was a friend of Thompson's who was a friend of Queen's who was a friend of Martin's who was a friend of Kane's.

Exasperated, Surratt finally exclaimed, "You know well I am a Southern man. If you cannot trust me, we will separate."

His hand called, Booth could delay no longer. He spoke of the suffering of Southern soldiers in Northern prisons and of the critical need of the South for these men. He had an undertaking at hand that would lead to their exchange. These words were followed by a long and, it seemed to Surratt, an ominous pause.

"Well, sir, what is your proposition?" demanded Surratt, breaking the silence.

Booth rose and looked under the bed, inside the wardrobe, out the door, and down the passage. "We have to be careful. Walls have ears." Drawing his chair close to Surratt, he whispered, "It is to kidnap President Lincoln and carry him off to Richmond."

"Kidnap President Lincoln?" Surratt shot back. He laughed nervously. "It is not feasible, and in the second place you do not realize the danger."

"I don't consider *that* for a moment," Booth countered. The actor then launched into a detailed exposition of his plot. Surratt listened, increasingly impressed by the planning Booth had done. He had thought the scheme through, from the topic of Lincoln's movements in the city down to the roles individual conspirators would play. And, just as he had with Sam Arnold, the actor stressed the relative ease with which the abduction could be accomplished.

When Booth finished his presentation, Surratt could see it might be doable, but "I confess I stood aghast at the proposition." He told Booth, "Inside of an hour, or, at the most, two hours, from the time we get possession of Mr. Lincoln's person the entire country will be in a furore."

Surratt thought the matter over for several days. He had the same reservations as Harbin. The courier wrote, "I looked upon Booth from the start as a hot-headed, visionary man," sincere in wanting to aid the South but of unsettled mind. Nevertheless, the war was at a crisis point. Something momentous had to be done. Maybe Booth's scheme *was* practical. It also seemed honorable. "Where is there a young man in the North with one spark of patriotism in his heart who would not have with enthusiastic ardor joined in any undertaking for the capture of Jefferson Davis and brought him to Washington?" Surratt asked in a public lecture in 1870.

"I told him I was willing to try it."

Surratt secured, Booth turned to prospects of his own. Visiting stars who played at Ford's often remarked that "there were several persons connected with this theatre whose violent sentiments in favor of the rebellion and its leaders have frequently been noticed."[21] It is not surprising, therefore, to find Booth at the 1864 Christmas dinner given by the Fords for their theatrical family.

Helen Truman, a novice actress, observed considerable intimacy between Booth and one player of Southerner birth, Edwin Emerson of Alexandria, Virginia.[22] Emerson was promising material. His older brother

Benjamin, a Confederate soldier, had died of wounds received in battle near Richmond in 1862. His younger brother Henry had been arrested in 1863 for running the Potomac blockade with medicines and goods and had languished for months in the Old Capitol Prison, refusing to take the oath of allegiance.[23] But Emerson, who had much to say about his friendship with Booth in later years, never mentioned being approached for the abduction team. If he had been, Emerson rebuffed him. A markedly religious man, he felt that the war had grown so brutal and demoralizing that neither side held the moral high ground.[24]

More is known about Booth's courtship of John Mathews, who took eccentric and character roles for Ford. Mathews had known Booth since boyhood days in Baltimore when they had run to fires on the trail of the hose companies, knowing a good fight between the companies was likely to ensue at their destination. The pair were "friends, chums, and comrades," according to a mutual acquaintance.[25] Since Mathews was unquestionably loyal, Booth attempted to recruit him. All he accomplished was frightening him. Mathews grew up in the home of a coroner and had seen enough of death. When he would not say yes but could not say no, Booth exploded, declaring that the fellow Marylander was a coward and not fit to live. Mathews was properly frightened of Booth, too, and promised silence. "I cowed him down," Booth boasted to Samuel K. Chester.[26] Mathews would ultimately be browbeaten into doing a few errands for the conspiracy.

Behind the scenes at the theater "they were all Secech," recalled Harry Hawk, the sole actor onstage when Lincoln was shot. Indeed, when Hawk came to work on the day of the assassination, the staff greeted him with the salutation "you damned Yankee."[27]

Booth's easy manner and his open-handedness at neighborhood taverns won him a large following among the theater's stagehands and roustabouts. One of these admirers was the scene shifter Edman Spangler, a family friend who had done carpentry work when Tudor Hall was built. Fat and jovial, with a high-pitched voice and a fondness for the bottle, the good-natured Spangler was the butt of practical jokes about the theater.[28] He presented the appearance of being an insubstantial drudge, victimized by his admiration for Booth. There may have been more to him, however. Spangler was a member of the Order of the American Knights, a secret antiwar organization with a militantly antiadministration edge.[29] "He was always one of the hardest kind of Copperheads," said a coworker at Ford's.

And he was constantly in Booth's company, holding his horse or blackening his boots with an obliging attention.[30] Thomas Harbin stated that Spangler was involved with their plot, but George Atzerodt, a subsequent member of Booth's team and one quick to implicate others, believed him innocent, as did Samuel Arnold.[31] It seems most likely that Spangler, like Mathews, knew what was afoot, though he took no part in it.

Booth's home county of Harford was also a promising recruiting ground. Maryland's new antislavery constitution failed at the polls here in October 1864, despite the fact that only citizens who took oaths of loyalty to the Union were permitted to vote. That Mudd's Charles County and Surratt's Prince George's voted against the constitution surprised no one. They were in southern Maryland and had much in common politically with adjacent areas of Virginia across the Potomac. But Harford, on the state line with Pennsylvania, had always enjoyed a more liberal reputation. The military draft was also detested in the county. Opponents conducted a campaign of arson attacks on the barns of enrollment officials. Authorities struck back with collective punishment, levying punitive fines on families judged disloyal whether or not a personal culpability in the attacks could be shown. Booth discovered great animosity over these matters, together with anxiety about the prospect of enforced racial equality, when he visited in Bel Air to fish the waters.[32]

The regulars at George Cook's store in Five Forks, a community fourteen miles northwest of Bel Air, were entirely disaffected from Lincoln. Cook, a widower with a large family, hated the war. Intently pro-Southern, he had no intention of traveling the abolitionist warpath, nor did the DeVoes, Gibsons, Russells, Whitefords, and other neighbors who gathered about Cook's hot stove on wintry mornings to share the latest news with Booth. Having often hunted in the area, Booth knew these men and talked to them with relative freedom. These farmers were serious people, not simply the usual ne'er-do-wells who always congregated to eat Cook's free crackers and drink his whiskey. "Many people prominent in Harford County were wont to gather and talk with Booth," recalled Cook's then eleven-year-old daughter Hannah, whom Booth would pull up to his lap for a kiss. "Booth was a fine young man."

"Father and a few of the neighbors and Booth blathered about the store stove and discussed the feasibility of removing Lincoln from the Presidency," said Hannah in an interview given about 1926. "His murder was not considered, but the kidnapping and removal to the Far South was tentatively agreed upon. There he was to be held for a king's ransom, all for the Southern cause." When pressed for details about the abduction plot, Hannah demurred, "Oh, well, the war is ended."[33]

Herman Stump was also active in Booth's plot, according to an unpublished family history drawing upon the recollections of Mary North Stump, a sister-in-law who lived with the attorney at his estate. "Deeply involved in the Southern cause, he worked in underground organizations outlawed by the Federal Government. If the South had been victorious, the members of these secret organizations would have been heroes and more information would have come down to us," the memoir states, "but as it was in defeat and [with] the probable involvement of some in the assassination of Lincoln, the result has been practically a blank."

Determined to preserve for history some details about all this, Herman Stump Murray, Stump's cousin and namesake, made a special trip from New York City in 1917 to interview Booth's old friend. Murray recalled that Stump acknowledged, by certain gestures he made, that he had been involved with Booth, then cut off further discussion of the topic by reminding his kinsman that he had been sworn to secrecy and must honor his oath. To assuage Murray's disappointment, the lawyer adopted the Hannah Cook principle. "It was a long time ago," Stump said philosophically, "and times have changed. What seemed right then may seem wrong now, and too many people would be hurt."[34] Silence had served Stump well. He went on to be elected to two terms in the U.S. House of Representatives and served as superintendent of immigration for President Grover Cleveland in the 1890s.

Edwin and June visited Stump and George Y. Maynadier, Stump's close friend and law partner, in Bel Air in 1867. The actors, who were old acquaintances of the attorneys and their families, spent a pleasant evening chatting with them in their office. The conversation was free, fun, and unrestrained—except on one topic. John Wilkes Booth's name was never mentioned. Maynadier observed that Stump did not bring it up. No one else did either.[35]

Years later Maynadier put another name before the public. George B. Love was Booth's classmate at Bel Air Academy and his intimate friend. "He was likewise the most notorious of all the boys and young men at school or in the village, as the ringleader of everything desperate and reckless," wrote Maynadier. Court-martialed for corruption while serving as a steward in a federal hospital, Love committed suicide days after Lincoln's death. Maynadier, who knew a great deal of the Southern network

in Maryland, thought that Love killed himself because he feared the consequences of his plotting with Booth. Or maybe not. Maybe it was just "a
curious coincidence," Maynadier teased readers in a 1902 reminiscence.
" 'I tell the tale as 'twas told to me' is all the comment I have to make." [36]

Booth was at Edwin's home in New York on Christmas Day 1864.
That night he drank heavily with Sam Chester at the House of Lords on
Houston Street. Afterward the men sauntered up Broadway and over to
Fourth. Chester was miserable working with Edwin and Clarke at the
Winter Garden, and Booth had enticed him to join in an unspecified but
"big speculation sure to coin money." At an unfrequented spot along the
street Booth said, "I want to tell you what this speculation is."

"I wish you would because you have worried me enough about it," replied Chester.

Making certain they were alone, Booth hemmed and hawed and finally
said, "It is a conspiracy against the government."

"To do what?"

"To capture the heads of the government at Washington and carry them
to Richmond, including Mr. Lincoln." The abduction party was nearly
ready, Booth explained. It would seize Lincoln while he attended a performance at Ford's Theatre. But Booth was frustrated, he said, in his efforts
to find help at that house. "He broached the affair to several but could not
get any to assist him in the theatre," Chester recalled. Hence this proposition. Booth needed Chester backstage to cut the gaslights, plunging the
theater into darkness, and to open the rear door of the theater onto an
alley for the capture team.

Chester, who thought Booth wished to discuss a speculation in Maryland farmland, was terrified by what he heard. The mild-mannered actor
played an effective heavy onstage, but he had no intention of taking that
role to the streets. Chester was a peaceful sort and so apolitical that he had
never even voted. He flatly refused Booth's request.

For an intense half hour Booth turned the full range of his powers on
Chester. The friend parried every appeal. Neither friendship nor patriotism nor money could touch him. Any involvement would ruin his family,
Chester pleaded. Booth countered by offering to leave behind for their use
three or four thousand dollars, the value of the bonds he kept in a safe at
Asia's home in Philadelphia. When Chester remained adamant, Booth grew
irritated, then threatening. He declared that he would destroy Chester in
the profession if he did not join in.

"I have facts in my possession that will ruin you for life," Booth said menacingly.

"It is very wrong [to say that], John, because I have always looked upon you as a friend and have never done you any wrong." Chester begged Booth to drop the subject and never mention it again.

"At any rate you won't betray me," Booth concluded. "I carry a derringer loaded to shoot every one that betrays us."

That said, they parted, Booth by no means finished with this conversation.

He reconnected with Arnold and O'Laughlen in Baltimore and purchased a buggy there. This vehicle was to be used to haul Lincoln away. Arnold and O'Laughlen drove it to Washington. They also got the balance of the group's weapons safely into the capital. Booth introduced them to young Surratt, and the two men took a room at a local hotel, awaiting orders.[37]

Booth checked back into the National Hotel on New Year's Eve and spent most of the month of January 1865 in Washington.[38] He found Surratt actively engaged in arrangements for their enterprise.

Richard M. Smoot, a Charles County farmer and blockade-runner, owned a large flat-bottomed bateau, painted the color of lead and capable of carrying fifteen people. Smoot found Surratt noticeably eager to purchase it, saying "the need of the boat would be the consequence of an event of unprecedented magnitude in the history of the country which would startle and astound the entire world."[39] Smoot inferred that this was the proposed abduction of Lincoln, a rumor of which had reached his ears. Mum about his purpose, Surratt smiled and told Smoot's brother Edward, "If the Yankees knew what [I am doing], they would stretch this old neck of mine." He jerked his head back to illustrate the point.[40]

Surratt and Smoot agreed on a price of $250. The courier directed that the boat be hidden up King's Creek, a small tributary of the Potomac, and held ready on a moment's notice. He also informed Smoot that he needed two other boats of similar size, each capable of transporting fifteen persons. These were to be kept at different points along the river. Three boats would give the abduction team considerable flexibility on the flight from Washington should unforeseen circumstances arise.

Surratt told Smoot to turn the boat over to George A. Atzerodt, a German immigrant and a blockade-runner whom he and Harbin had recruited. A swarthy man with long dark-brown hair and a narrow receding chin and forehead, Atzerodt had a look that invited suspicion. "This fellow might safely challenge the rest of the party as the completest personification of a low and cunning scoundrel," thought the journalist Noah Brooks.[41] Appearances aside, "Atzerodt was a man full of fun, country humor, and quaint stories," said Surratt's friend Weichmann. It was necessary to recruit a man like Atzerodt because, as the conspirators knew, "the Potomac was closely guarded, and it was a serious matter to get across." Atzerodt's muscular shoulders, indicating considerable strength gained by rowing, showed that he knew the river well. He crossed so frequently with contraband, "both rebel and federal, and picked up so much money in that way that he was very saucy," thought one traveler on his way to Richmond. As far as Atzerodt's politics went, "he always hated the niggers."[42]

Charles Yates of Charles County was to have direction of the rowing party on the river. Yates was a skilled boatman as well as a crack shot.[43] If Yates and his crew were ready and river conditions optimal, the Potomac could be crossed within an hour of the time it was reached. Once they reached the Virginia shore, two Confederate Signal Corps camps were near at hand, and locals like Benjamin B. Arnold of King George County, Virginia, a courier at one of the camps, pledged to hurry Lincoln to the rebel capital. In good weather the trip from the Potomac to Richmond might be made in one day. Given the myriad of complications that could arise, the certainty of a fierce pursuit, and the reprisals that would surely follow, Arnold had it right when he told his family that the undertaking would likely be "a very dirty job."[44]

Thomas A. Jones, Harbin's brother-in-law, was alerted to the plot. Jones handled underground operations on the Potomac's Maryland shore opposite one of the Confederate signal stations. Shrewd and daring, Jones dispatched rebel mail and agents and watched the river. He did not meet Booth personally until after the assassination, when he undertook the exceedingly dangerous job of hiding him and crossing him into the Old Dominion, but the involvement of professionals like himself and Harbin indicated the increasing sophistication of the planning. Jones recalled that Lincoln was to be chloroformed if necessary, that the kidnappers would be dressed in federal uniforms to pass checkpoints, and that relays of fresh horses were to be kept along the route to allow the abductors to outpace their pursuers.[45]

Clearly, a sizable corps of supernumeraries was cast in Booth's abduction drama, lending credibility to his boast to Chester that there was "an immense party connected with it, a party of fifty or a hundred." "Plenty of parties in Charles County knew of the kidnapping affair," confessed Atzerodt when captured and examined by authorities after the assassination. One Northern reporter who studied Booth's plot wrote in disgust, "Its accessories were so numerous that the trouble is not whom to suspect, but whom not [to] accuse."[46]

THOMAS LISTER OF BOSTON published a horoscope of Abraham Lincoln in September 1864. The astrologer forecast that "in January, 1865, some deep, base plot will be got up against the President as shown by the transit of the evil planet Mars."[47] The New York astrologer L. D. Broughton agreed. During the election period Lincoln enjoyed the beneficent influence of Jupiter "transiting over his ascendant in good aspect to Venus' place and a secondary direction of the Moon to Jupiter." This was clear. But a danger to Lincoln now arose. The reason Lister knew this, Broughton continued, was that he had lifted the horoscope, without acknowledgment, from Broughton's own *Monthly Planet Reader and Astrological Journal*.[48] Broughton's indignation suggested that if Lister continued his career as a plagiarist, Lincoln would not be the only person in peril.

Be that as it may, John Wilkes Booth, personifying malevolent Mars, was now together with Arnold and O'Laughlen in Washington. Since winter weather curtailed Lincoln's visits to the Soldiers' Home, the trio began to shadow the President for other opportunities. "Each watched, as far as practicable, the movements of Lincoln, being cautious not to draw the attention nor arouse the suspicions of the numerous hordes of detectives and spies who at that time thronged every thoroughfare," recalled Arnold. On one occasion Arnold sent word to Booth that the president and his coachman had just crossed the Anacostia River on a drive. Only one guest accompanied them. Arnold thought the moment extraordinarily opportune for a strike. Incredibly, Booth failed to respond to this and to a second equally favorable opportunity. Arnold was frustrated, but his complaints met a curt response.[49]

Booth had other ideas. Why chase the president when he would come to them? Lincoln could be abducted while he attended a performance at Ford's. Booth took Arnold and O'Laughlen to reconnoiter the theater. They looked particularly at rear entrances. A man from New York (evidently Chester) would cut off the gas and create the confusion necessary for their escape across the stage, out the back, and down the alley at the theater's rear. When Arnold expressed doubt about their chances in a crowded theater, Booth refused to listen.

Booth was constantly in and about the theater during these weeks. William Ferguson, Ford's callboy, saw him often there or across Tenth Street in the house of the tailor William Petersen, where John Mathews and Charles Warwick of the stock company rented a back bedroom. Delivering parts of a play for these cast members to study, Ferguson found half a dozen actors in the room, all chatting in high spirits. "Lying lazily on the bed, a pipe in his mouth, his handsome hair disheveled, was John Wilkes Booth," Ferguson recalled. He rested on the bed in which Abraham Lincoln would later die.[50]

Booth intended to take Lincoln during the engagement of Edwin Forrest.[51] The great Forrest, though past his prime, remained *the* preeminent American actor, and his name on the marquee would bring Lincoln to the door, as Booth knew. Judge Barnett of the *National Intelligencer* wrote that during Forrest's engagement it was "quite an ordinary thing to witness the President and members of his cabinet, Foreign Ministers, Senators, Representatives, and distinguished strangers, as well as the world of literature of Washington, ornamenting the private boxes and orchestra chairs."[52] Harry Ford said that "when Forrest was there, [Lincoln] came very often—4 nights out of 6."[53]

Forrest's visit reunited Booth with John McCullough, who toured with the aging star and took second leads. McCullough detested the war, declaring "he would never fight against the South—that if drafted, would die first—those who were fighting in the Union cause were d—— fools and men of no brains—and Lincoln was too ignorant for the position and should be put out of the way."[54]

"Booth, no doubt, would have opened his heart to McCullough and endeavored to draw him into that general plan of abducting or killing Mr. Lincoln," wrote Townsend, who interviewed Booth's brother actor extensively in later years, but he knew it would have been wasted effort. The amiable Irishman was a poor hater.[55] He wanted humanity to laugh and to love. Nevertheless, Booth gained some advantage from sharing his room at the National Hotel with McCullough and with Joseph McArdle, Forrest's manager.[56] This kept him informed on the daily ins and outs of Forrest's engagement.

At the same time, Booth continued familiarizing himself with his southern Maryland flight path. "He visited the houses of the people, paid no little attention to the girls, stood unlimited whiskey to the men, and made himself generally popular."[57] He became acquainted with John Lloyd, the hard-drinking tenant who leased the tavern from Mary Surratt. Booth and Lloyd were "mighty thick," according to Rachel Hawkins, a former slave who cooked for the Surratts. Hawkins remembered the actor fondly for his liberality to the servants. That same generosity bought drinks and confidences from the locals at T.B., an oddly named village south of Surrattsville on the road to Bryantown. And Booth was on the best of terms with Father Peter Lenaghan, the parish priest of the Mudd family. Lenaghan warmly recommended Booth to his congregants, not surprising for a clergyman who subscribed to the fiercely anti-Lincoln *New-York Freeman's Journal and Catholic Register.*[58]

Meanwhile Booth stepped up the pressure on Chester. He prevailed on Matthew Canning to urge John T. Ford to employ Chester at Ford's Theatre, even offering to pay the actor's salary. Chester was talented, so Ford agreed if Chester could get clear of his Winter Garden commitment.[59] "You *must* come to Washington. We cannot do without you," Booth wrote Chester during the first week of January. Chester refused, and Booth replied by return mail, "You *must* come." He sent fifty dollars for Chester's traveling expenses and directed his friend to be in Washington by the evening of Saturday, January 14, 1865.

Surratt, for his part, had been unable to secure leave from his job at the Adams Express Company.[60] He decamped on the fourteenth for the town of Port Tobacco in Charles County, where he met with Harbin and Atzerodt. M. E. Martin, a New York broker attempting to cross the Potomac to purchase cotton and tobacco, saw Surratt eat a quick supper, then hurry off on his return to the city on a night ride.[61] Surratt made it back to Washington safely, but he never returned to his office and even failed to pick up his final paycheck. To the puzzled Weichmann, Surratt made clear that there were things more important than money. He told the friend that if he succeeded in his current speculation, "his country would love him forever and that his name would go down green to posterity."[62]

Martin, who was paying a liberal retainer to Atzerodt to get him across the river, overheard enough of the boatman's conversation with Surratt to realize he had just been bumped off the priority list. The New Yorker confronted Atzerodt at the Port Tobacco hotel, complaining that he had paid plenty and received nothing in return. Atzerodt denied that anyone was crossing at that time due to high winds and ice in the river. When

Martin repeated his charge of duplicity and called Atzerodt a scoundrel, the boatman disclosed that on Wednesday, January 18, a large party of ten to twelve persons would cross. He had been engaged all day in preparations for it. "They were going to have relays of horses on the road between Port Tobacco and Washington." Atzerodt said he would be absent perhaps ten days as he was to meet this group in Washington and accompany it all the way to Richmond.

Anticipating Martin's next remark, Atzerodt added, "It would be impossible for [you] to cross with this party."

"What does this mean?" asked Martin.

"O, I cannot tell you," was the reply.

Martin guessed aloud that a group of Confederate officers were about to escape prison and cross. Atzerodt paused for a moment. "Yes," he responded dismissively. "That is it, and I am going to get well paid for it."[63]

On January 18, as Atzerodt and the boat team stood by, Edwin Forrest starred in *Jack Cade*. One of Forrest's signature plays, it brought the largest audience of the season to Ford's. Lincoln was expected to be present, according to Helen Truman, the stock company's fledgling who carefully noted the president's visits to the theater.[64] But the only unscripted excitement occurred when a drunken patron loudly insisted that it was his right as an American citizen to screech and holler from his seat in the audience.[65] The kidnappers, wherever they were, made no move.

Why? One theatergoer stated that Lincoln went to Grover's that night and to Ford's the following evening; if so, the conspirators' plans were foiled by the president himself. Thomas A. Jones wrote that the plot failed due to the roads, made impassable by rain and the traffic of heavy army wagons.[66] Booth complained that other people had let him down. One would think that he referred to Chester, who failed to come to Washington as summoned, but Booth made the comment *to* Chester, indicating that he put the blame elsewhere. Whatever operation was intended, and whatever complication arose, the plot simply never got off the ground. Mrs. Surratt went out to the tavern to inform Harbin, Atzerodt, and John, who were readying the route below Washington, to stand down.[67]

Discouraged, Booth returned to New York. He renewed his courtship of Chester. Rebuffed again, he relieved his friend enormously by releasing him from the plot. "He said he honored my mother [Lydia, of Baltimore] and respected my wife [Annie, an actress] and told me to make my mind easy," Chester declared. "He would trouble me about it no more."

The conspiracy had cost him four thousand dollars out of pocket, Booth grumbled. Earlier he had told Chester to keep the fifty he sent, but now, short of cash, he retrieved it. Booth spoke of giving up the entire project.

"Thank God for your sake, John," exclaimed Chester. "I always liked you and am glad that you are clear of it."

Booth remained determined to quit the North, however. "I am going to Richmond," he declared firmly.[68]

Frustrated in his efforts to nab Lincoln, Booth had at least proven adept in capturing someone else. Lucy Hale was the younger daughter of Senator John P. Hale and his wife, Lucy Lambert. Hale was a three-term New Hampshire Republican who had been the antislavery candidate for president on the Free Soil Party ticket of 1852.[69] He resided with his wife and their daughters, Elizabeth and Lucy, at the fashionable National Hotel, located on Pennsylvania Avenue as did Booth. Daughter Lucy was one of Washington's great beauties. Nature had blessed her with lustrous black hair, lovely blue-gray eyes, and a flawless complexion. These complemented a spirited and social temperament. One minute a cool aristocrat, the next a singer of silly songs, the next a romping playmate with her dogs, Lucy combined radiance, remarkable charm, and powerful seductiveness. Young men clamored for her dance card. John Hay, one of Lincoln's private secretaries, and Oliver Wendell Holmes Jr., officer of a Massachusetts infantry regiment, were among those who sought Lucy's attention. Suitors of such quality were so plentiful, in fact, that the vivacious young woman was heedless of them. She threw her dazzling smiles about freely, but they meant far less to her than to the lucky man upon whom they fell.[70]

Lucy met Booth during his Washington performances in 1863, when she rewarded his Charles De Moor with a bouquet of flowers.[71] Now, both were living at the National, and Lucy could scarcely be missed as she maneuvered her sweeping skirts past him on the hotel's broad staircase.

Her interest in Booth needs little explanation. A Washington journalist who saw him at the hotel wrote that he was "a handsome, dark, melodramatic fellow, and among a certain set here he was a great favorite socially." Since Lucy went against type, his interest in her is intriguing. At twenty-four she was older than those who customarily caught Booth's eye. And James R. Ford, business manager of Ford's Theatre, who boarded at the National, added ungallantly that she was "rather stout." Ford backpedaled to explain he meant only that she was a little larger than her older sister, Elizabeth.[72] A photograph of Lucy, her head on Lizzie's shoulder, confirms this. But it also shows the perfect face and come-hither look that overwhelmed all other considerations.

One evening there was a dance at the National. Chairs were aligned along the black marble pillars of the lobby for parents and chaperones, while tables were cleared away in the grand dining room to create a dance floor for the young and the young-at-heart. "The hotel was a blaze of light," recalled a guest who watched Booth and Lucy dancing. "Between the waltzes everyone was good-naturedly gossiping at the devotion of a couple who walked up and down the rooms, apparently oblivious of place and surroundings. They were a very attractive pair. There were some who caviled at her choice, but the young girl's sweet face seemed excuse for any infatuation."

There is no truth to an 1878 story that at this or another ball Robert Todd Lincoln, the president's son, stole Lucy's favor in front of a glowering Booth. Lincoln specifically denied this tale. "I never saw John Wilkes Booth in my life," he stated.[73] The younger Lincoln, an officer on Grant's staff at the front in Virginia, was rarely in Washington that winter. Anyway, he loved and perhaps was already engaged to Mary Harlan, an Iowa senator's daughter whom he later married. More to the point, Booth was not one to pout on a dance floor. "He was not a man to act toward a rival in any such manner," scoffed John Mathews at this story. "He was bold and daring and would have assaulted him openly had such been his intention."[74]

Mathews witnessed the agony this distracting romance with Lucy caused Booth. "Were you ever in love?" Booth asked him one afternoon in Mathews's room at Petersen's.

"No, I never could afford it," the friend responded.

"I wish I could say as much. I am a captive. You cannot understand how I feel."

"Booth loved her as few men love," explained Mathews. "He had a great mind and a generous heart, and both were centered upon this girl." Booth said that Lucy had told him her only objection to him was that he was an actor, and he had told her his only objection to her was she was an abolitionist. But love conquers all, Booth continued, and he intended to marry her.

Throwing himself on Mathews's bed, Booth exclaimed, "If it were not for that girl, how clear the future would be to me! How easily could I grasp the ambition closest to my heart—the release of the Confederate prisoners. If it were not for her, I could feel easy. Think of it, John, that at my time of life—just starting [over] as it were, I should be in love. I am. I am in love!"[75]

9

. . . .

COME WEAL OR WOE

JOHN YATES BEALL, a daring Confederate agent based in Canada, was executed at Governors Island in New York harbor on February 24, 1865. Beall had been captured at Niagara Falls after attempting to derail a train in order to rob it and free rebel prisoners of war in transit. He sought to establish himself as a lawful combatant by virtue of his rank as an acting master in the Confederate navy. A military commission rejected this justification, however, and condemned Beall for spying and waging "irregular and unlawful warfare as a guerrilla." Beall's last words were "Tell my mother that you saw her son die without craven fear and without bravado. I die in the service and defense of my country."[1]

Surprisingly, President Lincoln had received extraordinary appeals on Beall's behalf from a number of prominent Northerners. Former U.S. senator Orville H. Browning, one of Lincoln's oldest and closest friends, brought the president a petition of clemency signed by eighty-five members of the House of Representatives and six members of the Senate. None of these Union men wished Beall freed, of course, but they sought a stay of sentence or possibly a commutation to imprisonment. Some felt his trial too hasty. Others wished Beall given time to appeal or to prepare to meet his Maker. Still others feared the rebels would seek revenge, as anonymous letters were sent to the president threatening his life if Beall were executed. Small wonder that the first thought Browning had upon learning of Lincoln's assassination was that Beall's friends had done it.[2]

Even Booth joined the clemency parade, according to an extraordinary but apocryphal story that sprang up after Lincoln's death. Being a bosom friend of Beall, Booth supposedly made a personal appeal to Lincoln for the agent's life. To add spice to the tale, Booth was accompanied on his White House visit by Senator Hale, Lucy's father. At an interview lasting until 4:00 a.m., Booth confessed his plot to kidnap the president. He knelt before Lincoln, clasping the president's knees with his hands, and, "weeping like a child, besought him to pardon Beall." Deeply moved, a tearful Lincoln agreed. But the next morning Seward or Stanton—pick a villain—coerced the kind-hearted but weak president into reneging on his promise. Stunned by Lincoln's perfidy, the story concludes, Booth greased his pistol.[3]

The facts are much less colorful.[4] Booth met the condemned man in 1859 when Beall sold provisions to the commissary office of the 1st Virginia Regiment at the time of John Brown's hanging. Far from being devoted friends, the pair were mere acquaintances. They did not room together at the University of Virginia, nor did Beall bankroll Booth's stage career, nor were they cousins, as Edwin Booth let the public know shortly after Lincoln's murder. Booth did recognize Beall's name, however, and remember him. Beall came to his attention often during the war as the rebel hero of naval exploits on the Chesapeake Bay and Lake Erie, and the actor empathized deeply with the doomed man as he awaited his fate. The story of Booth and Beall as entwined souls of the Damon and Pythias variety persisted for years, however. It appealed to the Copperhead editor and the Confederate memorialist because it made sense of the assassination. Revenge for a friend was a motive everyone could understand, if not approve, and it eased the consciences of those whose hatred of Lincoln had fed the flames of fanaticism.

Lincoln acted shrewdly in the Beall case. He threw the question of mercy back to General John Adams Dix, who oversaw Beall's trial, and Dix, still seething over the attempted arson of New York, let the execution proceed. The details of Beall's death were gruesome. He was hanged on a bizarre device that jerked his body upward, breaking his neck. Few who read the account of his last moments were unmoved. In Virginia, Confederate Major Robert W. Hunter, who had known both Beall and Booth at Charlestown in 1859 at the time of John Brown's execution, introduced a resolution in the state's House of Delegates denouncing Beall's death as an outrage to humanity. A Canadian friend of the dead man promised, "We'll make the damned Yankees howl."[5]

Booth was concerned enough with this case to make an effort—the substance of which is unknown—to effect a pardon, and when his effort failed and Beall was executed, it hit him hard. He fainted, according to Beall's fiancée, Martha O'Bryan, and then had an attack of "brain fever," understood as a lapse into a frantic and disordered state of mind.[6] It was similar to the mental disturbance that struck him in Montgomery, Alabama, during the secession winter of 1860. His enmity toward the president hardened, Joe Simonds informed their oil-country friend A. W. Smiley. John McCullough, a man with whom Booth was intimate, said, "Booth damned Old Lincoln for a murderer and said somebody would one day give it to him."[7]

Booth was at the National Hotel in Washington on the afternoon that Beall was executed. Once again he was sharing digs with McCullough, and it was there in room 231 where his fellow actor heard these remarks. Booth had wasted most of February, his principal accomplishment being the composition of a Valentine's Day poem for Lucy Hale. His anger at the execution and the approaching second inauguration of Lincoln seemed to reenergize him. With the exception of the occasional interlude for romance, Booth would be increasingly absorbed with the conspiracy thereafter.

New recruits joined the crew. David E. Herold was a small, slightly stooped young man with black hair and a spray of mustache. Weichmann described him as "a seedy, frowzy, monkey-faced boy."[8] A native of the District of Columbia, he grew up in a middle-class family living near the Navy Yard, where his father, Adam, worked as a clerk. After preparatory studies at Georgetown College and Rittenhouse Academy, Herold worked at pharmacies in the city. He met Booth in 1863 when the actor underwent surgery. Herold was one of those people to whom Booth jested that the tumor Dr. May removed from his neck was actually the bullet Canning had fired into his thigh. Good-natured Davy seemed younger than his twenty-two years.[9]

Adam Herold had died the preceding fall, an event that unsettled his son and put him at loose ends. Refusing to get a job, he spent his days hunting partridge in southern Maryland. His mother, Mary, tried tough love, locking him out of the house for the night if he was not at home by ten, but, as Herold laughed, "I am ahead of the old lady."[10] Nothing deterred him from gunning and tramping. His political opinions were unknown, probably even to himself, but he was a hardy, happy youth who loved adventure, knew the roads along the abduction route, and had friends at almost every farmhouse on the way.[11] Surratt recommended him to Booth, and Booth asked him if he "would like to go into an enterprise to make money." Herold joined the team over a glass of ale as the men stood on the porch of the Metropolitan Hotel. "Booth is a good fellow," Herold told a friend.[12]

Lewis Powell, a native of Alabama, was twenty-one. He enlisted at the outset of the war with the 2nd Florida Infantry and served continuously until wounded and captured at Gettysburg in July 1863. While detailed as a prisoner-nurse in Baltimore, he escaped to Virginia and joined Mosby's guerrillas. Lonely, war-weary, and far from home, he reentered Union lines at Fairfax Court-House on January 13, 1865. Posing as a refugee named Lewis Paine, he took the oath of allegiance, sold his horse, and headed back to Baltimore. There he called at a boardinghouse run by Mrs. M. A. Branson and renewed his acquaintance with her daughters, Maggie and Mary, whom he had met while a prisoner.[13]

The series of events by which Powell was introduced to Booth has never been made clear, and at this point it is probably past recovering. One may reject, as a deception conceived to protect the Branson family, Powell's claim that the two met at the Richmond Theatre early in the war.[14] Booth was not in Richmond at any time during the war. Equally implausible is the speculation that Powell was assigned by Confederate intelligence officials to contact and work with Booth.[15]

The most likely scenario is that the Bransons introduced Powell to D. Preston Parr, a Baltimore china dealer, and Parr passed him along to Surratt, with whom he engaged in smuggling and espionage activities. Surratt found the young Floridian destitute and adrift, smarting with self-reproach for deserting a cause in which he deeply believed. Powell needed purpose. He was ready. All the conspirators needed to do was decant him. Their plot restored his dignity by allowing him to "still claim to be a confederate soldier."[16]

More than six feet tall, a muscular young man with blue eyes and a thick black shock of hair brushed off a broad forehead, Powell had an appealing sense of self-possession. "I liked [Powell]," said Captain Christian Rath, the Michigan officer who was to be both Powell's jailer and hangman. "He was a magnificent man—big, strong, kind, generous, with an iron resolution, and a voice and manner as soft as a woman's. He would have murdered a dozen men—would have waded through blood—and yet I believe he was thoroughly unselfish. The Confederacy was all and everything to him."[17]

After the assassination Lincoln's secretaries John G. Nicolay and John Hay described Powell, Herold, and the other members of Booth's ensemble as "a small number of loose fish." Townsend agreed. "The Company of which [Booth] was President might well be labeled 'limited,'" quipped the journalist. "They were a miserable parcel of country tools. There was a lamentable lack of material for any such eccentric episode as Booth had hit upon."[18] These harsh assessments indicate that Booth's associates seemed commonplace to their contemporaries. They hardly seem the skilled "covert action team" of modern writers who posit Lincoln's death as part of a grand Confederate strategy.

In truth, Booth's new comrades fit neither characterization very well. Herold, at first glance a trifling ragamuffin, was quick-thinking, remarkably loyal, and a fine shot. His attorney's attempt after the assassination to make him look stupid, thus easily manipulated by Booth, was merely a legal strategy. School chums thought him a boy of above-average intelligence. "He was naturally quick and smart," said a detective who chased him.[19] And Powell, characterized by a Union officer as "a cross between a big booby and a sullen animal," was a battle-hardened veteran who played chess and read medical books.[20] In summary, the members of Booth's gang were individually more substantial than they seemed, if less in aggregate than conspiracy buffs might wish them to be.

THE EVENING OF MARCH 3, 1865, was festive. Lincoln's second inauguration would occur the following day, and the city teemed with excitement. There seemed to be faces in every window, flags on every building. Crowds milled about the streets, and bands played patriotic airs. It was too memorable a night to remain indoors, so Booth, Surratt, and Weichmann set off to see the preparations for the big event.

As the trio made its way to the House of Representatives and ascended to the Capitol gallery, Booth stopped suddenly. "Who is that?" he asked.

Booth was staring at a bust of Lincoln on a pedestal in a corner. It seemed inconceivable to him that a likeness of any living politician would be permitted in such a hallowed place. It smacked of deification. "What's *he* doing in here before his time?" Booth demanded angrily. Weichmann had no answer but was struck by the hostility of the remark. It was the first time Booth had spoken of Lincoln to him in an unfriendly manner.[21]

In his position as a clerk in the office of the commissary general of prisoners, Weichmann was proving useful to the conspirators. Fatty, as Surratt was wont to call him, gave Booth data on Confederate prisoners in federal hands and allowed Booth to use his office for meetings. "This corrupt scoundrel betrayed his official trust," wrote William P. Wood, superintendent of Old Capitol Prison.[22] Excited by the prospect of an adventure, Weichmann even wished to join the team. Booth remained suspicious of him, but Surratt spurned Fatty, who waddled when he walked, for a practical reason: "He could neither ride a horse nor shoot a pistol."[23]

Inaugural day commenced disagreeably. It had rained through the night, and the rain continued, blown about by strong winds. The public was undeterred. As the parade down Pennsylvania Avenue to the Capitol formed near the White House, a mass of people gathered "upon sidewalks and at every window, door, balcony, step, and on many of the roofs" along the route, wrote a Baltimore journalist. It was the largest crowd ever to witness an inauguration. The scene was tumultuous but noticeably less anxious than in 1861, when there were sharpshooters on the same rooftops and threats of revolution in the air.[24]

The procession started forward down the muddy avenue. One mile long, it took an hour to pass any given point. Military units on horse and foot were featured. There were black soldiers among them, another startling contrast to Lincoln's first inauguration. The presidential carriage, drawn by two horses, was in its appropriate place, but Lincoln was not seated in it. He was already at the Capitol, where he had gone earlier in the day to sign bills. Mrs. Lincoln, her son Robert, and Iowa senator James Harlan (Robert's future father-in-law) sat in the president's place.[25] Preceding the carriage was a troop of federal marshals, distinctively attired with white scarves. Firemen from Washington and Philadelphia followed with gaily decorated engines, and still farther back a delegation from the Navy Yard hauling a replica monitor with revolving turret. A number of rebel prisoners under transfer accidentally merged with the procession at one point, "giving it somewhat the character of a Roman pageant, when captive enemies added by their misery to the triumph."[26]

Booth watched this cavalcade somberly from a spot on the embankment at the north wing of the Capitol near where the president's carriage would pass. He was dressed casually as if ready to ride, with his pants tucked into the tops of his boots and an old felt hat drawn over his forehead. Anxious and moody, Booth ignored a friend who shouldered through the crowd to greet him. As Lincoln's carriage passed, he turned away from the friend and walked off.[27]

The day's formalities were to begin in the Senate Chamber, where, with the president in attendance, Andrew Johnson would be sworn in as the new vice president. Then the president and party were to be escorted through the Rotunda to the east front of the great building, where Lincoln would take the oath and deliver his inaugural address. The public were welcome on the grounds, but entrance into the Capitol was tightly controlled. Every door to the building was closed except the east door of the north wing. Admission was to ticket holders only.[28]

Booth had secured a ticket from Lucy Hale, one of a number given to her father for family and friends.[29] It was a small rectangular card of stiff paper with a printed notice to "Admit the Bearer" signed by George T. Brown, the Senate's sergeant at arms. "She gave the ticket innocently," concluded John A. Bingham, an Ohio congressman who later investigated the matter.[30] It was anyone's guess what privilege this card conveyed. Perhaps two thousand people, far more than could ever be accommodated, had cards of admission. Roswell Parish's ticket allowed the tourist to spend four hours to get from a line of soldiers at the door to the Senate itself.[31] Inside, he found the chamber floor packed with the official party, cabinet secretaries and their top assistants, members and former members of the House and Senate, justices of the Supreme Court, judges of the federal courts, distinguished military officials, governors and ex-governors of the states, key mayors, the diplomatic corps, and other persons of importance. The families of these men and the press jostled for space in the gallery.

Impressively, Booth elbowed close enough to witness the swearing-in of Johnson. When the ceremony was completed, the actor rushed for the Rotunda. "That man must be in a hurry," a friend said to Otis S. Buxton, assistant doorkeeper of the House of Representatives, as Booth shot past them. "That is Wilkes Booth," responded Buxton.[32]

In the Rotunda a double line of Capitol policemen created a corridor from the north to the east door by which the president would pass to the outside for his inauguration. Ticket holders gathered to watch the procession. Ward H. Lamon, marshal of the District of Columbia and a longtime friend of Lincoln's, led the way. He was followed by the former presidents and vice presidents, the justices of the Supreme Court, Sergeant at Arms Brown, and the inaugural committee. Warm applause sounded as Lincoln, with Johnson, appeared behind them. Those parties admitted to the floor of the Senate Chamber were to have followed the president in specified order. Protocol by rank collapsed due to the size of the crowd. The procession into the Rotunda became pell-mell according to Charles Adolphe Pineton, marquis de Chambrun, a French nobleman who inserted himself into the official parade.[33]

Booth was standing on the south side of the police line near the exit to the portico. As Lincoln passed by and through the great doors to the outside, the actor suddenly broke through the police line and attempted to join the procession only a few feet behind the president. John W. Westfall, the nearest policemen, seized Booth by the arm, and a struggle ensued. "He was very strong," recalled Westfall, who shouted for help. "His resistance was so determined that he succeeded in dragging [me] from the line and at one time broke loose from [my] grasp."[34]

Benjamin B. French, the commissioner of public buildings, had charge of security. Seeing the disturbance, he ordered the huge doors shut. They closed, muffling a thunderous cheer for Lincoln as he emerged before the throng outside. Inside, the procession staggered to a halt. Westfall regained a hold on Booth, and other officers rushed to assist him. French came over, put both of his hands on Booth's chest, and ordered him back beyond the lines.

Scowling, Booth swore at French and "said he had a right to be there and looked very fierce and angry that we would not let him go on." For an instant French was taken aback. He ordered Westfall to release Booth. Neither man recognized the actor, and, given Booth's vehement demand to proceed, it occurred to the commissioner that the interloper might be one of the new congressmen recently arrived in the city. French did not yet know all their faces.

But Booth's manner was just too troubling. "He gave me such a fiendish stare," wrote the commissioner.[35] Westfall thought he was "a lunatic or out of his right mind—he looked so wild and seemed so unnecessarily excited." French decided to order him off. Booth was forcibly thrust behind the line and melted away among the spectators. The doors were reopened; the procession resumed. French gave no further thought to the incident. Not so the men who had grappled personally with Booth. One fellow officer who helped Westfall throw Booth back into the crowd said, "The intruder meant mischief."

A day or two after the assassination Westfall brought French a photograph of Booth. Studying it, the two realized for the first time who it was they had dealt with on inauguration day. "My God, what a fearful risk we ran," exclaimed the commissioner. "The man was in earnest and had some errand. My theory is that he meant to rush up behind the President and assassinate him." Added Marshal Lamon: "A tragedy was planned for that day which has no parallel in the history of criminal audacity. It is amazing that any human being could have seriously entertained the thought of assassinating Mr. Lincoln in the presence of such a concourse of citizens. And yet there was such a man in the assemblage."

Several weeks later Booth and Chester were having a drink at the House of Lords in New York City when Booth suddenly slapped his hand down on the table and blurted out, "What a splendid chance I had to kill the President on the 4th of March!" As Chester told it, "He said he was as near the President on that day as he was to me. I said something to him about being a foolish fellow, crazy or something of that nature. What good would it do him to commit an act like that? He said he could live in history if he committed it."[36]

Whether such an attack was planned for that day is a question whose answer was buried with Booth. Given his impulsive nature and the extraordinary occasion, it could have happened. "All that day he was saying queer, luny things," declared McCullough. Intruding upon Booth in his room, he found his old friend in a trancelike state. Booth's eyes were staring vacantly, his mouth working wordlessly. A large revolver sat before him.[37] But Booth had no death wish. He talked big and acted boldly, but to the very end he was determined to survive the consequences of his actions. As disturbed as he was becoming, he may have appreciated Lamon's observation that "nothing can be more certain than this—that the murder of Mr. Lincoln on that public occasion would have been instantly avenged. The infuriated populace would have torn the assassin to pieces, and this the desperate man doubtless knew."

Booth walked back from Capitol Hill to the National with Walter Burton, the hotel's night clerk. His composure had returned. Burton loved Lincoln and "in all his association with John Booth never knew that the actor was not also a loyal admirer of the President." He recalled, "I never heard Booth speak a word against Lincoln. I never suspected that he was less pleased [with the day's events] than I was."[38]

THE DAY AFTER the inauguration, Booth and Lucy ended their courtship. The timing suggests that his odd behavior had attracted the notice of her family. Or their parting may have been due to the fact that the Hales were leaving Washington. His term in the Senate having expired, Hale was moving his family to prepare for his new assignment as American minister to Spain.[39]

Booth and McCullough had shared their room during the inaugural crunch with John Parker Hale Wentworth, Lucy's first cousin. Wentworth proved a handy go-between for their courtship. Now he offered a final service. He handed Booth an envelope from Lucy. If there was a letter inside, it is long gone. The envelope survives. On it Lucy copied the celebrated lines from John Greenleaf Whittier's poem "Maud Muller."

> *For of all sad words from tongue or pen*
> *The saddest are these—It might have been.*
> *March 5th 1865*

Wentworth gave the envelope to Booth, who added his own sentiment just above Lucy's:

> *Now in this hour that we part,*
> *I will ask to be forgotten never.*
> *But in thy pure and guileless heart,*
> *Consider me thy friend, dear, ever.*
> *J. WILKES BOOTH*[40]

Congressman Bingham thought Booth's courtship of Lucy had been calculated in furtherance of his plot.[41] But evidence is abundant from the Booth and Hale families that the couple were seriously attached. Moreover, Lucy was not close to the Lincolns. As a source of information, she knew no more about the president's movements than any other belle in the city. Booth had better sources of intelligence, one of them a remarkable individual whose story has never been investigated in studies of the assassination.

Spiritualism was one of the more interesting social phenomena of the nineteenth century. The glad tidings of this movement—that the dearly departed were ever present and ready to offer comfort and advice to the living—were powerfully appealing. Critics denounced it as a superstition and a fraud, but the movement attracted great interest, amplified by the grief that the war brought to countless American homes. Spiritualist newspapers proclaimed the faith, and circles of believers established themselves in the leading cities. The Washington circle counted among its members a number of government officials. Warren Chase, a lecturer and missionary of the movement, thought the interest shown in spiritualism was greater in the capital than in any other place.[42]

Prominent among the mediums who served the movement was Charles J. Colchester.[43] This English-born spiritualist, alleged to be the illegitimate son of a duke, had remarkable powers. He could read sealed letters, cry out the names of visitors' deceased friends, cause apparitions to appear, and produce words on his forearm or forehead in blood-red letters. To the faithful he was an extraordinarily gifted intermediary with the other side. To skeptics he was a con man who employed sleight of hand, hypnosis, and sideshow magic in darkened rooms to fill his pockets at the expense of the troubled and the brokenhearted.

Still, spiritualism was in its adolescence, and until the movement was fully understood, who could say what it was that Colchester actually offered? The civil and military elite, from General Grant on down, all flocked to witness his manifestations.[44]

Mary Lincoln grew interested in the miracles of the séance table when her son Willie died in 1862. She met with a number of "spirit ministers" afterward.[45] Dutiful husband that he was, the president tagged along with her on occasion. It seemed prudent, and it could be entertaining. However, he was not a believer, referring whimsically to the spirit world as "the upper country." His secretaries Hay and Nicolay were indignant at claims that their chief took the hocus-pocus seriously.[46]

Colchester set up shop in Washington during the closing months of the war and before long was working his wizardry at the White House and the Soldiers' Home. There, at private sittings, the handsome young soothsayer mystified the Lincolns. The president's friend Noah Brooks, aware of the influence Colchester was establishing with the first lady, sought out the scamp, caught him cheating, and threatened him with arrest. Lincoln, intrigued with what he was seeing, determined to understand the material basis of these phenomena. He asked Colchester to submit to an examination by Joseph Henry, secretary of the Smithsonian Institution. The medium agreed, and a chagrined Henry reported back to the president that he had no immediate explanation for Colchester's phenomena.[47]

Colchester was trouble. Chronically short of cash, he was honest if he liked a client but admitted to Chase that "he often cheated the fools, as he could easily do it." Colchester struck Brooks at a séance. He tried to black-mail Mrs. Lincoln. And he drank. Asked out for a glass by friends, the convivial Colchester would reply that he must first consult the spirit world for guidance. With an earnest look he would slap his hand on a nearby lamppost, commune intently, then announce that the spirits had authorized a libation. A regular on the Washington social circuit, he soon met Booth.[48]

The actor's interest in spiritualism began in 1863 when his sister-in-law Molly died. He attended a number of séances with Edwin that year.[49] Later he was strongly attached to the remarkable Ira and William Daven-port, seeing the brothers in private séances as often as he could when their paths crossed his in 1864.[50] In addition Booth was friends with Lottie Fowler, the seer who prophesied within days the date of the assassination of Czar Alexander II of Russia in 1881.[51]

These facts provide a background to Booth's connection with Colches-ter, but one additional fact may explain it more fully. Besides his ability to contact the dead, Colchester was also a prophetic medium. He could foretell the future—an ability useful to Booth, who was beginning to think the unthinkable. The pair spent a considerable amount of time in each other's company, said George W. Bunker, the National's room clerk, and they often went out together. Bunker observed that Colchester was not merely Booth's friend. It was more than that. He was his "associate."[52]

One wonders (the record is mute on this point) what Colchester learned of Booth's plans. His actions suggest he was alarmed. For all his faults, Col-chester was only a master of misdemeanor—he had no felony in his heart—and to his credit he warned Lincoln of his danger. This became clear a few days later when someone urged Lincoln to be mindful of his personal safety. The president responded, "Colchester has been telling me that."[53]

While warning Lincoln was a stock-in-trade for mediums, here was one mystic in a position to know what he was talking about. Colonel Henry H. Wells, a top military policeman, was understandably interested in having a talk with Colchester after the assassination. Bunker, the room clerk, gave Wells a detailed description of the man and added that he had moved on to the Washington Hotel. But Wells was unable to find Col-chester there or anywhere else in the city. Brooks wrote, "I never saw or heard of him afterward."

Booth had a more serious problem than Colchester's big mouth. Arnold, who considered himself the most committed member of the team, was unhappy. "How inconsiderate you have been!" he wrote Booth not long after the inauguration. Arnold was tired of Booth's high-handed and uncommunicative manner. He also resented wasting time in Washington and deceiving his family about his activities. Arnold went on to complain that Booth, although a passionate private, was a poor commander. The actor promised "he would furnish all the necessary materials to carry out the project." But, Arnold complained, "I am, as you will know, in need. I am, you may say, in rags, whereas today I ought to be well clothed. I do not feel right stalking about with[out] means, and more from appearances a beggar."[54]

"We were sadly in want of money," confessed John Surratt, "our expenses being very heavy." As Harbin would later tell Townsend, "Booth had to provide the money to keep this band together, and they were all drinking, expensive people."[55] Booth had only twenty-five dollars left in his checking account at Jay Cooke & Company, Bankers, after the January plot fizzled. True, there was the four thousand dollars in bonds in Asia's safe, and there was the Canadian money. But the former were for his mother, the latter getaway money. To keep the plot going Booth borrowed five hundred dollars from Simonds, another five hundred from O'Laughlen, additional sums from Canning and McCullough, and still more from an unidentified party in Washington. He also traveled to New York City to raise cash.[56]

At the same time, two members of the abduction team were telling friends that they would soon be rich. Herold informed his cronies that he would shortly have "a barrel of money." Atzerodt declared to pals in Port Tobacco that "if he ever came back [here], he would be rich enough to buy the whole place." The greasy boatman also informed his sister Catherine that "she would either hear of him being hung or making a good deal of money—a fortune." Atzerodt seemed particularly boastful on the subject.

Booth, too, spoke of the money to be made in his undertaking. He brought it up as early as December 18, 1864. While pitching the abduction to Thomas Harbin, he stated, "There is not only glory, but profits in the undertaking." To Sam Chester, Booth promised "there would be money in it after the thing is done." Chester continued, "He said there was plenty of money in the affair; that if I would do it, I would not want again for as long as I lived, that I would never want for money."[57]

Was this salesmanship? Was it self-deception? Or was it evidence that the Confederate government promised Booth money to abduct or attack Lincoln? The South did fund all manner of secret service operations, like the compensation it provided late in the war to "bodies of men for the capture and destruction of enemy property on land and sea." Richmond authorities paid a man named Edward Frazor and his associates fifty thousand dollars for burning steamboats on the Mississippi River.[58]

As is often the case when facts on a topic are few, speculation has run rampant. To state the obvious, a president is not a steamboat, and it would be surprising if the bureaucrats who administered the rebellion had treated him like one. These men, Lincoln's political peers, were not fools. They understood and feared the principle of retaliation. Davis wrote Lincoln in July 1863 that "one cannot contemplate [reprisals] without a feeling of horror." Nevertheless, the frightening practice was "our only means of compelling the observance of the usages of civilized warfare." It restrained the belligerents, as Lincoln indicated when he told Norman B. Judd, the former minister to Prussia, "It is always possible for the other fellow to retaliate, and we have had to think of that in this war."[59]

Significantly, most of Booth's co-conspirators evinced no financial motive for their actions. Townsend, impressive in his knowledge of the conspirators and their motives, believed Powell was not in it for money, nor was O'Laughlen. Two of their comrades specifically denied any such thing for themselves. Surratt maintained that patriotic feelings alone motivated him, as did Arnold, who declared that he acted without "promise of pay or reward."[60] The latter never even heard his fellow plotters mention money.

There are less melodramatic interpretations of the money talk. It seems commonsensical that Booth would seek to energize members of the cadre like Atzerodt in such a manner. Booth's promise of twenty thousand dollars to the boatman clearly earned his allegiance.[61] As for Booth himself, it is always possible that something he heard in Canada led him to hope he might get a reward from a grateful Confederate government. It is equally possible that he intended to parlay the public acclaim that would come his way into wealth on the Southern stage.[62] Or it is possible that the actor, who had a great deal of ego tied up in making money, was just like many other people when the topic came up. The less he had, the more he talked about it.

The question of money is part of the larger issue of the relationship, if any, between Booth and the Confederate government. Federal authorities sought hard to prove one in 1865. They failed. In the 1980s able authors revived the charge, raising several valuable points. As the war went badly, the Confederacy grew frantic and engaged in increasingly irregular and desperate operations. This was at the time when southern officials were outraged in March 1864 by the Dahlgren raid on Richmond, regarded by the South as an attempt to murder Jefferson Davis. Rebel soldiers subsequently hunted Lincoln on occasion. There was the plan for a raid on the Soldiers' Home in the summer of that year. A few months later Captain Thomas N. Conrad, a Confederate agent, entered Washington to develop a scheme to seize the president. The former plan was aborted, the latter abandoned when Conrad saw how well Lincoln was guarded. It was roughly at this time when Booth commenced his intrigue with Harbin and Surratt, men who ran confidential errands for Davis and his secretary of state, Judah Benjamin. Surely, it was reasoned, the leadership knew and approved of Booth's undertakings.[63]

The key associates of Booth deny that this was the case, and their statements explain why the conspirators were broke. "This scheme of abduction was concocted without the knowledge or the assistance of the Confederate government in any shape or form," wrote Surratt, second only to Booth in the operation. "They never had anything in the wide world to do with it. In fact, the question arose among us as to whether after getting Mr. Lincoln, if we succeeded in our plan, the Confederate authorities would not surrender us to the United States again for doing this thing without their knowledge or consent." Similarly, though Booth told Chester that he felt assured of an assist from certain "parties on the other side" (probably meaning Harbin and his associates), he never said that the rebel government had sanctioned what he was doing.[64]

Booth wrote an extensive political tract justifying the abduction. Known from its salutation as the "To Whom It May Concern" letter, it detailed his alienation from the North, hatred of abolitionism, and determination to assist the South as its fortunes faded. Of exceeding interest is the letter's close. Booth signed himself as "a Confederate at present doing duty upon his own responsibility." The phrase "at present" suggested that he might seek an official connection with the rebels at a later date. The letter was written at the commencement of his plot in August 1864. He sealed it and placed it in Clarke's safe in Philadelphia. Later, possibly in

January 1865 (the final time he is known to have had access to the document), he deleted the words *at present*. The letter, discovered and published a few days after the assassination, read in its final edit "a Confederate doing duty upon his own responsibility."[65] Could anything be plainer?

The money crisis threatened their independence. Booth told Chester "that he was very short of funds—so very short that either himself or some member of the party must go to Richmond [in order] to obtain means to carry out their designs."[66] Arnold urged Booth to adopt just such a course. As Arnold reminded him diplomatically, it had been Booth's own initial inclination, expressed during their inaugural meeting at the Barnum City Hotel the preceding year. "I prefer your first query, go and see how it will be taken in R[ichmon]d," Arnold phrased his advice. "Do not act rashly or in haste." In the end Booth and Surratt decided to keep their own counsel. "We were jealous of our undertaking and wanted no outside help," explained the latter.

Surratt demonstrated the fierce independence of the conspirators in his reaction to the discovery of a rival conspiracy against Lincoln. The young courier was resting one evening in the reading room of the Metropolitan Hotel when several men came in. It was dusk, and the gaslights had yet to be turned on. Believing they were alone, the men began to talk about some plot parallel to Surratt and Booth's. Partially concealed behind a writing desk, Surratt became an uninvited but vitally interested earwitness to their conversation. He informed Booth, who said that he, too, was hearing whispers to the same effect. "It only made us all the more eager to carry out our plans at an early day for fear someone one should get ahead of us," recalled Surratt.

Advocates of a grand Confederate conspiracy, unable to discredit Surratt's characterization of the plot as an autonomous operation by freelance agents, simply ignore it. Yet it was independently confirmed by Arnold, who denied being a member of the Confederate Secret Service. "There never was any connection between Booth and the Confederate authorities," wrote Arnold in the 1890s. "The scheme originated in Booth's own visionary mind [and] Richmond authorities, as far as I know, knew nothing [about] it. I was in Booth's confidence and had anything existed as such, he would have made known the fact to me." Federal officials wanted a different answer, and one would think that if Arnold could have given it to them in good conscience, he would have done so. It would have put an imprimatur of legitimacy on his actions and lifted some of the opprobrium that embittered his later life.

Booth and Surratt frequently discussed their lack of funds. There was money out there; making it would be risky, but Booth found it necessary to attempt it. A prominent Washington druggist, whose name is unknown, had high-grade quinine for sale to the rebels. He turned the drug over to Booth, who carried it south hidden in horse collars. The two men shared the profits. On a single trip Booth earned one thousand dollars.[67] "Nights of rowing," Booth responded wearily when Asia asked about the roughness of his palms.[68] It was exhausting and dangerous work.

He attempted to discuss this with Clarence Cobb, a former schoolmate from Milton Academy with an interest in medicine. The friend refused to listen. Marylander though Cobb was, "I told him that I did not wish to know anything about it, as my sympathies were with the government," wrote the friend in 1885. Booth replied that he respected that and turned to a denunciation of Vice President Johnson.

Late on the night of March 15, 1865, Booth called a team meeting. The conclave was held at Gautier's, a restaurant on Pennsylvania Avenue popular with the after-theater crowd.[69] Money was no problem that evening. Booth reserved a private dining room, ordered a supper of oysters, wine, whiskey, and cigars, and reserved a hack for his guests' convenience. There was talk of oil deals, playing cards were in hand, and when waiter John Thomas Miles cleared the table and withdrew with his one-dollar tip, he thought a gambling party was about to get under way.[70]

This event was the first and only gathering of all the principal conspirators.[71] Arnold was present with O'Laughlen. It remained to be seen if the latter had been able to comply with Booth's wishes and bring the former along in a positive frame of mind. The two men had never met Powell or Atzerodt, so they were introduced. Surratt had brought Powell, and in life's rich irony the young Confederate wore Weichmann's blue military coat.[72] Herold rounded out the guest list. Too many people, thought Arnold.

It was well after midnight before their host got down to business. All was in readiness, Booth explained. They needed only to consider the roles of each at the theater. Arnold was on record as opposing any theater attempt as dangerously complicated. It was his opinion, as well as that of the very shrewd Confederate agent Thomas A. Jones, that Lincoln should be nabbed on one of his nightly walks, often taken alone, from the White House to the War Department building, a block to the west. The president could then be hurried through the White House garden to the relatively isolated Van Ness mansion nearby. This huge old home, owned by the elderly rebel sympathizer Thomas Green, a friend of Parr's, was available for their use. It had large vaults accessible by trapdoors. These had been dug out for use as a wine cellar and an ice house. Lincoln might be safely chilled there, too.[73]

New complications to any abduction effort had arisen in recent weeks, however. Surratt thought that "the government had received information that there was a plot of some kind on hand." This explained why it was constructing a stockade on the Navy Yard Bridge, the most expeditious route into southern Maryland and on to Richmond. He was confident the government was onto them. "The best thing we could do," concluded Surratt, "would be to throw up the whole project." Booth sat silently as Surratt spoke, but others around the table murmured in assent. Arnold added a salient point. He had come into the conspiracy with the sole motive of forcing a renewal of the prisoner exchange. The North was now permitting exchanges in cases of sickness and extreme hardship, so "the object to be obtained by the abduction had been accomplished," he explained.

These remarks might as well have been addressed to Gautier's mahogany sideboard, for all their effect on Booth. What would happen, he explained, was that Arnold would seize Lincoln in his theater box, and Booth and Atzerodt would handcuff him and lower him to the stage, where Powell would catch and hold him until everyone joined them and fled the building. They would then join Surratt and Herold, waiting as guides, beyond the Anacostia River. Then the plan was changed. Booth and Powell would seize Lincoln in the box, O'Laughlen and Herold put out the lights, Arnold hold the president onstage, and Surratt and Atzerodt stand ready beyond the bridge to hurry them through the countryside to the boat.

This was all folly, thought Arnold. It was perilously complex, unworkable, and foolhardy. "To me it seemed like [it] would lead to the sacrifice of us all without attaining the object for which we combined together." The plan was, in fact, irrational. Lincoln could not be hustled away in the presence of hundreds and hundreds of theatergoers, many of whom would be soldiers. How absurd the plan seemed outside the hothouse atmosphere of their well-lubricated meeting was shown a few months later after Arnold had been arrested for conspiracy and placed on trial. When Detective Eaton G. Horner recounted the conspirator's confession that his assignment was to grab Lincoln on the stage, incredulous laughter rippled through the courtroom. Despite the fact that his neck was being measured for a noose, Arnold had to laugh, too.[74] The idea was preposterous.

Tonight no one was laughing. Earlier in the evening Surratt and Powell had attended a play at Ford's, where they studied the layout from seats in the upper box customarily used by the president.[75] Now they sat like lumps, listening without dissent to Booth. Everyone else was equally silent. "No discussion was had about failure," stated Atzerodt, "and what to do in that case."[76] No one was thinking this through, wrote Arnold in his memoirs, "they being completely spellbound by the utterances of Booth, not looking at the consequences which would follow."

Exasperated, Arnold listened to no more. The thing could not be done, he declared forcibly. O'Laughlen was about to concur when Booth cut him off and growled at Arnold, "You find fault with everything concerned about it."

Arnold recalled, "I said no, I wanted to have a chance [of getting out alive], and I intended to have it—that he could be the leader of the party, but not my executioner. I wanted a shadow of a chance for my life."

Booth responded angrily, "Do you know you are liable to be shot [for breaking] your oath?"

"If you feel inclined to shoot me, you have no further to go," retorted Arnold heatedly. "I shall defend myself."

The men glared at each other. For a second it was unclear what would transpire. "Two stubborn natures had met," wrote Arnold, "and it looked very much as if the meeting would be dissolved with serious consequences attending it." More seconds passed, the antagonists calmed themselves, and order was restored. The theater idea was finished, however, and it would not be revived. The showdown ended what Arnold described as Booth's "only thought by day and, from his conversation, his frequent dreams by night."

Frustrated, Booth rose to his feet. Slamming his fist down on the table, he exclaimed, "Well, gentlemen, if the worst comes to the worst, I shall know what to do." Everyone at the table understood his statement as a threat to kill Lincoln, and the remark evoked alarm. "They had looked upon the plot as a melodrama and found, to their horror, that John Wilkes Booth meant to do murder," wrote a contemporary journalist.[77] No one had agreed to that game.

"I am opposed to it. I will not stay in it," exclaimed Surratt.[78] Others agreed, rising and reaching for their hats. Seeing he had gone too far,

Booth sought to calm them. "Too much champagne," he explained lamely. It was five in the morning before the exhausting and ill-favored conference came to a conclusion. Booth walked out into the chilly dawn with an ultimatum from Arnold on his mind. If the abduction was not attempted this week, the outspoken friend would sever all ties with the conspiracy.

The two scarcely spoke when they met that afternoon. Arnold stood about sullenly, Booth managed an apology of sorts, and the two shook hands. Arnold had to admit that Booth worked tirelessly on their behalf. "He was always busy and in motion," the fellow conspirator said. Harbin and Joseph Baden, his associate, were summoned from Virginia to stand by. With them came word that the roads and the time were propitious. Booth had Mathews dispatch a trunk, through intermediaries in Baltimore, to Dr. Mudd. It was filled with potted meat, sardines, crackers, flasks of brandy, and toilet articles. These were intended for the use of Lincoln and the abduction party on their flight. Booth wished to treat the president as respectfully as the extraordinary situation of his captivity permitted, or so believed Mathews, the chief conspirator's faithful friend and apologist.[79]

Arnold wanted action. Providentially it appeared. Campbell Hospital was a large military facility on Seventh Street at the northern boundary of the city. A collection of frame and canvas buildings, it served about 640 sick or wounded soldiers. The convalescents had an amateur acting troupe. Government officials attended its weekly shows, and professional actors dropped by occasionally to raise spirits with a free performance.[80] E. L. Davenport, Booth's old patron, and his partner, J. W. Wallack, promised to bring their company from the Washington Theatre on Friday afternoon, March 17, to perform the comedy *Still Waters Run Deep*.[81]

Lincoln had recently visited the hospital, helping himself to a slice of shortcake in the kitchen, and Booth showed up shortly afterward for a reconnaissance. The actor made himself agreeable, playing whist with Helen Cole, a nurse, and looking around.[82] Lincoln, he learned, would be present at Friday's performance.

Early on the afternoon of the seventeenth, St. Patrick's Day, Booth gave the long-awaited signal. Herold departed Washington in the buggy with the carbines to await the others in the country, while the rest of the party, mounted and well armed, headed out Seventh Street in pairs. Their route passed quickly from residential neighborhood to farmland, not as isolated as the road to the Soldiers' Home but acceptable terrain for a quick strike. Arnold and O'Laughlen were the first to arrive at the rendez-vous point, the brewer Louis Beyer's restaurant in a grove of trees near the hospital. After a short time Atzerodt and Powell rode up, followed by Booth and Surratt. The men pretended their encounter was accidental. Introductions were made, and hands were shaken.

While the party took a drink, Booth rode over to the hospital grounds. In the garden adjoining the large hall that served as chapel, lecture room, and theater, he found Davenport stretching his legs. Booth greeted him and asked, "Who is in the house? Did the old man come?"

Davenport said no, and Booth turned away. "It seems to me you are in a great hurry, John," the friend called after him.

"Yes," replied Booth. "I am trying a new horse, and he is rather restive."

Booth looked around. The hospital grounds were fenced, gated, and guarded. Had he walked into a trap? Alarmed, Booth returned immediately to the restaurant. He was highly excited and advised the party that "he feared our movements were being overlooked," wrote Arnold. Urging great caution, Booth ordered them to separate and return to the city by different routes.[83]

If the president actually intended to visit Campbell Hospital, it would have made for a busy afternoon. He was scheduled to take part in a ceremony at which Indiana soldiers presented O. P. Morton, their governor, with a rebel garrison flag recently captured at Fort Anderson, North Carolina. Shortly after 4:00 p.m. Lincoln emerged on the veranda of the National Hotel with Morton at his side. The large Southern banner was unfurled to display to the two thousand people who filled the street, the poet Walt Whitman among them. As the flag rolled out over the balcony, it caught on a gilded eagle mounted above the hotel's front doors. It took several tugs to free it. That a secession flag should be impeded by a national symbol caught Lincoln's attention, and he observed to laughter, "The eagle objected to having the flag put over it."[84]

Historians have heaped scorn on Booth for not knowing what anyone with three cents for the morning newspaper knew that day. While he was riding the countryside looking for Lincoln, the president was speaking at Booth's own hotel. Of course the actor knew this. He was back in town and in the crowd. As Lincoln's carriage rolled to a stop before the hotel doors, Booth pushed frantically forward to reach it. The press of the crowd threw him back. Thomas E. Richardson, a Booth friend, saw him retire in disappointment among the spectators.[85] From the veranda Governor

Morton saw him, too, as Booth, arms folded and face upturned, leaned against an ornate lamppost that was a local landmark and gazed up at Lincoln.[86]

"There are but few views or aspects of this great war upon which I have not said or written something whereby my own views might be made known." Lincoln began. "There is one—the recent attempt of our erring brethren, as they are sometimes called"—laughter rang out—"to employ the negro to fight for them. The great question with them was whether the negro, being put into the army, will fight for them. I have in my lifetime heard many arguments why the negro ought to be a slave, but if they fight for those who would keep them in slavery, it will be a better argument than any I have yet heard."

Richardson turned to Booth, who had joined him, and asked, "Don't you think Mr. Lincoln looks pale and haggard and much worn?" "Yes, he does," responded Booth. "Can we hear well from here?" The agent noticed that Booth looked more pallid than usual himself.

"I will say one thing with regard to the negro being employed to fight for them that I do know," Lincoln continued. "I know he cannot fight and stay home and make bread, too. One is about as important as the other to them. They have drawn upon their last branch of resources, and we can now see the bottom. I am glad to see the end so near at hand."

Booth had fixed Lincoln with an intense stare. His features twitched involuntarily, and "his face was the very embodiment of tragedy, every feature distorted [into] one of the most demoniacal expressions I have ever seen on the face of mortal on or off the stage," recalled Richardson. The agent was unable to look away. For five full minutes this bizarre display continued. Richardson thought at first that the actor was just hamming it up for the crowd. He was certainly drawing notice. Far from histrionic, however, this was something disturbingly real. Booth stood transfixed and transported. He did not even hear Richardson when the agent attempted to speak to him. When the ceremony concluded and Lincoln prepared to leave, Booth recovered himself and again attempted to approach the carriage. Again he was rebuffed.

"Three cheers for the old flag, three cheers for the president!" someone cried.

CHAOS REIGNED AT THE SURRATT HOUSE when Weichmann returned from work that evening.[87] Mrs. Surratt, weeping bitterly, kept repeating that her son had gone away and told her lodger he must do the best he could for his supper. Equally upset, Anna held a table knife in her hand and swore that she would kill Booth if anything happened to her brother. Weichmann stepped back. Having once been knocked flat by Anna when he attempted to steal a kiss, Fatty had a proper appreciation for the young woman's volatility.[88]

Distressed and confused, Weichmann retreated to his room. He had just settled down with Dickens's *Pickwick Papers* when the door burst open and John Surratt rushed in. The young man was still booted and spurred from the day's ride, and he seemed completely unnerved. Waving a small revolver around in his hand, he cried, "I will shoot anyone that comes into this room." He leveled the pistol at Weichmann. "My prospects are gone, my hopes are blasted," he exclaimed. "I want something to do. Can you get me a clerkship?"

In a few minutes Powell charged into the room. He said nothing but was clearly agitated. As he adjusted his waistcoat, Weichmann observed a large revolver on his hip.

Minutes later Booth appeared, riding whip in hand, and rushed frantically around the room in circles. Weichmann hardly knew what to make of this extraordinary parade, but his eye caught one odd fact. Powell's face was red with excitement. Booth's was white.

"You here?" declared Booth, catching sight of him at last. "I did not see you." Booth motioned, and the three men left the room and climbed the stairs to the small back attic where Powell slept. They stayed some thirty minutes and left the house together without a word to Weichmann.

The gang was bitterly disappointed with the outcome of the day's events, but if they felt that their identities had been revealed, it showed great sang-froid or thick-headedness that they were back in public the following evening. On Saturday, Booth played Pescara for John McCullough's benefit at Ford's. Surratt secured a pair of complimentary tickets from Booth and brought Weichmann. They found Herold and Atzerodt in the audience. Booth, in fine form, thrilled the house, which cheered and stamped the floor in its appreciation of his performance. Weichmann wrote, "Never in my life did I witness a man play with so much intensity and passion as did Booth on that occasion."[89] It would be Booth's last professional appearance.

The crew now scattered. Surratt went to Richmond as escort for a stranded rebel agent, then on to Canada with dispatches. Arnold and

O'Laughlen went to Baltimore, Powell went to New York, Herold went home, and Atzerodt went wherever Atzerodts go. Booth headed north.

The actor said it was time to lie low, and perhaps it was. For the past several weeks Weichmann had relieved his conscience by throwing out hints at his office about the strange activities at his boardinghouse. He mentioned Booth by name and identified him as a rebel sympathizer. Frightened by what he witnessed, Weichmann opened up, wondering aloud if the group didn't intend "the assassination of all the officers [of the government]."[90] Meanwhile, Powell was in trouble for beating a servant at the Branson house in Baltimore. He was arrested, named as a spy in the *Baltimore Sun*, and ordered north of Philadelphia for the duration of the war. The Floridian was subject to arrest on sight in Washington.[91] Meanwhile, Atzerodt aroused the interest of detectives in Baltimore by indiscreet talk about how he would soon be rich.[92] Finally, Augustus Howell, a rebel agent from Maryland, was arrested at the Surratt tavern in Prince George's County. This was worrisome to Booth because Howell was party to the plot. A federal detective, backtracking, showed up at the boardinghouse asking for Surratt.[93] The government was nibbling at the edges of the conspiracy.

Booth made it to New York without incident and ran into June. The elder brother had learned that John's oil adventures were not as successful as he had represented. When June scolded him for his deception, John replied that there was a woman whose love "was worth more to him than all the money he could make." The engagement with Lucy Hale was back on, and he had come to see her.[94] She was spending time in the city at the Fifth Avenue home of friends, taking Spanish lessons and preparing for her family's relocation to Europe in May.[95] Lucy would go with her parents, and what this meant for their relationship was unclear. It had everyone thinking, however. Herold told a friend that "the next time the boys heard of him he would be in Spain. There was no extradition treaty between the United States and Spain."[96]

Booth visited his mother. Mary Ann always feared her son would become a soldier and die for his country, and during the winter she dispatched June to Washington in an unsuccessful effort to retrieve him. Weeks of frightful dreams about him ensued. Now the worst seemed realized. John's talk and manner were highly alarming, and she was distraught as he departed. After he left, she wrote him a troubled letter. "I did part with you sadly, and I still feel sad, very much so.... I feel miserable enough," it read. "I never yet doubted your love and devotion to me, but since you leave me to grief, I must doubt it. I *am* no Roman mother. I love my dear ones before country or anything else. Heaven guard you is my constant prayer."[97]

When Booth returned to the capital on Saturday, March 25, he learned of the absence of Surratt and the arrest of Howell. Despite this, and despite the order he had given his men to disperse for a month, the increasingly erratic leader began anew. He summoned Powell from New York and telegraphed O'Laughlen in Baltimore to come with or without Arnold.[98] Monday's *Evening Star* announced that the president would attend an opera at Ford's Theatre. Mrs. Lincoln had secured tickets for Wednesday, March 29. Booth discovered this and informed O'Laughlen, "We sell that day for sure."[99]

Lincoln was not in Washington on March 29, however, having left the city the previous week to visit the front. He lingered there, not returning until April 9. Booth had failed again, and these repeated disappointments were wrecking his team. Yates and the boat party on the Potomac were exasperated with him. Herold spoke about traveling to the Idaho Territory to prospect for gold, Surratt dared not return to Washington for fear of the detectives, and Arnold was at his wit's end.[100] He poured out his unhappiness in a long letter to Booth, blasting his friend's poor leadership and urging him again to seek Richmond's approval for their plot. Anyway, "you know full well that the G[overmen]t suspicions something is going on there. Why not, for the present, desist?" Arnold sweetened the letter with a vague promise to rejoin Booth later, but for the present he announced that he was getting a job. The letter had an appropriate salutation— "Dear John."[101]

All was civil when Arnold and O'Laughlen met Booth at the National Hotel a few days later. O'Laughlen came to collect the five hundred dollars Booth owed him and brought Arnold along for backbone. Booth had promised that if the latest effort failed, he would give up the plot. Now, at last, even he seemed defeated. He told the two men that he intended to return to his profession. He was wrapping things up. He would sell the getaway buggy. When Arnold asked what he should do with their weapons, Booth replied he should keep them, sell them, or do anything he chose with them. The enterprise to abduct Abraham Lincoln was over.[102]

10

· · · ·

THIS ONE MAD ACT

"FOR SIX MONTHS we had worked to capture," Booth wrote. "But, our cause being almost lost, something decisive and great must be done."[1] While Booth made this decision rather late, the certain "something" had been in his thoughts for many months.

It stemmed from Booth's belief that Lincoln was a tyrant and a dictator. One element in this conviction was a historical coincidence. It so happened that during Booth's lifetime no president had ever had a second term. Prior to the constitutionally imposed limit of two terms that went into effect in 1951, it was easy for Lincoln-haters to believe that the president, seeking reelection, secretly yearned for kingship. George Washington, Thomas Jefferson, and Andrew Jackson had been attacked as aspiring monarchs when they took a strong hand, and their powers seemed paltry compared with Lincoln's. "You'll see," Booth told Asia, "you'll see that re-election means succession. This man's re-election, I tell you, will be a reign!" "That will never come to pass," she replied. "No, by God's mercy," exclaimed her brother, leaping to his feet. "Never *that*!"[2]

No less of a personage than Attila the Hun assured Lincoln "of regal power and a dictatorship for life." At least that was how the gossip of Lincoln's foes reported the word from the Georgetown spiritualist circle befriended by the president's wife.[3] The claim revealed their deep distress at the unprecedented manner in which Lincoln administered the government. "The most powerful monarch in Europe would not dare commit the outrages which have been put upon us by the Lincoln administration," wrote an editor in the president's hometown of Springfield, Illinois.[4] The draft, the income tax, military supervision of voting, arrests of civilians, confiscation of property, suppression of newspapers, trials by military commission, and travel and trade restrictions constituted an unparalleled expansion of federal power. Emancipation and the suspension of the writ of habeas corpus, a principle declared by Supreme Court Chief Justice Salmon P. Chase in 1868 to be the crown jewel of American liberty, were truly breathtaking measures.[5] These revolutionary steps would have been inconceivable to Lincoln himself before the war, but now he felt they were necessary to win it and preserve the nation. "So long as I have been here, I have not willingly planted a thorn in any man's bosom," Lincoln told a White House audience shortly after his reelection.[6]

Opponents were not consoled. New York Democrat Gaylord J. Clarke bemoaned "the gross usurpation and blundering incompetency of the vulgar joker who disgraces the chair once occupied by the immortal Washington. Abraham Lincoln [can say] with as much truth as the Roman monster Caligula, 'I have power in all things and over all persons.'"[7] Adversaries north and south joined in comparing Lincoln to Bonaparte, to Louis XIV, to Cromwell, to Caesar, or to the pharaohs. In this vein Josephine Seaton, daughter of the founding editor of the *National Intelligencer*, wrote to former president James Buchanan during the war that he had been the nation's last constitutional president. The future belonged to despotism. "We will never have another presidential election," lamented an Indiana Democratic Party leader, W. P. Davis, in 1864. "Lincoln will be proclaimed Emperor long before his term expires."[8]

A contemporary expression of the hatred of tyranny was the Latin motto "Sic semper tyrannis," meaning "ever thus to tyrants," adopted by Virginia in 1776 and placed on the obverse of the state's great seal. The motto appeared below a prostrate tyrant, his crown fallen away and his despotic chains broken, as he lay vanquished at the foot of Virtus. As an element of the great seal, the phrase could be seen on state commissions, grants of land, letters of credential, and the like. It appeared on the flag of the Richmond Grays at the John Brown execution in 1859 and then on the official state flag as the struggle for Southern independence opened. With the war, the words appeared widely, incorporated into the masthead design of the

Richmond Whig and, shortened to "Sic semper," in the lyrics of the pro-Southern anthem "Maryland, My Maryland."[9] A search of the Surratt house turned up a souvenir card depicting the arms of the state of Virginia, two Confederate flags and the lines "Thus will it ever be with tyrants/Virginia the mighty/Sic semper tyrannis." The card lay openly on a mantelpiece.[10]

Charles Lobdell of the La Crosse, Wisconsin, *Democrat* thought Lincoln deserved the full sic-semper treatment. Denouncing the president as a traitor and murderer, Lobdell wrote in August 1864, at about the time Booth got his abduction plot under way, that "if [Lincoln] is elected to misgovern for another four years, we trust some bold hand will pierce his heart with dagger point for the public good."[11]

This was an extreme statement even for a Copperhead newspaper, but it highlights a critical point: Lobdell himself did not attempt such a deed, nor did countless others. It was one thing for the disaffected and the rebellious to complain about arbitrary power and to employ phrases evocative of the struggle against George III, America's last king. It was quite another to put the doctrine of tyrannicide into practice. Lincoln was the duly elected president of a democratic nation. His survival through four years of war indicated that even his enemies understood this meant something. There was a line not to be crossed. Whether from motives of morality or prudence or fear, it stayed the hand of the assassin. William Seward's observation that "assassination is not an American practice or habit, and one so vicious and so desperate cannot be engrafted into our political system" seemed true—unless a hotheaded young Marylander of limited prudence, little fear, heroic instincts, and the certitude of a fanatic was handy.[12]

One will always wonder to what extent life imitated art that night at Ford's Theatre. Weichmann suggested it when he asked Booth shortly before the assassination why he was not playing. "He answered that the only play he cared to present was *Venice Preserved*." The reply meant nothing to Weichmann until years later when he read the work, the story of a plot to murder members of the Venetian senate for their betrayal of the people's liberty.[13]

The actor John M. Barron, an early friend of Booth's, was convinced that the plays in which Booth appeared were a disastrous influence on him. Barron referred to the unreality of the stage's idealized characters and gratifying endings. Contemporary plays were a fountain of inspiration for anyone wishing to give evil its due. Villains were always punished on the nineteenth-century stage, and heroes rewarded. Barron thought "the characters he assumed, all breathing death to tyrants, impelled him to do the deed."[14]

A previously unrecognized example of this is found in *Wept of Wish-ton-Wish*, dramatized from the 1829 novel by James Fenimore Cooper. This historical romance of the seventeenth-century frontier was a set piece for Maggie Mitchell, and Booth played it with her during his years in Richmond. As the Mohegan warrior Uncas, he put Conanchet, the leader of his enemies, to death. Central to the play was the mysterious Major Gough, one of the fugitive regicides who had condemned Charles I to death. Gough was sympathetically presented as a virtuous man who acted on his conscience. "What said I, in the judgment I pronounced, but that you were an enemy to England's liberty and peace, and so should die," Gough tells the king in a reverie.[15] Gough was inspired by the true story of William Goffe, one of the regicides who, tradition asserts, sought refuge in Judges' Cave on West Rock in New Haven. It was said that Goffe put the words "Sic semper tyrannis" at the cave's entrance.[16] "Heaven knows, I spoke but for my country, not myself," Gough says in the play.

While such examples might be multiplied, no play held higher pride of place in this grim genre than Shakespeare's *Julius Caesar*. The work seems uncannily apt as a template for Booth. Lincoln starred as Caesar, a leader seduced by power, with Booth as Brutus, a lover of tradition and of the old Republic that Caesar threatened. The casting seems eerily complete, down to the spiritualist Colchester, who warned Lincoln and thus reprised the role of the Soothsayer who gave warning to Caesar.

Shakespeare provided the would-be assassin with a flattering role model in Brutus.[17] The humanity and high motives of Caesar's assailant were compelling. His patriotism and decency were beyond question. An individual as noble as Caesar himself, Brutus furnished a ready symbol of legitimacy for the political murder that Booth had in mind. Importantly, however, Booth seems less like Shakespeare's Brutus than his Cassius, the play's principal supporting conspirator. Brutus loved Caesar. He was conflicted and "with himself at war" over his course of action. Cassius hated Caesar from the outset. It was he who drew Brutus into conspiracy, much as Booth drew others in with him. "Cassius symbolizes eternal justice," Booth said of his favorite character in the play.[18]

That Shakespeare's Brutus, and not history's, inspired Booth is plain. Asia wrote that her brother read Plutarch, the classical author who was Shakespeare's principal historical source for the play. But Booth's writings and conversations reveal no knowledge of the actual historical assassination. A letter he wrote justifying the Lincoln assassination illustrated this.

When Booth quoted Brutus on the necessity of assassination, he employed lines from act 2 of Shakespeare's play.[19]

"There is no doubt that his study of and meditation upon those characters had much to do with shaping [his] mental condition," thought his Richmond friend E. A. Alfriend. That was simply because, "in the 'book and volume of [an actor's] brain,' there live all the characters he has impersonated. And ever and anon *they rise up and salute him.*"[20]

One could misinterpret the significance of the stage influence, however. Chester, Mathews, and McCullough were actors. They often took the same roles as Booth, but none of them attacked the president. Nor did his actor-brothers, who shared not only the identical parts but the same parents and family environment. Clearly, to the framework of theatrical imagery and rationalization a further factor must be added. Critical in importance yet incalculable of measure, it was the element of Booth's unique personality. As Barron observed, the stage influence became destructive only when steeped in "the terribly earnest and emotional temperament" that his friend possessed.

One such element was the way that great men and women owned Booth's imagination. He worshipped figures of heroic mold, according to Harry Langdon. While he and Booth roomed together in Richmond, the latter read excerpts from John S. C. Abbott's biography of Napoleon I published in *Harper's Magazine* and grew enraptured with the French emperor. "It so excited him that he would go and kiss a picture or bust of Napoleon if he saw it anywhere, in a shop window, or a saloon, or among the properties of a theater," Langdon recalled.[21] His mother gave him a set of the Abbott volumes as a present.[22] The fact that Napoleon was a dictator was an inconsistency lost on Booth in his respect for the magnitude of the emperor's accomplishments.

On the darker side, Booth admired Charlotte Corday, who stabbed Jean-Paul Marat, the French revolutionary leader, in 1793.[23] And the more contemporary name of Felice Orsini worked magic on him. Orsini was an Italian nationalist who attempted unsuccessfully to assassinate Napoleon III in 1858, when Booth was in his first acting season in Philadelphia. Orsini was captured and beheaded. When news of his execution reached New York City, a nighttime procession in his honor through the principal streets of the city was given by two thousand people carrying torches and red flags. His memory so inspired Maryland's rebels that Cipriano Ferrandini, head barber at the Barnum City Hotel, Booth's Baltimore home away from home, offered himself in 1861 as his state's Orisini to kill Lincoln. Booth also admired Orsini but boasted immodestly that if he had undertaken such a job, he would not have bungled it.[24]

Booth had in his makeup the same "elements of character that have made or marred the fortunes of [these] heroes and adventurers," thought Michael F. Tiernan, who knew the actor in St. Joseph, Missouri, in 1864. Tiernan never knew a man more completely under the influence of such forces. It manifested itself in a desperate preoccupation with Lincoln. And there was that disquieting look familiar to anyone who has ever locked eyes with a fanatic. Tiernan called it "the kindling eye, full of emotion, which reflected the intensity of his feelings and sympathies."[25]

The price for such distinction was hefty, but Booth seemed ready to pay it. Several weeks before the assassination he told a friend that he would do "something which the world would remember for all time."[26] He said the same thing to a half-dozen other people. This craving was not comparable to any professional ambition. It was a longing for a renown that would outlive the grave and make him an ornament in the history of his country. The desire intensified as history swept past, leaving Booth to witness the greatness others achieved. Fueled by this ambition and fired by guilt over his failure to become a soldier, Booth burned to effect some defining act of heroism.[27] As he told friends in Baltimore, "he was going to do something that would bring his name forward in history."[28]

Asia noticed a curious childhood trait in her brother. Just as he had read in Bunyan's *Pilgrim's Progress*, where virtues and vices were embodied by human characters, Booth imagined inanimate challenges as physical opponents. A list of difficult spelling words, for example, John might imagine as a battalion of enemy soldiers. Her brother, personalizing a problem into a human adversary, would then attack it with a military spirit. "I always come out in victory," he told her. Pretending something is a reality in form and life, as he put it, "I lay my demon."[29]

Ralph Waldo Emerson noted that times of crisis push forward an individual from leader to symbol to icon.[30] Events had hurried Lincoln along this road, and Booth held him responsible for every wreck along the way. "Our country owed all our troubles to him," he wrote in his diary after the assassination.[31] A. W. Smiley, Booth's oil country friend, was one of many people struck by the actor's focus on Lincoln's person. While ferocious battles were being waged in the early summer of 1864, Booth said little on military matters, but he constantly expressed a hatred of Lincoln as bitter as if the president were a personal foe. Booth fixed the depth of his antagonism in Smiley's mind by offering the vivid statement "I would rather have my right arm cut off at the shoulder than see Lincoln made president again."[32]

It is hardly surprising that Booth daydreamed about attacking the president long before he gathered the courage to do it. At a rehearsal in Chicago in 1863, Booth exclaimed, "What a glorious opportunity there is for a man to immortalize himself by killing Lincoln!"

The remark ignited a debate. "What good would that do?" McVicker, the theater's manager, asked.

Booth responded with a quotation. "'Fame not more survives from good than evil deeds./The ambitious youth who fired the Ephesian Dome/ Outlives in fame the pious fool who reared it.'" The lines referred to Herostratus, who set fire to the Artemision at Ephesus in 356 BCE in order to gain renown. The quotation was widely familiar from act 3 of Colley Cibber's adaptation of *Richard III*.

"Well, who was that ambitious youth?" McVicker continued. "What was his name, John?"

"That I don't know," sputtered Booth.

"Then where's the fame you speak of?"

Perplexed, Booth responded only that "though the name was lost, the record of the deed would live throughout all time." There was immortality in such acts, he felt assured.[33] Returning to the topic on a subsequent occasion in Cleveland, he insisted to a friend that "the man who killed Abraham Lincoln would occupy a higher niche of fame than George Washington."[34]

AS THE YEAR of 1865 got well under way, Booth seemed more unsettled than ever. He was moodier, edgier, and increasingly erratic. He slapped away the hand of a federal officer whom Stuart Robson wished to introduce. He snubbed Jacob Cuyler of Albany, with whom he once had been intimate. He threatened George Wren of Marshall Theatre days and then smiled and spoke sweetly to him the following day.[35] "I hardly know what to make of you this winter," wrote Joe Simonds, "so different from your usual self. What is the matter?"[36]

Even the devoted Simonds fell victim to reproach. When Chester remarked over drinks at a chophouse that he heard Booth had made eighty to one hundred thousand dollars in oil, Booth lashed out at his former partner. If it had not been for Simonds, Booth snapped, he could have made twice that sum.[37] Similarly, he grew angry with Harry Ford, a younger brother of John T. Ford whose admiration for Booth was boundless. No more was heard of Booth's promise to celebrate Harry's twenty-first birthday with a benefit performance after the two quarreled over politics in Mathews's room at the Petersen house.[38] Booth was snarling at his best friends.

Chester touched a nerve mentioning money. "My beloved precious money," Booth once said.[39] Most people thought he was rich, and it flattered him to let them believe it, but he had much less than anyone knew. Recently Booth had suffered a financial blow so severe even family members could hardly drag the truth out of him. The theatrical wardrobe he left in Montreal for shipment to Richmond was consigned to the Canadian schooner *Marie Victoria*. En route to Nassau, the ship wrecked near Bic on the Lower St. Lawrence River. The captain abandoned ship, and salvers helped themselves to the waterlogged residue. What had been a magnificent theatrical wardrobe was left a molder of ruined costumes, boots, caps, doublets, gloves, and piles of playbooks with Booth's own carefully written-out stage directions. The product of years of work and accumulation disappeared overnight. An authority stated that the original value of the cargo ran into the thousands.[40]

If one adds to this sum the six thousand dollars spent in the oil fields and the cost of the abduction effort, estimated to total between six and ten thousand dollars, it can be seen that Booth lost most of his fortune in the final months of his life.[41] In a manifesto penned at the outset of the abduction effort, Booth stated that when he finally went south, he was willing to "go penniless to her side." Intended as a literary flourish, the words had become a hard truth.[42]

Not surprisingly he was drinking more than ever. Powell and Weichmann, Harbin and Mathews, Mudd and the Fords—all of them commented on it. Jeannie Gourlay of Ford's was right to say that Booth was no barroom loafer, but, seen over the course of years, the change in his habits from the relatively abstemious Richmond days was troubling. The billiards champ John Deery saw Booth tipple brand freely at his bar and billiards hall above the National Theatre. Deery observed, "It was more than a spree." Unfortunately, Booth never seemed to get drunk. Liquor energized him. It worked like an accelerator, not a brake. It fired his volatility. McCullough believed it brought out the bandit in him.[43]

WHEN THE EXPRESS TRAIN finally crossed the international border into Canada, James Gordon lost all restraint. "Hurrah for Jeff Davis and the

Southern Confederacy!" the lanky Confederate colonel cried aloud. He turned to face the federal detective who had followed him from New York City and said, "The next time you come around close to me, I will stab you to the heart." So ended an exhausting six weeks that commenced when Gordon, returning from a secret mission in Europe, was captured on a blockade-runner at Fort Fisher, North Carolina, on January 25, 1865. Posing as a Scottish traveler, he got loose in the North and commenced a cat-and-mouse game with federal agents. Safely out of their reach at last, Gordon made his way to Montreal. He checked into the St. Lawrence Hall and reported to his fellow Mississippian Jacob Thompson, who was his wife's uncle, for orders.[44]

"I met Wilkes Booth in Montreal," Gordon wrote, "and as he sympathized with the South in her struggle, we became intimate friends on a brief acquaintance."[45] Gordon was developing a plot to abduct Lincoln and hold him as a hostage to force peace talks. Booth had taken the overnight train up from New York to discuss the matter with Gordon and receive his benediction to pursue the project. Assassination was not discussed. The men parted with kind words and hearty handshakes, Gordon later acknowledging that he failed to see the desperate and revengeful spirit raging in his new associate.[46] Their meeting would weigh on the consciences of those involved. Jacob Thompson told a confidential friend in postwar years "that he would be sorry to the day of his death that he ever had anything to do with the kidnapping plot, as he felt that possibly had it not been for such a thing, the assassination might not have occurred."[47]

Booth traveled on to Boston and was there on April 5, 1865. "He was in a most unsettled frame of mind," wrote his actor-friend McKee Rankin, who spoke with him at the Parker House.[48] As the city celebrated the capture of Richmond two days earlier, Booth expended his energy in a basement shooting gallery near the hotel. He fired over his shoulder and under his arm, then capped the performance with an amazing throw shot between his legs. It hit the target dead center. Moody and misanthropic, Booth declared that he hoped to put his skills at the service of the faltering Confederacy.[49] His fellow marksman Joseph H. Borland, a commercial traveler from Pittsburgh, had Southern sympathies of his own, and Booth confessed to him a hatred of Lincoln so intense that Borland said it had the feeling of insanity.[50]

The actor made two additional stops in Boston. Calling at Orlando Tompkins's drugstore, Booth presented Lody (as he called him) with a bloodstone ring and a request that he wear it in remembrance of their friendship.[51] "I may never see you again," he told the druggist. It sounded like a farewell, as did a stop at the Boston Theatre, where Edwin was engaged.

"Well, Jim," Booth said to Jim Brown as the young man sat with Edwin in his dressing room, "Richmond has fallen at last. What do you think of it?"

"Yes, poor Richmond," replied Brown, who grew up in the city and had family there.

"[Are you] sorry, you rascal?" Edwin broke in. "You ought to be glad. It has been a great blessing to mankind that it has fallen."[52]

Politics again. "You and I could never agree upon this question," John said, his last words to his brother. "Goodbye, Ned."[53]

One could not reason with Edwin, John complained to Chester over ale and Welsh rabbit at the House of Lords in New York. Booth was talking loudly, drinking heavily, and telling stories about his brother. He mentioned their terrible fight the previous summer when Edwin threw him out of the house for expressing his opinions. Months had passed, but that still rankled. How pathetic to be unable "to express my thoughts or sentiments even in my own home."[54] It was on this occasion that Booth also mentioned to Chester the opportunity he had had to kill the president on inauguration day.

Chester changed the topic to a ring that Booth kept kissing. Sam pried out the fact that Booth was engaged to be married, and he even learned Lucy Hale's name. Since Booth had a reputation as a professional bachelor, Chester laughed at the thought—"I presumed that was another of his crazy ideas"—but Booth assured Sam that this was serious. Information about the engagement is conflicting. The final report from Boston said that John and Lucy broke up over his political extremism. This explained why Lucy was leaving her purported fiancé behind as she departed for Spain with her family. Their sailing date was announced as May 10, John's twenty-seventh birthday.[55] While this sounds like a breakup, Booth's family believed otherwise. Asia understood that Lucy intended to return after one year and marry him, and she added that Edwin later received heartbreaking letters from Lucy expressing her devotion to John.[56]

Chester was ready for this peculiar outing to end. The tab was called for, and Chester offered to split the bill. Booth would not hear of it. "Petroleum pays for this," he boasted.

BOOTH CHECKED BACK into the National Hotel on April 8. In the parlor of the Surratt house he reacted excitedly to Weichmann's jibe that the fall of Richmond meant the end of the Confederacy. "No, it is not gone up yet," he argued. Taking out a map, Booth showed Weichmann the routes by which Lee and General Joseph Johnston, commander of a rebel army in North Carolina, could get to the mountains and continue the fight.[57]

Nevertheless, prospects were bleak, and Booth wept over the South's reverses. Asked to take a drink by a friend, the actor readily agreed. "Anything to drive away the blues," he said.[58] His increased drinking, irritability, fatigue, restlessness, bouts of silence, and mood swings were classic signs of depression. So was his difficulty concentrating, shown when he asked Henry Merrick, a clerk at his hotel, whether the year was 1864 or 1865. The question was so absurd that Merrick thought Booth was joking.[59] Booth also experienced sleep disturbances. One night McCullough was awakened by tears falling from the eyes of someone standing over him. It was Booth. "Why, what is the matter?" McCullough exclaimed. "My God," Booth responded in a pathetic tone, "my God, how peacefully you were sleeping. I cannot sleep."[60]

While Booth tended his torments, a "Mr. Kincheloe" passed the hours in a third-story room at the Herndon House near Ford's Theatre. Surratt had arranged lodgings for this individual, whom he described to the landlady as a delicate gentleman whose uncertain health required that his meals be delivered to his room. The odd thing was that the purportedly enfeebled guest fell on his food like a hungry wolf. The waiter who brought the meals thought the man could have easily eaten a small pig, bones and all. The invalid, if he may be so described, was Lewis Powell, back from New York, and the delicacy of his situation was legal, not physical. Liable for arrest on a laundry list of charges, the young man sat and awaited his next misadventure with Booth.[61]

It was quick in coming. Powell was the only conspirator whose hatred of Lincoln approached his own, so Booth urged the hotheaded Southerner to murder the president. While later a prisoner, Powell informed Thomas T. Eckert, acting assistant secretary of war, that one night he armed himself for that purpose and hid in the shrubs along the brick walkway between the White House and the War Department. Seeing Lincoln approach in company, he fled. Booth suggested the direct approach. Send in a card requesting a moment of the president's time, and when admitted, slay him on the spot. When Powell spurned the idea, the actor berated the combat veteran as a coward.[62]

The laurels of Brutus were costly, and there were moments when Booth seemed willing to let others earn them. Robert E. Farrell was a teenager from Canada who shared Booth's love of horses. He fought on both sides during the war and was—like Powell—an alumnus of the fierce Mosby school of partisan warfare. Whether his presence in Washington was coincidental or part of some operation has never been determined. Farrell was to shoot Lincoln as the president rode by in a carriage. The young man proved capable of murder, as his later life showed, but he lost this opportunity when the president did not appear as expected.[63] Farrell's association with Booth escaped notice, but it explains an intriguing remark Powell made to Eckert. The young Floridian steadfastly refused to implicate others in his misfortune, saying of the federal dragnet only, "All I can say about that is that you have not got the one-half of them."

IF BOOTH ACTUALLY did read Plutarch, he might have remembered the ancient author's admonition that the success of any great enterprise requires one indispensable ingredient—time. By April 1865, the clock had run out for the South. Richmond was taken, and Lee, pressed at every turn by Grant, fled west. Lincoln, who had been visiting with the army for the better part of two weeks, entered the shattered Southern capital on April 4. "This must be President Davis' chair," he said, sitting down at the desk of the fugitive Confederate chief executive.[64] He returned to Washington by steamer on April 9 and during the night learned the news of Lee's surrender. The following morning church bells rang, and cannon at the forts encircling the city spread the word that the end was at hand. "The streets were in jubilee over the glorious news," wrote Secretary Seward's daughter Fanny in her diary. "All department employees had a holiday—happy people, marching about with flags and bands of music."[65] Bonfires and torches extended the glorious day into night for the crowds of excited citizens who surged along the avenues with shouts and serenades.

Lincoln's Richmond tour provoked Booth. For some reason, he believed the president threw a leg ostentatiously over the arm of Davis's chair and fouled his office by spitting tobacco juice, neither true. A few days later, when prisoners from the rebel capital arrived in Washington, one group marching past the War Department was stoned and abused by onlookers. Police broke up the assault and scattered the culprits, but Booth was enraged over the mistreatment of these defenseless men. He spoke of it with great bitterness and excitement on the morning of the assassination.[66]

Distressing as these events were, the news from Appomattox was a catastrophe. "Lee should *never* have given up his sword," he declared to Harry Ford. "I don't like the way he surrendered." Since Lee received the sword for the defense of Virginia in a solemn ceremony at the Capitol in Richmond, he told Harry, he should have died upon it. The actor spoke of Lee as if he were now an enemy, telling a friend "the whole Southern Confederacy was managed by a set of cowards."[67]

Booth, with Powell and Herold in tow, joined a throng besieging the executive mansion on the evening of Tuesday, April 11.[68] "It was a dark night and rain was falling," recalled Joshua Brigham, one of two thousand people in the audience to hear the president's first formal response to the rebel collapse. "Hundreds of umbrellas massed together made an imperfect covering for the shivering crowd. The dim lights from the outdoor gas jets and from the mansion gave a weird appearance to the occasion, and the hollow sound of raindrops falling upon the canopy of umbrellas accentuated the strangeness of the scene."[69]

Around 8:00 p.m. Lincoln emerged at a second-story window under the north portico of the mansion. "The White House was brilliantly illuminated, and the figure of the President stood out in full relief to the immense crowd below, who stood in the darkness to listen to his speech," wrote Clara Harris, the daughter of a New York senator who stood with Mrs. Lincoln at a nearby window.[70] Shoot him, Booth ordered Powell. "No, I will not do it," Powell replied. Booth argued that the crowd, which filled the north lawn and stretched back onto Pennsylvania Avenue, was so large he could escape detection. Insisting it was too risky, Powell walked off.

If the audience contained any rabble wanting rousing, they were disappointed. Lincoln had no stump speech for them. His agile mind was already at work on postwar problems, and he served up common sense on his reconstruction efforts in Louisiana. After the ordeal of the past four years, however, nothing could be amiss between orator and audience on this long-awaited night. The celebrants would have cheered if Lincoln merely thrust an arm out the window. It was victory's sweet moment. "Gloom had given way to light and hope," wrote a Chicago reporter. "The Union had been preserved, and it was a triumph for Abraham Lincoln if for any man."[71] The president, recalled T. R. Fitch of Boston, appeared, "through the mist of my moistened eyes, in a halo of glory." The rays of light streaming from the large window through the evening's mist seemed to give Lincoln a divine aura.[72]

To avoid any misunderstanding of his views, Lincoln prepared written remarks. He read them by the light of a candle held by Noah Brooks; Tad, at his father's feet, collected the pages as the president dropped them. Among the vexing issues upon which Lincoln touched was black voting. It would have been morally indefensible for the government to deny suffrage to African American soldiers, who helped preserve the nation, when peace would bring demands to reenfranchise their former masters, who sought to divide it. Aware of that fact and recognizing the dissatisfaction of some "that the elective franchise is not given to the colored man" in Louisiana, Lincoln stated, "I would myself prefer that it were now conferred on the very intelligent and on those who serve our cause as soldiers."

Lincoln's remarks snapped the last line holding Booth to the ground. "That means nigger citizenship," Booth muttered to Herold. "Now, by God! I'll put him through." From this moment on, Herold later told his attorney Frederick Stone, Booth was determined to kill the president. It would only be a matter of opportunity. When the two of them caught up with Powell, Booth uttered a prophecy of his own. "That is the last speech he will ever make."

Race was consuming him. "We are all slaves now," he informed Harry Ford and two staffers in the box office of the theater the next day. Booth had always viewed African Americans with a dismissive condescension, but he was completely unsettled by the change in their status produced by the war. He was shamed, he told Harry, to see black soldiers guarding prisoners passing through Washington in transit to camps in the North. "We are all slaves now."

Harry, who enjoyed twitting Booth, replied that his comment made no sense. Hadn't Lee himself wanted black soldiers for the Confederate army? "If a man were to go out and insult a nigger now," retorted Booth, "he would be knocked down by the nigger, and nothing would be done to the nigger." Thomas Raybold, who helped out with ticket sales at the theater, interjected that in that case he should not insult one. When Booth kept harping on the topic, the men turned their attention elsewhere, and the actor wandered away.[73]

"Booth's hobby" was what Mathews called Booth's morbid fixation on Lincoln. The hobby deserved a far more menacing name. "Somebody ought to kill the old scoundrel," Booth said to E. A. Emerson the day before the assassination. As he held Emerson's cane at either end behind his head and across his shoulders, he snapped it to pieces in a violent motion.[74] Booth would pay Lincoln for betraying the prewar Union. And, as his cry of revenge at the theater would indicate, he also intended to punish the North as a whole. "What I want, and I am as good a Union man as anyone, is peace," he said. "I can't see why there should be such great rejoicing."[75] The North's gloating was a contemptible kick of a wounded brother. Why should it celebrate while others wept? Why should it not share the pain and humiliation he and others like him felt? "It's impolitic to goad an enemy to madness," he wrote in a rare moment of self-awareness.[76]

Despite his obsession with Lincoln, Booth was still rational enough to understand that the president's death must be part of a greater whole if it were to help the remnants of the rebellion. On Thursday, April 13, 1865, Booth pushed his way into the office of C. D. Hess, manager of Grover's Theatre, and urged him to invite Lincoln and his key subordinates to a performance. Booth seemed particularly anxious "that Mr. Lincoln should be attended by his cabinet advisors," Hess recalled. Booth's manner was uncharacteristically intrusive—he interrupted the reading of a play—but it reminded Hess that he had intended to invite the president for the night of April 14. The manager wrote an invitation addressed to Mrs. Lincoln, as was his custom, and a messenger, Thomas Quantrille, set out with it to the White House.[77]

Sending Atzerodt to snoop around the Kirkwood House, where Vice President Johnson lived, Booth and Powell scouted the home of Secretary of State Seward on Lafayette Square near the White House. Seward had fractured his jaw and broken an arm in a nasty carriage accident on April 5. He was confined to bed, and George F. Robinson, a convalescent soldier, was assigned as his night nurse. Robinson noticed Powell at the dining room window and investigated. The young Southerner explained that he wished to know how Seward was feeling, leading Robinson to conclude he was just a solicitous family friend.[78] Meanwhile, Booth was cooing questions and pitching woo to Margaret Coleman, Seward's housekeeper. She was a pretty Irish lass, and Booth was of a mind to give her his diamond pin. Margaret rather liked Powell's looks, however. "As big as two men," she said, "he was very handsome."[79]

A grand illumination of the capital occurred Thursday night. Fireworks boomed, flags waved, bands played, and steam fire-engine whistles screamed. By prearrangement, lanterns, lamps, and gas jets were turned on at government offices, hotels, shops, and homes throughout the city. At City Hall as many as sixty tallow candles decorated some individual windows. The word *PEACE* dazzled forth in fiery letters on the front of the War Department building. Other buildings were similarly illuminated, many with patriotic mottoes or devices. Two dozen large bonfires added further brilliance to the scene. The principal avenues looked like rivers of flame to the thousands of admiring men, women, and children who moved along them. "The city was literally a blaze of light from eight to ten o'clock in the evening," one reporter observed. To soldiers stationed at the circle of lonely forts surrounding the city, "it must have seemed as though Washington was on fire."[80]

Booth was stupefied by the celebration. He told a fellow guest at the National that he hoped the candles would start fires and burn every house in the city to the ground. "I would rejoice at the sight," he said, adding self-consciously, "I guess I'm a little desperate. Do you know I feel like mounting my horse and tearing up and down the streets, waving a Rebel flag in each hand?"[81] He gave his mother a more restrained reaction. "Everything was bright and splendid," Booth wrote her in a letter headed two o'clock on the morning of April 14. "More so in my eyes if it had been a display in a nobler cause. But so goes the world. Might makes right."[82]

It has never been determined where Booth spent that night, if he slept at all. He breakfasted late at his hotel. About noon he appeared at Ford's to check his mail. Harry Ford was at the lobby door. Seeing him approach, Harry declared loudly enough for all to hear, "Here is a man that don't like General Lee." Booth rose readily to the bait and said again that Lee should not have surrendered. "General Lee is a good general," Ford snapped, "and I guess he knows what he ought to do."

Earlier in the day the White House had reserved the state box for the Lincolns and General Grant for the evening. Booth had pestered Harry for weeks with inquiries as to when "the old bugger" would be in attendance, so Harry kept after him. "The President is going to be here tonight with General Grant. They've got General Lee here as a prisoner," he teased. "We're going to put him in the opposite box."

Booth looked startled. "Never!" he cried. "Lee would not let himself be used as Romans used their captives and be paraded." It was a jest, Harry assured him, but Lincoln *was* coming. James R. (Dick) Ford, Harry's elder brother, who ran the theater's business affairs, had already given the tickets to a messenger from the executive mansion.[83]

Booth spun the cardboard plan of the house around. Sure enough, boxes seven and eight, joined together to make the large State Box on evenings when the Lincolns were in attendance, were crossed off. A note in pencil indicated that the president and party were expected. Booth showed no discernable excitement at what he saw.[84]

Breaking the seal on a letter from his morning mail that Raybold handed him, Booth turned away and settled on the gallery steps. It was a letter of four or eight pages, evidently written in a female hand. Booth looked up several times and laughed while reading it. "The damned woman," he was heard to remark. Booth was gone the next time Ford looked.

Down Tenth Street Booth ran into Dick Ford, who had been out to see about advertisements and decorations for the evening. With Ford was John F. Coyle of the *National Intelligencer* and Major Thomas Donoho, a friend of Booth's father. The actor renewed his lamentations over the surrender, then asked abruptly what would happen if Lincoln and his cabinet were swept away by bold hands. "What would be the result of an earthquake?" Donoho replied. Coyle chuckled and added, in one of the most ill-considered remarks of the century, "They don't make Brutuses nowadays."[85]

The next hours seemed like a blur. Booth dropped in on Mrs. Surratt, who was going to her country place on business, and asked her to tell her tenant Lloyd to ready the weapons secreted there since March. He called at the Kirkwood House for Vice President Johnson, an apparent attempt to learn his whereabouts. And he rented a saddle horse from a livery stable near the National Hotel. Little wonder that when Merrick asked him later if he had made a thousand dollars that day, Booth replied, "No, but I have worked hard enough to have made ten times that amount."[86]

Sometime during the afternoon Booth pulled to hand several sheets of ordinary business stationery and wrote a letter defending his intentions. He addressed it to Coyle, whose conservative politics and sympathy with the South were well known. The missive was about three pages in length. According to John Mathews, the only person ever to read it, the letter had the tone of a run-of-the-mill Copperhead editorial. Only the concluding paragraph was portentous. "For a long time I have devoted my energies, my time and money to the accomplishment of a certain end," wrote Booth. "I have been disappointed. Heartsick and disappointed, I turn from the path which I have been following into a bolder and more perilous one. Many will blame me for what I am about to do, but posterity, I am sure, will justify me." Booth signed his name and added those of Powell, Herold, and Atzerodt, "men who love their country better than gold or life." Booth sealed the letter, stamped it, and pocketed it.[87]

About four in the afternoon Booth rode his rented horse down Pennsylvania Avenue. Seeing Mathews by the curb, he headed over for a few words with him. Some 440 prisoners from General Richard Ewell's corps captured on the retreat to Appomattox at Sailor's Creek on April 6 had just passed by. The bedraggled rebels attracted much attention—although little hostility in this instance—as they trudged along. There were even a few good-natured remarks shouted to them by Union men relieved to see the end of the war. Other spectators averted their eyes. It was painful to see the broken looks of so many gaunt and exhausted warriors who had fought to the end.[88]

Booth watched this spectacle in horror. If he had looked closely, he would have seen much more than he wanted. In the group was Richmond's local defense force. Friends from the Confederate capital were present, even members of the old Richmond Grays. There was John Pitt, whom Booth had accompanied to Charlestown at the time of the John Brown affair. There, too, was their old captain Wyatt M. Elliott, now a rebel lieutenant colonel, who had allowed Booth to join the unit and witness Brown's execution.[89] The funeral march of Booth's world was in progress.

Having never been on a battlefield, Booth had not seen a Confederate army in defeat or surrender, and the grim parade stunned him. Placing a hand upon his forehead, Booth cried out to Mathews, "Great God! I have no longer a country! This is the end of constitutional liberty in America."

Gathering the reins of his horse in his left hand, Booth leaned over and with his right hand clasped Mathews so firmly that he felt Booth's nails dig into his arm. Mathews could tell he had been drinking, but he was not drunk. He was highly excited, hence "pale as a ghost."

Booth had a favor to ask. "Perhaps I may leave town tonight, and I have a letter here which I desire to be published. Please attend to it for me unless I see you before ten o'clock tomorrow; in that case I will see to it myself." Booth handed the letter to Mathews, who put it in the pocket of his frock coat.[90]

Booth summoned the faithful few to an eight o'clock meeting at the Herndon House.[91] Lincoln had proven impossible to catch. "It's no use to try any longer," he explained. Wheeling around, he declared that they must kill him. "It would be the greatest thing in the world," he enthused. But there could be no botching the job. "I'll take the 'Old Fox' myself."[92]

His announcement did not surprise Powell. The two men were like knife and sheath. "Booth was the only one in earnest," Powell knew. Herold was a little blabbermouth, "the rest women and babies."

"You take Seward," Booth told him. Powell did not flinch. During his years in the army a conviction had grown on Powell that a deep dishonor had been done to the South. As part of that wound he believed— incorrectly—that he had lost both of his brothers in the war. Seward's death would help redress that terrible imbalance and perhaps bring a measure of peace to himself and his homeland. Powell would do whatever Booth wished. He had no particular animus toward the secretary, but "he was sworn to perform the duty allotted to him," he later explained, "and that was his portion of the work."

Herold had an idea. Physicians were trooping in and out of the Seward home. Dr. T. S. Verdi had called three or four times the previous day. The former pharmacy clerk explained to Powell that he could gain access to the house by posing as a deliveryman with medicines from the doctor.

"You take Johnson," Booth ordered Atzerodt. The vice president's hotel room was the first one on the right-hand side at the landing on the second floor of the Kirkwood. Nothing could be easier than reaching the door of "the dirty tailor from Tennessee," as Booth called him. The resourceful Herold had obtained a letter to Johnson from a printer. He said that the vice president could be approached under the pretext of delivering it.

In ordering the blockade-runner to kill Johnson, Booth completely mistook his man. "Atzerodt talked valiantly while the rum was in his throat, promised gloriously, galloped fiercely, and looked daggers," joked his attorney William E. Doster, but he was a coward in the trenches. He was known in Port Tobacco for jumping out a tavern window to avoid a fight. Doster later produced witnesses who testified that Atzerodt, despite fierce mien and manner, was a harmless fellow. He would never have attacked the vice president or anyone else. "I told [Booth] I would not do it," he said, "that I had gone into the thing to capture, but I was not going to kill."

Then he was a fool, countered the actor. "It was death for every man that backed out," Booth said. Furthermore it was too late for such thoughts. As deeply involved as he was, he was sure to be hanged anyway. No, no, the German pleaded, "I did not come for that and was not willing to murder a person."

"Boy, boy," said the actor, coming menacingly toward him. Booth slapped his hand heavily on Atzerodt's chest. "What is to become of you?" Suddenly, Booth struck him. Atzerodt fell to the floor. "You *must* kill Johnson!" Booth shouted. Atzerodt would do it, Booth exclaimed, or he would blow his brains out. Back on his feet, Atzerodt was wild-eyed and speechless. "What will become of you?" Booth repeated in disgust. "Herold has more courage than you." *He* would kill Johnson, Booth continued, and Atzerodt would help. Realizing the only way out was further in, Atzerodt nodded his consent.

"Get your horse," Booth growled.

WAS JOHN WILKES BOOTH ILL? The ingenue Jeannie Gourlay, playing Mary Meredith in *Our American Cousin*, looked out and saw him standing at the rear of the parquet. He was a friend, yet she scarcely recognized him. "Over the heads of the audience, his face showed as pale as death," she thought. Moments later, when she finished her lines with Harry Hawk's Asa Trenchard, Booth was gone.[93]

It was 10:10 p.m. as Booth mounted the steps to the dress circle, humming to himself as he went. Booted and spurred, he wore an ordinary business suit of dark color and a finely quilted slouch hat. He was inconspicuously armed with a single-shot derringer. The pistol, with its handsome walnut stock and silver mountings, had a large-bore rifled barrel.[94] It was a deceptively powerful weapon, smaller than a man's hand, yet capable of inflicting a fearsome wound at close range. Booth also carried a large bowie knife.

Upstairs, Booth walked leisurely along the rear wall toward the State Box on the south side of the theater. He passed his friend Abner Brady without a nod. Booth exercised regularly at Brady's gym, and Brady thought the slight odd. He also passed without greeting George Blauvelt, another acquaintance.[95] Farther on, and only six or so feet from the outer door to the box, sat Alexander M. Crawford and Theodore McGowan, two army officers. They effectively blockaded the aisle. Booth insisted on passing, so the men had to readjust their chairs to let him by. *Here is an ill-bred fellow,* thought McGowan. *Drunk,* thought Crawford. They gave Booth hard looks. He returned them with a glare.[96]

Stepping down a level, Booth paused, removed his hat, and leaned back against the wall. He remained there for a minute, looking nervously at the audience.[97] He could see the house was well filled but not packed, perhaps because it was Good Friday. Many soldiers and sailors in uniform were present. From his position Booth could not see Lincoln or the other occupants of the box, which formed part of the proscenium. An elevation of eleven-plus feet separated where they sat from the stage floor. The distance was no trifle, but Booth had made leaps of similar height to the same stage. The orchestra, not needed until the conclusion of the play, had departed at the end of the second intermission, and their chairs were empty. The stage was free of encumbering furniture, and Hawk would soon be alone on the set, as Booth was well aware. "He knew just what he was going to do and how much time he had," stated Harry Ford.[98]

Charles Forbes, the presidential messenger, sat before the outer door to the State Box. Mrs. Lincoln had ordered him to remain there in case he was wanted. Earlier in the play, after the Lincoln party settled in, Forbes had slipped off for a quick drink with Francis Burke, the president's coachman, and John F. Parker, the White House policeman who escorted the presidential party to their seats. Whistles wetted, Forbes was now back in his chair, and Burke was at his station atop Lincoln's carriage on Tenth Street in front of the theater. Parker's whereabouts are unknown.[99]

Booth took another step down to the level where Forbes sat. Seeking a pretext for admission, he pulled a small pack of visiting cards from his pocket, carefully selected one, held it thoughtfully, then presented it to the attendant. The fateful card bore a distinguished name well known to Forbes. The name was not revealed in the evening's aftermath. In fact, the card disappeared. Nothing has ever been learned of it.

Lucy Hale believed it was her father's card. A spur-of-the-minute expedient by Booth? A grim joke? Payback? Forbes knew Hale well and would never have mistaken Booth for the portly former senator. The card would simply have accorded the bearer attention.[100]

Forbes was an immigrant American, a penniless lad from Ireland who entered government service and rose to the position of Lincoln's faithful footman. But he was not a bodyguard. He was not there to seal the box off to traffic. He was a valet, armed only with good intentions. "Anyone could have passed in without molestation," said S. P. Hanscom, a journalist who called at the box earlier to deliver a dispatch. The stocky attendant would have fought for the president had he any reason to think his life was in danger. Seeing nothing amiss with Booth, Forbes motioned for him to proceed. Forbes felt profound remorse for this decision, later telling false stories of his own whereabouts and throwing blame on Parker.

When Booth tried to open the door, it stuck. Placing a knee against it, he popped it free, entered, and closed it behind him.[101]

He stood in an empty corridor about eight feet long and four feet wide. The dim space concealed a wooden plank. Booth wedged one end of this pine board against the door and the other into a mortise he had previously prepared in the wall. The fit was so tight that anyone attempting to gain entry with this brace in place would have to break down the door. Although Booth employed this precaution effectively, he was so nervous that later he could not remember if he had actually done it.[102]

Two small doors, neither with working locks, led into the State Box. There was a peephole in the door to Booth's immediate left, while the door at the end of the passage was actually ajar.[103] A glance through either revealed

Lincoln bundled up in his overcoat in a large rocker. The president was the closest of the box's four occupants to the entryway, largely out of sight of the audience, but almost close enough to Booth for him to lean out and touch. Mrs. Lincoln sat on his right. Seven or eight feet farther right were Mrs. Lincoln's young friend Clara Harris and Major Henry Rathbone, her stepbrother. A redhead with imposing muttonchops, Rathbone was an army paymaster about Booth's age. He was dressed in civilian clothes, his back to the door.

Hawk's folksy American character was delivering a homespun rebuke to an aristocratic English lady who had just left the stage in a huff. As always, a loud laugh would follow Hawk's line.

The moment was at hand for the performance of a lifetime.

"I care not what becomes of me," Booth would write. "I struck boldly for my country and that alone."[104]

Mrs. Lincoln laughed. The president looked down toward the orchestra seats as if he saw a familiar face. Booth stepped swiftly behind him. "Freedom!" cried the actor, just as the conspirators cried when they attacked Caesar, and he fired his pistol at Lincoln's head.

There was a flash and the sharp report of the shot throughout the building as a large lead bullet smacked Lincoln behind the left ear. The president's right arm flew up convulsively and he slumped forward in his chair, his head dropping forward on his chest. He made no sound, not even a sigh, and looked as if he had merely fallen asleep.[105]

Dropping the pistol, Booth rushed past Mrs. Lincoln, brushing her shawl to the floor as he moved to the front of the box.

Rathbone, startled by the pistol's explosion, looked around to see the assassin moving like a specter through the enveloping gunsmoke. As Booth put a boot on the cushioned balustrade, the major leapt toward him. Wrapping his arms around the assassin from behind, he dragged him back from the railing.

Booth would have to fight his way out of the box, and it would be serious business. A combat veteran, Rathbone was a courageous man, tall and agile, but Booth was stronger, desperate, and frenzied. The assassin twisted himself around in Rathbone's grasp. For the first time the men were face-to-face, and Booth's countenance sent a shudder through the major.

"Let go of me, or I will kill you!" gasped Booth.

"No, I will not!" cried Rathbone, clutching Booth's throat with a hand. Later the major recalled, "I grasped him with all my strength, which was doubly increased by the horror of the scene, but I might as well have attempted to hold a giant. He seemed endowed with sinews of steel."

With a sudden jerk Booth freed his right arm. Rathbone looked up and saw the knife in Booth's hand. As the actor slammed it downward, Rathbone threw up his left arm to deflect the blow. The blade sliced deeply into the officer's arm below the shoulder, and he fell away.

Booth moved again to the front of the box. Putting a hand on the balustrade, he swung himself onto it.

"Sic semper tyrannis!" he cried in a loud, clear voice. At the same time he began a half-jump, half-drop to the stage.

As he pushed off, Rathbone reappeared, reaching out to seize his coat. Booth was too far gone, however, and came free. Clutching one of Booth's buttons in his hand, Rathbone fell away again.[106]

The major's tug did its work. It threw Booth off balance, and the folds of patriotic bunting that decorated the box reached out to entangle the rowel of the spur on his right heel. A ripping noise sounded as Booth pulled a ribbon of flag down with him and slammed with a cry onto the green baize stage carpet.[107] He hit so hard that the noise was as distinct backstage as the shot had been.

Booth landed awkwardly on his right knee and thigh. Pitched forward, he caught himself as best he could with both hands. For a suspenseful second he remained there as if frozen in a crouching position. "Kind of crumpled up," thought William H. Flood, a naval officer in an orchestra seat.[108]

The assassin's left foot was bent beneath him. Slammed violently in the fall, the fibula of that leg broke above the ankle joint. A burst of pain swept his body, followed by sudden light-headedness and nausea. "I felt I was going to swoon upon the stage," he would tell a friend. Fortunately the break of this smaller of the two leg bones was a serious but not a disabling injury.[109] Had he broken the larger tibia, he would have been effectively immobilized. Because the fibula bears little weight, Booth would be able to walk, and walk he must, for there were sixty-four feet between where he lay and the alley behind the theater where his horse awaited. With what Booth later said was all the determination he could muster, he composed himself, got to his feet, and started for the wings.[110]

"Booth did not seem to run very fast," said the actor John L. Debonay, standing at the first entrance on stage left, not far from where Booth fell. "He seemed to be stooping a little [as he went]." "He stalked in the old fashion tragedy stalk, moving the leg more from the hip than the knee," thought the playwright A. R. Cazauran.[111]

Almost to a person playgoers thought they were witnessing an innovation in the evening's entertainment. They sat perfectly still, "so still you could have heard the rustle of a kerchief," continued Cazauran. The scene was a front scene, set as close to the audience as possible, and it brought Booth near the footlights.[112] As he reached center stage, his face turned toward them. He flung his arm dramatically overhead. The wide blade of his knife reflected the light of the gas jets as if it had been a diamond. His eyes glittered brightly.[113]

"The South is avenged!" he cried. Lowering his head, he continued his flight. "In a very stagy stride, still pale, serious, and intense, he went right across the stage," said Charles Hamlin, seated just beyond the orchestra railing.[114]

"Stop that man!" Rathbone cried shrilly from the box. "Stop him!" Hawk was the only person in a position to do so, but that actor, certain only that Booth was coming at him with a knife, had another idea. "I ran," Hawk explained unheroically.[115]

Unimpeded, the assassin continued, "staggering across the stage in a tragic manner," declared the bartender James P. Ferguson, who had watched the tragedy unfold from a catbird's seat in the front of the dress circle directly opposite the State Box. Looking up, Booth noticed his friend. As their eyes met, Booth shook his knife over his head once more and exalted breathlessly, "I—I—I have done it!"[116]

Fleeing to the first entrance, Booth came upon Laura Keene and William J. Ferguson rehearsing their lines at the prompter's desk. Without pause he pushed between them. "His lips were drawn against his teeth, and he was panting," recalled young Ferguson.[117] Backpedaling, Ferguson imagined as he retold the story that he felt the assassin's hot breath on his cheek. Keene seemed in a daze as she bumped hands with Booth as he passed.

Booth came to the north wall of the theater after hurrying through the first entrance as rapidly as he could. He threw out both hands to steady himself briefly on its brick, then turned right into a passageway leading directly back to the alley door. This passage was always kept clear during *Our American Cousin*, in which the ladies appeared in full dress, for it was very narrow. It was three feet wide, even less in places, and two people could not pass along it side by side.[118]

Unexpectedly a figure in a blue-black swallowtail coat filled the passage near the alley exit. The orchestra leader, William Withers, ignorant of what had transpired, chatted with Jeannie Gourlay, his girlfriend. Withers's back was to Booth.

"Let me pass! Let me pass!" cried the assassin.

Withers looked around and saw Booth rushing at him. "If I live a thousand years, I will never forget that ten seconds of my life spent between John Wilkes Booth and his liberty," said the maestro. "His face was wild and haggard, his hair stood on end, and his eyes were bolting from his head."

"Let me pass!" Booth repeated. Withers did not move. "I was completely paralyzed. I was glued to the floor, dumbfounded and speechless."

The men collided. Withers spun around. "Damn you!" said Booth, and he swept his knife twice in Withers's direction. With a ripped collar and a slight flesh wound to the neck, the music man sprawled to the floor, very content to be there.[119]

Passing through the stage door into the alley, Booth looked for his horse. He had left her with Spangler, but there stood Joseph Burroughs, the theater's bill-carrier and flunky, with the reins. The pistol shot had roused Burroughs from his lounging spot on a carpenter's bench, and he was ambling up to the door with the animal when it flew open.

"Give me that horse!" cried Booth. Burroughs complied, but as Booth seized the reins, the smallish teenager stood on helpfully holding the bridle. Booth reached out and smacked him in the chest with the butt of his knife. The blow sent Burroughs flying, but it was not malicious. "He was merely pushing me away," Burroughs later told authorities.[120]

Booth now commenced the painful task of mounting with a broken leg. His horse's skittishness compounded the challenge. Burroughs described the little bay as "very spirited, very uneasy, scratching against the bench." The mare's stamping was so distinct it drew the attention of Mary Jane Anderson, gawking out the window of her tenement on the alley.[121] Booth was unfamiliar with the animal, a horse he had rented that afternoon when his favorite sorrel was unavailable.

To Anderson it appeared that Booth mounted instantly. To Burroughs his difficulty was apparent.[122] To Booth himself the process seemed interminable. "Nearly five minutes," he told Herold, an absurd exaggeration explainable only by the anxiety he felt at the firestorm on his heels.[123]

Spooked by the excitement and by Booth's awkward ascent, the restless animal circled hard to the left as the powerfully built assassin struggled up. It seemed for a moment that Booth would lose control of her. Such was the hope of Joseph B. Stewart, an audience member who emerged from the door in pursuit of the fugitive. But, as Stewart grudgingly acknowledged, "Booth maintained his reason nor did his wonderful nerve desert him."[124] Shortening the right rein, Booth forced her back and skillfully headed her up. Heavily spurred, the horse lunged forward. Booth crouched over the saddle, and the bay dashed off, flinging dirt from her hooves into Stewart's face. The rattling of her feet on the stones of the alley echoed in the moonlit pathway. In seconds horse and rider were gone.

Back inside the theater, the frightful shrieks of Mrs. Lincoln and cries for water and a surgeon awoke the audience to the tragedy. "Perhaps you can judge of the scene that followed, but I doubt it," Wesley Batchelder, seated in the dress circle, wrote his mother. The audience broke and parted like a wave on a rock. Some spectators sat stunned. Some hurried from the building. Others, transfixed in the aisles, spoke in frightened whispers, while a few cried for vengeance and threatened to burn the theater. The bolder members of the audience swarmed the stage, where the players, creeping out from the wings, huddled together in alarm. Absolute chaos, thought Kathryn Evans, who played a maid in the evening's production.

The tumult fell to a hush as the gravely wounded president was carried to the door of the box. A funereal procession assembled. Wailing, Mrs. Lincoln looked ghastly in her blood-covered dress. "For God's sake, gentlemen, let the poor lady pass," someone shouted to the pressing crowd. Clara Harris looked equally dreadful, her dress, hands, and face speckled with gore. Rathbone, his countenance deathly, was shaken, wounded, and deeply agitated.

Charles H. Jones was a young navy sailmaker with a reverence for Lincoln so profound that he had yet to grasp the reality of the situation. "Do you think it is serious?" he asked Rathbone.

"Serious?!" replied Rathbone incredulously. "Look!" he cried, thrusting out his gore-flecked hand. "That is his brain!"[125]

11

....

EXIT BOOTH

SERGEANT SILAS T. COBB'S WAR to save the Union was ending with a whimper, not a bang. He had been a bootmaker before the conflict, and he would resume his trade when it was over, but for the present he was master of a rough-hewn structure of bark-covered timbers from which he and a tiny detail of Massachusetts soldiers served out their enlistments at the Washington end of the Navy Yard Bridge across the Anacostia River. This guardhouse, to honor it with a name, had loopholes through which Cobb and his men could fire on rebel raiders.[1] None ever came, and at this point in time none ever would, so the sergeant and his squad had little to fear or indeed to do except wave through army wagons, poke into produce trucks, and check the passes of fellow soldiers with guilty faces. For the most part they stood and looked about. Cobb had learned one lesson that every soldier in every war must know and know well. He knew how to wait.

Shortly before 11:00 p.m. Cobb heard a commotion coming down Eleventh Street. It was Booth, riding rapidly. As the actor came up, the sergeant halted him.

"Who are you, Sir?" Cobb asked.[2]

"My name is Booth." It was best to tell the truth. The newly minted assassin had papers on his person that, if examined, would put a lie to any other name. Anyway, he was ahead of the news. With luck he would stay that way.

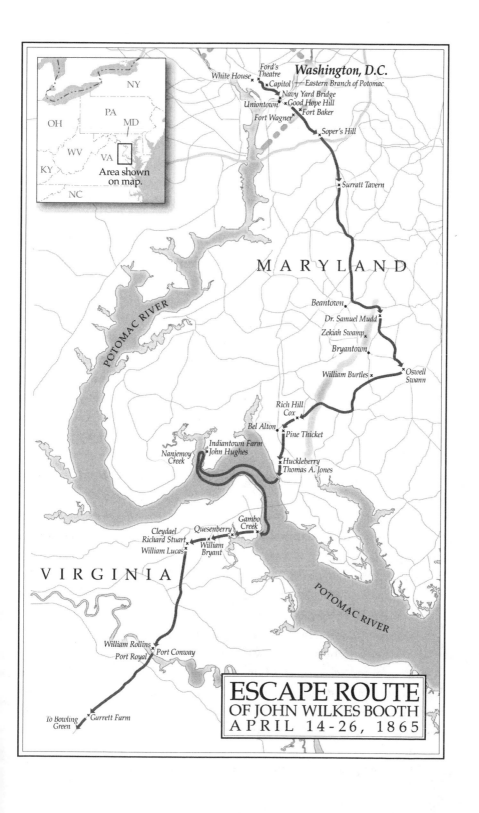

ESCAPE ROUTE
OF JOHN WILKES BOOTH
APRIL 14-26, 1865

"Where are you going?" asked Cobb.

"I am going home." Booth's horse, ridden hard, was restive and stirred uneasily before the sergeant. By contrast its rider seemed calm and self-possessed. He addressed Cobb as friend, and Cobb returned the civility. Uncharacteristically light and high-pitched, Booth's voice betrayed anxiety but would have done so only to those who knew him well. "I live close to Beantown, but do not live in the town," he continued.

Cobb said that he didn't know a place named Beantown.

"Good God!" replied Booth good-naturedly. "Then you never was down there."

The questioning continued. Where had Booth come from? Where had he been? Why had he been out so late? Didn't he know the rules about crossing at night? Four agonizing minutes of this blather continued.

Cobb had served nearly two years in a second-line unit without having been on a battlefield or fired a shot in anger. Unsuspecting, he was finally face-to-face with danger. Booth told Arnold that he would shoot his way across the bridge if anyone delayed him. This boast proved as idle as most. It was useless to shoot Cobb or bolt past him for the simple reason that the bridge was guarded at both ends. Across the river at Uniontown a heavy gate, barring all traffic, had been closed earlier in the evening. The gate abutted a blockhouse with its own squad of soldiers. Only words would get him across.

"Didn't you know, my friend, that it [is] against the laws to cross here after nine?"

"No. It is news to me," answered Booth.

"What is your object to be in town after nine o'clock when you have so long a road to travel?"

"It is a dark road, and I thought if I waited a spell I would have the moon." The answer made sense. The moon had risen only thirty minutes earlier. Four days past full, it was quite bright under a sky with thin, light, curling clouds. The evening was pleasant, with temperatures in the midfifties and a light wind.[3] It was a fine night for travel.

The sergeant studied the horseman anew by the lamplight at the guardhouse door. "Booth seemed to be gentlemanly in his address and style and appearance," Cobb later explained. "What I thought was that he was some rich man's son who lived down there. I thought he was a proper person."

"I will pass you," Cobb finally said, "but I don't know as I ought to."

"Hell! I guess there'll be no trouble about that," laughed Booth, and he turned his horse onto the planks.

The Navy Yard Bridge, one-quarter mile in length, was a haphazard affair, very unevenly floored and in poor condition. The rule was for riders to walk their horses across the span.[4] Booth complied while in Cobb's sight, but once over the draw he upped the pace. Private George Drake, who was on post at the Uniontown end, cried out, "Walk that horse!" Booth ignored the order, and Drake yelled, "Damn you, walk that horse!!" Booth quickly checked her speed.

Private Frederick A. Demond, also on the night shift, lazed out of the blockhouse. He looked at Booth, then helped Drake push open the gate. "We had no orders to stop any one coming from Washington as the guard on that end of the bridge was supposed to know who they passed," lamented Demond. "Oh, if only I knew. I would have shot [Booth] as quick as I would a mad dog." As it was, Demond watched Booth put spurs to the mare and ride off.[5]

Booth made the long haul up Good Hope Hill at a frantic pace. He rode as if he were being chased, thought Polk Gardner, a youngster heading in the opposite direction. Seeing Gardner, Booth reined in his horse and asked the youth if he had passed another traveler riding rapidly. Booth was looking for Herold, who was to have met him at the bridge. Gardner said no, and Booth rode on.[6] Looming ahead were Forts Baker and Wagoner, two jewels in the defensive crown of the city. They flanked the road to left and right. The forts were connected by telegraph to 22nd Army Corps headquarters in Washington, but such was the confusion in the capital that it would be another hour before they received the frightful news.[7] Booth passed between them without incident. At the hill's summit the lights of the city seemed almost at his feet, the Capitol dome silvered by moonlight. An open road south lay before him.

"HE IS A DAMN PRETTY fellow," Herold complained. "He promised to meet me here."

"What is going on tonight?" Drake wondered aloud as once more he swung open the gate to Uniontown. Herold rode through past Drake, past Demond, past a convoy of army wagons, past teamsters idling at the curb, past Gardner and up the hill. He was five or ten minutes behind Booth, and his steady roan was closing the distance. Booth's mare had great speed, but, according to her owner James W. Pumphrey, from whose stable the horse was being stolen, she had limited endurance. At ten or so miles, if pushed hard, she would break down.[8]

Herold found Booth at the foot of Soper's Hill beyond the District line in Maryland. Never was star happier to see best supporting actor.

"Dave," cried Booth in relief as Herold rode up. "Dave, I've done it! I've killed the tyrant!"[9]

Herold later told his family that he never dreamed Booth wished to harm the president. Shocked beyond measure at what he heard, "I begged Booth to let me leave." Booth responded by threatening to kill him if he did.[10] If anyone besides his family believed such a claim, that person has yet to be found. In for a penny, Herold was in for a pound. In fact, he had news of his own. He had remained near Seward's house long enough to know that Powell was doing bloody work inside. For their escape Herold had shown Powell the bridge neighborhood that afternoon, but in the aftermath of the attack on the secretary of state, Powell, a relative stranger to Washington, had gotten lost in the maze of city streets.[11] He would not be joining them.

Before they rode on, the pair swapped horses. Booth had boasted earlier in the day that his little mare was so lively she could almost kick him in the back.[12] That was no advantage to a man who could not put the foot of his broken left leg into the stirrup.[13] With great difficulty Booth was mounted on the roan, and Herold took the bay. Herold's horse, Charley, was a gentle creature customarily rented to ladies. It was "a large single-foot racking horse—the easiest horse to ride," explained Allison Nailor, from whose stable Herold took his mount. "It has a very easy gait—the motion being like that of a cradle."[14] Charley offered less bounce at the trot and little side-to-side sway, and was capable of being ridden comfortably for hours under normal conditions. Racing was not normal, however, and it was taking a toll. Examined the next morning, the roan was found to have a badly swollen shoulder, and the bay was lame in her left foreleg, from which a chunk of skin was missing.[15]

It was about three miles to the Surratt Tavern, and midnight found Herold pounding violently on its door. John Lloyd let him in and hurried to retrieve two carbines hidden at the house, as well as a pair of field glasses Mrs. Surratt had brought out earlier in the day. Herold quaffed some whiskey and took the bottle out to Booth, who remained mounted. Booth took a few slugs of his own. Between the two of them they put quite a dent in the contents, giving the stout and sulky landlord one dollar for the damages.

Herold took a carbine, but Booth refused one, taking only the field glasses. "Booth said he could not carry his carbine," Lloyd stated. "It was as much as he could do to carry himself."[16]

"I have broken my leg," he explained.[17]

Lloyd had been drinking all day, drank more that night, vomited, and was passed out when aroused by Herold. Friends described the Virginia native as "a drinking, swearing, talkative Southern sympathizer with a bad memory—when sober—of what he said when drunk."[18] Something was about to occur, however, that was not the sort of thing one forgets.

"I will tell you some news," called out Booth as he and Herold turned to leave. "We have assassinated the President and Secretary Seward."

As drunk as he was, Lloyd heard this. The words hit him like a slap in the face. He was a former District of Columbia policeman, and he instantly took in the gravity of Booth's statement and his own culpability in the affair.

"God damn you!" the astonished innkeeper exclaimed to the horsemen. "Get away from here a thousand miles as fast as you can go!"[19]

As they galloped away from the tavern, the pain in Booth's leg was becoming unbearable. He described feeling as if the bones of his leg tore the flesh at every bound of the horse. It was imperative to find medical help. Booth asked Lloyd about a physician, but the only one whom he knew no longer practiced. The assassin posed the same question to two locals tending a broken wagon near Surrattsville. They were equally unhelpful but later told authorities that they thought that the horsemen inquired for Samuel A. Mudd.[20]

Mudd's house was seventeen miles farther on and a challenge for any nightrider to find. "The road becomes very lonely, and the country wears a desolate and deserted look," wrote a journalist who retraced their steps.[21] Groves of pine stood on one side, marsh on the other. Stumps of trees dotted the occasional field. Here was a darkened church, there a cemetery. The way was winding, narrow, and washed by rain. On a sunny summer day Booth could not have found Mudd's on his own. Happily, Herold knew the roads "better than he knew the Lord's Prayer." He also knew that the route was well out of the way. Given their circumstances, Herold strongly opposed taking any such detour. Booth replied that he *must* see a doctor.[22] At the injured man's insistence, Herold dutifully led them down Beantown Road, then turned east.

The young man was a godsend. Booth would not have seen another sunset without him.

"I TOOK A KNIFE and split the leg of his boot down to the instep, slipped it off and the sock with it," recounted Mudd. Herold, between whispers to Booth, urged the doctor to be quick, and Mudd did the best he could after being startled awake at 4:00 a.m. "I felt carefully with both hands down along his leg. At first I could discover nothing. After a second investigation I found on the outside near the ankle, something that felt like indurated flesh, and then for the first time I concluded it was a direct and clear fracture of the bone." The fibula had broken the way a stick of candy might break, snapped in half and forming two smooth surfaces. The grating of these ends was distinctly observable when Booth moved.

The break was located about two inches above the ankle. Fortunately, it was not compound, nor was the adjoining tibia fractured. Having no proper splints, Mudd cut up an old hatbox for that purpose. The box, with its absurdly incongruous decorative pattern, was fashioned into a pasteboard expedient extending from the arch of the foot to a point just below the knee. Forming a sort of boot firm enough to keep the lower leg rigidly straight, it was serviceable for the present, but the injury required redressing after several days of rest—if Booth remained at rest. If moving, he took great risks from striking the leg or falling on it.[23]

Although Mudd later told detectives that he did not regard the break as particularly dangerous or painful, his patient's condition was alarming. Booth was shaking, moaning, nearly prostrate. Gulping air as if exhausted, he complained of severe back pain. "Booth's eyes had a most unnatural expression, either from excessive drinking or excessive mental excitement. His hair was in disorder, his clothes covered with mud, and he appeared unable to stand," recalled Mudd's wife, Sarah, who tore cloth strips for bandages.[24] Booth had a black mark down one side of his face—like Cain.

Herold and Mudd helped Booth to an upstairs bed. As he was lowered into it, the doctor noticed that the injured man had two revolvers concealed in his clothes.

Booth spent the dawning day attempting to sleep. It was the only thing that brought relief. He refused both breakfast and lunch brought to his room by a servant. Concerned when the second meal was returned untouched, Mrs. Mudd prepared a tray with cake, oranges, and wine and carried it up herself. "I guess you think I have very little hospitality," she said brightly. "You have been sick all day and I have not been up to see you." She asked how he was feeling. "My back hurts me dreadfully," he replied.[25]

Throughout the day Mudd called several times to check on his patient. He brought Booth a razor, soap, and water, following Herold's suggestion that a shave might raise the invalid's spirits. (Unsaid was its added benefit of removing Booth's trademark mustache.) He also whittled two arm pieces for a rough pair of crutches. Hearing the injured man say that he did not think he could travel on horseback, he agreed to help Herold find a buggy.

In the early afternoon Mudd, mounted on his favorite gray, and Herold, on the mettlesome bay, rode to the nearby home of Mudd's father in search of a carriage. Having no luck there, the two headed for Bryantown. Herold was anxious and charged ahead, but as they drew within sight of the village, he stopped and turned back. He seemed deeply engaged in thought when Mudd met him. "I believe I will get my friend to go on horseback," he announced. A vanguard of the 13th New York Cavalry had just arrived in Bryantown.[26] Herold might have seen them, or he could have stopped upon realizing the irrationality, in their circumstances, of running for his life in a coach-and-four. There were no easy roads in their future. It was trail and swamp and thicket for them.

Mudd continued on to Bryantown to purchase a few household items for his wife. Surprised to find a federal swarm in the village, he asked a picket what had happened and was informed that Lincoln had been shot by a man named Booth. Mudd was horrified. Booth had told him that he was returning from a trip to Virginia when injured. "Dr. Sam Mudd was a rather intense man, not very broad-minded and not cool," the Confederate agent Thomas A. Jones believed.[27] At this critical moment, his heart and head in a mad race, the doctor managed an outward calm. He commenced a deliberately slow retreat home, chatting with neighbors about the news as he collected his thoughts. His impulse was to turn Booth in. But Mudd, who knew little enough about the assassin, knew one thing for certain—"Booth would never be taken alive."[28] The heavily armed fugitive was in his home with Mudd's wife and four young children. Mudd simply could not risk a shootout in the family parlor. He would return, run Booth and Herold off, and pray for the best.

"Treachery!" exclaimed Mudd, ripping into his guest. Booth "had come with a lie on his tongue which would be certain to have him in serious trouble." Outraged, Mudd said he had a mind to throw the assassin and his Man Friday to the wolves.

Booth had no fight left in him at this point, and he wilted before the doctor's assault. Speaking confidentially to a friend years later, Mudd said

"Booth appealed to him in the name of his mother, whom he professed to love so devotedly," not to do that. Booth pleaded and "acted and spoke so tragically" that Mudd finally relented on the condition that the men leave his place at once. Booth thanked him and gave him twenty-five dollars for his services.[29]

Darkness and the threat of rain had gathered as Booth worked his way on his new pine crutches to the horses. "His face presented a picture of agony," recalled Sarah Mudd, and she cautioned Herold about his condition.

"If he suffers much, we won't go far," promised the young man.

OSWALD SWAN, A BLACK TOBACCO farmer, had been hailed from the darkness outside his home by two white men on horseback. One he described as a little squirt, the other a larger man with a broken leg. It was Herold and Booth, and the pair, hungry and lost, wanted bread and whiskey and Swan's services as guide through Zekiah Swamp to Rich Hill, the estate of Samuel Cox. It was a three-hour trip in the gloom, but, circling below the dangers in Bryantown, Swan got them safely to Cox's about one in the morning. He received twelve dollars for his trouble and a piece of advice. "Don't you say anything," warned Herold. "If you tell that you saw anybody, you will not live long."[30]

Herold slammed the large brass knocker on Cox's front door, and the sound rang out in the quiet of the night like a cannon shot. The household was instantly aroused, and the formidable Samuel Cox in his slippers answered. "How do you do?" he asked as he fought to protect his flickering lamplight from the chilly night wind.[31]

Tall, large-voiced, and imperious, Cox was the local squire. The fugitives sought him out as an individual whose rebel bona fides were so pronounced he was under suspicion throughout the war. A brief conversation ensued, after which Cox blew out his light and brought the men inside for food and drink. Looking through the dining room windows from the yard, Swan fancied, improbably enough, that he saw oysters and champagne on the table.

Cox had learned of the assassination the previous day. Booth now confirmed the fact and acknowledged that he had done it. Since Booth did not know Cox personally, the assassin established his identity by showing the planter his tattoo. Cox had seen the elder Booth perform and thus knew the Booth name, but this was no time to reminisce. Though Cox was practically deaf in his left ear, his right ear was registering much. As the night wore on, so did the realization that it would not do for Booth and Herold to remain at Rich Hill. Cox could hide them in the woods, feed them, and try to get them across the Potomac, but the pair had to leave his house before sunrise announced them to the neighborhood.

The cocks were crowing as Booth and Herold were shown the door. Mary Swann, a servant, wrapped some food in a red handkerchief for Booth to take along. *What pretty black eyes this man has*, she thought.[32] Oswald Swan, waiting patiently outside, put his hand under the armrest of the injured man's crutch and helped get the assassin atop his horse. Booth was grumbling all the while about Cox's lack of hospitality. "I thought Cox was a man of Southern feeling," he said indignantly.

Dismissing Swan, Booth and Herold exited the gate of the Cox estate. Fences, framed by flower beds in the first blush of spring, guided them down a lane to the road. As they passed the stables, Samuel Cox Jr. watched them carefully from his bedroom window. He was suspicious that the travelers might attempt to steal fresh mounts. The two had nothing on their minds except their eviction and exile to the brush, however. Mary recalled, "They went away cussin' and swearing."

Franklin Robey, Cox's overseer, joined the fugitives and led them west about one and a half miles into a thick stand of pines.[33] Shrewdly, Cox put them on a neighbor's property. This thicket was uncomfortably close to the road, but it was so dense it looked as impenetrable as a briar patch. Inside it one could see no farther than thirty or forty feet, about the length of the front porch at Tudor Hall. Robey told Booth and Herold to wait there. Someone would be sent to them as soon as possible. For the present they had food and blankets. A nearby spring would furnish water. They were to stay perfectly quiet and listen for a particular whistle, which their visitor would make as he approached them.

Booth selected a spot and made himself as comfortable as he could on a mat of pine needles. The ground was cold and wet. After putting down his pistols, knife, crutch, and hat, he drew a blanket over himself and settled back. It was a bright and pleasant Easter Sunday morning.

Well before noon Herold heard a noise. Taking the carbine, he left to investigate and returned with a lean and plain-looking stranger. The man's face was glum, suggesting that its owner would rather be anywhere else than in these pines. But here he was because Cox asked it, and Cox, his foster brother, was both family and best friend. The two had turned to each other since childhood, and now Cox had called again, this time for an enormous favor from Thomas A. Jones.[34]

At first glance Booth might have been disappointed with his new guardian angel. The homespun Mr. Jones appeared dull-witted and indolent. He impressed one as a plebeian with limited awareness, much less sagacity, about events that swirled around him. Nothing could have been more misleading. Jones was a crafty rebel agent and a veteran river-crosser so successful that he had been caught only once in the war. While he was in prison, Union soldiers moved into his house. Jones's wife, Jane, the sister of Thomas Harbin, was driven with her children into a small back room while the troops took what they wanted and acted as they wished. Jones returned home to discover that Jane, ill and overworked, had died in childbirth. "My wife was the best woman I could ever have," the widower lamented, and her death turned a foe into an inveterate enemy. "He sincerely hated the Yankees," recalled a friend.[35] The years had been so hard on Jones that, although middle-aged, he looked old to the assassin.

"Booth seemed to be suffering intense pain from his broken leg," wrote Jones in an 1893 memoir, and he did not attempt to rise. Introducing himself, he acknowledged proudly what he had done, asked what the public thought of it, and expressed an urgent desire to cross the Potomac. Booth returned repeatedly to the point that if he could only get across the river, he could receive proper medical care. In Virginia all would be well. "His voice was pleasant, and his manner was courteous and polite," recalled Jones. "A determined man, not boasting."

Jones replied that the death of Lincoln was good news. For his part he would bring Booth food and newspapers. Since the country was filling up with soldiers and detectives, nothing could be done about crossing the river for the present. It was too dangerous to attempt it. Be patient, counseled Jones, and be assured that he would do all he could to help.

"He held out his hand and thanked me," said Jones. A grimace accompanied movements even so slight, and Jones was touched by the helpless man's plight. "I did not know Booth, but how could I give up the life of that poor devil?" he explained. "I determined to die before I would betray him."[36]

True to his word, Jones returned the following morning. He brought ham, fish, bread, coffee, whiskey, and other things his kitchen furnished. Robey visited, and so did the Coxes *père et fils*. The amount of provisions hauled from Rich Hill into the thicket led employees at Cox's mill to speculate that someone important was hiding there.[37] "They fixed him up the best they could," recalled one of Cox's former slaves.

The nourishment Booth most craved came bundled in a small roll. Booth was eager to know the consequences of his actions, so Jones brought him newspapers, unidentified by title but doubtless from Baltimore or Washington. From them Booth learned that Lincoln died early Saturday morning at an hour when the assassin rested at the Mudd house. Powell knifed Seward, injuring him seriously but not fatally. Atzerodt made no attempt on the life of Johnson. Upon Lincoln's death the nation did not flounder or fall into revolution. Order prevailed, and a constitutional transition of power occurred. The country was shaken to its depth by the murder, but, as Brevet Colonel Henry L. Burnett of Ohio, a judge advocate, said, "We stand guard, and the government shall not die."[38]

Such were the cold facts of Booth's act, but the emotions his deed produced leapt shrieking from the page. Monster crime! Demon deed! Appalling! Iniquitous! Barbaric! Chicago: "The crime of the ages has been committed. It is hard to conceive of any event which would occasion sorrow so profound and apprehension and foreboding so painful." Boston: "The nation is bowed in anguish. The oppression would beggar human power to properly describe." Philadelphia: "The most intense horror has spread over this city. All kindly feeling toward the Rebels has been obliterated." Cincinnati: "The universal feeling is one of terrible wrath." New York: "People appear perfectly horrified, and the utmost rage is felt toward all known secessionists and rebel sympathizers."[39] Baltimore: "Great woe! Every place was in mourning, all business suspended, a death-like stillness pervaded the community." Washington: "The feeling of the populace has been one of the deepest and most intense indignation against the perpetrators."[40]

The folly of Booth's act almost matched its infamy. "There was not, in all of Mr. Lincoln's constitution, the smallest element either of the usurper or the tyrant," wrote a Western editor. "Never was there a man in any high place to whom such a phrase [as 'Sic semper tyrannis'] was less appropriate."[41] The assassin was a devil, added the publisher Coyle in a stinging personal rebuke in the *Intelligencer*. "Booth was no cavalier, no romantic knight seized with monomania. On the contrary he was a cold, cautious, cowardly planning knave who knew well the good and gentle character of his victim. The monster wretch, compared with whose foul deed the records of all other assassins pale, committed a deed without a single manly motive, engendered of cowardice, cruelty and loathsome egotism."[42]

Butcher! Wretch! Sanguinary fiend! Dastard murderer! The assassin's personal and political friends turned on him in fury. Frank Queen in the

New York Clipper proclaimed Booth a bloody-handed cutthroat.[43] John T. Ford and John Sleeper Clarke denounced him, as did nationwide meetings of Booth's fellow actors, who joined the condemnation with their professional passion. The recently loyalized *Richmond Whig* characterized the assassination as "an atrocity which will shock and appall every honorable man and woman in the land."[44] "A hellish crime," declared Confederate General J. R. Jones.[45] Robert Ould, the South's agent for the exchange of prisoners, thought that in its harm to the rebel states "it is the worst— Lee's surrender was nothing to it."[46] A leading Copperhead journalist wrote, "It seems marvelous that there should live one human being so warped in judgment, so steeped in wickedness, so hardened in devilish fanaticism as to be capable of this deed."[47]

Booth carried a pocket memorandum book purchased in St. Louis in 1864. He used its pages to jot down names, addresses, business notes, and the like. To pass the time in the thicket he fashioned a daily calendar, commencing on April 17 and extending optimistically through mid-June.

Shaken to the core by the charges of wickedness and cowardice, Booth turned to a blank page in the volume, took out his stub of a pencil, and defended himself. "I struck boldly and not as the papers say. I walked with a firm step through a thousand of his friends, was stopped, but pushed on," he wrote. "Our country owed all her troubles to him, and God simply made me the instrument of his punishment. I can never regret it."[48] Blaming others for the broader plot's failure and praising his own courage in escaping with a broken leg, he bemoaned the failure of the *National Intelligencer* to publish the letter he left with Mathews, not knowing that Mathews had read the document in secret after the assassination and burned it.[49]

The sentiments of Brutus were cheered at the Winter Garden five months earlier—he heard it—but apparently the world was not a stage after all. Booth wrote despairingly of his future. He was ready to die with the rebellion, he told Jones. The fisherman attempted to lift his spirits, as best a man who apparently did not know how to smile could do, but he also raised an unpleasant issue that Booth must face.

The horses could not be cared for in the present circumstances, and they might disclose the hiding place by reacting to his pursuers' mounts, whose pounding and neighing along the road were unmistakably audible. The troublesome bay, whose name is not recorded, had broken loose several times. She sealed her fate and that of Charley. Booth must kill them.[50]

The assassin liked horses more than he did most people, but he knew the truth of Jones's advice. "If we can hear those horses, they can certainly hear ours, uneasy from want of food and stabling," he explained to Herold, and he gave a pained consent. Cox told Herold where to take them, then watched the young man and Robey ride them off at night toward the swamp. Taking the horses through a cutting tangle of undergrowth, the two rode them into a bog. Robey shot each horse once in the head, and the animals sank into the muck, saddles and all. The overseer pocketed as a souvenir of this dismal business a martingale ring from one horse's tack, broken off as it fought for life in the mire.[51] Cox, anxious the thing be done properly, later searched the area carefully. He discovered no trace of what happened there.

Monday morning was cold, Tuesday afternoon windy, but in a piece of good luck the weather was generally mild during Booth's residence in the thicket. Nights dipped into the forties, however, and were dark, cheerless, and uncomfortable. Booth had a touch of pleurisy, for which sleeping on the ground was no prescription, and Herold's health was reduced, too, by hunting trips during which he lay out on winter nights in duck blinds, putting a lingering chill in his bones and affecting his eyes.[52] But the men do not appear to have pieced together a makeshift shelter from the elements, as later reported.[53] Jones, who would know, gave no such impression. The agent believed that the assassin, whose pain was more or less unabated, did not move from one spot at any time during his stay there.

Herold was a sight. His light-colored trousers were filthy, his fancy necktie askew, and his feet hurt. While Booth displayed his tattoo with pride, Herold busied himself attempting to rub away his initials, tattooed on his left arm.[54] The only boy in a family with seven sisters, the smooth-faced young man with the helmet of hair may have been a trifle spoiled, but at least he was companionable and compliant. Aggression and cruelty were alien to him. He could curse with the best, of course, but a friendly manner and an ability to talk his way out of trouble were his true weapons. So was a cleverness that few saw behind his dark blue eyes. He was also unflinchingly steadfast. With numerous opportunities to desert Booth, he never did. Whatever Herold's shortcomings, no one could have been more loyal.

Booth wrote in his pocket notebook that Herold prayed often. Well he might! A manhunt of unprecedented scope was under way, and it was meeting with great success. Powell, Atzerodt, Arnold, O'Laughlen, Spangler,

Mrs. Surratt, and Lloyd were arrested while Booth was in the coppice, and Mudd soon followed.[55] The pursuit, ranging initially as far afield as New York, Pennsylvania, and even Missouri, focused increasingly on southern Maryland. Ships guarded the river, and troops combed the swamp. "The whole country is full of wild cavalrymen shooting at everything they see," complained one detective. "The lunatics are flying around with sabers, the air full of bullets."[56] Soldiers searched Rich Hill. "So help me Gawd," Cox told them, "I know nothing about it." Unable to find Booth there, they emptied Cox's smokehouse as consolation.[57] Once they came close enough for Herold to hear a soldier with a message for Captain Stephen D. Franklin of the 20th Pennsylvania Cavalry Regiment shout out the captain's name as he called to Franklin on the road.

"TAKE CARE HOW YOU APPROACH THEM, Tom," cautioned Cox. "They might shoot you through mistake." Jones had never visited Booth at night, and he weighed Cox's words as he approached the fugitives. Thursday, April 20—a dreary, drizzly day—had finally closed. With the darkness the clouds grew denser, the dampness more intense, and a fog floated up from the swamp to shroud the area. All was intently dark. One could scarcely see ten feet ahead. It was no night for the fainthearted, but Jones had to come. The nearest search party, responding to an erroneous sighting of Booth, had thundered south to St. Mary's County. *Now or never*, thought Jones.

"Friends, this is your only chance," Jones told the fugitives. "The night is pitch dark, and my boat is close by. I will get you some supper at my house and send you off if I can." Jones and Herold put Booth onto his horse, an old mare named Kit. Every movement wrung a groan from the assassin, in spite of what Jones termed Booth's stoic attitude.

The distance from the thicket to the river was about three and a half miles. It took them down a cart path to the public road and then along that road to Huckleberry, Jones's farm, where his fields could be crossed and the river accessed. Jones walked slowly ahead of the fugitives. When all seemed safe, he halted and whistled. Herold then led Kit forward to where he waited. Jones advanced again to scout farther and repeat the pattern. The pace was unnervingly slow, leaving their imaginations prey to every whirr of a whippoorwill's wings, and it left them exposed to travelers who might approach from behind, but there was no other way to do it.

Two houses close to the highway posed hazards. One usually had a large number of children milling about. The other had dogs. Both places were passed uneventfully, however. Perhaps because of the weather, the men saw no one. Sometime after nine the travelers made it safely to Jones's place, where the farmer had them tie up to a pear tree near his stable and wait.

"Please let me go to the house and get some of your hot coffee," Booth said.

Jones looked up at the assassin. For nearly a week Booth had lived without the shelter of a roof, the comfort of a fire, or the taste of hot food. The crippled man, whom the world seemed ready to roast on a spit, wanted the cheer of a home, if only for a moment. Jones experienced a rush of pity for him. "My friend, it wouldn't do," Jones responded with a lump in his throat. "It would not be safe. I have negroes at the house and if they see you, you are lost and so am I. This is your last chance to get away."

"So be it," the assassin sighed dispiritedly.

Jones left Booth and Herold to the damp night and went inside. After supper with his children, he gathered food for the fugitives and rejoined them.

Three abreast, the men picked their way down a steep cliffside path leading to the Potomac. Jones and Herold were compelled to carry Booth along the narrow track, which ran through a heavy laurel undergrowth. Footing was difficult in the darkness as they struggled along, but soon the lapping of the river's waves could be heard. Jones thought the noise sounded particularly mournful and unwelcoming.

Marsh grass near the river concealed a lead-colored skiff. Jones got the boat into the river, then helped Herold get Booth on board. The assassin would navigate and steer from the stern while first mate Herold would row from amidships. It would be tough going, as the closest point on the Virginia shore was imperceptible. Indeed, the men could scarcely see each other. Jones lit a candle. Shielding it with a coat from any possible on-looker, he pointed out on Booth's small boxed compass a heading that would carry them to a creek on the Virginia side, and he gave them the name of a party there who might assist them.

"Goodbye," Jones said. He was beginning to shove them off when Booth cried, "Wait a minute, old fellow." The fugitive wished to pay him something for his trouble. Jones said no. This had never been about money. He could take only eighteen dollars, the cost of his boat, which he would not see again.

Booth's voice choked with emotion as he replied, "God bless you, my dear friend, for all you have done for me."

"The night was ink black," recalled Jones. "I could see nothing, and the only sound was the swish of the waves. I pushed the boat off. There was a moment's sound of oars on the water—and it glided out of sight."

Then, from the darkness, Jones heard a voice. "Goodbye, old fellow," the assassin called out.

HEROLD ROWED STEADILY forward into the current. Booth, dripping candle wax on the compass face, headed him right and left. Their objective, the mouth of Machodoc Creek in Virginia, was a distant six miles. It was an almost straight shot south by west down the Potomac, but the tide had set in against the travelers, and the river swirled with dangers. In the thick, moonless soup the men could see little, certainly not Virginia's shoreline. The experience was akin to swimming with one's eyes closed. Given their circumstances, the two landlubbers, equipped only with one paddle and one broken oar, made the best of their situation and plowed ahead. When water lapped into the boat, Herold stopped rowing and bailed it out with his hat.[58]

Suddenly a light cut the darkness. A Union patrol ship was in front of them. It was the USS *Juniper*, a military steamer. Eighty feet in length, it was a formidable vessel with a complement of twenty-six men and a heavy gun with a one-mile range. The voices of those on board were alarmingly distinct. Booth thought that with his oar he could have reached out and tapped the ship's hull.[59]

The chase was on—or was it? There is no evidence the ship noticed the little skiff in the fog. The *Juniper* was actually at anchor, the imagined searchlights only bow-lamps for the anchor. Booth feared the worst, however, and turned upriver. By first light, time and tide had carried him back to Maryland. Herold recognized their whereabouts as Nanjemoy Creek. They were near Indiantown Farm, the residence of John J. Hughes, where Herold had hunted.

More than a century later a grandson of Hughes claimed that the farmer received the fugitives with kindness and fed them. Herold painted a different picture of Nanjemoy hospitality: "We went to a man's house [probably Hughes] and wanted to buy some bread. He said he hadn't baked and would not bake any. He said he had nothing to eat either. I said we were wet and would like to have something to drink. I had a bottle and asked if he would sell me some whiskey. He said he would not do it." Then how about a glass of water? Herold asked sarcastically. A child finally sold

Booth a quarter's worth of milk. Questioned by his wife, Victorine, about what was going on, Hughes snapped, "You take care of the house, and I will take care of the outside."[60]

Spurned by people he thought would embrace him, Booth hit a new low. "After being hunted like a dog through swamps, woods, and last night chased by gun boats till I was forced to return [to Maryland], wet, cold, and starving, with every man's hand against me, I am here in despair," he wrote. "And why? For doing what Brutus was honored for, what made Tell a hero. And yet I, for striking down a greater tyrant than they ever knew, am looked upon as a common cutthroat. Behold the cold hand they extend to me. I think I have done well, though I am abandoned with the curse of Cain upon me, when, if the world knew my heart, that one blow would have made me great, though I did desire no greatness."

Rejection had done something to Booth that no amount of argument could have accomplished. It put into his hot head the suspicion that he might have made a mistake. The evidence is nuanced but clear. "I do not repent the blow I struck. I may before my God, but not to man. I bless the entire world. Have never hated or wronged anyone. This last [act of mine] was not a wrong unless God deems it so, and it's with Him to damn or bless me. God *cannot* pardon me if I have done wrong. I am sure there is no pardon in Heaven for me since man condemns me so."

At this point Booth was less worried about Lincoln's life than about his own. "Tonight I try to escape these bloodhounds once more. Who, who can read his fate? I have too great a soul to die like a criminal. Oh, may He, may He spare me that and let me die bravely. I do not wish to shed a drop of blood, but 'I must fight the course,'" concluded Booth, echoing Macbeth. "Tis all that's left me."[61]

At sundown on Saturday, April 22, the two men attempted the river once more. Herold rowed out of the Nanjemoy, passed an unmanned lightship, and headed for Virginia. The weather was breezy and afforded better conditions than two nights earlier, but there was the damnable *Juniper* again. The gunboat, having spent most of the day hauling detectives about, was back off Mathias Point on the Virginia shore at the spot where the Potomac turns south toward Booth's destination. This cape had to be turned. Happily it was cloudy and the moon had set, so the fugitives decided to run the gauntlet. They passed unnoticed within three hundred yards of the vessel.[62] Whether exhausted, confused, or spooked, the pair put in at their first port of opportunity, a tidal estuary named Gambo Creek.

Herold helped Booth ashore, then set off to reconnoiter. In a clearing in the pines he discovered the small farm of William Bryant, an older man, coarse and common, who occupied the bottom of the local social ladder.[63] Although it was Sunday morning, Bryant was at work in his field when Herold came up. Bryant was not interested in selling his horses, he quickly told the visitor. Food was another matter. Booth was got to the spot by some means and deposited under an oak tree inside a wormwood fence that enclosed what passed for Bryant's front yard. He was exhausted and agonizingly sore under his arms from the crutches. A pillow was fetched for him and his leg set at rest.[64]

A pallet of grass seemed a better choice than Bryant's shack. That ramshackle structure was little more than a plank hut, the inside of which looked dirty and uninviting. A black woman named Susan McGee lived here with Bryant. She was his housekeeper and, if rumor be true, his concubine as well. McGee busied herself preparing food. Booth was not hungry, even for the special things she whipped up to tempt his palate. He appreciated her solicitude, however, and, as he was wont to do, left behind as a keepsake one of his handkerchiefs.[65]

Meanwhile Herold set off to find Cottage Farm, the home of Elizabeth Quesenberry. Jones had directed the fugitives to call there because his brother-in-law Thomas Harbin, an early member of Booth's abduction team, ran his operations from a small schoolhouse on the lawn of Mrs. Quesenberry's home.

Walking up through the fields, Herold asked for the lady of the house. "Herold was covered with dirt, filth, and grime, unwashed, uncombed, the picture of a vacant-minded tramp," recalled one of those present. In a few minutes Mrs. Quesenberry rode up on horseback. As the stranger introduced himself and asked to buy horses or at the least to secure a conveyance in which to travel upcountry, she frowned. Her impulse was to order him off.[66] But the vagabond claimed to be an escaped soldier tending a brother with a broken leg, and Mrs. Quesenberry had a good heart, so she sent her governess to fetch Harbin, who was down by the river.

Harbin learned of the assassination several days earlier and knew who did it. When he saw the visitor, whom he knew on sight, his heart sank. With this man came a world of trouble.

"Herold, where's Booth?" the agent asked.

"He's over at the next farm, and you must go and see him." Seemingly on the point of collapse, Herold blurted out the story of his adventures. Everyone within hearing, including the servants, got an earful.

Harbin had a tender regard for Mrs. Quesenberry, a widow with four young children, and he was determined to protect her if he could. Drawing her aside, he said, "You must not sell this man a horse. There are circumstances connected with him which make it my duty to tell you to give him nothing more than something to eat."

"Herold was a mass of dirt," recalled Harbin, so while Mrs. Quesenberry started on their meals, Harbin and his associate Joe Baden walked Herold down to the schoolhouse for a scrub and brush. Mission accomplished, Herold was fed, and food for Booth was stuffed into a carpet sack.

At two o'clock in the afternoon of a beautiful breezy day, the young man commenced retracing his steps across the extensive fields behind the Quesenberry house. Watching him go, Harbin had to acknowledge that Herold, "of whom he expected so little, should show so much pluck. Herold's apparent courage was first rate." As the young man disappeared into the woods toward Bryant's place, something occurred to Harbin. There was no frost on the ground. In the odd way people notice an insignificant detail in a moment of crisis, Harbin realized that spring was truly here.

Harbin arrived at Bryant's about four and found Booth under the oak where Herold had left him. The assassin's appearance was striking. He was dirty and gaunt in appearance. His black suit was streaked and spotty. A pair of roughly built crutches was nearby, and an open shoe with leather laces, which Dr. Mudd supplied to replace his boot, revealed a swollen lower leg. There was no doubt who he was.

"John," Harbin called out pleasantly. Booth returned the greeting and said simply that, despite appearances, he thought the worst of his trip was over "and that while his journey thus far had been attended with much danger, he anticipated little difficulty over the remainder of the course as he soon expected to be among friends." After all, he was in Virginia. Booth displayed no signs of nervousness or apprehension, although his mouth occasionally twitched in pain as he spoke.

Harbin was eager to talk to Booth but unable to do so due to Bryant. The inquisitive farmer, who had a mercenary look, hung near them, unsure what to make of his guests but determined to advance his own interests when he did.

With Harbin's help, arrangements were speedily made. Bryant agreed to carry the fugitives on horseback to their next stop on two conditions.

First, he would be paid in greenbacks. He had always said, he informed the Southerners, that Confederate money would not be worth a damn. Second, he would be paid in advance. He wanted ten dollars for the eight miles.[67] "Fagin!" thought another visitor who dealt with him. "Physically and intellectually a good personation of Fagin. Money is his god."[68] Short of options, Booth agreed.

The assassin hobbled to a step in the fence, got himself on it, and pulled himself with a grimace onto a horse. He wore no spurs and left his broken leg out of the stirrup. Herold saddled up with Bryant. Harbin mounted his own animal. About twilight the quartet got moving. Their route was along a little-traveled series of gated lanes, down into deeply gouged streams, and up hills. The country was heavily wooded and had a gloomy look.

The ride was befittingly solemn, but as Herold and Bryant pulled ahead, Booth and Harbin got their chance to talk, and Booth spoke freely. "He had no regret. He was not remorseful," recalled Harbin, "rather took a rude joy in his act." The failure of the larger plot was not his, Booth claimed. It belonged to his associates, and he upbraided them. Surratt ran for his mother the moment assassination was mentioned, and those who stayed behind were not workmen at their tasks. "He only failed through the miserable agents he had been compelled to rely on." Booth said nothing about needing money or a doctor or anything else. His sole focus was on getting farther south. He hoped to reach the Confederate army in North Carolina, which was still in the field, and from there make his way to Mexico. "He was steady and hopeful and self-reliant. He possessed all of his courage."

"John, you will not be able to get very far," Harbin warned. "The Government is hunting you on all sides. They will capture you or shoot you."

"They will never capture me," replied Booth.

At a crossroads several miles from Bryant's house, Harbin stopped to turn for home. "They will get you," he repeated.

"No," said Booth, patting one of his pistols. "If I get in a tight place, I will take my life with this."

Harbin had a sentimental streak. He knew Booth well and regarded him as a decent person but one whom hatred and excess had driven mad. Never was anyone more clearly the author of his own tragedy. As Harbin rode back to Cottage Farm, he felt tears on his cheeks.

DR. RICHARD H. STUART WAS having none of this, and he glowered at Herold and his importunities. Tall, large, and well fed, the laird of Cleydael was a splendid-looking man in his late fifties and a wonderful incarnation of the old Virginia aristocrat. No one's blood ran bluer. During the war, which was waged for the benefit of Stuart and his fellow grandees if for anyone, he had done his share. He had smuggled drugs, harbored agents, languished in prison, lost slaves, buried children, and mourned relatives killed in combat.[69] His friend and distant kinsman Robert E. Lee had now surrendered. Even the redoubtable Mosby had thrown in his hand. The war was over at Cleydael.

"We are Marylanders," continued Herold.[70] He explained again that he and his brother were weary, hungry, and in need of accommodations.

"It is impossible. I have no accommodations for anybody," Stuart replied. Cleydael was a summer house with wide hallways for breezes and accordingly a relatively small number of rooms. There were already nine adults and two children inside. Every bed was taken. Stuart had turned away another group of Marylanders that day. Now dirty old Will Bryant wanted to drop off more driftwood at his front door. It really was too much.

Dr. Mudd had recommended them, persisted Herold. The brother had a broken leg.

"I don't know Dr. Mudd. Nobody was authorized to recommend anybody to me." Furthermore, added Stuart, he was a physician, not a surgeon, and thus unable to help with such an injury. "I did not really believe he had a broken leg," Stuart later told authorities. "I thought it was all put on. I did not like their appearance. I did not like the manner in which they urged the thing on me."

"If you will listen to the circumstances of the case, you will be able to do it," countered Herold.

"If you have any secrets, keep them. I don't want to know anything about you," the doctor rejoined. He would feed them; that was all.[71]

The family had just finished supper, so Booth and Herold came in and replaced them at table. Herold was loquacious. Booth was reserved, although eager to speak with Stuart privately. The doctor evaded the pleasure.

Major Robert W. Hunter, the fiancé of Stuart's daughter Margaret, was present. He was a recently paroled rebel officer. On the field with Lee at Appomattox two weeks earlier, he carried forward one of the truce flags that signaled the surrender. Hunter had been a friend of John Yates Beall and present when John Brown was hanged in 1859. He recognized Booth from that occasion and finally said, "I know you, sir."[72]

Booth opened up. He was indeed John Wilkes Booth. What they had heard about Lincoln was true. He had originally intended to capture the president, he explained. That failing, he planned the assassination in a single night and then did the deed.

Greatly disturbed, Hunter went to Stuart and told him he must get these men out of the house immediately. "I expect to enter your family, and I feel that I ought to interfere in this matter for your protection," he told the doctor.

The two were of one mind. Stuart grabbed his hat and set out to chase down Bryant while Hunter went back into the dining room. "Without any further discussion or controversy, I must tell you that you must leave this house at once and for good," he said to Booth. The subdued assassin, a heavily fringed gray shawl falling in folds from his shoulder, tottered to the door and passed outside into the chilly night.[73]

Bryant was pressed back into service, this time to take Booth and Herold to the cabin of William Lucas, a free-born black farmer and neighbor of Stuart whom the doctor thought might put the men up for the night. The family dogs, a neighing horse, and strange voices calling his name woke Lucas, but, given the unsettled times, he was unwilling to open the door. "People had been shot in that way," he said.[74] Finally, realizing Bryant was among the party, he ventured out.

"We were sent here," said the visitors as they pushed forward. "We have been knocking about all night and don't intend to any longer. We are going to stay."

"You cannot do it," protested Lucas. "I am a colored man and have no right to take care of white people. I have only one room in the house, and my wife is sick."

"Dave, we will not go on any farther, but stay here," declared Booth. Turning to Lucas, the assassin said, "We understand you have good teams." The men wanted a ride south to the ferry on the Rappahannock River in the morning, and Lucas would take them.

"Gentlemen, you have treated me very badly."

By the time Lucas said this, Booth was seated and in no mood to argue. He replied, "We offer to pay you for your accommodation and if you will not accept pay, we will take your horses, your wagon and we will compel you to take us where we want to go." When Lucas continued his protest, saying he needed his horses to put in his corn crop the next day, the assassin grew menacing. "Fellow, do you know we are some of Mosby's men?" Booth responded. The assassin pulled back his coat, revealing his revolvers and knife.[75] Lucas was frightened, as he should have been, and the dispute ended.

The farmer wisely changed the topic, asking Booth where he was from. Danville, replied Booth. He had escaped from the Yankees in Washington. Attempting to flee a gunboat, he had fallen from his horse and broken his leg. Now he simply wanted to get home. Lucas believed none of this, of course, but had heard enough stories about Mosby to fear that the crippled man might murder him, take the horses, and decamp. Booth was dangerous, and Lucas prudently decided to keep his distance. He and his wife sat on the stoop of their cabin until daybreak, afraid to sleep.

As he settled in for the night, Booth seethed with indignation. He had been specifically directed to Cleydael by friends in Maryland. Bryant offered to take him elsewhere, suggesting doctors closer by, but Booth said no. He had been determined to call on Stuart, whose welcome for fellow rebels was legendary on the other side of the river. Cox, Jones, Harbin, Mudd's in-laws, and many other Marylanders had enjoyed it. And yet the wealthy Virginian gave him a bum's rush to a black man's shanty. Booth, whose exhausting day started on the other side of the Potomac, had not slept under a roof in more than a week. Now he had been humiliated by those who should acclaim him. Worn out, mortified, and dishonored, he let Stuart have a piece of his mind.

"Dear Sir," he wrote on a page from his diary.[76]

Forgive me, but I have some little pride. I hate to blame you for your want of hospitality; you know your own affairs. I was sick and tired, with a broken leg, in need of medical advice. I would not have turned a dog from my door in such a condition. However, you were kind enough to give me something to eat, for which I not only thank you but on account of the reluctant manner in which it was bestowed, I feel bound to pay for it. It is not the substance but the manner in which a kindness is extended that makes one happy in the acceptance thereof. The sauce in meat is ceremony; meeting were bare without it. Be kind enough to accept the enclosed two dollars and a half (though hard to spare) for what we have received.

Yours respectfully,
Stranger
April 24, 1865

Tearing out the page, Booth rolled up the note with the money inside and closed it with a straight pin. Lucas would carry it to Stuart's house the following day. Reading it, the doctor exploded in anger. He had no intention of taking lessons in good manners from a murderer. He threw the letter across the room toward the fireplace.[77]

Monday morning was cool and clear and the sun well above the horizon when Lucas put his wretched-looking horses in their traces. Booth and Herold were finished with the breakfast Lucas's wife had prepared and were ready to depart.

If Lucas can be believed, Booth's plan was for Herold to drive the team to Port Conway and then, apparently, just keep going. In other words, he intended to steal the horses. Herold vetoed the idea. "You have a large family and a crop on hand. You can have your team back again," the younger man said. Charlie, Lucas's son, could drive the ten miles to the Rappahannock and return with the team.

Booth paid Mrs. Lucas twenty-five dollars for the family's forced hospitality, and by 7:00 a.m. he was under way. The assassin was very tired. He lay down in the back, attempting to sleep amid a load of old furniture, which provided some concealment.[78] Other than a frequent "Hurry up!" thrown Charlie's way, he said little as the cart rolled south.

The wayfarers arrived at Port Conway about noon. Herold jumped down and asked for water from an old-timer standing beyond the gate of a rail fence at one of the few buildings in the forlorn-looking village. A tin dipper full was handed him. Booth, sitting up in the wagon bed, called out, "Bring it down here."[79]

William Rollins, a fisherman with a broad sunburned face, came around the corner of the house as Herold was returning with the dipper. The young man asked him if there was anyone who could take them west to Orange Court House. Booth cautioned that they would have to bypass Fredericksburg "as the damn Yankees were too thick there." Well, Rollins replied, he had a wagon for hire. He never went as far off as Orange, however. In fact, he did not even know how far that was. He could take them south to Bowling Green. That town had a hotel where Booth could rest and gain easy access to the railroad. Rollins would carry them there for ten in gold. Too much, countered Booth, but he might go ten in paper. Or, the fisherman continued, if they just wanted over the grayish Rappahannock, he could take them in his fishing boat for ten cents.[80] Whatever they decided, they would have to cool their heels for a while. The tide was rising and he had nets to attend to.

As Rollins headed off, three horsemen crested a small hill nearby and rode directly down toward the landing. It looked as if they were heading straight for the fugitives. Herold tensed and slipped a hand inside his coat to rest on his pistol. The men rode up and passed him without a word. They were Confederate soldiers!

The three were Lieutenant Mortimer Ruggles, the son of a Southern general, Private Absalom Bainbridge, Ruggles's cousin, and Private Willie Jett, their boyhood friend. Ruggles and Bainbridge were soldiers in Mosby's command, while Jett belonged to the 9th Virginia Cavalry. All were young, younger than Herold. They were returning from the Piedmont after learning that Mosby had disbanded his soldiers instead of surrendering them.[81] They had come home to visit, seek paroles, and make their peace with the new order.

Gray wool meant one thing to the fugitives. They had reached the Confederacy, or at least some shred of it, and Herold lost no time in speaking to the men. Identifying himself by the last name of Boyd, he told them that his brother had been wounded near Petersburg. Lucas refused to take them any farther in the wagon, he complained, and they needed the soldiers' help to cross the river and continue south. Herold appeared anxious and overly inquisitive, and the men grew wary. They declined his offer to take a drink. Summoning the ferryboat from the opposite shore, the three rode back to Rollins's house to tie up and wait. Herold followed.

Bainbridge was a superb-looking fellow, tall, broad-shouldered, and narrow-waisted. Looking much like his athletic cousin, Ruggles was an even larger man and equally handsome. Between them the slight, dark-haired Jett sat like an afterthought, his face long and drawn. The eighteen-year-old had been shot in the abdomen in a cavalry skirmish the preceding summer. The wound nearly killed him. Perhaps because Jett appeared less intimidating than his companions, Herold tapped him on the shoulder and asked for a word in private.[82]

The two walked back to the wharf, where Herold renewed his petition for help. If the soldiers were raising a command to go south, or even to Mexico, he and his brother wished to go along.

Mexico? All this sounded quite odd to Jett. "I cannot go with any man that I do not know anything about," he replied. "Who *are* you?"

This was too much for Herold. His voice trembling, he said, "We are the assassinators of the President." Pointing to Booth, who was hobbling their way, he added, "Yonder is J. Wilkes Booth, the man who killed Lincoln."

The words rendered Jett nearly speechless.[83] All he could manage to do was to motion for Ruggles, who was watering his horse nearby. "Here is a strange thing," Jett finally stammered to the lieutenant.

"I suppose you have been told who I am?" said Booth as he joined them.[84] Given the huge rewards being offered for him, the assassin was displeased that Herold had identified him to strangers, but there was no retreat now. Booth looked directly at the men and added provocatively and with a display of his pistols that he was worth a lot of money to the men who captured him.

The soldiers stared back in awe. They knew of Lincoln's death, of course. Mosby had spoken approvingly of the assassin and even exclaimed, according to Jett, "By God I could take that man in my arms."[85] But they thought that Lincoln's assassin had already been captured. "We were greatly surprised [to meet him]," said Ruggles. "The calm courage of the man, in the midst of his great peril, and while racked by suffering, impressed me in spite of myself, for there was no braggadocio about him. The man won our admiration for we saw he was wounded, desperate, and at bay." Be that as it may, they were not the type of men to take blood money, and Ruggles said so. Booth relaxed on hearing his words and thanked them.

Herold asked their names, and introductions commenced. The assassin dropped all pretenses. His shawl, normally employed to conceal his tattooed initials, fell away, revealing plainly that Booth was who he claimed to be. "This brand would betray me," mused Booth, looking thoughtfully at the letters, then continued, "If I had captured Mr. Lincoln for a hostage, the South could have commanded peace. But it was not to be, and I had but one course left. I took it. It is done. If I have done wrong, then I am the one to meet the consequences." Rollins, who had returned from the river, was not close enough to hear these words but saw clearly that the soldiers were excited.

"We will help you," Ruggles said. "We will take you across the river." Bainbridge pledged to help as well, and Jett added, "I want to do the best I can for you."

"God bless you," Booth replied with emotion.[86]

With Ruggles's help Booth mounted Old Whitie, the lieutenant's horse, and rode it onto the old flatboat.[87] Jett and Bainbridge followed on their mounts, and Herold and Ruggles walked on, the latter holding the assassin's crutches. Booth sat squarely astride his horse and gazed expectantly at the village of Port Royal on the opposite shore. He pulled nervously on the scraggly beginnings of his new mustache. The group fell quiet, as the ferryman, Jim Thornton, was black and seemed to eye them closely as he poled along.

Booth looked bad, thought Ruggles. "His face was haggard, pinched with suffering, his dark eyes sunken but strangely bright, and upon his lip and face was a beard of some days' growth," recalled the officer. "His wounded leg was greatly swollen, inflamed and dark, as from bruised blood. That he suffered intense pain all the time there was no doubt, though he tried to conceal his agony both physical and mental."

"Whatever you deem best to do with me, my friends, I'll agree to be satisfied with," said Booth as the boat struck the wharf.

"Jett understands this country, and I think it will be well to act as he directs," responded Ruggles.

"Do with me, boys, as you think best" was the reply.

Booth's spirits were plainly brightening right in front of them. Surratt had told him that he would be safe if he only could get beyond the Rappahannock, and sure enough it was true. Things were turning up. He laughed heartily at his improved fortunes as the young soldiers clustered around him. "I'm safe in glorious old Virginia, thank God!" he cried.

12

....

THE LAST DITCH

"NOW WHICH WAY?" asked Booth.

That was a good question. Sarah Jane Peyton of Port Royal had opened her door to the cripple. Booth hobbled in, then hobbled back out when Miss Peyton decided it would be improper, in the absence of her brother, to have a strange man in the house. Across the street G. W. Catlett was not at home, while other potential hosts were unavailable or unaccommodating. There seemed to be no refuge for the assassin along the broad streets of the village.[1]

"I propose to take our friend Booth up to Garrett's house. I think they'll give him shelter there and treat him kindly," Jett said to the group.

"I'm in your hands," replied Booth.

The invalid was remounted on Old Whitie, Jett took Herold up with him, and Ruggles took Bainbridge. Riding up a series of hills that climbed to a plateau, the group headed south on the road to Bowling Green.

His black hat pulled down over his forehead, Booth had little to say as they rode along, but Herold was as talkative as ever. He informed Jett that Booth was not the only person with a tattoo. He had them, too. He had a heart and anchor, the symbols of love and of safety, hope, and salvation, on his right arm. Rolling up his sleeve, Herold showed them to his saddle mate.[2]

In midafternoon they arrived at the gate to the Garrett farm. Here the party split up. Herold stopped to wait with Bainbridge since he intended going with the soldiers to Bowling Green to buy a new pair of shoes. Jett, Ruggles, and Booth turned off the main road and headed toward Garrett's. As he rode off, Booth suddenly turned his horse around and, lifting his hat above his head, waved it at the pair. "Come and see me again," he called playfully to Herold and Bainbridge. "I shall always be pleased to see you."

"I'll be with you soon, John," responded Herold. "Keep in good spirits."

"Have no fear about me. I am among friends now." With that Booth wheeled about and galloped after Jett and Ruggles.

Bainbridge never forgot what Booth had just done. "Without a parole as I was and in my own country, our own homes near, among the friends of boyhood, among scenes with which I had been familiar since childhood, I felt the dread of capture. If he felt any premonitions of danger, he gave no signs of them. He seemed as light-hearted and careless as a schoolboy just released from his studies. Booth impressed me at that moment as the most reckless man I had ever met."[3]

Several hundred yards down a country lane, the riders came to the home of Richard H. Garrett. The farmer was summoned by a barking dog to the front yard, where he discovered the men on horseback awaiting him.

"Mr. Garrett, I suppose you hardly remember me," said Jett. "No, sir. I cannot recall you," was the response.[4] Jett had never been introduced to Garrett, although he knew him on sight and felt certain Garrett knew his father, whose name the soldier mentioned by way of introduction. Jett also knew the farmer had Southern sympathies to which an appeal could be made. "Here is a wounded Confederate soldier," the private explained. The man had been injured in the fighting near Petersburg. His name was Boyd. He was a Marylander and an individual of good character. "We want you to take care of [him] for a day or two. Will you do it?" Jett asked.

"Yes," said Garrett. "Certainly." Blessed by the safe return of his own sons Jack and Will from the war, Garrett could not refuse. The hospitable old fellow was willing to take in any suffering stranger so introduced. It was the neighborly thing to do.

Booth made his way up a sandy walkway to the porch. Taking a drink of water, he made himself comfortable in an armchair that was brought out of the house for his use. As supper was not served until dark, he napped until called. Once fed, he returned to the porch and settled on its broad low steps. Calling for some tobacco and a light, he fired up his pipe and chatted away the balmy spring evening. Lincoln's death was but one of many rumors swirling about the countryside, and it was not mentioned. At about ten Jack suggested they retire for the night.[5]

Jack and Will shared an upstairs bedroom to which Booth made his way. Unbuttoning his coat and vest, Booth removed his armaments. Without discussion Booth claimed Jack's bed and draped his small arsenal of two revolvers and a bowie knife on the bedstead. Eyeing them, Jack pulled the boot off the assassin's right leg. Swollen and bandaged, the left leg looked dreadful. "Riding jarred it," Booth said, but it was not very painful unless touched.[6]

"Good night," Booth said abruptly. He turned over in the bed and in a moment was sound asleep. "I thought that I had never seen so sweet and sound a sleeper," recalled Will.[7]

It was late on the morning of April 25, 1865, when Booth woke, and he discovered the household already astir. Will had left to turn out the cattle, Jack to run errands. Their sturdy little brother Richard was there to attend him. Tardy for the summons to breakfast, Booth was told not to concern himself. Soldiers were privileged characters, he was told, and might eat when they got ready.

Booth's hosts lived in a whitewashed two-story house framed with large bookend chimneys, not a manor by any means, but a comfortable country home set in a grove of locust trees. Fruit trees in bloom lay before it, and wooded gullies ran on either side. A pleasant pastoral feeling pervaded the property. Garrett, his wife, Fannie, and their large family had a nice place. They were nice people. Richard later wrote Edwin Booth that his family "did everything in their power to make your brother comfortable even when they did not know who he was, and, had they known, it would have made no change in them."[8]

It was as if the Garretts had granted Booth a sanctuary. Reveling in his newfound sense of safety, Booth left his pistols in the sons' room and ventured unarmed—for the first time in months—onto the porch for his morning smoke. The smells of the day's baking greeted him. Booth hobbled through a gate in a crossed-rail fence and made his way toward a weather-beaten barn. Beyond it were corncribs and a cattle shed.

Back on the porch, he stretched out on a bench. He was always fatigued from his injury and soon dozed off. When he awoke, Will was nearby. The twenty-year-old was drawn to Booth as "the finest-looking man I ever saw" and asked his story. The wayfarer was happy to comply. He explained that he was from Annapolis. Attempting to go home after the surrender, he learned that he had to take the oath of allegiance to do so. That he would never do. He decided to return to whatever was left of the army and take his chances. Falling in with a cousin, he took off on a drinking spree and ended up shooting it out with federal cavalry. After hiding in Maryland's swampy pines, he slipped back into Virginia. Now here he was, disabled, disheveled, and nearly broke after paying an extortionist for a boat. This fantastic concoction of falsehoods seasoned with a pinch of fact seemed to satisfy young Will.

The day was warm—the warmest in months—and the invalid moved out to lounge in the yard. He lay down on a carpet of spring grass so green and thick that it felt like velvet. Lilly, Hettie, and Cora—ages nine, six, and three respectively—gathered near the stranger. "We were full of romp and frolic," said Lilly, and she and her sisters danced around him, pulling on his shirt sleeves. The girls noticed his tattoo, so he explained it to them; the letter *J* stood for James, he said. That was his name. Pulling out his pocket compass, he showed them how it worked. Their puzzlement when he made the needle move by holding the point of his pocketknife above it made him laugh. "Pretty good sort of man," thought their brother Robert, who was seven. As they lounged about, an occasional white blossom from the apple tree overhead fluttered past them like a snowflake.[9]

The innocence of the children put him in a wistful mood. He spoke of his mother, with a sort of childlike tone that seemed odd in an adult. It was noticeable that his frame of mind was erratic. Despondent one moment, he was elated the next. He grew feverish and asked for water as his leg began to pain him again. He remained polite, however, and the Garretts charitably ascribed his flightiness to his injury and other war-time experiences.[10]

The dinner bell brought everyone inside, but more than food was on the table. Jack said that while he was out he met a man with a recent Richmond newspaper. It reported that Lincoln was indeed dead and a large reward was being offered for the capture of his killer.

"What reward?" asked Booth.

"$140,000," replied Jack.

Booth asked Jack to repeat the figure, which he did. "I would sooner suppose $500,000," Booth responded. With professional composure, the actor gave no sign of uneasiness as he spoke.

"I wish he would come this way," laughed Will. "I'd like to get that amount."[11]

Booth, sitting opposite Will at the table, could hardly believe such a remark from a young man still wearing a Confederate uniform. "I hadn't taken you for that bloodthirsty kind of man." responded Booth incredulously. "Would you do such a thing?" The assassin turned toward him, smiled, and waited for an answer.

"I would indeed," replied Will, adding that times were hard.

"Not as hard as hearts," countered Booth.[12]

"He is young and foolish," interrupted the father. "He does not mean what he says." The father had the final word on the murder—"No good will come of it"—and the conversation turned to other topics.

Later, on the porch, the Garretts' daughter Annie told Booth that it was unfortunate the assassination happened at a time when Southern prospects were so poor. Attempting to put a better face on things, Booth disagreed, asserting that since Johnson was a drunkard, "it would cause a revolution and be the best thing for the South."[13] "Well," she continued, "I suppose there were a good many people in the North as well as the South who were anxious to get rid of the President." She had little doubt they paid the assassin for his work. "No, Miss, it is my opinion he was not paid. He did it for notoriety's sake," countered Booth, mocking newspaper reports of his motive.[14]

Nevertheless the family's remarks depressed him. "The ship's gone down, down, down, never to rise again," he was overheard whispering sullenly. "Down, down, down."[15] It was hard for him to hear Southerners express indifference or antagonism to his act. To deal with the rebuke, Booth could only fall back on the standard response of reactionaries in every era. He believed that the public had grown too degraded and corrupt to appreciate his sacrifice. "I cannot see any wrong [I have done]," he wrote in his diary, "except in serving a degenerate people."

One statement brought out this attitude vividly. It also revealed that Booth's long-standing love affair with Virginia was at an end. He told the family, "Men are all selfish, North and South. You might as well die for a nation of Yankees as of Virginians."[16]

Booth noticed a large map of the United States hanging in the house. His mind back on his business, he asked Jack to take it down and put it on a table. Booth studied the map with care, taking notes as he drew a pencil line down to Norfolk, then on to Charleston, to Savannah, and through the Gulf of Mexico to Galveston. Richard, who stood watching, asked him where he wanted to go. "To Mexico," replied Booth.[17] But such a route was a fantasy, given Union control of the coast. More practically he renewed with Jack his interest in getting west to Orange. Having heard that there were rebels from Maryland there, he hoped to secure a horse from them and reach Johnston's army in North Carolina.

The day had grown hot. Booth returned to the porch, sitting in his shirtsleeves and writing in his diary. Jack sat nearby on the steps.

"There goes some of your party now," said the brother, pointing to a group of riders passing along the main road about a quarter mile east of the house. Booth rose and looked out at the horsemen. He had no *party* and immediately sensed trouble. "Will you please go and get my pistol," he said. When Jack hesitated, Booth commanded, "You go and get my pistols!"

Jack went upstairs, saw the horsemen heading away, and returned to tell Booth. Richard followed with the heavy belt of weapons.

"Why are you so nervous?" the older brother asked.

"I feel safer when I am armed" was his answer.[18]

The riders proved no danger. It was only Ruggles and Bainbridge heading back to Port Royal and to their homes across the river in King George County. They had stopped to deposit Herold, and in a few moments his familiar form came down the lane. Carrying a Spencer carbine slung over his shoulder on a homemade cotton strap, he limped along, a sore-footed hobo.[19]

Booth was relieved to see him. Meeting Herold at the gate, he drew him away from the house for a talk.

Herold's twenty-four-hour furlough had given him a taste of freedom, and he relished it. "I am sick and tired of this way of living," he announced. "I would like to go home." He said the words as if picking up his former life were a simple matter. "What do *you* intend to do?" he asked Booth.

"Well, I intend to stay here all night," responded the assassin.[20]

Herold following, Booth returned to the house, where he introduced the newcomer as a cousin. "Can I stay here?" the younger man asked Jack.

Garrett grimaced. Having been on twenty-one battlefields over four years of war, he had an instinct for anything amiss. He was suspicious of Booth's behavior on the porch, and now here was a new ragtag seeking hospitality. Herold was relaxed and bantering, but all was not right, Jack realized. He put the men off by saying that he would have to speak to his father. Jack's tone was not welcoming.

Only minutes elapsed before a thunder of hooves sounded. Ruggles and Bainbridge reappeared, riding hard down the lane toward the house.

"Well, boys, what's in the wind now?" Booth called out.

"Marylanders, you had better watch out," shouted Ruggles. "There are forty Yankee cavalry coming up the hill. You must seek refuge in the ravines. Get over there at once and hide yourself."

A determined look swept Booth's face. He bit his lip. "I will do as you say and go at once," said the assassin, straightening himself. He held out his hand in thanks, first to Ruggles, then to Bainbridge. "It will never do for you boys to be found in my company, so leave me. I thank you from my heart for what you have done, and God bless you."

Herold, who had stepped away, was back, and someone from the house pointed them to a secluded area. "I will *never* be a prisoner," Bainbridge heard Booth mutter as the two fugitives hurried off.[21]

Booth headed to a heavy stand of pine and scrub oak at the rear of the barn. Plunging into it, the assassin took cover. Had he found his vaunted "last ditch"? The phrase originated with William of Orange during that prince's seemingly hopeless resistance to a French invasion of the Netherlands in 1672 when he said memorably that there was one certain way to ensure that he never saw his country lost: "I will die in the last ditch."[22] Southerners revived the expression to indicate their willingness to fight to the bitter end, and even Grant echoed it in 1864 when he wrote that the rebels, in their dogged defense of the Old Dominion, seemed to be digging that ditch at last.[23] During the heady days of the abduction conspiracy Booth wrote, "They say [the South] has found that 'last ditch' which the North have so long derided and been endeavoring to force her into. Should I reach her in safety and find it true, I will proudly beg permission to triumph or die in that same 'ditch' by her side." Ingloriously, this ditch was a pile of underbrush.[24]

After five suspenseful minutes Herold ventured back to the yard to determine if the report of cavalry was true. A passing rider confirmed it, and soon Herold and Jack saw a torrent of mounted bluecoats flow past on the road to Bowling Green. While Herold deliberated that sobering sight, Jack told him that he was uncomfortable with the men's presence on the farm. They needed to leave.

"We will not get you into any trouble," Herold laughed. The young man was bright and reassuring. And he was hungry, too, he wanted Jack to know, and ready for something to eat. Herold's cheerfulness stemmed from a childlike conviction of his own innocence. After all, he had not shot anybody. By his road-weary logic he had done nothing over the past two weeks more egregious than lie about Booth's identity. "That is the worst thing I have done."

It was indisputably time to get moving, however, and Herold implored Jack to help them find the means to do so. The latter went to see a neighbor who occasionally rented a wagon. Having no luck, he returned home, bringing with him the realization he would have to transport the men himself if he wanted to get rid of them. Herold gave Jack a ten-dollar note to sweeten the prospect, and Jack promised to take them toward Orange in the morning.

As night fell, Booth lingered in the brush, and old man Garrett told Herold matter-of-factly, "You had better go down and tell Mr. Boyd to come up and get his supper." The young man went and called for Booth, and the assassin wobbled forward from the woods. He handed Herold the carbine to carry, and, taciturn and pale, he made his way to the house and joined the family.[25]

Having overstayed his welcome, Booth found the Garretts less sociable than the previous night. Jack thought the invalid suspiciously interested in the family's horses, while Herold's claim of service in the Confederate army seemed demonstrably false. The latter was a liar, the former a potential horse thief. This was all wrong.

"I don't want you to stay in the house," Jack told the men as they gathered on the porch after eating.

"Well, what's in that barn, then?" asked Herold. "We'll sleep in there."

It was well after eight when the Garretts and their guests walked out toward the looming square structure. The family called this building its tobacco house, although it had been some time since it served that purpose. The wicket door, creaking on its hinge when opened, revealed to Booth a planked floor filled on one side with hay and corn fodder for the farm's livestock and on the other with a wheat-threshing machine, a wheat fan mill, cradles, scythes, hoes, rakes, and plows, together with furniture from homes in Port Royal stored here for safety.[26] The space was chilly and uninviting, and as they entered it a bat fluttered above Booth's head.

Gathering a pile of corn husks and straw, Booth fashioned himself a pallet and said good night. Jack departed, still suspicious that the men might attempt to steal horses in the night. He lingered outside the barn, hoping to overhear Booth and Herold's conversation, but the fugitives talked in whispers and he learned nothing. Meanwhile, Will locked the door, effectively trapping the men inside. If the pair attempted to come out under those circumstances, they would raise a racket. As an added precaution, Jack and Will took blankets and settled down near the barn in a shed where feed was stored.

A bed of dry corn blades proved just as uncomfortable as it sounded, and Booth was unable to sleep. While Herold slumbered away, he tossed and turned. His groaning and grumbling were audible to the sons in the corn house, a restlessness that reminded them of a distressed animal.[27] Sometime after 2:00 a.m. the assassin heard noises—barking dogs, galloping horses, shouts, footsteps.

Not all nightmares occur when one is asleep, as it now—and most plainly—unfolded. Herman Neugarten, a broad-shouldered corporal in the 16th New York Cavalry, was outside the barn. The Prussian-born soldier, with shot and saber wounds of the leg, hip, hand, and face, was there in the manner of an undertaker. He was directing half a dozen men to surround the barn and outbuildings.[28] They were part of a force of twenty-nine, led by Lieutenant Edward P. Doherty, who, along with two federal detectives, Everton Conger and Luther B. Baker, swarmed the farm. These were the same men Herold had seen on the road that afternoon.

They were pointed that way because Rollins, the fisherman at the Port Conway ferry, and his wife, Bettie, had fingered Jett. That teenager, discovered and threatened at a hotel in Bowling Green, led the cavalrymen to the farm. The troopers, determined to learn the whereabouts of the strangers, were on the point of extracting the information from the elder Garrett by lynching him when Jack emerged from the shuck house. "Don't injure father," he exclaimed. "I will tell you all about these men. They are in the barn."[29] He pointed off into a night so dark the soldiers could scarcely see the building beyond his finger.

Will produced a candle, and its uncertain light flickered on Jack as the older brother, pushed by Baker and dragged by Doherty, stumbled toward the barn. A revolver was at his head. The soldiers surged at the building, encircling it. Booth woke Herold. "Don't make any noise," he whispered. "Maybe they will go off, thinking we are not here." Herold stirred to life, however, making little attempt to conceal himself. The rustling of straw and the thumping of planks as he walked about were unmistakably audible to the cavalrymen.

"You men had better come out of there," shouted Baker. "We know who you are."

There was silence, the summons was repeated, and Booth answered, "Who are you?" He spoke in a voice strong enough to be heard by the Garretts they clustered at the door of the family home.

"Never mind who *we* are," replied Baker. "We know who *you* are and you had better come out and deliver yourself up."

"This is a hard case, I swear. Perhaps I am being taken by my own friends," responded Booth hopefully.

His remark gave Baker an idea. Jack was Booth's landlord, dinner companion, and hostler. He knew Booth and, dressed in his Confederate uniform, was plainly gray inside and out. Let him do the job. Go into the barn, Baker ordered, and demand the fugitive's surrender. If he wouldn't come out, the barn would be burned over his head. Understandably frightened, Jack attempted to explain that the fugitives were desperate, but the men outside the barn were proving desperate as well. They had been on the chase for thirty-five straight hours. Edgy and exhausted, the party was short on patience, good humor, and possibly good judgment. Baker unlocked the door and pushed Jack through.

It seemed darker inside the barn than out, if that were possible, and Jack could distinguish little as he inched toward the area where he believed Booth to be. A form rose in front of him. "The cavalry are after you," he said to the dim presence.

"Damn you! You have betrayed me!" cried Booth. Jack hastened to explain "that the barn was surrounded, resistance was useless, and he had better come out and deliver himself up." "Get out of here!" was the response.

Doherty, having dismounted his men and positioned them around the barn, returned to the door as Jack exited. The lieutenant was displeased at what he saw. He had men enough, and they had courage enough, to handle this. At first light he intended to rush the barn from every entrance, overpowering its occupants. Detectives Conger and Baker had another plan. Doherty and his cavalrymen were so many dull cleavers. A fine hand might flush even a rabid villain like Booth out of his hole. Under the direction of Conger, a former lieutenant colonel, Baker would attempt to talk him out.

Doherty had an additional problem, this time with Sergeant Boston Corbett. An English immigrant and naturalized citizen, Corbett had been a journeyman hat finisher before the war. Once the fighting broke out, he served several short hitches before joining the 16th. Captured by Mosby in 1864, he was sent to the infamous Camp Sumter at Andersonville, Georgia. Nearly dead, he emerged from captivity on crutches.[30] Not unexpectedly, the sergeant hated the Confederacy and its cruel jailers. He hated the Southern aristocracy who authored the rebellion. He hated Richmond, where he was shunned for his eccentricities and his denunciations of slavery. And he hated the theater as "the school which made Booth an assassin."[31] No two men were less alike than Booth and this mad hatter, yet in the element of fanaticism their natures were similar.

The acting orderly sergeant of the troop, Corbett was a short man with a keen and determined look. His hair, parted down the middle in imitation of popular depictions of Jesus, rather overwhelmed a scruffy doorknocker beard and mustache. A decent, honest, and plain-mannered man of thirty-two, Corbett possessed a decidedly odd nature. He was a religious zealot—a preaching and praying machine. He believed in the duty of Christian perfectionism, following its tenets even to the point of self-mutilation. His outspoken faith alternately amused and annoyed his comrades, but they readily acknowledged his courage and martial qualities.[32] He was a fine soldier, yet often in trouble for making conscience his guide in all matters, military as well as civil.[33]

Corbett had a proposal for Doherty. He wanted permission to enter the barn alone and confront Booth. He would either take him or run him out of bullets, allowing for his capture. Corbett had often expressed a desire to die for freedom, and here was a plan suicidal enough to achieve that end. Doherty, who admired Corbett's soldiering, flatly refused the request. He had no intention of risking his ranking noncommissioned officer on such a mission. Towering over the little sergeant, the lieutenant turned him away with the words "Never mind. We'll get him."

Booth opened a parlay. "What do you want? Who do you take us for?"

"We want you," replied Baker. "We know who you are. Give up your arms and come out. If you don't come out, we will set the barn on fire and burn you out."

"Give me five minutes to consider."

"Very well," responded Baker. "Take the time."

"Come on," Booth whispered to Herold. The pair sneaked up to the door. Finding it locked, they moved to the back of the barn. With luck they could kick off a board and crawl out. The scheme had merit, but unfortunately the old slat wall seemed set in stone and the men were unable to budge it. "Let's kick together," urged Booth. Again, nothing.[34]

More than five minutes had elapsed when Baker yelled, "We have waited long enough. Surrender your arms and come out. You cannot escape."

"This is hard," replied Booth. "We are guilty of no crime. If I have done anything, I did it for the good of my country. At least I fancied so."

"I want you to surrender. If you don't, I will burn the barn down."

"I am a cripple and alone. Give me a chance for my life. Be fair and give me a show. Draw off your men fifty yards, and I will come out and fight you."[35]

"No," Baker replied, "I did not come to fight. I came here to capture you. I have fifty men, and I propose to do it."[36] If Booth came out and surrendered, no harm would come to him. If he did not come out, they would take him out, one way or the other.

"You have spoiled my plans. I was going to Mexico to make my fortune," responded Booth cavalierly.

Ten, twenty, thirty minutes went by in such talk. "Many words, to and fro," grumbled Corbett. Impatient with all this palaver, he was back at Doherty's elbow. The men were too exposed, he complained. They could not see Booth, but as the night waned away the assassin—crazed and dangerous—could see them. Let *him* enter the barn now, Corbett pleaded, and deal with the matter. He was not afraid to go in. "It was time the man was shot," the sergeant, with remarkable candor, later said.

With two Colt revolvers and the Spencer carbine, Booth had twenty rounds at his disposal.[37] "I could have picked off three or four of your men already if I wished to do so," the assassin called out to Baker. "I have had half a dozen opportunities to shoot you." That was certainly true. The detective stood near Will's candle. Conger pointed out the foolhardiness of that to Baker, and Baker hastily moved the light away from the building. Later, in thinking over these events, Baker concluded, "He did not appear to want to shoot anyone. I do not think Booth wanted to kill anybody except in an open, fair fight, [but in that case] I think he would have come out and fought the whole command till he died."

Doherty, not knowing their priceless prey's state of mind, again refused his sergeant's request. Frustrated, Corbett went to Conger and put his proposal to the lead detective and ringmaster. Corbett's station was at a large crack in the wall at the rear of barn. Get back there, Conger barked.

"Yes, sir," grumbled Corbett.[38]

Inside the barn Booth and Herold talked, whisperings at first that escalated into loud voices. "You had better give up," said Herold. "No" was Booth's reply. "I'll die like a man."[39] "Let me go out and give myself up," begged the young man.

"I never thought you would desert me," complained Booth. "I wouldn't leave a dog under such circumstances."

"I don't intend to be burnt alive." He laid down his pistol.

"Certainly!" cried Booth scornfully. "Get away from me. You are a damned coward and mean to leave me in my distress. I don't want you to stay." For an instant Herold wavered, but Booth regained his composure and Corbett heard him say, "Oh, go out, my boy. Save your life if you can."[40] Herold rose to leave, and Booth shouted, "There is a man in here that wants to surrender very bad." As Herold reached the portal, Booth added, "I declare before my Maker that this man is innocent of any crime whatever." It was the only gift Booth had to give him.

"I have no arms," Herold said. "Let me out." Jack opened the door, and Herold stuck his hands out as directed. In a flash Doherty grabbed him by the wrists and jerked him forward. The lieutenant passed him to Neugarten for searching.

Booth's voice rang out from inside: "Well, my brave boys, prepare a stretcher for me." Then, "Make quick work of it. Shoot me through the heart!" Such remarks dispelled any hope that Booth might surrender.

Realizing that the crisis was at hand, the assassin watched the walls for trouble, and there it was. Conger had forced Rebel Jack to pile kindling up to the barn. "Young man, I advise you for your own good not to come here again," said Booth in a threatening tone. Jack fled. Arms loaded with dry brush, Will was similarly run off. Meanwhile Neugarten went to pile hay against the building. "Come back here and I will put a bullet through you," Booth warned the corporal.[41] Taking matters into his own hands, Conger walked past Corbett at the back of the barn, made a twist of straw, lit it, and thrust it through a gap in the planks onto a pile of stubble. The dry material caught fire immediately. The barn lit up, and the cavalrymen drew in to the walls. The glowing interior made Booth visible to them through the gaps between the boards of the old tobacco house, while it prevented him from seeing them. Gun barrels leveled on the figure in the fiery footlights.

Booth was leaning against a haymow, attempting to rise on his crutches, when he noticed the flames spreading through a pile of straw in a corner. Wisps of nearby hay caught fire, exploding like match heads. "In an instant the whole interior of the place was light as day," recalled Private John Millington. Startled and confused at first, the assassin recovered and rushed as best a cripple could toward Conger's bonfire, a carbine in one hand and a crutch in the other. Watching this incredible drama unfold, Private Frederick Dietz recalled, "Misguided murderer that he was, there was something in Booth's manner which commanded our respect, if it did not win our admiration. His cool nerve in the face of such desperate odds was something wonderful."[42]

The assassin peered at the walls, his carbine poised for any intruder. Seeing none, he turned his attention to the fire. At first he attempted to trample it out, impossible with his broken leg. Then he grabbed a table lying bottom side up and made an effort to throw it on the fire, hoping to snuff out the blaze.

The fire spread, however. The hungry flames licked the walls and reached for the ceiling. Smoke billowed from the floor beneath Booth's feet. Hissing sounds came from all sides. It was too late. Realizing the futility of his efforts, he dropped the table, then turned away, coughing heavily, and headed back toward the center of the barn. No words could express the look of hatred and heroism that mingled on Booth's face, thought Corbett.[43]

The last ditch!

Baker, seeing Booth distracted by the fire, removed the lock and peeked inside. Noticing the door ajar and having no wish to roast, the assassin turned to face it. Framed by fire, he drew himself up to his full height. His eyes were lustrous as if he were feverish. His lips were pressed together. He swept the fingers of his right hand through his hair as if to compose himself.[44] "One more stain on the old banner," he cried in a loud, clear voice. "Do your worst!" Throwing down the crutch, he took out a pistol. With it in one hand and the carbine in the other, he took a halting step toward the exit. "If there was anything in the assassin's career which prompted admiration, it was his courage," said Conger. "I was twice wounded in the war, was under fire at many of the most disastrous battles, led my command right through the teeth of almost certain annihilation, and yet this exhibition of sublime courage, with death lurking in every corner, was a lesson to me."[45]

Corbett could stand this no longer. Satisfied that the assassin intended to fight his way out, the sergeant decided that Booth would not take another life.[46] Four years earlier, at the war's commencement, Corbett's hand had shaken that of Abraham Lincoln as the president, with tears of gratitude in his eyes, thanked the hat finisher and his comrades in the New York City militia for coming to the rescue of the capital. Now, at the war's end, Corbett beseeched God to make that same hand the one to avenge the president's death.[47] On the manhunt he had prayed for this privilege, and the Lord now answered back. "I heard the voice of God calling on me to fire," recalled Corbett.[48] "God commanded me do it."[49] With divine help directing his aim to give Booth the wound that Booth gave Lincoln, Corbett steadied his Colt revolver on his arm, uttered an audible prayer for his target's guilty soul, and fired.

A dull boom sounded in the barn. Corbett's bullet hit Booth in the neck, tore through it, flew across the barn, and smacked against a wall, falling to the floor in a little puff of dust. A low scream of pain like that produced by a sudden throttling came from the assassin, and he pitched headlong to the floor.[50] "Booth dropped like a log," recalled Millington.

Baker charged in. As Booth struggled to turn over, he pounced on him and pinned him to the floor. The assassin had a death grip on the pistol, and Baker wrenched it from his hand. Doherty piled on, pulling the knife from Booth's belt and seizing the carbine. Then the men realized there was no fight in their captive. His eyes were closed, his head drooping. He was helpless. He seemed lifeless.

"Kill the ——! Kill him!" shouted the soldiers as they rushed in on the officers' heels. "Let him alone," cried Private Emory Parady. "He's near enough dead now." Hovering over the body, Baker and Conger began to dispute what had just happened. Had Booth shot himself or been shot? As important as that question was, the answer had to wait. The fire was beginning to consume the barn. Jack, who rushed past the men in an effort to put out the flames, rushed back, his hair and eyebrows singed by burning hay falling from the rafters. The fire was forming into sheets. The room would soon be a furnace. Everyone had to get out immediately. Neugarten held Booth's head, Parady wrapped his arms under Booth's knees, and with an assist from Baker, Conger, and Dietz, they carried him outside to a grassy spot about twenty-five feet from the barn.

Shattered, Booth was not yet dead. The muscles of his mouth quivered, and someone shouted, "The damn rebel is still living." Baker sprinkled water on his face and he revived. The assassin's eyes opened, glazed and brilliant in the light of the fire. His sweat-soaked hair lay in ribbons across his forehead. Through his collar were bullet holes, in on his right side and out his left, where a cone-shaped slug about the size of a small grape had punched through the neck. There was little blood.

Booth struggled to speak, but his voice was very feeble. "You have finished me" was a guess at his words. He tried to speak again. Parady heard "Mother, Mother" before Baker pushed the private away and took his place. "Tell Mother," gasped Booth, swooning away, then returning. Conger elbowed in and pressed his ear close to Booth's lips. The assassin's words were unmistakable. "Tell my mother I die for my country."[51]

The lack of powder burns on Booth's collar indicated that the assassin had not shot himself. But what had occurred? The debate resumed until Corbett stepped forward and said simply, "I shot him." The little sergeant leaned in to inspect his handiwork. Corbett was a marksman, but in attempting to give Booth Lincoln's wound he was off the mark several inches. Nevertheless, he was satisfied. In fact, he was convinced he had hit Booth in the exact spot where Booth's shot had hit the president. When Corbett saw the track of his bullet, he said to himself, "What a God we serve!"

Herold, tied up by Millington, witnessed all this with trembling excitement.[52] As he always did when he got into trouble, he began to talk. There must be some mistake, he said. He was a simple Confederate soldier. His name was not Herold. He was unaware that the other man was an assassin. He believed the man's name was Boyd, not Booth. He had tried to get him to surrender and the man threatened to kill him. He wished to God his barn mate had never been born. He had always liked Mr. Lincoln. He loved the late president's jokes. He wanted the ten dollars he gave Jack returned. The rope hurt his hands.[53] "Young, green, weak-minded," Parady told a reporter forty-five years later. "I was sorry for him and have always felt that way."

The barn was blazing like a burning haystack, and the heat forced a retreat to the house, where Booth was placed on the veranda, his head near the large double doors.[54] He seemed to revive a bit, although any movement was very painful and he whispered, "No—no," when he saw a straw mattress being brought from inside. "Let me lie here," he pled. "Let me die here." Despite the protest, Baker raised him up, the mattress was folded double, and Booth's head was laid upon it.

Conger tore open Booth's shirt collar, and Baker took a cloth and water and bathed the assassin's wound. Although the haggard-looking fugitive was much changed, there was no doubt who he was. Conger knew Booth on sight, and so did Doherty.[55] But, in an abundance of caution, the officers formally identified their man. They read the printed description of the fugitive from the reward poster, put photographs beside his face, and examined his tattoo. Everything confirmed Conger's judgment from the moment he entered the barn: "It *is* Booth."

The assassin had asked the soldiers to make quick work of him, but they botched the job. Corbett's bullet fractured Booth's fourth and fifth cervical vertebrae, cutting the spinal cord and driving bone fragments into the muscles.[56] Immediate paralysis of the body below the injury resulted. The respiratory muscles were affected, and Booth could only breathe in labored gasps. Feeling as if he were choking, he asked to be turned on his side. This was done several times, but the change afforded no relief, and each time he asked to be turned back. Miserable, Booth muttered, "Oh, kill me, kill me."

"We don't wish to kill you," Baker replied encouragingly. "We hope you will get well."

Spreading a handkerchief on the porch, the detectives held Booth up and searched for spoils. Baker discovered the assassin's compass, pipe, tobacco, and matches in the coat. Oddly Booth's pocket also contained a handful of small onions. Conger found his diary, keys, and pocketknife, a small silver horseshoe charm, the Agnus Dei medal, the Montreal bank draft obtained in Canada the previous autumn, and a few greenbacks. The small amount of money they found led someone to observe that if that was all Booth had, he did not get rich for what he did. Conger also found cartes de visite of five women (one of Lucy Hale) and, on Booth's undershirt, a diamond stickpin presented to the assassin by the minstrel Dan Bryant. Conger tied these items up in a bundle and stuffed them in his own pocket.

"Kill me," Booth implored again in a whisper.

"No," replied Conger.

One of the soldiers stated that "he never saw a man suffer more or die harder," and through it all Booth could do nothing but lie there and endure it.[57] His mind was clear. He was aware of his surroundings. He was conscious of his suffering. It was as if he had become a witness to his own execution.[58] Soldiers wanting revenge had it that morning. A full pound of flesh.

What could be done for him was done. Brandy and ice were brought to the porch, and nursing devolved to the tender hands of Fannie Garrett and her sister Lucinda Holloway, while Fannie's daughter Kate fetched items as needed. Aunt Lue bathed the grievously wounded man's face.[59] Booth was unable to swallow, so she pressed a linen cloth soaked with water and brandy to his lips. The assassin opened his eyes at her touch and attempted to smile.

Meanwhile Conger and Baker seated themselves on either side of the body, ready to hear any confession. Aunt Lue knelt nearby, wearing an apron as if she were about her housework. Richard and Robert lurked behind her, the latter having dressed so hurriedly that he had his pants on backward.[60] Exhausted soldiers sagged on the waist-high porch or against its brick pillars. Herold was strapped to a locust tree in the yard, while the troopers' horses stood tethered to the fence beyond him. The scene was completed by the elder Garrett, still in his nightclothes and guarded by two soldiers, sitting on a block of wood and fortunate that, as Booth's host, it was his rear end and not his neck on the stump.

Shot at about 3:15 a.m., Booth clung tenaciously to life. Dawn came, then sunrise, and he held on. For most of the time his eyes were closed and his teeth were clenched in pain. He gasped as if trying to remove an obstruction from his throat. He talked little, and that almost all in the first hour, and his words were very faint. Once, hearing Baker mention Jett, he managed to say, "Did that man betray me?" "Hands," he gasped on another occasion, and, when they were held up, mumbled, "Useless, useless."[61] These words have been interpreted as a jab at Herold, a refusal of water, a comment on his paralysis, even a self-criticism of his life. The soldiers who attended him found his remarks mostly incoherent and unintelligible. There was no need to ponder the meaning of one thing Booth muttered, however. "I die for my country. I did what I thought was best."[62]

About 6:00 a.m., Dr. Charles Urquhart arrived from Port Royal. The old gentleman was flustered by what he saw. "He was used to war and bloodshed, but the scene seemed to startle him," recalled Private Carl John Anton Steinbrigge, one of the command. Composing himself, Urquhart set to work, applying stimulants to his patient. With a fastidious touch he opened his box of surgical instruments. Producing a probe, the physician examined the wound, searching for the bullet. Baker told him he was wasting his time. The slug had traversed the neck. Urquhart's initial optimism about Booth's condition gave way immediately, and in a professorial manner he explained that the wound was mortal. Booth would die within the hour.[63]

As the end approached, the assassin's skin became cool to the touch. His lips grew blue and drawn. Aunt Lue's warming massages of his temples availed little; in fact, she could feel his pulse fade away. At times his heart stopped, as Booth courted death, only to have the beat return.

Lengthier and lengthier intervals passed between breaths—literal minutes, followed by a noisy desperate gasp. Booth's body shut down. He asphyxiated. A spectral pallor took his face. Shortly after seven there was a shiver and a gurgle. Booth's head pitched back, he seemed to collapse, and life fled. It was over.

The death watch concluded, Doherty asked for a needle and began fashioning a coarse gray shroud of two blankets sewn together like a sack.[64] Conger departed to carry the news to Washington. Baker went about securing a wagon to bring the body along as soon as possible. The doctor clipped a lock of hair from Booth's forehead and handed it to Aunt Lue. "A sweet memento," she thought.[65]

It was morning, a clear warm morning, and time for breakfast at the farm, time for hot biscuits and good country butter all around.

Herold—God bless him—ate heartily.[66]

TO FIRST CLASS BOY Fred Oatley, nestled in his hammock beneath the spar deck, it sounded as if elephants were tramping across the iron face of the USS *Mahopac*.[67] Curious, he jumped up to observe the heavyweights. Brigadier General Joseph Holt, Judge Advocate General of the U.S. Army. Congressman John A. Bingham, Republican stalwart from Ohio. Colonel Lafayette C. Baker, head of the National Detective Police. Dr. Joseph Barnes, Surgeon-General of the United States. Major Thomas T. Eckert, Stanton confidante and chief of the War Department telegraph office. Stanton and Secretary of the Navy Gideon Welles had dispatched these men to the Washington Navy Yard to examine the remains of Booth, which reposed on the nearby *Montauk*.[68] Since one reached the *Montauk* by use of the *Mahopac*'s small cutter, Oatley was pressed into duty as ferryman for the officials.

Surgeon General Barnes stepped onto the deck of the *Montauk* as if he owned it. Without reporting his presence, showing his authority, or displaying any other regard for military etiquette, the physician walked directly to the carpenter's bench that served as Booth's bier. Taking a knife, he cut away the wrappings around the corpse.[69]

"That's it," said Patrick Stafford, one of the *Montauk*'s firemen standing nearby. "That's Booth."

"Look at that," said Dr. George B. Todd, the vessel's surgeon, pointing to the marks on Booth's left hand. "What do you make that out to be?"

Stafford leaned in to take a look, then straightened up. "J.W.B."[70]

Barnes had doubts that the soldiers had caught their man, however, and a close look at what the New York newspapers delighted to call "the whilom fop" hardly reassured him.[71] The owner of this body was no dandy. He looked as if he had been flushed out of a gutter. His clothing was soiled. His remains smelled. His hair was ineptly clipped and badly matted. There was no mustache at all, just a stubble of beard. And that face! It was wild and worn and older than its years. The lower part was discolored by extravasation of blood. Curiously, it was freckled.

Hundreds of other people wanted a look-see as well. Most were turned away at the Navy Yard gate, but dozens got their opportunity. A stream of officers, sailors, marines, yard employees, carpenters hammering on a coffin, mechanics working on an engine, and lucky civilian visitors all pressed toward the afterdeck. Despite the efforts of Barnes to prevent souvenir taking, several got close enough to obtain items from the body, such as Acting Master William Crowninshield, who secured a lock of hair for his sister Mary.[72]

The identity of the corpse was soon established. Seaton Munroe, lawyer and man-about-town, got aboard the *Montauk* because his brother Frank was a Marine Corps captain. Eckert invited him back to see the body. "I was soon gazing at the remains which needed no long inspection to enable me to recognize them," Munroe wrote. When Eckert realized that the attorney knew Booth socially, he escorted him to the ship's cabin to give a statement to the military commissioners. "I am confident that it is the dead body of J. Wilkes Booth," he told Holt and company. Before he left the *Montauk*, Munroe saw Herold, shackled hand and foot, emerge from a hatchway en route to have his photograph taken.[73]

Dr. John Frederick May, the most important of five official witnesses, was less certain than Munroe about the body's identity, at least initially. He knew Booth, having removed the fibroid tumor from Booth's neck in 1863. The handsome patient came to May's office daily thereafter to have the wound dressed, and the men became friendly. Booth presented him with complimentary tickets, and May, who admired the acting of Booth's father, attended a performance.

The doctor was dumbfounded when Barnes pulled back the tarpaulin covering the body. He would write, "Never in any human being had a greater change taken place, from the man I had seen in the vigor of life and health, than that of the haggard corpse which was before me, with its yellow and discolored skin and its whole facial expression sunken and sharpened by the exposure and starvation it had undergone!"[74]

"There is no resemblance in that corpse to Booth," May exclaimed to Surgeon General Barnes. "I cannot identify this body."

A shock went through the crowd. May, the most highly regarded surgeon in the nation's capital, was an individual of exceptional integrity. His words had weight. Detective John L. Smith, who happened to be a brother-in-law of Atzerodt, felt certain it was Booth, but May's positive tone alarmed him. "We all thought there must have been a great blunder somewhere," he recalled.

Barnes responded excitedly, "You have been his physician, doctor. Are there not some marks on his body? Is there not some physical peculiarity that you have noticed in the past that might serve as a mark?"[75]

May reflected for a moment, then asked, "Is there a scar upon the back of its neck?" Shortly after the operation Booth's wound tore open under the clutches of an actress during a performance. It left a large cicatrix formed by the process of granulation. Describing the injury to Barnes before looking at it, May said it would appear as an ugly scar or a burn rather than a proper surgical incision. Barnes discovered the mark on the neck precisely where May stated it would be found. "You have described the scar as well as if you were looking at it," remarked the surgeon general.

At May's request the body was placed in a sitting position. He studied the face. Slowly, inescapably, the familiar features came into focus.

"It is the body of J. Wilkes Booth. I have no doubt."[76]

The day was pleasant. It had none of the summer sizzle that could turn the iron plate of the *Montauk* into a griddle, but for the convenience of the official party an awning had been stretched overhead between Booth's catafalque and the hazy sky.[77] Under it, at 2:00 p.m., Surgeon General Barnes handed his hat to his steward and began the autopsy. First, he removed the dressing around the body's left leg. Marine Private Henry Landes, eyeing the soiled pasteboard, took out his pocketknife.[78] Other hungry hands moved toward the bandages Mrs. Mudd had prepared and the pins her husband used to secure them. "Gentlemen," directed the doctor sharply, "you will please not take anything from this body."[79]

Swollen and black to the knee, Booth's leg looked dreadful. A small artery had ruptured, resulting in considerable hemorrhaging under the skin.[80] Reporters who spoke with Surgeon General Barnes also stated that the fractured bone had cut its way through the flesh and protruded. The wound had become gangrenous, and "Booth could not have lived many days more in any event," five or so in the opinion of one.[81] Barnes mentioned nothing about this in his official statement, however.

The corpse was raised again so that Barnes and his assistant, Dr. J. J. Woodward, could measure the wound to the half inch. Then the body was reclined and a narrow piece of board put under the shoulders so that the head hung down backward, exposing the neck. Woodward opened his large postmortem case.[82] From its ghastly assortment of saws, hooks, hammers, and scalpels, he took dissecting scissors and a spine chisel and went to work. The neck was opened and the affected vertebrae excised. "Mutilated bone and viscera and blood-stained rags" was all Munroe's glimpse showed him and all he wished to see. It looked like a decapitation. "First man I seen without a head," Private Landes wrote imperturbably in his diary.[83]

The doctors duly noted the obvious. Booth was killed by a bullet fired at a distance of a few yards. The ball fractured the vertebrae and perforated the spinal cord, traveling through the neck with a slight inclination downward and to the rear. The large blood vessels were untouched. General paralysis was immediate, and death from asphyxia followed in course.[84]

"Booth must have suffered as much as if he had been broken on the wheel," observed Woodward.[85]

Now it was time for some official souvenir taking. Vertebrae three to five, as well as a piece of whitish spinal cord, were wrapped in stout brown paper, destined for the Army Medical Museum. Surgeon General Barnes gave George Hallowell, his messenger, a piece of muscle tissue with embedded bone fragments.[86]

Snick! Barnes heard the grit of a busy pair of scissors. Wheeling around, he discovered Marine Sergeant John M. Peddicord standing close to the body, and he sent the soldier a withering look. Peddicord, reasoning happily that a prohibition against *gentlemen* taking mementoes did not apply to enlisted men like himself, had grabbed the scissors from the autopsy table and snipped a strand of hair from the top of Booth's head. Perhaps it was Peddicord's somber face that saved him, perhaps his quick thinking, but the result was an amusing bit of theater. "You men get back there!" exclaimed the sergeant, cleverly deflecting attention from himself, and he turned about to chase away several sailors who had approached the bench. Barnes returned to conference with the other officers. His steward, who observed the episode as he cleaned the autopsy instruments, simply giggled.[87] The body was resewn into its shroud.

Detective Luther Baker was on the *Montauk* giving the commissioners a statement of events at the farm. When he finished, Colonel Baker, his boss, pulled him aside. "Stanton wants me to dispose of Booth's body," said the senior man, who was also the detective's cousin. "He doesn't care where it is put, only so that it will not be found until Gabriel blows his horn. He don't want the Rebs to get it and make an ado over it."[88]

The colonel was impatient to get going. Abruptly, and with little civility to his Navy Yard hosts, he took the corpse and moved it to a rowboat. Conspicuously, a heavy ball and chain were also put aboard. Onlookers concluded that the body was about to be sunk in the Eastern Branch of the Potomac. That impression seemed confirmed when Baker left the assassin's coffin behind. Throughout the day much interest attended the construction of this box.[89] Workmen scrambled for the privilege of driving a nail into its dressed pine surface. So many took part in this ritual that the nails, driven together, formed thick black bands around the sides and ends of the box. But what need was there for a coffin if Booth would be anchored to the river bottom?

A touch of the oars sped the Bakers' small vessel onto the river. Spectators, expecting to see the body dumped, followed eagerly along the shore to witness the historic event. They had no way of knowing that the boat's actual destination was the nearby Washington Arsenal, clearly visible from the Navy Yard, and the Bakers made every effort to conceal the fact.[90] The officers ordered their four-man crew, borrowed from the *Montauk*, to head in one direction, then veer off in another. At last a marsh cut off the crowd's pursuit, and the boat—unobserved—reached the area of the large horse depot at Giesboro Point, where the Eastern Branch joins the main course of the Potomac.

"It was a moonless and starless night," Detective Baker recalled. "We quietly ran our boat into a cove in the river bank and rested our oars. Old, condemned government horses were brought here and killed. We did not think any boat that might be following us would come to this dismal slaughter ground. All was still on the river. No sounds came to our ears but the hoarse croak of the bullfrog. Presently we began pulling slowly back [upriver]. Soon, against the clouded sky, we could discern the grim old penitentiary walls. We were before a door, seemingly let into the solid wall and almost at the water's edge."

Baker's recollections, given soberly in lectures to audiences in the 1880s, were hokum. The officers removed the corpse from the *Montauk* before 3:00 p.m. and, even with their deceptive navigation, covered the mile and a quarter to the Arsenal well before dark. They found no "door-of-the-damned" gaping along the Potomac like Traitor's Gate on the Thames. Quite the contrary. They pulled up to a pier at which stood an attractive summer house set scenically on the river for the enjoyment of officers and their families. Booth's remains were off-loaded—none too gently—into a corner of this arborlike structure.

Ellen Scott, who lived on the Arsenal grounds, was fishing with two girlfriends when the launch arrived. Major James G. Benton, the post's commandant, was also on the scene and saw at once that the inquisitive Ellen knew who was inside the bundle. "Do not mention it to anyone," he ordered.[91]

The Arsenal stood on Greenleaf Point at the southern end of the city.[92] During the war its large workshops churned out a variety of ordnance for the armed forces. The facility expanded in 1862 when the adjacent Washington Penitentiary was closed, its inmates sent elsewhere, and its massive three-story brick building transferred to the Arsenal as an arms warehouse. This old prison was to be Booth's new home, and the colonel set off with Benton to make arrangements. Detective Luther Baker was left to watch with the body—and the girls.

Night fell, and the last workmen left for the day. When all was quiet, Dr. George L. Porter, the post's medical officer, came to the dock.[93] He was joined by E. M. Stebbins, the Arsenal's storekeeper, and four enlisted men. One of the soldiers led a team and cart; another held a lantern. The remaining two men entered the summer house to retrieve Booth's body. Groaning at the unexpectedly heavy weight of their parcel, they hauled it out and deposited it in the back of the wagon. With Porter and the light-bearer leading the way, the small party set out toward the old prison. The soldiers marched on either side of the cart, and Stebbins brought up the rear.

Their route, leading north from the wharf, was the pride of the post. It was a stately tree-lined boulevard. Great dismounted guns, light artillery batteries, and pyramids of cannonballs dressed the right-hand side of the avenue. On the left, and extending to the Potomac, was a beautifully maintained lawn upon which stood several large ballistic pendulums used to measure bullet velocity. The flickering rays of the lantern cast fantastic shadows on this gallery of war as the party moved forward in silence. No one said a word. There was only the crunch of wheels, shuffle of feet, and rattle of hoofs on the gravel way.

This place was hallowed to Porter by the hours the late president spent here witnessing experiments with small arms, and it was odd that his murderer now traveled the road. Earlier in the day an estimated fifty thousand people in Buffalo paid homage to Lincoln's remains, part of the phenomenal total of seven million Americans who witnessed Lincoln's long trip home from Washington to Springfield.[94] Now six strangers were Booth's pallbearers as they hauled him to an ignoble grave. The occasion seemed poignant to Porter. As the years went by he felt its awe and solemnity even more.

Stebbins unlocked an enormous vaultlike door into the central section of the prison building and admitted the burial detail to the large wareroom. The wagon rumbled across a brick floor, past stout cedar columns, and stopped in a corner. Earlier a team of three men had attempted to dig a grave in one of the prison's suffocatingly small cells. They reported that the floor was stone rubble laid in cement. They might as well try to dig through a rock wall. That site was abandoned, leaving little doubt why no convict had ever tunneled out of this place, and the trio went to work here. Removing the bricks from the floor, they dug a pit, which in Porter's words "could not be dignified by the term *grave*." Booth's body was placed in an old arms case and lowered into the ground. The excavation was filled and the bricks replaced.

As the work was under way, Porter looked around the room. In such a large space a lantern threw little more light than a candle, and the thought occurred to the doctor that some important official might be watching them from behind an ammunition case in the dim recesses. But no, Porter concluded. Of course not. Stebbins had unlocked the door to let them in. He relocked it when they left. This was just what it seemed to be—a cold, bleak place, a hole in the ground, a tomb.

EPILOGUE: A GREEN
AND NARROW BED

FOR TWO AND ONE HALF YEARS John Wilkes Booth's remains moldered beneath the floor of the Old Penitentiary storeroom. Overhead his principal confederates went on trial in a courtroom on the third floor of the building. David Herold, Lewis Powell, George Atzerodt, and Mary Surratt were found guilty of conspiring with Booth to murder Abraham Lincoln and others, and they were condemned to death. "The hanging of one woman and three imbeciles," as an unsympathetic reporter phrased it, took place in the prison courtyard on July 7, 1865.[1] The four were buried near the scaffold.

Samuel Arnold, Michael O'Laughlen, and Samuel Mudd were sentenced to life at hard labor. Edman Spangler got a six-year term. John Surratt escaped to Europe, where he remained at large for more than a year. Captured in Alexandria, Egypt, he was returned to Washington, where the federal government prosecuted him. Luckily for Surratt, the rage for retribution had spent itself by then, and that, combined with sympathy over his mother's fate, carried the day. After two years of contentious legal proceedings, he left the court a free man.[2]

Bainbridge, Ruggles, and Jett were arrested along with Dr. Stuart and the two Garrett sons. Cox and Jones were also rounded up, while

Harbin, although under suspicion, evaded arrest. Stanton had warned persons harboring Booth or assisting him to escape that they would be subject to a military trial and death. Yet of this group, only Mudd went to prison. The rest were ultimately discharged. The Garrett boys left Washington with a Bible, a handshake, and twenty-five dollars from Boston Corbett. Jones returned home as silently as he left it, and the public did not learn of his role in Booth's escape until twenty years later when the fisherman told his story to Townsend. All it cost him at that late date was a government job.[3]

Perhaps these men had earned a share of trouble, but the same could not be said of the Booth family. "I can give you no idea of the desolation which has fallen upon us," Asia wrote Jean Anderson. "The sorrow of John's death is very bitter. The disgrace is far heavier." June was arrested when the War Department grew suspicious of a letter he had written John. He was deposited in Old Capitol Prison, and John S. Clarke was brought in for good measure. Joe Booth, en route from California when the assassination occurred, was detained upon his arrival in New York City. An examination before General Dix revealed the younger brother's utter ignorance of affairs—Joe did not even seem to know how old he was—and he was released. Edwin was taken to Washington when it appeared his testimony might be required. It was not, and the avowedly unionist brother was not further inconvenienced. Clarke and June were released before the trial of the conspirators concluded. The former emerged bellowing for a divorce from Asia to free himself from the family shame, while the latter counseled patience to the family. "Time is the only cure for our ills," he wrote Edwin. "Time will bring all things right—that is, as right as we have any right to expect." In his diary June turned to April 14, 1865—Good Friday, the day of the murder—and scratched out the word *Good*.[4]

In the autumn of 1867 the central portion of the prison was demolished as part of a renovation of the Arsenal. This necessitated the removal of Booth's body.[5] Stanton sent over the wareroom door key, which he had kept in his possession, and a team of laborers entered to exhume the assassin's remains. The men took the coffin box to a fifteen-foot-long trench dug in a nearby warehouse. Here a common grave had been prepared for the relocated remains of Powell, Herold, Atzerodt, Surratt, and Booth, and of Henry Wirz, commander of Fort Sumter prison at Andersonville, Georgia, who had been hanged two years earlier. At the head end of

Booth's box his name was painted in black letters using a tin template such as packers employed to label their goods. Each body was identified in this manner, and the location of each grave charted by order of Grant, then interim secretary of war.[6] The work was done in such secrecy that few were aware of what transpired, although by this time the word was out that Booth was at the Arsenal.[7]

Booth's remains were disturbed yet again in 1869. Mary Lincoln, in her anguished widowhood, imagined that Andrew Johnson had a hand in her husband's death.[8] She was not alone in this belief. Although his name was on Booth's hit list, Johnson was investigated by the House Judiciary Committee, some of whose members thought (or at least hoped) he was a co-conspirator. Other charges led to his impeachment, and he narrowly escaped removal from office. A few weeks before leaving the White House, the lame-duck Johnson, having no popularity to lose, decided to conclude assassination matters by pardoning Mudd, Arnold, and Spangler. (Mike O'Laughlen had died the previous year.) Released from a military prison off the Florida Keys, the men returned to their homes.[9]

Would Johnson, in pardoning the living, pardon the dead as well? Would he bring an end to what the *New York World* journalist St. Clair McKelway termed "the long war of the government of the United States against a corpse"?[10] Edwin requested John's body within weeks of his death, dispatching Stuart of the Winter Garden to fetch it.[11] The manager was curtly rebuffed. "It would be a source of irritation to the loyal people of the country if his body was permitted to be made the instrument of rejoicing at the sacrifice of Mr. Lincoln," Stanton explained.[12] By November 1865, attitudes had changed, and Edwin received indirect word from Stanton (delivered through the New York political boss Thurlow Weed) that it would be possible in the fullness of time.[13] An eager response brought no reply.

Despite this, "Edwin never desisted from his patient and quiet endeavor to recover the body," recalled the playwright Edward Alfriend, the brothers' Richmond friend.[14] Booth approached Grant through Adam Badeau, who served on the general's staff. The elder brother stressed his strongest suit, namely the consolation this would bring Mary Ann. "I appeal to you on behalf of my heart-broken mother that she may receive the remains of her son," he wrote the general in September 1867. "What a consolation it would be to an aged parent to have the privilege of visiting the grave of her child."[15] Once again no bones were forthcoming.

Edwin was performing in New York on February 10, 1869, when the *Times* of that day published the startling news that President Johnson had given Anna Surratt her mother's remains for reburial. Edwin wrote immediately to the president, renewing his plea for the body and promising secrecy in the affair. The letter was entrusted to John H. Weaver, sexton of Christ Church, Baltimore, whom Edwin commissioned to handle the arrangements.[16] Weaver was also an undertaker and had buried both Booth's father and grandfather.

On Monday afternoon, February 15, Johnson was chatting with the *World's* McKelway in his private office at the White House when the president took up a single card from among many brought to him. The card belonged to Weaver. "A moment's trivial business," said the president, interrupting their chat.

The door opened, and Weaver, attired in somber sable colors, glided into the office. Slim, solemn, impassive, mournful, and mechanically polite, Weaver seemed a caricature of his profession. If this man *isn't* an undertaker, McKelway chuckled to himself, he missed his calling. Johnson gave Weaver's note a quick scan. "It is all right," remarked the president, "but see that the matter is done quietly." Bowing to Johnson as though he were a pharaoh, Weaver backed away.[17]

Accompanied by Richard Harvey of the Washington firm of Harvey and Marr, Weaver went to the Arsenal, claimed the body, and loaded it in a small red express wagon. To avoid an inquisitive crowd gathering in front of his establishment, Harvey returned to the rear. The back entrance shared the alley behind Ford's Theatre by which Booth escaped. The thought was inescapable: the murderer had returned to the scene of the crime.

It had grown dark, and Harvey's lamp was called for. Its yellow light revealed that Booth's gun box, set up on trestles for inspection, was much decayed. The corpse was lifted out and placed into a plain unpainted coffin. In less than an hour the body was at the depot awaiting the 7:30 p.m. train to Baltimore.[18] It arrived there later that same night and was taken to Weaver's funeral home on Fayette Street opposite the rear door of John T. Ford's Holliday Street Theatre. "Successful and in our possession here," Ford telegraphed Edwin.[19]

The rollicking burlesque *Ixion; or, The Man at the Wheel* was in rehearsal on Wednesday when Ford came onstage and whispered something to the comedian Charles Bishop.[20] To everyone's surprise Ford then dismissed the company. Walking over to Blanche Chapman, his goddaughter,

Ford took both of her hands in his and said, "Blanche, I want you to keep your eyes and ears open and your mouth shut." The manager escorted the teenager across the street to Weaver's. Bishop, who had run John-related errands for Edwin in the past, followed with Blanche's younger sister, Ella. Accompanying them were Harry Ford, his niece Annie Ford, Holliday stage manager Thomas A. Hall, doorkeeper Basil Moxley, property man Billy Ballauf, and others.[21] The actor Frank Oakes Rose, not about to be left out, scaled the fence around Weaver's and added himself to a party of about twenty-five, several of whom were army officers.[22]

In the half-light of two gas jets flickering feebly at either end of a darkened room, Blanche recognized Mrs. Booth and Rose. Shaking with excitement, she went forward to greet them. Nearby were Joe Booth and the actor Joe Whiting, his close friend.[23] Blanche knew the Booths well, having stayed several weeks at their home when she and Marion, June's daughter, were dismissed from Eden Hall School, operated by the Society of the Sacred Heart near Philadelphia, for being the children of actors. Blanche made herself memorable by wolfing down pancakes, appropriating Edwin's hair tonic, and generally unsettling the household.[24]

The cadaver that all had come to see was scarcely recognizable. The mass of blackened bones reposed in the clothes in which the assassin died. A search of the garments uncovered two buttons and a pistol cartridge in a vest pocket. On the right foot was a heavy riding boot. Dr. Mudd's brogan, split open to accommodate swelling, was on the left. The broken leg was disjointed at both the knee and ankle. The skull was entirely detached. A small amount of flesh clung to the face, with a hole about the size of a dime in each cheek. This indescribable substance crumbled into nothingness at the touch. The sockets of the eyes seemed filled with something resembling damp sawdust. Booth's hair was surprisingly full. The dead man's teeth were set tightly together as if he were still in agony. One look at the remains made Blanche's head swim.[25]

The body was housed in a case of special design patented by Weaver during the war. It featured an intermediate glass cover that could be closed and still permit viewing of remains sealed below.[26] The splendid casket, made of reddish-brown mahogany, had silver mountings, moldings, and handles. A lining of white silk merino cradled the corpse, while the interior of the outer lid was upholstered with white satin. No one could say the heap of decay and rotting clothes that was John Wilkes Booth was not elegantly coffined.

Joe Booth, Ford, and Weaver came forward. When the room grew quiet, Joe said, "If this is the body of my brother John, I can identify it by a gold-plugged tooth on the right side of the jaw next to the eye tooth."

Weaver produced a drawing of the molar. Pushing down the jaw, the undertaker located the tooth and pointed it out for all to see. "The teeth were beautiful and perfect, save [that] one," wrote Norval Foard, an editor of the *Baltimore Sun*, whom Ford had invited to the examination.[27] Ford announced that this peculiarly shaped filling was conclusive proof of identification in his mind. Besides, he added, the firm lower jaw could have belonged to no other man than Booth. As Ford spoke, the skull was passed from hand to hand as if it belonged to some Yorick and all were there Hamlet-like to meditate upon it.

Blanche had never met Booth and wondered how Ford could be so certain. She asked Harry, whom she was to marry, if he was equally sure about this.

"I knew Booth better than I know you," he replied. "There's no need of doctor or dentist. One look told me."[28]

William H. Burton, another fence-jumper, broke a hush. "That boot looks like a pair John used to wear when we went skating. If it is one of the pair, there will be a hole in the heel made by the screw of the skate." What Burton meant was that a skate's iron runner was secured to a shoe by boring a hole for an affixing screw with a gimlet. The skate was then stamped on and strapped to the foot. The boot on Booth's right leg was examined. Sure enough, there on its heel were two telltale indentations cut for just such a purpose.[29]

Mrs. Booth would not approach or even look upon the remains, so Weaver asked Ella to cut a lock of hair for the mother. The young woman shrank back, however, and Blanche took her sister's place, snipping a large curl from the forehead. It fell into a paper held by Ford.[30]

"I shall never forget that moment," wrote Blanche of standing before the mother. "The sorrow in Mrs. Booth's face. The tears dropping in her lap as she separated the strands of hair." She gave Ella and Blanche each a small lock. As she did, a faint moan came from her lips.[31]

Back at the coffin Blanche picked up a loose piece of blanket and stuffed it in her handbag.[32]

Baltimore was Booth's hometown, and it was not surprising that news of the body's presence stirred the city. People gathered expectantly at the Baltimore Cemetery, where the *Sun* had announced that Booth would be interred. Others assembled at Weaver's. By afternoon the curious, the sympathetic, and the unreconstructed around the funeral home numbered several hundred. Seeking mementoes, those admitted cut to pieces the blankets enclosing the body. There was talk of organizing a funeral demonstration. The police came by.

Weaver, who had promised the family utmost privacy, complained angrily to the *New York Times* that no unruly crowd had stormed his establishment in the manner its reporter described or had taken souvenirs from the body. Only a handful of people saw the body, and those solely for purposes of identification.[33] Its correspondent had not seen what he had seen, Weaver claimed. Not so, countered the *Sun*'s Foard. "*Many* persons saw the remains. Some with a fondness for souvenirs tore off pieces of the blanket and secured locks of hair."

When the family left the funeral parlor and returned to their rooms at Guy's Monument House down the street, Weaver completed his arrangements.[34] Customarily he placed a metallic tablet-plate bearing the deceased's name in the center section of the interior surface of the outer cover. This refinement was dispensed with, however, and the rough plank containing the assassin's name was placed on his breast. The inner and outer doors of the casket were closed and locked.

On the chilly morning of Thursday, February 18, 1869, Weaver took the body to Green Mount Cemetery. Fearing a hearse would attract attention, he transported the remains in an ordinary wagon. The undertaker had a receiving vault at Green Mount, a holding tomb dug in a hillside where the body could be kept until winter passed, a final burial place prepared, and a time for the family to gather determined. No other persons were present as Weaver and his assistants carried the casket through the flat-arched entrance of this temple-fronted vault. Inside, among family members like Weaver's late wife, Margaret, and strangers accruing the two-dollar-per-month storage charge, Booth was left to slumber under the gaze of a marble statue of the Angel of Resurrection mounted above the door.[35]

The Booth family had intended to bury John in Baltimore Cemetery. The elder Booth was buried there under a handsome stele Edwin had had erected in 1858. Grandfather Richard was there, too. But Green Mount was a more attractive place. It was a new "rural cemetery." This did not mean that it was located in the country, rather that, in contrast with crowded urban and church cemeteries, it was a place with spacious

landscaped grounds and affecting commemorative monuments conducive
to a sense of peace and reflection. Chartered in 1838, the year of John's
birth, Green Mount had a pastoral beauty overseen by an attractive Gothic
Revival chapel on a hill. People strolled its tree-lined paths as if it were a
public park.

Mary Ann purchased a double lot, roughly thirty by forty feet, in the
Dogwood section of Green Mount on June 13, 1869.[36] Junius Sr. and old
Richard were unearthed from their places of rest and reburied here.[37] At
Rose's request, dear old Aunty Rogers told Weaver how to locate the
graves of the children at the farm, and he exhumed the dust of Frederick,
Elizabeth, and little Mary Ann. Placed in a common coffin, their traces
were brought to the city.[38] The father's large monument was also moved
to Green Mount and reerected. On the reverse surface of the stele a stone-
cutter added the name "John Wilkes" in one-and-a-half-inch-tall sans
serif font. The names of the Harford children and of Henry, who died in
London in 1836, were incised below his.

Despite these preparations, several former rebels who welcomed Booth
home to Baltimore feared he would be denied Christian burial. As the
story goes, the bevy of ex-Confederates who visited Weaver's included the
journalist Foard, an infantry veteran and clerk in the Treasury Department
in Richmond; John W. McCoy, manager of a rebel gunpowder firm in
North Carolina; Henry C. Wagner, Booth's friend who gave the first musical performance of the rebel hymn "Maryland, My Maryland"; Thomas
W. Hall, editor of Baltimore's *The South* newspaper and Confederate major;
and William M. Pegram, Southern cavalryman, aide to J. E. B. Stuart,
and former resident of the Old Capitol Prison.[39] It was said that they decided to take matters into their own hands. Led by Pegram and Wagner, a
party of Southerners removed the remains from the vault at night, carried
them by torchlight to the Booth lot, and buried them in an unmarked
location.[40] This story would be repeated well into the twentieth century
by historians, but it was entirely fanciful.

The uneasy pilgrimage of John Wilkes Booth ended less dramatically
on June 26, 1869. The cloudless summer day was oppressively hot, with
a temperature in the low nineties, when shortly after noon a closed carriage swung through the Tudor-style gateway of Green Mount and
stopped just past the great elms.[41] Out stepped Mrs. Booth, Edwin, June,
and Rose. (Asia was with Clarke in England, where they immigrated the
previous year; Joe's whereabouts are unknown.) Mary Ann wore deep

mourning as dictated by Victorian custom. The black crepe of her dress was so dull it reflected no light, an apt metaphor for her sorrow. "The mother was much overcome," stated a reporter for the *New York Clipper*, "and the family much stricken."

About fifty family friends, mostly ladies, were gathered at the gravesite. The faithful John Mathews stood among them.[42] The sympathy of the attendees was palpable. "Oh, Poor John," wrote Aunty Rogers, who seemed to know their thoughts. "Dear boy, good boy. Sorryfull for such a Hansom boy [as] he was to let the enemy of souls Cheat him out of so much pleasure, as he could have done so much good in this world for he was A gentleman. Poor fellow. I hope the lord had mercy on his soul. It may be that [his] act and his suffering brought him to the savour. The lord herd the Cryes of the thief on the Cross."

Six pallbearers drawn principally from Baltimore theatrical circles removed the body from the vault and carried it down the hill to the gravesite. None of these men had been a particular friend of the deceased except Samuel Linton, whose supper table in an apartment at the Holliday Theatre often accommodated a merry Booth.[43] The group carried the casket to the southeast face of the obelisk. Below the names of John and his siblings an open grave yawned. The excavation was lined with brick, a customary precaution to keep the ground from sinking. A seven-foot stone slab resting nearby would be placed over the brickwork after the casket was lowered to help maintain an even appearance at the site.[44]

The Reverend Thomas U. Dudley, minister of Christ Church, where the Booths had been nominal members during their Baltimore residence, was asked to perform the service. Because he was otherwise engaged, Dudley turned the request over to his ministerial colleague and houseguest Fleming James, a recent graduate of seminary. Both men were Richmond natives with Confederate credentials, and neither saw anything amiss in reading the burial order. Indeed, James, said to have been present at Pickett's charge at Gettysburg, did not hide his Southern feelings even in New York City, where he served as assistant pastor at St. Luke's Hospital. The young minister was present in gown and surplice.[45]

The service commenced at one o'clock. "Forasmuch as it hath pleased Almighty God, in his wise providence, to take out of this world the soul of our deceased brother, we therefore commit his body to the ground," intoned James as he stood at the head of the grave.[46] The service, taken from the Episcopalian *Book of Common Prayer*, was simple and unostentatious but thoroughly impressive, thought Foard. The day's work cost James his Manhattan pastorate, as he would be forced out by hospital authorities and turn to the more congenial climate of Baltimore as rector at St. Mark's.[47]

"Earth to earth, ashes to ashes, dust to dust; looking for the general Resurrection in the last day, and the life of the world to come through our Lord Jesus Christ, at whose second coming in glorious majesty to judge the world, the earth and the sea shall give up their dead."

John's remains were lowered into the grave. The box containing the children, their names engraved on a silver plate, was laid on top of his coffin. Mary Ann stood at the mouth of the grave, watching and sobbing as she clung to June's arm. After the spade men filled the grave, several women came forward and distributed bouquets over it.[48]

The government did not order the family to leave the grave unmarked. This oft-told story seemed credible to the public because of the stigma attached to an uncommemorated resting place. Such was the criminal's end as a reward for a life of shame, a life unworthy of remembrance. But the absence of a headstone on John's burial spot was due entirely to Edwin's wishes. The older brother had the lot beautified with flowers and arbor vitae trees. In time he permitted the planting of small rosebushes at the head and foot of his brother's grave. A one-foot-tall wooden cross was erected there. But Edwin was dead set against any permanent memorial. Henry W. Mears, a Weaver employee, discussing general lot improvements with the brother several years later, asked him, "And John Wilkes' grave? What about John Wilkes?" He regretted the words as soon as he said them. A shade came over Edwin's face. There was a pause. "Let it remain as it is. Place no mark there," said Edwin.[49]

All was done as Edwin wished. But if he meant to keep the grave's location hidden from the public, he failed. The site of John's green and narrow bed became the worst-kept secret in Baltimore. The grave was easy for interested parties to find.

In the early summer of 1870, the following year, family and friends of Confederate soldiers buried at Green Mount came to the cemetery to garland the graves of their dead. The *Baltimore American* reported that "the grave that exceeded all the rest in its profuse decorations was that of J. Wilkes Booth." A pyramid of flowers covered his mound. The adjacent graves of Booth's father and grandfather bore not a single petal, indicating this tribute had not been placed by family members. These flowers were placed by strangers. "This was the day set apart to do honor to the Southern soldiers," the story concluded, "and if the richness and profusion of the emblems is to be taken as the measure of affection in which the deceased soldier is held, John Wilkes Booth is the greatest hero of them all."[50]

THE FEDERAL GOVERNMENT did a satisfactory job identifying Booth's body when it arrived in Washington, but then it made a major mistake. Secretary of War Stanton knew that "every hair of his head would be a valued relic to the sympathizers with the south," and he directed that the remains be secretly buried. Colonel Lafayette Baker, boarding the *Montauk* to carry out the secretary's orders, was incensed to see people—including known secessionists—taking souvenirs from the body. He had to twist a lock of Booth's hair from the hand of one woman who refused to relinquish it. The indignant colonel determined to put the body—and hopefully all thought of it—beyond the reach of rebel idolaters, so he misled the public about the disposition of the remains.[51] He told Townsend, whose reports on the assassination were the most widely read in the nation, that he sank the body in the Potomac. Frank Leslie published in his popular illustrated New York newsweekly a dramatic engraving of Baker dumping the corpse into the river.[52]

Baker hoped the matter would rest there, but the fact that Booth was gone before most people knew he was even in town made the government's haste look suspicious. Why the hurry? Were Stanton and Baker, both highly controversial figures, hiding something? Speaking on the floor of the U.S. Senate in July 1866, Garrett Davis of Kentucky said, "I have never seen myself any satisfactory evidence that Booth was killed. I want it proved that Booth was in that barn. Why was not his body brought up publicly to Washington and exposed to the gaze of the multitude, that it might be identified? Why so much secrecy about it? It may be he is dead, but there is a mystery and a most inexplicable mystery to my mind about the whole affair. He may come back some of these days and murder someone else."[53] Such silliness amused the soldiers who ran Booth to ground. Returning to Washington by boat with the body in April 1865, Private Andrew Wendell and his fellow cavalrymen had filed past the corpse to inspect their handiwork. "Some people—and big people—said we had the wrong man and that Booth wasn't dead," Wendell told a reporter in 1908. "He was dead enough when we looked at him."[54]

The belief that Booth escaped his captors took root, defying common sense. It allowed some Southerners to feel that although they might have lost the war, they got in the last punch by putting Lincoln into the ground. "We greeted his death in a spirit of reckless hate," wrote Booth's Richmond friend John S. Wise. "We had seen his face over the coffins of our brothers and relatives and friends, in the flames of Richmond, in the disaster at Appomattox. We were desperate and vindictive."[55] The belief that Booth killed the president *and* got away with it doubled the delight of Lincoln haters, believed Walter Benn, who performed with Booth at the Boston Museum. While he scoffed at the notion that Booth survived Garrett's barn, Benn acknowledged that the assassin did live on "in haunting thought, in wild erratic memory."[56]

By 1885, twenty years after Booth's death, the escape story had developed considerable texture. The influential *Atlanta Constitution* reported from sources in Alabama that Booth had hired an Irishman to take his place on his flight from Ford's Theatre. Misidentified as Booth, the unfortunate substitute was killed at Garrett's. Willie Jett knew the truth, but he hated Lincoln and was paid to keep his mouth shut. Meanwhile, the story continued, Booth was hiding in the Washington foundry of Clark Mills, the sculptor who created the equestrian statue of Andrew Jackson across from the White House in President's Park. Booth was later heard from in Memphis, Tennessee, where he was arrested for public drunkenness. Despite the fact that this event was reported in the local newspapers, he was allowed to escape and flee to France. Later he visited Japan. Wherever he went, he sent photographs of himself in native costume to friends in the United States to assure them of his well-being. As of October 1885, when this article was published, Booth was said to be alive and well. "He is in the service of the Khedive of Egypt and owns over one hundred camels."[57]

John T. Ford hated such talk. "If you listen to idle gabble and wild assertions, a hundred Wilkes Booths are wandering mysteriously over the American continent," he grumbled at the time. "The talk is a silly and at times a wicked falsehood."[58]

The escaped Booth was initially an icon of the Lost Cause, a postwar cultural movement that sought meaning in the defeat of Confederacy. It took on an added dimension when the story moved west and merged with the tradition of celebrating the fugitive outlaw and the wandering desperado. John St. Helen, a saloonkeeper in Granbury, Texas, purportedly confessed to being Booth before disappearing in the 1870s. David E. George, an Oklahoma inebriate, made a similar statement before committing suicide in 1903. A Tennessee lawyer, Finis L. Bates, claimed that St. Helen and George were the same person and that the Booth mystery had finally been solved. Despite the fact that George was taller than Booth, had different eye color, and lacked the identifying neck scar, bullet wound, tattoo, and slightly bowed legs, he was close enough for the credulous Bates, who took George's mummified body and displayed it at carnivals.[59] The exhibit joined no fewer than five alleged skulls of Booth already touring the country.[60]

The various survival stories, added to the loss of knowledge inevitable with the passage of time, confused the public enough by 1911 for the journalist Edward Freiberger to write in the *Washington Post*: "Although there are 90,000,000 people in the United States, not 500 could tell you what became of the body of the assassin of Abraham Lincoln. Some will tell you that John Wilkes Booth was burned to ashes in the Virginia barn in which he was captured. Others will express the opinion that the remains of the misguided actor were cut to pieces and mysteriously dropped into the sea. Then, to add interest to the mystery, someone will claim to have positive information that Wilkes Booth is still alive and living comfortably and quietly in any one of a dozen cities—Louisville, Denver, San Francisco, Albuquerque, New Orleans, or Montreal."[61] The escape hypothesis was so ridiculous to Freiberger's colleague Isaac Markens that he satirized the mythmakers by assuring them that "Booth lived for many years and enjoyed life. In London one day and Paris the next, he journeyed on the Nile, took in the Pyramids and the Sphinx, kissed the Blarney stone, and, in his native land, was frequently seen at Saratoga, Coney Island, Yellowstone Park. He chauffeured his machine through Dixieland in winter and New England in summer."[62]

Undeterred, Bates and his successors exhibited the mummy at sideshows throughout the 1920s and 1930s. Mr. George, brown as a hickory nut, was displayed in a setting with faux Egyptian columns, suggesting the wisdom and authenticity of the ages, while above the body was a sign with the words "For the Correction of History." The Reverend Clarence True Wilson, a Methodist minister interested with the story, gave it what feeble intellectual cover he could in his position as a nationally known prohibition advocate.[63] A second escaped Booth was featured in the 1977 book and film *The Lincoln Conspiracy*. In this laughable historical muddle

Booth fled to Europe after a bizarre plot in which the assassin conspired against Lincoln on the orders of the president's own top subordinates.[64]

In May 1995 the escape theorists finally had their hour. They prevailed on several distant Booth family descendants (including a great-great-granddaughter of Edwin) to ask for an exhumation and formal identification of John's body. Green Mount Cemetery refused the request, claiming that the story of Booth's escape was a hoax and that an exhumation would violate its obligation to respect the repose and protection at law and equity afforded to the remains of the dead. A four-day trial in Baltimore City Circuit Court resulted, litigating the escape theory. The national media flocked to Booth's hometown to cover an event made memorable by its gathering of forensic experts, anthropologists, folklorists, historians, actors, assassination buffs, a Lincoln impersonator, a mummy expert, and a brother-in-law of President John F. Kennedy.

Legends of an escaped Booth, all proper in their way as local tall tales, did not fare well as fact against the phalanx of historians that Green Mount assembled on its behalf. The cemetery's witnesses demonstrated conclusively that Booth died in 1865 and was interred in Green Mount four years later. Judge Joseph H. H. Kaplan agreed with this view and, understanding that the remains would be in an unsuitable condition for examination due to soil and water conditions at the site, ruled against the petitioners. A three-judge panel of the Court of Special Appeals of Maryland upheld Kaplan's verdict in 1996. Its decision ended the case and let John Wilkes Booth remain where his mother placed him on that hot summer afternoon in 1869. He rests there today.[65]

"I think the escape crowd enjoyed their day in the sun less than they expected," chuckled James O. Hall, elder statesman of Green Mount's team of expert witnesses, when the verdict was announced. Hall recalled a statement of Prince Nicholas Romanoff, a cousin of Czar Nicholas II of Russia, when DNA testing in 1994 revealed that the woman who claimed for decades to be the Grand Duchess Anastasia, the czar's youngest daughter, was an imposter. "People look for exceptional events to change the past," Romanoff said. "But history is brutally effective in its solutions, and brutally simple."[66]

"I KNOWED THEY'D KILL HIM," the seventy-six-year-old Sarah Bush Lincoln said when the news of her stepson's assassination reached her cabin on the Illinois prairie. "I ben awating fur it."[67]

Many others had long feared such a tragedy and wondered only about the timing of it. What possible benefit could the act have for the cause Booth espoused? "Had this taken place a year or two ago when the rebels might possibly have turned the temporary derangement of our national machinery to their advantage, it would seem probable, but now, when all is lost, when there is no hope, it staggers belief," Navy Assistant Paymaster William F. Keeler wrote to his wife.[68] Why didn't Booth see this, wondered Carl Schurz, a major general in the Union army? "Nothing could have been more obvious to any sane mind," he wrote. "This crime could not possibly be of the least benefit to the Southern people in their desperate straits, but would only serve to inflame the feelings of their victorious adversaries against them."[69]

To make matters worse for the rebels, "they have killed their best friend," wrote Charles Deamude, a corporal in Company K, 150th Regiment, Illinois Volunteers, the day after Lincoln's death.[70] Most white Southerners did not agree with that assessment, at least immediately. John S. Wise, one of Virginia's fieriest rebels, rejoiced at the news of Lincoln's death. "In mature years I have been ashamed of what I felt and said when I heard of that awful calamity," he wrote in his book *The End of an Era* (1899). "Time taught us that Lincoln was a man of marvelous humanity."[71] With Lincoln dead, and the experience of Reconstruction a bitter postscript, it was easier for Southerners like Wise to adopt a friendly perspective on the late president. The belief that Lincoln would have rolled their way on postwar issues was wishful thinking, but few seemed to doubt it. The Georgia editor James Ryder Randall wrote ten years after the war, "The killing of Lincoln was a blunder as well as a crime for he was an amiable and kind hearted man animated by a sincere love of the union but without malice to any who fought against it. He would not have sanctioned the adoption of harsh measures against the Southern people. He was powerful enough with his party to have defeated proscription and, if his life had not been taken, there is every reason to believe the southern people would not have endured many of the evils which they have been afflicted with since the termination of the war."[72]

ADOLPHE, MARQUIS DE CHAMBRUN, a French attorney who met Lincoln during the final months of the president's life, wrote that the assassination lent "a tragic prestige" to its victim.[73]

The Reverend Nathan H. Chamberlain explained this phenomenon to his congregation at St. James Church in Birmingham, Connecticut, in a sermon on April 19, 1865. Booth was still a fugitive, hidden in the thicket near Samuel Cox's farm in Maryland, when Chamberlain told his congregation that the assassin had failed. Yes, he had killed a man, but he had done so under such circumstances as to apotheosize the victim. Lincoln was now elevated above daily political squabbles and vexatious controversies over war and reconstruction. "Martyrdom for duty lifts a man out of days to become a citizen of the ages," said Chamberlain.[74] The American diplomat John Bigelow thought similarly, writing from Paris to Secretary of State William Seward, "Mr. Lincoln could not have surrendered his life on terms more advantageous to his country or to his own fame. The manner of his death has transfigured him in the eyes of all mankind."[75]

Lincoln's ascent to Olympus began with the extraordinary events attending the return of his remains for burial to his hometown of Springfield, Illinois. The body left Washington on April 21, 1865, and made a thirteen-day, 1,700-mile trip through the principal cities of the North. Millions of Americans turned out to meet it in displays of grief and sympathy. The occasion was the most-shared event of the century—absolutely unparalleled in the nation's history.[76]

"Look at that face and remember it," said a grandfather as he held up his grandson to gaze at Lincoln's remains during their display at Independence Hall in Philadelphia. "As you grow up you will see it in stone and bronze. Then you will be thankful that I brought you here today."[77]

Memorials for the president followed, notably a striking monument in Springfield erected over his tomb. At the monument's dedication ceremony in 1874, Governor Richard J. Oglesby, a close Lincoln friend, declared the structure a fitting tribute for "the obscure boy, the honest man, the illustrious statesman, and great liberator and the martyr President."[78]

Key literary figures crafted Lincoln's legacy during the remaining years of the century. Walt Whitman shared his love of the president throughout the 1880s with a highly popular lecture on the president's death. It was so convincingly presented that listeners thought mistakenly that Whitman had been present at Ford's Theatre on April 14, 1865. The poet told his audiences that Lincoln, whom he saw often during the war, was an authentic American who was down-to-earth, fraternal and democratic—one of them. In the following decade Lincoln's secretaries John G. Nicolay and John Hay coauthored their massive *Abraham Lincoln: A History* (1890). If history was indeed biography, they asserted, in the heft that only ten volumes can supply, then Lincoln's life was the life of the nation. "He is now the greatest of all Americans," agreed the marquis de Chambrun.

The centennial of Lincoln's birth occurred in 1909. It led the prominent journalist Horace White to reflect, "Abraham Lincoln has been in his grave more than forty-two years, and we should have expected that a considerable amount of dust would have settled upon his tomb. This is a busy world. Each generation has its own problems to grapple with, its own joys and sorrows, its cares and grief to absorb its thoughts and compel its tears," White continued. "Time moves on, and each particular thing in it dwindles in size. So also do most men. But some men bulk larger as the years receded. The most striking fact of our time, of a psychological kind, is the growth of Lincoln's fame since the earth closed over his remains."[79]

Plans for a grand memorial on the National Mall began in 1911. Before his death six years earlier, John Hay had urged that the monument be given this eminent location for one reason. "Lincoln of all Americans next to Washington deserves this place of honor," he claimed. "He was of the Immortals." The Lincoln Memorial was dedicated in 1922. Above the president's immense statue the inscription reads: "In This Temple as in The Hearts of the People for Whom He Saved the Union the Memory of Abraham Lincoln Is Enshrined Forever." This building has become one of the most familiar structures in the world and a symbol of the nation's capital.

The twentieth century brought a cultural outpouring of Lincolniana, not just formal histories and biographies but also films, plays, poetry, portraits, musicals, and sculpture. Over the years, and down to the present, Lincoln meant many and often conflicting things to the American people, and their understanding of him grew more nuanced, informed, and occasionally critical. Nevertheless, all who claimed him for one purpose or the other responded to his honesty, faith in democracy, devotion to law, and essential kindness.

By the time of the two-hundredth anniversary of his birth in 2009, Lincoln had become ubiquitous. He had been depicted on the ten-dollar demand note in 1861 and the fifteen-cent stamp in 1866. But when he appeared on the iconic Lincoln penny in 1909 and the five-dollar bill in 1914, his likeness was distributed in quantities that made his image one of the most recognizable on earth. In 2012 alone, six billion pennies were minted and nearly 730 million five-dollar bills were printed by the government he served. Little wonder that people around the world with no idea who he is know the features of his face. Having conquered Earth in this fashion, Lincoln moved on to Mars when a penny was taken recently to the Red Planet (as part of a camera calibration target) by NASA's Mars rover Curiosity.

BERT SHELDON, A WASHINGTON, D.C., policeman and Lincoln enthusiast, wrote in 1945, "When Lincoln made his ascent into immortality, he took J. Wilkes Booth with him."[80] One would imagine that each found the other's presence disagreeable.

George Alfred Townsend thought differently. No contemporary of the assassin spent more time reflecting on the life of this odd young man than did Townsend. He watched Booth's first acting performances in Philadelphia in 1857, followed his remarkable career during the war, and talked him to only weeks before the assassination in 1865. The journalist subsequently wrote the first popular book on the assassination and the first important novel about it. Townsend spent fifty years investigating and reporting the Booth story.

Although born in a slave state, Townsend was a strong Lincoln man, a political radical, and a tireless critic of Southern leaders and society. He loved poking fun at "the rubes," as he expressed it. Despite that, he was accused of being friendly to Booth in his 1865 articles on the conspiracy. He defended himself by replying, "Much as I denounce and deprecate his crime—holding him to be worthy of all execration, and so steeped in blood that the excuses of a century will fail to lift him out of the atmosphere of common felons—I still stand back in surprise and terror at the wonderful resources and extraordinary influence of one who I had considered a mere thespian. There must have been something in this man capable of extension and perseverance above the common. What a tragedy for a man of beaming presence—bold and agreeable—to be so insanely ignorant of the consequences of the crime he committed, a crime that would make the remotest nations give him up to be hanged."

Booth's irrationality allowed Townsend to view the assassin with pity. "Booth was the last genius of the rebellion," he wrote, "and he committed an imperial crime." But his act was so heinous and absurd that Townsend wondered if even Lincoln himself would fail to feel a touch of compassion for the fool who did it. The assassination, he concluded, was "the greatest crime in the western world, done by a morbid, revengeful, melodramatic, ambitious and irregular young man of bold and almost insane purpose. It made Mr. Lincoln the most beloved memory in our country, adding to his great services the crown of martyrdom. In Abraham Lincoln's beautiful and enduring fame, even his assassin seems embraced and forgiven."[81]

ACKNOWLEDGMENTS

. . . .

Over the quarter century of research that went into making *Fortune's Fool*, I accrued a heavy debt to friends and colleagues who advised and assisted me. While many of these individuals are cited in the endnotes, I wish to take special notice here of their contributions—both academic and personal—to my work.

James O. Hall, a retired federal government worker and the most senior of the "Boothies," as Booth buffs were known, first encouraged me to write a Booth biography. From day one he never wavered in his support of my efforts. While we did not always agree in our interpretations of people or events, he was as supportive of me as if my project were his own. I cannot put into proper words my feelings of gratitude to him. I can only hope that every author may have such a friend. Sincerely thankful, I dedicate this book to his memory.

I take pleasure in also acknowledging:

Laurie Verge, Joan Chaconas, and Sandra Walia (for making the Surratt House a "must" stop for researchers, writers, and thousands of visitors each year);

John Sellers, Clark Evans, and Michelle Krowl (for assistance at the Library of Congress);

Ed Steers, Tom Turner, Bill Hanchett, Blaine Houmes, and Pep Martin (for noteworthy scholarship on the people and events of April 14, 1865);

Michael Burlingame, Joan Cashin, and Ron Soodalter (for generosity and bonhomie);

James Swanson, Michael Kauffman, Steve Miller, Richard Sloan, and John Elliott (for original and stimulating studies of the assassination);

Tom Bogar, Don Wilmeth, and David Grimsted (for exceptional knowledge of the nineteenth-century stage);

Louise Taper, James L. Woods, Susan Lemke, James Cornelius, Tom Schwartz, and Tom and Connie Spande (for love of history);

Douglas L. Wilson, William C. Harris, Don Kennon, and Paul Tetreault (for service to the Abraham Lincoln Institute);

Trevor Plante and Mike Musick (for help at the National Archives);

James McPherson, Mark Neely, Frank Williams, Allen Guelzo, Harold Holzer, and Jason Emerson (for inspirational writing and lecturing);

Andy Waskie, Roger Hunt, Henry Deeks, Lewis Leigh, Jan Wade, Matthew Pinsker, Bob Lucas, and Mike Murtaugh (for devoted study of the Civil War);

John W. Stump, Jim Chrismer, and Tom Fink (for insights into the history of the Booth family in Harford County, Maryland);

Mark Greenough (for knowledge of Virginia militia history), Angela Smythe (for steadfastness in seeking the answers to difficult questions), and Scott S. Taylor (for assistance at Georgetown University's Lauinger Library);

Wally Hutcheon, Charles Poland, Kathy Lloyd, Bill Fleming, and Bruce Mann (for camaraderie at NOVA);

Bruce Leggat, Bob Lesman, Marion Barnwell, and Nelson Lankford (for careful reading and criticism of the manuscript);

Dan Watermeier, Ray Wemmlinger, Steve Archer, and Jim Wollon (for faithful custody of the Booths and their story);

Susan Ferber, Joellyn M. Ausanka, Andrew Varhol, Lauren Hill, India Cooper, and Owen Keiter (for guidance through the briar patch at Oxford University Press);

And to Jane, David, and Carey Alford and to Suzanne Gilbert (for loving support over the years).

A few friends did not live to see the book published. Their steady interest in my task always encouraged me, and as I completed the work, my thoughts often turned to them. I recall them, with fondness: Bertram Wyatt-Brown, Sheldon Meyer, John K. Lattimer, John C. Brennan, Dinah Faber, Dorothy and Howard Fox, Constance Head, Cameron Moseley, Gordon Samples, and Art Loux. Thank you all, dear comrades.

NOTES

....

ABBREVIATIONS

HRHRC   Harry Ransom Humanities Research Center, University of Texas, Austin

HSHC   The Historical Society of Harford County Inc., Bel Air, Maryland

HTC   Harvard Theatre Collection, Houghton Library, Harvard University, Cambridge, Massachusetts

JOH   James O. Hall Papers, Hall Research Center, Surratt House Museum, Clinton, Maryland

LFFRC   Lincoln Financial Foundation Research Collection, Allen County Public Library, Fort Wayne, Indiana

LOC   Library of Congress, Washington, D.C.

LOV   Library of Virginia, Richmond (Archives Division)

MdHS   Maryland Historical Society, Baltimore, Maryland

NA   National Archives and Records Services, Washington, D.C.

NA M599   "Investigation and Trial Papers Relating to the Assassination of President Lincoln," a collection of statements of evidence, letters, court records, and related papers from the War Department's Judge Advocate General's Office and found in Record Group 153. It is available as Microcopy 599 (16 reels, published in 1965). In the notes, items are cited with reel and page number, e.g., 4/410–11, NA M599 (reel 4, pp. 410–11).

OR   U.S. War Department. *The War of the Rebellion: A Compilation of the Official Records of the Union and Confederate Armies*. 128 vols. Washington: GPO, 1880–1901.

RG   Record Group

VHS   Virginia Historical Society

VRHC   Valentine Richmond History Center, Richmond, Virginia

INTRODUCTION

1   John E. Washington, *They Knew Lincoln* (New York: E. P. Dutton, 1942), pp. 28–29, 38–40; *Washington Post*, Feb. 8, 1942.
2   *St. Paul and Minneapolis Pioneer Press*, Feb. 20, 1887.
3   "Howard's Letter," clipping, n.d. [Oct. 1885], Booth Files, HTC.
4   Gobright, *Recollection of Men and Things at Washington during the Third of a Century* (Philadelphia: Claxton, Remsen, Haffelfinger, 1869), p. 348.
5   *Baltimore American*, Dec. 8, 1902.
6   John Wilkes Booth to Mary Ann Booth, n.p., n.d. [1864], Letters Received (1809–1870), Records of the Attorney General's Office, General Records of the Dept. of Justice, RG 60, NA.
7   William Hanchett, "Booth's Diary," *Journal of the Illinois State Historical Society*, vol. 72 (Feb. 1979), pp. 39–56.
8   Asia Booth Clarke, *John Wilkes Booth: A Sister's Memoir*, ed. Terry Alford (Jackson: University Press of Mississippi, 1996), p. x.
9   *Denver Post*, Jan. 7, 1899.
10 William J. Ferguson, *I Saw Booth Shoot Lincoln* (Boston and New York: Houghton Mifflin, 1930), p. 14.
11 *Richmond Times Dispatch*, June 29, 1924.
12 *Philadelphia Press*, Sept. 7, 1901.
13 Charlotte M. Martin, ed., *The Stage Reminiscences of Mrs. Gilbert* (New York: Charles Scribner's Sons, 1901), pp. 57–58.
14 Booth Scrapbook, Fawcett Theatre Collection, Hodges Library, University of Tennessee, Knoxville; *Detroit Free Press*, Dec. 15, 1901.

CHAPTER 1. BRIGHT BOY ABSALOM

1   HSHC, Ella V. Mahoney Papers, including drafts of an unpublished manuscript that Mrs. Mahoney coauthored with her friend and amanuensis Helen Covey Milius titled "The House That Booth Built: The House That Fell with Lincoln"

(ca. 1940–42); Willard H. Wright, "Tudor Hall—House of the Booths," *Mentor,* vol. 17 (Feb. 1929), pp. 15–18.

2   Irving Dilliard, "Three to Remember: Archibald MacLeish, Stanley Kimmel, Phillips Bradley," *Journal of the Illinois State Historical Society*, vol. 77 (Spring 1984), pp. 50–56; *Washington Evening Star*, Jan. 9, 1936. Kimmel's papers at the Macdonald-Kelce Library, University of Tampa, contain his 1934 research notebook (quoted here), among other significant items. Thanks to Art Bagley.

3   George A. Townsend, "A Visit to the Maryland Home of the Booths," *St. Louis Post-Dispatch*, May 8, 1880; Michael E. Ruane, "Birthplace of Infamy," *Washington Post*, Feb. 4, 2001; *Baltimore Sun*, March 6, 1938.

4   Kimmel, notebook, p. 23; Stanley Kimmel, *The Mad Booths of Maryland* (New York: Bobbs-Merrill, 1940), p. 67; Mahoney and Milius, "House," pt. 1, pp. 139–40, and fragments; *Bel Air Aegis*, Sept. 6, 1935.

5   Asia Booth Clarke, *John Wilkes Booth: A Sister's Memoir*, ed. Terry Alford (Jackson: University Press of Mississippi, 1996), p. 33. Written in 1874, this memoir was first published under the title *The Unlocked Book: A Memoir of John Wilkes Booth by His Sister Asia Booth Clarke*, ed. Eleanor Farjeon (New York: G. P. Putnam's Sons, 1938). The original manuscript, which I examined courtesy of Arthur and Deirdre L. Kincaid, has no title.

6   John T. Ford comment in Mahoney to Milius, Tudor Hall, July 9 and 17 [1938], author's collection.

7   *Forney's War Press* (Philadelphia), April 25, 1865.

8   *Boston Journal* clipping, n.d., laid into copy of *The Elder and the Younger Booth*, Brown Collection, Manuscripts Department, Boston Public Library; clipping, n.d., Albert Davis Collection, HRHRC.

9   Stephen M. Archer, *Junius Brutus Booth: Theatrical Prometheus* (Carbondale and Edwardsville: Southern Illinois University Press, 1992), an indispensable book for information on Booth's parents; Asia Booth Clarke, *Booth Memorials: Passages, Incidents, and Anecdotes in the Life of Junius Brutus Booth (the Elder)* (New York: Carleton, 1866), pp. 77–79.

10 Liber HD, No. 7, Folio 407–10 (June 4, 1824), and Liber HDG, No. 8, Folio 261 (March 15, 1825), Office of the Clerk of Court, Harford County Courthouse, Bel Air, Md. Junius could own real property only if he declared his intention to become a citizen of the United States and then became one within twelve months. Bernard C. Steiner, *Citizenship and Suffrage in Maryland* (Baltimore: Cushing, 1895), p. 20.

11 Elizabeth Rogers to W. Stump Forward, Baltimore, Md., Aug. 16, 1886, Miscellaneous Manuscripts, Manuscript Division, LOC.

12 *St. Louis Post-Dispatch*, May 8, 1880; James T. Wollon Jr., "Harford County Architectural Notes: Tudor Hall, Fountain Green: Home of the Booth Family,"

Harford Historical Bulletin, no. 3 (Spring 1973), p. 11; Walter E. McCann, "The Booth Family in Maryland," *Frank Leslie's Popular Monthly*, vol. 17 (April 1884), p. 407.

13 Dinah Faber, "Interior Decorations at Tudor Hall While the Booth Family Was in Residence ca. Spring 1853–Spring/Summer 1857," typescript, n.d., courtesy of the author; Asia Booth Clarke, *The Elder and the Younger Booth* (New York: James R. Osgood, 1882), pp. 66–67; *New York Tribune*, May 12, 1865.

14 Asia Booth Clarke, *Personal Recollections of the Elder Booth* (London: printed but not published, n.d. [1880?]), pp. 24–25.

15 Mahoney and Milius, "House," p. Ad-5, and untitled notes in Mahoney Papers, HCHS; Ella V. Mahoney, *Sketches of Tudor Hall and the Booth Family* (Bel Air, Md.: author, 1931), pp. 11–13; *Bel Air Aegis*, May 26, 1899; Mahoney, untitled manuscript on Booth's burial, p. 17, Mahoney Papers, HCHS.

16 Clarke, *Booth*, p. 64.

17 *New York Mercury*, Sept. 17, 1887.

18 John T. Ford, draft of letter to *Baltimore Gazette* [1867?], Ford Papers, MdHS.

19 Birth years for Henry, Mary Ann, Frederick, and Elizabeth are given, with limited confidence, from Kimmel, *Mad Booths of Maryland*, p. 340. There appears to have been an eleventh child named Mary who died at birth in Boston in 1828. Arthur W. Bloom, *Edwin Booth: A Biography and Performance History* (Jefferson, N.C., and London: McFarland, 2013), p. 6. The family Bible, located at the Museum of the City of New York, gives no birth years.

20 Mahoney and Milius, "House," p. 76; Mahoney, "Disposal of Body," manuscript (1930s), HSHC.

21 Clarke, *Booth*, p. 113; Francis Wilson, *John Wilkes Booth: Fact and Fiction of Lincoln's Assassination* (Boston and New York: Houghton Mifflin, 1929), p. 7.

22 William Winter, *Vagrant Memories: Being Further Recollections of Other Days* (New York: George H. Doran, 1915), p. 169.

23 Frank A. Burr, "The Life of a Great Actor," clipping [ca. 1890], Booth Family Files, HTC.

24 Mahoney and Milius, "House," pt. 1, pp. 100, Ad-4.

25 Anne Hartley Gilbert, *The Stage Reminiscences of Mrs. Gilbert*, pp. 57–61.

26 Mahoney and Milius, "House," pp. 102–4, and untitled notes in Mahoney Papers, HSHC.

27 Mahoney and Milius, "House," pt. 1, p. 66; *New York Christian Advocate and Journal*, April 8, 1852; Methodist ministers on Harford Circuit courtesy of John H. Pearce Jr.

28 *Baltimore Sun*, June 1, 1887; *Baltimore American*, July 12, 1896; Mahoney, *Sketches*, p. 35; *Bel Air Aegis*, May 26, 1899; Mahoney and Milius, "House," p. 100; W. Stump Forward, "Junius Brutus Booth," manuscript (1887), p. 98, MdHS.

29 Kimmel, notebook, p. 44; Mahoney and Milius, "House," p. Ad-6; note in hand of Milius, Mahoney Papers, HCHS; Forward, "Junius Brutus Booth," p. 121.

30 Dinah Faber, "Joseph and Ann Hall: Behind the Scenes at Tudor Hall," *Harford Historical Bulletin,* no. 104 (Fall 2006), passim; Mahoney and Milius, "House," pp. 25, 50; Clarke, *Personal Recollections,* p. 40.

31 Clarke, *Personal Recollections,* p. 17. Archer's fine biography provides an extended list of his ups and downs.

32 Edwin Booth to William Winter, Boston, July 17, 1886, in *Between Actor and Critic: Selected Letters of Edwin Booth and William Winter,* ed. Daniel Watermeier (Princeton, N.J.: Princeton University Press, 1971), pp. 274–77.

33 "Booth Letter," *History Detectives,* July 6, 2009 (season 7, episode 3), www.pbs.org/historydetectives, accessed Nov. 5, 2013. Thanks to the enlightening research of Prof. Dan Feller.

34 Archer, *Booth,* pp. 150–51.

35 *Baltimore Sun,* May 3, 1838.

36 [Thomas Hall], *The Actor; or, A Peep behind the Curtain* (New York: William H. Graham, 1846), p. 141.

37 [Hall], *The Actor,* pp. 93–43.

38 Mahoney, *Sketches,* pp. 24–25: Mahoney and Milius, "House," pt. 1, p. 24.

39 Clarke, *Booth Memorials,* p. 94.

40 *Baltimore American,* July 12, 1896.

41 Clarke, *Personal Recollections,* p. 28.

42 *Boston Daily Globe,* March 7, 1909.

43 Mahoney and Milius, "House," pp. 58–60; *Bel Air Aegis,* March 7, 1902.

44 *St. John (New Brunswick) Daily Telegraph,* March 30, 1874, courtesy of Daniel F. Johnson; *Baltimore Sun,* Sept. 7, 1850. The Register of Degrees at King's College, Windsor, Nova Scotia, lists four degrees conferred on Arnold between 1825 and 1836, the final being a D.C.L. Edwin Arnold, *Arithmetical Questions on a New Plan* (New York: Cady and Burgess, 1850), p. iii.

45 "Academies," clipping, Joseph F. Hughes Scrapbook Collection (1945–49), HSHC.

46 Clarke, *Booth,* p. 35.

47 Booth to Joseph H. Simonds, Philadelphia, October 9, 1861, in *"Right or Wrong, God Judge Me": The Writings of John Wilkes Booth,* ed. John Rhodehamel and Louise Taper (Urbana and Chicago: University of Illinois Press, 1997), p. 72. A few additional letters have been discovered since this book was published.

48 James Shettel, typescript, n.d., James Shettel Papers, York County Historical Society; George Alfred Townsend, *The Life, Crime, and Capture of John Wilkes Booth* (New York: Dick and Fitzgerald, 1865), p. 20.

49 Clarke, *Unlocked Book,* p. 168.

50 Clarke, *Booth*, p. 57.

51 *Cincinnati Enquirer*, Aug. 3, 1884.

52 *Philadelphia Tribune*, June 27, 1929.

53 Ernest C. Miller, *John Wilkes Booth in the Pennsylvania Oil Region* (Meadville, Pa.: Crawford County Historical Society, 1987), p. 63.

54 *Dallas Morning News*, Feb. 23, 1908.

55 *Washington Evening Star*, Aug. 18, 1906.

56 Mahoney and Milius, "House," pt. 1, pp. 16–17; *Baltimore Sun*, March 6, 1938; *St. Louis Post-Dispatch*, May 8, 1880.

57 Clarke, *Booth Memorials*, p. 79; Forward, "Junius Brutus Booth," pp. 147–54.

58 After renting various places, Junius took a ninety-nine-year lease on the house on Exeter (formerly Green) Street on September 26, 1845. Deed Books AWB-357-265 and AWB 381-452. Formerly kept at the Register of Deeds Office in Baltimore, these volumes are now online at MDLandRec.net.

59 McCann, "Booth Family in Maryland," p. 408; *Baltimore Sun*, Dec. 12, 1898.

60 Faber, "Interior Decorations"; Clarke, *Personal Recollections*, p. 16.

61 Clarke, *Booth*, p. 6; *Baltimore Sun*, June 18–19, 1888; *Daily Alta California* (San Francisco), July 15, 1888; Bloom, *Edwin Booth*, p. 7.

62 James J. Williamson, *Prison Life in the Old Capitol and Reminiscences of the Civil War* (West Orange, N.J.: n.p., 1911), p. 79.

63 Clarke, *Booth*, pp. 35, 45. Booth may have attended school for a brief period in York, Pennsylvania, as well.

64 McCann, "Booth Family in Maryland," pp. 409–10; Henry Tyrrell, "Edwin Booth," clipping, n.d. (ca. 1886), Booth Files, HTC; "Mr. Edwin Booth's Birthday," clipping, n.d. (ca. 1885), Dielman File (Oversize), Booth Files, MdHS.

65 Clipping, n.p. [Jan. 2, 1897], Hamilton File, HTC; *Nashville American*, Dec. 25, 1898.

66 *Baltimore Sun*, Feb. 26, 1925.

67 *Allentown (Pa.) Sunday Call-Chronicle*, Feb. 12, 1956.

68 *Baltimore American*, July 27, 1903; Celia Logan, "These Our Actors," clipping, n.d., Booth Files, HTC.

69 Stuart Robson, "Memories of Fifty Years: Chapter 1," *Everybody's Magazine*, vol. 3 (July 1900), p. 87.

70 Townsend, *Life, Crime, and Capture*, p. 21.

71 John Locke, "Of Cruelty," in *Some Thoughts Concerning Education* (1693), at www.animalrightshistory.com, accessed Oct 10, 2013.

72 *Diagnostic and Statistical Manual of Mental Disorders*, 5th ed. (Washington and London: American Psychiatric Publishing, 2013), pp. 469–75.

73 John J. McLaurin, *Sketches in Crude-Oil* (Franklin, Pa.: author, 1902), p. 105; Cornell Greening and Richard Match, "New Evidence," *Blue Book*, vol. 86 (Feb. 1948), p. 20; Clarke, *Booth*, p. 55.

74 "The Booth Family Mystery," clipping, n.d., n.p., Booth Family Files, MdHS.

75 "A Sad Romance Recalled," n.d. [Baltimore, 1891], n.p., Booth Family Files, MdHS; *Boston Daily Globe*, March 7, 1909.

76 *New York Press*, Aug. 9, 1891.

77 Mahoney and Milius, "House," pp. Ad-3, 13, 18, 94; Kimmel, notebook, pp. 13–14.

78 Clarke, *Personal Recollections*, pp. 24–25.

79 J. B. Booth, Adelaide Booth, and Richard J. Booth, Agreement, Baltimore, May 7, 1847, J. B. Booth Papers, MdHS.

80 *Chicago Evening Journal*, April 19, 1865; *Cincinnati Daily Commercial*, April 18, 1865.

81 *Cleveland Leader*, May 6, 1884.

82 "Tombs of the Booths," clipping, n.d., July 26, 1891, JOH.

83 Mahoney and Milius, "House," pp. Ad-13, 14; Mahoney, "Chronology of John Wilkes Booth's Life," undated manuscript, Mahoney Papers, HCHS.

84 Mahoney, "Why Booth Shot Lincoln," typescript (1940), Mahoney Papers, HCHS.

85 Bloom, *Edwin Booth*, p. 6.

86 *Cincinnati Daily Commercial*, April 18, 1865.

87 Clarke, *Booth*, p. 45; Mahoney, *Sketches*, p. 14; *Washington Evening Star*, March 21, 1891.

88 John E. and Eli M. Lamb, *Circular of Milton Boarding School...* (Baltimore: James Lucas & Son., 1859), pp. 7, 11; *Friends' Intelligencer and Journal*, vol. 42 (July 18, 1885), p. 361; Francis Lamb, "The Lambs," typescript, n.d., p. 9, and Elizabeth Lamb to James [no last name], n.p., Sept. 12, 1959, both in Folder 14, Box 2, Lamb-Booth-Miller Family Papers, Friends' Historical Library, Swarthmore College. My thanks to Father Robert L. Keesler for his early work on Booth's education.

89 David Allen, "The Milton Inn Connects Shakespeare, Lincoln," *North County News* (Baltimore), Feb. 13, 1997, p. 17; Milton Inn/Lamb's School, Maryland Historical Trust Inventory of Historical Properties, Inventory Form.

90 James W. Shettel, "J. Wilkes Booth at School," *New York Dramatic Mirror*, vol. 75 (Feb. 26, 1916), p. 3; "More Reminiscences of Wilkes Booth," *Washington Evening Star*, May 2, 1885.

91 Esther L. Cox and George E. Cox to David R. Barbee, Baltimore, Aug. 31, 1940, Folders 203 and 204, Box 4, David Rankin Barbee Papers, Special Collections, Lauinger Library, Georgetown University.

92 Clarke, *Booth*, pp. 39–43.

93 Mahoney and Milius, "House," pp. 33–34; Clarke, *Booth*, p. 43–44, 66. Gypsies also frequented the neighborhood of Woolsey's blacksmith's shop near the farm.

94 Clarke, *Booth*, p. 38.

95 *Friends' Intelligencer*, vol. 80 (Dec. 22, 1923), p. 861; T. Chalkley Matlack, "Brief Historical Sketches Concerning Friends' Meetings," typescript (1938), vol. 4, p. 994, Friends' Historical Library, Swarthmore.

96 Entry for Sept. 9, 1850, Marriages Volume (1775–1950), Gunpowder Monthly Meeting, Baltimore Yearly Meeting, pp. 183–84, Friends' Historical Library, Swarthmore.

97 *Towson (Md.) Jeffersonian*, Dec. 26, 1931; *Philadelphia Inquirer*, Jan. 8, 1934; Thomas P. Slaughter, *Bloody Dawn: The Christiana Riot and Racial Violence in the Antebellum North* (New York: Oxford University Press, 1991), pp. 3–7.

98 Rhodehamel and Taper, *"Right or Wrong, God Judge Me,"* p. 107.

99 Mahoney and Milius, "House," pt. 1, p. 46.

100 "Edwin Booth's Real Self," *Theatre*, vol. 24 (Dec. 1916), p. 360.

101 *Booth versus Booth*, Libel, Boston, May 12, 1851, Record Book for the Supreme Judicial Court, Suffolk County, Nov. 1851 Term, Case Docket 513, p. 318. Her mother stated in this document that Blanche was ten years of age. *New York World*, Jan. 11, 1925.

102 Winter, *Vagrant Memories*, p. 169; "Drawing to an End," clipping, ca. 1889, Edwin Booth File, HRHRC; "Booth's First Play," clipping, n.d., Booth Files, HTC; *Baltimore American*, July 27, 1903.

103 Kimmel, notebook, p. 33; Mahoney and Milius, "House," p. Ad-11; Townsend, *Life, Crime, and Capture*, p. 20.

104 *New York Herald*, Nov. 1, 1903.

105 *St. Louis Post-Dispatch*, May 12, 1881; Wilson, *Booth*, p. 7; Clarke, *Booth*, pp. 33–34, 56; draft of "This One Mad Act," p. 131, Izola F. Page Collection, examined at Keene, N.H., courtesy of my friends Marjorie Page Colony and Izola Page Allen; Townsend, *Life, Crime, and Capture*, pp. 20–21.

106 *New York Mercury*, Oct. 5, 1884.

107 Inventory and nomination forms for Tudor Hall, National Register of Historical Places (1972–82), HSHC; Archer, *Junius Brutus Booth*, p. 198; Wollon, "Tudor Hall, Fountain Green," p. 11.

108 Clarke, *Booth*, p. 9.

109 *Baltimore Sun*, Nov. 4, 1852, and Nov. 2, 1889; Isobel Davidson, *Real Stories from Baltimore County History* (1917; rpt. Hatboro, Pa.: Tradition Press, 1967), p. 172; Amy A. Stirling (Van Bokkelen's great-granddaughter) to Mrs. Cain, Baltimore, Feb. 12, 1928, JOH.

110 Booth to Joseph Simonds, Washington, D.C., April 19, 1863, in Rhodehamel and Taper, *"Right or Wrong, God Judge Me,"* p. 88.

111 *A Circular Describing the Mode of Discipline and the Course of Studies in the Junior and Senior Departments of St. Timothy's Hall* (Baltimore: Joseph Robinson, 1852);

Rules and Regulations for the Government of the Students at St. Timothy's Hall (Baltimore: Joseph Robinson, 1852), pp. 11–14; Erick F. Davis, "Saint Timothy's Hall," [Baltimore County Historical Society] *History Trails*, vol. 11 (Spring 1977), pp. 11–15. The Episcopal Diocese of Maryland Archives in Baltimore holds correspondence, class lists, pamphlets, sermons, and other material on the school in this period.

112 *Baltimore Sun*, March 29, 1925.

113 Clarke, *Booth,* p. 35.

114 *New York Clipper*, April 29, 1865; *Atlanta Journal*, Jan. 20, 1924.

115 *Chicago Post*, April 16, 1865; "Wilkes Booth," clipping, n.d. [1865], LFFRC.

116 Michael W. Kauffman, ed. [Samuel B. Arnold], *Memoirs of a Lincoln Conspirator* (Bowie, Md.: Heritage Books, 1995), p. 42.

117 *Philadelphia Press*, Dec. 27, 1881, which also has the stories of Booth's bush-house adventures, his boyhood ambitions, and the student revolt; *Baltimore Sun*, Sept. 20, 1852.

118 Townsend, *Life, Crime, and Capture*, p. 20.

119 J. Edward Leithead, "Colonel Prentiss Ingraham," *Dime Novel Round-Up*, vol. 32 (Jan.–Feb. 1964), pp. 2–6, 10–14.

120 *Philadelphia Press*, Dec. 27, 1881.

121 Clarke, *Booth*, p. 45.

122 *Catonsville Times*, March 14, 2001; Clarke, *Booth*, p. 46; *Philadelphia Press*, Dec. 27, 1881; *Announcement for the 10th Annual Session of St. Timothy's Hall* (1853), courtesy of Pep Martin.

123 *Wheeling (W. Va.) Register*, Sept. 14, 1877; *Columbus (Ga.) Daily Enquirer*, Sept. 5, 1877; *New York Sun*, March 28, 1897; *Boston Daily Advertiser, Boston Evening Transcript,* and *Boston Daily Globe*, all Sept. 18, 1883; Clarke, *Booth*, p. 117.

124 Augustus Thomas, *The Print of My Remembrance* (New York and London: Charles Scribner's Sons, 1922), p. 75; J. B. Booth Jr. Scrapbook, p. 36, William Seymour Family Collection, Princeton University Library.

125 Clarke, *Booth*, pp. 85, 117.

126 Clarke, *Booth Memorials*, p. 148.

127 Clarke, *Elder and Younger Booth*, pp. 106–7; Archer, *Junius Brutus Booth*, pp. 215–16; Clarke, *Personal Recollections*, p. 33.

128 Clarke, *Elder and Younger Booth*, p. 106; Clarke, *Booth Memorials*, pp. 153–54.

129 Ella V. Mahoney to Helen C. Milius, Bel Air, Md., Jan. 31, 1939, author's collection.

130 *Kansas City Star*, Nov. 8, 1897.

131 Entry of Dec. 11, 1852, Merchants' Exchange Reading Room Record Books, Arrivals Series, Box 12, Call No. MS 610, MdHS; *New York Dramatic News*, March 4, 1882.

132 Clarke, *Personal Recollections*, pp. 33–35.

133 Church register, St. Timothy's Episcopalian Church, entry for Jan. 23, 1853, examined courtesy of the Rev. W. Terry Sweeney.

134 Clarke, *Booth*, pp. 127–28.

135 *Washington Post*, June 8, 1903; *New York World*, April 26, 1891; G. W. Baird to A. D. Bulman, Washington, D.C., May 1, 1914, in Federal Hill Antiques catalog, issue of Nov. 10, 1997, JOH.

136 John Mathews in George A. Townsend, *Katy of Catoctin; or, The Chain-Breakers* (1886; rpt. Cambridge, Md.: Tidewater Press, 1959), p. 531.

137 Miller, *John Wilkes Booth in the Pennsylvania Oil Region*, p. 69.

138 Campbell MacCulloch, "This Man Saw Lincoln Shot," *Good Housekeeping*, vol. 84 (Feb. 1927), p. 115.

139 Michael W. Kauffman, *American Brutus: John Wilkes Booth and the Lincoln Conspiracies* (New York: Random House, 2004), p. 92; John T. Ford, statement, Washington, D.C., April 28, 1865, in *The Lincoln Assassination: The Evidence*, ed. William C. Edwards and Edward Steers Jr. (Urbana and Chicago: University of Illinois Press, 2009), p. 527; Lance Gifford (Gifford's great-great grandson) to author, Baltimore, Md., Nov. 30, 1993.

140 *Bel Air Southern Aegis*, July 18, 1857.

141 Mahoney and Milius, "House," p. 82.

142 Mahoney, undated memoir [1940], Mahoney Papers, HCHS; Clarke, *Booth*, pp. 46–78.

143 Clarke, *Booth*, pp. 49–50.

144 Clarke, *Booth*, pp. 71–72; entry for July 30, 1854, in Merchants Exchange Reading Rooms, Arrivals Series, Box 12, Call No. MS 610, MdHS; *Washington Post*, Jan. 10, 1917.

145 Booth letter, Tudor Hall, August 8, 1854, in Rhodehamel and Taper, *"Right or Wrong, God Judge Me,"* p. 38.

146 *State vs. John Booth*, July 31, 1854, Harford County Court Records, HSHC. Congratulations to Alice Williams, who discovered this document, and special thanks to John A. Lupton for his skillful interpretation of it.

147 Rhodehamel and Taper, *"Right or Wrong, God Judge Me,"* pp. 36–43.

148 Mahoney and Milius, "House," pt. 1, pp. 2, 66.

149 Townsend, *Katy of Catoctin*, p. 267.

150 *Population of the United States in 1860, Compiled from the Original Returns of the Eighth Census* (Washington: GPO, 1864), p. 215. For context, see David Grimsted, *American Mobbing, 1828–1861: Toward the Civil War* (New York: Oxford University Press, 1998).

151 Booth letter, Tudor Hall, Nov. 12, 1855, in Rhodehamel and Taper, *"Right or Wrong, God Judge Me,"* p. 43; Asia Booth to Jean Anderson, Tudor Hall, Sept. 10,

1856, Asia Booth Clarke Letters, BCLM Works on Papers Collection, ML 518, Box 37, MdHS.

152 Clarke, *Booth*, pp. 53, 75–76.

153 Clarke, *Booth*, pp. 81, 88–89.

154 *St. Louis Post-Dispatch*, May 8, 1880.

155 Clarke, *Booth*, pp. 67–68.

156 *Booth History Spotlight*, no. 21 (Fall 2013), pp. 2–3; Clarke, *Booth*, p. 95.

157 *Washington Evening Star*, March 27, 1897; *Baltimore American*, Jan. 19, 1896; Edwin M. Royle, "Edwin Booth as I Knew Him," *Harper's Magazine*, vol. 132 (May 1916), p. 845; "Booths, Father and Son," clipping, n.d. [1893], LFFRC; *New York Times*, March 19, 1882; William Winter, "Edwin Booth," *Harper's New Monthly Magazine*, vol. 63 (June 1881), p. 65.

158 Edwin Booth to Nahum Capen, New York, N.Y., July 28, 1881, in Edwin B. Grossman, *Edwin Booth: Recollections by His Daughter* (New York: Century, 1894), p. 227; "Edwin Booth's Real Self," *Theatre*, vol. 24 (Dec. 1916), p. 360.

159 Clarke, *Booth*, p. 71.

160 *Bel Air Southern Aegis*, July 18, 1857.

161 Clarke, *Booth*, p. 50.

162 Clarke, *Booth*, pp. 71, 76–77; *Baltimore Sun*, Aug. 14, 1855.

163 *Wilkes-Barre Times*, Dec. 19, 1894.

164 Clarke, *Booth*, pp. 51, 54, 77–78.

CHAPTER 2. THE MUFFIN

1 Townsend, *Life, Crime, and Capture*, p. 21.

2 *Philadelphia Daily News*, Aug. 13, 1857.

3 George Alfred Townsend, "The Crime of Lincoln's Murder," manuscript (1914), p. 2, author's collection.

4 *New York Clipper*, March 26, 1910.

5 *Theatre Magazine*, vol. 17 (June 1913), p. 180.

6 *Boston Daily Advertiser*, May 12, 1862; *Philadelphia Daily News*, April 17, 1865.

7 *Boston Evening Transcript*, May 9, 1898; Gordon Samples, *Lust for Fame: The Stage Career of John Wilkes Booth* (Jefferson, N.C., and London: McFarland, 1982), p. 71.

8 *New York Clipper*, March 5, 1910.

9 *Baltimore Sun*, Feb. 10, 1907; *Richmond Whig*, March 11, 1859.

10 "Muffins," *New York Clipper*, Aug. 28, 1859.

11 Cast list in *Philadelphia Daily News,* Aug. 13, 1857.

12 *New York Clipper*, Aug. 13, 1859.

13 *Philadelphia Public Ledger*, Aug. 11, 1857.

14 *New York Clipper*, April 20, 1861.

15 *Philadelphia Daily News*, Aug. 15, 1857.

16 *Philadelphia Sunday Dispatch*, Aug. 16, 1857.

17 Clarke, *Booth*, p. 78.

18 Townsend, *Life, Crime, and Capture*, pp. 21–22.

19 *Baltimore Sun*, June 8, 1893.

20 Samples, *Lust for Fame*, p. 171.

21 Playbill for Feb. 19, 1858, copy in T. Allston Brown Scrapbook Collection, vol. 2, p. 189, Van Pelt Library, University of Pennsylvania, Philadelphia; Townsend, *Life, Crime, and Capture*, pp. 21–22.

22 Clipping, n.d., McCullough File, Museum of the City of New York.

23 Clipping, "Winning Fame," [Philadelphia, 1880s?], Booth Files, HTC.

24 Townsend, *Life, Crime, and Capture*, pp. 21–22; *Wilkes-Barre Times*, Dec. 19, 1894.

25 Joseph Whitton, *Wags of the Stage* (Philadelphia: G. H. Rigby, 1902), p. 31.

26 Bruce E. Woodruff, " 'Genial' John McCullough: Actor and Manager" (Ph.D. dissertation, Speech and Dramatic Art, University of Nebraska, 1984), chap. 1.

27 *Cincinnati Enquirer*, July 2, 1885; *New York Dramatic News*, Aug. 26, 1882.

28 *Philadelphia Evening Telegraph*, April 15, 1865.

29 "Winning Fame."

30 Finis L. Bates, *Escape and Suicide of John Wilkes Booth, Assassin of President Lincoln* (Memphis: Pilcher, 1907), p. 226. Kudos to my student Diana Vera for correctly identifying Bates's Gay as Gray.

31 *Baltimore Sun*, Nov. 23, 1899.

32 "Winning Fame."

33 *New York Clipper*, Oct. 31, 1857.

34 *Philadelphia Sunday Dispatch*, Nov. 15, 1857.

35 *New York Clipper*, March 6, 1858.

36 Clarke, *Booth*, p. 79.

37 *Baltimore Sun*, Feb. 10, 1907.

38 Dorothy E. Stolp, "Mrs. John Drew, American Actress-Manager, 1820–1897" (Ph.D. dissertation, Speech, Louisiana State University, 1952), p. 338n.

39 *Philadelphia Daily News*, Feb. 10, 1858.

40 *Philadelphia Sunday Dispatch*, April 4, 1858.

41 Manuscript draft of "This One Mad Act," chap. 19, p. 2, Izola F. Page Collection; Booth to Booth, Baltimore, n.d. [1858], HTC. *Philadelphia Daily News*, April 17, 1865: "He failed to give any evidence of talent for the stage."

42 Rosalie Booth to J. B. Booth Jr., Baltimore, July 12, 1858, HRHRC.

43 Guest Register No. 18, entry for July 13, 1858, New-York Historical Society.

44 Clarke to Jean Anderson, April 29, 1860, March 3, 1861, and May 24, 1865, Clarke Letters, MdHS.

45 Clarke, *Booth*, p. 78.

46 James H. Stoddart, *Recollections of a Player* (New York: Century, 1902), p. 117. Booth was billed as "Wilks Booth" in *Baltimore American and Commercial Advertiser,* Aug. 27, 1858.

47 Quoted in David Rankin Barbee, "Lincoln and Booth," p. 237, unpublished manuscript, Folders 821–26, Box 16, Barbee Papers, Lauinger Library, Georgetown University.

48 Charles F. Fuller Jr., "Kunkel and Company at the Marshall Theater Richmond, Virginia, 1856–1861" (M.F.A. thesis, Ohio University Graduate College, 1968), passim. For Booth's time here, see Deirdre Barber, "A Man of Promise: John Wilkes Booth at Richmond, 1858–1860," *Theatre in the Antebellum South*, in *Theatre Symposium: A Journal of the Southeastern Theatre Conference,* vol. 2 (Tuscaloosa: University of Alabama Press, 1994), pp. 113–29.

49 Beth A. Kunkel, "The Partnership of Kunkel and Moxley" (Honors History Paper, Northern Virginia Community College, 1992), passim; *Baltimore American and Commercial Advertiser* and *Baltimore Sun,* both Jan. 26, 1885; *Richmond Daily Enquirer*, Dec. 17, 1859; *New York Clipper*, Feb. 16, 1861, and July 12, 1890; *Baltimore Sun*, July 8, 1890.

50 *New York Clipper*, Aug. 1, 1857.

51 *New York Clipper*, Feb. 13, 1858.

52 Quincy Kilby, "Some Newly-Collected Facts about John Wilkes Booth," typescript, n.d. [ca. 1914], Seymour Collection, Princeton University Library.

53 Photostat of the playbill for *Adrienne*, Nov. 19, 1858, VRHC, and for *De Soto*, cited in note 73 below.

54 Boniface interview (1905), Brown Theatrical Scrapbook Collection, vol. 4, Manuscripts Department, Boston Public Library.

55 Samples, *Lust for Fame*, p. 26.

56 Booth to Booth, Richmond, Sept. 10, 1858, in Rhodehamel and Taper, *"Right or Wrong, God Judge Me,"* p. 45.

57 Weather data from the journals of Richard Eppes and William F. Wickham in the collections of the Virginia Historical Society, kindly provided me by Frances Pollard.

58 Herbert T. Ezekiel and Gaston Lichtenstein, *The History of the Jews of Richmond from 1769 to 1917* (Richmond: Ezekiel, 1917), p. 223; *Richmond Dispatch*, July 2, 1890.

59 *Atlanta Constitution*, Dec. 31, 1887. James Beale Wahoske, Mary Bella's grandson, graciously contributed to my research on his family.

60 *Atlanta Journal*, Jan. 20, 1924; John B. Clapp and Edwin F. Edgett, *Players of the Present* (New York: Benj. Bloom, 1971, from the first edition, 1899–1901),

pp. 303–4; clipping, "With Players in War Times," n.d. [Richmond, 1907?], VRHC.

61 "Reminiscences of Samuel Knapp Chester," an interview conducted Aug. 15, 1902, in the "Alonzo May Dramatic Encyclopedia," MdHS.

62 "Memorandum of Evidence Against J.W.B./ Statement of Samuel K. Chester," April 28, 1865, 4/410–11, NA M599.

63 *New York Times*, March 1, 1869.

64 Booth to Booth, Richmond, Sept. 10, 1858, in Rhodehamel and Taper, *"Right or Wrong, God Judge Me,"* p. 45.

65 George A. Townsend's interview with Harry Langdon, clipping, n.d. [1883], LFFRC.

66 Townsend's Langdon interview, LFFRC; *Philadelphia Daily News*, April 17, 1865.

67 Kitty Blanchard (Mrs. McKee Rankin), "The News of Lincoln's Death, Including Two Stories of John Wilkes Booth," *American Magazine*, vol. 67 (Jan. 1909), p. 259.

68 Manuscript on stock companies, n.d. [1930?], Seymour Collection, Princeton University Library.

69 William Norris researched Murdoch's career and kindly furnished text for the play *DeSoto*.

70 Edmund H. Russell, manuscript biography of Murdoch, pp. 590, 639, James E. Murdoch Collection, HTC.

71 *Baltimore Sun*, Nov. 25, 1906.

72 Clarke, *Booth*, p. 79.

73 *De Soto*, March 21, 1859, original in author's collection and available in Champ Clark, *The Assassination: Death of the President* (Alexandria, Va.: Time-Life Books, 1987), p. 34. Murdoch's line to Booth is in *Gems from George H. Miles* (Chicago: J. S. Hyland, 1901), p. 173.

74 *New York Mercury*, Jan. 15, 1887; *Cincinnati Daily Times*, Nov. 11, 1868.

75 Russell biography, pp. 351, 1744ff., HTC.

76 *Atlanta Constitution*, Dec. 31, 1887.

77 *Philadelphia Daily News*, April 17, 1865.

78 *Richmond Whig*, Dec. 21, 1858, quoted in Fuller, "Kunkel and Company," p. 112.

79 Quoted under the date of Oct. 1, 1858, in notes of Edward V. Valentine, Valentine Museum, Richmond.

80 John S. Wise, *The End of an Era* (New York: Thomas Yoseloff, 1965), pp. 93–94.

81 *Baltimore American*, June 8, 1893.

82 Edward M. Alfriend, "Recollections of John Wilkes Booth," *The Era: An Illustrated Monthly Magazine of Literature and General Interest*, vol. 8 (Oct. 1901), p. 604.

83 Alfriend, "Recollections," p. 604.

84 Francis Wilson, *John Wilkes Booth: Fact and Fiction of Lincoln's Assassination* (Boston and New York: Houghton Mifflin, 1929), p. 18.

85 *Minutes of the General Assembly of the Presbyterian Church in the United States of America...A.D. 1860* (Philadelphia: Presbyterian Board of Publications, 1860), p. 21.

86 "Reminiscences of John Wilkes Booth in His Theatre Days," clipping, n.d. [Cincinnati, 1890s], Booth Scrapbook, formerly at Baltimore's Peale Museum. William errs in dating this incident.

87 *Richmond Whig*, Oct. 15, 1856, quoted in Fuller, "Kunkel and Company," p. 78.

88 Frank Fenton, "San Francisco Theater, 1849–1859" (Ph.D. dissertation, English, Stanford University, 1942), pp. 238–39.

89 Alexis de Tocqueville, *Democracy in America* (Garden City, N.Y.: Anchor, 1969), chap. 19.

90 Whitton, *Wags of the Stage*, p. v.

91 John H. Hewitt, *Shadows on the Wall; or, Glimpses of the Past* (Baltimore: Turnbull Bros., 1877), pp. 60–61.

92 Fuller, "Kunkel and Company," p. 102.

93 "A Noted Southern Theatre Gone," *Illustrated American*, vol. 19 (April 18, 1896), p. 521.

94 *Philadelphia Press*, April 22, 1917; *Atlanta Constitution*, March 11, 1888; *Richmond Daily Times*, Feb. 27, 1887; George Wren, statement, April 19, 1865, 6/491–96, NA M599.

95 Valentine theatrical memoranda, VRHC; *Richmond Times-Dispatch*, June 29, 1924.

96 Alfriend, "Recollections," pp. 603–4; entry for Thomas M. Alfriend, Henrico Co., Va., Census of 1860, p. 427. My understanding of Alfriend owes much to Patricia C. Click and Kevin C. Ruffner.

97 Fuller, "Kunkel and Company," p. 105; Samples, *Lust for Fame*, p. 30.

98 "Friend's Warehouse," vol. 4, Family History Folio Collection, Jones Memorial Library, Lynchburg, Va.

99 Edward A. Wyatt IV, "Three Petersburg Theatres," *William and Mary College Quarterly Historical Magazine*, vol. 21 (April 1941), pp. 106–8; *Richmond Daily Enquirer*, Nov. 12, 1859.

100 *Baltimore Sun*, Dec. 9, 1906.

101 James Branch Cabell, *Let Me Lie: Being in the Main an Ethnological Account of the Remarkable Commonwealth of Virginia and the Making of Its History* (New York: Farrar, Straus, 1947), p. 151.

102 James Branch Cabell, *Ladies and Gentlemen: A Parcel of Reconsiderations* (New York: Robert M. McBride, 1934), pp. 267–69. The pack of cards is owned by the Virginia Historical Society.

103 *New Orleans Daily True Delta*, Jan. 17, 1861; *Spirit of the Times*, June 28, 1862.

104 *Spirit of the Times*, June 28, 1862.

105 *Baltimore Sun*, Nov. 11, 1906.

106 *Atlanta Journal*, Jan. 20, 1924.

107 Iline Fife, "The Theatre during the Confederacy" (Ph.D. dissertation, Louisiana State University, 1949), p. 28.

108 Leonard Grover, "Lincoln's Interest in the Theatre," *Century Illustrated Monthly Magazine*, vol. 77 (April 1909), p. 943. I have reversed Grover's sentences for clarity.

109 *Baltimore Sun*, Feb. 10, 1907.

110 Samples, *Lust for Fame*, p. 205.

111 *Richmond Daily Times*, Feb. 27, 1887.

112 *New York Clipper*, May 7, 1859. The license was issued under the name of John Clarke Sleeper. Issue Book LSN (1851–65), Folio 568, dated April 25, 1859, Marriage Licenses Issues, Baltimore City, Md., Hall of Records, Annapolis.

113 Asia to Jean Anderson, n.p., n.d. [Philadelphia, July 1859?], Clarke Letters, MdHS.

114 Clarke, *Booth,* p. 79.

115 "Notable Players of the Past and Present, No. 42," *New York Clipper*, Oct. 15, 1910.

116 *New York Clipper*, April 30, 1859, and May 5, 1860.

117 Robert M. Sillard, *Barry Sullivan and His Contemporaries: A Histrionic Record* (London: T. F. Unwin, 1901), vol. 2, p. 20.

118 Alfred Bates, ed., *The Drama: Its History, Literature, and Influence on Civilization*, 20 vols.) (New York: AMS Press, 1970), vol. 19, p. 133.

119 Sillard, *Barry Sullivan*, vol. 2, p. 20.

120 Wilson, *Booth,* p. 17.

121 Diary note of Oct. 6, 1891, Valentine theatrical memoranda, VRHC.

122 *Philadelphia Times*, June 7, 1893; *San Francisco News Letter*, Sept. 9, 1876.

123 *Philadelphia Times*, June 7, 1893; clipping, Booth Scrapbook, p. 195, Fawcett Theatre Collection, Hodges Library, University of Tennessee, Knoxville; *The Season* (New York), Jan. 14, 1871.

124 Alfriend, "Recollections," p. 604.

125 Wilson, *Booth*, p. 18.

126 *Richmond Whig*, May 2, 1859.

127 *New York Clipper*, May 7, 1859.

128 William Winter, *Life and Art of Edwin Booth* (New York: MacMillan, 1893), pp. 194–95.

129 Samples, *Lust for Fame*, p. 34.

130 Clapp and Edgett, *Players of the Present*, p. 304.

131 *Richmond Times-Dispatch*, Sept. 14, 1924.

132 Townsend's Langdon interview, LFFRC.

CHAPTER 3. LIONS AND FOXES

1   Alfriend, "Recollections," p. 604.

2   Cast list in *New York Clipper*, Aug. 20, 1859; Fuller, "Kunkel and Company," pp. 131, 134.

3   *New York Daily Tribune*, Oct. 29, 1877; playbill of May 24, 1859, Medford Town Hall, Medford, Mass., American Antiquarian Society, Worcester, Mass.

4   Adams to "Dear Reakirt," Long Branch, N.J., 2/59–63, NA M599.

5   *Baltimore Sun*, Jan. 20, 1907.

6   Arthur Byron to David R. Barbee, n.p., March 11, 1939, Folder 265, Box 5, Barbee Papers, Georgetown University Library.

7   Samuel J. T. Moore Jr., *Moore's Complete Civil War Guide to Richmond* (Richmond: Moore, 1978), pp. 71–72. Later known as Ford's Hotel, it is the site of the State Library.

8   *Second Annual Directory for the City of Richmond, 1860* (Richmond: W. E. Ferslew, 1860), p. 52.

9   *Richmond Dispatch*, Sept. 5, 1859; *Richmond Daily Examiner*, Sept. 5, 1859.

10   *New York Clipper*, Sept. 10, 1859; playbill in Fuller, "Kunkel and Company," pp. 134–35.

11   George Colman, *The Heir at Law: A Comedy, in Five Acts* (New York: S. French, 1872), pp. 67–71.

12   *Richmond Enquirer*, Sept. 8, 1859.

13   *New York Clipper*, Oct. 1, 1859.

14   *Richmond Enquirer*, Sept. 8, 1859; *New York Clipper*, April 22, 1865.

15   Townsend, *Life, Crime, and Capture*, p. 22.

16   *Baltimore Sun*, Jan. 20, 1907.

17   Alfriend, "Recollections," p. 604.

18   Beale File, Folder 280, Box 5, Barbee Papers, Lauinger Library, Georgetown University.

19   *Richmond Dispatch*, Feb. 2, 1902.

20   Crutchfield to Valentine, Richmond, July 5, 1909, VRHC.

21   Louis H. Manarin and Lee A. Wallace Jr., *Richmond Volunteers: The Volunteer Companies of the City of Richmond and Henrico County, Virginia, 1861–1865* (Richmond: Westover, 1969), pp. 248–51; Lee A. Wallace Jr., *1st Virginia Infantry* (Lynchburg, Va.: H. E. Howard, 1984), p. 6; Philip Whitlock, "Recollections," manuscript (1908–13), VHS. The Grays roster included Elliott, Alfriend, Phillips, Caskie, the three Bossieuxs, and Whitlock himself.

22 George W. Libby, "John Brown and John Wilkes Booth," *Confederate Veteran*, vol. 38 (1930), p. 138.

23 Agnes M. Bondurant, *Poe's Richmond* (Richmond: Poe Associates, 1978), 143n.; scrapbook of J. M. Bossieux, VRHC.

24 Whitlock, "Recollections," p. 90.

25 *Richmond News Leader*, Feb. 12, 1937; Wirt Armistead Cate, "A History of Richmond, 1607–1861," unpublished typescript (1943), p. 924, VRHC; *Richmond Daily Enquirer*, July 30, 1859; *Richmond Times-Dispatch*, May 6, 1933.

26 *Richmond Daily Enquirer*, Oct. 19, 1859; T. P. August, Col., First Regt. of Va. Vols., to Gov. Wise, Richmond, Oct. 20, 1859, "Executive Papers/John Brown's Raid/Expenses," Box 472, LOV; James O. Hall, "John Wilkes Booth and John Brown," *Surratt Courier*, vol. 11 (Nov. 1985), p. 1. For a well-written overview, see Tony Horwitz, *Midnight Rising: John Brown and the Raid That Sparked the Civil War* (New York: Henry Holt, 2011).

27 R. H. Sherar, autographical manuscript, Paola, Kans., June 13, 1914, Boos Collection, courtesy of Bill Luetge.

28 *New York Sun*, Feb. 13, 1898.

29 John H. Claiborne, *Seventy-Five Years in Old Virginia* (New York and Washington: Neale, 1904), p. 141.

30 Alfriend, "Recollections," p. 603.

31 Clarke, *Booth*, p. 108.

32 Grover, "Lincoln's Interest in the Theater," p. 943.

33 Russell, manuscript biography of Murdoch, pp. 1744ff, HTC.

34 *Atlanta Constitution*, March 11, 1888; Beale File, Folder 280, Box 5, Barbee Papers, Lauinger Library, Georgetown University.

35 *New York Times*, Oct. 27, 1859.

36 *Richmond Enquirer* (weekly ed.), Nov. 29, 1859.

37 This correspondence may be seen in Boxes 473–77, LOV. Arson, in *Richmond Daily Enquirer*, Nov. 19, 1859.

38 Libby, "John Brown and John Wilkes Booth," p. 138.

39 *Richmond Dispatch*, Feb. 2, 1902.

40 *New York Clipper*, Dec. 3, 1859.

41 *Richmond Dispatch*, Feb. 2, 1902. The assistance of Valentine W. Southall Sr. is gratefully acknowledged.

42 Barnes interview with Carter W. Wormeley, in "With Players in War Times" (1907), clipping in VRHC.

43 Russell biography of Murdoch, pp. 1744ff., HTC.

44 *Richmond Daily Enquirer*, Nov. 7, 17, 1859; *New York Clipper*, Dec. 3, 1859.

45 Interview with Mr. and Mrs. Logan B. Shutt, n.p., Aug. 31, 1938, Micou-Daniel Papers. Collected by the Rev. Paul Micou and his nephew Richard M. Daniel in the 1930s, these papers consist of research notes and interviews, many with

older residents of Charlestown. They are used with the kind permission of Mrs. Richard M. Daniel. My dear friend Cameron Moseley was characteristically generous in bringing them to my attention.

46 Libby, "John Brown and John Wilkes Booth," p. 138; *Richmond Times-Dispatch*, July 7, 1929; Alexander W. Weddell, *Richmond, Virginia, in Old Prints, 1737–1887* (Richmond: Johnson, 1932), p. 203.

47 *Richmond Times Dispatch*, July 2, 1916; John O. Taylor, "John Brown," typescript, n.d., p. 1, VHS.

48 Crutchfield to Valentine, July 5, 1909, VRHC.

49 Henry Hudnall, "Organization of First Company and John Brown Raid," *Contributions to a History of the Richmond Howitzer Battalion*, pamphlet no. 1 (Richmond: Carlton McCarthy, 1883).

50 *New York Herald*, Dec. 26, 1859; *Richmond Times-Dispatch*, May 1, 1904, courtesy of Angela Smythe.

51 J. Lucius Davis to the Ladies of Charlestown, Richmond, Va., Jan. 30, 1860 (printed), Gibson Papers, Jefferson County Museum, Charles Town, W. Va.

52 Redman and Gibson, bill to Captain Elliott, Nov. 20, 1859, with statement of George W. T. Kearsley, Charlestown, June 7, 1860, in Box 452, Auditor of Public Accounts, Harpers Ferry Fund, Accounts and Vouchers, Entry 145, RG 48, LOV.

53 *Norfolk Southern Argus*, Dec. 9, 1859. Taylor, "Brown," p. 2, identifies the place as an old tin shop.

54 Alfriend, "Recollections," p. 603.

55 Libby, "Brown and Booth," p. 138.

56 *Detroit Free Press*, Jan. 5, 1897.

57 Alfriend, "Recollections," p. 603.

58 *New York Daily News*, Nov. 25, 1865.

59 Booth's service is documented in his pay claim (April 14, 1860) in Box 448, Harpers Ferry Fund, Accounts and Vouchers, Auditor of Public Accounts, Entry 145, RG 48, LOV.

60 Bill of Nov. 20, 1859, in Box 450, Auditor of Public Accounts, Harpers Ferry Fund, Accounts and Vouchers, Entry 145, RG 48, LOV.

61 Taliaferro to Wise, Charlestown, Nov. 27, 1859, in Box 477, Executive Papers, John Brown Raid, Expenses, RG 3 (Wise), LOV.

62 *Richmond Enquirer* (semiweekly ed.), Nov. 29, 1859.

63 *Richmond Daily Enquirer*, Nov. 24, 1859.

64 Libby, "Brown and Booth," p. 138, which also contains the Collier anecdote.

65 "A Reminiscence of John Wilkes Booth," *Texas Siftings* (Austin), Aug. 4, 1883.

66 "A Town under Marshall Law," *Richmond Daily Enquirer*, Nov. 25, 1859; T. G. Pollock to Elizabeth L. Pollock, Charlestown, Nov. 21, 1859, *Fireside Sentinel* [Lloyd House Newsletter, Alexandria, Va., Library], Jan. 1989, p. 3.

67   Gibson Papers, Jefferson County Museum, Charlestown, West Virginia.

68   Regimental morning reports in RG 46, Virginia Department of Military Affairs, LOV.

69   Lucy Johnston Ambler, *When Tidewater Invaded the Valley* (Charles Town, W. Va.: Spirit of Jefferson Press, 1934), unpaginated.

70   *Richmond Enquirer*, semiweekly ed., Nov. 29, 1859.

71   Boxes 448–50, Auditor of Public Accounts Records, Harpers Ferry Fund, Accounts and Vouchers, Entry 145, RG 48, LOV.

72   Berkeley W. Moore to Isaac Markens, New York, N.Y., April 9, 1910, Markens Papers, VHS.

73   Taylor, "John Brown," p. 1.

74   *Spirit of Jefferson*, Aug. 18, 1874.

75   *Texas Siftings*, Aug. 4, 1883.

76   Cameron Moseley, *John Yates Beall: Confederate Commando* (Great Falls, Va.: Clan Bell International, 2007, Special Memorial Printing), brings together many new facts.

77   The records of the Auditor of Public Accounts, Harpers Ferry Fund, contain receipts for forage furnished by Beall commencing Nov. 28, 1859, and a "Consolidated Return of Provisions" received and issued at Charlestown by George W. T. Kearsley, Feb. 4, 1860, documents sales of beef starting Nov. 29, 1859. Boxes 448–49, RG 48, Entry 145, LOV.

78   *Pomeroy's Democrat*, Sept. 14, 1870; *Confederate Veteran*, vol. 9 (Jan. 1901), pp. 3–4; *New York World*, Feb. 8, 1925; *Nashville Tennessean Magazine*, Feb. 5, 1950.

79   *Cincinnati Enquirer*, July 2, 1885. Joseph H. Simonds, another longtime Booth friend, also stated that Booth and Beall were acquaintances. Interview of A. W. Smiley in Miller, *John Wilkes Booth in the Pennsylvania Oil Region*, p. 72.

80   Box 449, Auditor of Public Accounts, Harpers Ferry Fund, Accounts and Vouchers, Entry 145, RG 48, LOV.

81   Isaac Cocke to Benj. Cocke, Charlestown, Dec. 2, 1859, VHS.

82   *New York Tribune* (semiweekly ed.), Dec. 2, 1859.

83   Angela Smythe has gathered an extraordinary amount of material on the Grays and these photographs as she seeks to identify Booth in the images. See her www.antebellumrichmond.com, a highly impressive site.

84   *Norfolk Southern Argus*, Dec. 9, 1859.

85   *Richmond Enquirer* (semiweekly ed.), Nov. 29, 1859; *New York Daily Tribune*, Dec. 1, 1859; *Baltimore American*, Nov. 26, 1859.

86   Libby, "Brown and Booth," p. 138; *Richmond Times-Dispatch*, July 7, 1929.

87   Alfriend, "Recollections," pp. 603–4.

88   *Spirit of Jefferson*, July 8, 1948; John A. Alfriend, *History of Zion Episcopal Church* (Charles Town, W. Va.: St. Andrew's Parish, 1973), unpaginated, quoting Keys's diary. Keys subsequently married Charles E. Ambler, the local Episcopalian

minister, and became the mother of Lucy Johnston Ambler, author of *When Tidewater Invaded the Valley. Charles Town Farmer's Advocate*, April 4, 1925.

89 Arthur W. ("Sunshine") Hawks Sr., "Hamlet with a Goatee and Moustache," *Spirit of Jefferson*, May 13, 1925. Hawks's great-grandson Marshall Hawks shared family recollections and allowed me to study a scrapbook owned by his ancestor.

90 *Richmond Enquirer* (semiweekly ed.), Nov. 29, 1859.

91 *New York Times*, Oct. 31, 1859.

92 *Richmond Enquirer*, Nov. 29, 1859.

93 Taylor, "Brown," p. 2.

94 *New York Sun*, Feb. 13, 1898.

95 Townsend, *Life, Crime, and Capture*, p. 22.

96 Clarke, *Booth*, pp. 88, 108; Henry A. Wise, *Seven Decades of the Union* (Philadelphia: J. B. Lippincott, 1881), p. 244.

97 *New York Daily Tribune*, Dec. 3, 5, 1859; *New York Semi-Weekly Tribune*, Dec. 6, 1859; *Norfolk Southern Argus*, Dec. 6, 7, 1859; *Charlestown Free Press*, Dec. 8, 1859; *Spirit of Jefferson* (Charlestown, Va.), Dec. 3, 1859; John Brown Reference File, Connecticut State Library, Hartford; John H. Zittle, "A Correct History of the John Brown Invasion at Harpers Ferry, Va., October 17, 1859," manuscript, n.d., VHS; and three letters written from Charlestown on Dec. 2, 1859, as follows: J. T. L. Preston to wife, in Elizabeth P. Allan, *The Life and Letters of Margaret Junkin Preston* (Boston and New York: Houghton Mifflin, 1903), pp. 111–17; T. J. Jackson to wife, in Mary Anna Jackson, *Memoirs of Stonewall Jackson* (Dayton, Ohio: Morningside, 1985), 130–32; and Thomas G. Pollock to mother in *Fireside Sentinel*, Jan. 1989, 5.

98 Bill of Redman and Gibson, Charlestown, to the regimental quartermaster, accepted Feb. 13, 1860, Auditor of Public Accounts, Entry 145, Harpers Ferry Fund, Box 449, RG 48, LOV.

99 William Couper, *One Hundred Years at V. M. I.*, 4. vols. (Richmond: Garrett and Massie, 1939), vol. 2, p. 20.

100 Elijah Avey, *The Capture and Execution of John Brown: A Tale of Martyrdom* (Elgin, Ill.: Brethren Pub., 1906), p. 38.

101 Affidavit of John Avis, Charlestown, W. Va., April 25, 1882, *Southern Historical Society Papers*, vol. 13 (1885), p. 341.

102 *Virginia Free Press* (Charlestown), Dec. 8, 1859.

103 Whitlock, "Recollections," pp. 87, 152.

104 Parke Poindexter, "The Capture and Execution of John Brown," *Lippincott's Monthly Magazine*, vol. 43 (Jan. 1889), p. 125.

105 Avis affidavit.

106 Wise to Taliaferro, Richmond, Nov. 24, 1859 (copy), in Box 477, Executive Papers, John Brown's Raid, Expenses, RG 3 (Wise), LOV.

107   Clarke, *Booth*, p. 81.

108   *Richmond News Leader*, Jan. 14, 1927.

109   *Wheeling Intelligencer*, Nov. 18, 1869; interviews with Cleon Moore, Charles Town, W. Va., Sept. 26, 1938, and B. D. Gibson, Charles Town, W. Va., July 5, 1938, Micou-Daniels Papers.

110   "Crime of Lincoln's Murder," n.p.

111   *Spirit of Jefferson*, May 13, 1925.

112   Hawks to Valentine, Ruxton, Md., June 4, 1925, Valentine Papers, VRHC; Hawks's biographical file in the Records of the Superintendent, Virginia Military Institute Archives, Lexington, Va.

113   *Washington Star*, Dec. 5, 1859; *Richmond Daily Enquirer*, Dec. 5, 1859.

114   *New York Press*, May 21, 1893; *Richmond Daily Enquirer*, Dec. 5, 1859; *New York Daily Tribune*, Dec. 5, 1859.

115   Clarke, *Booth*, p. 81; Oswald G. Villard, *John Brown, 1800–1859: A Biography Fifty Years After* (1910; rpt. Gloucester, Mass.: P. Smith, 1965), pp. 284–85.

116   Clarke, *Booth*, pp. 81, 88, 108; Rhodehamel and Taper, *"Right or Wrong, God Judge Me,"* p. 60.

117   "The John Brown Raid," *Wheeling Intelligencer*, n.d. [1869], copy in T. T. Perry Papers, VHS; Townsend, *Life, Crime, and Capture*, p. 22; *Charlestown Free Press*, Nov. 25, 1869.

118   *Boston Daily Globe*, March 7, 1909.

119   *New York Clipper*, Sept. 4, 1858; *Baltimore Sun*, Jan. 26, 1885; Kunkel, "Partnership of Kunkel and Moxley," pp. 6ff.

120   *Boston Transcript*, Oct. 7, 1905.

121   Mary Devlin to Edwin Booth, n.p., Nov. 28, 1859, in *The Letters and Notebooks of Mary Devlin Booth*, ed. L. Terry Oggel (Westport, Conn.: Greenwood, 1987), p. 22.

122   *New York Press*, May 21, 1893.

123   Alfriend, "Recollections," p. 603.

124   *Richmond Enquirer*, Nov. 29, 1859.

125   *Baltimore Sun*, Nov. 4, 1906.

126   *Richmond Times*, March 24, 1895.

127   *New York Clipper*, April 10, 1858.

128   Jefferson's remark in Bates, *The Drama*, vol 19, p. 19.

129   *New York Mercury*, Oct. 15, 1887, and Sept. 13, 1891; *New York Play-Bill*, April 21, 1865.

130   Robert F. Batchelder graciously furnished me with a copy of the acrostic. White in *New York Clipper*, June 30, 1860.

131   *New York Clipper*, Dec. 24, 1859; *Richmond Enquirer*, Sept. 8, 1859; Fife, "The Theatre during the Confederacy," pp. 138, 339. Jennifer D. Lee, "The Wren

Family" (Honors History Paper, Northern Virginia Community College, 1989), author's collection, contains an interview with Eliza's great-granddaughter.

132 *Pittsburgh Gazette Times*, July 14 and Aug. 4, 1907; *Washington Capital*, April 11, 1880. There is no evidence Booth was ever married.

133 *Richmond Whig* and *Richmond Enquirer*, both Feb. 4, 1859; *Second Annual Directory for the City of Richmond 1860*, p. 186; *Richmond Enquirer* and *Examiner,* Feb. 22, 1868. Nancy Lowry, a Redford descendant, and Emma Coley, custodian of records for the Central United Methodist Church, Manchester, were most helpful in my research.

134 John did not tell Rose what the insult was, and there are no additional details of the incident. Rose Booth to Edwin Booth, Philadelphia, March 12, 1860, Booth-Grossman Family Papers, Billy Rose Theatre Library, New York Public Library.

135 *New York Clipper*, June 23, 1860. The couple was living in the Richmond home of Joseph Myers at the time of the 1860 census, where Kunkel and Moxley were also found.

136 Dissolution Agreement, April 19, 1860, John F. Sollers, "The Theatrical Career of John T. Ford," (Ph.D. dissertation, Stanford University, 1962), p. 116. Newspaper advertisements indicate the departure of Ford several weeks previous to the date of this agreement.

137 Fuller, "Kunkel and Company," pp. 145–48; *New York Clipper*, March 3, 1860.

138 Oggel, *Letters and Notebooks of Mary Devlin Booth*, p. 45, with spelling modernized.

139 Voucher No. 7421, Accounts and Vouchers, Auditor of Public Accounts, Entry 145, Harpers Ferry Fund, Box 448, RG 48, LOV. Booth served eighteen days, counted as nineteen in this document, from Nov. 19 to Dec. 6, 1859. However, he was paid three months' salary (at $21 per month) plus $1.58 clothing allowance. The file also contains certificates dated April 13, 1860, by R. A. Caskie, acting quartermaster of the 1st Regiment, stating, "John Wilkes Booth did serve in the Quarter-Master department of the 1st Reg. of Va. Volunteers while on duty at Charlestown," and by Col. Thomas P. August declaring, "I saw Mr. Booth frequently at the Department, and I am satisfied from the certificate of Mr. Caskie that he performed service for the time mentioned in his certificate."

140 *Philadelphia Daily News*, April 17, 1865.

141 *Daily Enquirer*, May 31, 1860.

142 *Daily Enquirer*, June 4, 1860; Barbee, "Lincoln and Booth," p. 247; *New York Dramatic News*, June 15, 1878. Kathleen M. Ward, "James W. Collier: A Man of Many Talents" (Honors History Paper, Northern Virginia Community College, 1990), author's collection, is an excellent review of this actor's career.

143 *New York Clipper*, April 22, 1865.

144 Clarke, *Booth*, p. 79, 85. Also contains "They loved him" and "idealized city."

145 Catherine Reignolds, *Yesterdays with Actors* (Boston: Cupples and Hurd, 1887), p. vii.

146 Petition of Miles Phillips et al., Richmond, April 3, 1850, HTC.

147 *Philadelphia Daily News*, April 17, 1865.

148 Mary Beale Wahoske to David R. Barbee, Portland, Oregon, Nov. 14, 1945, Folder 280, Box 5, Barbee Papers, Georgetown University Library.

149 Townsend, *Life, Crime, and Capture*, p. 22.

150 Wilson, *Booth*, pp. 38–39.

151 *New York World*, April 16, 1865.

CHAPTER 4. THE UNION AS IT WAS

1 Marriage record of Edwin Booth of Philadelphia, Pa., and Mary Devlin of [no town given], N.J., July 7, 1860, Municipal Archives, City of New York.

2 Oggel, *Letters and Notebooks of Mary Devlin Booth*, p. xxviii; Chester autobiography in Alonzo May, "May's Dramatic Encyclopedia of Baltimore," MdHS.

3 Asia B. Clarke to Jean Anderson, Philadelphia, July 11, 1859, Clarke Letters, MdHS.

4 *Baltimore Sun*, Dec. 30, 1906.

5 Adam Badeau, "Edwin Booth on and off the Stage: Personal Recollections," *McClure's Magazine*, vol. 1 (Aug. 1893), p. 263.

6 Alfriend, "Recollections," p. 604 (emphasis added); "Edwin Booth's Domestic Troubles," n.d., n.p., laid into a copy of *The Elder and the Younger Booth*, Brown Collection, Boston Public Library.

7 Alex. K. Johnston in *Philadelphia Item*, Sept. 3, 1890; *New York Dramatic Mirror*, Sept. 6, 1890; *Philadelphia Sunday Dispatch*, Aug. 9, 1857; *Washington National Republican*, Feb. 16, 1874.

8 *New York Clipper*, Sept. 3, 1859.

9 *Cincinnati Enquirer*, Jan. 19, 1886; *New York Clipper*, Oct. 21, 1860; Capt. John H. Jack, 186th Penn. Vols., statement, n.d. [April 1865], 5/49–57, NA M599.

10 *Baltimore American*, Feb. 12, 1909; "The Stage," clipping, n.d., Booth Scrapbook, p. 192, Fawcett Theatre Collection, Hodges Library, University of Tennessee, Knoxville; Ward, "Collier," pp. 3–4.

11 John H. Jack, statement, n.d. [1865], 5/49–57, NA M599; *New York Clipper*, Oct. 21, 1860.

12 Helen B. Keller, "The History of the Theater in Columbus, Georgia, from 1828 to 1865" (M.A. thesis, University of Georgia, 1957), p. 142.

13 Richard and Kellie Gutman, *John Wilkes Booth Himself* (Dover, Mass.: Hired Hand Press, 1979) contains more than three dozen photographs of Booth. Several others have been discovered since the book's publication.

14 Clarke, *Memoir*, p. 77.

15 *New York Clipper*, Nov. 24, 1860.

16 Sources agree the shooting was accidental. The *Daily Sun*, Oct. 13, 1860, identifies Dr. Stanford and states that Canning "was loading the pistol and when pressing on the cap it discharged, the contents entering Mr. Booth's thigh, causing a severe wound." *Albany Atlas and Argus*, April 19, 1865; *Columbus Daily Enquirer-Sun*, Sept. 15, 1885.

17 "Brief Biography of J. Wilkes Booth, found on the person of M. W. Canning when arrested by the Provost Marshal, D.C.," n.d. [April, 1865], 2/36–39, NA M599.

18 "Wilkes Booth Myth Is Still Food for Thought," clipping, n.d., *Birmingham Age-Herald*, Louise Wooster Scrapbook, Birmingham, Ala., Public Library Archives. According to an acquaintance of Charles F. Crisp, whose father was Canning's partner, "the two men were in a bedroom having a friendly tussle" when the accident happened. "Murmur of the World," clipping, n.d., in Nellie J. Spinks, "Every Star a Drop of Blood," manuscript (1970), Birmingham Public Library Archives. Frank P. O'Brien, "Passing of the Old Montgomery Theatre," *Alabama Historical Quarterly*, vol. 3 (Spring 1941), p. 9.

19 Keller, "History of the Theater in Columbus," p. 147; *Daily Sun*, Oct. 15, 1860; recollections of Arthur Benoit of the Holliday Street Theatre in *Baltimore American*, Feb. 14, 1909.

20 *Philadelphia Daily News*, April 17, 1865.

21 *Philadelphia Item*, Sept. 3, 1890.

22 Keller, "Theater in Columbus," p. 150.

23 *Montgomery Advertiser*, Nov. 15 and 24, 1907.

24 *New York Clipper*, June 30, 1860; La Margaret Turnipseed, "The Ante-Bellum Theatre in Montgomery, Alabama, 1840–1860" (M.S. thesis, Auburn University, 1948), for context.

25 Arthur F. Loux, "The Accident-Prone John Wilkes Booth," *Lincoln Herald*, vol. 85 (Winter 1983), p. 263.

26 *Wilkes' Spirit of the Times*, Feb. 23, 1861.

27 E. D. Saunders to J. B. Fry, Philadelphia, April 24, 1865, 2/197–98, NA M599.

28 *Montgomery Weekly Post*, Oct. 31, 1860.

29 Samples, *Lust for Fame*, p. 49.

30 *Philadelphia Daily News*, April 17, 1865, *New York Clipper*, Dec. 15, 1860.

31 *New York Graphic*, June 12, 1875.

32 Canning, "Brief Biography."

33 "James Lewis," clipping in Scrapbook 1, p. 101, General Mss., Laurence Hutton Papers, Princeton University Library.

34 Lynda L. Crist, ed., and Mary S. Dix, coeditor, *The Papers of Jefferson Davis*, vol. 6 (Baton Rouge: Louisiana State University Press, 1989) accounts for his time elsewhere. I am indebted to Ms. Crist for help on this point and many others.

35 Whitton, *Wags of the Stage*, p. 71; Reignolds, *Yesterdays with Actors*, p. 136.

36 *Montgomery Daily Mail*, issues of Nov. 15 and 16, 1860.

37 *New York Mercury*, Nov. 12, 1887; Kate's characterization in *New York Dramatic Mirror*, Dec. 31, 1913.

38 *Philadelphia Inquirer*, June 6, 1865; *Washington Sunday Herald*, Jan. 25, 1874. Of particular value is Gayle Harris, "Sir Henry Irving's Favorite Leading Lady," a speech given on July 15, 1995, at the Theatre Museum, London.

39 Booth to "Dear Miss," Montgomery, Ala., n.d., copy courtesy of my late friend John K. Lattimer.

40 "James Lewis," Hutton Papers, Princeton University Library.

41 *Burlington (Vt.) Free Press and Times*, March 21, 1874.

42 Will. McMinn to "Dear Sir," Montgomery, Nov. 27, 1860, printed letter with envelope addressed to Booth, 7/242, NA M599.

43 Samples, *Lust for Fame*, p. 51.

44 Crutchfield to Edward Valentine, Richmond, July 5, 1909, VM.

45 *New York Clipper*, March 16, 1861. "Montgomery is said to be noted for presentations. Taking the population of Montgomery into consideration, the city is said to be the best theatrical place in the South."

46 *New York Clipper*, Nov. 24, 1860.

47 *Washington Post*, Jan. 5, 1902.

48 "Lincoln Assassination," clipping from the "Cincinnati Correspondence of the Courier-Journal, July 1, 1882," LFFRC.

49 Wooster's interview, *St. Louis Globe-Democrat*, April 20, 1890, and *Pittsburgh Dispatch* of the same date. Copies of both articles, together with other Booth matter, were compiled by Wooster in a scrapbook housed in the Birmingham, Ala., Public Library Archives. *The Autobiography of a Magdalen* by "L. C. W." (Birmingham: Birmingham Pub. Co., 1911) is important. Her 1890 interview contains serious historical errors absent in the autobiography. James L. Baggett, ed., *A Woman of the Town: Louise Wooster, Birmingham's Magdalen* (Birmingham: Birmingham Public Library Press, 2005) reprints the autobiography with valuable biographical details.

50 "Lou," as she was known, was the most famous Alabama courtesan of her generation. The federal census of Montgomery (1st Division, p. 88), enumerated on July 16, 1860, found Louise and her sister Margaret living with Jenny Davis, a madam. The only residents of this house were eight young women ranging in

age from eighteen to twenty-five and identified—delicately—as seamstresses. In the 1870 Montgomery census (5th Ward, p. 506) Louise, named as a schoolteacher, resides in a brothel with a number of other young women. By their names the census taker has written "House of Ill-Fame" in the margin. She was recorded as a "Bawdy House Keeper" in Birmingham in the Jefferson County census of 1900.

Wooster threw her home and purse open to nurse the sick during the 1873 cholera epidemic in Birmingham. Her courage and generosity at the time won admiration, even from those who shunned her socially. She died a wealthy although an unhappy woman. Obituary in *Birmingham News*, May 17, 1913, mentioning Booth. W. Stanley Hoole, "The Madame Was a Lady," *Dixieland* (the magazine section of the *News*), May 3, 1970. Alabama friends Sandy Watson and James Walker contributed useful insights on this topic.

51 *Washington Constitution*, Nov. 3, 1860; *Philadelphia Public Ledger*, Nov. 5, 1860.

52 *Montgomery Advertiser*, Dec. 24, 1917, and Jan. 13, 1918; Hill Ferguson, "John Wilkes Booth and Louise C. Wooster," unpublished typescript (1952), Hill Ferguson Papers, Birmingham Public Library Archives; Idah McGlone Gibson, "In My Portrait Gallery," *Woman Beautiful Magazine*, vol. 2 (Feb. 1909), p. 20; *Montgomery Advertiser*, March 4, 1920; *Palm-Beach Post*, Dec. 7, 1929.

53 *The Assassination and History of the Conspiracy* (Cincinnati: J. R. Hawley, 1865), p. 56; Booth Scrapbook, Folger Shakespeare Library.

54 "The Stage Memories of John A. Ellsler," pp. 111, 114, typescript, n.d., Western Reserve Historical Society Library, Cleveland, Ohio.

55 "Sketch of John Wilkes Booth, the Murderer of the President," unidentified clipping [April 1865], Booth Scrapbook, p. 12, Folger Shakespeare Library; *New York Herald*, April 16, 1865.

56 W. Jonathan Dickson, *La guerre d'Amerique, 1860–1865...avec un Appendice contenant la biographie de J. Wilkes Booth* (Paris: Librairie des Communes, 1865), p. 203, reading "Il passait pour fou."

57 "The Stage Memories of Ellsler," p. 129.

58 *Wilkes' Spirit of the Times*, Dec. 22, 1860.

59 *Autobiography of a Magdalen*, p. 52.

60 John T. Ford, testimony, May 25, 1867, *United States House of Representatives, Committee on the Judiciary, Impeachment Investigation. Testimony Taken...in the Investigation of the Charges against Andrew Johnson*, 39th Congress, 2nd Session, and 40th Congress 1st Session (Washington: GPO, 1867), p. 535; *New York Clipper*, Dec. 15, 1860; *New York Times*, Dec. 10, 1860.

61 *Wilkes' Spirit of the Times*, Dec. 22, 1860.

62 Asia to Jean Anderson, Philadelphia, Dec. 16, 1860, A. B. Clarke Papers, MdHS.

63 *Philadelphia Press*, Dec. 14, 1860. Booth's speech shows the influence of several of these orators. It mentioned approvingly speaker Theodore Cuyler, president of the Select Council, who opined that abolitionists were abusing freedom of speech, and his fear that abolitionist teachings, having reached the slaves, endangered the lives of slave-owners. George W. Woodward of the Pennsylvania Supreme Court rebuked Henry Ward Beecher by name and took issue with the idea that slavery was a sin.

Brown, who handled legal affairs in Philadelphia for the elder Booth in the 1830s, worked to have J. B. Booth, Jr., released from prison in 1865. See J. B. Booth Jr., diary, June 22, 1865, Special Collections, Mugar Memorial Library, Boston University; Clarke, *Booth*, p. 125n.

64 Daniel W. Crofts, *Reluctant Confederates: Upper South Unionists in the Secession Crisis* (Chapel Hill and London: University of North Carolina Press, 1989), pp. 196–200.

65 The manuscript of this speech was owned by the Players, New York City, for many years until sold by the club in 2007. Edwin noted on the first page of the manuscript that it "was found (long after his death) among some old play-books & clothes left by J. W. B. in my house."

The text was published in Rhodehamel and Taper, *"Right or Wrong, God Judge Me,"* pp. 55–64. This book contains a valuable context for the document. It should be supplemented by Jeannine Clarke Dodels, "John Wilkes Booth's Secession Crisis Speech of 1860," in Arthur Kincaid, ed., *John Wilkes Booth, Actor: The Proceedings of a Conference Weekend in Bel Air, Maryland, May 1988* (North Leigh, Oxfordshire: Editor, 1989), pp. 48–51; and Dodels, "Water on Stone: A Study of John Wilkes Booth's 1860 Political Draft Preserved at the Players Club" (1992 revision), copy supplied me by Ms. Clarke Dodels.

I present the speech here with some text rearranged for clarity.

66 *Rochester Evening Express*, Jan. 26, 1861.

67 *Portland Sunday Telegram*, April 13, 1902, quoting from the *Advertiser* of April 29, 1861, with "shuttlecock" quotation; James Moreland, "A History of the Theatre in Portland, 1794–1932," 2 vols., typescript (1938), vol. 1, p. 231, Portland Public Library.

68 "Booth as Othello," n.d., in J. B. Booth Jr., scrapbook, Seymour Collection, Princeton University Library.

69 *New York Clipper*, Feb. 9, 1861.

70 *New York Clipper*, Feb. 9, 23, 1861; *Albany Atlas and Argus,* Feb. 18, 1861; *New York Sunday Mercury*, Aug. 15, 1886; Henry D. Stone, *Personal Recollections of the Drama* (New York: B. Blom, 1969, from the 1873 ed.), p. 70.

71 Henry P. Phelps, *Players of a Century: A Record of the Albany Stage* (New York: B. Blom, 1972, from the 1890 2nd ed.), p. 326.

72 *Albany Evening Journal*, Feb. 18, 1861.

73 Phelps, *Players of a Century*, pp. 324–26, with Cuyler's remark on Booth's mood change.

74 Frank A. Burr, "John Wilkes Booth: The Scene of the Assassin's Death Visited," *Boston Sunday Herald*, Dec. 11, 1881.

75 Orders went out from city and state officers on the night of April 19 for the destruction of the North Central and the Philadelphia, Wilmington, and Baltimore Railroads. Troops from Philadelphia were unable to reach the city on April 21. The White House did not receive New York newspapers, then three days old, until April 23. There was only mail from the South on April 24 "on account of the stoppage of the trains on the Northern Rail Roads," wrote John Hay. "A few letters and papers" from the North arrived on April 25, and the situation improved thereafter. Michael Burlingame and John R. Turner Ettlinger, eds., *Inside Lincoln's White House: The Complete Civil War Diary of John Hay* (Carbondale and Edwardsville: Southern Illinois University Press, 1997), pp. 3–12.

76 *Albany Evening Journal*, April 19, 1861.

77 A. D. Doty to the *Washington Chronicle*, n.d. [April 1865], in L. C. Baker, *History of the United States Secret Service* (Philadelphia: author, 1867), pp. 549–50.

78 "Jocko, the Brazilian Ape," performed by Canito on April 24 and characterized in "A Monkey in Love," clipping, n.d., "Scrapbook of Drama," author's collection; *New York Times*, Jan. 22, 1875; *Albany Atlas and Argus*, April 24, 1861.

79 T. Allston Brown, *History of the American Stage* (New York: Dick and Fitzgerald, 1870), p. 191; *New York Sunday Mercury*, Nov. 12, 1881. Maria Irving's first stage appearance was at Troy, New York, in 1859. *New York Clipper*, Dec. 3, 1859. My student Kimberly R. Moss provided me with numerous facts on Irving's life.

80 *New York Clipper*, June 12, 1858.

81 Townsend, *Life, Crime, and Capture*, p. 24.

82 *Madison (Ind.) Daily Courier*, May 11, 1861, copy courtesy of Cynthia Faunce, Indiana State Library.

83 *Cincinnati Enquirer*, January 19, 1886.

84 *New York Sunday Mercury*, May 21, 1893.

85 The books were a two-volume set of John S. C. Abbott's *The History of Napoleon Bonaparte* (1859). John K. Lattimer owned the books and allowed me to examine them and many other treasures in his collection.

86 H. C. Young to Edwin Stanton, Cincinnati, Ohio, April 20, 1865, 2/33–35, NA M599.

87 *New York Clipper,* May 25, 1861; *Wilkes' Spirit of the Times,* May 25, 1861. Neither rebuked him severely. The latter newspaper reported the story with a certain light-heartedness.

88 James Hall to William H. Herndon, St. Denis, Md., Sept. 17, 1873, in Douglas L. Wilson and Rodney O. Davis, eds., *Herndon's Informants: Letters, Interviews, and Statements about Abraham Lincoln* (Urbana: University of Illinois Press, 1998), p. 582.

89 Thomas F. Cotter, "The Merryman Affair," [Baltimore County Historical Society] *History Trails,* vol. 24 (Winter 1989–90), p. 7.

90 *The South* (Baltimore), April 22, 1861.

91 Burlingame and Ettlinger, eds., *Inside Lincoln's White House,* p. 8; James O. Hall, "Butler Takes Baltimore," *Civil War Times Illustrated,* vol. 17 (Aug. 1978), pp. 4–10, 44–46.

92 William A. Howell, "Memories of Wilkes Booth," *Baltimore Sun,* Nov. 23, 1899; *San Antonio Express,* Feb. 27, 1913. For Howell at the Holliday, see *New York Clipper,* Sept. 22, 1860. I am indebted to Donaly E. Brice, Texas State Library, for helpful information on Howell.

93 "May's Dramatic Encyclopedia," entry of May 12 [actually 21], 1861, MdHS.

94 *Washington Post,* Jan. 5, 1902.

95 G. W. Booth, *Personal Reminiscences of a Maryland Soldier in the War between the States, 1861–1865* (Baltimore: Fleet, McGinley, 1898), p. 9.

96 Ralph W. Powell, "George Proctor Kane: Hero or Traitor?" (Honors History Paper, Northern Virginia Community College, 1990), author's collection. Banks's "To the People of the City of Baltimore," Headquarters, Dept. of Annapolis, June 27, 1861, in *OR,* ser. 1, vol. 2, chap. 9, pp. 140–41. Kane obituaries in June 24, 1878, issues of the *Sun* and *Gazette* (of Baltimore).

97 *New York Dramatic News,* July 1, 1882.

98 *New York Dramatic Mirror,* Aug. 15, 1896.

99 *OR,* ser. 2, vol. 1, pp. 666–67; Mark Neely, *The Fate of Liberty: Abraham Lincoln and Civil Liberties* (New York: Oxford, 1991), pp. 16–28.

100 Robert H. Rhodes, ed., *All for The Union: The Civil War Diary and Letters of Elisha Hunt Rhodes* (New York: Vintage, 1992), p. 12.

101 *The South* (Baltimore), Aug. 20, 1861.

102 *The South* (Baltimore), May 17, 1861.

103 *The South* (Baltimore), Aug. 27, 1861.

104 Clarke, *Booth,* p. 66; Clarke to Jean Anderson [Philadelphia], June 27, 1861, Clarke Letters, MdHS. *St. Louis Post-Dispatch,* May 8, 1880, for the raid and Booth's warning Stump.

105 Book listed as item 56, R. M. Smythe Sale 216 (Nov. 29, 2001).

106 Militia Appointment Records, volume for 1822–62, page 41, Records of the Adjutant General of Maryland, Maryland Hall of Records, Annapolis; *Men of*

Mark in Maryland, vol. 1 (1907), pp. 359–62. *Bel Air Aegis and Intelligencer*, Jan. 22, 1886, courtesy of James Chrismer and John W. Stump, contains highly interesting information on Stump's activities, Booth's ride to his assistance, and the concealment of county arms. Stump in 1861 in *St. Louis Post-Dispatch*, May 8, 1880.

107 *Baltimore Sun*, Jan. 16 and Dec. 25, 1860, Jan. 15, 1861; contemporary copies of Hicks to E. H. Webster, Annapolis, Nov. 9, 1860; Webster to Hicks, Bel Air, June 6, 1861; and Stump to Webster, Bel Air, June 17, 1861, Archives Division, HSHC.

108 *OR*, ser. 2, vol. 2, p. 332.

109 Hunter C. Sutherland, "Biographical Sketch of George Washington Archer (1824–1907)," *Harford Historical Bulletin*, no. 38 (Fall 1988), p. 106; *Bel Air Southern Aegis and Intelligencer*, July 20, 1861.

110 Glenn A. Porter, "Union and Anti-Negro Sentiment in Harford County, 1858–1868" (M.A. thesis, Morgan State College, 1971), p. 40, mentioning also the reward for Stump. The soldiers withdrew about 10:00 a.m., July 14, "amid the most deafening cheers for Jefferson Davis and groans for Lincoln."

111 *St. Louis Post-Dispatch*, May 8, 1880.

112 *New York Tribune*, May 5, 1865.

113 Clarke, *Booth*, pp. 67, 82–83.

114 *Chicago Times*, April 25, 1865.

115 Clipping, n.d. [St. Louis, Mo., April 1865], Booth File, Manuscript Department, Illinois State Historical Library; *New York Times*, April 21, 1865. Correspondent J. R. Hamilton reported these little-known facts from Richmond in an article filed April 18.

116 "Sketch of John Wilkes Booth," clipping, n.d. [1865], Booth Scrapbook, Folger Shakespeare Library.

117 Reid Mitchell, *Civil War Soldiers* (New York: Viking, 1988), p. 17.

118 *Providence (R.I.) Literary Subaltern*, Jan. 15, 1830.

119 B. F. Morris, *Memorial Record of the Nation's Tribute to Abraham Lincoln* (Washington: W. H. & O. H. Morrison, 1865), p. 33.

120 *New York Play Bill*, April 21, 1865.

121 *Kansas City Star*, Nov. 8, 1897; *St. Louis Sunday Republic,* clipping, n.d., Box 6, F. L. Black Papers, Special Collections, Kresge Library, Oakland University; Clarke, *Booth*, p. 39.

122 Edwin Booth to Capen, Windsor Hotel [London], July 28, 1881, Grossman, *Edwin Booth*, p. 227; June in Clarke, *Booth*, pp. 118–19.

123 *Trial of John H. Surratt*, 2 vols. (Washington: GPO, 1867), vol. 2, p. 1229.

124 *Richmond Times Dispatch*, June 18, 1938; Roman mother in two versions emanating from John T. Ford, draft of letter to the editors of the *Baltimore*

Gazette, n.d., Ford Mss., MdHS, and *Trial of Surratt*, vol. 2, p. 1229, remarks of Joseph H. Bradley Sr., attorney for John H. Surratt Jr., on Aug. 2, 1867. Lillian W. Aldrich, *Crowding Memories* (Boston and New York: Houghton Mifflin, 1920), pp. 72–73, reports, "[He] had only been held from joining Lee's army and fighting against his country by the promise given in answer to his mother's prayer."

125 Asia B. Clarke to Jean Anderson, Philadelphia, n.d., Clarke Letters, MdHS.

126 *Baltimore American*, June 8, 1893.

127 Grossman, *Edwin Booth*, p. 227.

128 Flag in collection of the Museum of the Confederacy (#0985.06.0126) with a note that it was "given to Mrs. Robert Nelson Hanna of Bel Air, MD., by John Wilkes Booth during the War."

129 "Herman left at 5 [p.m.], intends leaving soon for parts unknown, the Federalists after him to imprison him for Southern principles, till the end of the war." Priscilla S. Griffith (Stump's sister), diary, Aug. 9, 1861, Alice Parker Collection, HSHC; *The South* (Baltimore), Aug. 27, 1861.

CHAPTER 5. SHINING IN THE ROUGH

1 Terry Alford, "Mary Ann Holmes, Actress?" *Surratt Courier*, vol. 16 (May 1991), pp. 5–6.

2 Clarke, *Booth*, pp. 44–45.

3 Thomas, *Print of My Remembrance*, p. 59.

4 *National Police Gazette*, April 22, 1865; *Baltimore Sun*, June 4, 1903.

5 "Sketch of John Wilkes Booth, the Murderer of the President," clipping, n.d. [April 1865], Booth Scrapbook, Folger Shakespeare Library.

6 *Buffalo Morning Express*, April 17, 1865; *Atlanta Constitution*, Jan. 2, 1885; L. C. Baker, "$30,000 Reward" poster, Washington, D.C., 1865, JOH.

7 Edwin Booth, passport application, Boston, Aug. 3, 1861, vol. 212 (1861), RG 59, NA.

8 *New York Times*, June 30, 1878.

9 John M. Barron's reminiscences, appearing in the *Baltimore Sun* between Nov. 4, 1906, and April 7, 1907, provide the quotes from Jefferson and Neafie.

10 John S. Mosby Jr., "The Night That Lincoln Was Shot," *Theatre Magazine*, vol. 17 (June 1913), p. 180.

11 DeBar Player Record-Book (1853–71), Ben DeBar Papers, A0368, Missouri Historical Society; *St. Louis Star and Times*, April 22, 1933; Charles A. Krone, "Recollections of an Old Actor," *Missouri Historical Society Collections*, vol. 4, no. 2 (1913), pp. 221–32.

12 Grant Herbstruth, "Benedict DeBar and the Grand Opera House in St. Louis, Missouri, 1855–1879" (Ph.D. dissertation, Graduate College of the State University of Iowa, 1954), for an overview of Ben and his theater.

13 *New York Clipper*, Nov. 17, 1860.

14 *Booth v. Booth*, Records of the Supreme Judicial Court, Suffolk County, Mass.; *New York World*, Jan. 11, 1925; T. Allston Brown Scrapbook Collection, vol. 4, p. 215, Van Pelt Library, University of Pennsylvania; Asia to Jean Anderson, Philadelphia, n.d., Clarke Letters, MdHS.

15 Booth to Joseph Simonds, Philadelphia, Oct. 9, 1861, in Rhodehamel and Taper, *"Right or Wrong, God Judge Me,"* p. 72.

16 *New York Dramatic Mirror*, Dec. 11, 1886; *Chicago Tribune*, Aug. 29, 1877; Margaret E. McConnell, "William Warren II: The Boston Comedian" (Ph.D. dissertation, Speech and Theatre, Indiana University, 1963), p. 98.

17 *St. Louis Sunday Republic*, April 19, 1903.

18 Reignolds, *Yesterdays with Actors*, p. 114.

19 *St. Louis Post-Dispatch*, May 8, 1880.

20 *Missouri Republican*, Jan. 8, 1862; Samples, *Lust for Fame*, pp. 66–67.

21 *Chicago Evening Journal*, Jan. 28–31 and Feb. 1, 1862; *Chicago Tribune*, Jan. 21, 1862.

22 "John Wilkes Booth," clipping, n.d. [1891], Jerome Howard Shorthand Collection, Manuscripts Division, New York Public Library; *Chicago Sunday Chronicle*, Oct. 31, 1897; *Chicago Tribune*, Dec. 21, 1898.

23 Emmett Dedmon, *Fabulous Chicago* (New York: Random House, 1953), p. 88.

24 Booth to Simonds, Baltimore, Feb. 18, 1862, in Rhodehamel and Taper, *"Right or Wrong, God Judge Me,"* p. 77.

25 "The 'Old Drury' of America," *The Era Almanack, 1874* (London: 1874), p. 40; Sollers, "Ford," p. 114.

26 *Baltimore Sun*, Oct. 9, 1860.

27 *Baltimore American*, June 8, 1893; *St. Louis Post-Dispatch*, Feb. 20, 1885; "Booth's Romance," clipping, n.d., LFFRC; statement of Ford, manuscript [Baltimore, 1880s], Ford Papers, MdHS.

28 Archer, *Junius Brutus Booth*, p. 198, 215; Phelps, *Players of a Century*, p. 325.

29 *Baltimore Sun*, Aug. 6 and Oct. 7, 1906; *Boston Sunday Herald*, Feb. 26, 1911.

30 Owen Fawcett, diary, Feb. 22, 1862, Fawcett Theatre Collection, Hodges Library, University of Tennessee, Knoxville.

31 Ferguson, *I Saw Booth Shoot Lincoln*, pp. 16–17.

32 *Baltimore Sun*, Feb. 16–March 8, 1862.

33 *Chicago Post*, April 16, 1865.

34 *Baltimore Sun*, March 17. 1906.

35 Nora Titone, *My Thoughts Be Bloody: The Bitter Rivalry between Edwin and John Wilkes Booth That Led to an American Tragedy* (New York: Free Press, 2010), p. 266.

36 *Baltimore American and Commercial Advertiser*, Feb. 24, 1862.

37 *Baltimore Maryland News Sheet*, March 7, 1862.

38 *Baltimore Sun*, Feb. 24, 1862.

39 *New York Times*, May 16, 1886; E. D. Saunders, statement, April 24, 1865, 2/197–98, NA M599.

40 *Cincinnati Enquirer*, Jan. 19, 1886.

41 Clipping, n.d., Booth Scrapbook, p. 193, Fawcett Theatre Collection, Hodges Library, University of Tennessee, Knoxville.

42 Junius Henri Browne, *The Great Metropolis: A Mirror of New York* (Hartford: American Publishing, 1869), p. 175, for all Browne quotes.

43 *New York Clipper*, Aug. 28, 1886; "Wilkes Booth as an Actor," *New York Dramatic News and Society Journal*, July 1, 1882; "Samuel Colville" [New York, 1882], biographical clipping file, HTC.

44 *Baltimore Sun*, Nov. 23, 1899.

45 *San Francisco Daily American Flag*, April 17, 1875; *Sacramento Daily Union*, April 17, 1865; John C. Brennan, "John Wilkes Booth's Enigmatic Brother Joseph," *Maryland Historical Magazine*, vol. 78 (Spring 1983), p. 25.

46 Clarke, *Booth*, pp. 134–38; Brennan, "Booth," p. 25; *San Francisco Bulletin*, April 19, 1865; *Sacramento Daily Union*, April 21, 1865; *Philadelphia Illustrated New Age*, May 27, 1865.

47 "Wilkes Booth as an Actor" (note 43 above) provides these McCloskey quotations, as well as information on Tilton's accident. McCloskey confused Tilton with Collier at places. Political argument in McCloskey, "Autobiography of an Old Player," typed manuscript (1904–5), untitled section, p. 31, courtesy of Jim and Kathy Murphy.

48 *New York Herald*, March 18, 1862; *New York Daily Commercial Advertiser*, March 18, 1862.

49 *Baltimore Sun*, Aug. 6, 1906.

50 *New York Daily Commercial Advertiser*, March 24, 1862; *Boston Journal*, Sept. 9, 1893; David Beasley, *McKee Rankin and the Heyday of the American Theater* (Waterloo, ON: Wilfrid Laurier University Press, 2002), p. 35.

51 T. Allston Brown, *A History of the New York Stage*, 3 vols. (New York: Dodd, Mead, 1903), vol. 1, p. 340, with "groundwork" quote; *Chicago Inter Ocean*, Aug. 27, 1893. Tilton was back at work within a few days.

52 *New York Sunday Mercury*, April 5, 1891.

53 *New York Mercury*, April 9, 1887.

54 William Seymour, "Some Richards I Have Seen," *Theatre Magazine*, vol. 32 (June 1920), p. 502.

55 *Boston Herald*, Jan. 5, 1890.

56 Krone, "Recollections," p. 223.

57 Winter, *Vagrant Memories*, p. 169.

58 *New York Times*, March 19, 1862, and May 3, 1869; *Times and Messenger*, March 22, 1862; *Tribune*, March 21, 1862; *Evening Express*, March 20, April 3, and April 5, 1862; *Herald*, April 3, 1862; *World*, March 31, 1862.

59 *New York Sunday Mercury*, April 5, 1891.

60 Barton Hill, "Personal Recollections of Edwin Booth," *New York Dramatic Mirror*, vol. 37 (Christmas issue, 1896), pp. 2–9.

61 *New York Sunday Mercury*, June 4, 1882; *New York Dramatic News*, Jan. 26, 1878.

62 *New York Herald-Tribune*, April 24, 1932.

63 Clipping, n.d., Davis Collection, HRHRC.

64 Clarke, *Booth*, pp. 77, 80. George L. Stout, a veteran actor and childhood friend of both men, said Edwin was unwilling for John to come to New York. *Baltimore American*, July 27, 1903.

65 Titone, *My Thoughts Be Bloody*, p. 261.

66 Reignolds, *Yesterdays with Actors*, p. 149; William H. Crane, *Footprints and Echoes* (New York: E. P. Dutton, 1927), p. 19.

67 Kate Ryan, *Old Boston Museum Days* (Boston: Little, Brown, 1915), pp. 4–12.

68 J. E. Buckingham Sr., *Reminiscences and Souvenirs of the Assassination of Abraham Lincoln* (Washington, D.C.: Rufus H. Darby, 1894), pp. 47–49; *Boston Post*, May 17, 1862.

69 Stanwood: "Wilkes Booth," clipping, n.d. [Boston, ca. 1895], Box 3, John T. Ford Papers, LOC; *Boston Evening Transcript*, May 13, 1862.

70 *Boston Courier*, May 31, 1874; *New York Clipper*, May 24, 1862; *Boston Daily Evening Transcript*, May 13, 1862.

71 *Boston Evening Transcript*, May 13, 1862.

72 *New York Clipper*, May 31, 1862.

73 Clipping, n.d. [Boston, 1862], Booth Files, HTC.

74 *Boston Daily Advertiser*, May 19, 1862; *Boston Evening Transcript*, May 15 and 20, 1905. For their thoughts on this review I am indebted to the distinguished critics Dan Sullivan, Michael Feingold, Ernest Schier, Holly Hill, Julius Novick, David Richards, and Elliot Norton.

75 "Notable Players of the Past and Present, No. 13," *New York Clipper*, vol. 58 (March 26, 1910); "Recollections of John Wilkes Boothe [*sic*]," manuscript, n.d. [1880s], Albert G. Porter Papers, Indiana State Library; *New York Sunday Mercury*, April 5, 1891.

76 *Boston Post*, May 17, 1862.

77 *Booth History Spotlight*, no. 21 (Fall 2013), pp. 2–3; *St. Paul and Minneapolis Pioneer Press*, Feb. 20, 1887, including "muttering" remark, LFFRC; McCloskey, "Autobiography," untitled section, p. 32; Mahoney and Milius, "House," pp. 26, Ad-7, HSHC.

78 Priscilla S. Griffith, diary, Feb. 25, 1862, HSHC; *OR*, ser. 2, vol. 2, p. 332; Alexander B. Stump, "Notes on the Children of J. W. Stump & Their Part in the

American Civil War, 1861–65," typescript [1978–79], copy in author's possession. The graciousness of Sally Stump and Mary Witt, her daughter, regarding this later document has been most helpful.

79 *New York Tribune*, May 5 and 12, 1865.

80 Terry Alford, "Wonderful and Mysterious: Edwin Booth's Search for His Dead Wife," paper delivered to the 14th Annual Surratt Society Banquet, Fort Lesley J. McNair Officers' Club, Washington, D.C., May 11, 1990, pp. 7–11.

81 Arch Street Theatre playbill, Feb. 23, 1863, copy courtesy of Abraham Lincoln Bookshop.

82 Fragment of a typescript, n.d., Mahoney Papers, HSHC; *Boston Globe*, June 7, 1893.

83 Stolp, "Mrs. John Drew," pp. 276–80, 317.

84 Rose Eytinge, *The Memoirs of Rose Eytinge* (New York: F. S. Stokes, 1905), pp. 244–45.

85 A. Frank Stull, "Where Famous Actors Learned Their Art," *Lippincott's Monthly Magazine*, March 1905, p. 374.

86 Stuart Robson, "Fifty Years of My Life, Part II," *Everybody's Magazine*, vol. 3 (Aug. 1900), pp. 190–91.

87 Booth to Simonds, Philadelphia, March 1 [1863], Princeton University Library.

88 Bonnie G. Satterfield Stowell, "Mrs. John Drew: Nineteenth Century American Theatre Manager" (M.F.A. thesis, Graduate School of the University of Texas at Austin, 1969), pp. 138–39.

89 Brown, *History of the American Stage*, p. 129; James W. Shettel, "J. Wilkes Booth at School," *New York Dramatic Mirror*, Feb. 26, 1916, p. 5.

90 Lewis C. Strang, *Famous Actors of the Day in America* (Boston: L. C. Page, 1900), pp. 297–303; *Springfield (Mass.) Republican*, March 31, 1901.

91 Clarke to Anderson [Philadelphia], March 3, 1863, Clarke Letters, MdHS.

92 *Philadelphia Evening Telegraph*, April 15, 1865; Clarke, *Booth*, pp. 81–82.

93 Eugenie Paul Jefferson, *Intimate Recollections of Joseph Jefferson* (New York: Dodd, Mead, 1909), p. 248.

94 *Philadelphia Press*, March 5, 1863; *North American Gazette*, March 14, 1863. Playhouse described in *Philadelphia Evening Bulletin*, July 10, 1936.

95 Titone, *My Thoughts Be Bloody*, p. 288.

96 Booth to Booth, Washington, D.C., Jan. 17, 1865, Princeton University Library.

97 *New York Sun*, March 17, 1925; Grover, "Lincoln's Interest in the Theater," p. 943; *Washington Evening Star*, January 17, 1867; *New York Sunday Mercury*, March 21, 1886.

98 *Washington Evening Star*, April 21, 1862; Alexander Hunter and J. H. Polkinhorn, *New National Theater, Washington, D.C.: A Record of Fifty Years* (Washington: Polkinhorn, 1885), p. 47; *Washington Post*, April 17, 1898; *National Intelligencer*, April 12, 30, May 8 and 9, 1863.

99   *Cincinnati Enquirer*, Jan. 19, 1886. May's statement, April 27, 1865, 4/360–65, NA M599; his testimony, June 24, 1867, *Surratt Trial*, vol. 1, pp. 270–71; his "The Mark of the Scalpel," manuscript (1887), pp. 3–5, Manuscript Division, LOC, and published in *Records of the Columbia Historical Society*, vol. 13 (1910), pp. 52–54; *Journal of the American Medical Association*, vol. 17 (July 18, 1891), pp. 121–23. Operation and date: *Washington National Republican*, April 17, 1863; testimony of Joseph K. Barnes, May 20, 1865, Benjamin Perley Poore, *The Conspiracy Trial for the Murder of the President*, 3 vols. (Boston: J. E. Tilton, 1865), vol. 2, p. 60.

100 Allen D. Spiegal, "Dr. John Frederick May and the Identification of John Wilkes Booth's Body," *Journal of Community Health*, vol. 23 (Oct. 1998), pp. 385–86.

101 *New York Journal*, July 22, 1905; William B. Styple, *The Little Bugler: The True Story of a Twelve-Year-Old Boy in the Civil War* (Kearney, N.J.: Belle Grove, 1998), p. 138. Thanks to Doug Pokorski.

102 *Theatre Magazine*, vol. 3 (Dec. 1903), p. 299; "Richelieu in War Time," clipping, n.d. [1890s], Booth Scrapbook, p. 135, Fawcett Theatre Collection, Hodges Library, University of Tennessee, Knoxville; *Lexington Herald*, Feb. 17, 1909.

103 Terry Alford, "When Booth Gave Lincoln Roses," speech delivered at 13th Annual Symposium of the Abraham Lincoln Institute, National Archives II, College Park, Md., and accessible at http://www.lincoln-institute.org/symposia/sym2010/videos/alford.htm.

104 *Washington Post*, May 4, 1913.

105 *New York Sun*, March 17, 1925; J. T. Ford, "Memoranda and statement of all matters," n.d. [1865], Ford Papers, MdHS.

106 *Chicago Times*, April 20, 1865.

107 *Chicago Inter Ocean*, June 16, 1901.

108 Edgar J. Goodspeed, *Funeral Discourse on the Death of Abraham Lincoln* (Chicago: The Trustees, 1865), p. 5; David B. Chesebrough, *No Sorrow like Our Sorrow: Northern Protestant Ministers and the Assassination of Lincoln* (Kent, Ohio: Kent State University Press, 1994), p. 38.

109 *New York Herald*, June 27, 1909.

110 Clarke, *Booth*, pp. 79–80.

CHAPTER 6. LIFE'S FITFUL FEVER

1   *Providence Daily Journal*, May 30, 1859; *Washington National Tribune*, Jan. 14, 1904.

2   Archer, *Booth*, pp. 227, 313; *Providence Evening Press*, March 18, 1859.

3   Kincaid, *John Wilkes Booth, Actor*, p. 53; *National Police Gazette* (New York), April 22, 1865.

4   *New York Clipper*, March 5, 1859. My appreciation to Joan Murphy, Randy Thomas, and the late Anne Thomas Cantrell.

5   *Chicago Daily News*, Feb. 11, 1926.

6   *Washington Evening Star*, June 27, 1891, for Forney quotations.

7   *Cincinnati Enquirer*, July 6, 1878.

8   Maria Bella Beale interview (1887), Folder 280, Box 5, David Rankin Barbee Papers, Georgetown University Library; *Atlanta Journal*, Jan. 20, 1924.

9   Townsend, *Life, Crime, and Capture*, p. 24.

10 Anon. to Booth, n.d., n.p., in Edwards and Steers, *The Lincoln Assassination*, p. 161.

11 Clara Morris, *Life on the Stage: My Personal Experiences and Recollections* (New York: McClure, Phillips, 1901), pp. 99–100.

12 *New York Mercury*, Oct. 12, 1890.

13 *New York Sun*, March 23, 1918.

14 Blanche Booth to Leslie Traylor, Minneapolis, Minn., May 12, 1925, Folder 5, Box 7, Earl H. Swaim Papers, Georgetown University Library; *Newark (N.J.) Sunday Call*, Feb. 6, 1939; Mitchell interview in "Lincoln's Assassination," clipping [1881?], Assassination File, Abraham Lincoln Library and Museum, Lincoln Memorial University, Harrogate, Tennessee; Blanche Chapman Ford statement to George S. Bryan (1938), in Bryan, *The Great American Myth* (New York: Carrick and Evans, 1940), p. 126.

15 *Manuscript Society News*, vol. 11 (Spring 1990), p. 46.

16 *New York Clipper*, Sept. 10, 1864, and Sept. 5, 1891.

17 *San Francisco Daily Dramatic Chronicle*, March 7, 1865.

18 L. L. Stevens, *Lives, Crimes, and Confessions of the Assassins* (Troy, N.Y.: Daily Times Steam Printing, 1865), p. 22. Compiled from newspaper accounts, interviews, and a fanciful imagination, this volume must be used with care.

19 *New York Clipper*, Nov. 21, 1863.

20 John P. Simonton, manuscript note on verso of Brown cabinet photograph [n.d., but before 1929], author's collection.

21 John A. Kennedy, statement, New York, N.Y., April 21, 1865, 3/691, NA M599.

22 F. W. Heath, diary entry of May 1, 1865, Huntington Cairns Papers, Manuscript Division, LOC. Courtesy of my friend Prof. Joan Cashin.

23 *Cincinnati Daily Enquirer*, July 6, 1878.

24 Starr to Booth, Washington, D.C., Feb. 7, 1865, 2/358–59, NA M599; *Portland (Me.) Eastern Argus*, May 31, 1865.

25 Rhodehamel and Taper, *"Right or Wrong, God Judge Me,"* pp. 106–17; Leah L. Nichols-Wellington, *History of the Bowdoin School, 1821–1907* (Manchester, N.H.: Ruemely Press, 1912), p. 177; *Boston Daily Globe*, Nov. 18, 1923.

26 Booth to Booth, New York, March 13, 1865, typescript in Ella Mahoney, "A Faded Letter," Mahoney Papers, HSHC.

27 *Boston Daily Globe*, Feb. 17, 1935.

28 A. F. Norcross, "A Child's Memory of the Boston Theatre," *Theatre Magazine*, vol. 43 (May 1926), p. 37.

29 *Boston Daily Globe*, March 7, 1909; "Sketches of the Assassins," "A Reminiscence of J. Wilkes Booth," and other articles in Booth Scrapbook, Folger Shakespeare Library; Townsend, "Crime of Lincoln's Murder."

30 *Richmond Times-Dispatch*, June 24, 1906; *New York Telegraph*, May 23, 1909.

31 Ferguson, *I Saw Booth Shoot Lincoln*, p. 13.

32 Ford, "Memoranda," MdHS; *Cincinnati Daily Enquirer*, June 24, 1878.

33 Annie A. Fields, diary, May 5, 1865, Fields Papers, Massachusetts Historical Society.

34 *New York Police Gazette*, April 22, 1865.

35 Kenneth Turan in *Los Angeles Times*, April 3, 2005.

36 Terry Alford, "John Wilkes Booth and George Alfred Townsend: A Marriage Made in Hell?" paper delivered to the Third Biennial Tudor Hall Conference, May 3, 1992, Aberdeen, Md.

37 *Chicago Times*, April 18, 1865; *Chicago Post*, April 16, 1865.

38 *Washington Chronicle*, Sept. 5, 1886.

39 *Baltimore Sun*, March 17, 1907.

40 E. L. Bangs to Ella Mahoney, Baltimore, Md., Nov. 28, 1927, Mahoney Papers, HSHC.

41 *Baltimore American*, July 15, 1905.

42 Clarke, *Booth*, p. 121; Rhodehamel and Taper, *"Right or Wrong, God Judge Me,"* p. 65.

43 *New York Clipper*, Sept. 16, 1865; *New York Telegraph*, May 23, 1909.

44 *Cincinnati Enquirer*, Aug. 3, 1884; John T. Ford, testimony, May 31, 1865, in *The Trial: The Assassination of President Lincoln and the Trial of the Conspirators*, ed. Edward Steers (Lexington: University Press of Kentucky, 2003), p. 103; *New York Police Gazette*, April 22, 1865.

45 Townsend, *Katy of Catoctin*, p. 343; Townsend, "Crime of Lincoln's Murder."

46 *Chicago Post*, April 16, 1865; *Baltimore Sun*, July 15, 1864.

47 *Denver Post*, Jan. 7, 1899.

48 "Booth Once Started Riot," clipping, n.d, Booth Vertical File, Enoch Pratt Library, Baltimore, Md.

49 Ferguson, *I Saw Booth Shoot Lincoln*, pp. 14–19.

50 "J. Wilkes Booth," clipping, n.d. [1865], LFFRC; *Chicago Post,* April 16, 1865.

51 George Ford, clipping, n.d. [Aug. 15, 1926], scrapbook titled "April Fourteenth, 1865," McLellan Collection, John Hay Library, Brown University.

52 John Mathews, statement, April 30, 1865, 5/302–14, NA M599.

53 *Chicago Post,* April 16, 1865.

54 Ferguson, *I Saw Booth Shoot Lincoln,* p. 14.

55 Lillian Woodman, *Crowding Memories* (Boston and New York: Houghton Mifflin, 1920), p. 61; Brennan, "Joseph Booth," p. 25.

56 *Boston Daily Advertiser,* Sept. 24, 1896; Norcross, "Child's Memory," p. 72.

57 *New York Daily Tribune,* June 7, 1903; "Saw Edwin Booth Identify Brother," clipping, n.d., Wooster Scrapbook, p. 14a, Birmingham Public Library Archives.

58 James Henry Hackett, *Notes and Comments upon Certain Plays and Actors of Shakespeare* (New York: Carleton, 1863), p. 93.

59 "Baize," clipping, n.d. [Boston, April 3, 1909], Julia Bennett Barrow File, HTC.

60 *Chicago Inter Ocean,* Aug. 27, 1893.

61 *Portsmouth Journal of Literature and Politics,* Feb. 14, 1863.

62 Quoted in C. Spencer Chambers, clipping, *Walton (Ky.) Advertiser,* March [no day given], 1929, Shettel Papers, York County Historical Society.

63 Oggel, *Letters and Notebooks of Mary Devlin Booth,* pp. 105–6.

64 *Boston Evening Transcript,* Nov. 30, 1894.

65 Charles H. Shattuck, *The Hamlet of Edwin Booth* (Urbana: University of Illinois Press, 1969), p. 14.

66 Reignolds, *Yesterdays with Actors,* p. 142.

67 Deirdre L. Kincaid, "Rough Magic: The Theatrical Life of John Wilkes Booth" (Ph.D. thesis, University of Hull, 2000), p. 68; *Chicago Tribune,* June 18, 1878; "Drawing to an End," clipping, n.d. [ca. 1889], Edwin Booth Biographical File, HRHRC.

68 Undated note in Kimmel Collection, Macdonald-Kelce Library, University of Tampa; David Carroll, *The Matinee Idols* (New York: Arbor House, 1972), p. 32.

69 Rock Brynner, quoted in *Washington Post,* June 18, 2006.

70 *St. Louis Sunday Republic,* clipping, n.d., Black Papers, Kresge Library, Oakland University.

71 *Chicago Post,* April 16, 1865; *Detroit Free Press,* Dec. 25, 1892.

72 Emerson, "The Night That Lincoln Was Shot," p. 179; *Boston Globe,* n.d. [Dec. 1895], Booth Files, HTC.

73 *Washington Post,* July 17, 1904.

74 "J. Wilkes Booth," clipping, n.d. [1861], John Wilkes Booth Biographical File, HRHRC.

75 Ferguson, *I Saw Booth Shoot Lincoln,* pp. 17–18.

76 *Boston Herald*, Jan. 10, 1890; Morris, *Life on the Stage*, p. 98, Townsend, *Katy of Catoctin*, p. 462.

77 *St. Louis Republic*, April 19, 1903; *New York Herald*, June 27, 1909; *New York Dramatic Mirror*, Feb. 12, 1898, and Oct. 3, 1908.

78 "The Actor's Fame," clipping, n.d., Seymour Collection, Princeton University Library.

79 Ellsler, "Stage Memories," p. 110.

80 *Cincinnati Enquirer*, July 2, 1885.

81 *Baltimore Sun*, April 7, 1907.

82 *Boston Herald*, Jan. 10, 1890.

83 *Washington Daily National Intelligencer*, March 18, 1865.

84 *New York Sun*, March 17, 1925.

85 *Washington Evening Star*, Nov. 14, 1891.

86 Jefferson, *Intimate Recollections*, p. 247.

87 Rhodehamel and Taper, *"Right or Wrong, God Judge Me."* p. 95.

88 *Pittsburg Dispatch*, April 20, 1890.

89 *St. Louis Star and Times*, April 22, 1933.

90 *Oregonian* (Portland, Ore.), Dec. 13, 1908.

91 Charles Pope, diary, Oct. 10–13, 1858, p. 335, "An American Actor's Diary—1858," ed. J. Alan Hammack, *Educational Theatre Journal*, vol. 7 (Dec. 1955), p. 335.

92 Robson, "Memoirs of Fifty Years," pt. 1, p. 88.

93 *Cincinnati Enquirer*, Jan. 19, 1886.

94 John T. Ford, testimony, May 31, 1865, in Steers, *The Trial*, pp. 102–4.

95 Morris, *Life on the Stage*, p. 103.

96 Ferguson, *I Saw Booth Shoot Lincoln*, p. 15.

97 *Baltimore Sun*, April 7, 1907; Reignolds, *Yesterdays with Actors*, p. 142.

98 *Chicago Tribune*, Jan. 21, 1862.

99 Morris, *Life on the Stage*, p. 103.

100 *Detroit Free Press*, Aug. 11, 1916.

101 *New York Press*, May 21, 1893; Poore, *The Conspiracy Trial*, vol. 2, p. 532; Weaver: *Chicago Inter Ocean*, Aug. 27, 1893.

102 *Baltimore Sun,* Feb. 12, 1926; *Detroit Free Press*, Aug. 11, 1916.

103 *Texas Siftings* (Austin), Feb. 13, 1886.

104 *New York Clipper*, March 26, 1910.

105 *Chicago Inter Ocean*, Aug. 27, 1893.

106 *New York Clipper*, Sept. 16, 1865; *Boston Herald*, Jan. 5, 1890.

107 Robson, "Fifty Years of My Life," pt. 5, p. 484.

108 Alfriend, "Recollections," p. 604.

109 Morris, *Life on the Stage*, p. 104.

110 *Washington Daily National Intelligencer*, Jan. 22, 1865.

111 "Wilkes Booth," clipping, n.d. [Boston, c. 1895], Box 3, John T. Ford Papers, LOC.

112 Stolph, "Mrs. John Drew," p. 320.

113 *Washington Daily National Intelligencer*, Nov. 9, 1863.

114 *Philadelphia Press*, Dec. 4, 1881; *Kansas City Times*, Feb. 23, 1885.

115 *Boston Sunday Herald*, April 11, 1897.

116 *Chicago Daily News*, Feb. 11, 1926.

117 *Washington Daily National Intelligencer*, April 30, 1863; T. Crugar Cuyler to Boyd B. Stutler, Wayside, Ga., June 11, 1949, in West Virginia Memory Database Collection, http://www.wvculture.org/history/wvmemory/index.html, accessed Sept. 4, 2012.

118 Louis J. Weichmann, *A True History of the Assassination of Abraham Lincoln and of the Conspiracy of 1865* (New York: Alfred A. Knopf, 1975), p. 115.

119 *Boston Sunday Gazette*, Jan. 24, 1863; *New York World*, text on verso of Kate Reignolds playbill, JOH.

120 *Washington Daily National Intelligencer*, April 28, 1863.

121 *Boston Saturday Gazette*, Jan. 24, 1863; Fawcett: *Detroit Free Press*, Dec. 15, 1901. Edwin did play the piece after this date, however.

122 Brown, *A History of the New York Stage*, vol. 1, p. 510. Booth played the Colley Cibber version, defended "as a good acting play, one for the stage and not for the library." Editor's note in Booth's own promptbook copy (New York: Samuel French, n.y.), HRHRC.

123 *New York Tribune* in "J. Wilkes Booth: Opinions of the New York Press," broadside [Boston, 1862], Edward Naumberg Gift Envelope, Booth Family Folder, Seymour Collection, Princeton University Library; *New York Times and Messenger*, March 23, 1862.

124 *Kansas City Times*, Feb. 23, 1885.

125 *New York Sunday Mercury*, n.d. [1891], Ford Papers, MdHS.

126 Ellsler, "Stage Memories," pp. 109–10.

127 "The Stage in America," *The Era Almanack and Annual for 1873* (London: Era, 1872), p. 45.

128 Booth to Keach, Chicago, Dec. 8, 1862, Gratz Collection, Historical Society of Pennsylvania; *Boston Courier*, June 14, 1874; *Kansas City Times*, Feb. 23, 1885.

129 Clipping, n.d. [1865], Atwater Scrapbook, Chicago Historical Society.

130 "Actor Owens's Successes," clipping, n.d., HTC.

131 Clarke, *Booth*, p. 108 (with hoarded comment, p. 81, and 5–20s, p. 130); *Baltimore American*, Dec. 8, 1902.

132 Boston Water Power Company Collection, Vol. AC-4, Transfer #7777 (Boston, May 30, 1864), Baker Library, Harvard University; *Boston Post*, April 28, 1864. Special thanks to Jennifer Turner.

133 Bradford [Pa.] *Evening Star*, Oct. 29, 1888; John J. McLaurin, *Sketches in Crude-Oil* (3rd ed., Franklin, Pa.: author, 1902), p. 105.

134 Booth to Simonds, Phila., Feb. 28, 1863, Andrew de Coppet Collection, Princeton University Library.

135 Richard and Kellie Gutman, "Boston: A Home for John Wilkes Booth?" *Surratt Society News*, vol. 10 (Sept., 1985), pp. 1, 6–7. Beth Carroll-Horrocks helped the author appreciate the lot's location.

136 *New York Herald*, Nov. 1, 1903.

137 Mary E. Shull, "A Scrapbook of Memories," a paper presented at the 1990 Tudor Hall Conference, author's copy. My appreciation goes to Mary Beth for her groundbreaking work on the Mitchell family.

138 Neely, *Fate of Liberty*, p. 26.

139 Harry Ide, "The Shooting of Jessie Wharton," at freepages.military.rootsweb .ancestry.com/-pa91/cc240001, accessed Feb. 20, 2013; *New York Herald-Tribune*, April 23, 1862; Washington *Daily National Intelligencer*, April 29, 1862.

140 Thomas Walter, "Personal Recollections and Experiences of an Obscure Soldier," *Grand Army Scout and Soldiers' Mail*, vol. 3, no. 35 (Aug. 9, 1884), p. 2.

141 St. Louis *Daily Missouri Democrat*, April 22, 1862.

142 Clarke, *Booth*, pp. 55–56; Asia B. Clarke to Jean Anderson, Tudor Hall, April 4, 1854, Clarke Letters, MdHS.

143 "John Overton Wharton," manuscript family genealogy, n.d. [c. 1900?], author's collection.

144 New York *Pomeroy's Democrat*, July 20, 1870.

145 *Goshen* [Indiana] *Times*, Sept. 10, 1868.

146 Clarke, *Booth*, p. 85.

147 *Washington Post*, July 17, 1904.

148 *Philadelphia Weekly Press*, Dec. 8, 1881.

149 *Kansas City Star*, Nov. 8, 1897.

150 Washington, *They Knew Lincoln*, pp. 90–91; Eric Foner, *The Fiery Trial: Abraham Lincoln and American Slavery* (New York and London: W. W. Norton, 2010), p. 240; *Chicago Daily News*, Feb. 12, 1916.

151 *New York Clipper*, Jan. 23, 1864; Denver *Rocky Mountain News*, Jan. 20, 1864; *New York Herald-Tribune*, Jan. 9, 1864.

152 Booth to Moses Kimball, St. Joseph, Mo., Jan. 2, 1864, in Rhodehamel and Taper, *"Right or Wrong, God Judge Me,"* p. 93; Booth to Ellsler, Louisville, Ky., Jan. 23, 1864, Western Reserve Historical Society.

153 *St. Joseph Morning Herald*, Jan. 3, 1864; *New York Clipper*, Feb. 21, 1874; Cameron *Observer*, Jan. 16, 1879; *Cincinnati Commercial*, Feb. 13, 1912. Thanks to my student Kathleen Mikitko, who studied Tiernan's life.

154 *St. Louis Republic*, Aug. 4, 1901; *Kansas City Star*, July 25, 1909; *Kansas City Star*, Jan. 3, 1912; identification of Bassett from "Operating Expense Record" (1863–64), pp. 60, 147, Hannibal and St. Joseph Railroad Company Records, Newberry Library, Chicago.

155 Krone, "Recollections of an Old Actor," p. 343.

156 John S. Kendall, *The Golden Age of the New Orleans Theater* (Baton Rouge: LSU Press, 1952), pp. 495–502; Henry Rightor, *Standard History of New Orleans, Louisiana* (Chicago: Lewis Pubs., 1900), p. 467.

157 *New Orleans Daily Picayune*, March 16, 1864; Samples, *Lust for Fame*, p. 81.

158 Booth to R. M. Field, Cincinnati, Feb. 22, 1864, in Rhodehamel and Taper, *"Right or Wrong, God Judge Me,"* p. 101; *New Orleans Times*, March 19, 22, and 27, 1864; Booth to Simonds, n.p., n.d. [1864], Coll. 420, Fogg Autograph Collection, Maine Historical Society; Alfred Stille, *Therapeutic and Materia Medica* (Philadelphia: Henry C. Lea, 1874), pp. 376–77.

159 *Boston Globe*, March 7, 1909; *The Civil War in America* (Washington: Library of Congress, 2012), pp 12–13.

160 Rhodehamel and Taper, *"Right or Wrong, God Judge Me,"* p. 126.

161 Peacock to John E. Boos, Massillon, Ohio, Feb. 25, 1914, quoted in undated catalog of the Autograph Alcove, Wauwatosa, Wisc., item 35602; Stephen B. Williams, "Precursor to Infamy: Encounter in New Orleans. A Soldier's Story" (1994), copy in author's possession.

162 Benj. F. Butler, *Butler's Book* (Boston: A. M. Thayer, 1892), p. 376; Kendall, *Golden Age of the New Orleans Theater*, p. 498.

163 *Boston Evening Transcript*, April 27 and May 17, 1864; *Boston Courier*, July 12, 1874.

164 *Boston Post*, April 17, 1865.

165 *New York Mercury*, Oct. 5, 1884.

166 Clarke, *Booth*, pp. 100, 116.

167 *Boston Evening Transcript*, Nov. 30, 1894.

168 New York *National Police Gazette*, April 29, 1865; *New York Daily Tribune*, April 17, 1865.

169 *New York Clipper*, April 22, 1865.

170 "The Murder of Lincoln," clipping, n.d. [1874?], HRHRC; *Chicago Daily Tribune*, June 23, 1878. Booth told the actor Charles Pope, "My voice is in bad shape." *New York Sun*, March 28, 1897.

171 Louis J. Mackey interviews (ca. 1894) with Franklin-area residents, copies at the Drake Well Museum, Titusville, Pa. The interviews are available, with some errors in transcription, in Ernest C. Miller, *John Wilkes Booth in the Pennsylvania Oil Country* (Meadville, Pa.: Crawford County Historical Society, 1987).

172 "An Incident in the Life of Titus Ridgway," from an interview with his great-nephew Lloyd Ridgway by Arthur M. Crawford, typescript (1988), courtesy of the Rev. Mr. Crawford; *Crawford* [Pa.] *Journal*, April 4, 1907.

173 Simonds to Booth, Franklin, Pa., Dec. 7 and Dec 31, 1864, 2/313–16 and 325–29, NA M599.

174 *Titusville (Pa.) Herald*, Aug. 22, 1934.

175 McLauren, *Sketches in Crude-Oil*, p. 105.

176 *Pittsburg Dispatch*, April 20, 1890.

177 *New York Clipper*, Jan. 21, 1874; MacCulloch, "This Man Saw Lincoln Shot," p. 115.

178 Ellsler, "Stage Memories," p. 113.

179 *St. Louis Post-Dispatch*, May 12, 1881.

180 Otis Skinner, *The Last Tragedian* (New York: Dodd, Mead, 1939), p. 136.

181 Arthur W. Bloom, *Joseph Jefferson: Dean of the American Theatre* (Savannah: Frederic C. Beil, 2000), p. 185.

182 Mary Ann Booth to Edwin Booth, New York, N.Y., June 10, 1862, Hampden-Booth Theatre Library, the Players; undated diary entry of English traveler, Catalogue 315 (1994), Henry Bristow of Ringwood, Hants, England.

183 Woodruff, "McCullough," pp. 537, 643 n212.

184 *New York Herald*, Nov. 1, 1903.

185 *St. Louis Republic*, Aug. 4, 1901.

186 Frank E. Jerome, "Recollections of J. Wilkes Booth in Leavenworth, Kansas, in December, 1863," manuscript (1886), Kansas State Historical Society Library, Topeka.

187 *Chicago Inter Ocean*, Aug. 27, 1893.

188 1884 Townsend interview; Mathews: *Boston Sunday Herald*, April 11, 1897.

189 *Detroit Free Press*, April 17, 1883.

190 Simonds to Booth, Franklin, Pa., Dec. 7, 1864, and Feb. 21, 1865, 2/309–29, NA M599.

191 *Philadelphia Inquirer*, April 18, 1865; "The Great Tragedy!" clipping, n.p., April 17, 1865, Booth Scrapbook, Fawcett Theatre Collection, Hodges Library, University of Tennessee, Knoxville.

192 *Chicago Post*, April 16, 1865. There is no evidence Booth ever married.

193 *Washington Post*, July 17, 1904; *Cleveland Plain Dealer*, Dec. 2, 1863.

194 Rhodehamel and Taper, *"Right or Wrong, God Judge Me,"* p. 130.

195 *Baltimore American*, June 8, 1893; Barbee, "Lincoln and Booth," p. 1059; Ford account, n.d., Mahoney Papers, HSHC.

196 Townsend, "Crime of Lincoln's Murder."

CHAPTER 7. MISCHIEF, THOU ART AFOOT

1   The meeting was held on or about August 9, 1864. Arnold, statement, April 18, 1865, in *Baltimore American*, Jan. 18, 1869; Arnold, statement, Dec. 3, 1867, Benj. F. Butler Papers, Manuscript Division, LOC; Arnold's narrative history written in the 1890s and published in installments in the *Baltimore American*, Dec. 7–20, 1902. These three documents are available in Kauffman's lucidly edited edition of Arnold, *Memoirs of a Lincoln Conspirator.* Arnold's *Defence and Prison Experiences of a Lincoln Conspirator* (Hattiesburg, Miss.: Book Farm, 1943), printed directly from the original manuscript, contains a few introductory remarks by Arnold edited out of the 1902 newspaper series, but it lacks the valuable 1865 statement or any explanatory notes. Willie Arnold and the Holliday in John T. Ford, statement, April 28, 1865, 5/455, NA M599; Merchants' Exchange Reading Room Record Books, Arrivals, vol. 20, MdHS.

2   *New York World*, May 19 and June 2, 1865; Robert G. Mowry, statement, April 17, 1865, 3/508–12, NA M599; Percy E. Martin, "Baltimorean in Big Trouble: Samuel Arnold, a Lincoln Conspirator," [Baltimore County Historical Society] *History Trails*, vol. 25, pt. 1 (Autumn 1990), pt. 2 (Winter 1990–91), and pt. 3 (Spring 1991), pp. 1–12; Martin, "Sam Arnold and Hookstown," *History Trails*, vol. 16 (Summer 1982), pp. 13–16.

3   *The Trial of the Assassins and Conspirators at Washington City, D.C., May and June, 1865, for the Murder of President Abraham Lincoln* (Philadelphia: T. B. Peterson & Bros., 1865), p. 21; Nettie Mudd, ed., *The Life of Dr. Samuel A. Mudd* (New York and Washington: Neale, 1906), p. 295.

4   "Abstract from monthly returns of the principal U. S. military prisons," July 1864, in *OR*, ser. 2, vol. 8, p. 997; Benjamin P. Thomas and Harold M. Hyman, *Stanton: The Life and Times of Lincoln's Secretary of War* (New York: Knopf, 1962), pp. 371–75; William A. Tidwell, James O. Hall, and David Winfred Gaddy, *Come Retribution: The Confederate Secret Service and the Assassination of Lincoln* (Jackson and London: University Press of Mississippi, 1988), pp. 145–49.

5   *St. Louis Post-Dispatch*, May 17, 1903; Clarke, *Booth*, p. 110.

6   W. W. Goldsborough, *The Maryland Line in the Confederate Army*, rev. ed. (Baltimore: Guggenheimer, Weil, 1900), p. 203. One of Johnson's officers, C. Irving Ditty of the 1st Maryland Cavalry, CSA, asserted after the war that he knew nothing of any Booth association with this plan. *Philadelphia Weekly Press*, March 13, 1880.

7   Henry Watterson, *"Marse Henry": An Autobiography*, 2 vols. (New York: George H. Doran, 1919), vol. 1, p. 76.

8   *New York Times*, Nov. 1, 1859.

9   *Washington Evening Star*, Dec. 7, 1870.

10 *Cincinnati Commercial*, Oct. 20, 1868.

11 Matthew Pinsker, *Lincoln's Sanctuary: Abraham Lincoln and the Soldiers' Home* (Oxford and New York: Oxford University Press, 2003), p. 5; minutes of May 30, 1859, and letter of Lorenzo Thomas to Sec. of War Edwin Stanton, May 21, 1862, "Records of the Board of Commissioners, Soldiers' Home," vol. 1 (1851–77), pp. 177, 190–92, consulted at the ADMIN Building, Soldiers' Home, Washington, D.C. In 1864 Lincoln lived here from early July until sometime after mid-October.

12 Kauffman, *Memoirs of a Lincoln Conspirator*, p. 42.

13 Henry T. Louthan, "A Proposed Abduction of Lincoln," *Confederate Veteran*, vol. 11 (April 1903), pp. 157–58.

14 Walt Whitman, "Washington in the Hot Season," *New York Times*, Aug. 16, 1863.

15 Smith Stimmel, "Experiences as a Member of President Lincoln's Body Guard, 1863–65," *North Dakota Historical Quarterly*, vol. 8, pt. 2 (Jan. 1927), p. 13.

16 *New York Times*, April 6, 1887. Despite this assertion, Lincoln continued to get out on his own from time to time.

17 Littleton Newman, testimony, May 18, 1865, in Benn Pitman, comp., *The Assassination of President Lincoln and the Trial of the Conspirators* (New York: Moore, Wilstach & Baldwin, 1865), p. 239.

18 Clarke, *Booth*, p. 84.

19 H. D. McLean, M.D., "Erysipelas," and R. B. Tunstall, M.D., "Erysipelas: Symptoms and Treatment," both manuscripts, n.d. [Philadelphia, ca. 1857], author's collection.

20 Booth to Sumner, New York [Aug. 27 or 28, 1864], in Rhodehamel and Taper, *"Right or Wrong, God Judge Me,"* p. 117.

21 J. B. Booth Jr., diary, Aug. 28, 1864, Folger Shakespeare Library. Erysipelas had a typical duration of ten to fourteen days. Robley Dunglison, *A Dictionary of Medical Science* (Philadelphia: Henry C. Lea, 1874), p. 374.

22 Clarke, *Booth*, pp. 118–19; Samuel K. Chester, testimony, May 12, 1865, in Poore, *The Conspiracy Trial*, vol. 1, p. 44.

23 Badeau, "Dramatic Reminiscences," *St. Paul and Minneapolis Pioneer Press*, Feb. 20, 1887; Alford, "Wonderful and Mysterious," p. 12.

24 Clarke, *Booth*, p. 84; Chester, statement, 4/140–70, NA M599.

25 *Boston Evening Journal*, April 15, 1865.

26 Thomas Y. Mears and wife to Joseph H. Simonds et al., September 29, 1864, Deed Book Z, p. 309; J. Wilkes Booth et al. to Junius B. Booth, Oct. 21, 1864, Deed Book CC, pp. 365–66, Office of the Register and Recorder, Venango County Courthouse, Franklin, Pa. The Oct. 29, 1864, deed to Junius is in the Pearce Civil War Collection, Navarro College, Corsicana, Texas.

27 *Titusville Morning Herald,* June 14, 1865.

28 Simonds to Capt. D. V. Derickson, Franklin, April 25, 1865, 2/738–40, NA M599; Simonds, testimony, May 13, 1865, in Poore, *The Conspiracy Trial,* vol. 1, pp. 39–42.

29 Booth to Moses Kimball, St. Joseph, Mo., Jan. 2, 1864, in Rhodehamel and Taper, *"Right or Wrong, God Judge Me,"* p. 93.

30 Miller, *Booth in the Pennsylvania Oil Region,* p. 69–70, which also recounts the Caleb Marshall incident.

31 "That Oil Company Joe S[imonds] and myself started…has gone up fine," Booth bragged to Orlando Tompkins from Washington on February 9, 1865. "Stock to day instead of being $1000, is $15000, per share." Letter courtesy of Richard and Kellie Gutman.

32 *Washington Union,* April 15, 1865.

33 Louis J. Mackey interview with Sarah Dodd (1894), Mackey Papers, Drake Well Museum.

34 W. H. F. Gurley, U.S. Consulate at Quebec, to Edwin Stanton, June 7, 1865, 7/228, NA M599; *Montreal Telegraph,* quoted in *Quebec Gazette,* April 24, 1865; *Quebec Gazette,* June 7, 1865; *New York Clipper,* July 1 and 29, 1865; *Quebec Morning Chronicle,* July 17, 1865; *New York Times,* April 18, 1890.

35 J. B. Booth Jr., statement, n.d. [Spring 1865], 4/117–20, NA M599.

36 *New York Daily Graphic,* March 22, 1876; *Minneapolis Tribune,* July 1, 1878.

37 Potter to William Seward, Montreal, March 31 and April 27, 1865, Letters of the U.S. Consul at Montreal, roll 6, T222 (microcopy), NA. John W. Headley, *Confederate Operations in Canada and in New York* (New York: Neal, 1906), is the account of an important rebel agent.

38 A copy of a portion of the guest register of the St. Lawrence Hall, Oct. 18, 1864, containing Booth's signature, is found in the Charles Bromback Collection, Manuscript Division, LOC.

39 *Montreal Star,* Feb. 12, 1902.

40 "When Wilkes Booth Was in Montreal," *Montreal Star,* Dec. 6, 1902, mentions cards with Westcott, billiards with Dion, the "Redcoat" comment, and Booth's scattering silver.

41 *Montreal Star,* March 8, 1902; *Toronto Globe,* May 8, 1865.

42 Hosea B. Carter, testimony, in Poore, *The Conspiracy Trial,* vol. 2, pp. 405–9; Harriette E. Noyes. *A Memorial of the Town of Hampstead, New Hampshire. Historic and Genealogic Sketches* (Boston: George B. Reed, 1899), vol. 1, pp. 339–41; *Concord Monitor,* March 31, 1900. Randall A. Haines generously shared his insights into Sanders's career. See his article "The Revolutionist Charged with Complicity in Lincoln's Death," *Surratt Courier,* vol. 13 (Sept. 1988), pp. 5–8, and (Oct. 1988), pp. 7–10.

43 John Devenny [*sic*], statement, April [n.d.] 1865, 4/264–69, NA M599; Poore, *The Conspiracy Trial*, vol. 1, pp. 34–37. Kieran McAuliffe kindly provided me with the proper name for Dolly's, rendered Jolly's and Dowley's in 1865 sources. Sala in *Toronto Globe*, May 10, 1865.

44 Peggy Robbins, "The Greatest Scoundrel," *Civil War Times Illustrated*, vol. 31 (Nov.–Dec. 1992), pp. 54ff.

45 Statement of Alfred E. Penn [pseudonym?], 7/419ff., NA M599.

46 *New York Tribune*, May 22, 1865. Similarly, Sanders and Beverly Tucker declared in a joint letter that "we have no acquaintance whatever with Mr. Booth or any of those alleged to be engaged with him. We have never seen or had any knowledge in any wise of him or them, and he has never written us a note or sought an interview with us." *Montreal Evening Telegraph*, May 5, 1865.

47 Iles, "John Wilkes Booth," manuscript (1935), Kimmel Collection, Macdonald-Kelce Library, University of Tampa.

48 *New York Times*, May 7, 1865; *Chicago Times*, May 10, 1865.

49 Robert A. Campbell, testimony, in Poore, *The Conspiracy Trial*, vol. 2, pp. 83–89.

50 John C. Thompson, testimony, in Poore, *The Conspiracy Trial*, vol. 2, p. 269; *Minneapolis Tribune*, July 1, 1878.

51 Clarke, *Booth*, pp. 84, 116, 119.

52 Clarke, *Booth*, p. 88.

53 Charles L. Wagandt, *The Mighty Revolution: Negro Emancipation in Maryland, 1862–1864* (Baltimore: Johns Hopkins University Press, 1964), pp. 256–61; Robert J. Brugger, *Maryland: A Middle Temperament, 1634–1980* (Baltimore: Johns Hopkins University Press, 1988), pp. 807–8.

54 Roy P. Basler, ed., *The Collected Works of Abraham Lincoln*, 8 vols. plus index vol. (New Brunswick, N.J.: Rutgers University Press., 1953–55), vol. 7, pp. 301–3; *Baltimore American* and *Washington Evening Star*, both April 20, 1864.

55 Townsend, *Life, Crime, and Capture*, p. 43.

56 Alford, "John Wilkes Booth and George Alfred Townsend," p. 19.

57 Eaton Horner, testimony, in Poore, *The Conspiracy Trial*, vol. 1, p. 435; *Baltimore American*, April 19, 1869.

58 Thomas N. Conrad, *The Rebel Scout* (Washington: National Publishing, 1904), pp. 62–65.

59 John C. Thompson, testimony, in Poore, *The Conspiracy Trial*, vol. 2, pp. 268–74; Judith Simms, "My Maryland Heritage: The Ancestry of William Queen" (M.A. thesis, College of Notre Dame of Maryland, 1963). I gladly acknowledge the research of my student Tim Chesser on the Queen and Thompson families.

60 *Georgetown College Journal*, vol. 23 (May 1895), p. 88.

61 Recollections of her grandson Eugene K. Lloyd in *Mudd Society Newsletter*, vol. 6 (Oct. 1985), p. 3.

62 "Then and Now" [1864], *Mudd Society Newsletter*, vol. 15 (Sept. 1994), p 3. Copy of original clipping graciously provided by Danny Fluhart.

63 Mudd, *Life of Mudd*, p. 65; *New York Tribune*, June 17, 1883; Richard Washington and Henry Simms, statements, Aug. 31, 1863, Provost Marshal's Two-Name File, File #6083, RG 109, NA; Mudd to Brownson, Bryantown, Md., Jan. 13, 1862, O. A. Brownson Papers, University of Notre Dame Archives.

64 Thompson, testimony, in Poore, *The Conspiracy Trial*, vol. 2, p. 271; *New York World*, May 19, 1865, quoted in *Surratt Courier*, vol. 24 (Feb. 1999), p. 7; James O. Hall, "That Letter of Introduction to Dr. Mudd," typescript (1998), p. 3, author's collection.

65 *Baltimore Catholic Mirror*, Dec. 17, 1892. The assistance of the Reverend Paul K. Thomas, archivist of the Archdiocese of Baltimore, has been most helpful.

66 *New York Daily Graphic*, March 22, 1876.

67 Edwin Booth to "my dear friend," July 23, 1864, *Collector*, vol. 83 (1970), p. 13.

68 Charles Shattuck, "The Theatrical Management of Edwin Booth," in *The Theatrical Manager in England and America: Player of a Perilous Game*, ed. Joseph W. Donohue Jr. (Princeton, N.J.: Princeton University Press, 1971), pp. 143–88.

69 The insights of Prof. Stephen M. Archer are gratefully acknowledged.

70 The playbill, a copy of which is located in the Booth Files, HTC, contains Stuart's quotations and a cast list. Latin translation courtesy of the High Reverend James L. Woods of Madison, Wisconsin, a friend *memor et fidelis*.

71 Carrie Alexander, "The Three Booth Brothers in Julius Caesar" (Honors History Paper, Northern Virginia Community College, 1992), has enriched my understanding of that evening.

72 *New York Herald*, Dec. 29, 1886; *New York Times*, Dec. 29, 1886.

73 *New York Sunday Mercury*, Dec. 26, 1886; Stuart biographical file, HTC.

74 "Stories about Booth from Stuart, His Old Manager," *New York Recorder*, n.d. [1893], HTC; Winter, *Life and Art of Edwin Booth*, p. 71.

75 *Pittsburgh Post*, June 7, 1893.

76 *New York Clipper*, Dec. 3, 1864; Brown, *A History of the New York Stage from the First Performance in 1732 to 1901*, 3 vols. (New York: Dodd, Mead, 1903), vol. 1, p. 460.

77 *New York Times*, Nov. 28, 1864.

78 Clarke, *Elder and Younger Booth*, p. 159; Clarke, *Booth*, p. 87.

79 "Winter Garden—The Shakspere [*sic*] Benefit," n.d. [Nov. 26, 1864], Booth Scrapbook, Folger Shakespeare Library; *Play Bill*, April 21, 1865.

80 Fawcett, "A Memorable Season: Winter Garden, New York, in 1864 & '65," Booth Scrapbook, pp. 193–96, Fawcett Theatre Collection, Hodges Library, University of Tennessee, Knoxville.

81 *Cleveland Plain-Dealer,* June 6, 1893.

82 *San Francisco Chronicle,* July 9, 1899.

83 Nat Brandt, *The Man Who Tried to Burn New York* (Syracuse, N.Y.: Syracuse University Press, 1986), and these city newspapers: *Evening Post,* Nov. 26, 1864; *Clipper,* Dec. 3, 1864; *Sun,* Nov. 26, 1864; *Times,* Nov. 27, 1864; *Leader,* Dec. 3, 1864; and *Daily News,* Nov. 28, 1864.

84 J. Frank Kernan, *Reminiscences of the Old Fire Laddies* (New York: M. Crane, 1885), p. 194.

85 *National Police Gazette* (New York), April 22, 1865.

86 Alexander Del Mar, "Prophecy of Antony," clipping, n.d. [1909], LFFRC.

87 *Chicago Sunday Inter Ocean,* Jan. 4, 1900.

88 *Boston Journal,* June 9, 1893. Brown's proper name was James Hope. Mary Ann Brown, his grandmother, hired him out to Kunkel at the Richmond Theatre, where he met Edwin. *Baltimore Sun,* June 10, 1893.

89 Undated typescript by James W. Shettel, p. 9, Shettel Papers, York County Historical Society, York, Penn.

90 Rufus Wright, manuscript, n.d., collections of the National Portrait Gallery, Washington, D.C., where it accompanies one of the two photographs. The second image, presented to Mrs. Booth, is in the HTC. Thanks to Eric Bartlett Wentworth, a descendant of Wright.

91 "The Booths," undated clipping [1864], HTC.

92 Charles Pike Sawyer, "Sixty Years and More of Shakespeare," unpublished manuscript (1930s), p. 2, author's collection. The much-esteemed Constance R. Spande, whose friendship cast its happy light my way for more than two decades, brought this document to my attention. Thank you, Connie.

CHAPTER 8. THE FIERY FURNACE

1 Booth to Booth, n.p., n.d. [1864], Letters Received (1809–1870), Records of the Attorney General's Office, General Records of the Dept. of Justice, RG 60, NA; Clarke, *Booth,* pp. 104–5.

2 John S. Clarke, affidavit, May 6, 1865, 7/408–12, NA M599.

3 Simms, "My Maryland Heritage," p. 58.

4 Arnold, *Memoirs,* pp. 23, 134.

5 All Harbin details from Townsend, "Crime of Lincoln's Murder"; *Cincinnati Enquirer,* April 18 and 23, 1892; "Booths, Father and Sons," clipping, n.d., LFFRC. Harbin described in M. E. Martin, statement, May 6, 1865, 5/328–37, NA M599.

6 *Washington Critic,* Nov. 19, 1885; "A Hotel Clerk with a History," clipping [1885], Atwater Scrapbook, Chicago Historical Society.

7   *Cincinnati Enquirer*, Aug. 3, 1884; George A. Atzerodt, statement, May 1, 1865, in Steers, *The Trial*, p. cv. Kudos to Joan Chaconas, who located this document in a private collection in 1977.

8   Mudd, *Life of Mudd*, p. 68.

9   Mudd told Samuel Cox Jr. in 1877 that he was "not favorably impressed with Booth" and that "he was particular in not inviting him to his house, but that Booth came that evening unsolicited." Marginal note in Cox's copy of Thomas A. Jones, *J. Wilkes Booth* (Chicago: Laird and Lee, 1893), MdHS; Louise Mudd Arehart, "Tid Bit," *Mudd Newsletter*, vol. 14 (Sept. 1993), p. 1. Booth *was* pushy in his dealings with people. It explains the statement of Mary Surratt to Louis J. Weichmann that "Dr. Mudd and the people of Charles [County] are getting tired of Booth, and they are pushing him off on John." *Trial of John H. Surratt in the Criminal Court for the District of Columbia, Hon. George P. Fisher Presiding*, 2 vols. (Washington: GPO, 1867), vol. 1, p. 372.

10 Thomas L. Gardiner, testimony, May 17, 1865, in Poore, *The Conspiracy Trial*, vol. 1, pp. 361–65; Samuel A. Mudd, statement, April 21, 1865, 5/212ff., NA M599.

11 *Philadelphia Press*, April 12, 1896; Osborn H. Oldroyd, *The Assassination of Abraham Lincoln* (Washington: author, 1901), p. 259.

12 Weichmann, *True History*, pp. 32–34; Weichmann, testimony, in Poore, *The Conspiracy Trial*, vol. 1, pp. 70–71, 94–101, 103–4, 135, 389–90; Weichmann, testimony, in *Trial of Surratt*, vol. 1, pp. 369–72. Weichmann's family spelled its name Wiechmann; he adopted the former spelling. In an April 3, 1898, interview with Hanson Hiss in the *Washington Post*, Surratt denied that Mudd introduced him to Booth "on the street or anywhere else." However, Mudd confirmed the meeting on two occasions. Pitman, *The Assassination of President Lincoln*, p. 421; *New York Times*, Aug. 4, 1865; Mudd, *Life of Mudd*, pp. 42–46.

13 Mudd, *Life of Mudd*, pp. 43–45.

14 "John H. Surratt," *New York Tribune*, May 20, 1867; Weichmann, testimony, in Poore, *The Conspiracy Trial*, vol. 1, p. 91.

15 *A Complete List of the Students Entered at St. Charles' College, Ellicott City, Maryland* (Mt. Loretto, Staten Is., New York: Im. Virgin Mission Press, 1898), unpaginated; Alfred Isacsson, "A Biography of John Surratt" (M.A. thesis, St. Bonaventure University, 1957), pp. 1–14; Weichmann, *True History*, passim. The late Father Isacsson's scholarship and friendship were invaluable.

16 *Washington National Tribune*, Oct. 29, 1885.

17 *Washington Evening Star*, Dec. 7, 1870.

18 "Innocence of Mrs. Surratt Declared," *Confederate Veteran*, vol. 18 (Oct. 1910), p. 474.

19 Weichmann, *True History*, pp. 28, 31.

20 This account of the Booth-Surratt interview is drawn from the 1870 lecture and Surratt's interview with Hiss.

21 *New York Clipper*, April 29, 1865.

22 *Los Angeles Times*, Feb. 11, 1923. Helen Coleman (Mrs. Frank Wynkoop) gave this interview as Helen Truman, although her name is spelled Trueman on Ford's Theatre playbills.

23 Karen L. Gunderson, "Edwin A. Emerson: History's Witness," manuscript (1990), copy in author's possession. Ms. Gunderson produced a superbly researched life of Emerson.

24 Author's interview with the late Douglas Lee Emerson (Edwin's grandson), July 20, 2000, Annandale, Va. Special thanks to my friend Doug Emerson, his son.

25 *Chicago Tribune*, June 30, 1878; *Boonville (Mo.) Weekly Advertiser*, May 20, 1881.

26 Samuel K. Chester, statement, April 28, 1865, 4/140–70, NA M599; Chester, testimony, May 12, 1865, in Poore, *The Conspiracy Trial*, vol. 1, pp. 45–48. All Chester material in this chapter comes from these documents. Coroner, Allegany Co., Md., Federal Census of 1850, p. 484, roll 277, NA M432. Mathews acknowledged his intermittent involvement to the anonymous author of "The Route Booth Rode," manuscript (ca. 1909), chap. 2, p. 18, JOH.

27 *Cincinnati Enquirer*, April 16, 1881.

28 "Assassination and Funeral of President Lincoln," C. C. Carrington Scrapbook, vol. 2, p. 56, John Hay Library, Brown University; Joseph Jackson interview of Jennie Gourley, *Philadelphia Ledger*, n.d., copy in James W. Shettel Scrapbook, pp. 8–12, Shettel Collection, Historical Society of York County, Pa.; William J. Ferguson, "Talks of an Old-Time Actor," manuscript (1920s), p. 77, collection of Esther Quinn, whose courtesies in providing information on Ferguson are much appreciated.

29 John T. Ford, testimony, June 9, 1865, in Poore, *The Conspiracy Trial*, vol. 3, p. 475.

30 Jacob Rittersback, statement, n.d. [1865], vol. 93, Joseph Holt Papers, LOC; *Providence Journal*, Aug. 14, 1865.

31 Townsend, "Crime of Lincoln's Murder"; "Booths, Father and Sons," clipping, n.d., LFFRC; *Baltimore American and Commercial Advertiser*, Jan. 18, 1869.

32 Wagandt, *The Mighty Revolution*, p. 256–60; C. Milton Wright, *Our Harford Heritage: A History of Harford County, Maryland* (Baltimore: French-Bray, 1967), pp. 376–78; Priscilla Stump Griffith, diary, Oct. 12–13 and 31, 1864, HSHC.

33 Hannah Cook Frey interview by William McGlanahan, "Woman Says Booth Plotted to Kidnap Lincoln at Her Home," clipping, n.d. [1926?], Anna Lee Smith Scrapbook, HSHC. *Blather* is misspelled *bather* in the original. See also *Harford Gazette*, June 16, 1950, courtesy of Jim Chrismer, whose knowledge of Civil War events in the county is unsurpassed. John R. Overmiller kindly assisted the author by interviewing Neva Frey Reisinger (Hannah's granddaughter) on

March 7, 1995. The assistance of Mary Jane Sopher in uncovering details of Cook's subsequent life in Iowa is appreciated.

34 Stump, "Notes on the Children of J. W. Stump & Their Part in the American Civil War, 1861–'65."

35 "Additional Reminiscences of the Booth Family," *Bel Air Aegis*, March 7, 1902.

36 Court-martial of George B. Love, Hospital Steward, File OO-509, Records of the Judge Advocate General's office, RG 153, NA; "The Suicide at Washington," clipping, n.d. [April 1865], Lincoln Obsequies Scrapbook, LOC.

37 Arnold, *Memoirs*, pp. 23–24.

38 Memoranda of George W. Bunker, clerk at the National Hotel, providing the dates of Booth's stays at the hotel. This valuable document provides a basis for the actor's comings and goings in Washington during the winter of 1864–65 and was an exhibit at the 1865 conspiracy trial. 15/260–63, NA M599.

39 Richard M. Smoot, *The Unwritten History of the Assassination of Abraham Lincoln* (Clinton, Mass.: W. J. Coulter, 1908), pp. 7–9; *Washington Daily Chronicle*, July 10, 1865. Smoot's book is handily available as *Shall We Gather at the River: The Unwritten History of the Assassination of Abraham Lincoln* (Rodeo, N.M.: Eco Publishing, 2011), with notes by its editor, Randal A. Berry.

40 Edward L. Smoot, testimony, June 20, 1867, in *Trial of Surratt*, vol. 1, p. 190.

41 Noah Brooks, "The Close of Lincoln's Career," *Century Illustrated Monthly Magazine*, May 1895, p. 26; *Morning Cleveland Herald*, May 24, 1865.

42 Clipping, n.p., Nov. 13, 1886, LFFRC; Weichmann, *True History*, p. 76; *Washington Star*, May 15, 1865; *New York Tribune*, July 17, 1881; "niggers" in *Detroit Advertiser and Tribune*, July 10, 1865.

43 Atzerodt statement of May 1, 1865; *Port Tobacco Times and Charles County Advertiser*, Dec. 2, 1858.

44 Oldroyd, *Assassination of Abraham Lincoln*, pp. 267–68, 283–84.

45 Jones, *J. Wilkes Booth*, p. 39.

46 Townsend, *Life, Crime, and Capture*, p. 39.

47 *Independent*, May 11, 1865.

48 *Broughton's Monthly Planet Reader and Astrological Journal*, vol. 5 (Nov.–Dec., 1864), p. 2, courtesy of Leanne Garland, Abraham Lincoln Library and Museum, Lincoln Memorial University; *Louisville Courier-Journal*, Feb. 12, 1940.

49 Arnold, *Memoirs*, pp. 24, 44–45, 134–35.

50 William J. Ferguson, "I Saw Lincoln Shot!" *American Magazine*, vol. 90 (Aug. 1920), p. 86.; H. Clay Ford, statement, April 20, 1865, 5/483ff, NA M599. My thanks to Benjamin Waite, who helped me understand Ferguson's career.

51 Evidence for a January 18, 1865, abduction effort rests on connecting Chester's testimony and Martin's account of Atzerodt with knowledge of the whereabouts of Booth, Lincoln, and Forrest.

52   Woodruff, "McCullough," pp. 151–53.

53   Ford, statement, 5/483ff, NA M599.

54   William J. Rainnie to Judge Joseph Holt, Camp near Annapolis, Md., May 19, 1865, 6/113–15, NA M599.

55   *Cincinnati Enquirer*, July 2, 1885.

56   George W. Bunker, testimony, May 12, 1865, in Poore, *The Conspiracy Trial*, vol. 1, p. 31.

57   "A Wild Ride for Life," clipping, n.d. [1869], LFFRC.

58   "A Wild Ride for Life," clipping, n.d. [1869], LFFRC. *Lenahagn* mangled into *Flanagan* in source. Subscriber information from issue of Nov. 5, 1864.

59   John J. Jack, statement, April [n.d.], 1865, 5/49–57, NA M599; John T. Ford, testimony, May 25, 1867, in *Impeachment Investigation,* p. 535.

60   Charles C. Dunn, testimony, July 1, 1867, in *Trial of Surratt*, vol. 1, pp. 436–37.

61   Martin, testimony, June 20, 1867, in *Trial of Surratt*, vol. 1, pp. 213–16, and statement, May 6, 1865, 5/328–37, NA M599.

62   Weichmann, testimony, May 18, 1865, in Poore, *The Conspiracy Trial*, vol. 1, pp. 388–91.

63   *Washington Capitol*, Feb. 1, 1874.

64   *Los Angeles Times*, Feb. 11, 1923.

65   *Washington Daily Globe*, January 19, 1865; Forrest to James Oakes, Washington, Jan. 27, 1865, Forrest Papers, Princeton University Library.

66   Jones, *Booth*, pp. 42–43.

67   *Cincinnati Enquirer*, Aug. 3, 1884.

68   Chester, statement, April 28, 1865, 4/140–70, NA M599, and testimony, May 12, 1865, in Poore, *The Conspiracy Trial*, vol. 1, pp. 45–48; *Detroit Advertiser and Tribune*, July 10, 1865.

69   Junius told the public about his brother's engagement to a "Miss Hale." *Chicago Times*, April 17, 1865; *New York Daily News*, April 21, 1865. The claim was promptly denounced as false. "Booth attempted to force his attention upon Miss Hale, but she always manifested a decided aversion to the handsome villain," claimed the *Washington National Republican*, quoted in the *Buffalo Morning Express*, April 28, 1865. This statement was incorrect and dishonest, of course, but not unexpected.

      Junius did not identify by first name the young woman with whom his brother was involved, and confusion over her identity existed for nearly a century. She was misidentified as Bessie Hale by Alexander Hunter (Chicago *Daily Inter Ocean*, June 18, 1878). For the identification of Lucy as Booth's fiancée, see Terry Alford, "Alexander Hunter and the Bessie Hale Story," *Alexandria History*, vol. 9 (1990), pp. 5–15.

There were two reasons why the journalistic jackals of 1865 did not chew Lucy to pieces. Many editors, due to a sense of propriety in dealing with women of Lucy's social class, simply let the story lie. It was, after all, deemed irrelevant to the murder. Hence the journalist Benjamin Perley Poore noted that her name "was honorably kept a secret." Poore, *Perley's Reminiscences of Sixty Years in the National Metropolis*, 2 vols. (Philadelphia: Hubbard Bros., 1886), vol. 2, p. 183.

No less important was a signal political victory for which Senator Hale has never been given credit. He met privately on April 15, 1865, with Andrew Johnson and apparently gave the new president a satisfactory explanation of his daughter's connection with Booth. The meeting, discussed subsequently in the endnotes of chapter 10, secured the influence of Johnson in keeping Lucy's name out of the government's investigation. A photograph of Lucy, one of five photographs of women found on Booth's body, was kept in War Department records relating to the assassination, yet as late as 1891 a newspaper reporter was informed hers was the one he could not copy. It was "the picture of the daughter of one distinguished Senator from a New England State [Hale] and the wife of another [William E. Chandler, whom Lucy married in 1874] now living from the same section." *New York World*, April 26, 1891.

The John Parker Hale Papers at the New Hampshire Historical Society, the principal collection of family papers, reflect a thorough family cover-up. They contain no documents casting any light on Lucy's courtship with Booth. In fact there is an entire absence of any family letters in the critical period of April–June 1865, suggesting a successful cull of material from the time. The papers of William E. Chandler, gathered at the Library of Congress and at the New Hampshire Historical Society, along with the Hale-Chandler Papers at Dartmouth College Library, are similarly unhelpful.

Richard H. Sewell's *John P. Hale and the Politics of Abolition* (1965) and Leon B. Richardson's *William E. Chandler, Republican* (1940) are political biographies. Good books, particularly Sewell's, they take no notice of Booth. However, when Richardson was doing his research, Admiral Lloyd Chandler, Lucy's stepson, informed him candidly that she "was infatuated with Booth." This was confirmed by George Moses, a U.S. senator from New Hampshire who was a close political ally of William B. Chandler and knew her. Richardson to Helen C. Milius, Hanover, N.H., Oct. 10, 1946, author's collection.

I am indebted to the late John Parker Hale Chandler Jr. and to his daughter Rose C. Daniels, worthy descendants of Lucy Hale, for their assistance in my investigation of this topic.

70 Richmond Morcom, "They All Loved Lucy," *American Heritage*, vol. 21 (Oct. 1970), pp. 12–15. My late friend Boo Morcom allowed me to examine Lucy

Hale's unpublished diaries and letters. See also *Concord Evening Monitor*, Oct. 15, 1915; *Washington Sunday Herald*, April 23, 1882.

71 "J. Wilkes Booth's Romance," clipping, n.d. [1870s], Varnum-Tenney Family Scrapbook, Perkins Library, Duke University; draft manuscript of "The House That Booth Built," pt. 3, Mahoney Papers, HSHC.

72 James R. Ford, testimony, July 9, 1867, in *Trial of Surratt*, p. 582.

73 Alford, "Hunter," p. 11. For Robert Lincoln, see Jason Emerson's fine *Giant in the Shadows: The Life of Robert T. Lincoln* (Carbondale: Southern Illinois University Press, 2012).

74 *New York Evening Post*, June 24, 1878; *New York Herald*, June 25, 1878.

75 "Booth's Romance," *Atlanta Constitution*, Jan. 15, 1882; F. A. Burr, "Booth's Bullet," *Washington Evening Star*, Dec. 7, 1881; Samuel A. Chester, statement, April 28, 1865, 4/163–64, NA M599.

CHAPTER 9. COME WEAL OR WOE

1 *New York Times*, Feb. 15, Feb. 25, and April 21, 1865; *New York Tribune*, Feb. 25, 1865; William G. Beymer, *On Hazardous Service: Scouts and Spies of the North and South* (New York: Harper and Bros., 1912), pp. 254–55.

2 Theodore C. Pease and James G. Randall, eds., *The Diary of Orville Hickman Browning*, 2 vols. (Springfield: Illinois State Historical Library, 1925–33), vol. 2, pp. 7–8, 19; Isaac Markens, *President Lincoln and the Case of John Y. Beall* (New York: author, 1911), passim; Joseph George Jr., "The Trial and Execution of Two Confederate Agents in New York," *Lincoln Herald*, vol. 89 (Fall 1987), pp. 102–111. John P. Hale was not one of the six senators who signed the petition to Lincoln.

3 D. F. St. Clair, "Why Booth Shot President Lincoln," *New Voice*, vol. 16 (June 10, 1899), pp. 1, 15. If the editor Mark Pomeroy, a veteran Lincoln hater, was not the father of this story, he was its favorite uncle. In 1870, when he did a major exposition on the topic, he wrote that he first became aware of Booth's Beall connection in 1867. The essence of his version was that "[Lincoln] lied to a dangerous man, and the dangerous man, with erratic ideas of chivalry, stung by the insult and broken faith, fired with grief-tinted anger, to avenge the death of a bosom companion." *Pomeroy's Democrat*, July 27 and Sept. 14, 1870.

For Hale's alleged involvement, see *Pomeroy's Democrat*, Aug. 24, 1870; *Washington Chronicle*, Sept. 5, 1886; *New York Times*, April 30, 1876; *New York Truth*, quoted in *Indianapolis Western Citizen*, January 11, 1882; Joseph George Jr., "And a Follow-Up on the John Yates Beall Subject," *Surratt Courier*, vol. 26 (Feb. 2001), pp. 3–4.

4   There was never any intimacy and apparently no contact between the two men after 1859. Daniel Lucas, Beall's biographer and closest friend, wrote, "The whole story about John Wilkes Booth and his connection with Beall is a fabrication without a particle of truth." Lucas's daughter Virginia noted that she found in her research "not an allusion in all [Beall's] correspondence, nor in his diary, nor in his prison experience to the name of Booth." Virginia Lucas, "John Yates Beall: An Appreciation. Notes Also on the Wilkes Booth-Beall Tradition," *Confederate Veteran*, vol. 35 (Aug. and Sept. 1927), pp. 301, 337–38.

      Isaac Markens, who wrote to Beall family members and wartime associates around 1910, heard the same thing. His papers at the Virginia Historical Society contain the statement of Beall's brother William, made to a cousin, that "he was certain that his brother John never met or knew Booth." Similarly, James H. McNeilly, an intimate friend and amanuensis of Beall's fiancée, Martha O'Bryan, wrote Markens, "I came to the conclusion that it was doubtful if Beall ever knew Booth. Certainly he never had an intimacy with him. I think the whole story was a fabrication for sensational purposes."

      Markens did well in demonstrating that Booth was not Beall's wartime associate and played no role in the pardon controversy. While regrettable, it is not surprising that he and his sources would have missed the association vouched for by McCullough (below). Booth was in Charlestown for two weeks only and not then an important enough personality to draw much notice among the mass of strangers in town. Edwin's denial in *Washington Constitutional Union*, April 21, 1865; *Philadelphia Evening Telegraph*, April 25, 1865.

5   Clipping, n.d., James T. Brady Papers, VHS; Baker, *History*, p. 544.

6   *Cincinnati Enquirer*, April 18, 1892; notebook, p. 91, Micou-Daniel Papers; Susan B. Eppes, *Through Some Eventful Years* (Macon, Ga.: J. W. Burke, 1926), p. 216.

7   A. W. Smiley, second interview with Louis J. Mackey in Miller, *Booth in the Pennsylvania Oil Region* (1987 ed.), p. 72. McCullough's statement, made to Townsend and published in the *Cincinnati Enquirer* on July 2, 1885, provides the key that allows historians to put the relationship between the two men in proper perspective.

8   *New York Tribune*, May 20, 1867.

9   J. E. Buckingham Sr., *Reminiscences and Souvenirs of the Assassination of Abraham Lincoln* (Washington: Rufus H. Darby, 1894), pp. 29–30; "Voluntary Statement of David E. Herold," Washington, D.C., April 27, 1865, 4/442–85, NA M599; Laurie Verge, "That Trifling Boy . . . ," *Surratt Courier*, vol. 27 (Jan. 2002), pp. 4–9; Jane E. Herold, statement, April 20, 1865, 4/402–10, NA M599; *New York Morning Advertiser*, May 16, 1895; *Christian Times* (Chicago), June 8, 1865; Noah Brooks, "Pen Pictures," clipping [1865], LFFRC.

10 Mudd, *Life of Mudd*, p. 31.

11 Oldroyd, *Assassination of Abraham Lincoln*, p. 274.

12 *Washington Evening Star Extra*, July 7, 1865; *Troy Weekly Times*, May 6, 1865.

13 Betty J. Ownsbey, *Alias "Paine": Lewis Thornton Powell, the Mystery Man of the Lincoln Conspiracy* (Jefferson, N.C.: McFarland, 1993), pp. 1–42. Powell was arrested, tried, convicted and executed as Lewis Payne, his actual identity not being determined until the conclusion of the trial. The statements of Mrs. Branson and her daughters, 3/188–205, and of Preston Parr, 5/517, NA M599; *Baltimore Sun*, Nov. 15, 1900; Betty J. Ownsbey, "Those Elusive Branson Ladies Again: Lewis Powell, the Seward Assassin, and His Baltimore Lady Loves," *Surratt Courier*, vol. 38 (Jan. 2013), pp. 3–17.

14 Argument in defense of Powell by his attorney, W. E. Doster, in Steers, *The Trial*, pp. 313–14.

15 Tidwell, Hall, and Gaddy, *Come Retribution*, p. 339.

16 Powell claimed to work in Parr's shop. Oldroyd, *Assassination of Abraham Lincoln*, p. 167; Ownsbey, *Alias "Paine,"* p. 39. The *Boston Post*, July 8, 1865, noted "he was led into the conspiracy by Booth and John Surratt." Powell "claimed to be acting as a soldier under Booth," whom he recognized as his superior officer, but he did not claim to "hold any grade or commission in the confederate army," nor was he aware that Booth held one. Thomas T. Eckert, testimony, May 30, 1867, in *Impeachment Investigation*, p. 674.

17 "Mrs. Surratt's Case," *St. Louis Globe Democrat*, n.d. [1888], LFFRC.

18 J. G. Nicolay and John Hay, "The Fourteenth of April," *Century Magazine*, vol. 40 (Jan. 1890), p. 432; Alford, "John Wilkes Booth and George Alfred Townsend."

19 Steers, *The Trial*, p. xlv; statement of Herold's boyhood friend W. M. Clarke, manuscript (1923), copy courtesy of my friend Bill Luetge; S. P. Currier, statement, n.d. [1865], 4/228–30, NA M599.

20 H. B. Smith, *Between the Lines: Secret Service Stories Told Fifty Years After* (New York: Booz Bros., 1911), p. 257.

21 Weichmann to Thomas Donaldson, Philadelphia, April 20, 1886, copy courtesy of Robert L. Keesler; Weichmann, *True History*, p. 88.

22 Curtis C. Davis, "In Pursuit of Booth Once More: A New Claimant Heard From," *Maryland Historical Magazine*, vol. 79 (Fall 1984), p. 226.

23 *Washington Evening Star*, Dec. 7, 1870. Weichmann denied foreknowledge of any conspiracy against Lincoln's person, but from conversations Spangler heard in the exercise yard from fellow prisoners Powell, Herold, and Atzerodt, the Ford's Theatre carpenter implicated him "in a knowledge of the original plot to abduct, and with furnishing information" from his office. C. C. Carrington Scrapbook, vol. 2, p. 193, John Hay Library, Brown University; Atzerodt, statement, April 25, 1865, 3/596–602, NA M599; *New York Tribune*, May 20, 1867.

24 *Baltimore Clipper*, March 6, 1865; *Morning Cleveland Herald*, March 6, 1865; miscellaneous items in scrapbook titled "Newspaper Clippings on the Assassination and Burial of Abraham Lincoln," Newberry Library, Chicago; *Washington Sunday Star*, March 7, 1915.

25 Mark H. Dunkelman, "For Old Abe and the Union, of Course," *Lincoln Herald*, vol. 98 (Fall 1996), p. 90; Michael Burlingame, *Abraham Lincoln: A Life*, 2 vols. (Baltimore: Johns Hopkins University Press, 2008), vol. 2, p. 765.

26 *Philadelphia Press*, March 6, 1865, also giving a description of the confused scene outside the Senate chamber. The tickets of most guests were "useless, [and] these wretched beings wandered about the passages, like Paris outside of Paradise, unable to hear or see."

27 *Philadelphia Evening Telegraph*, April 17, 1865; *National Police Gazette*, April 29, 1865.

28 *Washington Evening Star*, March 3, 1865. Ladies could enter from the terrace through the principal western door of the Capitol.

29 Chester, statement, April 28, 1865, 4/163–64, NA M599. Chester errs in stating that Booth was on the stand, as statements of those in the Rotunda make clear.

30 A sample ticket is in the collections of the Illinois State Historical Library. Bingham in *Chicago Daily Tribune*, Nov. 23, 1873. Donald R. Kennon, chief historian of the U.S. Capitol Historical Society, was generous in helping with matters dealing with the Capitol's history and personalities.

31 Roswell Parish, diary, March 4, 1865, Bartlett Collection, Mugar Memorial Library, Boston University.

32 The original 1876 affidavits of Buxton and of four Capitol policemen who witnessed John W. Westfall's encounter with Booth are gathered in the Ward Hill Lamon Papers, Huntington Library. Lamon published them in "The Real Lincoln," *Washington Critic*, Sept. 17, 1887. The historian Benson J. Lossing revived Westfall's story in an article titled "A Reminiscence," *Independent*, vol. 36 (Feb. 14, 1884), pp. 3–4. Also: Weichmann, *True History*, pp. 90–94; D. Mark Katz, "Booth's First Attempt," *Incidents of the War*, vol. 1 (Spring 1986), pp. 8–11, 18.

33 Marquis de Chambrun, "Personal Recollections of Mr. Lincoln," *Scribner's Magazine*, vol. 13 (Jan. 1893), p. 26.

34 Westfall, affidavit, May 13, 1876, was owned by Osborn H. Oldroyd and is in the collections of the Ford's Theatre National Historic Site.

35 French to Frank O. French, Washington, D.C., April 24 and 30, 1865, Benjamin B. French Family Papers, LOC.

36 Chester, statement, April 28, 1865, 4/140–70, NA M599; Poore, *The Conspiracy Trial*, vol. 1, p. 49.

37 *Washington Daily Morning Chronicle*, Nov. 8, 1873.

38 *Washington Star*, undated citation [ca. 1909] on Clara E. Laughlin's Washington interviews, Folder 223, Box 4, Barbee Papers, Georgetown University Library; Laughlin, *The Death of Lincoln* (New York: Doubleday, Page, 1909), pp. 41–42.

39 The Senate *Executive Journal* reveals that Lincoln submitted Hale's nomination on March 10, 1865, and that the Senate approved it by unanimous consent on the same day. Thanks to Donald A. Ritchie.

40 Lot 63 (text illustrated on p. 219), Parke-Bernet's sale of the Oliver R. Barrett Lincoln collection, Feb. 20, 1952. Wentworth in John Wentworth, *The Wentworth Genealogy: English and American*, 3 vols. (Boston: Little, Brown, 1878), vol. 2, p. 730.

41 *Daily Chicago Tribune*, Nov. 23, 1873.

42 Burton G. Brown Jr., "Spiritualism in Nineteenth-Century America" (PhD dissertation, Boston University, 1972); Mary F. Bednarowski, "Nineteenth Century Spiritualism: An Attempt at a Scientific Religion" (PhD dissertation, University of Minnesota, 1973); Emma H. Britten, *Nineteenth Century Miracles: A Complete Historical Compendium* (New York: Wm. Britten, 1884), and *Modern American Spiritualism: A Twenty Year Record* (1870; rpt. New Hyde Park, N.Y.: University Books, 1970).

43 Terry Alford, "Charles J. Colchester's Life among the Spirits," *Northern Virginia Review*, vol. 5 (Spring 1990), pp. 1–6.

44 *Buffalo Commercial Advertiser*, Aug. 24, 1865.

45 Jean H. Baker, *Mary Todd Lincoln: A Biography* (New York: W. W. Norton, 1987), pp. 217–21; Jennifer Fleischner, *Mrs. Lincoln and Mrs. Keckly: The Remarkable Story of the Friendship between a First Lady and a Former Slave* (New York: Broadway Books, 2003), pp. 258–60; Wayne C. Temple, *Abraham Lincoln: From Skeptic to Prophet* (Mahomet, Ill.: Mayhaven, 1995), pp. 196–201.

46 Jay Monaghan, "Was Abraham Lincoln Really a Spiritualist?" *Journal of the Illinois State Historical Society*, vol. 34 (June 1941), pp. 209–32; *Decatur (Ill.) Daily Republican*, Oct. 24, 1891, courtesy of Michael Burlingame.

47 Nettie Colburn Maynard, a trance medium befriended by Mrs. Lincoln, mentioned the president's meetings with Colchester, as did Warren Chase, who claimed that Lincoln sent for Colchester frequently. Nettie Colburn Maynard, *Was Abraham Lincoln a Spiritualist?* (Philadelphia: R. C. Hartranft, 1891), pp. 92, 178, 254; Noah Brooks, *Washington in Lincoln's Time* (New York: Century, 1895), pp. 64–66; Warren Chase, *Forty Years on the Spiritual Rostrum* (Boston: Colby and Rich, 1888), p. 96; "Lincoln's Spiritualism," clipping [1891], LFFRC; Thomas Coulson, *Joseph Henry, His Life and Work* (Princeton: Princeton University Press, 1950), pp. 308–9. Henry subsequently learned how Colchester produced noises in different parts of a room when he had a chance conversation with a maker of

electrical instruments who provided the medium with a special concealable apparatus for that purpose.

48 Maynard, *Lincoln*, p. 173; *Buffalo Commercial Advertiser*, Aug. 19, 1865; Earl W. Fornell, *The Unhappy Medium: Spiritualism and the Life of Margaret Fox* (Austin: University of Texas Press, 1964), p. 122. Boston's *Banner of Light*, the leading spiritualist journal, asserted that although Colchester led thousands to spiritualism, he was unprincipled. Issue of May 19, 1866; Brown, "Spiritualism," p. 149.

49 Alford, "Wonderful and Mysterious," pp. 14–18.

50 *Nashville Dispatch*, April 25, 1865; T. L. Nichols, *A Biography of the Brothers Davenport* (London: Saunders, Otley, 1864), for a contemporary account. Arthur Conan Doyle, *The History of Spiritualism*, 2 vols. (New York: George H. Doran, 1926), devoted a chapter to these brothers, "probably the greatest mediums of their kind the world has ever seen" (vol. 1, p. 226).

51 *San Francisco Chronicle*, January 26, 1941; *Boston Evening Transcript*, July 28, 1899; *Banner of Light*, Aug. 5, 1899.

52 Bunker, testimony, June 26, 1867, in *Trial of Surratt*, vol. 1, pp. 329–30; exhibit 4 of the conspiracy trial, 15/260–63, NA M599.

53 Sylvan J. Muldoon, *Psychic Experiences of Famous People* (Chicago: Aries, 1947), p. 153. Nettie C. Maynard corroborates the fact that Colchester warned Lincoln, but for Lincoln's statement about that warning one needs Muldoon's source, which the author has been unable to learn. It parallels Maynard's account (pp. 181–82) but is not drawn solely from it.

54 Arnold to Booth, Hookstown, Md., March 27, 1865, 15/343–46, NA M599; Arnold, *Memoirs*, pp. 9–10, 23.

55 *Cincinnati Enquirer*, Aug. 3, 1884.

56 Booth's bankbook, preserved at the Chicago Historical Society, shows deposits of $1,750, all but $25 withdrawn by January 18, 1865. Joseph Simonds to Booth, Franklin, Penn., Dec. 31, 1864, 2/314–16, and Thomas H. Carmichael, statement, [1865], 4/198, both NA M599; *Detroit Free Press*, April 17, 1893; Arnold, *Defence and Prison Experiences*, p. 25; Townsend, *Life, Crime, and Capture*, p. 23.

57 James O. Hall with Michael Maione, *"To Make a Fortune." John Wilkes Booth: Following the Money Trail* (Clinton, Md.: Surratt Society, 2003). The authors present details of Booth's finances and of the monetary expectations of certain team members. However, they fail to prove their central thesis that "Booth was promised a large reward—a fortune—if he captured Lincoln and delivered him to Richmond as a hostage." They cite no evidence as to when, where, or by whom such a promise was made.

58 Edward Frazier, statement, June 8, 1865, in Poore, *The Conspiracy Trial*, vol. 3, pp. 424–31; Tidwell, Hall, and Gaddy, *Come Retribution*, pp. 166–67.

59 Davis to Lincoln, July 2, 1863, *Papers of Jefferson Davis*, vol. 9, p. 254, and Davis's emendation of letter to George W. Randolph, July [n.d.] 1862, vol. 8, p. 292; Judd in Don E. Fehrenbacher and Virginia Fehrenbacher, eds., *Recollected Words of Abraham Lincoln* (Stanford: Stanford University Press, 1996), p. 93.

60 Kauffman, ed., *Memoirs of a Lincoln Conspirator*, pp. 12, 34, 42, 127–28, 136.

61 *New York Herald*, Sept. 4, 1904.

62 Booth told Atzerodt that he would open a theater in Richmond. *Detroit Advertiser and Tribune*, July 10, 1865.

63 Tidwell, Hall, and Gaddy, *Come Retribution*, and William A. Tidwell, *April '65: Confederate Covert Action in the American Civil War* (Kent, Ohio, and London: Kent State University Press, 1995).

64 Booth did not tell Chester that the rebel government would pay him for Lincoln, but Chester concluded, from the tenor of their conversation, that such was his plan. This led Colonel Henry S. Olcott, Chester's inquisitor, to leap to the conclusion that his scheme "had the knowledge and cooperation of the insurgent leaders." Chester, testimony, May 12, 1865, in Poore, *The Conspiracy Trial*, vol. 1, p. 47.

65 Booth to "My dear Sir," n.p., n.d. [1864], Records of the Attorney General's Office, General Records, Letters Received Files (1809–1870), General Records of the Department of Justice, RG 60, National Archives, Archives II, College Park, Md. Conveniently available in Clarke, *Booth*, pp. 106–10, where the writer believes he erred in dating the letter to November 1864.

66 Chester, testimony, May 12, 1865, in Poore, *The Conspiracy Trial*, vol. 1, pp. 48.

67 "V" [Clarence Cobb], "More Reminiscences of Wilkes Booth," clipping [1885], laid inside copy of *The Elder and the Younger Booth*, Brown Collection, Manuscripts Department, Boston Public Library.

68 Clarke, *Booth*, pp. 82–83, 85.

69 *Washington Daily Constitutional Union*, January 18, 1865. Ann H. Holcombe, a Gautier descendant, generously provided information about this well-regarded Washington family and business. Frederick Hatch, "The Meeting at Gautier's Restaurant," *Journal of the Lincoln Assassination*, vol. 26 (2012), pp. 2–9.

70 Statements of Miles and of Thomas Manning, both May 5, 1865, 5/285–94, NA M599.

71 *Washington Evening Star*, Dec. 7, 1870; Arnold in his *Memoirs* and his *Defence and Prison Experiences*; John Horner, *Lincoln's Songbird: Wilson G. Horner (1834–1864), a Brief Life of Melody and Harmony* (Gettysburg, Pa.: author, 1998), p. 40.

72 Weichmann, *True History*, p. 98.

73 *The Trial of the Assassins and Conspirators at Washington City, D.C., May and June, 1865, for the Murder of President Abraham Lincoln* (Philadelphia: T. B. Peterson & Bros., 1865), p. 20; *Boston Daily Globe*, Dec. 25, 1904. Green denied his home was part of the planning. *Washington Star*, May 24, 1890. James M. Goode,

Capital Losses: A Cultural History of Washington's Destroyed Buildings, 2nd ed. (Washington and London: Smithsonian Books, 2003), p. 34.

74 Steers, *The Trial*, p. 390; Eaton G. Horner, testimony, May 18, 1865, in Poore, *The Conspiracy Trial*, vol. 1, p. 432; John C. Brennan, "The Three Versions of the Testimony in the 1865 Conspiracy Trial," *Surratt Society News*, vol. 8 (March 1983), p. 4.

75 Honora Fitzpatrick, testimony, June 21, 1867, in *Trial of Surratt*, vol. 1, p. 234, and her testimony, May 22, 1865, in Poore, *The Conspiracy Trial*, vol. 2, pp. 89–91; Thomas J. Raybold, testimony, June 2, 1865, in Poore, *The Conspiracy Trial*, vol. 3, pp. 39–40.

76 *Baltimore American and Commercial Advertiser*, Jan. 18, 1869.

77 *Brooklyn Daily Eagle*, May 3, 1865.

78 *Cincinnati Enquirer*, Aug. 3, 1884.

79 Col. H. H. Wells to Col. J. H. Taylor, Headquarters, Military District of the Patuxent, April 28, 1865, 458/408, M619 NA; Victor L. Mason, "Four Lincoln Conspiracies," *Century Illustrated Monthly Magazine*, vol. 51 (April 1896), p. 895; *Washington Evening Star*, Dec. 7, 1881; Atzerodt's statement of May 1, 1865.

80 *Washington Daily National Intelligencer*, March 22, 1865; *Washington Evening Star*, Sept. 20, 1892, and April 28, 1940; *Washington Star*, Sept. 17, 1944; *Boyd's Washington and Georgetown Directory…1865* (Washington: Hudson, Taylor, 1865), pp. 39, 137.

81 Cast list in the *Intelligencer*, March 18, 1865.

82 *Rhinelander (Wisc.) News*, Feb. 12, 1927.

83 Arnold, *Defence and Prison Experiences*, pp. 47–48; Weichmann, *True History*, pp. 111–16; Davenport in *Chicago Inter Ocean*, Aug. 27, 1893; William Hanchett, "The Ambush on Seventh Street Road" (1981), rev. ed., in *In Pursuit of… Continuing Research in the Field of the Lincoln Assassination* (Clinton, Md.: Surratt Society, 1990), pp. 151–61. The Park Hotel is located on the A. C. E. Boschke map (1859) at 7th Street and Boundary Avenue line.

84 *Washington Daily National Intelligencer*, March 18, 1865; *New York Herald*, March 18, 1865; Walter Lowenfels, ed., *Walt Whitman's Civil War* (New York: Alfred A. Knopf, 1960), pp. 261–62.

85 "The Lincoln Tragedy," *New York Herald*, June 19, 1878.

86 William D. Foulke, *Life of Oliver P. Morton*, 2 vols. (Indianapolis and Kansas City: Bowen-Merrill, 1899), vol. 2, pp. 4–5.

87 Weichmann, *True History*, pp. 101–2, and his testimony in *Trial of Surratt*, vol. 1, pp. 399–400.

88 *Washington Evening Star*, Feb. 12, 1951. The punch could have happened during a political dispute.

89 Weichmann, *True History*, p. 119.

90 D. H. L. Gleason, statement, April 18, 1865. 4/374–80, NA M599.

91 Ownsbey, *Alias "Paine,"* pp. 45–50.

92 Provost Marshal James L. McPhail to C. A. Dana, Ass't Secretary of War, Baltimore, Md., April 15, 1865, 458/337–39, M619 NA.

93 James O. Hall, "The Saga of Sarah Slater," *Surratt Courier*, vol. 7 (Jan. 1982), pp. 3–6, and (Feb. 1982), pp. 2–6; Atzerodt's statement of May 1, 1865.

94 J. B. Booth Jr., diary, March 25, 1865, Mugar Memorial Library, Boston University; J. B. Booth Jr., statement, May 5, 1865, in Clarke, *Booth*, pp. 119–20.

95 Lizzie Hale to father, New York, N.Y., March 27 and 31, 1865, and to mother, same, March 30, 1865, Hale Papers, New Hampshire Historical Society.

96 *Providence Journal*, May 3, 1865; *Brooklyn Eagle*, May 3, 1865. An extradition treaty was ratified and entered into force in 1877, providing specifically for the delivery of persons charged with assassination.

97 Clarke, *Booth*, p. 66; Arnold, *Defence and Prison Experiences*, p. 21; Mary Booth to J. W. Booth, New York, N.Y., March 28, 1865, 2/352, NA M599. In opening the envelope containing this note, Booth tore away letters from several words along the right-hand margin of the page. I have reconstructed these.

98 Martha Murray, testimony, June 22, 1867, in *Trial of Surratt*, vol. 1, pp. 246–47; Booth telegrams of March 23 and 27, 1865, in Steers, *The Trial*, pp. 118, 121, 223.

99 *Washington Evening Star*, March 27, 1865; Mary T. Lincoln to Charles Sumner, Executive Mansion, March 23, [1865], in *Mary Todd Lincoln: Her Life and Letters*, ed. Justin G. Turner and Linda L. Turner (New York: Knopf, 1972), pp. 209–10.

100 Townsend, "Crime of Lincoln's Murder"; B. H. Strother, statement, April 22, 1865, 4/413–16, NA M599.

101 *Washington Evening Star*, Dec. 7, 1870; Arnold to Booth, Hookstown, Md., March 27, 1865, 15/343–46, NA M599.

102 Arnold, *Memoirs*, pp. 28–29.

CHAPTER 10. THIS ONE MAD ACT

1 On his escape Booth made entries in a small memorandum book commonly known as his diary. The original volume is in the care of the National Park Service at Ford's Theatre. The text may be found as part of the testimony of Everton J. Conger, June 25, 1867, in *Trial of Surratt*, vol. 1, pp. 310–11. William Hanchett reproduces the text with useful notes in "Booth's Diary," *Journal of the Illinois State Historical Society*, vol. 72 (Feb. 1979), pp. 39–56.

2 "Presidential reelections have of late years been utterly disregarded. A popular sentiment had set in against them which almost had the force of constitutional

law." *New York Times*, May 28, 1864. Joseph George Jr., "Trial of Mrs. Surratt: John P. Brophy's Rare Pamphlet," *Lincoln Herald*, vol. 93 (Spring 1991), p. 20; Clarke, *Booth*, p. 88. For background, see Noel Henning Mayfield, *Puritans and Regicide: Presbyterian-Independent Differences over the Trial and Execution of Charles (I) Stuart* (Lanham, Md.: University Press of America, 1988), pp. 65–66; Francis J. Bremer, "In Defense of Regicide: John Cotton on the Execution of Charles I," *William and Mary Quarterly*, 3rd ser., vol. 37 (Jan. 1980), pp. 103–24; Robert V. Remini, *Andrew Jackson and the Course of American Freedom*, vol. 2 (New York: Harper & Row, 1981), pp. 371, 377–78, and illustration facing p. 257. In the 1840s Whigs sought to limit the presidential tenure of office to four years. Frank L. Klement, "'Brick' Pomeroy and the Democratic Processes: A Study in Civil War Politics," *Transactions of the Wisconsin Academy of Sciences, Arts, and Letters*, vol. 51 (1962), p. 160.

3 Fayette Hall, *The Copperhead; or, The Secret Political History of Our Civil War Unveiled* (New Haven: n.p., 1902), p. 47.

4 *Illinois State Register* (Springfield), Aug. 7, 1864, quoted in Michael W. Kauffman, "Booth, Republicanism, and the Lincoln Assassination" (Special Scholars thesis, University of Virginia, Dec. 1980), p. 32.

5 Neely, *The Fate of Liberty*, pp. xii–xvi; Frank L. Klement, *The Copperheads in the Middle West* (Chicago: University of Chicago Press, 1960); John Niven, *Salmon P. Chase: A Biography* (New York: Oxford University Press, 1995), p. 395.

6 Basler, *The Collected Works of Abraham Lincoln*, vol. 8, p. 101.

7 *New-York Freeman's Journal and Catholic Register*, March 16, 1863.

8 Charles Warren, "Lincoln's 'Despotism' as Critics Saw It in 1861," *New York Times*, May 12, 1918; Terry Alford, "Why Booth Shot Lincoln," in *Lincoln and His Contemporaries*, ed. Charles M. Hubbard (Macon, Ga.: Mercer University Press, 1999), pp. 123–24.

9 Edward S. Evans, *The Seals of Virginia: Published as a Part of the Report of the Virginia State Library for 1909–1910* (Richmond: State of Virginia, 1911), pp. 31–46; *Chicago Evening Journal*, April 23, 1865.

10 William M. Wermerskirch, testimony, July 2, 1867, in *Trial of Surratt*, vol. 1, p. 488.

11 Ruth Anne Tucker, "M. M. 'Brick' Pomery: Forgotten Man of the Nineteenth Century" (Ph.D. dissertation, History, Northern Illinois University, 1979), p. 99. Lobdell wrote and published the editorial containing this sentence while Pomeroy was absent in Chicago. Pomeroy, customarily identified as the author of these words, did not disavow them.

12 Hanchett, *Lincoln Murder Conspiracies*, p. 25. In a similar vein, Thomas N. Conrad resolved early in the war to assassinate General Winfield Scott. Discouraged by rebel authorities, Conrad concluded that "sober second thought would not

justify the course." Terry Alford, "The Silken Net: Plots to Abduct Abraham Lincoln during the Civil War," speech delivered to the Lincoln Group of the District of Columbia, Washington, D.C., April 21, 1987. "All nations in all ages have refused to admit private murder as a lawful mode of waging war upon a public enemy," stated a *New York Times* editorial on April 18, 1858.

13 Weichmann, *True History*, p. 131. Thomas Otway's tragedy *Venice Preserved; or, A Plot Discovered* (1681) was performed through Europe and in the United States. Booth did the play on March 27, 1858, at the Arch Street Theatre.

14 Transcription of an account by Barron, Box 4, Alonzo May Papers, MdHS.

15 Bates, *The Drama*, vol. 19, p. 268.

16 Douglas C. Wilson, "Web of Secrecy: Goffe, Whalley, and the Legend of Hadley," *New England Quarterly*, vol. 60 (Dec. 1987), pp. 515–48, and communication from Mr. Wilson, Dec. 12, 1987, on this theme in nineteenth-century New England fiction.

17 The Everyman Shakespeare edition of this play (London: J. M. Dent, 1993), with its stellar editor's introduction and text notes by my friend John F. Andrews, is most valuable. See also Andrews's remarks at the symposium "Lincoln: Leader and Martyr," Chambersburg, Pa., Feb. 11, 1995; his "Blame It on Shakespeare," *Humanities*, vol. 10 (March–April 1989), pp. 30–32; and his "Was the Bard behind It? Old Light on the Lincoln Assassination," *Atlantic Monthly*, vol. 266 (Oct. 1990), pp. 26, 28, 32.

18 "Saw Lincoln Shot," clipping, n.p. [1934], Assassination File, Abraham Lincoln Library and Museum, Lincoln Memorial University; MacCulloch, "This Man Saw Lincoln Shot," p. 115.

19 Clarke, *Booth*, p. 55; Rhodehamel and Taper, *"Right or Wrong, God Judge Me,"* p. 150.

20 Alfriend, "Recollections," p. 604; *Baltimore Sun*, Jan. 20, 1907.

21 "Lincoln's Assassination," n.d. [1883], Abraham Lincoln Library and Museum, Lincoln Memorial University.

22 The set of Abbott's *Napoleon Bonaparte* mentioned in chap. 4.

23 Clipping, n.p. [1865], Atwater Scrapbook, Chicago Historical Society.

24 *New York Times*, April 18, 1858; Norma B. Cuthbert, ed., *Lincoln and the Baltimore Plot, 1861, from Pinkerton and Related Papers* (San Marino, Calif.: Huntington Library, 1949), p. 37; *Morning Cleveland Herald*, April 28, 1865.

25 *New York Clipper*, Feb. 21, 1874.

26 *New York Clipper*, April 29, 1865.

27 *Baltimore American*, June 8, 1893.

28 James F. Moulton Jr. to his uncle William, Baltimore, April 17, 1865, in *Surratt Courier*, vol. 16 (Feb. 1991), p. 5.

29 Clarke, *Booth*, pp. 35–36.

30 Ralph Waldo Emerson, "Journal GL" (1861–62), in *The Real War Will Never Get in the Books*, ed. Louis P. Masur (New York: Oxford University Press, 1993), p. 121–41.

31 Hanchett, "Booth's Diary," p. 40.

32 Miller, *Booth in the Pennsylvania Oil Region*, p. 72; *Philadelphia Press*, April 17, 1865.

33 *Chicago Post*, April 16, 1865; John T. Stafford interview, *New Orleans Times-Democrat*, Jan. 11, 1891. "The ambitious youth" is actually "the aspiring youth" in Cibber's version.

34 *Cleveland Leader*, April 17, 1865.

35 Robson, "Memories of Fifty Years," chap. 1, p. 88; Phelps, *Players of a Century*, p. 326; *Pittsburgh Gazette Times*, Aug. 4, 1907.

36 Simonds to Booth, Franklin, Pa., Feb. 21, 1865, 7/38, NA M599.

37 Chester, statement, April 28, 1865, 4/140–70, NA M599; *National Police Gazette* (New York), April 22, 1865.

38 John T. Ford, "The 14th of April, 1865," *Washington Evening Star*, April 18, 1885; Harry Ford, statement, April 20, 1865, 5/484, NA M599.

39 Clarke, *Booth*, pp. 81–82.

40 *Montreal Witness*, June 7, 1865; Department of Marine, RG 42, A 1, vol. 177, p. 131, Public Archives of Canada, Ottawa; *Quebec Gazette*, June 7, 1865; "Wilkes Booth's Wardrobe," *New York Times*, Nov. 15, 1891; W. H. F. Gurley to Edwin Stanton, Quebec, June 7, 1865, 7/225ff., NA M599.

41 Lewis J. A. McMillan, testimony, July 2, 1867, in *Trial of Surratt*, vol. 1, p. 483, and Stephen F. Cameron, testimony, July 16, 1867, in *Trial of Surratt*, vol. 2, p. 794.

42 *Washington Evening Star*, Dec. 7, 1881; "To Whom It May Concern" letter, Clarke, *Booth*, p. 110.

43 *Minneapolis Journal*, April 27, 1914; *New York Telegraph*, May 23, 1909; *Cincinnati Enquirer*, July 2, 1885.

44 *New York Herald*, April 10, 1910; *Washington Times*, Feb. 27, 1910; "Biographical Memoranda" (1903) in Gordon's hand, Gordon Subject File, Miss. Dept. of Archives and History, Jackson. For the Jan. 25, 1865, capture of the *Blenheim* by the USS *Tristram Shandy*, and his name as a prisoner transferred to the USS *Rhode Island* on Feb. 17, 1865, see the logs of these vessels in RG 24, Stack Area 18W4, NA; *New York Herald*, Feb. 1, 1865. Gordon registered at St. Lawrence Hall on March 8, 1865, per the hotel register (Public Archives of Canada, Ottawa, from microfilm copy, JOH). My interview with Dr. Robert L. Gordon, James Gordon's grandson, on Jan. 2, 1988, was highly informative. To the late Bob Gordon and his gracious wife, Caroline, I am also indebted for the opportunity to examine family documents as well as photographs of Gordon and Thompson and for many other courtesies. I happily acknowledge a particular gratitude for the friendship, assistance, and hospitality of Dr. Forrest T. Tutor, owner of Lochinvar, the Gordon

home near Pontotoc, Mississippi. Tutor's *Gordons of Lochinvar* (Lulu.com, 2008) brings numerous Gordon documents together.

45 James Gordon to Mildred L. Rutherford, Okolona, Miss., Aug. 11, 1894, *Miss Rutherford's Scrapbook*, vol. 2 (Jan. 1924), p. 4; clippings in Gordon Scrapbook (1909–12), compiled by Ella N. Gordon, copy in author's possession. It has not been recognized that Booth made this second trip to Montreal.

46 C. B. Whitford, "Some Sportsmen I've Known: Col. James Gordon," *American Field*, vol. C (May 12, 1923), p. 691.

47 Thompson's remarks given in several phrasings in drafts of an unfinished manuscript by James N. Wilkerson, n.d. [1930s], and Wilkerson to Swiggett (retained copy), Kansas City, Mo., July 16, 1935, Wilkerson Papers, LFFRC.

48 McKee Rankin, "The Story of J. Wilkes Booth's Wardrobe," typescript (1909), pp. 1 2, Chicago Historical Society. Booth told Rankin he had just come from Montreal.

49 *New York Clipper*, April 29, 1865; *New York Telegraph*, Dec. 4, 1910, John Wilkes Booth Scrapbook (1862–1936), Billy Rose Theatre Library, New York Public Library; *Springfield (Mass.) Republican*, April 18, 1865.

50 *Boston Post*, April 17, 1865.

51 *Boston Globe*, April 15, 1905; Kilby, "Some Newly Collected Facts about John Wilkes Booth," Seymour Collection, Princeton University Library.

52 Chester, statement, April 28, 1865, 4/140–70, NA M599, for all Chester material cited here.

53 L. L. Stevens, *Lives, Crimes, and Confessions of the Assassins*, p. 23.

54 Booth to mother [n.d., 1864], Clarke, *Booth*, p. 104.

55 *Boston Daily Evening Voice*, April 17, 1865. This newspaper had good sources among Booth's friends in the Boston theatrical community.

56 Asia B. Clarke to Jean Anderson, Philadelphia, May 22, 1865, Clarke Letters, MdHS; Clarke, *Booth*, p. 128.

57 Weichmann, *True History*, p. 131; Weichmann, testimony, June 27, 1867, in *Trial of Surratt*, vol. 1, p. 388.

58 Statement of Henry B. Phillips, April 15, 1865, *While Lincoln Lay Dying* (Philadelphia: Union League of Philadelphia, 1968), unpaginated; *New York Herald*, Sept. 4, 1904; *Philadelphia Inquirer*, April 18, 1865; *Philadelphia Evening Telegraph*, April 17, 1865.

59 "John Wilkes Booth—His Movements on the Day of the Murder," clipping, n.d. [April, 1865], Booth Scrapbook, Folger Shakespeare Library; *Albany Evening Journal*, April 17, 1865.

60 William R. Alger, *Life of Edwin Forrest, the American Tragedian*, 2 vols. (Philadelphia: J. B. Lippincott, 1877), vol. 2, p. 546.

61 Weichmann, *True History*, pp. 121–22.

62 Powell's hatred for Lincoln grew during his service years. *Washington Evening Star*, Dec. 3, 1887. David H. Bates, *Lincoln in the Telegraph Office* (New York: Century, 1907), pp. 384–87. Thomas T. Eckert, testimony, May 30, 1867, *Impeachment Investigation*, p. 674, also containing the "half of them" remark.

63 "Lincoln's Assassination," clipping, n.d. [May 1896?], LFFRC; *Maysville (Ky.) Daily Bulletin*, July 25, 1884.

64 Nelson Lankford, *Richmond Burning: The Last Days of the Confederate Capital* (New York: Viking, 2002), p. 163.

65 Patricia C. Johnson, ed., "'I Have Supped Full on Horrors': The Diary of Fanny Seward," *American Heritage*, vol. 10 (Oct. 1959), p. 96, diary entry of April 10, 1865.

66 *New York Herald*, March 3, 1922; *Washington Post*, March 30, 1902; "J. Wilkes Booth's Crime," clipping, n.d. [May, n.y.], LFFRC; Harry Ford, statement, April 20, 1865, 5/466, NA M599; Barbee, "Lincoln and Booth," p. 681.

67 T. D. Crothers, "The Insanity and Inebriety of J. Wilkes Booth," *Alienist and Neurologist*, vol. 32 (1911), p. 49.

68 George A. Townsend, manuscript of *Katy of Catoctin; or, The Chain-Breakers*, p. 995n., Townsend Papers, Maryland Hall of Records, Annapolis; Eckert, testimony, *Impeachment Investigation*, p. 674; Bates, *Lincoln in the Telegraph Office*, p. 384.

69 "Living Lincoln Links," typescript, n.d. [ca. 1936], John Hay Library, Brown University.

70 William H. DeMotte, "The Assassination of Abraham Lincoln," *Journal of the Illinois State Historical Society*, vol. 20 (Oct. 1927), p. 423; Burlingame, *Abraham Lincoln*, vol. 2, pp. 800–803; Clara Harris to friend, n.p., April 29 [1865], *New York Independent*, June 20, 1889.

71 Clipping, *Chicago Inter Ocean*, n.d. [April 1905], author's collection.

72 *Boston Evening Transcript*, April 14, 1890; "Last Public Address," April 11, 1865, in Basler, *Collected Works of Abraham Lincoln*, vol. 8, pp. 403–4; Burlingame, *Abraham Lincoln*, vol. 2, pp. 800–802.

73 Harry Ford, statement, April 20, 1865, 5/459–61, NA M599.

74 *New York Herald*, June 25, 1878; "Recalls Lincoln Shot," clipping, *Chicago Daily News*, n.d., LFFRC; Emerson to R. D. Bowen, Alexandria, Va., April 21, 1920, copy in Julian Raymond Papers, U.S. Army Military History Institute, Carlisle Barracks, Pa.

75 *New York Clipper*, April 29, 1865.

76 Clarke, *Booth*, p. 110.

77 *Washington Evening Star*, April 15, 1865; C. D. Hess, testimony, May 31, 1865, in Steers, *The Trial*, p. 99; "Quantrall, 82, Reviews Lincoln Assassination," *Washington Herald*, Oct. 12, 1930, Assassination File, Abraham Lincoln Library

and Museum, Lincoln Memorial University. Rilla E. Clem, Quantrille's grand-daughter, states that his name is misspelled in this article.

78   George F. Robinson, statement, covered by letter of H. H. Seward to Col. Wells, Washington, April 21, 1865, 6/94–95, NA M599; *Springfield (Mass.) Daily Republican*, April 20, 1865. On Seward's injury see John K. Lattimer, *Kennedy and Lincoln: Medical and Ballistic Comparisons of Their Assassinations* (New York: Harcourt Brace Jovanovich, 1980), p. 91; John M. Taylor, *William Henry Seward: Lincoln's Right Hand* (New York: HarperCollins, 1991), p. 241; and testimony of Robinson, May 19, 1865, in Steers, *The Trial*, p. 155.

79   *Washington Evening Star*, June 4, 1887; Atzerodt, statement, May 1, 1865, in Steers, *The Trial*, p. cvi.

80   *Washington Daily Morning Chronicle*, April 14, 1865; *Boston Commonwealth*, April 22, 1865; Rev. William James, "On the Night Lincoln Died," clipping [1901], Booth Scrapbook (formerly in Peale Museum), MdHS; H. A. Dobson, typed copy of speech (ca. 1928), Last Days File, Abraham Lincoln Library and Museum, Lincoln Memorial University; *Washington Post*, April 14, 1895.

81   Jesse W. Weik, "A New Story of Lincoln's Assassination: An Unpublished Record of an Eye-Witness," *Century Illustrated Monthly Magazine*, vol. 85 (Feb. 1913), p. 561.

82   Booth to Mary Ann Booth, Washington, April 14, 1865, *New York Herald*, April 30, 1865.

83   *Cincinnati Commercial*, Oct. 20, 1868; *Washington Evening Star*, Dec. 7, 1881, and April 18, 1885. Lincoln reservation from James R. Ford, testimony, May 30, 1865, in Steers, *The Trial*, pp. 100–101; *Washington Evening Star*, April 15, 1897. Years later Harry's son George acknowledged that his father had contributed to the tension of the day with his ill-advised teasing of Booth. *Dallas Morning News*, Nov. 23, 1951.

84   Emerson to Bowen, April 21, 1920, Raymond Papers; Boston *Sunday Herald*, April 11, 1897.

85   *New York Times*, April 23, 1886; *Washington Post*, April 17, 1898.

86   John M. Walton Jr., *Historical, Architectural, and Archaeological Research at the Surratt Dwelling House-Tavern, Clinton, MD* (Alexandria, Va.: Contract Archaeology, 1973), pp. 62–63; *Springfield (Mass.) Daily Republican*, April 18, 1865; *Albany Evening Journal*, April 17, 1865.

87   *Washington National Intelligencer*, July 18, 1867; F. A. Burr, "Booth's Bullet," *Washington Evening Star*, Dec. 7, 1881, with some rearrangement of text. When Mathews reached his lodgings after the murder, he opened and read the letter. Horrified at being associated with the document, he destroyed it. The original, therefore, does not exist. These words are Mathews's reconstruction. He told John T. Ford in 1865 that the document made reference to "famous assassinations

of history to justify the deed," and Ford added in 1878 that Booth excused his act "by Roman precedent." John T. Ford, testimony, May 25, 1867, *Impeachment Investigation*, p. 533; *Missouri Republican* (St. Louis), June 18, 1878; *New York Herald*, June 23, 1878; *New York Evening Post*, June 24, 1878; *Washington Post*, April 20, 1902, and Jan. 7, 1905.

88 *Baltimore Clipper*, April 15, 1865; *Chicago Tribune*, Feb. 7, 1909.

89 R. A. Brock, *Virginia and Virginians*, 2 vols. (Richmond and Toledo: Hardesty, 1888), vol. 2, p. 565.

90 John Mathews, testimony, July 16, 1867, in *Trial of Surratt*, vol. 2, p. 821; "The Defense of Booth," clipping [*Chicago Tribune*, 1881], Assassin File, Abraham Lincoln Library and Museum, Lincoln Memorial University; Mathews, testimony, July 1, 1867, *Impeachment Investigation*, p. 783.

91 Martha Murray, landlady at the Herndon House, testified that Powell checked out at 4:00 p.m. on April 14, raising doubt that the murder meeting occurred at that location, at least on that day. But Powell and Atzerodt informed their attorney William E. Doster that the plot was hatched at an eight o'clock meeting at that location. Doster, *Lincoln and Episodes of the Civil War* (New York: G. P. Putnam's Sons, 1915), pp. 269, 274, 305.

92 This recreation from Atzerodt's statements together with Doster, in Steers, *The Trial*, pp. 302–5, 314; *Cincinnati Commercial Gazette*, Jan. 24, 1891; Ownsbey, *Alias "Paine,"* p. 14; Townsend, "Washington: The Issues of Summer," clipping [1868–69], scrapbook, #128, p. 60, Townsend Collection, Maryland Hall of Records, Annapolis; Eckert testimony, *Impeachment Investigation*, p. 674; William H. Payne to Bradley T. Johnson [Washington, D.C.], Sept. 6, 1894, typescript, Eppa Hunton Papers, VHS; *Washington Evening Star*, Dec. 3, 1887; *Boston Post*, July 8, 1865; *New York World*, July 10, 1865: *Washington Evening Star*, May 2, 1885; Capt. Frank Munroe, affidavit, April 23, 1865, 2/45–47, NA M599; *Baltimore American*, Dec. 21, 1903; *New York Herald*, Sept. 4, 1904.

93 *Minneapolis Journal*, April 27, 1914; Gourlay interview, clipping, n.d. [1906], LFFRC.

94 My friend Douglas M. Wicklund, senior curator, National Firearms Museum, examined the pistol while working at the National Park Service Conservation Center at Harpers Ferry. I am indebted for his valuable observations.

95 Clipping, n.p., June 18, 1922, Assassination File, Abraham Lincoln Library and Museum, Lincoln Memorial University.

96 Crawford statement [April 15, 1865], *While Lincoln Lay Dying*, unpaginated; *New York Commercial Advertiser*, April 17, 1865; New York *Daily Tribune*, April 17, 1865.

97 *New York Herald*, April 15, 1865.

98 *New York Post*, July 8, 1894; Thomas A. Bogar, *Backstage at the Lincoln Assassination: The Untold Story of the Actors and Stagehands at Ford's Theatre* (Washington: Regnery History, 2013), passim.

99   *Albany Evening Journal*, April 18, 1865; Frederick Hatch, "Lincoln's Missing Guard," *Lincoln Herald*, vol. 107 (Fall 2005), pp. 106–17; Paul Kallina, "The Case of the Missing Coachman," *Lincolnian*, vol. 8 (March–April 1990), pp. 2–3.

100   *New York Daily News*, April 16, 1865; *Forney's War Press*, April 22, 1865. Lucy's grandson John Parker Hale Chandler Jr. wrote to Helen C. Milius that it was well understood in his family that Booth used Hale's card (January 25, 1942, letter in author's collection). Irving Bell, a journalist and publisher whose work the author is pleased to acknowledge, was told by Chandler that Booth "had a thousand chances to pick up one of the Senator's cards." Author's copy of Bell, "John Wilkes Booth and the Senator's Daughter," unpublished manuscript (1962), p. 14; *Concord Monitor-Patriot*, June 24 and October 8, 1963. The author learned the same from Chandler in an interview, November 9, 1990. The special correspondent of the *Chicago Times* reported on April 15 that Booth "gave the name of some distinguished gentleman." *Weekly Jacksonville Sentinel*, April 28, 1865. This claim is buttressed by the statement of an eyewitness, Helen A. Bratt DuBarry, that Booth presented "a card with the name of a Senator written on it." Letter to her mother, April 16, 1865, Manuscripts Collection, Abraham Lincoln Presidential Library, Springfield. It is noteworthy that Hale, present at Johnson's inauguration the following morning, held a private meeting with the new president shortly before his swearing-in. "It was of a strictly confidential character, and therefore he had no right to communicate what passed between them," Hale told the public. The ex-senator evidently explained away Booth's association with his family, as he came out of the meeting loudly proclaiming his confidence in Johnson's leadership. *Dover Gazette*, April 21, 1865; *Dover Morning Star*, April 26, 1865; *Dover Enquirer*, April 27, 1865. One speculates that this tête-à-tête explains why Lucy's name is entirely absent from investigation records and why Forbes was not called at the conspiracy trial to identify the individual he admitted to the box or to produce the card. Incredibly, Forbes himself does not even appear to have been called upon to give a statement to investigators.

101   *Cincinnati Enquirer*, April 14, 1892.

102   David Herold, statement, April 27, 1865, 4/442–85, NA M599; John T. Ford, untitled manuscript [1865], Ford Papers, MdHS.

103   Thomas Raybold, testimony, June 2, 1865, in Steers, *The Trial*, pp. 109–11.

104   Hanchett, "Booth's Diary," pp. 41–42.

105   *New York Times*, April 18, 1865; *Chicago Evening Journal*, April 19, 1865, containing Hawk's letter to his parents; *Washington Post*, Dec. 30, 1883; Abott A. Abott, *The Assassination and Death of Abraham Lincoln* (New York: American News, 1865), pp. 4–7; Horatio N. Taft, diary, April 30, 1865, Manuscript Division, LOC.

106 Henry Rathbone, affidavit, April 17, 1865, and his testimony, May 15, 1865, in Steers, *The Trial*, p. 78; "The Murder of Lincoln," clipping [1896], F. L. Black Papers, Oakland University; *Washington Post*, Nov. 13, 1898; *Chicago Tribune*, July 3, 1878.

107 *Washington Star*, May 23, 1915; *New York Herald*, Feb. 25, 1922.

108 *New York Sun*, Aug. 30, 1897; *New York Times*, Feb. 28, 1909; *Boston Sunday Herald*, Feb. 7, 1909.

109 Surgeon General Joseph K. Barnes to E. M. Stanton, Wash., D.C., April 27, 1865, Records of AGO, Entry 623, File D, RG 94, located in the Treasure Room, NA. When captured, Herold said, "Booth injured his leg by jumping on the stage and not by falling off his horse as has been stated." *New York Tribune*, April 28, 1865. Mudd found the fracture "direct and clean." *Washington Daily National Intelligencer*, April 6, 1869; "Booths, Father and Sons," clipping, n.d. (1893), LFFRC. While it is generally understood that the fibula is a not a weight-bearing bone, it does carry some load. With the ankle joint in neutral position, there is a weight distribution to the fibula of 6.4 percent. A low fibula fracture is essentially an ankle fracture, both extremely painful and difficult to walk upon. K. Takebe, A. Nakagawa, H. Minami, H. Kanazawa, and K. Hirohata, "The Role of the Fibula in Weight-Bearing," *Clinical Orthopaedics and Related Research* 184 (April 1984) pp. 289–92. Thanks to Dr. Nitin Goyal of the Anderson Orthopaedic Clinic of Arlington, Va., for his review this material.

110 Morris, *Memorial Record*, p. 33; C. C. Carrington, comp., "Assassination and Funeral of President Lincoln," scrapbook, 2 vols. (1871), vol. 1, p. 36, John Hay Library, Brown University; Townsend, *Katy of Catoctin*, p. 510n.

111 John L. Debonay, testimony, May 31, 1865, in Steers, *The Trial*, p. 105; Roeliff Brinkerhoff, *Recollections of a Lifetime* (Cincinnati: Robert Clarke, 1900), p. 168; Cazauran, "The Murder of Lincoln," HRHRC. Confusion about what was happening saved Booth more surely than the speed of his exit. "There were many people in the orchestra [seats] who might have caught him if they had immediately pursued him," thought barkeep Ferguson.

112 After identifying (by name) some 353 eyewitnesses, the author drew this account from the most trustworthy of their statements. Given over a period of eight decades, these vary considerably in quality. See also *New York Sun*, Feb. 9, 1913; *New York Times*, April 18, 1915. Timothy S. Good, ed., *We Saw Lincoln Shot: One Hundred Eyewitness Accounts* (Jackson: University Press of Mississippi, 1995), is a handy compilation.

113 *Dorchester Beacon*, April 11, 1896; Charles A. Leale, statement enclosed in a letter to Benj. F. Butler, New York, N.Y., July 20, 1867, Butler Papers, LOC.

114 James S. Knox to father, April 16, 1865, in Good, *We Saw Lincoln Shot*, p. 40; *Chicago Daily Inter Ocean*, July 11, 1883; Isaac Jaquette, "Reminiscences of the

Assassination of President Lincoln," manuscript [n.d.], courtesy of James E. Houghton.

115 Hawk to his parents, Washington, April 16, 1865, *Chicago Evening Journal*, April 19, 1865; Hawk interview, clipping [Aug. 1894], LFFRC.

116 James P. Ferguson, statement [April 15, 1865], *While Lincoln Lay Dying*; his statement, April 15, 1865, 4/339ff., NA M599; his interview of April 15, in *New York Times*, April 18, 1865; his statement, April 18, 1865, in clipping [1928], File Notebook 23A, F, Lauriston Bullard Papers, Boston University; his testimony, May 15, 1865, in Steers, *The Trial*, pp. 76–77; *Cincinnati Enquirer*, July 6, 1878. Albert Daggett also heard this remark.

117 *Baltimore Sun*, Feb. 12, 1926; Ferguson, "I Saw Lincoln Shot!" *American Magazine*, Aug. 1920, p. 15; *Independent*, April 4, 1895, p. 430, courtesy of my friend Michelle Krowl; *New York Herald*, April 15, 1865.

118 James J. Gifford, testimony, May 19, 1865, and John T. Ford, testimony, May 31, 1865, both in Steers, *The Trial*, pp. 102, 117; *Washington Star*, April 15, 1915.

119 *San Francisco Call*, May 1, 1892; Withers, testimony, May 15, 1865, in Steers, *The Trial*, p. 79; *New York World*, Feb. 12, 1911; *New Orleans Times-Picayune*, Dec. 28, 1879; *New York Sun*, Feb. 11, 1917. Richard Sloan, "John Wilkes Booth's Other Victim," *American Heritage*, vol. 42 (Feb.–March 1991), pp. 114–16, is a fine overview.

120 Burroughs, statements of April 15 and 24, 1865, 4/65–70 and 4/135–37, NA M599.

121 Mary J. Anderson, testimony, May 16, 1865, in Steers, *The Trial*, p. 75.

122 *Washington Critic*, April 17, 1885.

123 *Washington Evening Star*, April 18, 1885.

124 Stewart, testimony of May 20, 1865, in Steers, *The Trial*, pp. 79–80, and of June 17, 1867, in *Trial of Surratt*, vol. 1, pp. 126–27; "The Route Booth Rode," manuscript (ca. 1909), p. 22, JOH.

125 *Philadelphia North American*, Feb. 11, 1911. Rathbone assisted others in getting Lincoln from his chair, according to William T. Kent. *St. Louis Globe Dispatch*, Dec. 3, 1891.

CHAPTER 11. EXIT BOOTH

1 "Washington," clipping, May 3 [1869], Townsend Scrapbook Collection, item 128, pp. 81–82, Townsend Collection, Maryland Hall of Records, Annapolis.

2 Silas Cobb, statement, n.d. [April 1865], 4/172–78, NA M599, and his testimony, May 16, 1865, in Steers, *The Trial*, pp. 84–85.

3 Sun and moon data for Washington, D.C, April 14, 1865, Astronomical Applications Dept., U.S. Naval Observatory, Washington, D.C., at USNO website; entry for April 14, 1865, "Meteorological Journal No. 26," Naval Observatory, Box 2, NC-3, Entry 63, Records of the Weather Bureau, RG 27, NA. This source provided all weather data in the chapter unless otherwise indicated. Thanks to Kevin Ambrose for his interpretation of this material.

4 *New York Herald*, March 31, 1869.

5 Frederick A. Demond, statement, Cavendish, Vt., June 12, 1915, Folder 13, Box 7, Swaim Papers, Georgetown University Library; Demond to George Demond, April 21, 1865 [Washington, D.C.], quoted in *Boston Traveler*, April 14, 1964.

6 Polk Gardner, testimony, May 16, 1865, in Steers, *The Trial*, p. 85, and his statement, n.d. [April 1865], 4/344–47, NA M599; *New York Times*, July 8, 1865.

7 Steers, *Blood on the Moon*, p. 136; Benjamin F. Cooling III and Walton H. Owen II, *Mr. Lincoln's Forts: A Guide to the Civil War Defenses of Washington* (Shippensburg, Pa.: White Mane Publishing, 1988), pp. 198–99, 207. Wally Owen provided insights on these points.

8 "Assassination and Funeral of President Lincoln, arranged by C. C. Carrington," scrapbook, 2 vols. (1871), vol. 1, p. 14, John Hay Library, Brown University.

9 Statement of Herold to Rev. Mark L. Olds, who attended him at his execution, and found in W. M. Clarke manuscript (1923), copy courtesy of my friend Bill Luetge.

10 *New York Morning Advertiser*, May 16, 1895; Herold, statement, April 27, 1865, 4/442ff., NA M599, containing all facts in this chapter related to him unless otherwise indicated.

11 M. P. Pope, statement, April 27, 1865, 4/511–15, NA M599.

12 James P. Ferguson, statement, 4/339ff, NA M599.

13 *Washington Sunday Gazette*, Feb. 22, 1885.

14 *Washington Star*, January 10, 1885; Kauffman, *American Brutus,* p. 63. JoAnn Dawson of Fairwinds Stables provided her insight into all manner of horse issues.

15 Thomas Davis, statement and interrogatory, April 29, 1865, 4/245–60, NA M599.

16 John M. Lloyd, statement, April 22, 1865, 2/199–209, NA M599; his interrogatory, April 28, 1865, 5/148–83, NA M599; and his testimony, May 13, 1865, in Steers, *The Trial*, p. 86; *Philadelphia Press*, May 8, 1896 ("stout and surly"); George Cottingham, testimony, May 25, 1865, in Poore, *The Conspiracy Trial*, vol. 2, page 193.

17 T. M. Harris, "The Case of Mrs. Surratt," *New York Sun*, n.d. 1901, LFFRC.

18 John T. Ford, manuscript statement, n.d. [on verso of 1880s stationery], Ford Papers, MdHS.

19 "The Route Booth Rode," p. 28, JOH. Based on a postwar interview, this document offers a different but perhaps more honest account of Lloyd's reaction than that he provided authorities in 1865.

20 Lloyd, testimony, June 24, 1867, *Surratt Trial*, vol. l, p. 284; report of A. R. Allen and W. W. Kirby to L. C. Turner, April 23, 1865, 7/369–73, NA M599.

21 "Wild Ride for Life," clipping, n.d. [1869], LFFRC.

22 "The Route Booth Rode," p. 24, JOH; Thomas Ewing to Andrew Johnson, July 10, 1865, Mudd Pardon File, RG 204, NA.

23 *New York Herald*, March 31, 1869; Mudd, statements [April 1865], 5/212-0239, NA M599; *Washington National Tribune*, May 6, 1915.

24 Paul Devere, "The Flight of J. Wilkes Booth," *No Name Magazine*, vol. 1 (July 1890), p. 182.

25 Mudd, *Life of Mudd*, pp. 30–33.

26 James O. Hall, *John Wilkes Booth's Escape Route* (Clinton, Md.: Surratt Society, 2000), p. 8.

27 *Boston Daily Globe*, Jan. 3, 1886.

28 *New York Times*, Aug. 4, 1865.

29 Samuel Cox Jr., manuscript notes (1893) of an 1877 conversation with Mudd, found in the margins of his copy of Jones, *J. Wilkes Booth*, MdHS; Oldroyd, *Assassination of Abraham Lincoln*, pp. 268–69.

30 Oscar (Ausy) Swan, statement, 6/227–29, NA M599.

31 Samuel Cox Jr. to Mrs. B. T. Johnson, Rich Hill, July 20, 1891, copy in Cox Files, JOH; H. H. Wells, statement, May 8, 1865, 4/207, NA M599; Cox Sr. interrogatory, Carroll Prison, April 28, 1865, vol. 92, Joseph Holt Papers, LOC; May (Mary) Swann, 6/160–64, NA M599; *Philadelphia Press*, May 8, 1896; Norma L. Hurley, "Samuel Cox of Charles County," *Record* [of the Historical Society of Charles County, Maryland] 53 (Oct. 1991), pp. 1–6.

    Cox and his son swore the fugitives never entered the house. Oswald Swan swore they did. Swann upheld Cox's story at the time, but later she reportedly told close friends the two were admitted and fed.

32 Cora Frear Hawkins, "John Wilkes Booth's Easter Sunday in Southern Maryland," *Baltimore Sun*, April 13, 1941, for Mary Swann's observations.

33 *Port Tobacco Times*, Dec. 25, 1896; *Washington Evening Star*, Dec. 22, 1896.

34 Jones, *J. Wilkes Booth*, passim; George A. Townsend, "How Wilkes Booth Crossed the Potomac," *Century Illustrated Monthly Magazine*, vol. 27 (April 1884), pp. 822–32; Oldroyd, *Assassination of Abraham Lincoln*, pp. 101–10.

35 *Boston Daily Globe*, Jan. 3, 1886; *Cincinnati Enquirer*, April 16, 1892.

36 *Washington Post*, Jan. 19, 1890; *Boston Daily Globe*, March 13, 1895.

37 James R. O'Beirne, diary, n.d. [April 1865], *New York Times*, Dec. 7, 1930; *Sunday Oregonian* (Portland), April 4, 1943, which also contains "So help me Gawd."

38 Thomas Reed Turner, *Beware the People Weeping: Public Opinion and the Assassination of Abraham Lincoln* (Baton Rouge and London: Louisiana State University Press, 1982), p. 45.

39 *Chicago Times*, April 15, 1865; *Chicago Evening Journal*, April 15, 1865; *Boston Post*, April 17, 1865; *Baltimore Clipper*, April 17–19, 1865; *Philadelphia Evening Telegraph*, April 15, 1865; Robert Herron, "How Lincoln Died in Cincinnati," *Bulletin, Historical and Philosophical Society of Ohio*, vol. 17 (Jan. 1959), p. 24. The grief was not universal. Someone in most towns, North and South, approved of Booth's deed. Northerners whose incautious utterances Booth read in the newspapers were there because they received rough handling or worse. Not unexpectedly, the farther south one went, the greater the approval, until one reached Texas, where satisfaction over Lincoln's death was most widespread. Booth did not live to learn that, of course. John S. Wise, serving with Johnston's army in North Carolina, wrote perceptively of his fellow Southerners: "Lincoln incarnated to us the idea of oppression and conquest. Among the thoughtless, the desperate, and the ignorant, [his death] was hailed as a sort of retributive justice. Among the higher officers and the most intelligent and conservative men, the assassination caused a shudder of horror at the heinousness of the act and at the thought of its possible consequences." Wise, *The End of an Era*, p. 454.

40 F. W. Heath, diary, April 19, 1865, Huntington Cairns Papers, Manuscript Division, LOC; *New York Daily Tribune*, April 17, 1865.

41 *Chicago Christian Times*, April 20, 1865.

42 Clipping [April 1865], Carrington Scrapbook, John Hay Library, Brown University; *Washington National Intelligencer*, April 26, 1865.

43 *New York Clipper*, April 22 and May 8, 1865.

44 *Richmond Whig*, April 17, 1865.

45 *Troy Weekly Times*, April 29, 1865.

46 Clipping, n.d., Booth Scrapbook, Folger Shakespeare Library.

47 *Columbus (Ohio) Crisis*, April n.d., 1865, author's collection.

48 Hanchett, "Booth's Diary," p. 40, with some textural rearrangement for clarity; *St. Louis Missouri Republican*, June 18, 1878; "The Crime of Lincoln's Murder," unpaginated.

49 *Washington National Intelligencer*, July 8–9, 1867.

50 Prentiss Ingraham, "Pursuit and Death of John Wilkes Booth," *Century Monthly Illustrated Magazine*, vol. 39 (Jan. 1890), p. 446n.

51 *La Plata (Md.) Crescent*, Dec. 25, 1896.

52 *Independent*, vol. 47 (April 4, 1895), p. 430; *Cincinnati Enquirer*, Jan. 19, 1886.

53 *Cincinnati Daily Enquirer*, June 28, 1878.

54 Verge, "That Trifling Boy," pp. 4–9; James L. Swanson, *Manhunt: The Twelve-Day Chase for Lincoln's Killer* (New York: William Morrow, 2006), p. 279; John C. Brennan, "Hobbledehoy David Edgar Herold," typescript (1986), author's

collection. Only John C. Brennan, bless his soul, could have conceived such an article at this. Eye color in Lt. Col. C. W. Davis to Col. Bernard Laibold, St. Louis, Mo., April 21, 1865, Letters Sent Relating to the Secret Service (184–65), vol. 559/1391, DMO, RG 393, NA. A second report says his eyes were hazel.

55 Steers, *Blood on the Moon*, p. 209.

56 "He Led the Pursuit of Booth," *Philadelphia Press*, May 8, 1896.

57 *Baltimore Sun*, April 13, 1941.

58 *Portland (Ore.) Telegram*, April 3, 1909.

59 Mason, "Four Lincoln Conspiracies," p. 905. A Washingtonian with connections to the War Department, Mason interviewed the Quesenberrys, among others. Log of the *Juniper*, April 20, 1865, noting "cloudy with thick foggy weather." The vessel anchored off Mathias Point at 8:30 p.m. and remained there until it started downriver the following morning. Bureau of Navy Personnel, RG 24, NA. Tide data for Mathias Point on April 20 courtesy of Todd Ehret, physical geographer, NOAA Tides and Currents Office, CO-OPS.

60 James O. Hall's interview with George C. Hughes, Dec. 31, 1975, and Willard C. Calkins Jr. to John Wearmouth, Ocean City, N.J., May 10, 1971, JOH. Herold's attorney Frederick Stone said Hughes refused Booth "bread or any human intercourse." *Washington Capitol*, Feb. 8, 1874.

61 Hanchett, "Booth's Diary," pp. 40–42, with some rearrangement of punctuation for clarity of reading.

62 Log of the *Juniper*, April 22, 1865; Herold, statement, 4/442ff., NA M599.

63 Herold's statement, also mentioning Booth's soreness.

64 Townsend, "Crime of Lincoln's Murder," n.p.; *Cincinnati Enquirer*, Aug. 3, 1884. The latter item has all Harbin quotes given here.

65 Oldroyd, *Assassination of Abraham Lincoln*, p. 282.

66 Elizabeth R. Quesenberry, deposition, May 16, 1865, 5/556–59, NA M599; Anderson C. Quisenberry, *Genealogical Memoranda of the Quisenberry Family and Other Families* (Washington: Hartman and Cadick, 1897), p. 34.

67 William L. Bryant, statement, May 6, 1865, 4/94–97, NA M599.

68 W. N. Walton, "Booth's Flight and Death," clipping [May 3, 1865], Booth Scrapbook, Folger Shakespeare Library.

69 Tidwell, Hall, and Gaddy, *Come Retribution*, pp. 460–61; *Boston Daily Globe*, Jan. 3, 1886.

70 Richard H. Stuart, statement, May 6, 1865, 6/205–11, NA M599.

71 Mason, "Four Lincoln Conspiracies," p. 908.

72 *Boston Daily Globe*, July 26, 1891; Booth's remarks in St. George T. C. Bryan, notes of conversation with Hunter, n.d. [before 1916], Grinnan Family Papers, VHS.

73 *Century Illustrated Monthly Magazine*, vol. 28 (Aug. 1884), p. 638.

74 William Lucas, statement, May 6, 1865, 5/144–47, NA M599.

75 *New York Herald*, May 4, 1865. This Lucas version of Booth's threatening behavior, not the subsequent and melodramatic knife-flourishing scene, was confirmed by L. B. Baker. *Impeachment Investigation*, p. 484.

76 Booth wrote two notes to Stuart, in the first of which he stated he was enclosing five dollars. Stuart received Booth's second note, lowering the amount enclosed as indicated. *Impeachment Investigation*, p. 677.

77 Statement of Stuart's niece to Ella Mahoney, manuscript (1930s), HSHC. His wife saved the paper from the fire.

78 Kimmel, notebook, (1934), p. 52, Macdonald-Kelce Library, University of Tampa.

79 William Rollins, statements of May 20, 1865, 457/550–61, NA M619, and of May 6, 1865, 6/78–82, NA M599.

80 *New York Herald*, May 4, 1865.

81 Willie Jett, statement, May 6, 1865, 4/86–99, NA M599, and his testimony, May 17, 1865, in Steers, *The Trial*, p. 90–91.

82 Turner Rose, "Rappahannock Ferry," *Washington Post*, March 13, 1938.

83 Everett C. Bumpus, "With Wilkes Booth in Maryland," clipping, n.d., HTC.

84 Ingraham, "Pursuit and Death of John Wilkes Booth," and Ingraham's companion piece, "The Tragedy of the Civil War," *Pen and Ink* (1902), Wilkerson Papers, LFFRC.

85 *Buffalo Morning Express*, May 10, 1865; *Troy Weekly Times*, May 13, 1865.

86 Lindsay G. Roach, "The Saddle of the Assassin Booth," *New York World*, Feb. 7, 1909.

87 Thomas N. Conrad, *The Rebel Scout* (Washington: National Publishing, 1904), p. 153.

CHAPTER 12. THE LAST DITCH

1 *New York Herald*, May 4, 1865.

2 Jett, statement, May 6, 1865, 4/86–99, NA M599.

3 Ingraham, "The Tragedy of the Civil War," LFFRC.

4 *New York Sun*, Feb. 11, 1917.

5 John M. Garrett and William H. Garrett, depositions, both May 20, 1865, 457/499ff., NA M619; John M. Garrett, testimony, June 25, 1867, in *Trial of Surratt*, vol. 1, pp. 302–5; *Brooklyn Daily Eagle*, Nov. 27, 1881.

6 "Last Days of Wilkes Booth," clipping, n.d., folder titled "Newspaper and Pictorial Accounts of Lincoln Assassination, No. 1," HRHRC.

7 *Washington Star*, May 24, 1890.

8 Bryan, *Great American Myth*, p. 269.

9 Betsy Fleet, ed., "A Chapter of Unwritten History: Richard Baynham Garrett's Account of the Flight and Death of John Wilkes Booth," *Virginia Magazine of History*

and Biography, vol. 71 (Oct. 1963), p. 393; *Boston Sunday Herald*, Dec. 11, 1881; *Brooklyn Daily Eagle*, Nov. 27, 1881.

10 *Utica Daily Observer*, Oct. 4, 1867.

11 William H. Garrett, "True Story of the Capture of John Wilkes Booth," *Confederate Veteran*, vol. 29 (April 1921), p. 129.

12 *Richmond News-Leader*, March 3, 1911.

13 Statement of William H. Garrett from a copy (1940) owned by his niece Kate G. Campbell, George S. Bryan Papers, New York Public Library.

14 Lucinda K. B. Holloway, "Capture of Booth," *Washington Evening Star*, April 10, 1897.

15 Jeanne Senseny, "Wilkes Booth's Death," [1895], Booth Scrapbook, Fawcett Theatre Collection, Hodges Library, University of Tennessee, Knoxville.

16 *Utica Daily Observer*, Oct. 4, 1867.

17 "Capture of Lincoln's Assassin," *Milwaukee Sentinel*, clipping, n.d. [1896?], LFFRC.

18 *New York Sun*, Feb. 11, 1917.

19 Edward P. Doherty, testimony, May 22, 1865, in Poore, *The Conspiracy Trial*, vol. 2, p. 94.

20 Statement of Herold, April 27, 1865, 4/442ff., NA M599.

21 Ingraham, "Pursuit and Death of John Wilkes Booth," and Ingraham, "The Tragedy of the Civil War," LFFRC. There is some confusion about who said what to Booth.

22 David Hume, *The History of England from the Invasion of Julius Caesar to the Revolution of 1688*, 6 vols. (Indianapolis: Liberty Classics, 1983–85), vol. 6, p. 214.

23 U. S. Grant, *Personal Memoirs of U. S. Grant*, 2 vols. (New York: Charles L. Webster, 1885–86), vol. 2, p. 584.

24 R. B. Garrett to A. R. Taylor, Portsmouth, Va., Oct. 14, 1907, JOH.

25 William J. Newbill to Ella Mahoney, Irvington, Va., Nov. 2, 1925, author's collection.

26 Richard H. Garrett to Grandison Warring, Sept. 5, 1866, copy courtesy of Francis J. Gorman; *Philadelphia Press*, April 12, 1896; *Claim of Richard H. Garrett* [1871–72], Report 743, pp. 1–8, U.S. House of Representatives, 43rd Congress, 1st Session.

27 *Utica Daily Observer*, Oct. 4, 1867.

28 Herman Neugarten, statement, May 29, 1865, Doherty Papers, Manuscript Collection, Abraham Lincoln Presidential Library, Springfield, Ill., as well as his service and pension records, NA; *Harrisburg Telegraph*, Nov. 26, 1910.

29 Accounts by Baker, Doherty, and Conger, differing in some details, provide the basics of Booth's capture and death. Doherty: testimony, May 22, 1865, in Poore, *The Conspiracy Trial*, vol. 2, pp. 92–94; report, Washington, D.C., April 29,

1865, in *OR*, ser. 1, vol. 46, pt. 1, pp. 1317–22; statement, n.d., 456/276, NA M619. Conger: testimony, May 17, 1865, in Poore, *The Conspiracy Trial*, vol. 1, pp. 312–22; testimony, May 14, 1867, *Impeachment Investigation*, pp. 324–33; testimony, June 25, 1867, in *Trial of Surratt*, vol. 1, pp. 305–14; statement, April 27, 1865, 455/728ff., NA M619. Baker: statement, April 27, 1865, 455/665–86, NA M619; testimony, June 25, 1867, in *Trial of Surratt*, vol. 1, pp. 315–23; testimony, May 22, 1867, *Impeachment Investigation*, pp. 479–90. These are supplemented by reports drawn from the participants in the *Washington Star*, *New York Times*, *New York World*, and *New York Herald*.

30   Steven G. Miller, "Boston Corbett: A Re-Evaluation," paper delivered at the "Crime of the Century, Part II" Surratt Society Conference, April 1, 2006; Corbett, copy of deposition, Cloud County, Kans., Nov. 1, 1883, Boston Corbett–George A. Huron Collection, Kansas State Historical Society.

31   *Rochester Democrat*, May 2, 1865; *Troy Weekly Times*, May 6, 1865; *Boston Daily Globe*, Feb. 20, 1887.

32   *Philadelphia Weekly Times*, April 14, 1877; Corbett, statement, April 29, 1865, 455/253–61, NA M619; John C. Collins, "Recollections of Boston Corbett by an Eyewitness of the Booth Shooting," clipping, n.d., LFFRC.

33   "The Assassin's End," *Harper's Weekly*, vol. 9 (May 13, 1865), p. 294.

34   *Telegram Magazine* (Portland, Ore.), Feb. 19, 1910, with Parady's "Kill him" remarks and characterization of Herold.

35   *Manchester (N.H.) Union Democrat*, May 2, 1865; *New York Tribune*, April 28, 1865.

36   Frank G. Carpenter, "John Wilkes Booth: A Talk with the Man That Captured Him," *Lippincott's Monthly Magazine*, vol. 40 (Sept. 1887), p. 450.

37   Wesley Harris, "Booth's Arsenal," posted Dec. 22, 2011, diggingthepast. blogspot.com, accessed April 15, 2013.

38   William L. Reuter, *The King Can Do No Wrong* (New York: Pageant Press, 1958), p. 43, based on a 1916 Conger interview.

39   William Byrne, deposition, May 29, 1865, Doherty Papers, Lincoln Presidential Library, Springfield, Ill.

40   Corbett stated that Booth did not attempt to stop Herold from leaving, "giving him a free chance to go, and encouraging him to do so, instead of threatening to shoot him as Herold said he did." Corbett, statement, May 1, 1865, 455/254–62, NA M619.

41   "Lincoln's Assassination," *St. Louis Republic*, n.d. [ca. 1895], LFFRC.

42   Steven G. Miller, ed., "A Trooper's Account of the Death of Booth," *Surratt Courier*, vol. 20 (May 1995), p. 7.

43   R. B. Hoover, "The Slayer of J. Wilkes Booth," *North American Review*, vol. 149 (Sept. 1889), p. 382, with "What a God" remark. Corbett would never have applied the adjective *heroic* to Booth; Hoover captures only the essence of his description.

44 *Chicago Globe*, April 3, 1889.

45 *Butte Evening News*, Sunday ed., April 3, 1910.

46 *Reading Eagle*, April 2, 1911; *Philadelphia Evening Telegraph*, May 16, 1865.

47 Richard Thatcher, "Boston Corbett's Prison Life," manuscript (1905), Corbett-Huron Collection; Thomas Goodrich, *The Darkest Dawn: Lincoln, Booth, and the Great American Tragedy* (Bloomington and Indianapolis: Indiana University Press, 2005), p. 255.

48 *Washington National Tribune*, Aug. 8, 1912.

49 Edward Kirk Jr., "Recollections and Reminiscences in Connection with Boston Corbett," manuscript (1905), Corbett-Huron Collection, which mentions shaking Lincoln's hand. Conger and Baker felt Corbett shot Booth "without order, pretext, or excuse." See their statement, Dec. 24, 1865, in Baker, *History of the United States Secret Service*, p. 537.

50 *Buffalo Commercial*, clipping, n.d. [ca. 1891], and *Brooklyn Daily Eagle*, clipping, n.d. [1922], both LFFRC; *Richmond Whig*, June 28, 1867.

51 *Atlanta Constitution*, May 21, 1886; *Galveston News*, July 19, 1893.

52 *Washington National Tribune*, April 7, 1910, and May 4, 1911.

53 *The Assassination and History of the Conspiracy*, p. 65; *Boston Herald*, April 28, 1865; *New York Tribune*, April 28, 1865.

54 *Atlanta Constitution*, Dec. 11, 1881.

55 Conger File, Beaverhead County Museum, Dillon, Montana.

56 Alfred A. Woodhull, comp., *Catalogue of the Surgical Section of the United States Army Medical Museum* (Washington: GPO, 1866), pt. 3, p. 58

57 *New York Mercury*, March 26, 1881.

58 *Philadelphia Press*, May 4, 1865.

59 *St. Louis Globe Democrat*, March 7, 1897, and July 25, 1943.

60 Ella Mahoney, "My Last Witness," her interview with Robert C. Garrett [1932?], Mahoney Papers, HSHC.

61 *Atlanta Daily Constitution*, Aug. 28, 1879; *Chicago Globe*, April 3, 1889.

62 *New York Clipper*, May 6, 1865; "The Killing of Booth," clipping, n.d. [April 1865], Booth Scrapbook, Folger Shakespeare Library.

63 *Chicago Times*, May 9, 1865; "Wilkes Booth's Death," clipping, n.d., Yale University Library.

64 Baker, *History of the United States Secret Service*, p. 507; *Washington National Tribune*, Feb. 13, 1890.

65 *Atlanta Constitution*, May 21, 1886.

66 *Richmond Times-Dispatch*, April 3, 1938; Steers, *Blood on the Moon*, pp. 204–5.

67 *Washington National Tribune*, March 11, 1915. This is Oatley's rank from the April 1865 muster roll of the *Mahopac*, where he served under the name of Fred S. Otis. Thanks to Trevor Plante.

68 Welles and Stanton to Commandant of the Washington Navy Yard, Wash., D.C., April 27, 1865, Mark Katz, *Witness to an Era: The Life and Photographs of Alexander Gardner* (Washington: Viking, 1991), p. 59; log of the USS *Montauk*, RG 24, NA; Leonard F. Guttridge, "Identification and Autopsy of John Wilkes Booth: Reexamining the Evidence," *Navy Medicine*, vol. 84 (Jan.–Feb., 1993), pp. 17–26.

69 H. B. Hibben, *A History of the Washington Navy Yard* (Washington: GPO, 1890), pp. 146–49.

70 *Baltimore and Ohio Magazine*, vol. 13 (Feb. 1926), p. 11.

71 William May to Dudley Knox, Wash., D.C., May 18, 1925, U. S. Naval History Division, *Civil War Naval Chronology, 1861–1865* (Washington: GPO, 1971), pt. 6, pp. 26–28; *New York Tribune*, April 28, 1865.

72 James O. Hall, "That Ghastly Errand," *Surratt Courier*, vol. 21 (Oct. 1996), pp. 4–5.

73 Seaton Munroe, "Recollections of Lincoln's Assassination," *North American Review*, vol. 162 (March 1896), pp. 431–34; Munroe, examination, April 28, 1865, 4/356–59, NA M599.

74 J. F. May, "The Mark of the Scalpel," *Records of the Columbia Historical Society*, vol. 13 (1910), p. 55, from the original 1887 manuscript, Manuscript Division, LOC; Barnes, testimony, May 20, 1865, in Poore, *The Conspiracy Trial*, vol. 2, p. 60.

75 *New York Herald*, Sept. 4, 1904.

76 John F. May, statement, 4/360–65, NA M599; Allen D. Spiegel, "Dr. John Frederick May and the Identification of John Wilkes Booth's Body," *Journal of Community Health*, vol. 23 (Oct. 1998), p. 397; *New York Clipper*, July 29, 1865.

77 *Harper's Weekly*, vol. 9 (May 13, 1865), p. 294.

78 *Washington National Tribune*, May 6, 1915.

79 John M. Peddicord's recollections, *Roanoke Evening News*, June 3, 1906; *Roanoke Times*, Jan. 8, 1921.

80 *Baltimore Daily Gazette*, April 29, 1865.

81 Barbee, "Lincoln and Booth," pp. 996–97; *New York Tribune*, April 29, 1865; *New York Mail and Express*, May 15, 1896.

82 John K. Lattimer, "Similarities in Fatal Woundings of John Wilkes Booth and Lee Harvey Oswald," *New York State Journal of Medicine*, vol. 66 (July 1966), p. 1786; John Weiss and Son, *A Catalogue of Surgical Instruments, Apparatus, and Appliances, Etc.* (London: M. S. Rickerby, 1863), plates 43, 43a.

83 Entry of April 27, 1865, courtesy of Joe Landes, his great-grandson; *Kansas City Journal-Post*, Feb. 7, 1932. Contrary to reports, "the bad head and wicked heart" of the assassin were not touched by the autopsy doctors. *Boston Herald*, quoted in *New York Clipper*, May 20, 1865.

84 Joseph K. Barnes, comp., *The Medical and Surgical History of the War of the Rebellion (1861–65)* (Washington: GPO, 1875, 2nd issue), pt. 1, p. 452; Barnes to Stanton, Wash., D.C., April 27, 1865, Entry 623, File D, RG 94, Treasure

Room, NA, courtesy of the late Len Guttridge, a valued friend; Alfred A. Woodhull, *Catalogue of the Surgical Section of the United States Army Museum* (Washington: GPO, 1866), pt. 3, p. 58.

85 *New York Daily Graphic*, April 13, 1876.

86 *Washington Evening Star*, Nov. 21, 1881; Gretchen Worden, "Is It the Body of John Wilkes Booth?" *Transactions and Studies of the College of Physicians of Philadelphia*, vol. 16, no. 5 (1994), p. 77; Harvey E. Brown, *The Medical Department of the United States Army from 1775 to 1873* (Washington: Surgeon General's Office, 1873), p. 225–26, 237.

87 Interview with John C. Watson, Peddicord's grandson, Alexandria, Va., June 2, 1995.

88 "End of J. Wilkes Booth," *Chicago Daily Tribune*, Feb. 17, 1889; L. B. Baker, "An Eyewitness Account of the Death and Burial of J. Wilkes Booth," *Journal of the Illinois State Historical Society*, vol. 39 (Dec. 1946), p. 445.

89 Frank G. Carpenter, "John Wilkes Booth," *Washington National Tribune*, Feb. 13, 1890; *Washington Evening Star*, May 12, 1897.

90 Baker's destination was not entirely a secret. John B. Montgomery, commandant of the Navy Yard, knew the body was taken to the Arsenal. Montgomery to Welles, Wash., D.C., April 27, 1865, HM 25253, Huntington Library, San Marino, Calif.

91 David Homer Bates, "Booth, the Assassin," typescript (1911), chap. 10, pp. 15–16, Bates Papers, LOC.

92 John B. Ellis, *The Sights and Secrets of the National Capital* (New York: U.S. Publishing, 1869), pp. 463ff.

93 George L. Porter, "How Booth's Body Was Hidden," *Columbian Magazine*, vol. 4 (April 1911), pp. 70–73; interview of Marcia Maloney, Porter's descendant, by my student Kay Washechek, Oct. 25, 2009.

94 *Chicago Tribune*, April 28, 1865, courtesy of Prof. Richard Fox.

EPILOGUE. A GREEN AND NARROW BED

1 "Baker, the Detective," clipping, n.d., LFFRC.

2 Andrew C. A. Jampoler, *The Last Lincoln Conspirator: John Surratt's Flight from the Gallows* (Annapolis, Md.: Naval Institute Press, 2008), for his escape, capture, and trial.

3 *Washington Evening Star*, January 3, 1890.

4 Clarke, *Booth*, pp. 12–15, 111–40; Booth, diary, Mugar Memorial Library, Boston University.

5 James M. Goode, *Capital Losses: A Cultural History of Washington's Destroyed Buildings* (Washington and London: Smithsonian Press, 2003), p. 341; Julian E. Raymond,

"History of Fort Lesley J. McNair, Washington, D.C., 1794-1951," typescript (1951?), p. 83, courtesy of my friend Susan Lemke, National Defense University Library, Special Collections, Archives and History Division, Fort McNair.

6 Frank H. Phipps to Thomas H. Ridgate Sr., Cobourg, Ontario, Canada, Aug. 16, 1919, JOH.

7 *Washington Evening Star*, Oct. 3, 1867; *Baltimore Sun*, Jan. 14, 1913.

8 Turner and Turner, *Lincoln*, p. 345.

9 Kauffman, *American Brutus*, pp. 387–90.

10 *New York World*, Feb. 16, 1869.

11 *Boston Journal*, May 20, 1865.

12 Edwin M. Stanton, testimony, May 18, 1867, *Impeachment Investigation*, p. 409.

13 Booth to Stanton, Philadelphia, Pa., Nov. 9, 1865, reel 10, E. M. Stanton Papers, LOC.

14 *Richmond Times-Dispatch*, Nov. 13, 1932.

15 Booth to Grant, Baltimore, Md., Sept. 11, 1867, in *The Papers of Ulysses S. Grant*, vol. 17, ed. John Y. Simon (Carbondale and Edwardsville: Southern Illinois University Press, 1991), pp. 315–16n.; *New York Times*, Sept. 19, 1867, and May 20, 1902.

16 Booth to Johnson, New York, Feb. 10, 1869, in *The Papers of Andrew Johnson*, vol. 15, *1868–69*, ed. Paul H. Bergeron (Knoxville: University of Tennessee Press, 1999), pp. 431–32.

17 *Brooklyn Daily Eagle*, Jan. 14, 1877.

18 *Washington Evening Star*, Feb. 16, 1869; *Washington Post*, March 25, 1901.

19 Ford to Booth [Baltimore, Md., Feb. 15, 1869], Hampden-Booth Theatre Library, The Players.

20 Feb. 16–19, 1869, issues of Baltimore's *Sun*, *Gazette*, and *Commercial Advertiser*.

21 Wilson, *Booth*, pp. 292–95.

22 *New York Daily Tribune*, June 7, 1903, also containing Joe Booth's remark about the filled tooth and Burton's comment on the boot.

23 "Identified Booth's Body," clipping, n.d. [1903], JOH.

24 *Newark Sunday Call*, Feb. 6, 1938.

25 *Baltimore Sun*, Jan. 14, 1903; *Wilkes-Barre Times*, Dec. 19, 1894; "Lincoln's Assassination," *Boston Traveler*, clipping, n.d, Townsend Scrapbook, LOC.

26 Patent No. 32,261, issued to Weaver on May 7, 1861, www.google.com/patents, accessed Jan. 14, 2010.

27 *Baltimore Sun*, June 4, 1903.

28 George Ford, *These Were Actors: A Story of the Chapmans and the Drakes* (New York: Library Publishers, 1955), p. 301.

29 The historian David R. Barbee found these marks when he examined the boot in 1940. Barbee memoranda, May 18, 1940, Folder 182, Box 4, Barbee Papers,

Georgetown University Library. *New York Clipper*, Feb. 16, 1861, explains how a skate was fixed in place.

30 "Saw Edwin Booth Identify Brother," clipping [1903], Wooster Scrapbook, Birmingham Public Library Archives.

31 Wilson, *Booth*, p. 295.

32 Chapman statement, Schenectady, N.Y., Dec. 31, 1912, Boos Collection, photocopy in author's possession.

33 *New York Times*, Feb. 18, 1869.

34 *Knoxville (Iowa) Journal-Express*, Feb. 11, 1920.

35 Entry of Feb. 18, 1869, Green Mount Cemetery Mortuary Stub Book, 1868–72, manuscript, fLin 2806.3, William Whiting Nolen Collection, Houghton Library, Harvard University, courtesy of my friend Thomas A. Horrocks. I am indebted to Elisabeth Potter for her insights into funeral iconography.

36 Certificate of ownership, June 13, 1869, copy in JOH.

37 *New York Clipper*, June 26, 1865.

38 Elizabeth Rogers to W. Stump Forward, Baltimore, Md., Aug. 16, 1886, Manuscript Division, LOC.

39 Identifications in *Baltimore Sun* of March 27, 1906; Aug. 21, 1889; July 6, 1901; June 30, 1907.

40 *Baltimore Sun*, Dec. 27, 1931.

41 Merchants' Exchange Reading Room Record Books, Arrivals, vol. 24, MdHS.

42 *Birmingham Age-Herald*, April 17, 1895.

43 *Baltimore Sun*, Feb. 5, 1897.

44 John H. Weaver's "second bill" to Green Mount Cemetery, Baltimore, June 26, 1869, for expenses at lots numbered 9–10, Dogwood Section, interment permit 16821, photocopy in JOH.

45 Dudley's statement to Mrs. DuPont Lee, n.d., Wilkerson Papers, LFFRC; *Baltimore Sun*, June 28, 1869; entry of June 26, 1869, Register of Marriages, Baptisms, and Burials, Christ Church (1828–1871), microfilm CR-Bal-2, MdHS.

46 The service was short, and the lesson, usually given in church, was dispensed with. The 1848 standard edition of *The Book of Common Prayer* was then in use.

47 *New York Times*, July 2, 1869.

48 *New York Clipper*, July 3, 1869; *Baltimore American*, March 2, 1902.

49 *St. Louis Post-Dispatch*, Nov. 6, 1886; *Baltimore American*, Sept. 30, 1901; *New York Sun*, Jan. 18, 1903; Kilby, "Some Newly-Collected Facts About John Wilkes Booth," Seymour Collection, Princeton University Library; Ella Mahoney, manuscript note, n.d. [1930s], from a conversation with Weaver, HCHS.

50 *Baltimore American*, June 9, 1870.

51 Baker, *History of the United States Secret Service*, pp. 507–8.

52 *Frank Leslie's Illustrated Newspaper*, May 20, 1865.

53 *Congressional Globe*, 39th Congress, 1st Session, July 28, 1866, p. 4292.

54 *Chicago Record-Herald*, Feb, 14, 1908.

55 Wise, *End of an Era*, pp. 454–55.

56 *Wilkes-Barre Times*, Dec. 19, 1894.

57 *Atlanta Constitution*, Oct. 21, 1885.

58 Ford, statement, n.d. [1885], Box 4, Ford Papers, LOC.

59 C. Wyatt Evans, *The Legend of John Wilkes Booth: Myth, Memory, and a Mummy* (Lawrence: University Press of Kansas, 2004); Finis L. Bates, *The Escape and Suicide of John Wilkes Booth* . . . (Memphis: Historical Publishing, 1907).

60 *St. Louis Democrat*, March 29, 1925.

61 *Washington Post*, Feb. 26, 1911.

62 *Louisville Courier-Journal*, Aug. 15, 1917.

63 C. Wyatt Evans, "Of Mummies and Methodism: Reverend Clarence True Wilson and the Legend of John Wilkes Booth," *Journal of Southern Religion*, vol. 5 (2002), accessed March 16, 2014, at http://jsr.fsu.edu/2002/Evans.htm.

64 William Hanchett, *The Lincoln Murder Conspiracies* (Urbana and Chicago: University of Illinois Press, 1983), pp. 226–33.

65 Francis J. Gorman, "The Petition to Exhume John Wilkes Booth: A View from the Inside," [University of Baltimore Law School] *Law Forum*, vol. 27 (Spring 1997), pp. 47–57.

66 *Washington Post*, Oct. 6, 1994.

67 Eleanor Atkinson, "Lincoln's Boyhood," *American Magazine*, vol. 65 (Feb. 1908), p. 369.

68 Robert W. Daly, ed., *Aboard the USS* Florida, *1863–5: The Letters of Paymaster William Frederick Keeler, U.S. Navy* (Annapolis, Md.: U.S. Naval Institute, 1968), p. 212.

69 Carl Schurz, *The Reminiscences of Carl Schurz*, vol. 3 (New York: McClure, 1908), p. 141.

70 Charles Deamude to father, Cleveland, Tenn., April 16, 1865, Manuscript Department, Illinois State Historical Library, Springfield.

71 Wise, *End of an Era*, pp. 454–55.

72 *Augusta (Ga.) Chronicle and Constitutionalist*, July 10, 1877.

73 *Impressions of Lincoln and the Civil War: A Foreigner's Account by the Marquis Adolphe de Chambrun* (New York: Random House, 1952), p. 102.

74 Nathan H. Chamberlain, *The Assassination of President Lincoln* (New York: G. W. Carleton, 1865), p. 20.

75 John Bigelow to William Seward, Paris, May 5, 1865, William Henry Seward Papers, Dept. of Rare Books and Special Collections, Rush Rhees Library, University of Rochester.

76 Scott D. Trostel, *The Lincoln Funeral Train: The Final Journey and National Funeral for Abraham Lincoln* (Fletcher, Ohio: Cam-Tech, 2002).

77 "Letters to SPK," Kimmel Collection, Macdonald-Kelce Library, University of Tampa.

78 Merrill D. Peterson, *Lincoln in American Memory* (New York and Oxford: Oxford University Press, 1994), for an overview of these themes. Hay quote at p. 206.

79 Horace White, "Abraham Lincoln in 1854," *Putnam's Monthly*, vol. 5 (March 1909), p. 728.

80 Bert Sheldon, "A Trip over the Booth Escape Route in July," Lincoln Fellowship Group of Washington, D.C., Assassination File, Abraham Lincoln Library and Museum, Lincoln Memorial University.

81 Alford, "Booth and Townsend"; Townsend: *Life, Crime, and Capture*, p. 40.

NOTE ON SOURCES

· · · ·

Abraham Lincoln Assassination Bibliography: A Compendium of Reference Materials (1997), compiled by Blaine V. Houmes, makes a traditional bibliography unnecessary. Houmes's book contains citations of some three thousand primary and secondary sources and is a necessary starting point for research.

If we don't "stand on the shoulders of giants"—largely because we can't get up there—we are certainly indebted to our predecessors for their pioneering research, and I found the collected papers of the following historians most useful and informative: David Rankin Barbee (the assassination), Georgetown University Library, Washington, D.C.; Ella Mahoney (Booth family), HSHC; George Bryan (the assassination), New York Public Library; James O. Hall (the assassination), Hall Center, Surratt House Museum, Clinton, Maryland; Stanley Kimmel (Booth family), Macdonald-Kelce Library, University of Tampa, Tampa, Florida; and Constance Head (John Wilkes Booth), author's possession.

While no comprehensive biography of John Wilkes Booth has been published until now, several valuable books treat aspects of his life. Asia Booth Clarke, his sister, wrote reminiscences of her brother in 1874. *John Wilkes Booth: A Sister's Memoir* (1996), which I edited, presents this text with a biography of the author. First published as *The Unlocked Book* (1938), her memoir is uneven, indulgent, and occasionally confounding, but it remains vital to understanding her brother's childhood. Arthur F. Loux's *John Wilkes Booth—Day by Day* (2014) reconstructs Booth's life in a calendar format with short biographical notes. *"Right or Wrong, God Judge Me": The Writings of John Wilkes Booth* (1997), edited by John Rhodehamel and Louise Taper, brings together Booth's letters and political statements. Deirdre L. Kincaid's "Rough Magic: The Theatrical Life of John Wilkes Booth" (Ph.D. thesis, University of Hull, 2000), with its perceptive interpretations, supersedes Gordon Samples's *Lust for Fame: The Stage Career of John Wilkes Booth* (1982).

Two Booth family members have been well served by biographers. Stephen Archer's *Junius Brutus Booth, Theatrical Prometheus* (1992) is the standard life of the father. Dan Watermeier's *American Tragedian: The Life of Edwin Booth* (2015), a volume long awaited by scholars, is a rewarding cradle-to-grave treatment of John's older brother. Arthur W. Bloom's *Edwin Booth: A Biography and Performance History* (2013) provides many new facts and interpretations. *Brothers* (2012), by George Howe Colt, reflects upon the nature of brotherhood among the Booth sons. David Grimsted's *Melodrama Unveiled: American Theater and Culture, 1800–1850* (1968) considers in masterly fashion the social and theatrical currents of the world in which Booth lived and worked, and Don B. Wilmeth's books provide a critical context to the theatrical aspects of this biography.

Studies of the Lincoln assassination contain special insights into Booth and his conspiracy. In *Blood on the Moon* (2001) Edward Steers Jr. presents a careful overview of Lincoln's murder while laying low many misconceptions about the event. Michael W. Kauffman's *American Brutus: John Wilkes Booth and the Lincoln Conspiracies* (2004) recounts Booth's intrigues and their aftermath in a highly original fashion. Anthony S. Pitch's *"They Have Killed Papa Dead!"* (2009) is an animated retelling of the assassination plot, execution, and aftermath. *My Thoughts Be Bloody: The Bitter Rivalry between Edwin and John Wilkes Booth That Led to an American Tragedy* (2010) by Nora Titone speculates on purported professional and personal conflicts between the brothers, set in the rich cultural panorama of the times. Timothy S. Good's *We Saw Lincoln Shot: One Hundred Eyewitness Accounts* (1995) is a handy sourcebook of witness statements, while Thomas A. Bogar's *Backstage at the Lincoln Assassination: The Untold Story of the Actors and Stagehands at Ford's Theatre* (2013), draws back the curtain on those inadvertently caught up in the murder of the president. James Swanson's *Manhunt: The Twelve-Day Chase for Lincoln's Killer* (2006) provides a riveting account of Booth's escape and the murder's expiation.

The assassination, broadly considered, is the focus of William Hanchett's *The Lincoln Murder Conspiracies* (1983), reviewing more than a century of historical writing on the assassination. Thomas R. Turner's *Beware the People Weeping: Public Opinion and the Assassination of Abraham Lincoln* (1982) examines the reaction of the American people and their government in the aftermath of the murder, as does Elizabeth D. Leonard's *Lincoln's Avengers: Justice, Revenge, and Reunion after the Civil War* (2004). One of Booth's acquaintances caught up by the dragnet following the murder is the subject of Kate Clifford Larson's *The Assassin's Accomplice: Mary Surratt and the Plot to Kill Abraham Lincoln* (2008). Jay Winik's *April 1865: The Month That Saved America* (2001) provides a sweeping narrative setting for this troubled time.

Notable Web resources include Angela Smythe's www.antebellumrichmond .com, a rich trove of facts and images connected with the host's efforts to identify Booth in group photographs of the Richmond Grays taken at Charles Town,

Virginia, in 1859. Also highly recommended are Roger J. Norton's www
.rogerjnorton.com/Lincoln.html, a lively board with features on many assassination topics, and Randal A. Berry's www.lincoln-assassination.com, with its variety of interesting material. Dave Taylor's blog, www.boothiebarn.com, is an
enjoyable read and gathering spot.

A helpful context for understanding Booth's actions is gained from Jonathan
W. White's *Abraham Lincoln and Treason in the Civil War: The Trials of John Merryman* (2011), which examines the challenge of disloyalty in Booth's home state
of Maryland. Jennifer L. Weber's *Copperheads: The Rise and Fall of Lincoln's Opponents in the North* (2006) thoughtfully analyzes the Northern antiwar movement,
which Booth fully supported. And David C. Keehn's *Knights of the Golden Circle:
Secret Empire, Southern Secession, Civil War* (2013) speculates on Booth's possible
connection with this secret Southern society.

James McPherson's *Battle Cry of Freedom* (1988), which covers the war with
exceptional clarity and acumen, gives us a full view of the national ordeal during
the period in which Abraham Lincoln became Booth's preoccupation, then his
obsession. To those who wish to understand who Lincoln was and what he meant
to contemporaries like his assassin, Michael Burlingame's *Abraham Lincoln: A
Life* (2008) is an absolute treasure. Ronald C. White Jr.'s *A. Lincoln: A Biography*
(2009) is a concise life by a thoughtful writer. Doug Wilson's *Lincoln's Sword: The
Presidency and The Power of Words* (2006) examines Lincoln's most formidable
weapon—timeless ideals, memorably expressed—while Doris Kearns Goodwin's
Team of Rivals: The Political Genius of Abraham Lincoln (2005) demonstrates how
he wielded those ideals to transforming effect among his own associates. Allen
Guelzo's *Abraham Lincoln: Redeemer President* (1999) skillfully delineates the mind
and spirit of Lincoln in the context of his times. *The Fiery Trial: Abraham Lincoln
and American Slavery* (2010) by Eric Foner traces with astute steps Lincoln's path
to emancipation and beyond, an illuminating contrast to the course of his assassin. John McKee Barr's *Loathing Lincoln: An American Tradition from the Civil
War to the Present* (2014) surveys Lincoln's image among those, like Booth, who
considered him a terrible president—if not a criminal who defied the Constitution. These studies may be supplemented by Frank Williams's *Judging Lincoln*
(2002), a series of essays with fresh perspectives on many facets of the president's
life, and Harold Holzer's *Lincoln at Cooper Union: The Speech That Made Abraham
Lincoln President* (2004), an insightful book about a critical moment in the career
of the great president's life.

INDEX

. . . .